DATE DUE FOR RETURN

Introduction to Risk Management and Insurance

NINTH EDITION

INTRODUCTION TO RISK MANAGEMENT AND INSURANCE

Mark S. Dorfman, Ph.D.

Ephraim, Wisconsin 54211

PEARSON

Prentice
Hall

UPPER SADDLE RIVER, NEW JERSEY 07458

Library of Congress Cataloging-in-Publication Data

Dorfman, Mark S.
    Introduction to risk management and insurance / Mark S. Dorfman. — 9th ed.
        p. cm.
    Includes index.
    ISBN 0-13-224227-3
        1. Insurance. 2. Risk (Insurance) 3. Risk management. I. Title.

HG8051.D65 2007
368—dc22   2007009301

Acquisitions Editor: Mark Pfaltzgraff
Product Development Manager: Ashley Santora
Project Manager: Mary Kate Murray
Marketing Assistant: Laura Cirigliano
Associate Director, Production Editorial: Judy Leale
Senior Managing Editor: Cynthia Zonneveld
Production Editor: Suzanne Grappi
Permissions Coordinator: Charles Morris
Associate Director, Manufacturing: Vinnie Scelta
Manufacturing Buyer: Michelle Klein
Design/Composition Manager: Christy Mahon
Cover Design: Bruce Kenselaar
Composition: ICC Macmillan Inc.
Full-Service Project Management: Mohinder Singh
Printer/Binder: Hamilton Printing Company
Typeface: 10/12 Times

Includes copyrighted material of Insurance Services Office, with its permission.
Copyright, Insurance Services Office, Inc. 1996, 2004.

1005070086

10 9 8 7 6 5 4 3 2 1
ISBN-13: 978-0-13-224227-1
ISBN-10: 0-13-224227-3

Mark S. Dorfman
April 14, 1945–December 22, 2006

Mark Dorfman was a stimulating teacher, a respected scholar and researcher,
a dedicated author, a beloved father and husband, and a man of honesty and
integrity. Since his first course in graduate school in 1966, he never ceased to be
excited about the subject of risk management and insurance. He loved his family,
his students, teaching and traveling in Austria, France, Germany, and Door County,
Wisconsin, eating delicious food, and listening to the blues. He leaves behind
friends and colleagues around the globe who will miss his smile, his wit,
his gracious habit of always saying "Thank you," and his ability to always see
the best in others.

To all the M's in my life, and to Dorothy, who know that
· *Love Is Reflected in Love*

Brief Contents

Contents

Preface

The ninth edition of this book is written for students who want to learn about risk management, insurance, and professional financial planning. This text also is written for instructors who, like the author, enjoy the challenges and rewards of classroom relations with students. As a reader would expect in an introductory textbook, presenting essential terminology and key risk management and insurance concepts are critically important goals. The manuscript has benefited from decades of exchanging ideas with students, colleagues all over the world, and risk management and insurance professionals. The best of these exchanges ended with "Now I understand."

WHY HAVE A NEW EDITION?

Students sometime ask their instructors if they really need to purchase the most recent edition of a textbook, or if the previous edition will do. I hope the following response to this question provides a persuasive answer that the purchase of this revision provides significant value to the reader and instructor. Clearly, the principles and vocabulary of risk management and insurance, the focus of this text, have not changed since the previous edition; however, some very important events have occurred in the past four years which provide new illustrations and applications of these concepts. One purpose of the following list of new material covered in this revision is to get readers excited about the subject they are about to study:

- The impact of the catastrophic 2004 and 2005 hurricane seasons has raised many challenges for the insurance industry, the Federal Emergency Management Agency (FEMA), for the risk management profession, and for the whole country. Chapter 2, "Defining the Insurable Event," discusses theoretical and practical questions concerning insurance for natural catastrophes. Chapter 3, "Risk Management," describes some of the risk management lessons learned from these disasters in a new section on crisis risk management.
- Product development in life insurance, especially in the area of guaranteed annuity options, has complicated and broadened the choices faced by consumers and professional financial planners. Chapter 15, "Annuities," describes many recent product developments in annuity offerings.
- The introduction of a prescription drug benefit for Medicare recipients has complicated and broadened the choices faced by eligible Social Security participants. Chapter 22, "Social Security," presents recent information about the Social Security program, including the Medicare prescription drug benefit.
- The U.S. health care delivery system has many critics and many unsolved problems, including the continuing problem of medical malpractice and financing the costs of medically caused injuries. Chapter 16, "Medical Expense and Disability Income Insurance," presents a comprehensive discussion of the health care

system, while Chapter 19, "Commercial Liability Insurance," discusses the medical malpractice problem and some solutions, including President George W. Bush's proposed cap on noneconomic damages (i.e., pain and suffering).

- The steady reduction of the number of defined benefit pension plans accompanied by the steady increase in the number of defined contribution pension plans, including 401(k) plans, have changed the retirement financing plans of many workers. Moreover, the bankruptcy of large employers in the steel, airline, and other industries has caused the financial impairment of the Pension Benefit Guarantee Corporation (PBGC), the federal agency that guarantees defined benefit plans. Chapter 21, "Employee Benefits," has a revised discussion of employee benefits, including pension plans.

- Ethical lapses involving the country's largest insurance brokers in recent years have led to significant readjustment in the business practices of this segment of the insurance industry. Chapter 5, "Insurance Occupations," covers this new material.

- The International Financial Reporting Standards (IFRS) prescribe how and when insurance companies should recognize profits and report the value of their assets and liabilities. The IFRS attach new importance to the efforts of insurance company accountants, insurance supervisors, and insurance financial rating agencies. References to the IFRS appear in several places in this revision.

This list of new topics covered in this edition is not complete. New articles containing new ideas or refinements of previous theories have appeared in academic journals since the previous edition, and many of these new contributions are summarized or footnoted in this edition. However, reading this description of some of the new material contained in this revision should help to persuade readers that the topics covered in this book are interesting and the descriptions of many important new subjects are current.

Among the significant revisions found is this edition are many new hyperlinks to Web sites. To recognize the importance of this new and extremely valuable avenue for learning, the author has added *Internet Research Assignments* to the end of each chapter. One purpose of these new assignments is to familiarize readers with the rich resources available on the Internet to risk management and insurance scholars. Like his students, the author has become adept at searching for information from this vast reference facility. He also has learned that some sites disappear, others change their addresses or names, and new sites appear frequently, so in some places, keywords for search engine use have been identified. When investigating the various topics on these sites, the reader is cautioned to be highly critical of the quality and timeliness of the information found. The Internet can be a rich source of quality information, but it can also provide misleading and biased information that sometimes is written solely to further the interests of the writer.

Given the foregoing discussion of the highlights of this new edition, I think it is important to note that the strengths of the previous eight editions of this book have been retained: a user-friendly writing style, coverage of important ideas that is full without adding tedious details, and interesting examples and illustrations, many coming from actual legal decisions.

IMPORTANT FEATURES OF THIS BOOK

In addition to the *Internet Research Assignments* already mentioned, this book contains several other features to help readers focus on main ideas. Each chapter begins with a list of *Learning Objectives* and includes a *Review* section that provides the reader with a self-test of the material covered in the chapter, as well as *Objective Questions* in a multiple-choice format. The *Objective Questions* give students a second opportunity to determine if they have mastered the material covered in the chapter and to prepare themselves for examinations. (Answers to the *Objective Questions* appear in Appendix D at the end of the book.) Each chapter also contains *Discussion Questions*.

Boldfaced words appear throughout the text and in the margins. The boldface type is meant to alert readers to important vocabulary. In addition, there is a *Glossary*, which provides brief definitions of most of the terms that appear in boldface throughout the text. Shaded boxes have been used throughout the text to alert the reader to important material, such as direct quotation of insurance policy language, judicial decisions, and quotations from other authors.

This book is divided into six parts and 23 chapters:

- Part 1 (Chapters 1 to 3) covers basic principles and terminology.
- Part 2 (Chapters 4 to 7) presents operational and regulatory background for the insurance industry.
- Part 3 (Chapters 8 to 11) covers basic insurance policy terminology and focuses on the personal insurance policies most likely to be purchased by readers—the homeowners policy and the personal automobile policy.
- Part 4 (Chapters 12 to 16) presents the topic of professional financial planning, including life and health insurance.
- Part 5 (Chapters 17 to 20) describes advanced risk management topics and commercial property and liability insurance.
- Part 6 (Chapters 21 to 23) covers employee benefits, Social Security, unemployment insurance, and workers' compensation.

ADDITIONAL RESOURCES

In addition to features within this book, a variety of resources are available for both instructors and students using this book.

For Instructors

Several instructors' resources accompany the ninth edition of this text and are available for professors at the following Web site: (*http://www.prenhall.com/dorfman/*). Professors must register on the Web site to access the book's resources.

Saul W. Adelman of Miami University of Ohio wrote the Instructor's Manual. Each chapter of the Instructor's Manual is broken down into six sections: (1) Suggested Classroom Time, (2) Chapter Overview, (3) Lecture Outline, (4) Answers to Review Questions, (5) Answers to End-of-Chapter Objective Questions, and (6) Ideas for Instructors and Teaching Methods. Professor Adelman also created the PowerPoint presentations for this edition.

Brenda Wells of the University of North Texas wrote the test bank, which includes true/false, multiple choice, and essay questions.

For Students

Students interested in using the Web sites referenced in this text first should go to the Web site (*http://www.prenhall.com/dorfman/*), where they can access all the Web sites that appear in the text without further typing, using the list of hyperlinks sorted by chapter and name.

WHY STUDY RISK MANAGEMENT AND INSURANCE?

In the words of a reviewer of this edition, "the world is a risky place." Individuals and businesses must face risk daily. Because we all face risks, and because the consequences of these risks can be destructive, individuals and businesses must manage risk and finance the costs that risk imposes. The text describes many ways risk can be managed, and it explains that insurance is just one of several ways to finance the cost of being exposed to risks.

The importance of studying risk management and insurance has been increased greatly because of the terrorist attacks of September 11, 2001, and Hurricane Katrina in August 2005. Each of these destructive events increased our focus on securing both individual and community assets from loss. Clearly, we will be spending more money and time on risk management activities in the future.

Students also may study risk management and insurance for personal reasons. Some students will pursue a risk management and insurance career; while others will pursue a career in other management areas that require an understanding of risk management. Some students will take advanced risk management and insurance courses and need the foundation provided by this book, and all readers are likely to purchase personal lines of insurance sometime in their lives.

Occasionally I have asked my students why they were taking a risk management and insurance course. Typical answers have been: "I know I'm going to buy insurance someday, so I thought I'd learn about it." "My friend told me to take the course because she liked it." "I'm planning on going into the insurance business, so I thought I'd learn about it in school." "I'm a business major, and I think all businesspeople should know about risk management." "My roommate was in an accident and didn't have the right insurance coverage." These are all good reasons for studying this book. After taking an introductory risk management and insurance course, students should have an understanding of how insurance helps to solve some personal financial problems. One purpose of this book is to introduce some basic insurance concepts from the consumer's viewpoint—both individual and corporate consumers—and to advocate intelligent, informed purchases of insurance.

ACADEMIC OBJECTIVES

The study of insurance can play a significant role in achieving the general goals of a broad-based undergraduate education. The author believes the study of insurance is a way to accomplish the following goals:

- To encourage critical thinking, including moral and ethical reasoning
- To facilitate the ability to use language effectively
- To aid in the understanding of human behavior
- To provide understanding of important societal problems
- To integrate knowledge across a broad range of subject areas, including mathematics, social science, philosophy, law, natural science, and economics
- To integrate knowledge across the business curriculum, including marketing, finance, accounting, management, and management information systems

Critical Thinking and Moral Reasoning

It would be difficult to teach risk and insurance courses without discussing logical alternative choices with students. The text discusses the following questions, among others: What distinguishes socially acceptable from socially unacceptable characteristics in setting insurance rates? Could a capitalistic society function without a private insurance system? Should health insurance be provided on a public basis, a private basis, or some combination of the two? Who should decide what types of treatments should be reimbursed under health insurance coverage? Should the insurance transaction be regulated at the federal or at the state level? How should an insurance agent or broker act when a conflict of interest arises with a client? These questions require critical thinking and logical analysis.

Effective Use of Language

Other than "business English," perhaps no course offered in U.S. business schools focuses more attention on the English language and its nuances than the introductory risk management and insurance course. The study of insurance policies is a study of English in action. Much learning occurs when students discover that the same words may mean different things to different people; that courts often are needed to interpret language when it is not used precisely; and that using ambiguous language can have very expensive consequences. Compensation for loss often depends on definitions of perils such as *explosion, collapse*, and *terrorism*. Discussion of legal cases throughout this book should leave the impression on readers that language must be used precisely to avoid unintended results. According to many curricular experts, understanding the importance of communicating effectively is one of the greatest lessons learned at the undergraduate level.

Understanding Human Behavior

Human behavior is a relevant topic in every insurance course because the insurance transaction is inevitably the result of human interaction. Many risk management questions have psychological explanations, including the following: Why are some exposures to loss insured while others are not? What role does human behavior play in causing or preventing losses? How can society encourage people to save for retirement and adequately insure their lives?

Societal Problems

The U.S. Congress and individual state legislatures discuss insurance issues regularly, and insurance issues frequently appear in the news. Among the important societal questions raised in this text are the following: How should health care costs be financed? How should we prepare for an aging society, including financing long-term care and providing adequate retirement income? How should the cost of catastrophic hurricanes, earthquakes, and floods be financed? How should the cost of repairing our damaged environment be borne? None of these problems can be addressed adequately without discussing insurance.

Insurance is one of society's most effective tools for financing some of its most difficult problems. Thus, the study of insurance will remain important so long as the problems that it solves remain important.

Integration Across the Curriculum

Risk management and insurance concepts cannot be taught effectively without reference to economics, mathematics, and law. Concern with potential losses, the focal point of the undergraduate risk management curriculum, is shared to some extent by all major divisions of business studies. Instruction in risk management and insurance often includes references to history, politics, architecture, engineering, medicine, psychology, and gerontology.

Conclusion

One purpose of this book is to provide readers with the vocabulary and information that will allow them to understand some important societal questions and form their own conclusions. Another purpose is to provide the background information needed to understand the types of problems that can arise from the individual's or firm's exposure to loss, and how these problems may be approached and solved. Many speeches have been given and many articles have been written about insurance, and recent political campaigns have focused on insurance-related issues, including health care and the future of Social Security. Perhaps if speakers and editorial writers knew that their audiences understood the questions, self-serving arguments would give way to more direct and honest discussion. Because insurance questions tend to be complex, many listeners have been kept in the dark. The author hopes that studying this text will let in some light.

THE AUTHOR

I have taught introductory risk management and insurance classes for more than 35 years at the following universities: University of Illinois, Miami University (Ohio), the University of Arkansas at Little Rock, the University of North Carolina at Charlotte, the Wirtschaftsuniversität Wien (The Business and Economics University of Vienna, Austria), the University of Ulm, Germany, and Audencia University in Nantes, France. I still enjoy teaching; in fact, sharing ideas with students remains one of my life's great joys. I hope readers who have come this far in the preface already realize that I believe teaching risk management and insurance to students is very important. I always keep students in mind when writing this book, and I hope they find the writing style "user-friendly."

I was born in Chicago and attended Chicago public schools. My undergraduate degree is from Northwestern University. The University of Illinois awarded my Master of Science and Doctor of Philosophy degrees.

I have held high offices, served on boards of directors of several academic and nonacademic institutions, and have written extensively in the major risk management and insurance academic journals.

ACKNOWLEDGMENTS

I treasure my friends as among my greatest joys. I have had the help of many friends in writing and revising this book. I am truly grateful for them and want to acknowledge their help and support. Readers might expect that after nine editions and all the assistance received, there would be no errors or omissions remaining. While I'd like this to be the case, when such problems are discovered, I am either the originator or a willing accomplice.

My intellectual companion of the past three decades, Saul Adelman, has made countless suggestions for improving the manuscript. Collaboration with Saul has enriched my thinking about many risk management and insurance issues, and I gratefully acknowledge his help and friendship.

My wife, Marcia, provided her consistent support, valuable proofreading skills, and talents as a professional librarian as this text has progressed through nine editions. Marcia's contributions appear throughout the book.

Special mention must be given to Professors Brenda Wells, A. Frank Thompson, and William Warfel, who all have shared many suggestions and ideas over several editions. Dr. Wells also wrote the computer test bank questions available to instructors who adopt this text.

I also am grateful to acknowledge the comments and criticisms made by several anonymous reviewers of the ninth edition. Many of their comments, suggestions, and insights have found their place in the ninth edition.

The following people, many of whom are distinguished classroom instructors or successful business practitioners, have made contributions to this or previous editions of the text. I have omitted their titles, affiliations, and degrees. To me they are friends, and their friendship and ideas have been essential to this thirty-year-long writing project:

Khurshid Ahmad	Robert J. Myers
Eugene Anderson	Robert Nagy
Robert Atchley	James R. Newell
Kenneth Black, Jr.	Max Oelschlaeger
Mark Cross	Daniel J. Pliszka
Karl C. Ennsfellner	Jochen Russ
John Fitzgerald	Barry Schweig
Robert P. Hartwig	Steven Tippins
Cheri Hawkins	Peter Townley
George L. Head	Peter Walters
David Marlett	Steven Weisbart

High on the list of contributors to this book are more than three decades of students. Many sharp-eyed students have found items to criticize, and many have suggested improvements that I have implemented. Other students have asked challenging questions that have led to further improvements. I take great pleasure in recognizing the help these students provided.

Mark S. Dorfman

CHAPTER 1

Fundamentals and Terminology

After studying this chapter, you should be able to:

■ Describe the legal and financial nature of insurance

■ Explain how an insurance system operates

■ Distinguish among a loss, a hazard, and a peril

■ List the components of an insurance premium

■ Discuss the advantages and disadvantages of insurance transactions from society's standpoint

The main purpose of this chapter is to introduce some of the vocabulary and concepts used throughout this text. Many of the technical words used by risk managers, professional financial planners, and other people working in risk management and insurance are introduced in this chapter.

Insurance is one of the most interesting and important transactions made by individuals and businesses. In the 1943 South-Eastern Underwriters Association decision by the U.S. Supreme Court, Justice Hugo Black wrote, "Perhaps no modern commercial enterprise directly affects so many persons in all walks of life as does the insurance business. Insurance touches the home, the family, and the occupation or business of almost every person in the United States." Clearly, insurance is important to people, and many aspects of the insurance transaction merit study and thought.

Readers must understand the mathematical foundation of insurance to appreciate the subject fully. The law of large numbers explains how losses can be predicted.

Governments must make laws that allow an insurance system to operate. Some societies operate no insurance system. Some societies, including our own, have outlawed certain forms of insurance. A discussion of society's benefits from and costs of operating an insurance system helps establish the importance of this transaction.

This chapter concludes by pointing out that when insurance companies pay for losses, they are using their insureds' premiums. The public often misunderstands this point. People assume that because the insurance company writes the check for insured losses, it is the company's money paying the losses. We shall see when we look at the case of arson that this conclusion is wrong.

INSURANCE DEFINED[1]

We begin our discussion by noting that experts do not always agree on the definitions of risk management and insurance terms. Nor is the question of defining terms carefully one of splitting hairs or counting the number of angels that might land on a pinhead.

---

[1] For an extended discussion of the definition of insurance and its regulatory implications see: Government Accountability Office, "Definitions of Insurance and Related Information" (February, 2006). (GAO-06-424R)

Questions involving definitions of insurance terms have required many court cases and can involve millions of dollars. Defining the term *insurance* is an issue courts have dealt with for decades. If a transaction is labeled as insurance, it is subject to regulations, accounting rules, and tax laws. Thus, the tax courts have had to determine which transactions qualify for the tax treatment accorded insurance transactions.[2] Also, state insurance regulators must determine whether a transaction such as service contracts that guarantee replacement of parts on appliances or automobiles fall within or outside the definition of insurance. The definitions to follow are generally accepted and lay the foundation for material covered throughout the text.

Financial Definition

Insurance

The first definition of insurance we examine is the financial one. **Insurance** is a financial arrangement that redistributes the costs of unexpected losses. Insurance involves the transfer of potential losses to an insurance pool. The pool combines all the potential losses and then transfers the cost of the predicted losses back to those exposed. Thus, insurance involves the transfer of loss exposures (or the uncertainty of loss) to an insurance pool and the redistribution of the cost of losses among the members of the pool. Certainty of financial payment from a pool with adequate resources and accurate ability to predict losses are the hallmarks of the insurance transaction.

Throughout human history, unexpected economic losses have occurred. Such losses would occur even if the insurance transaction never had been developed. Through the operation of an insurance system, however, combined losses can be predicted. The predictability of losses is basic to an insurance system's operations. Because insurance allows a group's (but not an individual's) losses to be predicted with reasonable accuracy, it allows the cost of losses to be financed and redistributed in advance.

An insurance system redistributes the cost of losses by collecting a premium payment from every participant (insured) in the system. In exchange for the premium payment, the insurer promises to pay the insured's claims in the event of a covered loss. Generally, only a small percentage of insureds suffer losses. Thus, an insurance system redistributes the costs of losses from the unfortunate few members experiencing them to all the members of the insurance system who pay premiums.

Figure 1–1 illustrates how a fire insurance pool redistributes the costs of losses. Assume that each member of the pool is exposed to loss of his or her home by fire. Each member willingly pays a $1,000 premium to the insurance pool. The insurer promises payment in the event of fire. Assume that homeowner 4644 loses his house in a fire. He collects $180,000, the insured value of his house, from the insurer. If no insurance pool existed, the unfortunate victim would lose $180,000. Instead, the members of the pool each paid $1,000 to provide funds to pay for losses. As you can now see, each insured paid a small part of the $180,000 loss experienced by one member. In one sense, the insurance company operates like a big checkbook. The insureds make the deposits (premium payments), and the insurer writes the checks to insureds suffering losses.

The $1,000 premium each insured paid in advance was calculated based on projected losses. When the year began, it was not predicted that home 4644 would burn, but rather that 33 houses from among the 5,000 insured would burn. From this prediction came the decision to charge each homeowner $1,000 for insurance.

---

[2] The tax courts have generally disallowed insurance-related deductions in the absence of a transfer of risk. The courts have applied this rule to premiums paid to wholly owned captive insurers, premiums paid for options, and premiums paid for retroactive liability insurance. These topics are discussed later in the text.

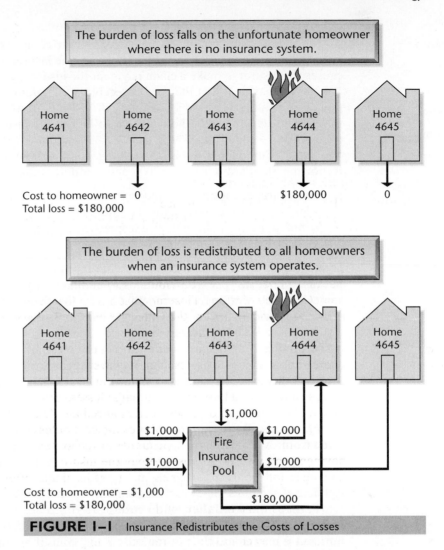

The burden of loss falls on the unfortunate homeowner where there is no insurance system.

Home 4641

Home 4642

Home 4643

Home 4644

Home 4645

Cost to homeowner =   0   0 $180,000   0
Total loss = $180,000

The burden of loss is redistributed to all homeowners when an insurance system operates.

Home 4641

Home 4642

Home 4643

Home 4644

Home 4645

$1,000

$1,000   Fire $1,000
                Insurance
$1,000   Pool $1,000

Cost to homeowner = $1,000
Total loss = $180,000 $180,000

FIGURE 1–1   Insurance Redistributes the Costs of Losses

Risk averse

Mathematically fair price

An insurance system can operate because all insureds are willing to substitute a relatively small certain outlay, the insurance premium, for a relatively large uncertain loss. We assume that most people find the possibility of suffering a large loss unpleasant to consider. Because they are **risk averse**, many people willingly pay an insurance premium that is greater than the mathematically fair chance of loss to be relieved of the uncertainty about a loss and to be compensated if the loss occurs. Thus, even if no loss occurs during a year, as will be the case for most insureds, value still has been received in the form of a reduced or eliminated unpleasant mental state—the anxiety about a loss. Not everybody is risk averse. Some people enjoy assuming risk; they are *risk seekers*. Other people will pay to be relieved of risk, but they will pay only the mathematically fair price. These people are *risk neutral*. The **mathematically fair price** is the probability of loss times the amount of the expected loss. Insurance is never a mathematically fair trade because the insurer adds operating and other costs to loss costs when it builds its premiums. We discuss the basics of premium construction later in the chapter.

Legal Definition

Insurance

Insurer

Insured

Policyholder

Policy owner

Premium

Policy

Exposure to loss

Insurance is a contract in which one party agrees to compensate another party for losses. We call the party agreeing to pay for the losses the **insurer**. We call the party whose loss causes the insurer to make a claim payment the **insured**, **policyholder**, or **policy owner**. We call the payment that the insurer receives a **premium**, call the insurance contract a **policy**. and call the insured's possibility of loss the insured's **exposure to loss**. We say that the insured transfers the exposure to loss to the insurer by purchasing an insurance policy.

The definition of *insurance contract* contained in the International Financial Reporting Standards (IFRS) in 2005 puts our definitions back together as follows:

> An insurance contract is a contract under which one party (the insurer) accepts significant insurance risk from another party (the policyholder) by agreeing to compensate the policyholder if a specified uncertain future event (the insured event) adversely affects the policyholder.[3]

Perhaps the most important phrase in this quotation is "significant insurance risk," because the IFRS specifically intends to eliminate from the term *insurance contracts* some contracts written by insurers that have a low degree of risk transfer. (We will discuss one example of these contracts in Chapter 3, "Risk Management," when we describe "Finite Risk Arrangements.")

Insurance is a branch of contract law. The insurance policy, like all contracts, is an arrangement that creates rights and related duties for those who are parties to it. For instance, the insurance contract creates the insured's right to collect payment from the insurer if a covered loss occurs. The insurer has a duty to pay for such losses. The insurance contract also creates other rights and duties. The insurer has the right to collect premiums, and those wanting their coverage to continue have the duty to pay them. The insurer has the right to specify the rules and conditions for participating in the insurance pool, and the insured has the matching duty to obey them if he or she expects to collect for losses. In analyzing an insurance contract, you should remember that a right created for one party represents a duty for the other party.

Perhaps the word *duty* is too strong a term to describe the obligations of an insured to an insurer. Generally, an insurer legally cannot force an insured to pay premiums, but it may cancel the insurance or deny claims if premiums are unpaid. Likewise, an insurer generally cannot force an insured to meet the conditions set forth in the contract, but if the insured does not meet the conditions, losses will not be paid. Thus, it seems fair to note that an insurance contract creates rights and corresponding obligations for both the insurer and the insured.

LOSS, CHANCE OF LOSS, PERIL, HAZARD, AND PROXIMATE CAUSE

The subject of insurance is more easily understood if we apply exact meanings to words used in the discipline. Terms such as *loss*, *chance of loss*, *peril*, *hazard*, and *risk* are often used in everyday conversation, but these words take on a particular meaning when used to describe insurance.

Loss

Loss

The word **loss**, as it is commonly used, means being without something previously possessed. We speak of "loss of memory" and "loss of time," for example. When the word

---

[3]Readers can find a description and discussion of the International Financial Reporting Standards (IFRS), including this definition of insurance contract, at the following Web site: (*http://www.iasplus.com/standard/standard.htm*).

is used in insurance, however, it takes on a more limited meaning. A typical insurable loss is an undesired, unplanned reduction of economic value. We use the word *expenses* to refer to planned losses such as burning of fuel or wear and tear.

Direct losses

Indirect losses

Insurable losses are categorized as direct or indirect losses. This distinction is important. **Direct losses** are the immediate, or first, result of an insured peril. **Indirect losses**, also called *consequential losses*, or *loss of use*, are a secondary result of an insured peril. For example, if fire destroys a home, the loss of the home is the direct loss. The expense of living in a hotel while the home is being rebuilt is an example of an indirect loss. If a tornado destroys a restaurant, the property damage is the direct loss; the loss of income during the period when the business is being rebuilt is the indirect loss. There must be a direct loss before there can be an indirect loss. Property insurance policies are specific when providing coverage for direct losses, indirect losses, or both.

Chance of Loss

Chance of loss

The concept of **chance of loss** is expressed as a fraction. The numerator is either the actual or the expected number of losses. The denominator represents the number exposed to loss. The chance of loss is the probability of suffering a loss. Each house in an insurance pool represents one exposure to loss. If we expect 3 houses out of 1,000 houses in an insurance pool to be destroyed by fire, the expected chance of loss is 3/1,000, or 0.003. The chance of loss in a given case may or may not be known accurately before a loss occurs. If we are referring to the predicted chance of loss, we divide the expected number of losses by the number of exposure units. This fraction is called the *a priori* chance of loss. If we are looking backward over time, we can divide the actual number of losses by the total number of exposures. This fraction is called the actual, or *ex post*, chance of loss.

It is the possibility or the chance of loss that creates the need for insurance. If there were either no possibility of loss or if losses were certain to occur, insurance would not exist. In the first instance, there would be no need for it. In the second, there would be no element of uncertainty about losses, and the result would be expenses rather than losses. Expenses should be handled by methods other than insurance.

Peril and Hazard

Peril

A **peril** is defined as the cause of the loss. Examples of perils include fires, tornadoes, heart attacks, and criminal acts. Insurance policies provide financial protection against losses caused by perils. Insurers call policies that specifically identify a list of covered perils **specified-perils** contracts. The alternative format is to cover all losses except those that are specifically excluded. Insurers call this type of policy an **open-perils** contract.

Specified-perils

Open-perils

Hazards

Hazards are conditions that increase the frequency or the severity of losses. Storing 55 gallons of gasoline in an oil drum in a garage is an example of a hazard. The storage of the gasoline generally will not cause a loss. The gasoline, however, will make fire losses that otherwise occur more severe. Poor lighting in a crime-prone area is a hazard, in that theft losses may be more frequent than would be the case if better lighting were available. The poor lighting by itself would not cause the loss, but to the extent that it makes theft more frequent, it is a hazard. Sometimes hazards increase both the frequency and severity of losses, as would be the case if an automobile is driven too fast for existing conditions.

Insurance fraud

Moral hazard

Two special hazards deserve additional definition: moral hazard and morale hazard. If an individual causes or exaggerates a loss to collect insurance proceeds, this is **insurance fraud**, and the loss results from the **moral hazard**. If somebody burns down a building to collect insurance, the fire causes the damage, but the moral hazard is responsible for the increased frequency of loss. If a thief steals $5,000 but the insured storeowner reports a $20,000 loss to the insurance company, the $15,000 fraud committed by the insured results from the moral hazard.

Morale hazard refers to an attitude of carelessness or indifference to loss created by the purchase of an insurance contract. The attitude, "Why should I care? I'm insured," is an example of the morale hazard. If a person remains unnecessarily in a hospital to collect health insurance benefits rather than returning to work, the morale hazard is responsible for the increased severity of the loss.

Insurers try to eliminate the moral hazard and minimize the morale hazard by selecting their insureds carefully and by including contractual provisions causing the insured to regret the loss despite the insurance coverage. For example, some contracts require insureds to pay the first specified number of dollars of a loss, and others require insureds to pay a percentage of each loss. In both cases, the insureds have reason to regret the losses while still receiving insurance compensation. Insurance contracts do not cover losses caused by an insured's fraud.

Proximate Cause

The proximate cause of a loss is an important concept in property insurance. In insurance terminology, the **proximate cause** of a loss is the first peril in a chain of events resulting in a loss. The loss would not have occurred without this step. Generally, if the proximate cause of the loss is an insured peril, the insurer will pay the claim and will pay for any subsequent damage. However, if the proximate cause of the loss is an excluded peril, the insurer will not pay the claim. (We explore the complicating factor of *concurrent causation*, or losses having more than a single cause, in Chapter 10, "Homeowners Insurance (HO).") In some cases, establishing the proximate cause of the loss can be difficult. After Hurricane Katrina, for example, determining whether the cause of destruction was wind (a covered peril) or flood (an excluded peril) was a very important issue for many homeowners. Because it raises questions of fact, sometimes it takes a court to determine the proximate cause of the loss.

Risk

The word *risk* is often used in connection with finance, banking, and insurance. No single generally accepted definition of risk exists, however. Of the many definitions, two distinctive ones commonly are used when writing and speaking about insurance. One defines **risk** as the variation in possible outcomes of an event based on chance. That is, the greater the number of different outcomes that may occur, the greater the risk. Another way of expressing this concept is to state: The greater the variation around an average expected loss, the greater the risk.

The second definition of risk is the uncertainty concerning a possible loss. People working in the insurance industry often use the term *risk* to mean the exposure to loss. So you may hear an agent say, "We'll insure that risk for $1,000."

The definition of risk as variability in possible outcomes is useful because it focuses attention on the degree of risk in given situations. The *degree of risk* is a measure of the accuracy with which the outcome of an event based on chance can be predicted. For now, it will serve our purpose to note that the more accurate the prediction of the outcome of an event based on chance, the lower the degree of risk. Conversely, the less accurate the prediction is, the higher the degree of risk. For example, predicting what flavor of ice cream a total stranger will choose from among the 30 possible choices at Wilson's Ice Cream Parlor is risky if 30 equally delicious outcomes are possible. If, however, you know something about the person, such as the fact that she always orders some variety of chocolate ice cream, you will be able to make a better prediction.

Morale hazard

Proximate cause

Risk

Predicting the outcome is now less risky. In our example, if only 6 out of 30 flavors had chocolate in them, you have narrowed the choice from 1 of 30 to 1 of 6 possibilities. The variability in the possible outcomes has been reduced. The risk is lower than in the original case, and the outcome more predictable, so we say a lower degree of risk exists.

Turning to an insurance example, if we were asked to predict how many houses will burn next year out of 5,000 houses randomly chosen from all over America, this situation is risky. There are 5,001 possible outcomes (no loss is the additional outcome). If, however, we know something about these houses relating to the frequency or severity of loss—for example, they were all family homes less than five years old, in good condition, and located no more than five miles from a fire station—we might narrow the range of our prediction. That is, the degree of risk has been reduced by the new information. If we know, based on past statistics, about 1 percent of an average group of homes with similar characteristics burned, we could make an even more accurate prediction. The added information has reduced the degree of risk again. Because insurance companies keep accurate statistics on losses that have occurred, they are better able to predict the number and total dollar amount of losses that will occur. Thus, one result of an insurance system's operations is increased accuracy in the prediction of losses—in other words, insurance reduces risk.

Although the variability concept of risk emphasizes the statistical aspects of risk and insurance, the uncertainty concept emphasizes the behavioral aspect of people exposed to risk. The definition of risk as uncertainty concerning loss is useful because it helps to explain why people purchase insurance. If Horace Mann does not purchase insurance, he may be uncertain about whether he will have to pay for fire losses to his home. He is uncertain because he does not know in advance if his house will burn or, if a fire occurred, how severe the damage would be. Once he has purchased fire insurance, it becomes certain that he will not have to pay for any fire losses to his home, because the insurance company will pay for such losses. In this case, the homeowner has transferred his uncertainty, or risk, to the insurance company.

Although insureds are no longer uncertain after they transfer their risk to the insurance company, neither is the insurance company uncertain about what losses, or claims for payment, it will experience. Because the insurance company combines the exposures of many homeowners, it can predict the total dollar amount of losses accurately. Because it can predict losses accurately, the insurance company has reduced the uncertainty about the number and dollar amount of losses that will occur. It has reduced the risk. Shortly we will discuss the law of large numbers, which allows an insurance system to reduce risk.

Pure, Speculative, and Operational Risk

Pure risk

It does or it doesn't (burn)

Pure risk refers to possibilities that can result only in either loss or no change. Nothing good can come from an exposure to pure risk. A factory's exposure to loss by fire is an example of a pure risk. A factory either burns or it does not burn. There is no gain potential from this possibility. Instead of the term *pure risk*, the term **operational risk** appears in banking literature. New international banking rules known as the New Basel Capital Accord, or Basel II, establish capital requirements for operational risk. That is, the greater a bank's exposure to operational risk, the more capital it must have to meet the Basel II solvency requirements. Banking examples of operational risk include losses related to fraud, computer crashes, natural disasters, and workplace safety.

Operational risk

workplace

Speculative risk

Speculative risk refers to those exposures to price change that may result in either gain or loss. Most investments, including those in the stock market, are classified as speculative risks. Other speculative risks result from the potential gains or losses associated with interest rate changes, price movements of foreign currencies, and price movements of agricultural and other commodities. Most speculative loss exposures are not subject to insurance. However, some speculative loss exposures may be financed using derivative securities and some modern financial techniques described in Chapter 17, "Advanced Topics in Risk Management."

Generally, insurance contracts cover only pure risks. However, some risk managers, and critics of risk managers, have questioned whether making the distinction between pure and speculative risk is appropriate. They suggest the function of the risk manager is to protect an organization from loss whether the source of the loss is a tornado (pure risk) or an unexpected devaluation of a foreign currency (speculative risk). When risk managers develop a plan to treat pure and speculative risks in a comprehensive plan while also considering the cost of capital implications of their risk management strategy, they call the process *enterprise risk management*. Chapter 17 describes enterprise risk management programs.

Risk Management

Risk management

Chapter 3 provides the details of the risk management process, so we will present only a limited definition of risk management here. **Risk management** is the logical process used by businesses and individuals to deal with their exposures to loss. It is a strategy of preloss planning for postloss resources. Risk management describes an ongoing process for dealing with the possibility of loss.

THE MATHEMATICAL BASIS FOR INSURANCE

Law of large numbers

An insurance system can operate successfully only when it can predict losses accurately. Predicting losses accurately reduces risk. Insurance pools reduce risk by applying a mathematical principle called the **law of large numbers**. Simply put, the law states that the greater the number of observations of an event based on chance, the more likely the actual result will approximate the expected result. For example, if a die were rolled six times, we would expect each face to appear once because each of the six sides has an equal chance of appearing on any given throw. The law of large numbers leads to the conclusion that the more often the die is rolled, the more closely the one-sixth probability of each face appearing will be realized.

Suppose an insurance pool expected 1 percent of its members to experience a loss, based not on reasoning as in the die example, but on historical records of losses. The law of large numbers states that the greater the number of exposures in the pool, the more likely the 1 percent loss figure will be realized. By applying the law of large numbers, the insurance company can predict accurately the dollar amount of losses that it will experience in a given period. The relative accuracy of the company's predictions increases as the number of exposures in the insurance pool increases. We can state this same idea with more mathematical rigor by noting that when the exposures in the insurance pool are independent and have the same loss potential, the riskiness of the pool, measured by the standard deviation divided by the average loss, tends toward zero as the number of exposures tends toward infinity. This calculation is called the **coefficient of variation**.

Coefficient of variation

If insurers can predict losses accurately, then the costs can be budgeted and shared in advance if the appropriate premium is charged. The substitution of a small certain premium in place of a large uncertain loss motivates many consumers and businesses to purchase insurance. We must emphasize that the law of large numbers only allows accurate predictions of broad group results. It does not allow us to predict accurately what will happen to a particular exposure (George's house or Sue's life) in the group.

TABLE I–I Barn Insurance Pool

Number of barns insured = 1,000
Value of each barn = $80,000
Total value of property in insurance pool = $80,000,000
Predicted losses at the rate of 1% of total value = $800,000
Predicted loss per farmer = $800,000/1,000 = $800
Loss per $100 of property value = $800,000/800,000 = $1

A MATHEMATICAL EXAMPLE OF AN INSURANCE SYSTEM'S OPERATIONS

Assume that 1,000 Ohio farmers wish to join together to form an insurance pool to protect themselves against the loss of their barns by fire. They learn that in the past, fire losses caused damage each year equal to 1 percent of the value of similar barns. That is, some barns were destroyed by fire, while others were damaged only partially. Taken together, the fraction (dollars of fire damage divided by the dollar value of exposed property) equaled the 1 percent figure. If each farmer has a barn worth $80,000, then 1,000 such barns will have a value of $80,000,000 (1,000 × $80,000). Using the 1 percent damage prediction, the expected losses for the pool will be $800,000 (0.01 × $80,000,000). If we assume that the pool has no operating expenses, that the actual losses equal the expected losses, and that no investment income is earned on premiums paid in advance, then the cost of membership in the pool is $800 per farmer. This premium can be calculated by dividing the $800,000 in losses by the 1,000 insured farmers in the insurance pool. (See Table 1–1 for a review of these numbers.)

Because it is unlikely each farmer's barn will be worth exactly $80,000, we can compute the cost of insurance based on each $100 of value. Each $100 of insurance should cost $1 ($800,000/800,000, or dollar value of losses per hundreds of dollars of exposures). Thus, a farmer with a $45,000 barn would pay $450 for a one-year membership in the pool (450 × $1, or hundreds of dollars of value times premium cost per $100). A farmer with a $65,000 barn would pay $650.

BUILDING BLOCKS OF AN INSURANCE PREMIUM

Four Basic Components

The assumptions we just made about expenses, investment earnings, and variation in loss experience are unrealistic. Insurers must hire people to manage the firm and acquire business. Assume that these administrative and acquisition expenses add 30 percent to the $1 insurance rate, making the rate $1.30 for each $100 of barn covered. Furthermore, although the pool expects losses equal to 1 percent of value, it is prudent to provide for losses greater than those predicted. Therefore, insurers must create a reserve for unexpected losses. Assume that this reserve adds another 10 percent to the $1 loss cost, making the premium $1.40 per $100 of barn value. Now assume that that the insureds pay premiums on January 1, and on average, the insurer pays claims on July 1; in that circumstance, an insurer earns one half-year's interest on premium deposits. At a 6 percent annual rate, 3 percent would be earned in one half-year, and these investment earnings reduce the premium to $1.37. Life insurance companies explicitly recognize the interest that they expect to earn when they calculate their rates. Property insurance companies indirectly allow for interest earnings when pricing their insurance,

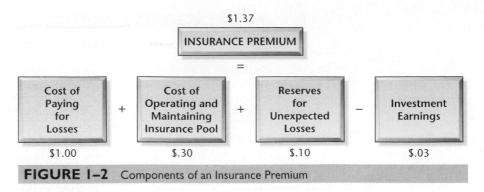

FIGURE 1–2   Components of an Insurance Premium

as we discuss in the next section. In summary, the four building blocks of an insurance premium are the following:

1. The estimated cost of the losses
2. The expenses of operating and maintaining the insurance pool
3. An allowance for unexpected losses, or the risk factor for the insurance pool
4. Earnings on investment   *interest*

Figure 1–2 summarizes this information.

Cash Flow Underwriting and the Underwriting Cycle

Is it possible for an insurance pool to pay $1.06 in claims for every $1 that it collects in premiums and still be profitable? The answer is yes, if investment earnings more than offset the cost of paying claims. In practice, the anticipation of investment earnings leads some companies intentionally to price their insurance below the level of expected losses for competitive reasons. Other insurers expect to make a profit on both their insurance and investment functions, but even these insurers allow expected investment income to modify their insurance rates.

Cash flow
underwriting

Cash flow underwriting describes the practice of trying to attract new business by pricing insurance "at a loss." The theory underlying cash flow underwriting is that investment income can more than offset underwriting losses. Although relatively high investment returns allow success with this strategy in some years, intense competition and lower available investment returns could cause insurers to experience net losses in other years. To see the effect of cash flow underwriting on industry operating results, we must define some important property insurance vocabulary.

Written premiums

Earned premiums

Written premiums are the total premiums collected by an insurer during a specific period such as a year. **Earned premiums** are the percentage of an advance premium payment belonging to the insurance company. The insurer may not earn some of the written premiums until many months after it receives the premium payment. For example, if an insured pays a year's insurance premium on January 1, by March 1 the insurer has earned only two months' worth of premiums. The difference between the written and earned premiums equals the **unearned premiums**. The premiums for March through December would be unearned in our example.

Unearned
premiums

Loss ratio

The **loss ratio** is the incurred losses (those losses reported to the insurer and adjustment expenses on these losses) divided by earned premiums. Simply put, the loss ratio is the percentage of the earned premium paid for losses and loss adjustment expenses. The **expense ratio** is the total expenses (except loss adjustment expenses) divided by written premiums. The **combined ratio** is the sum of the loss and expense ratios. It summarizes, in one number, the underwriting experience of

Expense ratio

Combined ratio

TABLE 1–2   Financial Results for the U.S. Property Insurance Industry ($ Billions)

	2000	2001	2002	2003	2004
Written Premium	299.7	323.5	369.7	404.4	423.3
Earned Premium	294.0	311.5	348.5	386.3	412.6
Losses Incurred[a]	201.0	234.5	238.8	238.7	246.4
Loss Adjustment Expense	37.8	40.9	44.8	50.0	53.2
Other Underwriting Expense	82.6	86.2	93.8	100.7	106.4
Policyholder Dividends	3.9	2.4	1.9	1.9	1.6
Underwriting Gain (Loss)	(31.2)	(52.6)	(30.8)	(4.9)	5.0
Investment Income	40.7	37.7	37.2	38.6	39.6
Operating Income (Loss)	9.9	(13.8)	5.6	33.8	44.1
Realized Capital Gains	16.2	6.6	(1.2)	6.6	9.3
Federal Income Tax	5.5	(0.2)	1.3	10.3	14.7
Net Income After Tax	20.5	(6.9)	3.0	30.0	38.7
Loss Ratio[b]	81.2%	88.4%	81.4%	74.7%	72.6%
Expense Ratio	27.6%	26.7%	25.4%	24.9%	25.1%
Combined Ratio	110.1%	115.9%	106.7%	99.6%	97.7%

[a]*Incurred losses include sums already paid and estimates of amounts to be paid.*
[b]*The loss ratio includes adjustment expenses.*
SOURCES: Insurance Services Office, *Best's Review*, Insurance Information Institute, *Business Insurance* and author's calculations. Figures may not balance due to rounding or omission of miscellaneous items.

the company or the industry.[4] If the ratio is below 100, the company's underwriting experience was profitable. If the ratio is more than 100, then the insurance underwriting was unprofitable.

The data in Table 1–2 presents the pattern of cash flow of the U.S. property insurance industry and the underwriting cycle.

Despite a combined ratio exceeding or only barely below 100 percent for all five years, the property insurance industry's after-tax net income was positive (that is, the industry earned a profit) each year except 2001. The profit came about because investment earnings exceeded underwriting losses. If companies expect their investment performance to be strong enough to overcome underwriting losses, they might quote lower prices for insurance and use "liberal" underwriting; industry commentators call this a **soft market**.

Soft market

Sometimes an unprofitable underwriting year coincides with an unprofitable investment year, as happened in 2001. The terrorist attacks on September 11, 2001, caused the most insured damage in history, and those losses also had a negative impact on an already weak investment market. When bad investment returns combine with unprofitable underwriting, capital usually leaves the insurance industry, leading to a **hard market**. In a hard insurance market, insurance companies raise their prices and are more "conservative" in their underwriting. Conservative underwriting means insurers are very careful and often do not offer coverage to the most risky exposures. For their good exposures, insurers may offer less coverage for a given premium or require a higher premium for continuing the same levels of coverage.

Hard market

Underwriting cycle

Readers can see the pattern of the **underwriting cycle** of the property insurance industry illustrated in the data in Table 1-2. The underwriting cycle involves a soft market leading to reduced industry profitability, which in turn leads to a hard market and

---

[4] Readers interested in the topic of evaluating insurance company operating results are directed to this article: "Measuring Underwriting Profitability of the Non-Life Insurance Industry," published by the Swiss Re, as Sigma No. 3/2006, at their Web site (*http://www.swissre.com/*).

increased profitability. The increased profitability means more capital is available in the industry and competition becomes more intense, which in turn leads back to a soft market and the cycle repeats itself.

THE BENEFITS AND COSTS TO SOCIETY OF INSURANCE SYSTEMS

Costs

What is the cost to society of operating an insurance system? Would it be represented by the $1.37 of premiums in our example? No, because $1 of the $1.37 premium represents the cost of losses. Presumably, these losses would occur even if no insurance system existed. The cost to society of operating an insurance system includes the cost of the resources that the system uses—the labor, the land, and the capital—but it does not include the cost of the losses. One exception is the losses that occur because of fraudulent attempts to collect insurance proceeds—those costs are a proper cost attributable to an insurance system. Experts estimate that the cost of property insurance fraud exceeds $40 billion annually, but of course, the actual number is unknown. Experts estimate that health insurance fraud losses are greater than property insurance frauds.[5] Some losses, however, are less frequent or less severe because the possibility of lower insurance premiums encourages loss prevention or loss reduction activities. For example, because of discounts insureds receive for employing security guards, or installing fire sprinklers and smoke detectors, society loses less of its resources because of fire or theft losses.

Benefits

What advantages does society gain from an insurance system's operation? How do these benefits compare with the resources used? One of the greatest benefits with which an insurance system rewards society is stability in families. Insurance prevents a family from experiencing the great hardships caused by unexpected losses of property or the premature death of the main income provider. Insurance allows a family to continue its activities in a much more normal fashion after a loss than would be the case if no insurance existed.

Insurance is also very useful to businesses. Insurance aids the planning process because the planner knows a property loss will not mean financial ruin, and the future of a business cannot be destroyed by a fire or the death of a key person.

Insurance aids credit transactions as well, because creditors are more willing to lend money if the debtor's death does not make collection of the loan difficult or impossible. Likewise, lenders are more willing to make property or real estate loans if they know a disaster cannot destroy the financial security behind their loan.

An economist would give an insurance system high marks because it functions as an antimonopoly device. That is, if no insurance system were available, only the largest businesses could sustain losses and remain in operation. Without insurance, there would be a tendency toward monopoly in many industries. For example, one of the nation's largest chains of grocery stores could probably lose one of its stores in a fire and remain in business, whereas smaller store chains could not sustain uninsured losses as well, and a mom-and-pop grocery would probably have to close permanently if an uninsured fire destroyed its only store. Insurance allows smaller operators in an industry to pool their exposure to loss and thus remain competitive.

---

[5] The Web site (*http://www.insurancefraud.org/*) provides details about insurance fraud, including a "Hall of Shame."

Financiers recognize that insurance availability tends to lower a firm's cost of capital because both creditors and investors would charge much more for the use of their money if it were subjected to the risks associated with natural disasters in addition to normal business risks. In addition, without insurance, firms would have to hold more money in relatively nonproductive near-cash reserves to protect themselves against a rainy day.

Insurance companies, and the organizations they support, contribute directly to society's welfare in many ways relating to loss prevention and medical research. Among the better-known company-sponsored loss prevention organizations are the National Safety Council (*http://www.nsc.org/*), Underwriters' Laboratories, Inc. (*http://www.ul.com/*), and the Insurance Institute for Highway Safety (*http://www.hwysafety.org/*). Many medical schools and other medical research facilities receive direct support for their work from life insurance companies.

Insurance companies are very important financial intermediaries. Annually, life insurance companies collect billions of dollars in people's savings and reinvest these amounts in the economy. Property insurers also maintain billions of dollars in their reserve accounts that are invested in our private-enterprise economy. Insurers provide a useful service to savers by evaluating and selecting sound investments, and they provide a service to businesses and governmental units at the local, state, and federal levels. In general, business and government borrowers do not find it practical to use the small savings streams of individuals, but they can effectively use the river of funds made available by insurance companies. In one recent year, insurance companies held an estimated $6 trillion in assets. Financial assets held by insurers include bonds (and other credit market securities), equity securities, cash, policyholder loans (life insurance companies), and mortgages. Financial services data may be found at the Insurance Information Institute Web site (*http://www.financialservicesfacts.org/financial/*).

In conclusion, although it costs society some of its scarce resources to operate an insurance system, and although some losses are caused in an attempt to collect insurance, the benefits that society receives from insurance operations far outweigh the costs.

ARSON: WHO REALLY PAYS FOR INSURED LOSSES

Earlier we stated that insurance functions to redistribute the cost of losses from the unfortunate few who experience them to all the members of the insurance pool who have paid premiums in advance. An understanding of this concept should dispel the mistaken but commonly held view that the insurance company uses its money to pay insured losses. True, the insurance company writes the check the insured receives, but it is usually the insureds' rather than the insurer's money being distributed. To make the point that the cost of insurance fraud is spread to all insureds along with the cost of legitimate claims, we examine the crime of arson for profit.

Arson   **Arson** for profit is defined as the deliberate, malicious burning of a building or other property to collect insurance proceeds. The actual amount of property damage done by arsonists is not known; however, experts recently estimated that arson, including automobile arson, caused property losses of more than $1 billion. (To find current data on this subject, use an Internet search engine with the keywords "insurance fraud," "arson statistics," or "arson for profit.")

It is estimated that a large percentage of all arson fires (though not all) involve insurance fraud. Other causes of arson include insanity (pyromania), covering up other crimes (murder and theft), juvenile delinquency, and political terrorism. (The National Fire Protection Association Web site, (*http://www.nfpa.org/*), provides a considerable amount of information about fires, including arson fires.)

Arson with the intent to commit insurance fraud may take many forms. In simple cases, unprofitable businesses such as restaurants and hotels often are suspected of being "sold back to the insurance company" by being deliberately burned. Sometimes elaborate schemes are involved. For example, some arson investigations have revealed a pattern of selling and reselling the same property between conspirators, each sale at a higher price, with the final, highly inflated "market" value being insured. Such a procedure produces a large profit for the conspirators when ultimately the building is deliberately burned and the insurance claim honored.

So insurance companies write hundreds of millions of dollars of checks each year to arsonists. It is unfortunate, as noted, that insurers pay these claims because insurers use the premiums of honest American homeowners and business owners to pay for arson losses.

When insurers distribute fire losses, including arson-caused losses, over all the members of an insurance pool by means of an insurance premium, each member contributes a share of each loss. This process was illustrated in Figure 1–1 and Table 1–1. The payment to the arsonist from the honest homeowner may be indirect because it travels through an insurance company first. Nevertheless, the insurer is using the homeowner's premium to pay the arsonist. It should be understood clearly that it is the insurance-buying public rather than insurers who bear the burden of insurance fraud. Likewise, not only are the costs of fraudulent insurance claims borne by insurance consumers, but so are the high-liability claims (the $1 million-and-larger injury lawsuits we often read or hear about). Thus, each insurance consumer has a clear self-interest in reducing insurance fraud and in promoting fair and practical loss settlements.

SUMMARY

Insurance is a financial arrangement for redistributing the costs of unexpected losses requiring a legal contract whereby an insurer agrees to compensate an insured for losses. A loss is an undesired, unplanned reduction of economic value. A chance of loss represents the probability of a loss. It is a fraction whose numerator represents the number of losses and whose denominator represents the number of exposures to loss.

A peril is the cause of a loss. Hazards are conditions that serve to increase the frequency or severity of perils. Moral hazards are the result of people trying to defraud the insurer, whereas morale hazards represent an attitude of indifference to loss created by the purchase of insurance. Direct losses refer to the loss of property. Indirect losses result from the loss of use of property.

Risk can be defined as the variability in possible outcomes of an event based on chance or uncertainty concerning loss. The degree of risk refers to the accuracy with which an event based on chance can be predicted. Pure risk, or operational risk, results when only a loss or an unchanged state occurs as the result of an event based on chance. If one may gain as a result of chance, the situation is described as a speculative risk.

The law of large numbers allows insurers to predict losses accurately. This mathematical rule states that the greater the number of observations of an event based on chance, the more likely the actual result will approximate the expected result.

The components of an insurance premium are the cost of losses, the expenses of operating the insurance company, the reserves needed for unexpected losses, and the investment earnings available when premiums are paid in advance. Insurance provides many benefits to society: stability in families and businesses, easier completion of lending arrangements, removal of one advantage of monopolies or large-scale businesses over small-scale operations, provision of capital to businesses and individuals, and active support of loss prevention research. With respect to the crime of arson for profit and other insurance frauds, it is the honest, premium-paying insured, not the insurer, who pays for the losses.

REVIEW TERMS

- Arson
- Cash flow underwriting
- Chance of loss
- Coefficient of variation
- Combined ratio
- Direct losses
- Expense ratio
- Exposure to loss
- Hard market
- Hazards
- Indirect losses

- Insurance
- Insurance fraud
- Insured
- Insurer
- Law of large numbers
- Loss
- Loss ratio
- Mathematically fair price
- Moral hazard
- Morale hazard
- Operational risk

- Peril
- Policy
- Premium
- Proximate cause
- Pure risk
- Risk
- Risk averse
- Risk management
- Soft market
- Speculative risk

REVIEW

1. The term *insurance* can be defined in both financial and legal terms. How do these definitions differ?
2. Describe the difference between direct and indirect losses. Give examples of each.
3. What is the difference between a hazard and a peril? Give examples of each.
4. Why is it the chance of loss, and not the loss itself, that creates the need for insurance?
5. What are the two definitions of risk discussed in this chapter? Are they actually different from one another?
6. How does insurance redistribute the costs of losses?
7. What is the difference between insurable losses and depreciation expenses?
8. How does a moral hazard differ from a morale hazard? Give examples of each.
9. Explain the term *proximate cause*.
10. Explain the difference between pure and speculative risk.
11. Define the law of large numbers. What are its implications for an insurance system?
12. List the four building blocks of an insurance premium. Why are investment earnings included in the calculations?
13. In what ways do insurance systems benefit society?
14. What are the major costs of insurance systems?
15. Why are the costs of losses not included in society's costs for operating an insurance system?
16. What is cash flow underwriting?

OBJECTIVE QUESTIONS

1. An insurable loss is:
   a. An event that has not been predicted
   b. An exposure that cannot be easily measured before the event has occurred
   c. An unexpected reduction of economic value
   d. Being without something one has previously possessed
2. Choose the true statement.
   a. Risk-averse people are willing to pay more than the mathematically fair price to transfer risk.
   b. Risk seekers are willing to pay more than the mathematically fair price to transfer risk.
   c. Risk-neutral people are willing to pay more than the mathematically fair price to transfer risk.
   d. Risk-averse people will not pay more than the mathematically fair price to transfer risk.
3. The definition of peril is:
   a. An event or condition that increases the chance of loss
   b. The uncertainty concerning loss
   c. A measure of the accuracy with which a loss can be predicted
   d. The actual cause of the loss
4. A moral hazard is:
   a. A loss of faith in the insurance company because of a denial of claims
   b. Illustrated by the loss of a wallet to a thief
   c. The increase of loss caused by attempts to defraud the insurer
   d. The potential for the insurance company to increase premiums after a loss

5. "A financial arrangement that redistributes the costs of unexpected losses" is the definition of:
   a. Derivative security
   b. Financial guarantee fund
   c. Mutual fund
   d. Insurance
6. A person storing 100 pounds of gunpowder in the basement so that he can load his own shotgun shells is an example of:
   a. A hazard
   b. A peril
   c. A loss
   d. Proximate cause
7. A pure risk is one where:
   a. The result can be only either a loss or no change.
   b. The result can be a gain, a loss, or no change.
   c. The result can be only either a gain or no change.
   d. The result cannot be predicted.
8. The expense ratio is defined as:
   a. Insured expenses divided by insured losses
   b. Total expenses divided by written premiums
   c. Combined expenses and losses divided by net income
   d. Net income divided by total expenses

DISCUSSION QUESTIONS

1. Provide some important examples of how a privately operated insurance system contributes to a market-based economy.
2. Develop a sequence of events in which the proximate cause of the loss is separated from the ultimate damage by at least five distinct events.
3. Explain why insurance fraud increases the cost of insurance for all policyholders.

INTERNET RESEARCH ASSIGNMENT

1. Update Table 1-2 with the most recent data available. Start your search at the site (*http://www.iii.org/*).
2. What are the most recent statistics on arson fires in the United States? Start your search at the site (*http://www. usfa.fema.gov/statistics/arson/*).

CHAPTER 2

Defining the Insurable Event

After studying this chapter, you should be able to:

■ Describe the characteristics of an ideally insurable loss exposure

■ Discuss the problem catastrophic loss potential creates for property insurers

■ Explain subsidization in insurance and why the government promotes it in some instances

■ Define the term *adverse selection*

■ Identify the main branches of the private insurance market

■ Describe the peril of negligence and understand why it is insurable

This chapter continues to take on more importance with every revision of the textbook. Since the previous revision, the bad hurricane season of 2004, followed by hurricanes Katrina, Rita, and Wilma in 2005, has again focused the nation's attention on the capacity of the private insurance industry to finance natural catastrophes. Consider this quotation from a U.S. Government Accountability Office (GAO) document:

> Although insurers and state governments have taken steps to enhance the industry's capacity to address natural catastrophe risk, a major event or series of events surpassing the over $20 billion in losses in Florida resulting from the 2004 hurricane season could severely disrupt insurance markets and impose substantial recovery costs on governments, businesses, and individuals.[1]

Unfortunately, the 2005 hurricane season produced far greater damage than the 2004 season. Thus, the question of how best to finance the reconstruction costs resulting from natural catastrophes requires continuing analysis and evaluation. This chapter provides a framework to understand the issues raised by this question. Several important insurance principles are introduced by focusing on the question "What is an insurable event?" Interestingly, this question is open for discussion; more interestingly, the answer is subject to change.

A sound insurance system requires *accurate* prediction of losses and *adequate* advance funding. By this strict definition of insurance, the peril of flood is not a good subject for *private* insurance because predictions are not very accurate; therefore, collecting an affordable, fair, and adequate advance premium is a problem. The emphasis on *accurate* and *adequate* means that these words are subject to discussion. The emphasis on *private* is to alert readers to the fact that in the United States, flood insurance is available, but only because the government participates in the market.

---

[1] GAO, "Catastrophe Risk: U.S. and European Approaches to Insure Natural Catastrophe and Terrorism Risks," (GAO-05-199; February 2005, p. 4.)

This chapter presents some of the most important insurance principles to define an insurable event. It begins by describing the elements of an ideally insurable exposure. Next, we will explore the question of why catastrophes generally are not insurable, at least not in the private insurance market. At this point, we describe terrorism insurance and some of the insurance problems arising out of the September 11, 2001, terrorist attacks. The discussion of risk classification brings the words *adverse selection* and *subsidization* to the reader's attention, while making the point that the costs of insurable events must be shared fairly. We follow by describing the traditional branches of the U.S. insurance industry because doing so provides a very practical answer to the question "What events are insurable?" The chapter ends with a discussion of legal liability insurance.

This discussion is presented early in the text for two reasons. First, the peril of legal liability probably is not as well known to most readers as the perils of fire or flood. Second, the concept of legal liability is required to understand material presented throughout the book, including the subjects of homeowners, automobile, and professional liability insurance, as well as the topic of Chapter 3, "Risk Management."

IDEALLY INSURABLE LOSS EXPOSURES

What kinds of loss exposures are ideal for insurance coverage? The criteria are as follows:

1. A large group of similar items exposed to the same peril(s)
2. Accidental losses beyond the insured's control[2]
3. Definite losses capable of causing economic hardship
4. Extremely low probability of a catastrophic loss to the insurance pool[3]

Although these criteria represent the ideal, in practice insurance companies provide coverage under less-than-ideal conditions. However, private insurance ventures that depart too far from the ideal are likely to fail. Government, or social, insurance programs, including flood, terrorism, and unemployment insurance, depart from these norms.

A Large Group of Similar Items Exposed to the Same Peril(s)

An insurance pool needs a substantial number of individual units to obtain predictive accuracy, which is the statistical benefit of the law of large numbers. A successful insurance system must reduce risk by predicting losses within an acceptable range. The insurer must predict both the mean frequency and the mean severity of losses accurately.

Large number

Predictive accuracy can be attained only when an insurance pool has a **large number** of insured exposures. Although the definition of a large number of exposures depends on several factors, a workable definition is a number of exposures that is large enough to allow for predictive accuracy. The critical test is whether the insurance pool is large enough to estimate results with sufficient accuracy to calculate a sound insurance premium.

---

[2] From the insured's standpoint, losses must be accidental. For example, if an insured deliberately took two different types of medicine that were incompatible with each other, the unintended fatal results would be accidental from the insured's standpoint. The term *accident* is difficult to define precisely, but unintended results are implied.

[3] Some commentators also specify an economically feasible premium, one that a sufficient number of average insureds can afford. An affordable premium allows the law of large numbers to operate. If premiums are high because the insurer cannot predict the risk with tolerable accuracy, only those most exposed to loss will purchase coverage. We discuss this problem later in this chapter.

The items in an insurance pool (known as the exposure units) need to be similar so the insurer can calculate a fair premium. The wind damage done to brick homes usually will be less than that suffered by mobile homes. It would be unfair to combine them in the same insurance pool and charge each insured the same premium rate based on the combined losses of the pool. If such an attempt were made, the rate developed would cause the owners of brick homes (less susceptible to loss) to pay too high a premium and the owners of mobile homes (more susceptible to loss) to pay too low a premium. Likewise, the perils faced by the exposures in the insurance pool should be the same. For instance, assume that some buildings in an insurance pool were especially susceptible to wind damage because they were located in a hurricane-prone area, while other buildings in the pool were not exposed to hurricanes. Charging all insureds in this pool the same rate would be unfair. The structures not exposed to hurricanes would be paying too high a premium. Unfair premiums cannot continue in a competitive insurance market, as we demonstrate in a later section of this chapter when we describe *subsidization*.

Accidental Losses Beyond the Insured's Control

Nonaccidental or expected reductions of economic value, such as wear and tear, are not insurable events because the insurance premium would have to include the costs of the losses plus the costs of operating the insurance pool. The result would be an uneconomical premium, higher than the original expenses.

Loss-causing events under the insured's control generally are not insurable either. If the insured could first cause a loss and then collect for the damage, the resulting claims would be far greater than if these self-inflicted losses were excluded. If self-inflicted losses were insurable, the premiums needed to fund the payments would be more than honest people would pay. In practice, insurance fraud is against public policy and also is excluded by the wording of insurance contracts. Thus, an insurance company will not pay for an insured's intentionally caused losses such as arson or theft, if discovered.

Accidental losses   Nonfraudulent losses arising from an insured's negligence are insurable. This is the case when, for example, an insured's bad driving causes an accident. A curious example of the application of the principle of **accidental losses** occurs with life insurance, where insurers consider suicide within a year or two of a policy's purchase an intentional loss. Insurers do not pay for these types of losses. If a suicide occurs after the first year or two, however, the loss is considered accidental, the result of mental illness.

Health and disability insurers also need to control self-defined losses, especially those attributed to malingering after an insured's illness or accident. Many health and disability policies cause each insured to bear a portion of the covered expenses to reduce the tendency to remain hospitalized unnecessarily. Likewise, policies replacing income while an insured is disabled replace only a percentage of the lost income, such as 66 percent, to provide an incentive to return to work. When losses produce no regret for the insured, there is strong evidence that claims go up.

Definite Losses Capable of Causing Economic Hardship

Insurable events must be definite and verifiable. Otherwise, insurer and insured would frequently argue about whether a loss has occurred. Thus, an individual can be insured against the loss of a house as the result of a fire but not as the result of its being haunted. More realistically, health insurers often limit payments for mental illness, in part because of the difficulty in determining the beginning, presence, or absence of the covered condition in many cases.

Termite damage usually is not insured by property insurance contracts because determining the time when the loss occurred and the extent of damage often is difficult. Termite damage, being gradual, also presents a morale hazard because homeowners with an infested residence might knowingly allow the damage to continue in anticipation of a large-scale replacement of an old structure with a new one. Termite exterminators often guarantee their work and agree to pay for subsequent damage if the treatment fails. However, they usually do so only after a thorough inspection and chemical treatment. Moreover, their guarantee is usually contingent on follow-up inspections. The whole transaction is more in the nature of a service contract or a warranty, neither of which is insurance in the legal sense, although some similarities among them exist.

The damage caused by insurable events also must be measurable in economic terms. The loss of a loved pet can cause a family much grief, but such discomfort cannot be measured economically. Thus, insurers exclude the loss of pets in homeowners insurance contracts. In contrast, the loss of racehorses or valuable livestock represents an insurable exposure because the damage can be measured economically. In fact, insurance companies write a significant amount of livestock insurance in the United States.[4]

Large-loss principle

Insurance operates most successfully when the potential damage caused by a peril is severe enough to cause economic hardship. Insuring inexpensive items, especially if losses are frequent, would result in premium charges equal to or greater than the potential damage, which makes such insurance unattractive. As a rule, insurance should be purchased only when losses are large and uncertain. This rule is known as the **large-loss principle**.

Low Probability of Catastrophic Loss

Catastrophic loss exposure

Loss exposures with catastrophic potential are not insurable events. Because we define a **catastrophic loss exposure** as a potential loss that is unpredictable and capable of producing an extraordinarily large amount of damage relative to the assets held in the insurance pool, the definition is open to interpretation. That is, despite the common convention of identifying any extraordinarily large loss as catastrophic, defining catastrophic loss from an insurance standpoint is more difficult because it depends on how "extraordinarily large" is defined.[5] For example, before Hurricane Andrew, many insurance companies felt that damage from one hurricane was not likely to be catastrophic because they did not expect the amount of damage to be great relative to the amount of assets in the insurance pool. Afterwards, many insurers changed their opinion and tried to withdraw this coverage from the market.

Insured catastrophes would occur if a single event, or a related series of events, could affect a large percentage of the loss exposure units in the insurance pool. That is, catastrophic loss potential exists when insured losses are not independent, or when a loss to one exposure unit implies a loss to many other exposure units.

Catastrophic losses from natural disasters have two general characteristics: (1) they are limited in geographic impact, and (2) they are not accurately predictable. Thus, earthquakes, volcanoes, and floods have catastrophic loss potential. Tornadoes, however, do not have this potential, even though they can create hundreds of millions

---

[4] This Web site contains some interesting information on this topic: (*http://www.agribizexpress.com/livestock.html/*).

[5] The GAO's definition of the term *catastrophe* is also open-ended: "Term used for statistical recording purposes to refer to a single incident or a series of closely related incidents causing severe insured property losses totaling more than a given amount." (GAO-05-199, cited in footnote 1, p. 69.)

of dollars of damage. There are several reasons for this. First, the geographic incidence of tornadoes is not limited because there is no state in the continental United States that has not experienced a tornado. Therefore, insured tornado damage can be spread across all insured property in the United States. Second, because windstorms (including tornadoes) occur frequently, the damage they cause can be predicted with reasonable accuracy. By contrast, earthquakes and volcanic eruptions are not reliably predictable. These events do not occur frequently (for which we can be grateful) and generally are limited to specific areas of the United States. Finally, compared to flood or earthquake losses, which can destroy entire cities or coastlines, tornadoes generally have a much more limited impact.

THE IMPACT OF RECENT CATASTROPHIC LOSSES[6]

To demonstrate that the answer to the question "What is an insurable event?" is subject to change, consider the insurance industry's reaction to the severe damage associated with hurricanes. One hurricane, Andrew, caused about $16 billion in insured losses (expressed in 1992 dollars, which would equal more than $20 billion today). Experts estimate the sum of the damage caused by the four hurricanes that hit Florida in 2004 to be more than $22 billion, and they have estimated the damage from Hurricanes Katrina and Rita in 2005 to be as high as $60 billion.[7] (An Internet search using the hurricanes' names will produce current estimates.) In light of these hugely expensive disasters, insurers have reconsidered their exposure to wind damage inflicted by hurricanes, and several insurers withdrew entirely from areas with high hurricane exposure. Other insurers tried to reduce their exposure by limiting the number of new or renewal policies issued in these areas. These losses also caused insurers to reconsider their pricing and reserving for catastrophic losses.

Catastrophic Computer Modeling

Insurance companies now use computer modeling to estimate the financial consequences of potential natural disasters. The computer models allow insurance companies (and state regulators) to manage their financial exposures better. Using computer models that combine information about the amount of property insurance the insurer has written in a specific area with estimates of storm frequency and severity, the insurer can estimate the effects of hurricane damage on its financial statements. Catastrophic computer models allow insurers to assess the financial effects of an event that is likely to happen once every 20 years or of an event likely to happen only once in 100 years. With this information, a company might limit the number of policies written in a specific area or arrange for reinsurance if its losses exceed some specified amount.

---

[6] A review of worldwide catastrophic losses occurring in 2005 can be found in this article, "Natural Catastrophes and Man-made Disasters 2005" published as *Sigma No. 2/ 2006* and found at this Web site: (*http://www.swissre.com/*).
[7] The Insurance Information Institute's Web site made an initial estimate of the hurricane losses as follows: "As of October 1, 2005, insured loss estimates for Hurricane Katrina range from $14 billion (lower end of Eqe cat range) to $60 billion (upper end of RMS range). The latter figure includes up to $25 billion in privately insured flood losses (mostly commercial), excluding NFIP policies. The lower estimate contains no estimate of privately insured flood loss. Hurricane Rita estimates range from $2.5 billion to $7 billion." More background and current information on the damage done by Hurricanes Katrina and Rita can be found at this Web site maintained by the Congressional Budget Office: (*http://www.cbo.gov/publications/collections/hurricanes.cfm/*).

Catastrophic Insurance Programs[8]

If private insurers reduce their exposures in catastrophe-prone areas, property owners then must look to state or federal insurance pools for coverage. Several states have established "wind pools" or "beach plans" to accommodate homeowners who are unable to purchase insurance in the private market, while the federal government operates a flood insurance program.[9]

Beach and Windstorm Plans

The states of Florida, Louisiana, Mississippi, North Carolina, South Carolina, and Texas have authorized insurance pools to provide property insurance (including for fire and windstorm perils) covering personal and business property in areas where private insurance companies do not accept the exposures voluntarily. One effect of beach plan insurance programs is to redistribute the losses of insuring hurricane-prone property to all property owners in these states. An Internet search using "windstorm insurance pools (plans)" as a keyword will provide more information on these programs. Information about the Florida Hurricane Catastrophe Fund, including information on the insured damage caused by the hurricanes of 2004, can be found at their Web site (*http://www.sbafla.com/fhcf/index.asp/*).

National Flood Insurance Program

Floods are the most common and destructive natural disaster in the United States. Much of the United States is exposed to the peril of flood. Areas along the coast exposed to hurricane storm surge or runoff from hurricane-caused rain face the risk of flooding, as does land in flood plains near waterways. Standard private insurance property forms exclude the peril of flood damage, but the federal government makes flood insurance available through the National Flood Insurance Program (**NFIP**).[10] The NFIP is part of the Federal Emergency Management Agency (**FEMA**), which in turn is part of the Department of Homeland Security (**DHS**).[11]

NFIP

DHS

The NFIP has three main goals:[12]

- To provide property flood insurance to property owners who would benefit from such coverage
- To reduce taxpayer-funded disaster assistance by making flood insurance coverage available
- To reduce flood damage through flood plain management, including the enforcement of building standards

The NFIP allows about 95 private insurers to sell flood policies, collect premiums, and adjust losses. If premiums and investment income are inadequate to pay claims, the government reimburses the insurers for the difference. If the insurers make a profit on the business, the government is entitled to this amount, but insurers are entitled to an expense allowance, including commissions for agents, for producing and servicing this

---

[8] An interesting academic discussion of the proper role of government in providing catastrophe insurance is provided by J. David Cummins, "Should the Government Provide Insurance for Catastrophes?," *Federal Reserve Bank of St. Louis Review*, July/August 2006, pp. 337–379. Cummins uses the terms *mega-catastrophe*, *cataclysmic*, and *globally undiversifiable* to identify events of the worst possible impact.

[9] In the interest of brevity, details on the California earthquake insurance program are not included in this section. These details can be found at the following Web site: (*http://www.earthquakeauthority.com/*).

[10] Congress reauthorized the NFIP in 2004, in the *Flood Insurance Reform Act of 2004*.

[11] The following Web sites provided detailed information on these agencies: NFIP (*http://www.fema.gov/nfip/*), FEMA (*http://www.fema.gov/*), and DHS (*http://www.dhs.gov/dhspublic/*).

[12] DHS Web site: (*http://www.dhs.gov/dhspublic/*).

business. The insurers pay flood losses from flood insurance premiums because the program operates mostly on a cash-flow basis. If losses exceed premiums, the insurers can borrow the additional amount needed to pay claims from the U.S. Treasury, but these loans must be repaid with interest.

By October 2005, FEMA had received about 193,000 flood insurance claims related to Hurricanes Katrina and Rita. The NFIP estimated it would pay $15 billion to $25 billion because of these storms. In its 35-year history before 2005, the NIFP had paid a total of about $15 million in claims, primarily from premium income. Because of the extent of the damage, Congress enacted legislation in November 2005 to increase FEMA's borrowing authority to $18.5 billion through fiscal year 2008.

The flood insurance program is not actuarially sound by design because Congress authorized subsidized (inadequate) insurance rates to encourage participation in the program. Many public policy critics question why the federal government provides subsidized flood insurance. They question whether this coverage encourages people to live in flood-prone areas, encourages mortgage lenders to make unsound loans, and causes taxpayers in non-flood-prone areas to subsidize people living in these areas. These critics also question whether the anticipation of federal disaster relief also encourages the unintended consequence of rewarding occupants of high-risk areas with taxpayer subsidies. Other critics note that "repetitive loss properties," properties with two or more claims in a 10-year period, make up only 1 percent of the NFIP-insured properties but account for 25 to 30 percent of all claims losses.

The counterargument to some of these critics is that if the NFIP charged risk-based premiums, it might reduce participation in the program, creating a greater need for federal (taxpayer-paid) disaster relief. FEMA estimates that every $3 of flood insurance claim payments save about $1 in disaster assistance payments. Moreover, it also estimates that its flood plain management efforts save about $1 billion in flood damage each year.

WHEN ONLY THE PEOPLE MOST EXPOSED TO A PARTICULAR LOSS WANT COVERAGE, THIS LOSS IS NOT AN INSURABLE EVENT

An insurance system operates successfully when many people or businesses faced with similar exposures transfer their potential losses to a pool, paying a relatively small premium for the right to collect loss payments from the pool. Using the law of large numbers, the pool can predict losses accurately and charge a premium appropriate to the risk. The system succeeds if the premium is small relative to the potential loss. Because they are risk averse, most people are willing to pay a relatively small, certain price to avoid a relatively large, uncertain loss. People have a price, however, beyond which they will not pay to transfer a risk.

Following this logic, if earthquake insurance was cheap—for example, $1 for $20,000 of protection—it is likely many people would purchase it. As soon as the price is raised, some people who think an earthquake is an unlikely source of loss to them will not pay the new price and will drop out of the insurance pool. Evidence suggests most non-Californians probably would not pay more than a nominal sum for earthquake insurance, despite the New Madrid fault in Missouri. The first group to drop out of the pool, therefore, will be those exposures most favorably situated relative to the peril. Their exit will force the premium rates upward.

As we described in Chapter 1, "Fundamentals and Terminology," insurance companies calculate their rates based on a fraction (the estimated dollar value of losses divided by the dollar value of insured property). When the most favorably situated exposures leave the pool, the denominator of the fraction becomes smaller while the numerator stays mostly unchanged. This effect produces the higher premium. For example, assume that $1 million worth of losses are to be spread over $100 million worth of property value. The cost of such insurance would be $1 for each $100 of property value. If $25 million worth of property were to leave the pool and if the losses were to remain the same, the $1 million of losses must be spread over $75 million of property, and this produces a premium of $1.33 for each $100 of property value.

The 33 percent increase in rates caused by the favored group leaving the pool has an identical effect on the next most favored group, and its members will leave the pool because the premium rates now exceed their valuation of the protection. As each of the marginal members of the pool leaves, the premium rates are forced upward, and every time more members leave the pool, yet another group of members sees the insurance protection as a poor value. This process becomes a vicious circle of premium increases, and it stops only when the pool contains just the members who will pay a high price to transfer their risk. These people will do so only because they are very susceptible to the peril.

At this point, an insurance system will break down completely because instead of transferring the cost from the few who experience it to a large pool of insureds, the pool must attempt to make the transfer among only those likely to experience loss. When the cost of operating the insurance pool is added to the cost of the losses transferred, the premiums will be too great relative to the potential loss, even for those wanting to remain in the pool. Thus, an insurance system will fail when only the most exposed to loss want insurance protection.

TERRORISM INSURANCE

Many of the concepts presented thus far in the chapter come into focus by examining the insurance market's reaction to the September 11, 2001, terrorist attacks. Readers can find current information on the tragedy using a search engine with these keywords: "insurance costs of September 11, 2001, terrorist attacks." Readers also can find the complete report of the 9/11 Commission that investigated the incident and the government's response at this Web site: (*http://www.gpoaccess.gov/911/index.html/*).

Insured Loss Estimates from the September 11 Terrorist Attacks

Until the last claim is settled, the final cost of the September 11 attacks to insurers will not be known. The following categories of losses provide a sense of the scope of the insurance claims.

1. **Aviation liability** claims arose from deaths, injuries, and property damage suffered because of claimed negligence by airlines, airports, security services, and others in not providing adequate security.
2. **Aviation hull** claims arose from the loss to the aircraft involved in the attacks.
3. **Life insurance** claims arose from the about 3,000 people killed in the attacks. Insurers paid claims for both group and individual policies.
4. **Property insurance** claims arose from the destruction of the World Trade Center towers, other buildings, and other property, including automobiles.
5. **Workers' compensation** claims arose from the thousands of employees killed or injured while at work in the areas affected by the attacks. Survivors of deceased workers are entitled to benefits, and injured workers are compensated for lost earnings and medical expenses.

6. **Business interruption** claims arose from the lost profits and extra and continuing expenses of businesses that were forced to close or relocate or else were unable to operate in a normal manner after the attacks.
7. **Event cancellation** claims arose from businesses in New York City and elsewhere that did not proceed with scheduled events because of the attacks.

The September 11 attacks also produced billions of dollars in uninsured losses, including the cleanup costs in New York, the damage to the Pentagon, and the uninsured business interruption losses suffered by the tourism industry throughout the world. Moreover, the cost of increased security to prevent or mitigate the cost of future attacks, and the cost reflected in the economy in general and the stock market in particular are real and must be added into the final estimate to the total damage caused by the terrorists.

The Impact on the Insurance Industry

Were the September 11 attacks an insurable event? Are subsequent acts of terrorism insurable events? Under the terms and conditions of many different types of insurance policies in place at the time of the attacks, insurance companies have paid their insureds for billions of dollars in losses. Therefore, the September 11 attacks were insured, whether or not they were insurable events. After the event, insurance companies and reinsurance companies excluded terrorism losses when policies were renewed at expiration, or when new policies were purchased. Consider the following testimony given to the U.S. House of Representatives:

> Prior to September 11, 2001, insured losses resulting from terrorism in this country were extremely infrequent. Insurance companies considered the risk so low that they did not identify or price potential losses from terrorist activity separately from the general property and liability coverage provided to businesses. But after the September 11th attacks, insurance companies recognized that their risk exposure was both real and potentially enormous. . . . Insurers pointed out that the experience with major terrorist events has been so limited, and the potential losses so large, that setting an actuarially sound price for such coverage is virtually impossible.[13]

After the attacks, insurance premiums for many businesses began to increase for several reasons. Some of the increases resulted from the insurance industry's loss of capital as it either paid or created reserves for the insured losses caused by the attack. However, data show that the industry lost more capital from the decline in its investment portfolios than from the attack. Some of the price increases resulted from a better understanding of the risk insurers and their insureds face from terrorism. Some of the increases resulted from a continuation of rising insurance costs that preceded the attacks. A significant reason for the increases in insurance premiums was the increases in the prices of the insurance premiums that insurance companies had to pay for rein-

Reinsurance   surance. When an insurance company buys insurance it is called **reinsurance**, and we cover this topic in Chapter 21, "Employee Benefits." Because of the international scope of the reinsurance arrangements, one effect of the attack was to spread the cost of the loss throughout the global economy.

---

[13] Richard J. Hillman, *Terrorism Insurance: Rising Uninsured Exposure to Attacks Heightens Potential Economic Vulnerabilities*, U.S. General Accounting Office, February 2002, p. 3. (GAO-02-472T)

Defining Terrorism

If insurers want to cover or to exclude the peril of terrorism, they must define the term clearly, should the wording be challenged in court. Industry groups and the National Association of Insurance Commissioners developed the following definition of terrorism:

Terrorism

Terrorism means activities against persons, organizations, or property of any nature that involve the following or preparation of one of the following:

a. use or threat of force or violence; or
b. commission or threat of a dangerous act; or
c. commission or threat of an act that interferes with or disrupts an electronic, communication, information or mechanical system;

when one or both of the following apply:

a. the effect is to intimidate or coerce a government or the civilian population of any segment thereof, or to disrupt any segment of the economy; or
b. it appears that the intent is to intimidate or coerce a government, or to further political, ideological, religious, social, or economic objectives or to express (or express opposition to) a philosophy or ideology.

The meaning of this definition may appear clear to the drafters, but as with most insurance language, it takes a court to determine how these words apply in particular cases. Moreover, global insurers and reinsurers may adopt their own definitions of terrorism that may be broader or narrower than this definition.

The November 2002 Federal Insurance Act

Terrorism Risk Insurance Act of 2002

Because of the terrorist attacks on the United States in September 2001, President George W. Bush signed the **Terrorism Risk Insurance Act of 2002** on November 26, 2002,[14] and he signed a two-year extension of this legislation in December 2005. The main features of the act (as amended) are the following:

1. The federal government, within the Department of the Treasury, will share losses from future terrorist attacks with the insurance industry.
2. The act is triggered when the Secretary of the Treasury certifies an event as an act of terrorism.
3. The act requires mandatory participation by property and casualty insurers, who must offer terrorism insurance to all policyholders.
4. Participating insurance companies pay the first dollars of losses before federal assistance is available. Federal payments are triggered if losses exceed $50 million in 2006 and $100 million in 2007.
5. When insurers' losses exceed their responsibility, the federal government pays for 90 percent of the excess insured losses. Insurers pay the additional 10 percent. The government's loss potential is limited to $100 billion.
6. The act allows insurers to charge a premium for terrorism coverage and they must disclose the charge clearly and conspicuously.

In conclusion, this section of the chapter demonstrates that the September 11 attacks transformed the peril of terrorism from a privately insured event to an event

---

[14] A comprehensive discussion of this act is provided in the following article: R. Glenn Hubbard, Bruce Deal, and Peter Hess, "The Economic Effects of Federal Participation in Terrorism Risk," *Risk Management and Insurance Review*, Fall 2005, pp. 177–209.

insurable only with federal government participation. Readers can see that terrorism is not an ideal loss exposure because the frequency and severity of claims are not predictable and loss potential is catastrophic.

RISK CLASSIFICATION AND INSURABLE EVENTS

A generally accepted principle of insurance is that each insured and each class of insureds should bear a mathematically fair share of the insurance pool's losses and expenses for an event to be insurable in the private market. Simply put, the mathematically fair price for insurance is found by multiplying the probability of loss for a given class of loss exposure by the average expected dollar loss, then adding a fair share of the insurer's expenses. Putting this principle into practice, however, is difficult and controversial. Without careful risk classification, many events that otherwise would be insurable would become uninsurable, as the following material reveals.

Subsidization

Subsidization

In theory, each insured's mathematically fair share of losses and expenses is based on the expected probability of loss for the risk class in which the exposure is placed. **Subsidization** occurs if each insured does not pay the mathematically fair price for insurance. If the insured is paying more than the mathematically fair price, the insured provides the subsidy. If the insured is paying less than the mathematically fair price, the insured receives a subsidy.

If significant subsidization occurs, the results would be so unfair to some insureds it would create an incentive either to switch insurers or forgo the insurance. For example, assume that the annual fair mathematical cost for $1,000 of life insurance for a 20-year-old man is $1.79, and that the cost for similar protection purchased by a 40-year-old man is $3.53. Assume that both people were joined by thousands of others of the same ages in one insurance pool, and every person in the pool was charged an average rate of $2.66 [($1.79 + $3.53)/ 2]. The 20-year-olds would be paying $0.87 too much and the 40-year-olds would be paying $0.87 too little. Now $0.87 might not seem too great a sum, but it is about 50 percent of the original price.

When the 20-year-olds realize they are subsidizing the 40-year-olds, they will seek and join another insurance pool designed specifically for 20-year-olds and charging a rate appropriate for 20-year-olds. When the 20-year-olds leave the original pool, the rate for the 40-year-olds must rise to its fair level. Significant subsidization cannot exist for long in a competitive insurance market because some insurers will offer lower rates to people paying too much for their coverage.

In practice, charging all drivers the same rate, reflecting average experience, results in good drivers subsidizing bad ones. Competition results in discounts for good drivers. Charging all 40-year-old men the same rate for life insurance would result in professors subsidizing crop dusters, so insurers charge people in hazardous professions higher premiums. Special life or health insurance rates for nonsmokers and discounts for insureds having smoke detectors demonstrate the rule that competition reduces subsidization in the insurance market.

The operation of this rule does have a limit. As insurers draw distinctions between risk classes more and more finely, the number of people assigned to each of the classes becomes smaller and smaller. At some point, the law of large numbers cannot operate satisfactorily. The insurance pool, as narrowly defined, becomes too small to allow sufficient predictive accuracy, which means some subsidization occurs in all insurance pools. Perhaps it could be shown that a driver with six accidents is a more favored exposure than one with seven accidents. If both drivers are charged the same rate, subsidization occurs. It is unlikely that competitive forces would produce an insurer specializing in providing insurance for people with exactly six accidents. Even if such a company were to appear, it is doubtful it could find enough exposures to combine for statistical accuracy in predicting losses, and it is likely that its administrative costs would be too great to spread over the small number of insureds in its pool. Therefore, competition serves to reduce or minimize subsidization, not to eliminate it. In practice, insurers try to achieve a balance between the small groups required for fairness and the large numbers of exposures needed for predictive accuracy.

Adverse Selection

Adverse selection

Antiselection

When one party to a transaction has more relevant information or more control of outcomes than another party to the transaction, the party with superior information or control can take advantage of the position. Insurance scholars call taking advantage of the possession of asymmetric information **adverse selection**, or **antiselection**. Actuarial Standard of Practice Number Twelve defines adverse selection a little more explicitly as "Actions taken by one party using risk characteristics or other information known to or suspected by that party that cause a financial disadvantage to the financial or personal security system *(sometimes referred to as antiselection)*."[15] For example, adverse selection occurs when people who know their health is deteriorating try to purchase health insurance to cover the cost of a needed operation. Another example would involve a person trying to purchase fire insurance immediately after a terrorist threatened his property. Adverse selection raises serious ethical and moral questions, but it is an ever-present fact in the insurance market.[16]

If insurers made no attempt to put applicants for insurance in different risk classes, a predictable result would occur. Applicants for insurance with a greater-than-average chance of loss would certainly apply for insurance. If these above-average-risk applicants succeed in purchasing insurance at average rates, the insurer is a victim of adverse selection. Adverse selection results in the insured not paying a rate that fairly reflects the insurer's exposure to loss. Insurers often accept exposures with a greater-than-average chance of loss but are careful to charge those insureds above-average rates. The purpose of insurance underwriting is to select insureds carefully and charge each a rate fairly reflecting the expected loss from each. In other words, one function of insurance underwriting is to prevent adverse selection.

PRINCIPLES OF RISK CLASSIFICATION

Insurers use risk classification to minimize subsidization and adverse selection. The guiding principle applied when establishing risk classes has been that each insured should bear the mathematical fair share of the pool's losses and expenses, but this rule can produce controversial results. In fact, using some measures that discriminate fairly in the mathematical sense produces results that most of society would consider offensive. Race is such a factor. Even though race can be shown to be a predictor of mortality, many people would object strongly to using it to set insurance rates.

---

[15] This standard can be found at the following Web site: (*http://www.actuarialstandardsboard.org/asops.htm/*).
[16] For an interesting and mathematical discussion of this topic see: "Risk Aversion and the Willingness to Pay for Insurance: A Cautionary Discussion of Adverse Selection," by Joseph G. Eisenhauer, *Risk Management and Insurance Review*, 2004, Vol. 7, No. 2, 165–175.

Some people find other variables objectionable, including age and gender. Critics object to these factors because they considered them beyond the insured's control. Thus, the courts, various state legislatures, and insurance companies have been debating which factors should or should not be used to set insurance rates.

Rate classification factors can be evaluated on the following four points: separation and homogeneity of the classes, reliability, incentive value, and social acceptability.

Separation and Class Homogeneity

If the insurer has constructed its risk classes carefully, each class will have a significantly different expected loss (separation). Moreover, each member of a given class will have approximately the same chance of loss (class homogeneity). This rule prevents combining males aged 20 and 40 in the same life insurance pool and causes a mathematically fair insurance exchange.

Reliability

If insurers decide to use a particular factor for classifying insureds, information about the factor should be obtained easily and not be subject to manipulation by the insured. The variables of age and gender would meet this standard, but asking an applicant how many miles he drives each year or whether he uses drugs or alcohol would not work as well because the insured can provide false information. When less-than-ideal criteria are used, insurers often seek independent verification of information provided by applicants.

Incentive Value

If insurers craft their risk classes carefully, insureds should be rewarded for maintaining clean driving records or for applying successful loss-prevention measures. Thus, factors used for risk classification should reward insureds with below-average loss potential with better insurance rates.

Social Acceptability

Social acceptability is the underwriting criterion that is the most difficult to handle. Who is to define social acceptability? The courts? Congress? Insurance commissioners? You and I? Moreover, this measure has the possibility of being at odds with the preceding risk classification criteria. How are such conflicting outcomes to be resolved? What do we do when the desirability of a mathematically fair insurance exchange conflicts with a socially desired outcome?

The social acceptability of using underwriting factors beyond an insured's control, especially gender, has historically been a difficult issue to resolve. Insurers voluntarily eliminated using race as an underwriting criterion because of the unacceptable social implications of this practice. Subsequently, the courts addressed the issue of using gender in two landmark pension cases. The result of these two cases, the **Manhart case** and the **Norris case**, was to equalize pension payments to similarly situated men and women and to disregard differences in life expectancies. These rules apply only to pension plans, not to individual life insurance and annuities, where gender-distinct mortality tables are still used.[17]

Manhart case

Norris case

---

[17] *City of Los Angeles, Department of Water and Power* v. *Marie Manhart*, U.S. Supreme Court, 1978 (434 U.S. 815). *Arizona Governing Committee for Tax Deferred Annuity and Deferred Compensation Plans, etc., et al. Petitioners Nathalie Norris, etc.*, U.S. Supreme Court, 1982 (No. 82-52).

Genetic testing

Among the controversial questions that continue to receive attention is the issue of genetic testing of insurance applicants. **Genetic testing**, using technology to examine an individual's genes, has the possibility of identifying people with a high potential for certain diseases. Whether insurers should be allowed to charge a 25-year-old man a higher-than-average premium because genetic testing suggests a greater-than-average chance of death by a heart attack when the man reaches age 45 remains a question of social policy. As this procedure becomes increasingly accurate (and change in this area has been very dramatic in recent years), society will have to weigh a fair insurance premium in the balance with social acceptability. Critics are concerned that people with the "wrong" genes will be unable to purchase life or health insurance at all. On the one hand, many people have a genetic predisposition to one or another potential illness, and society may find excluding or discouraging large numbers of people from purchasing insurance too high a price to pay for more accurate underwriting. On the other hand, insurers are concerned that people with knowledge of their genetic predisposition to disease may engage in adverse selection.

Credit scoring

Using a person's credit history to underwrite insurance, or **credit scoring**, is another area of controversy. On the one hand, evidence suggests that people with a bad credit history also produce more losses for homeowners or automobile insurance and therefore should pay higher insurance premiums. On the other hand, the results of credit scoring tend to raise the insurance costs of low-income and minority people more than other groups. In recent years, many states have passed laws that restrict the use of credit information in the insurance underwriting process. Most of these laws prohibit insurance companies from making an unfavorable decision based solely on an applicant's credit history. The following Web site provides a discussion of this controversy and includes recent court cases and legislation: (*http://www.iii.org/media/hottopics/insurance/creditscoring/*). Keywords using an Internet search engine would be "insurance," "credit scores," and "credit scoring."

BRANCHES OF INSURANCE

Figure 2–1 presents a simple diagram of the main insurance branches in the United States.

This chapter has presented several insurance principles to provide the basis of an answer to the question "What is an insurable event?" The focus of our discussion has been on private insurance markets that meet the criteria for ideally insurable loss exposures. Addressing the question of defining the government's role in providing insurance in a private market economy goes beyond the scope of this introductory textbook. However, we noted that the government sometimes provides insurance when the criteria for an ideal loss exposure are absent and the government becomes the insurer of last resort. The discussion of catastrophic losses presented examples of this role of government insurance. Other reasons for government insurance are related to maintaining the economic fabric of our society. This latter category includes providing subsidized insurance for people who could not otherwise acquire insurance in the private market. This category includes people in poor health (for example, the Medicare and Medicaid components of Social Security provide insurance coverage without risk-based premiums or exclusions) or low income (for example, Social Security provides a minimum retirement benefit, and the benefit is weighted in favor of low-income workers).

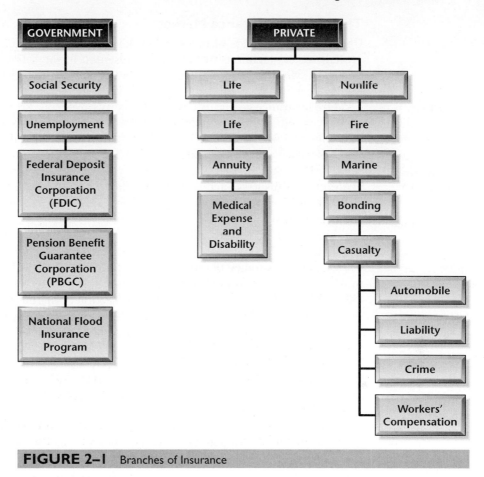

FIGURE 2–1   Branches of Insurance

Government Insurance Activities

A recent government report identified "71 activities that provide federal insurance to entities other than the federal government."[18] The following programs are among the better-known federal insurance activities:

- The U.S. Social Security Administration administers the trust funds paying retirement, disability, and survivor benefits (*http://www.ssa.gov/*).
- The Federal Deposit Insurance Corporation insures bank deposits up to $100,000 (*http://www.fdic.gov/*).
- The U.S. Department of Agriculture operates several insurance programs to indemnify farmers suffering losses from crop damage (*http://www.rma.usda.gov/fcic/*).
- The Department of Labor administers the Pension Benefit Guarantee Corporation and the Unemployment Trust Fund (*http://www.pbgc.gov*, *http://www.dol.gov/dol/topic/unemployment-insurance/index.html*).
- The Department of Homeland Security administers the NFIP (*http://www. fema.gov/nfip/*).

---

[18] U.S. Government Accountability Office, "Catalogue of Federal Insurance Activities," March 2005. (GAO-05-265R)

The Private Insurance Market

Categorizing the fields or branches of the private insurance market is difficult. Comprehensive explanations of the topics presented in the following text appear later in this book, with one or more chapters applying to each main branch of the insurance industry.

Fire insurance

Fire insurance generally covers stationary property, also called real estate, but land is not covered. Another simple way of putting it is that fire insurance generally covers buildings and their contents. In addition to the peril of fire, more broadly based property insurance policies provide payment for damage caused by such perils as windstorm, riots, and vandalism. Another type of coverage associated with property insurance is **business income (interruption) coverage**, which provides payment for indirect losses associated with damage done by fires and other covered perils.

Business income (interruption) coverage

Marine insurance

Marine insurance generally covers mobile property. Ocean marine insurance covers ships and their cargoes. Inland marine insurance covers property moving on planes, trains, and trucks. This category is often called *transportation insurance*.

Casualty insurance

Casualty insurance describes several different fields of insurance, including automobile insurance, liability insurance, crime insurance, workers' compensation, and accident and health insurance. The following section of this chapter provides an extended discussion of liability insurance because this concept is likely to be unfamiliar to some readers, and it is very important in the United States, where there are more lawsuits than elsewhere in the world.

Bonding

Bonding is a special type of protection in which one party (the surety) guarantees the performance (surety bond) or the honesty (fidelity bond) of a second party to a third party. If the second party's poor performance or dishonesty results in a loss to the third party, the surety must pay.

Life insurance

Life insurance describes insurance based on human life contingencies. If the covered peril is death, we call the contract *life insurance*. If the peril is survival, we call the contract an *annuity*. The annuity guarantees that the insured will not have to survive without money. If the covered peril is sickness, we call the coverage **medical expense insurance**. If the covered peril is disability, we call the coverage **disability income insurance**.

Medical expense insurance

Disability income insurance

In addition to these standard categories of coverage, insurers sell other interesting types of insurance. The following list is meant only to convey the scope of available insurance possibilities.[19]

1. *Weather-related insurance.* Payments can be made for crop-hail damage, rained-out concerts, or too much or too little snow.
2. *Change-of-law insurance.* Payments are made if new regulations increase construction costs after contracts are signed.
3. *Municipal bond insurance.* This coverage guarantees principal and interest payments on municipal securities, the type of debt issued by cities, states, and their agencies, and whose income is usually free of the federal income tax.
4. *Motion picture completion bonds.* Insureds receive payment if the film is not completed on time. The death of a star or other unforeseen events could cause the insurer to pay.
5. *Boiler and machinery insurance.* Many property insurance contracts specifically exclude damage caused by exploding steam boilers. Some insurance companies

---

[19] For more information about these interesting coverages, do an Internet search using the various types of coverages as keywords. For example, typing "boiler and machinery insurance" in a search engine produced more than 500,000 items.

sell this type of coverage, but in practice what insureds pay for, in addition to the indemnity agreement, is regular inspections of their boilers.

6. *Wedding insurance.* Many American weddings cost about $25,000. Wedding insurance covers losses arising from cancellation or postponement because of illness of the bride or groom, loss of wedding gifts, or failure of vendors to perform. The insurance provides reimbursement for nonrecoverable expenses, payment of extra expenses, or payment for lost or damaged wedding rings, gifts, or wedding clothes.

7. *Credit insurance.* Credit insurance is an example of insurance coverage for a speculative risk. In a **credit insurance** arrangement, the insurance company provides payment to its insured (the lender) if the insured's credit losses exceed a specified amount. In other words, the insurer pays the lender if the lender loses money because its debtors fail to repay their debts. Bankruptcies may leave lenders holding uncollectible account receivables, and credit insurance can reimburse the lender for its losses. Because it insures a speculative risk and is subject to adverse selection, insurance companies underwrite this coverage carefully.

Credit insurance

In addition to providing insurance for losses arising out of insolvencies, the insurer can provide insureds with information on the financial strength of existing and potential debtors. This financial information can be a very valuable service to the lender and a strong motivation to purchase the credit insurance. Such financial information and credit insurance protection can be especially useful for exporters, especially small to medium-sized companies dealing with unfamiliar customers.

Consider a recent credit insurance arrangement that guaranteed an aircraft manufacturer would receive about $1 billion in lease payments when it leased airplanes for 15 years to several airline companies throughout the world. The aircraft manufacturer without this coverage might not have received full payment of the leases if one or more of the airlines were badly managed or if unfavorable economic conditions ruined an airline operator's earnings. From the manufacturer's standpoint, leasing the planes represented a speculative risk. Purchasing credit insurance transferred this risk to an insurer. The insurer must have felt that because of safeguards in the credit insurance contract, the manufacturer had strong incentives not to lease planes to unqualified operators. Thus, the insurer defined this speculative exposure as an insurable event.

LIABILITY INSURANCE

Legal liability insurance provides protection against the financial impact of lawsuits. Simply put, if an insured's negligence results in another person's injury, the insurance company agrees to pay for the damage. Readers often do not grasp liability losses as easily as property losses. You cannot see the loss a lawsuit represents in the same sense as you can see a burned home or a damaged car. Yet a $100 million loss resulting from a negligent act is a substantial direct loss of property.[20]

Legal Background

Before describing legal liability insurance, we must spend some time examining the nature of the peril by learning some interesting legal background. The peril of **legal liability** arises out of the general rule of (English common) law that people are

Legal liability

---

[20] Readers can find current information on the cost of the tort (legal) liability system in the United States at this Web site: (*http://www.towersperrin.com/tillinghast/publications/reports/Tort_2004/Tort.pdf/*).

responsible for any loss (injury) they cause another to suffer. The law creates three categories for describing situations in which one person injures another:

- Breaches of contracts
- Criminal acts
- Torts, or civil wrongs

Breach of contract

Criminal acts

Torts

Breach of contract involves a failure, without a legal excuse, to perform contractual duties. Local, state, and federal laws define **criminal acts**, which in general are wrongs against society. **Torts**, or civil wrongs, involve unreasonable conduct toward another person. The same action, for example, battery (touching another person without permission), may be both a criminal and a civil wrong. Reckless driving is another act that could be both a civil and a criminal wrong. Although the punishment for a criminal wrong may include making restitution to the injured victim, generally it does not. The injured victim must undertake civil litigation in an appropriate court to collect payment for injury.

Civil litigation (often called lawsuits) begins in a court called a *civil trial court*. The designation of civil trial courts varies in different jurisdictions. They may be known as *circuit court*, *superior court*, *court of common appeals*, or *district court*. Appellate courts can review the decisions of trial courts if the losing parties believe trial procedures were unfair or if the law was improperly applied in their case. Appellate court rulings can be appealed to state (or sometimes federal) supreme courts on the same grounds.

Negligence

Negligence

Reasonable person

Put simply, **negligence** involves doing something a reasonable person would not do, or not doing something a reasonable person would do, that results directly in some injury to another person. A review of many court cases in which the concept of the reasonable person has been applied leads to the definition of a **reasonable person** as one who has normal possession of all faculties and senses; who thinks, speaks, and acts based on reason; and who is honest and moderate in all activities. The question of whether an individual has acted reasonably is usually a question of fact. Violating the reasonable person standard can result in a court imposing legal liability for a person's direct acts or omissions of actions.

Vicarious liability

Courts can also impose liability for the negligent acts of other parties. **Vicarious liability** means a person is liable because of another person's acts. For example, assume that Jack B. Nimble lends his car to Johnnie B. Good, and Johnnie then causes an accident with Jack's car. Jack might be held liable if it can be shown he was negligent in lending his car to someone he knew or should have known was a poor driver. (Johnnie also would be liable in this example.) More commonly, vicarious liability arises for businesses when parties hired as contractors injure others.

Joint-and-several liability

The rule of **joint-and-several liability** means that if a party is one among several responsible for a loss, even if its contribution was the slightest of all, it is fully responsible for making restitution to the injured party if the other defendants are financially unable to do so. For example, assume that four parties, A, B, C, and D, are responsible for injuring E. Even if A's actions contributed only 10 percent to E's injuries, if B's, C's, and D's assets are inadequate to compensate E, A will have to pay the balance of the claim, perhaps 99 percent of the total.

Negligence Lawsuits

When a case goes to court, the purpose often is to determine the facts. After reviewing the evidence, judges or juries determine the facts, and once that has happened, a judge applies the appropriate legal remedy. Two different juries may view the same evidence and reach different conclusions about the facts. One jury may feel a person's actions are reasonable; another may find the same actions unreasonable. Actions that are considered reasonable in rural North Carolina may be unreasonable in New York City. The point, however, is that the outcome of a legal contest cannot be determined until a jury settles the *questions of fact.* The facts are what a jury says they are.

Consider the instructions an Arkansas judge is required to give to a jury in a negligence case:

> When I use the word *negligence* in these instructions, I mean the failure to do something which a reasonably careful person would do, or the doing of something which a reasonably careful person would not do, under circumstances similar to those shown by the evidence in this case. [It is for you to decide how a reasonably careful person would act under those circumstances.] [To constitute negligence, an act must be one from which a reasonably careful person would foresee such an appreciable risk of harm to others as to cause him not to do the act, or to do it in a more careful manner.]

Plaintiff

Defendant

There are two parties to a negligence lawsuit. The **plaintiff** is the party claiming injury, while the **defendant** is the party from whom recovery is sought. In addition to human beings, businesses, government units, and other organizations may be plaintiffs or defendants in lawsuits.

Establishing Negligence and Damages

To establish a case of negligence, the law requires the plaintiff to prove all the following points:

1. The defendant had a legal duty to protect the plaintiff.
2. The defendant failed to perform that duty.
3. The plaintiff suffered an injury as a result of the defendant's failure to perform that duty.

Among the endless examples of negligence, consider the following claims:

- A stone thrown by a lawn mower injures a neighbor. The neighbor claims negligent operation of the mower caused the injury.
- A guest at a motel is injured because a light bulb in a hallway is burned out, causing the guest to trip over a chair. The injured guest's suit claims the motel operator was negligent in not replacing the bulb and leaving a chair in the middle of a hallway.
- A child is injured while playing on some outdoor equipment in a neighbor's backyard. The homeowner is sued for damages resulting from the child's injury. The injured child's parents raise the doctrine of **attractive nuisance**. This doctrine places a very high standard of care on property owners whose property may prove attractive to children. The property owner has the burden of proving that every reasonable step was taken to protect children from injury.

Attractive nuisance

Judgment

If each of the three elements of a negligent act is established to the satisfaction of the judge and jury, the plaintiff is entitled to a favorable judgment, usually a specific sum of money. A **judgment** is the official decision of the court as to the rights of the parties to a suit. It is enforceable by officers of the court. Thus, if the court finds that the defendant must pay the plaintiff $300,000, the plaintiff can expect the court to enforce this decision. The plaintiff need not try to collect. However, if the plaintiff fails to establish any one of the elements of negligence, or if the defendant establishes a successful defense, the court will not award the plaintiff a favorable judgment.

In some cases, a court will allow a plaintiff recovery for two different types of damage: compensatory damages for personal injuries and punitive damages.

Compensatory Damages

Courts award compensatory damages to put the victim in the same financial condition after an injury as he or she was in before the occurrence. Insurance policies may cover the following three categories of loss: bodily injury, personal injury, and property damage.

Bodily injuries include medical (or funeral) expenses resulting from a loss, wages lost while the plaintiff was recovering from the injury, estimated future income the injury prevents the plaintiff from earning, and pain and suffering caused by the injury. **Personal injuries** include damages suffered when a person is deprived of his or her rights. For example, slander or false imprisonment may deprive a person of his or her good reputation. **Property damage** includes destruction and loss of use of tangible personal property. Examples of property damage include destroying an automobile in an accident or putting a toxic (poisonous) substance on another's property.

Putting a dollar amount on these items ranges from easy to quite difficult in practice. If a person suffers an injury, incurs $50,000 in medical expenses, and loses one month's earnings, the total amount of damage may not be difficult to prove. However, valuing the mental stress a plaintiff suffers because of permanent disfigurement can be a difficult task for a jury.

Punitive Damages

Punitive damages are awards made to plaintiffs not as compensation for injuries suffered, but as a means of punishing defendants for outrageously offensive acts. What constitutes such an act is a question of fact. The insurer usually agrees to pay the amounts that its insureds become legally liable to pay for injuries inflicted by negligence. Punitive damages usually imply **gross negligence**, something for which the insurer may not have contemplated making payment. Also, punishing an insurance company (and thereby its pool of insureds) may not satisfy the courts' purpose of punishing wrongdoers. Thus, in a few states, state law prevents insurers from providing compensation for punitive damages. Again, we have another insight on insurable events—if insurance would frustrate public policy, an event becomes uninsurable.

The U.S. Supreme Court addressed the issue of punitive damage awards in April 2003.[21] In this case, a Utah jury awarded the plaintiffs $2.6 million in compensatory damages and $145 million in punitive damages. The Supreme Court found the relationship between the compensatory and punitive damages to be "irrational and arbitrary." The Supreme Court then returned this case to the Utah courts for reconsideration. In an earlier case, the Supreme Court found a 4-to-1 ratio of punitive to compensatory damages close to the line of being constitutionally improper.[22]

Res Ipsa Loquitur

In some cases, the plaintiff's injury is the obvious result of the defendant's activity. In such cases, the court may apply the doctrine of *res ipsa loquitur*, which is a legal doctrine of evidence allowing the jury to infer negligence on the part of the defendant. The translation of this Latin phrase is "the thing speaks for itself." It means the plaintiff is

Bodily injuries

Personal injuries

Property damage

Punitive damages

Gross negligence

Res ipsa loquitur

---

[21] *State Farm Mutual Automobile Ins. Co. v. Campbell*, WL 1791206 U.S. (2003).
[22] *Pacific Mut. Life Ins. Co. v. Haslip*, 499 U.S. (1991).

relieved of the duty of establishing the three required elements of the defendant's negligence, as the court is presuming the defendant was negligent. The doctrine does not mean that defendants cannot defend themselves, as would be the case with strict liability. It means, however, that the plaintiff is relieved of the initial burden of identifying which negligent act of the defendant caused the injury. The court applies the doctrine of *res ipsa loquitur* only when the following circumstances exist:

- The plaintiff's injury could not happen in the absence of negligence.
- Something exclusively in the control of the defendant caused the injury.
- It was impossible for the plaintiff's negligence to cause the injury.

Examples of situations in which this doctrine might be applied include commercial airplane crashes, sponges left inside surgery patients, and certain injuries resulting from unsafe products.

Defenses in a Negligence Suit

A defendant has two main lines of defense against a charge of negligence: contributory negligence and assumption of the risk. The jury also will find in favor of the defendant if the plaintiff fails to prove any of the three elements of a negligent act.

Contributory Negligence

Contributory negligence

Assuming that the plaintiff establishes the defendant's negligence, the defendant may counter with a defense of **contributory negligence**. If it can be shown that the plaintiff's own negligence contributed to or led to the injury sustained, the court will not allow recovery of damages from the defendant under the contributory negligence rule. This fact does not mean that the existence of some measure of negligence on the plaintiff's part relieves defendants of their duties. It means that because both parties are at fault, neither will be allowed recovery from the other. For example, assume that the plaintiff fails to signal a turn and the plaintiff's car is hit in the side by an oncoming car that was speeding. Assume that the defendant, the driver of the speeding car, establishes that the plaintiff's negligence in failing to signal led to, or at least contributed to, the loss. In this circumstance, neither plaintiff nor defendant could recover from each other under the contributory negligence rule.

Comparative Negligence

Comparative negligence

The contributory negligence rule is harsh; even slight negligence on a plaintiff's part can relieve a grossly negligent defendant of responsibility for an accident. Today, most states apply a modification of the contributory negligence rule called the doctrine of **comparative negligence**. The comparative negligence doctrine allows plaintiffs some degree of recovery even if they contributed to their own injuries.

Different states have different comparative negligence rules. Some states allow the plaintiff to recover damages proportionate to the defendant's negligence. Other states allow the plaintiff to recover only when the plaintiff is responsible for 49 percent or less of the damage. One state allows the plaintiff to recover only when a jury decides the plaintiff's contribution was "slight" while the defendant's contribution to the injury was "gross." In all cases, the comparative negligence rule allows the plaintiff a better chance for recovery than the contributory negligence rule.

As an example of recovery under the comparative negligence rule, assume that the plaintiff, Moe D'Laun, a landscape architect, sustains $100,000 damage in an automobile accident, and a court decides that Moe was 30 percent responsible for the accident. Under the comparative negligence rule, Moe would recover $70,000. Under the contributory negligence rule, Moe would recover nothing.

Last Clear Chance

Last clear chance

The doctrine of **last clear chance** is another modification of the contributory negligence rule. In general, when a plaintiff's negligence contributes to the loss, nothing may be collected if the court applies the contributory negligence rule. The last clear chance doctrine is an exception to the contributory negligence rule. This doctrine states that if the defendant had a clear chance to avoid injuring the plaintiff, then the plaintiff can collect despite having made a contribution to the loss. For example, assume the plaintiff, Denton Fender, was waiting to make a left turn but failed to use his turn signal. Assume the defendant, Manuel Transmission, had a clear chance to avoid the accident but hit Denton anyway. In this case, the sequence of events in court would likely be that (1) the plaintiff, Denton, establishes negligence; (2) the defendant, Manuel, establishes contributory negligence on Denton's part; and (3) the plaintiff then establishes that the defendant had a clear chance to avoid the accident despite the plaintiff's negligence. Assuming no further legal steps by the defendant, the plaintiff would receive full recovery.

Assumption of the Risk

Assumption of the risk

A second line of defense involves establishing that the plaintiff knowingly assumed the risk of injury. If the defendant establishes **assumption of the risk**, the plaintiff will not be awarded a judgment. For example, if the plaintiff challenged the defendant to a wrestling match, the plaintiff may not collect damages when his arm is broken during the contest. As we shall see shortly, the risks that one assumes, either expressly or by implication, can be a question of fact. To illustrate the issue, consider a hockey player. He assumes the risk of being struck by a puck or being checked forcefully by opponents. But does engaging in this sport also imply that he assumes the risk that an irate opponent will use his stick to split open his skull? If the injured player takes the aggressor to court, can the aggressor legitimately raise the assumption of risk defense? The question is for a judge and jury to decide.

Legal Judgments

If a judgment is favorable to a plaintiff, the defendant must pay the damages specified in the judgment. At this point liability insurance enters the picture. A liability insurance policy promises to pay (up to the limit of the policy) on behalf of the insured "all sums that the insured shall become legally obligated to pay as damages." Thus, the insurer agrees to pay the judgment on behalf of its insured. The legal process involved in a negligence suit is outlined in a simplified fashion in Figure 2–2.

ETHICS, LIABILITY INSURANCE, AND THE INSURABLE EVENT

The alert reader may question whether liability insurance, which relieves insureds from paying for the damage they cause others, violates the ethic of individual responsibility for one's own actions. The answer is that it does to some extent. If one purpose of the tort liability system is to punish wrongdoers, liability insurance defeats this goal. Other legal scholars maintain that the primary goal of the tort liability system is not punishment, but victim compensation, in which case liability insurance is an efficient remedy. Without liability insurance, many negligent parties would be bankrupt before the court's judgment could be satisfied. Such bankruptcy would leave an injured victim only partially compensated. Thus, liability insurance increases the welfare of injured parties who otherwise would not be able to collect their judgments from defendants.

If, however, liability insurance causes people to behave more recklessly than they would otherwise, society's welfare is adversely affected. Although liability insurance

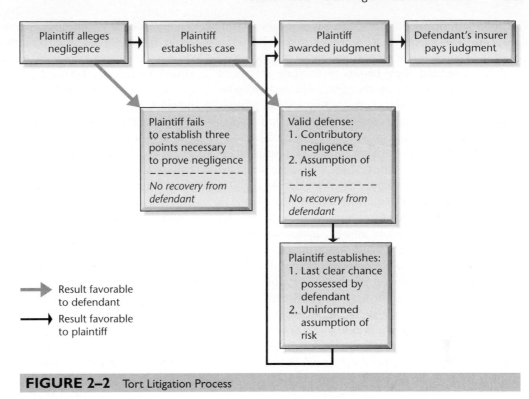

FIGURE 2–2   Tort Litigation Process

may create some morale hazard, it has not been shown that the availability of liability insurance causes a significant number of additional losses. One explanation lies in the fact that negligence, by definition, is accidental. Insurance payments generally are not made for intentional injuries inflicted on another person. From this perspective, unintentional negligence is the same as an accidental fire.

A second restraint on the morale hazard is the premium increases or outright rejections for coverage experienced by repeatedly negligent people. It is well known that drivers with frequent accidents pay more for their automobile liability insurance than good drivers. This knowledge probably works to restrain some people from risky driving behavior.

SUMMARY

An insurance system works best when the following four criteria are met:

1. A large number of similar items in the insurance pool are exposed to the same peril(s).
2. The losses insured against are accidental.
3. The losses are definite once they occur and of sufficient severity to cause economic hardship.
4. A low potential for catastrophic losses exists, especially ones likely to occur in a limited geographic area.

Exposures to catastrophic losses in a limited geographic area cannot be insured privately because when only the most exposed to loss want coverage, the insurance system breaks down. The premium becomes unacceptably high, and the large numbers needed for predictability are not present.

The terrorist attacks of September 11, 2001, caused several different categories of insured losses, including property damage, business interruption, aviation hull, life insurance, and workers' compensation insurance losses. The attacks also caused billions of dollars in uninsured losses throughout the world. After the attacks, insurers and reinsurers realized the peril of terrorism was unpredictable in its frequency and severity, and they began to exclude this peril from coverage. In November 2002, the federal government passed legislation providing federal participation in funding the costs of catastrophic terrorist attacks. This legislation was renewed in 2005.

Subsidization in an insurance pool results when the better risks pay more than their fair share to compensate for losses while the poorer risks pay too little. Two forces work to minimize subsidization: (1) competition from insurers who will appeal to the people paying too much, and (2) insurance regulation that operates to provide consumers with rates that are adequate, not excessive, and not unfairly discriminatory. However, in some situations, insurance regulators and the courts have forced insurers to cause subsidization in insurance pools to promote alternative social goals. Adverse selection implies that applicants for insurance attempt to pay a rate that does not fairly reflect their actual chance of loss.

Successful insurance transactions have been made in several distinct branches, or categories, of the private insurance industry. Liability insurance, which provides compensation for an insured's negligence, is an important branch of the U.S. insurance market.

Liability insurance provides coverage when insureds are sued because their actions or lack of actions are held by a jury to be unreasonable. To collect for damages, the injured party (the plaintiff) must establish that the other party (the defendant) had a legal duty to protect the plaintiff; that the defendant failed to perform this duty; and that, as a direct result of this failure, the plaintiff was injured.

If the defendant can establish that the plaintiff knowingly assumed a risk or the plaintiff contributed to the loss by some personal action, then the defendant may not have to pay a judgment. If a plaintiff can show that, despite the plaintiff's contribution to the loss, the defendant had a last clear chance to avoid causing the injury, the plaintiff may collect for damages anyway.

REVIEW TERMS

- Accidental losses
- Adverse selection
- Assumption of the risk
- Attractive nuisance
- Beach plans
- Bodily injuries
- Bonding
- Breach of contract
- Business income (interruption) coverage
- Casualty insurance
- Catastrophic loss
- Catastrophic loss exposure
- Comparative negligence
- Contributory negligence
- Credit insurance
- Credit scoring

- Criminal acts
- Defendant
- Disability income insurance
- Fire insurance
- Gross negligence
- Insurable interest
- Joint-and-several liability
- Judgment
- Large-loss principle
- Large number
- Last clear chance
- Legal liability
- Legal liability insurance
- Life insurance
- Manhart case
- Marine insurance
- Medical expense insurance

- National Flood Insurance Program (NFIP)
- Negligence
- Norris case
- Personal injuries
- Plaintiff
- Property damage
- Punitive damages
- Reasonable person
- Reinsurance
- Res ipsa loquitur
- Subsidization
- Terrorism
- Terrorism Risk Insurance Act of 2002
- Tort
- Vicarious liability

REVIEW

1. Which of the following exposures to loss would be a likely basis for an insurance system? Explain why the exposures would or would not qualify as a basis for insurance.
    a. The potential loss of domestic pets
    b. The potential loss of farm animals
    c. The potential loss of a college student's textbooks
    d. Insufficient snow to operate a ski resort
    e. The potential loss of receipts at an outdoor concert if it were to be rained out
    f. The potential loss of a valuable stamp collection
    g. The potential loss of a person's memory
2. What is the definition of a catastrophic loss?
3. Why are certain crime losses, such as the theft of furs and jewelry, a more difficult exposure to insure than fire loss? (Refer to ideal insurance transactions.)

4. What difficulties would be present in combining a group of men and women of the same age in the same life insurance pool?
5. What would happen to an insurance system in which the insureds were indifferent to the occurrence of losses?
6. Why are floods and earthquakes difficult to insure in a privately operated insurance system?
7. Describe who would be providing and who would be receiving a subsidy if an insurer created a special insurance pool combining all people causing two or more serious automobile accidents in the past ten years.
8. What is adverse selection? How do insurers try to prevent adverse selection?
9. Explain the statement that adverse selection causes subsidization.
10. List and describe the various branches of the private, life, and non–life insurance industries.
11. Explain the four major principles of risk classification.
12. What is meant by incentive value in a risk classification scheme?

13. Why is social acceptability of risk classification criteria such a difficult concept on which to get general agreement?
14. Describe the difference between a civil wrong and a criminal act. Give some examples of each and give some examples of acts that may fall into both categories.
15. Explain the purpose of strict liability laws.
16. Define a reasonable person.
17. List the plaintiff's duties in a negligence suit.
18. Considering the instructions to the Arkansas jury, how can we know what a "reasonably careful person would foresee" in a given case?
19. How does the term *bodily injury* differ from the term *personal injury*?
20. List some good defenses in a negligence suit. Give some examples of each defense.
21. What are the court's requirements before applying the doctrine of *res ipsa loquitur*?
22. What are punitive damages, and what purpose do they serve?

OBJECTIVE QUESTIONS

1. The criteria for ideally insurable losses include all the following except:
   a. Definite losses
   b. Accidental losses
   c. A small carefully defined group of exposures
   d. Low probability of catastrophic loss
2. One reason that floods have not been insured in the United States is:
   a. The potential damage is catastrophic.
   b. The federal government wants to discourage people from living in flood plains and thus has invalidated all flood insurance coverage.
   c. People would not purchase flood insurance, even if it were available at a low or moderate price.
   d. Insurance companies do not know how to define the peril of flood.
3. Credit insurance:
   a. Is mostly sold to bankers
   b. Repays lenders if their debtors fail to repay their debt
   c. Insures college students against failure to get credit when they transfer schools
   d. Insures people or business firms if they have a bad credit rating
4. If an insurance payment is based on the peril of human survival, the contract is called:
   a. Disability insurance
   b. Medical expense insurance
   c. An annuity
   d. Life insurance
5. The statement that insurance should be purchased only when losses are large and uncertain expresses:

   a. The central limit theorem
   b. The rule of adverse selection
   c. The law of large numbers
   d. The large-loss principle
6. If only those most exposed to loss try to purchase insurance, the insurance pool will fail because:
   a. Insurance agents will not sell the coverage.
   b. The coverage will be too cheap for insurance companies to make money.
   c. The premiums are likely to be more than most people could afford—perhaps even greater than the cost of the losses.
   d. The potential for fraudulent losses will undermine the insurance underwriting.
7. Which of the following statements is true regarding the Terrorism Insurance Act of 2002?
   a. The act is triggered when the president certifies that an event is an act of terrorism.
   b. The Department of the Treasury pays for all insured losses after a certified act of terrorism.
   c. Participation of property and casualty insurers is mandatory.
   d. The act lasts for 20 years.
8. Incentive value in a risk classification scheme means:
   a. Insureds have a financial incentive to prevent losses.
   b. Insurers have a financial incentive to find a better class of insureds.
   c. Agents have an incentive to sell more insurance.
   d. Insureds have an incentive to purchase the cheapest insurance.

DISCUSSION QUESTIONS

1. List some examples of exceptions you have heard of or read about to the guidelines set forth for ideal insurance exposures. Do these exceptions have any features in common?

2. Should the government provide catastrophic loss insurance for hurricanes, volcanic eruptions, and earthquakes?

3. Explain why the answer to the question "What is an insurable event?" may change over time.

INTERNET RESEARCH ASSIGNMENTS

1. Collect the most recent data on the NFIP, including the dollar amount of losses for the most recent five years. Start at this Web site: (*http://www.fema.gov/nfip/pcstat.shtm/*).

2. Present some information on "dog bite liability" or another currently interesting insurance issue. Start at this Web site: (*http://www.iii.org/*).

3. Search the Internet for the current estimate of losses caused by Hurricane Katrina.

4. Research the status of the following laws (or insurance rules)—if any apply—for your state:

    a. Any legislation limiting the use of credit ratings for underwriting purposes. Start your search at this site: (*http://www.namic.org/reports/credithistory/credithistory.asp/*).

    b. Any legislation regarding the use of genetic testing. Start your search at this site: (*http://www.ncsl.org/programs/health/genetics.htm/*).

5. Search the Internet and see if you can find an insurance company offering coverage for the business income losses associated with a labor strike. Comment on the implications of your discovery as related to the insurability standards presented in this chapter.

CHAPTER 3

Risk Management

After studying this chapter, you should be able to:

- Explain the role of risk management

- List the steps in the risk management process

- Identify the elements of a loss control program

- Describe six risk financing alternatives

- Apply the risk management process to a case study

One purpose of this chapter is to put insurance in a much broader perspective—a perspective called *risk management.* Seen in this context, insurance is one solution among several alternatives to the problem of risk financing. As readers will soon learn, other risk financing techniques include a pay-as-you-go approach called *risk assumption* and capital market arrangements often involving derivative securities. The chapter on advanced risk management presents a discussion of financial risk management and modern hedging techniques, while this chapter retains its focus on more traditional losses and solutions to the problems they present.

Risk management

We define **risk management** as the logical development and implementation of a plan to deal with potential losses. The purpose of a risk management program is to manage an organization's exposure to loss and to protect its assets. Risk management benefits all types of organizations facing potential losses, including businesses, nonprofit organizations, individuals, and families. Among the many lessons learned from the catastrophic hurricanes of 2004 and 2005 were the importance of preparing to control and finance losses before they occur, and the fact that losses strike city governments, museums, zoos, and hospitals as well as businesses of all sizes.

The risk management process begins when somebody asks, "What kinds of events can damage my business, how much damage can be done, and what should I do about it?" After evaluating the answers to these three questions and making decisions to solve the problems, the risk manager will ask, "Did I make the right decisions? Were my choices too expensive? Have circumstances changed sufficiently so that past decisions no longer apply?" Simply put, risk management is a three-step process. First, identify and measure potential losses; second, develop and execute a plan to manage this loss potential; and, third, review the plan continuously after it has been put in operation.

Risk management is a dynamic process. Large corporations change frequently: They introduce new products or services, merge divisions, acquire or sell operations, and increase or decrease capital costs. Change is also the rule for city governments, museums, hospitals, public universities, and other nonprofit institutions. Each time an organization changes significantly, it should review and, if necessary, update its risk management plan.

THE RISK MANAGEMENT FUNCTION

Trained specialists typically carry out the risk management function. The training of risk managers varies greatly. Many risk managers have insurance backgrounds; some are loss control engineers; some are attorneys; some are accountants; and some come to the risk management assignment with a liberal arts background. In recent years, the focus on financial risk management has seen more financiers, mathematicians, and others with special skills in derivative securities join the ranks of risk managers.[1]

Risk Management Staff

Because they face a wide variety of expensive potential losses, most large U.S. businesses employ a staff of people to conduct their risk management programs. A large risk management staff would be headed by a manager with overall responsibility. The staff would include one or more of the following positions: insurance expert, financial risk manager, claims manager, loss control engineer, employee benefits specialist, and financial analyst. Insurance experts are needed to work with insurance brokers in purchasing and renewing the organization's commercial insurance and reinsurance. With more firms participating in international commerce, many companies have hired specialists to protect property in foreign locations and property moving between domestic and foreign locations. Claims managers track and process claims from the time of loss until the claim is settled by the insurer. Loss control engineers manage losses arising from such things as defective products, employee injuries, and environmental pollution. Employee benefits specialists design and administer group life, health, disability, and pension plans. Financial analysts perform an increasingly important risk management function as many firms now realize that risk financing and financial risks can have a noticeable impact on an organization's profitability.

Small firms as well as large firms engage in risk management. The government classifies three-fourths of all U.S. companies as small, and some of these small firms are among the country's most profitable and rapidly growing organizations. They have the same types of property and liability exposures as large firms, though on a different scale. Many such firms engage in risk management activities but often do not employ a full-time risk manager or staff. Independent insurance agents can supply these small firms with checklists and loss control audits. Full-service insurance brokers can supply complete risk management services.

RIMS (*http://www.rims.org/*) and PRIMA (*http://www.primacentral.org/*)

The Risk and Insurance Management Society, Inc. (RIMS), is a professional organization for risk managers of both profit and nonprofit organizations. RIMS helps risk managers become aware of new problems and possible solutions through educational classes, publications such as its monthly journal, *Risk Management*, and its computer network.

The Public Risk Management Association (PRIMA) is a nonprofit association offering risk management educational programs, management information, and publications to people involved in public sector risk management. PRIMA members represent about 1,800 local governments.

---

[1] The topics of enterprise risk management (ERM) and the position of chief risk officer are described in Chapter 17, "Advanced Topics in Risk Management."

Statement of Objectives and Principles

A risk management program begins with a statement of general objectives, or a strategy. A statement of procedures or tactics designed to achieve these objectives follows.

Survival, Growth, and Responsibility

The first objective for the risk manager is to make sure the organization can survive losses. Ideally, the risk management program should allow the firm to continue to grow after a loss as if the loss had not occurred. In addition, the risk management plan should allow the organization to continue to behave responsibly toward the environment, its employees, suppliers, and customers, and the communities in which it operates.

Efficiency and Compliance

Another essential objective is to operate efficiently in a risky environment. This objective requires the firm to choose the appropriate balance among loss prevention, insurance, and other risk management tools. Efficiency means that risk management procedures operate smoothly. For example, the risk manager should be sure that loss control classes are held and that employees are motivated to perform their assignments safely.

In many firms, risk managers are responsible for keeping the firm in compliance with government regulations (such as safety and environmental laws). They also must be sure their organization complies with the requirements of its insurance contracts.

Risk Management Manual

The foregoing objectives, principles, and procedures were stated in general terms. In practice, each organization should develop a written manual with objectives and procedures related to its particular exposures. For example, a bank's risk management manual might emphasize security issues, while a manufacturing firm's manual might have many sections dealing with loss control procedures and a hospital's manual might focus on hygiene. While the risk management department often develops a statement of objectives, principles, and procedures, the organization's chief executive officer and the directors should approve this statement. Approval by chief operating officers and directors provides an endorsement of the plan and written recognition that the risk manager is empowered to insure, or leave uninsured, specified amounts of potential losses.

One large manufacturing company's risk management manual includes the following general guidelines:

1. Engage in loss prevention activities as if all chance of loss remained with the company.
2. Assume all risks that are not significant in relation to the company's financial strength.
3. Insure all risks that are not assumed.

Specific rules follow these general guidelines. For example, general guideline #2 results in identifying the following exposures to be assumed:

1. Losses to buildings and contents equal to or less than $1 million
2. Losses from physical damage to company-owned motor vehicles
3. Losses to products in transit

The $1 million risk assumption specified in point #1 is an amount related to this firm's financial capacity to bear loss. A much smaller firm might not be able to bear this size of loss, whereas a much larger firm might safely assume losses greater than

$250 million. Chapter 17, "Advanced Topics in Risk Management," presents some rules for setting risk assumption limits.

Guideline #3 leads to the following specific categories of exposures to be insured:

1. Losses to buildings and contents in excess of $1 million
2. Liability losses of the public
3. Employees' workers' compensation claims

We will briefly summarize several pages of another company's risk management manual, which makes the following points under the heading "Protecting the Company's Property Against Fire and Associated Perils."

- *Commitment to loss control:* This company genuinely is committed to loss control. Its management strongly endorses effective and efficient loss prevention and control. It expects its employees to be involved in enforcing loss prevention measures.
- *Good housekeeping:* Good housekeeping is a key component in the loss prevention and control program. Good housekeeping includes prompt waste disposal and proper material handling, especially in storage areas. Special care should be taken to avoid buildup of combustible wastes.
- *Sprinklers:* The company will install automatic fire sprinkler systems wherever needed.
- *Adequate water supply:* The company will maintain an adequate water supply to preserve the efficiency of the fire sprinkler system and fight all fires.
- *Emergency organizations:* The company will train employees to respond to all emergencies ranging from natural disasters to manmade disasters.
- *Regular inspections:* The company's property will be inspected by the risk management department on a regular basis. The inspections will result in written documentation. Inspectors will examine housekeeping, conditions of fire alarms, and sprinkler systems.

THE RISK MANAGEMENT PROCESS

Risk management activities occur before, during, and after losses. Most planning is done before losses occur. Losses involving natural disasters and other emergencies also require action while losses are happening. After a loss, the risk manager must file insurance claims and analyze loss patterns.

The risk management process requires the following steps:

1. Identify and measure potential loss exposures.
2. Choose the most efficient methods of controlling and financing loss exposures and implement them.
3. Monitor outcomes.

At this point, we can provide a more comprehensive definition of risk management: An ongoing process that requires the organization to identify the level of risk it wants to retain, to identify the risk it currently retains, and to make insurance and other financial arrangements to make the desired and the actual level of risk the same.

Estimation of Maximum Loss

When developing a risk management program, the risk manager should have a good notion of the maximum possible loss and the maximum probable loss. The *maximum possible loss* refers to the total amount of financial harm a given loss could cause under the worst circumstances. The *maximum probable loss* is the most likely maximum amount of damage a peril might cause under typical circumstances. In many cases, it may be that nothing economically feasible can be planned for the worst possible scenario. It may give the risk manager bad dreams contemplating the worst disaster that could possibly face a firm, but expending time and money to deal with the worst possible case usually will not be an efficient or practical use of the firm's limited resources. However, planning for the maximum probable loss that a firm might face every 50 or 100 years can be a valuable risk management exercise. Often, a risk manager can make efficient plans for large-scale losses. Moreover, thinking through a whole sequence of events leading to such a loss could serve as a review of all the pieces of the risk management program.

The losses caused by Hurricane Katrina in August 2005 proved to some firms that even though their risk management programs functioned well in the face of ordinary or even extraordinary losses, they could be overwhelmed by maximum probable losses. For example, many firms backed up important data: some firms kept backups in the same building, some in nearby buildings, and some in buildings 30 miles distant. In each of these cases, however, access to the original and the backup data was lost for days, weeks, or even longer. Firms facing weeks or months without electricity, phone service, Internet access, or gasoline for company vehicles could not function normally. Moreover, many, if not most, risk management plans called for resuming operations in the same building or location; neither alternative was possible for many firms. Another lesson many organizations learned from this incident was that maintaining their workforce in the aftermath of a disaster that destroyed their workers' homes was a missing link in risk management plans. Thus, even firms whose property could be reestablished physically could not resume operations in the absence of their trained workforce.

CRISIS MANAGEMENT—EMERGENCY PLANNING—DISASTER RECOVERY[2]

Crisis

The preceding discussion of some of the lessons learned from Hurricane Katrina provides an excellent beginning of a discussion of crisis management or emergency planning. Risk managers define a **crisis** as any event or series of events that have a severe negative impact on an organization. The negative impact could affect the firm's financial results, its brand value or reputation, or its relationships with its employees, customers, or suppliers.

Emergency planning is an integral part of a thorough risk management program. The first step in a crisis management plan is prevention. Before making prevention plans, a firm must analyze its vulnerability to various types of catastrophes and assess its capabilities and assets for dealing with emergencies. After this analysis is complete, risk managers should implement cost-efficient plans to reduce loss exposures wherever possible. Despite the best prevention plans, it is likely a firm will face some sort of crisis and therefore require an emergency response.

Disasters often require quick action. Plans should be in place in advance to deal with such things as natural disasters, terrorism, extortion plots (especially those involving computer and communication security), kidnapping of executives, explosions, chemical leaks, or any catastrophe where the amount of damage can be reduced by the action of an emergency response team. Firms with international operations should

---

[2] An Internet search using "crisis risk management" as keywords will produce an abundance of useful information on this quickly changing topic.

have personnel available to travel to any location where disaster threatens or has occurred.

Recovery plans often center on having good information and data. Firms should have a complete and current inventory of their buildings and their contents, including communications and computing hardware and software. They should have complete organization charts, including phone numbers of managers and employees. Good recovery plans identify contractors, equipment suppliers, insurance companies, and insurance brokers and other professionals whose services are needed after an emergency.

A crisis management plan involves prevention, preparation, and recovery strategies. It involves the creation of a crisis management team and procedures for communications with the public, employees, customers, and suppliers. Many firms now are arranging for backup facilities with replacement computer and communications networks at distant locations. Perhaps most importantly, a good crisis management strategy requires the imagination to prepare for the next crisis, not for the previous one.

Step One: Identification and Measurement of Exposures

Logically thinking about loss begins with categorizing the possibilities into four distinct classes:

- Direct property losses
- Losses of income and extra expenses following a property loss
- Losses arising from lawsuits
- Losses caused by the death, disability, or unplanned retirement of key people

It is well to remember that before a loss occurs, measurement is merely an estimate. Not all preloss estimates will reflect accurately the actual amount of damages or the actual exposure to loss.

Direct Property Losses

Risk managers can identify potential direct property losses in different ways. A walking tour of a factory, store, or hospital can reveal many property loss exposures. Risk managers often arrange regular interviews with knowledgeable employees such as production managers or accountants to identify significant changes in property holdings. The risk management procedures manual should establish a system for notifying the risk management department when property is acquired or sold. An analysis of financial statements, as well as the supporting accounts, can highlight assets exposed to loss, as can an analysis of past losses.

Checklists

Many insurance organizations provide a property checklist that may be used to identify and value potential property losses. A partial checklist appears in Table 3–1.

Flow Charts

A flow chart graphically represents the production or distribution process. Flow chart analysis displays a firm's relations with suppliers, customers, utilities, and methods of transportation. Risk managers analyze flow charts to spot production bottlenecks, sole-source suppliers, or concentrations of valuable property. Flow charts also help reveal the consequential impact of losses. For example, a loss of raw material inventory in a storage facility might stop the entire production process if the inventory cannot be replaced easily. Loss of shipping docks, however, may be overcome with temporary facilities. Losses at nonowned property, such as a sole-source supplier, or a key transportation

TABLE 3–1 Property Insurance Checklist

Identify and value:
- Owned buildings, equipment, and land
- Property leased from others
- Property leased to others
- Stationary inventory (average cost)
- Inventory being transported (average cost)
- Property under construction
- Owned or leased vehicles

Identify special perils to which property is exposed:
- Terrorism
- Radiation
- Explosion
- Flood
- Earth movement
- Theft
- Contamination

facility such as a bridge or tunnel, also could have a significant impact on production. Figure 3–1 illustrates a hypothetical flow chart.

Valuing Property

Risk managers must know the property's replacement value to estimate potential property losses. Because replacement cost often is unrelated to accounting book value (acquisition cost minus depreciation), risk managers should keep a current price and source list for their property. Estimating replacement costs might be a difficult problem when property must be custom-built and contracting costs change rapidly.

In an inflationary economy, the replacement cost of physical equipment is likely to be higher than its historical cost, and the risk manager should attempt to protect this greater value. During rapid inflation, some slow-moving inventories also may have market values significantly greater than their historical cost. Many insurance companies will insure for replacement value but pay only depreciated value until the

FIGURE 3–1 Operations Flow Chart

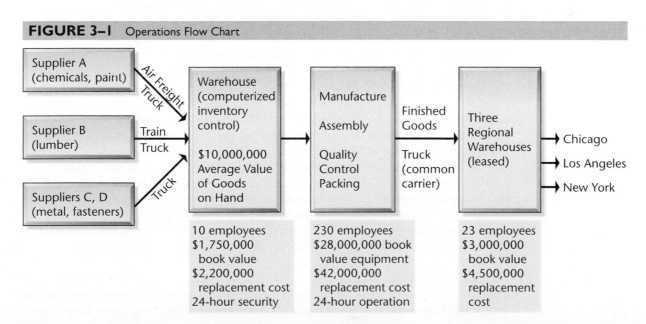

property is replaced. Insurers impose this strict condition to prevent firms from receiving the replacement value in cash and then not replacing the property.

International Operations

Firms with international operations may have property and employees in several different countries. These firms must devote special attention to identifying all their property, including property being transported between locations. Valuation of property in foreign countries may prove to be difficult due to currency fluctuations. Lack of local insurance facilities can be another problem. Thus, international businesses need specially trained staff to implement their risk management programs. Chapter 17 describes some of the special risk management problems of international business firms.

Loss of Income

Indirect losses

Indirect losses are more difficult to identify than direct property losses. We can see a machine and measure its value, but we cannot see the lost profits if the machine is unavailable for three months. Often, it is difficult to estimate how long a machine or a building will be unavailable after a loss, or whether a loss will occur during a busy season or a slack period. Despite these difficulties, risk managers must make careful estimates and judgments about the potential size of indirect losses.

Direct loss

The process begins with a forecast of expected income under normal circumstances. A second estimate of post-loss income follows. The difference is the potential income loss following a **direct loss**. The risk manager should ask informed people how long it would take to resume physical operations if a total or partial loss occurs. The accountant should estimate how much income would be lost in addition to how much in fixed and continuing expenses would occur before normal operations resume. If the business is seasonal, a loss of three months' production during the slower part of the year will not have the same consequences as a loss of production during the three busiest months of the year. Imagine the extent of the seasonality problem for businesses such as toy manufacturers or resort hotels.

The risk manager considers the fact that every direct loss of property usually has the potential for causing an indirect loss of income. In some cases, the indirect loss could be far worse than the direct loss. For example, if the information on a $250 computer storage device containing the record of a firm's accounts receivable were lost, it could cost more than $10,000 to restore it, and restoration is not possible in every case. (A backup storage device or a duplicate record stored at different locations seems appropriate, or even necessary, in cases involving data storage losses.)

For some businesses, quick resumption of operations after a loss is especially important. Examples include newspapers, broadcasting stations, retail stores, banks, and other businesses where customers are quickly and perhaps permanently lost if operations are not continuous. Included as a part of loss reduction programs for such businesses are knowledge of alternative sites for operations, knowledge of subcontractors and salvage operations, and awareness of alternative sources of funds that may be needed if operations are to be resumed in the shortest possible time. For businesses requiring continuous operations, the extra expenses to remain in operation following a direct loss represent an indirect income loss. For example, if a television station must rent facilities after its own are lost to fire, the difference between pre-loss and post-loss property rental or mortgage payments represents an indirect cost of the fire.

Liability Losses

Liability losses arise from three sources. First, an organization responsible for negligently injuring somebody must pay legal damages awarded by a court to the injured

TABLE 3–2   Typical Sources of Liability Loss

- Bodily or personal injury to employees, customers, clients, or guests
- Property damage to the real or personal property of others
- Intentional injury to people or their reputation, including illegal accusation or restraint of alleged shoplifters
- Wrongful hiring, termination, sexual harassment, or invasion of privacy of employees or job applicants
- Vicarious liability arising when a firm hires or authorizes another party to act on its behalf and this party injures a third party

party. Second, a legal defense costs money and time. A defense can be expensive even in cases where a court finds the alleged victim's claims groundless, false, or fraudulent. In some cases, the legal defense costs more than the damages awarded to parties claiming injury. The cost of loss prevention is a third source of loss arising from potential legal liability.

Risk managers spend considerable time trying to identify potential liability problems so they may be handled appropriately. Identifying possible liability losses requires current legal expertise. Most risk managers are not attorneys, but they must work with attorneys to manage liability losses. Risk managers must maintain some current legal knowledge because acts or omissions that would not have produced lawsuits twenty years ago may result in large claims for damages these days. In an age when a liability claim may represent nothing more than the imagination of the plaintiff's attorney, managing the liability risk becomes one of the risk manager's most challenging assignments. Table 3–2 presents a categorization of the bases of the most frequently encountered lawsuits.

Several types of liability losses are of increasing concern to both for-profit and nonprofit organizations. Workers' compensation claims arise from injury to a firm's employees while they are at work. Product liability occurs when a firm's products allegedly injure the public. Environmental impairment liability arises from violating federal or state statutes designed to protect the environment or from lawsuits from parties claiming injury caused by a firm's improper handling of toxic substances. Employment practices liability describes the loss potential arising from lawsuits from employees or job applicants alleging wrongful hiring, promotion, demotion, termination, and sexual harassment. We cover each of these special liability problems in Chapter 19, "Commercial Liability Insurance."

Loss of Key Personnel

Key person

If a business loses a **key person** by unplanned retirement, resignation, death, or disability, the effect may be felt in lost income. If several key employees are killed, disabled, or leave simultaneously, the results could devastate a firm. Identifying key employees can be a difficult assignment for risk managers because key employees may occupy almost any position: research scientist, president, salesperson, or treasurer. When the success of a business—or, in some instances, its existence—depends on one or more persons, the risk manager must identify these people and be ready to take steps to solve the problem if a loss occurs.

Measuring the potential loss arising from the key-employee exposure also can be difficult in some cases. Part of the problem is developing an estimate of where, at what cost, and how quickly a replacement may be hired and trained. The cost of the replacement would give the firm an estimate of the value of its exposure to loss. After making this estimate, the organization then could purchase life and disability insurance in this amount to finance this loss exposure.

Two other estimates that risk managers sometimes use to evaluate the cost of losing a key person are the following:

1. A multiple of the key person's salary; for example, purchasing life and disability insurance using a multiple between six and eight times salary would provide a firm considerable liquidity to hire an experienced replacement at a higher salary than the key person and provide some time for the replacement to become efficient.

2. An estimate of lost profits; for example, in a smaller firm, one or two people may contribute an estimated 20 percent of the annual profits. If these key people were to die or become disabled, the firm would have to replace those lost profits, perhaps for a few years, if the business were to survive the loss and be in about the same position as if the loss had not occurred.

Key employees should have well-trained subordinates when possible. In some cases, however, this may not be possible. For example, a movie production company may lose its investment if a movie star dies during filming. Thus, life and disability insurance on key employees (with the company named as beneficiary) may be a part of the risk management program. The insurance proceeds may not solve the immediate problem of replacing the employee's services caused by death or disability, but the settlement may provide the company more time to develop a solution.

Because not all key people are lost by death or disability, the risk manager is interested in the whole area of personnel administration, including questions of retirement policy, compensation policy, and the employee benefits program. To illustrate, consider a case involving a very expensive machine, critical to a manufacturing process, that only one employee knew how to maintain. This undesirable situation came to management's attention only after the employee retired and the machine broke down shortly thereafter. The losses caused by the downtime of the machine far exceeded the maintenance person's salary. This problem illustrates how difficult it can be to identify key employees. It also illustrates the dimensions of the risk management assignment.

Risk managers may identify key personnel using an organizational chart or a flow chart. Estimating the cost of key-employee losses is difficult because finding and training a replacement is a function of the job market. In some cases, trained substitutes can be found easily. In other cases, especially those involving salespeople who have built relationships with clients over long periods, resumption of the same level of performance may take years.

STEP TWO: LOSS CONTROL AND RISK FINANCING

All organizations incur costs because they are exposed to unexpected losses. Paying insurance premiums, paying for uninsured losses, paying for driver training programs, or paying for installing a fire sprinkler system—each represents a cost of being exposed to loss.

The risk manager has some ability to control the amount and timing of these costs. Successful loss control efforts reduce the amount of loss costs. Given that some losses occur even when loss control efforts are effective, an efficient risk financing program minimizes the impact of these losses on profits.

Loss Control

Loss control activities are designed to reduce loss cost and include the following risk management tools: risk avoidance, loss prevention, and loss reduction.

Risk Avoidance

Risk avoidance

Sometimes the best method of dealing with an exposure to loss is to avoid all possibility of the loss occurring. **Risk avoidance** means the chance of loss has been eliminated. In practice, it may mean not introducing a new product, ending the production of an existing product, discontinuing some operations, or selecting a business location where a particular peril is not present. For example, there are foreign countries in which U.S. firms will not make investments. The firms prefer to avoid the risks, such as confiscation of property or having employees held hostage, rather than attempt to make a profit. Individuals practice risk avoidance in their choice of careers when they avoid occupations that involve a significant chance of death or disabling injuries. Other people choose to avoid careers in which the chance of financial failure appears great to them.

Some risks are unavoidable. For example, firms or individuals cannot avoid the risk of bankruptcy, the risk of a liability suit, or the risk of premature death. The exposure to loss can often be reduced but not eliminated. For other exposures, avoidance is the only reasonable alternative. The basic rule is that when the chance of loss is high and loss severity is high, avoidance is often the best, and sometimes the only, practical alternative.

Loss Prevention

Loss prevention

Successful **loss prevention** activities lower the frequency of losses. So long as the benefits exceed the costs, firms should use loss prevention to treat all exposures, whether assumed or transferred to commercial insurers. The foremost purpose of loss prevention is to preserve human life. That is, a risk manager's first goal in a loss prevention program is to reduce or eliminate the chance of death or injury to people.

Large businesses often employ loss control engineers to identify sources of loss or injury and to institute corrective actions. Some losses can be attributed to workplace hazards such as poor layout of machines, inadequate lighting or ventilation, poor maintenance practices, or insufficient computer security. Other losses are more directly related to human shortcomings and errors, such as bad judgment, inadequate training or supervision, or lack of attention to safety requirements. Good loss control programs can be developed and implemented to deal with all these problems, but it takes a strong commitment by management and constant attention by the risk manager to reach the desired goals.

A close connection exists between loss prevention activities and insurance premiums: the more effective the loss prevention, the lower the insurance premiums. Therefore, the risk manager frequently has responsibility for overseeing loss prevention activities.

Examples of loss prevention activities include the use of tamper-resistant packaging, security guards in banks, driver training and safety education programs, and warnings printed on drugs and dangerous chemicals. As a rule, when the frequency of loss is high, risk managers should consider loss prevention activities as one alternative for dealing with the problem. Loss prevention measures are feasible, however, only so long as the benefits realized from fewer occurrences of loss are greater than the cost of the loss prevention measures. Because many loss prevention measures reduce death or injuries, establishing engineering solutions or using cost-benefit analysis raises the ethical problem of measuring the benefits of saving human lives. With many loss prevention activities, such as providing immunizations, economic benefits may not be realized for many years and may be quite difficult to measure.

Loss Reduction

Loss reduction

Successful **loss reduction** activities reduce loss severity. Despite the best loss prevention efforts, some losses occur. Loss reduction activities aim to minimize the impact of losses. An excellent example of a loss reduction device is the automatic fire-sprinkler system. This system is not designed to prevent fires but, rather, to prevent the spread of fires (that is, reduce a fire's severity). Clearly, it introduces a new peril to the environment—water damage. Nevertheless, sprinklers often pay for themselves in a short time through reduced fire insurance premiums. Other examples of loss reduction devices include firewalls and doors, instructions for treating people who have swallowed poisons, the training of replacement personnel, and salvage operations. When the severity of loss is great, and when the loss cannot be avoided, loss reduction activities are appropriate. As with loss prevention, loss reduction efforts can be justified only so long as the savings they produce exceed the cost of the efforts.

Among other loss reduction activities, *physical separation* deserves special mention. From an engineering standpoint, it may be preferable to build a 100,000-gallon-a-day ice cream plant rather than two 50,000-gallon-a-day plants. However, if the dairy built two plants, they could be separated by sufficient distance so that a loss to one plant would not jeopardize the functioning of the other. The same reasoning holds true for optimal warehouse size or even truck size. The point is that when choosing the size of an operating unit, risk considerations must be included along with engineering, marketing, and other factors.

Federal Loss Control Regulation

Occupational Safety and Health Act of 1970 (OSHA)

Loss control engineering became increasingly important in the United States with the passage of the **Occupational Safety and Health Act of 1970 (OSHA)**. Readers can view the entire act at the OSHA Web site, (*http://www.osha.gov/*). This federal law promotes a safe working environment for employees.

OSHA creates two duties for employers. One is to remove all recognized hazards from the work environment. The second is to comply with the standards for a safe working environment as published in bulletins from the Department of Labor. Because OSHA provides heavy fines for noncompliance with these standards, and even has a provision for imprisonment in some cases where employees' injuries are fatal, loss prevention activities have taken on added importance.

The OSHA program provides for on-site reviews by OSHA inspectors. It also requires extensive record keeping by employers detailing occupational injuries that result in death, injury, or significant medical treatment. The law also requires that employers enforce safety regulations rather than merely posting signs or providing safety equipment.

Consumer Products Safety Act of 1972

Comprehensive Environmental Response Compensation Liability Act of 1980

The **Consumer Products Safety Act of 1972** requires notification of the Consumer Product Safety Commission (CPSC) by manufacturers and retailers of any product hazard of which they become aware. The commission has an electronic network for sharing information about dangerous products (*http://www.cpsc.gov/index.html/*). In addition, the commission sets safety standards for some products such as lawn mowers. Once CPSC have developed the standards, makers of these products must certify that their output complies with these standards. Noncompliance can result in fines, penalties, and even imprisonment.

Superfund Amendments and Reauthorization Act of 1986

Clean Air Act

Water Pollution Control Act

Various federal environmental protection acts—including the **Comprehensive Environmental Response Compensation Liability Act of 1980** (CERCLA, often referred to as Superfund), the **Superfund Amendments and Reauthorization Act of 1986** (SARA), the **Clean Air Act** (as amended in 1990), and the **Water Pollution Control Act**—impose additional loss prevention duties on businesses, especially companies using toxic chemicals. The U.S. Environmental Protection Agency (EPA) (*http://www. epa.gov/*) regulates firms whose activities may damage the environment. The amended Clean Air Act, for example, requires organizations emitting pollutants into the air to get a permit from the EPA. If the organization does not get the required permit and subsequently pollutes the air, the EPA can shut down the establishment. If a firm gets the required permit but violates the provisions of the Clean Air Act, the EPA can impose fines up to $25,000 each day a violation occurs.[3]

Risk Financing

Risk financing determines when and by whom loss costs are borne. Risk financing includes the following alternatives:[4]

- Risk assumption
- Risk transfer other than insurance
- Self-insurance and financed risk retention
- Insurance

Risk assumption

Risk Assumption   Risk assumption means that the consequences of a loss will be borne by the party exposed to the chance of loss. Often risk assumption is a deliberate risk management decision. That is, firms assume some risks with the full understanding of the consequences of a potential loss, and with the understanding that these consequences will be borne by the firm. Deliberate risk assumption is typical when loss costs are small and will be financed from current cash flow. For example, firms often assume the risk of losing items of relatively small value such as hand tools or plates used by a restaurant. The ability to assume risk is a function of a firm's financial capacity. Thus, a large international oil company might assume the loss of a $250 million super oil tanker if its quarterly profits average $8 billion.

Sometimes organizations must assume risks. For example, deductible provisions contained in insurance policies force the insured to assume the risk for the first specified number of dollars of a loss. In addition, businesses sometimes must assume risk because commercial insurance is unavailable or unaffordable. For example, firms generally must assume catastrophic loss exposures, such as earthquake, volcano, or tsunami damage, because there is no other practical alternative.

Sometimes firms assume risk because they did not identify the potential loss before it occurred. Other firms find that they have assumed risks because of gaps in their insurance program or because somebody neglected to purchase needed coverage; none of these omissions represents effective risk management practice.

Businesses also assume risks when they operate a self-insurance or finite risk program. We describe these two topics shortly.

Funded risk assumption implies a firm has set aside a cash, or near-cash, investment fund that it can use when losses occur. This funding may supplement a plan to finance small losses from current cash flow. It provides an extra margin of safety if several assumed losses occur in a short period or if assumed losses arise during a period of reduced cash flow. Many large and medium-sized firms self-fund some of or all their health insurance or workers' compensation costs because they can predict these losses accurately.

Some firms may give accounting recognition to the expenses of assuming risk by maintaining an unfunded loss reserve account. This bookkeeping entry provides no cash in the event of loss, nor are there any tax deductions available until a loss occurs. The purpose of this approach is to give accounting accrual recognition to the cost of assumed risks, and to provide a more realistic view of the firm's financial position.

---

[3] An Internet search with the various federal acts as keywords will produce current information on each act mentioned in this paragraph.
[4] Chapter 17 describes some additional risk financing alternatives associated with financial risk management.

Self-Insurance   Readers should not confuse risk assumption, deliberate or un-planned, with the concept of self-insurance. Although **self-insurance** requires risk re-tention, it also requires a business to combine a sufficient number of its own similar exposures to predict the losses accurately. Furthermore, a self-insurance plan requires a firm to make adequate financial arrangements in advance to provide funds to pay for losses when they occur. Unless the self-insuring firm calculates and makes adequate payments to its self-insurance fund, a true self-insurance system does not exist. More-over, a self-insurance system must meet all criteria for any insurance system, as pre-sented in Chapter 2, "Defining the Insurable Event."

The Captive Insurance Company

One approach to self-insurance involves establishing a separate company formed to write insurance for a parent, called a **captive insurance company**. The captive's parent may be one company, several companies, or an entire industry. One motive in forming a captive is to save the overhead and profits earned by commercial insurers. A second incentive is to earn the investment income available on advanced funding. A third, and controversial, motive is to recognize insurance premium payments as a current busi-ness expense to parents while the captive insurer reports insurance income, thus allow-ing firms to capture the favorable tax differential between regular corporations and insurance companies.

Under federal income tax procedures, a firm cannot deduct self-insurance funding until losses occur, while it can deduct commercial insurance premiums when paid. The Internal Revenue Service (IRS) has tried to limit or eliminate the deduction of pay-ments to captive insurers, claiming there is no risk transfer. The *Carnation Company* case (1981) is the landmark decision in this area and sustained the IRS position. The *Mobil* case (1985) also upheld the government's view. In the early 1990s, the courts ap-parently moderated the government's strict position, allowing self-insurance premiums to be deducted currently by a few corporations whose captive insurers provided sub-stantial coverage to other parties.

Captive insurance companies appeal to some organizations because the organiza-tions see one or more of the following potential advantages:

- *Improved loss prevention incentives.* This advantage offers a chance to reap directly the benefits of successful loss control.
- *Improved claims settlements.* This advantage includes the ability to cover or exclude claims with more flexibility than a commercial insurer has.
- *Improved profitability.* This advantage includes the investment potential from investing cash flow or avoiding premium taxes.
- *Economies of scale.* A captive insurance operation also allows companies with many subsidiaries to combine the insurance needs of these subsidiaries under one insurance program. In areas such as the automobile liability exposure, a self-insurance facility combined with reinsurance might allow considerable savings compared to the cost of each subsidiary company purchasing its own coverage.

Although a captive insurer may offer a business some advantages, other factors must be taken into consideration when a business is deciding whether to use this ap-proach. First, commercial insurance companies often provide their customers with valu-able services in both loss prevention engineering and claims settlement. These services must be purchased or provided internally if a captive is used. Second, a business must hire competent management to administer the captive insurer. Third, the cost of capital required to operate the program represents a cost. Fourth, careful risk managers do not assume a risk before the funds are available to pay for the loss. The reader will remember from the description of insurance premiums in Chapter 1, "Fundamentals and Terminology," that most of the savings from a funded or unfunded risk assumption program must come from the expense and profit factors in the insurance premium. The cost of the losses remains the same whether the risk is assumed or insured.

Deductible

Retention

Some companies have taken a middle-of-the-road position between commercial insurance and forming a captive insurer. They do this by careful use of the deductible provision in their insurance policies. The **deductible** provision, or the **retention**, determines the amount that an insured must deduct from an insurance claim before determining the amount that the insurer must pay.[5]

As an example of this use of a deductible to lower insurance premiums, assume that the California Gold Company has a $100,000 deductible in its fire insurance policy. The insurer will pay claims only when the amount of loss exceeds $100,000, and then the insurer pays only the amount in excess of the deductible. Thus, a $1,000,000 insured loss produces a $900,000 payment. The rule is that the higher the deductible, the lower the insurance premium for a given exposure. Many people know that increasing the deductible on their automobile or homeowners insurance from $250 to $500 or $1,000 produces considerable savings in premiums. Businesses also save on their insurance premiums by increasing the deductible. The process must not be carried on to the point at which the risk assumed becomes too great relative to the financial capacity of the individual or firm, however. Chapter 17 presents an extensive discussion of the trade-offs involved when choosing the deductible size that maximizes premium savings without leaving unacceptable levels of risk.

Finite Risk Programs

Finite risk contract

Another approach to risk financing is multiple-year insurance arrangements. Seen in its most simple form, the **finite risk contract** commits the insured to transfer premium payments to an insurer in an amount equal to the aggregate policy limit. The transfer takes place in even installments over a specified number of years. If large losses occur in the early years of the program, the insurer in essence makes a loan to the insured until future premium payments cover the losses incurred. If the insured has no losses during the payment period, the insured is entitled to a refund.

A quick review of the foregoing description makes it clear the insurer has accepted very little risk. For this reason, the International Financial Reporting Standards (IFRS) and the IRS have concluded that where there is no risk transfer, there is no insurance. Thus, to qualify for tax benefits, or for accounting treatment to count as insurance, finite risk transactions must involve some appreciable amount of risk transfer.

Risk Transfer

Risk transfer

Risk transfer means the original party exposed to a loss can obtain a substitute party to bear the risk. Risk transfer is a feature of all insurance transactions because the uncertainty of who will pay for the loss is transferred from the individual to the insurance pool. Some methods of risk transfer, however, do not involve insurance. The distinction between insurance and noninsurance risk transfer is that insurance involves not only the mere transfer of risk but also the reduction of risk through the increased predictability provided by the law of large numbers.

Hedging

Hedging is an example of a noninsurance transfer of risk. Suppose Alex bets Tania a dollar that heads will appear when he flips a coin. If tails appears, he loses a dollar.

---

[5] Some authorities make a distinction between deductible and retention provisions, especially as they apply to liability insurance.

After some thought, Alex decides that the bet is making him uneasy. Therefore, he makes a second bet with Thomas on the same flip of the coin, but takes an opposite position. That is, he will win a dollar from Thomas if he flips tails but will lose a dollar if he flips heads. This balance is the nature of hedging: to take two simultaneous positions that offset each other so that no matter what the outcome of some event based on chance, the hedger neither wins nor loses.

More practical illustrations of hedging occur in the commodities and stock markets. Risk managers of financial institutions such as banks and mutual funds and of firms dealing in commodities, such as grain companies, cereal manufacturers, and soft drink bottlers, include hedging as an important risk management tool. In general, these firms try to offset potential losses caused by the increased cost of essential inputs, with gains arising from price increases on such financial instruments as commodities futures or derivative securities. **Financial risk management** includes the arrangements made to manage the loss exposures presented by currency fluctuations, interest rate changes, and commodity price changes. The futures market for commodities, currency futures markets for companies dealing in foreign currencies, and the options market for stocks allow speculators, investors, and businesses exposed to loss to enter into simultaneous transactions that limit the gains or losses arising from future price changes. We present some of the vocabulary of financial risk management and describe its increasing importance in Chapter 17.

Two other examples of noninsurance risk transfer involve leases and hold-harmless agreements. Leasing property allows the user of property to transfer the risk of the obsolescence of the property to the owner, usually for a price added to the lease payment. The transfer of the risk of obsolescence may be an important factor in the lease of technologically advanced equipment.

Hold-harmless agreements are contracts entered into prior to a loss, in which one party agrees to assume a second party's responsibility should a loss occur. For example, a railroad may require a manufacturer to assume all responsibility for accidents before building a spur line on the manufacturer's property. In other cases, vendors request hold-harmless agreements before selling a manufacturer's goods. Likewise, contractors may require subcontractors to provide the contractor with liability protection if they are sued because of the subcontractor's activities.

Insurance

From the risk manager's viewpoint, **insurance** represents a contractual transfer of risk. From society's viewpoint, insurance is more than mere risk transfer; it is risk reduction because the pooling of numerous risks allows better loss predictability.

Insurance is an especially appropriate risk management tool when the chance of loss is low and the severity of a potential loss is high. Many situations facing both firms and individuals meet these two criteria, and thus insurance is widely purchased. For small and medium-sized business firms, insurance is the foundation of their risk management program. Most large firms also face circumstances requiring commercial insurance. In some cases, the law requires insurance. In other cases, a large firm still may need the insurer's services, such as loss control inspections or loss settlement expertise. Finally, exposure to extremely large potential losses generally requires insurance.

After deciding to insure a particular loss exposure, the risk manager still faces many decisions, including choosing an insurance company, choosing an insurance agent or broker, and choosing an insurance policy. If the risk manager decides to use the services of an insurance broker, the risk manager and the broker often will work together to develop specifications for the insurance program. After arranging the insurance coverage, the risk manager's work is still not complete. As mentioned earlier in this

Financial risk management

Hold-harmless agreements

Insurance

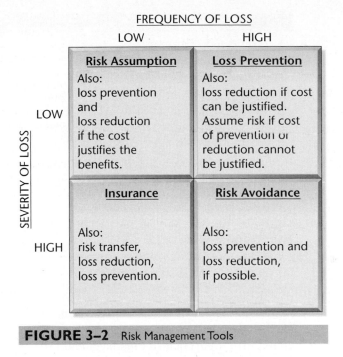

FREQUENCY OF LOSS

	LOW	HIGH
LOW	**Risk Assumption** Also: loss prevention and loss reduction if the cost justifies the benefits.	**Loss Prevention** Also: loss reduction if cost can be justified. Assume risk if cost of prevention or reduction cannot be justified.
HIGH	**Insurance** Also: risk transfer, loss reduction, loss prevention.	**Risk Avoidance** Also: loss prevention and loss reduction, if possible.

SEVERITY OF LOSS

FIGURE 3–2   Risk Management Tools

chapter, the risk manager must make sure the company does not violate any of the terms of the insurance agreement. If the contract is conditioned on the company employing a security guard or maintaining a fire sprinkler system, the risk manager must be sure that these conditions are met so that the contract is not breached.

Once a loss has occurred, the risk manager must report the loss promptly to the insurer and comply with all the post-loss contractual requirements. If adjusting the loss presents problems, the risk manager, acting with the company's legal staff, must negotiate the problems with the insurance company. It should be clear that the wise use of insurance as a risk management tool involves much more than purchasing an insurance policy.

Figure 3–2 summarizes the risk management tools and their appropriate uses.

STEP THREE: REGULAR REVIEW OF THE RISK MANAGEMENT PROGRAM

After all potential sources of loss have been identified and plans to deal with them implemented, the risk manager must review the program regularly to be sure that it meets current needs.

Over time, conditions change in every business. New assets are acquired, old assets lose their value, inventories increase or decrease, new production processes are used, new products are marketed, new personnel are hired, and laws are changed. Each change in the business might represent a new exposure to loss or might alter an existing source of loss. The risk manager also must be aware of all significant changes in the firm's legal environment and must be able to assess correctly their impact on the firm's risk management program.

A review of existing risk management plans is always useful. The risk manager must measure the actual results of the plans against the original objectives. Has the insurance company provided all the services expected of it and paid losses promptly? Has the loss prevention program actually resulted in fewer losses? Have the exposures

TABLE 3–3 Fundamental Risk Management Responsibilities

- Identify loss exposures.
- Select the most efficient methods to deal with loss exposures.
- Choose an insurance broker to provide needed services and insurance coverages.
- Prepare specifications for insurance quotations.
- Negotiate with the insurance broker to purchase and renew insurance contracts.
- File claims with insurers in the event of a loss.
- Develop and implement self-insurance and other retention programs.
- Maintain a database of insured and uninsured losses and loss claims against the risk. manager's firm. Regularly analyze the data and take needed corrective action.
- Review lease agreements, contracts and other documents for loss exposures.
- Develop and put into operation loss prevention and loss control programs.

the company assumed produced losses as expected? The risk manager answers these questions by a regular review of the risk management program.

The development and maintenance of accurate details on losses are important. These details include the date of the loss, the amount of damage caused, the cause of the loss, and what steps were taken to prevent future occurrences. OSHA provisions require keeping extensive records of losses. Even if loss recording were not the law, however, analysis of loss data permits the appraisal of loss prevention procedures and enables the diagnosis of problems in their early stages. Thus, maintaining loss records is an important part of a risk management program.

After the risk manager develops a loss prevention program, all affected employees should know the plan's aims and what role they are expected to play in the program. The risk manager must remain alert to any advances in loss control engineering that may make a given operation, plant, or store a safer place in which to work.

The risk manager should be satisfied that a decision has been made concerning each identified potential source of loss, including direct and indirect property losses, liability losses, and key personnel losses. Even if the firm chooses to do nothing about a particular source of loss, this decision should be noted. It might be desirable to review the decision if a loss occurs, or the decision might have to be revised as circumstances change.

Readers have come to the end of a long chapter filled with many topics. Table 3–3 presents a summary of some of the risk manager's usual activities.

SUMMARY

All firms and individuals face uncertainties caused by the possibility of loss. A risk management program is an organized method for dealing with risks. The program begins with identifying and measuring exposures to loss. The second step is choosing an approach from among the risk management alternatives and then implementing the decision. The third step is reevaluating and updating previous decisions.

An estimate of the total potential loss that a given peril could cause is an important step in the risk management program. The maximum possible loss is the damage that could be caused under the worst possible circumstances. The maximum probable loss is the most likely maximum amount of dam-age a firm might sustain from a loss given normal circumstances. Estimating the maximum probable loss involves considering both the direct and the indirect consequences of a loss. Once the risk manager has estimated the maximum potential for loss, he or she can develop an integrated plan to deal with it.

The identification process begins with recognizing four categories of losses:

- Direct losses of property, such as the loss of a machine in a fire
- Indirect losses of income, such as the loss of income if a business cannot operate because its most important machine burned

- Liability losses, such as being sued for negligently injuring a customer
- Loss of key personnel, such as the loss of a research scientist who has been responsible for several important inventions

The development of a risk management program includes choosing the most appropriate combination of risk management tools for a given exposure to loss. Once a solution is chosen, the risk manager must see to it that the decision is implemented carefully. If insurance is purchased, the conditions of the contract must be fulfilled. If loss prevention programs are drawn up, they must be made widely known.

Every risk management decision should be reviewed regularly to adjust to changing circumstances. Losses that were assumed years ago, for example, now may have to be insured. Conversely, losses insured for years now may be capable of being assumed. Furthermore, all decisions should be reviewed in light of the outcomes expected when the decisions were made.

There are seven ways to deal with risk. Risk avoidance means eliminating the chance of loss by not exposing oneself to the peril. This tool is appropriate when both the chance of loss and loss severity are high. Risk assumption means that one must pay for the loss oneself if it occurs. Risks may be assumed because they are of slight consequence or be-

cause one does not realize that there is a p of loss. A self-insurance program requires cc many similar risks so that losses may be predi.... ... curately. Self-insurance also requires adequate funds to be set aside in advance of losses.

Loss prevention activities lower the chance of loss. Loss prevention is mandated by OSHA and several other federal laws. Loss reduction activities are designed to reduce the severity of losses. A good example is an automatic fire-sprinkler system that does not stop fires from starting but slows their spreading.

Risk transfer means that one party finds another party to bear the consequences of an exposure to loss. Risk transfer is distinguished from insurance because insurance involves pooling and the predictability of losses in advance of their occurrence. Hedging is an example of risk transfer, as are hold-harmless agreements and many leasing agreements.

Insurance is an appropriate risk management tool when the chance of loss is low and the severity of loss is high. Insurance involves combining many similar exposures to loss to achieve predictability. Insurance allows the purchaser to substitute a small certain premium for a large uncertain loss. The risk manager's function involves much more than the purchase of an insurance contract. The risk manager must see that all contractual conditions are fulfilled and must represent the company's interest after a loss.

REVIEW TERMS

- Captive insurance company
- Consumer Products Safety Act of 1972
- Deductible
- Direct loss
- Financial risk management
- Finite risk contract
- Hedging

- Hold-harmless agreements
- Indirect loss
- Insurance
- Key person
- Loss prevention
- Loss reduction
- Occupational Safety and Health Act of 1970 (OSHA)

- Retention
- Risk assumption
- Risk avoidance
- Risk management
- Risk transfer
- Self-insurance

REVIEW

1. List and explain three desirable risk management goals likely to be found in a statement of objectives and principles.
2. Describe some purposes served by a risk management manual.
3. Explain three alternative methods a risk manager may use to identify and measure direct property losses.
4. Do all firms face liability losses? Explain your answer.

5. What is the best measure of the loss of a key person?
6. List and explain the three main categories of loss control activities.
7. What are the potential advantages of a self-insurance program? What are the potential disadvantages?
8. What are the steps in developing a risk management plan? Why is the order of the steps important? Which step is the most difficult to accomplish?
9. Describe four categories of loss. Give an example of each category, using a large automobile manufacturer as your example. Give an example of each category that might be found in a small business.
10. Why is the quick resumption of operations a problem for some businesses? Give examples to explain your answer.
11. What are the requirements for a self-insurance plan as opposed to simple risk retention?
12. What is OSHA? What is the connection between OSHA and a firm's risk management program?
13. How is loss prevention different from loss reduction? Give some examples of each.

OBJECTIVE QUESTIONS

1. Direct property losses would include each of the following except:
   a. Losses to owned buildings
   b. Losses to leased buildings
   c. Losses of inventory
   d. Loss of income after inventory is destroyed by fire
2. To estimate the value of potential property losses, risk managers should focus on:
   a. The purchase price of the property
   b. The property's book value
   c. The property's replacement cost
   d. The property's fair market value
3. Typical sources of liability losses include all the following except:
   a. A worker allows a machine to be destroyed by improper maintenance
   b. Losses caused to workers injured on the job
   c. Losses caused to the real property of others
   d. Losses caused by bodily injury to customers in a store
4. Risk avoidance:
   a. Means measures are taken to eliminate the loss exposure
   b. Means measures are taken to reduce loss severity
   c. Means insurance has been purchased and the risk transferred to an insurance company
   d. Is never a useful risk management tool

5. "The logical development and carrying out of a plan to deal with potential losses" is the definition of:
   a. Loss control
   b. Risk management
   c. Emergency response team
   d. Risk financing using derivative options
6. The purpose of a risk management flow chart is to represent graphically the production and distribution process to help the risk manager identify:
   a. Insurance policies
   b. Liability losses
   c. Nearby fire departments
   d. Production bottlenecks
7. Business firms face liability lawsuits when their: (choose best answer)
   a. Products injure consumers
   b. Customers steal their inventory
   c. Unions go on strike
   d. Attorneys fail to file legal documents
8. The federal law that promotes a safe working environment for workers is:
   a. Superfund
   b. Equal Opportunity Act
   c. OSHA
   d. CERCLA

INTERNET RESEARCH ASSIGNMENT

1. Identify three recent recalls of dangerous products by the Consumer Products Safety Commission. Start your search at this site: (*http://www.cpsc.gov/index.html/*).
2. Describe three current employment opportunities for risk managers; what are the salary offered and the education requirements? Start your search at this site: (*http://www.rims.org/*).
3. Investigate several "hot topics" that currently concern risk managers. Start your search at this site: (*http://www. iii.org/media/hottopics/*).
4. What is a risk retention group? Start your search at this site: (*http://www.captiveassociation.com/*).

TEXAS BANK TORNADO[6]

In March 2000, at 5:30 P.M., a tornado hit several major buildings in downtown Fort Worth, Texas. Among the buildings damaged by the windstorm was a tall glass tower that a large bank had leased mostly for administrative offices for its 600 employees, but that also had public banking facilities on the lower floors. Because the tornado hit just after the end of the workday, there was no loss of life, but property damage to the building and its contents was extensive. Because the bank did not own the building, the bank had to arrange for access to the property after the loss through the building's owners. Moreover, the city of Fort Worth's building inspectors declared the building to be imminently dangerous. After the building was labeled imminently dangerous, the bank's officers and employees had no access to it for over a week. During this week, wind and rain caused further damage to the furniture, equipment, and valuable papers.

The bank's risk manager had made prior arrangements with a disaster recovery facility in a remote location that allowed the bank to use the emergency facility's computers, phones, and fax machines after a disaster. This facility provided workspace for about one-third of the bank's critical personnel. The bank's risk manager also made arrangements for a shuttle bus service between the loss location and office space available in nearby Dallas, Texas. Employees were not able to retrieve critical papers from the loss site until two weeks after the tornado struck, by which time the glass windows in the tower had been replaced or boarded over with plywood.

The company had planned to replace all the destroyed furniture, carpeting, and electronic equipment, as well as to repaint its entire premises before reoccupying the damaged property. While the building was unusable, the bank had to find and rent alternate locations for many of its employees. It also had to continue the expensive shuttle service to Dallas and to provide many employees with an allowance for their commuting expense. In addition, the bank experienced much inefficiency, such as the inability to hold needed conferences and meetings that normally would have taken place in the damaged location. Perhaps the greatest complication arose when the building owner declared that it was too expensive to repair the building and therefore it was terminating all the leases. Leasing the same amount of space in a new location would likely cost the bank about twice what it had been paying at the damaged location.

Based on the information provided, complete the following assignments:

1. Identify all the direct losses the bank experienced.
2. Identify all the indirect losses the bank experienced.
3. In a maximum probable loss event arising from a tornado, identify the additional losses that you would expect to see.
4. How could the bank's risk manager use each of the following risk management tools in this case?
   a. Risk assumption
   b. Loss prevention
   c. Loss reduction
   d. Insurance
   e. Risk transfer

RISK MANAGEMENT AT A TELEVISION STATION

Television station WMSD is located in a Midwestern city of 1,750,000 people. The station is incorporated, with the majority of the stock owned by one family. The grandfather, age 68, who founded the station, already has begun to make gifts of the stock to other family members. His daughter, age 47, is currently the vice president and will manage the station after her father retires or dies. The station is affiliated with one of the major television networks.

WMSD has 156 employees. Of these, 20 appear on the air, 7 are managers or officers, and 129 are

---

[6] Judy A. Rogers, Assistant Vice President, Bank One Corporate Insurance and Risk Management, helped develop this case.

clerical, production, or marketing employees. The payroll for a recent year amounted to $43,550,000. WMSD's assets include buildings and a transmission tower valued at $47.5 million on the books but having a replacement value of $62 to $64 million. The station's equipment, including cameras, videotape machines, six cars, three trucks, a leased helicopter, and sophisticated electronic equipment and computers, has a book value of $52.6 million and a replacement cost of $73.5 million.

In recent years, the station's earnings after taxes were as follows: Year 1, $58 million; Year 2, $65 million; Year 3, $40 million. The income came from selling commercials in the local market and from network revenue. In recent years, one sales representative was responsible for almost one-quarter of the local advertising revenue. WMSD is the second-ranked station in the market and has become

aggressive in the past three years in trying to increase its market share. The station management has faced an uphill battle in gaining ground on the number-one station, and there is concern that both stations have lost earnings to cable television. The station's cash flow is seasonal, with maximum receipts occurring during December. Any losses before special events, such as sporting championships, would have a major impact on profitability.

Your assignment is to develop a risk management plan for WMSD. You are to consider all types of loss exposures and all the risk management alternatives discussed in this chapter. Give at least one example of how the risk management techniques of avoidance, assumption, loss prevention, loss reduction, and insurance may be used, explaining why each technique is appropriate.

Appendix: Personal Risk Management

In describing risk management, our emphasis has been on solving business problems. Families and individuals can benefit from developing a risk management program covering their personal exposures to loss. The risk management process remains the same:

1. Identify and measure potential loss exposures.
2. Develop and implement a risk management plan.
3. Review the plan regularly.

The personal risk management plan has more limited options than those of a business, and insurance is a more likely risk financing result than other risk management tools. Loss prevention, risk avoidance, and loss reduction can all play important roles in personal risk management. In the current legal and economic environment, with its increased chances of liability and crime losses, a personal risk management plan, or a personal financial plan as we often call it, is very desirable. Much of the information covered later in this book, especially the material on homeowners insurance, automobile insurance, and life insurance, must be understood before developing sound personal financial plans. The material presented here is only an outline of the risk management process.

People face three basic categories of losses: (1) property losses—direct and indirect, (2) liability losses, and (3) income losses related to human life contingencies.

Direct property losses arise from many perils: Fire, theft, and windstorm damage are frequent causes of such losses. Indirect property losses include extra living expenses during a period when a home is rebuilt after a fire and car rental expenses after a vehicle is stolen. Most people insure their real and personal property with a homeowners insurance policy. This policy also provides some extra living expenses and liability coverage and can be quite flexible when endorsements for special situations are attached to the basic policy.

Some people own large amounts of valuable property not found in average homes. Insurers recommend covering such property as valuable stamp or coin collections, artwork, furs, and jewelry with inland marine, personal property floater policies on a scheduled basis. A good insurance agent can provide checklists to help people identify their property loss exposures. For some property, expert appraisers are needed to determine value. In all cases, evidence of ownership and purchase price information is desirable. Replacement cost estimates are useful for property with rapidly changing values. Thorough identification and measurement of all potential property losses are critical steps in the personal risk management process.

Personal liability loss exposures increase each year as legal doctrines change. Exposures that did not exist twenty years ago (for example, social host liquor liability) confirm this trend. Identifying and measuring liability exposures are difficult. These exposures are covered ordinarily as a part of the homeowners policy, but people should be aware that this policy contains important exclusions from coverage. Liability arising from business pursuits is a good example of an important homeowners policy exclusion. People with business pursuits either should have their homeowners policy endorsed to cover such activities or should purchase an appropriate supplement policy.

Estimating the potential liability loss is almost as difficult for people as it is for businesses. Million-dollar claims for injury are almost commonplace. For this reason, many people add personal liability umbrella policies to their other insurance policies. These umbrellas provide coverage if underlying (homeowners and automobile) policies are exhausted. A $1 million personal liability umbrella usually is moderately priced, costing about $150.

Measuring and identifying income losses caused by adverse human life contingencies, such as death and disability, are difficult problems. Adequate health insurance in this period of $1,000+-a-day hospital bills is a necessary part of a personal risk management plan. Most people obtain their health insurance coverage as a part of an employee benefit plan.

In summary, each person or family should develop a risk management plan. They should identify and measure all loss exposures. Written decisions, legal documents (such as wills), and other valuable papers should be maintained in a secure place. Adequate amounts of insurance should be purchased. Risk avoidance, loss prevention, and loss reduction alternatives also should be considered. Finally, the program should be reviewed. The scientific approach to the loss exposure problem is essential to individuals and families in today's complex and changing financial environment.

CHAPTER 4

Insurance Companies

After studying this chapter, you should be able to:

- Describe the most important characteristics of the stock insurance company

- Describe the most important characteristics of the mutual insurance company

- Explain why many mutual companies transformed themselves into stock companies

- Explain the importance of the Gramm-Leach-Bliley Act to the insurance industry

This chapter begins by describing the Gramm-Leach-Bliley Act, the federal law that allows the creation of financial services holding companies. We then describe the two most important types of insurance companies, the stock insurance company and the mutual insurance company. In the past decade, many large mutual insurers have changed their form to become stock insurers, and we describe this process, which is called *demutualization*. Next, we describe Lloyd's of London and several forms of legal organizations that insurers use in this country. The chapter concludes with some data about the insurance industry. The appendix to this chapter presents some of the author's research on the transformation of the insurance industry in Central and Eastern Europe from a state monopoly to a market-based industry. This appendix highlights the role private insurance plays in a market economy.

FINANCIAL SERVICES REGULATION IN THE UNITED STATES

Gramm-Leach-Bliley Act (GLB)

In November 1999, the **Gramm-Leach-Bliley Act (GLB)**, which is also known as the Financial Services Reform Act of 1999, became law in the United States. Readers can find the entire act at this site: (*http://www.senate.gov/~banking/conf/confrpt.htm/*). This act marked a milestone of sufficient importance to the insurance market that we must describe it before providing information about the different kinds of legal organizations that now sell insurance. GLB allows banks, security dealers, and insurance companies to combine to form financial services holding companies. GLB allows banks to acquire insurance companies, insurance companies to acquire banks, banks to open their own insurance companies, and insurance companies to open banks. The law requires most of these combinations to be in the form of holding companies so that firewalls preclude capital flowing between the component parts. In general, it remains the responsibility of the various states to supervise and maintain the solvency of insurance companies, while the federal government has the main responsibility for supervising and maintaining the solvency of the banks and security dealers. Because of their separate status for regulatory purposes, it is still possible to describe the characteristics of insurance companies, even when they are a component part of a larger financial services company.

More than six years have passed since GLB became law, and commentators have drawn some initial conclusions about GLB's impact on the potential for combining

TABLE 4-1   Types of Insurance Organizations
• Stock Insurance Companies
• Mutual Insurance Companies
• Advance Premium
• Assessment
• Factory
• Perpetual
• Lloyd's of London
• Reciprocal Exchange
• Fraternal Insurers
• Savings Bank Life Insurance

banking and insurance services. In general, the "one-stop financial services firm" has not become the popular result some analysts expected when the law was passed. The following quotation makes this point:

> In sum, of the nearly 500 financial holding companies, only a handful of them have significant investment banking and insurance operations. . . . The lack of activity provides circumstantial evidence that the synergies between these activities are relatively weak.[1]

Table 4–1 presents an outline of organizations that sell insurance.

THE MOST IMPORTANT TYPES OF INSURANCE COMPANIES

The most important types of insurance companies are the mutual insurance company and the stock insurance company. These types of insurers write either life or non–life (property and liability) insurance coverage. Because of state laws regulating solvency and other matters, a single insurance company cannot sell both life and non–life insurance. Insurance holding companies, however, can combine both life and non–life insurance companies in one organization but must keep their operations separate. Thus, families of insurance companies can provide a broad range of coverage, including both life and non–life, personal, and commercial coverage. Property insurers that provide **Multiple-line insurers** more than one type of coverage, such as a company selling fire, inland marine, liability, workers' compensation, and automobile insurance, are called **multiple-line insurers**.

Stock Insurance Companies

Stock insurance company

A **stock insurance company** is similar to all other corporations where stockholder-owners provide the capital to establish and operate the corporation. These owners are entitled to the financial results, whether favorable or unfavorable. By exercising their right to vote, they elect the management of the corporation. Also, the owners may sell their shares (ownership interest) in the company if they choose to do so. The buying and selling of corporate shares is one of the hallmarks of a capitalistic economy. To buy or sell an interest in a publicly owned stock insurance company [a few of which have their stock traded on the New York Stock Exchange (NYSE) and many of which are listed in the National Association of Securities Dealers (NASD) market], both buyers and sellers would contact a representative of security brokerage firms.

---

[1]Federal Reserve Bank of St. Louis, "The Regional Economist," October 2005, p. 7.

Mutual Insurance Companies

Mutual insurance companies are nonprofit corporations. The owners of a mutual insurance company are the policyholders insured by the corporation. Policyholders of a mutual insurance company have rights similar to owners of for-profit corporations. For example, they can vote to elect the directors of the corporation. The directors, in turn, appoint the management to operate the corporation. Policyholders can also vote on important business matters, such as changes in the corporation's bylaws or changing the organization to a stock insurance company. The major subcategories of mutual insurance companies are advance premium mutuals, assessment mutuals, and factory mutuals.

One significant difference between stock and mutual insurance companies is that it is possible to own an interest in a stock company and not purchase insurance from it. Also, it is possible to be insured by a stock insurer and not have an ownership interest in the company. Neither of these positions is possible in a mutual insurer.

A second significant difference between these two forms of insurers is that in a stock company, additional funds not provided by past or present insureds, but by owners, can be used to absorb losses and expenses not covered by premiums. In some cases, these additional funds could prove to be a benefit to the insured of a stock company.

While mutual insurance companies legally are nonprofit corporations, this does not mean that they are run inefficiently. Quite the contrary—many of these companies operate as efficiently as any for-profit company. The author has had experience with several large mutual life insurers and has found them to employ the latest techniques in effective business management. As is typical of other forms of insurance companies, mutual insurers show considerable variation in performance.

The Web site of the National Association of Mutual Insurance Companies (NAMIC), a trade association of mutual property insurance companies, is (*http://www.namic.org/*). This site contains information about recent insurance legislation and other areas of interest to mutual insurance companies and their insureds.

Advance Premium Mutual

In terms of volume of insurance written, the most frequently encountered kind of mutual insurance company is the **advance premium mutual**. Under the advance premium system, policyholders pay their premiums when their insurance begins and become eligible for a dividend when the insurance period ends. Mutual insurance companies pay dividends only when they have favorable operating results. Favorable operating results occur when the insurance company experiences fewer losses or lower expenses than it predicted or has greater investment earnings than projected. If a mutual insurance company experiences greater losses or expenses than predicted, its ability to pay dividends is diminished. For example, if a mutual life insurance company were to incur substantial losses on its investments or to experience an unusually high number of losses, the insured-owner's dividends would be lower. If it continued to experience large losses, the insurer's surplus account eventually would be depleted. When individuals or businesses purchase insurance from a mutual insurance company, they become owners and share in the financial outcome of ownership, whether favorable or unfavorable. Advance premium mutual insurance companies, however, cannot assess their policyholders for unmet claims.

In the case of mutual life insurance companies, favorable operating results are the norm. As a rule, a built-in dividend arises because the annual premium is higher than needed to pay all expected losses and expenses. When, as anticipated, fewer losses occur than were predicted, the policyholder receives a dividend.[2] Unlike dividends from profit-making corporations, this dividend does not represent new income to the policyholder; rather, it represents the return of part of the premium. In this sense, the initial premium from a mutual company has a safety factor that can be returned to the policyholder if nothing unexpected occurs during the year. The Internal Revenue Service (IRS) calls the dividends paid by mutual insurance companies a return of premium, and they are not subject to federal income tax.

Assessment Mutual

Assessment mutuals do much less business than do advance premium mutuals. Under the assessment system, insured members may or may not pay a premium when the insurance period begins, but they become liable to pay their fair share of the insurance company's losses and expenses when the period ends. An insured's liability in an assessment mutual may or may not be limited, and potential purchasers from such a company should determine their maximum liability before purchasing insurance. Assessment mutuals provide primarily fire and windstorm insurance for small towns and farmers.

Factory Mutual

The **factory mutual** is a third type of mutual insurance company. An important distinction of this type of insurer is that it provides substantial loss prevention services, including regular inspection of the insured premises. Only those exposures meeting rigid safety and construction qualifications (for example, those with fire sprinkler systems) can qualify for coverage. Risk managers call this type of exposure a **highly protected risk**. Only a limited number of exposure units—large, well-constructed, carefully maintained exposures—are eligible for insurance by the factory mutual.

Many factory mutuals have required the advance deposit of the entire premium for multiyear policies. When the opportunity cost of tying up funds is high, this provision makes the insurance coverage more expensive. Nevertheless, because of selective underwriting standards, the losses, and hence the insurance costs, may be significantly lower for firms able to get insurance from a factory mutual. Readers can find more information about factory mutual insurance at the following Web site: (*http://www.fmglobal.com/*).

Perpetual Mutual

Perpetual mutuals are of historical significance. Although a few companies still operate on the perpetual basis, they are not a relevant factor in the insurance marketplace. The perpetual mutual requires each insured to contribute a large initial premium, with no future premiums required. The insurance pool is run from the earnings on the initial deposit. This type of insurance operation was organized by Ben Franklin in Philadelphia in the eighteenth century.

Demutualization

Demutualization occurs when a mutual insurer changes its legal form to that of a stock company. One reason for making this switch is to overcome a section of the Deficit Reduction Act of 1984 that places a limit on the amount of policyholder dividends that a mutual insurer can deduct on its federal tax return, causing an increased tax liability. A second motive for conversion was the financial weakness that some life insurers experienced in the early 1990s. The stock form allows other insurers to add capital to these weakened mutual companies through stock ownership. The troubled companies were

Margin notes:
Assessment mutuals
Factory mutual
Highly protected risk
Perpetual mutuals

---

[2] Some stock insurers also pay policyholder dividends as well as shareholder dividends.

able to issue stock to new investors after they demutualized. The new investors' capital provided funds needed to stabilize financial operations and to renew the insureds' confidence.

A more recent development encouraging demutualization is GLB, because stock insurers can be acquired and can make acquisitions more easily than can mutual insurance companies. While the process of demutualization is still arduous, with GLB companies had strong competitive reasons to go through the process. In fact, since 1995, many of the largest mutual life insurance companies have demutualized.[3]

Stock insurers have more flexible capital structures than mutual insurers. A stock company can raise capital by selling common or preferred stock or by issuing long-term bonds. The mutual company can increase its capital only by favorable operating results and does not have comparable flexibility in generating capital. Lack of flexibility in raising funds may prove to be a problem if a mutual company needs large amounts of funds to arrange mergers or acquisitions or to offset bad investment results. Stock companies also can use their more flexible financial structures to set up downstream subsidiary companies or upstream holding companies, or provide securities for an incentive compensation plan for executives.

Much controversy has surrounded some of the demutualizations announced in recent years. Some commentators claim that the current policyowners, who technically "owned" the company, have not received full value for their share of the company in the demutualization process. The critics say that when companies decided to demutualize, the boards of directors of the mutual companies switched terminology from "ownership rights" to "membership rights." There is no answer to the question "Who owns a mutual company, if not the policyowners?" Consumer groups have criticized the insurance supervisors, who are responsible for the demutualization process, for approving demutualization plans where current insured-owners have not received the fair market value of their interests in cash. These groups claim that a fair demutualization would distribute voting stock only to existing policyowners, while allowing the financial markets to set the value of each share. Subsequent changes in the company's capital structure then could be voted on by its current shareholders.

A second method used to demutualize is called a *mutual holding company*. These plans take on many forms and are quite complicated transactions; but, simply put, a mutual insurance company forms and owns a stock insurance company, and then the policies in the mutual company are swapped for stock in the stock company. The result is that the policyowners are not compensated for their ownership position and lose their ownership rights while the policies are transferred to the stock company.

LLOYD'S OF LONDON

Lloyd's of London Historically, **Lloyd's of London** (*http://www.lloyds.com/index.asp/*) has been one of the world's most important markets for marine, aviation, and other lines of insurance. Since the late 1980s, however, Lloyd's has reported billions of pounds in losses. A recent estimate suggests that about 3 percent of global non–life insurance premiums and perhaps 10 percent of the market for large industrial insurance still trades at Lloyd's. Because of its historical fame, and because its underwriters continue to be major global providers of marine and aviation insurance and reinsurance, the Lloyd's market remains interesting.

---

[3] Readers can find a listing of some large mutual and stock insurers at this Web site: (*http:// en.wikipedia.org/ wiki/Mutual_insurance/*). Readers can find more information on demutualization at this site: (*http://www. insurance-finance.com/demu.htm/*).

Lloyd's of London Is an Insurance Market

Curiously, Lloyd's of London is not an insurance company; it is a large insurance marketplace. Lloyd's is a meeting place where sellers (underwriters) meet buyers (organizations with exposures to loss). Like the NYSE, which does not sell stock, Lloyd's provides a place where buyers and sellers can meet and negotiate sales. At the NYSE, broker meets broker to arrange the purchase or sale of a client's stock. At Lloyd's, broker meets underwriter to arrange the transfer of a client's loss exposure.

The operations at Lloyd's have evolved since 1688, when Lloyd's of London was a coffeehouse operated by Edward Lloyd. Since that date, numerous changes in policy and membership have occurred. In 1969, foreigners were allowed to become *names* (underwriters) at Lloyd's. An act of Parliament, appropriately called the Lloyd's Act of 1982, currently governs Lloyd's. The membership composition has changed since the early 1990s. Now, Lloyd's admits corporations to the underwriting syndicates. Thus, U.S. insurers can participate in the Lloyd's market.

Each underwriting syndicate is a separate legal entity that accepts loss exposures for its own account. The General Insurance Standards Council of Lloyd's provides internal government for the Lloyd's underwriters, but each syndicate is relatively free to accept, reject, and price its own exposures.

Lloyd's provides internal control through an annual audit of each underwriter. Also, all premiums initially are placed in a premium trust fund, with claims and expenses being paid from the fund. After a delay of three years, the underwriters receive their profits from the fund or are forced to meet assessments if resources are inadequate.

OTHER LEGAL FORMS OF INSURANCE COMPANIES

The Reciprocal Exchange

Reciprocal exchange

A **reciprocal exchange** is like a mutual insurance company because the policyholders insure each other on a nonprofit basis. The difference between the two is that a reciprocal exchange is unincorporated. One definition of the word *reciprocal* is "mutual." In a reciprocal exchange, each insured insures every other insured and in turn is insured by every other member of the exchange.

Reciprocal exchanges provide a considerable amount of automobile insurance in some areas of the country, particularly the west. In a recent year, Farmers Insurance Exchange of California, a reciprocal exchange, was the third largest automobile insurer in the country, behind State Farm Mutual and Allstate. When compared with the whole property insurance market, reciprocals do not provide a large proportion of the total insurance written in the United States.

Attorney-in-fact

An **attorney-in-fact** manages a reciprocal exchange. This person is responsible to the policyholders for providing all the administrative services needed to operate the organization. While a reciprocal exchange is a nonprofit organization, the manager is paid for providing the services. Thus, the manager has an incentive to see the operations of the exchange grow and prosper.

Fraternal Insurers

Some fraternal orders or societies, such as the Aid Association for Lutherans or the Knights of Columbus, provide their members with life insurance protection. The amount of life insurance that these fraternals provide is not large compared with the total amount of life insurance owned by the American public. In a recent year, the amount of fraternal life insurance in force amounted to less than 2 percent of all life insurance.

Savings Bank Life Insurance

Savings bank life insurance

In New York, Connecticut, Massachusetts, and other East Coast states, consumers can purchase **savings bank life insurance.** The following quotation comes from the Savings Bank Life Insurance Company (SBLI) of Massachusetts Web site (*http://www.sbli.com/*):

> SBLI has the largest amount of life insurance in force in the state of Massachusetts. SBLI insurance products are now available to consumers in Connecticut, Maine, New Hampshire, New Jersey, Pennsylvania, Rhode Island, and Virginia.

Health Insurance Providers

Because most health insurance providers, including Blue Cross and Blue Shield (*http://www.bcbs.com/*), health maintenance organizations (HMOs), and preferred provider organizations (PPOs) are narrowly focused on providing health care coverage and financing, we describe these organizations in Chapter 16, "Medical Expense and Disability Income Insurance."

INSURANCE INDUSTRY

In a recent year, there were about 1,200 life insurance companies and more than 2,500 property insurers. Both the life and the property insurance markets are concentrated (oligopolistic), with most of the sales made by the largest 20 competitors. Few barriers to entering the insurance business exist. Each state determines its own qualifications for starting an insurance company. Usually these qualifications require a minimum amount of capital and founders of acceptable moral character. (The standards for passing the moral character test vary by state. However, moral character generally goes beyond the lack of a criminal record.) The minimum capital needed in most states is less than what is necessary to build most industrial plants.

The Insurance Information Institute (III) provides these and other insurance industry facts at its Web site (*http://www.iii.org/*).

SUMMARY

The financial services industry, including the insurance industry, has undergone dramatic change with the passage of the Gramm-Leach-Bliley Act of 1999. This act allowed the formation of financial services holding companies that can combine the products and services of banks, insurance companies, and security brokerage firms.

Legally, an insurance organization may take several different forms. It may incorporate as a stock or a mutual insurance company, or it may be unincorporated as a reciprocal exchange. The insureds may be the owners, as they are in the mutual insurance company. The owners need not purchase insurance from the company they own, as is the case in a stock insurance company. Regardless of the form of legal organization, the function of any insurance system is to redistribute the costs of the losses from the few insureds that experience them to all who are exposed to them.

Lloyd's of London is not an insurance company but an insurance market where individual underwriters accept risks for their own account.

REVIEW TERMS

- Advance premium mutual
- Assessment mutual
- Demutualization
- Factory mutual
- Fraternal life insurance
- Gramm-Leach-Bliley Act (GLB)
- Highly protected risk
- Lloyd's of London
- Multiple-line insurers
- Mutual insurance companies
- Perpetual mutual
- Reciprocal exchange
- Savings bank life insurance
- Stock insurance company

REVIEW

1. When was the Gramm-Leach-Bliley Act passed, and what was its purpose?
2. Is the legal organization of an insurance system important to the consumer? Explain your answer.
3. Why are the dividends on mutual insurance company policies not subject to the federal income tax, while dividends paid by stock insurers to their owners are subject to the federal income tax?
4. How does an advance premium mutual insurer differ from an assessment mutual?
5. What are the special characteristics of the type of exposure insured by factory mutual insurers?
6. What arguments might encourage a mutual insurer to demutualize?
7. How are reciprocal exchanges managed?

OBJECTIVE QUESTIONS

1. The Gramm-Leach-Bliley Act is important to the insurance industry because:
   a. It provides for federal regulation of the insurance industry.
   b. It allows banks, insurance companies, and securities dealers to combine and form holding companies.
   c. It requires insurance companies to provide coverage at reduced cost to people that can't afford health insurance.
   d. It ends the ability of property insurers to share their loss data with rating bureaus.
2. Stock insurance companies have all the following characteristics except:
   a. Ownership by people who are not necessarily insureds of the company
   b. Management elected by owners
   c. All profits and losses from insurance operations passed on to the insureds
   d. Being incorporated
3. The largest and most frequently found form of mutual company is the:
   a. Assessment mutual
   b. Factory mutual
   c. Perpetual mutual
   d. Advance premium mutual
4. Property insurers providing more than one type of coverage are called:
   a. Joint capacity insurers
   b. Double indemnity carriers
   c. Multiple-line insurers
   d. Joint underwriting organizations
5. The _____ mutual requires each insured to contribute a large initial premium, with no future premiums required:
   a. Perpetual
   b. Hybrid
   c. Multiline
   d. Assessment
6. Lloyd's of London remains a very important source of what type of insurance coverage?
   a. Fire
   b. Marine
   c. Life
   d. War
7. The reciprocal exchange is managed by:
   a. An attorney-in-fact
   b. An agency supervisor
   c. A superintendent of administration
   d. A director of insurance
8. The Gramm-Leach-Bliley Act allows banks, security dealers, and insurance companies to combine to form:
   a. Mega-surety firms
   b. Manufacturing companies
   c. Financial services holding companies
   d. Reciprocal insurance exchanges

DISCUSSION QUESTIONS

1. If you were to begin a bicycle insurance company to insure all the bikes in the United States, what form of organization would you choose? Explain your answer.

2. Do you think the Gramm-Leach-Bliley Act will cause more or less product innovation in the insurance industry? Explain your answer.

INTERNET RESEARCH ASSIGNMENTS

1. Describe the position of the National Association of Mutual Insurance Companies on some recent issue such as the government provision of catastrophic insurance coverage. Start at this site: (*http://www.namic.org/*).

2. How many insurance companies operated in the United States in the most recent year for which data is available? Start your search at this site: (*http://www.iii.org/*).

3. Type the keyword "reciprocal insurance exchange" into an Internet search engine. Identify two different reciprocal insurance exchange companies.

4. Identify recent criticisms of the GLB Act. Start your search by typing "GLB Act" in a search engine.

Appendix: Insurance and Private Enterprise: The Potential for Eastern Europe

Introduction

This appendix provides a simplified review of an important topic: the need for private insurance in a free-market economy. My purpose is to bring together many different concepts presented in the first four chapters to increase the understanding of the importance of risk management and insurance to a private enterprise economy. I also am pleased to share some of my research on this interesting topic with readers who might not read the academic journals where my work has appeared.

I remain unsure of the most appropriate designation for the "former Communist" or the "Eastern European" countries that are the subject of this appendix. To avoid confusion, the countries I am referring to include Estonia, Latvia, Lithuania, Poland, Hungary, the Czech Republic, the Slovak Republic, Slovenia, Bulgaria, Russia, Ukraine, and a few other bordering countries. In reference to their recent history, and not entirely to their geographic location, I will call these nations "Eastern European countries," though a glance at a current map shows that a few of them are farther west than Finland or Austria, which are usually considered "Western European" countries. More importantly, despite my combining these countries into one category, it is essential to remember each country is unique in its pre-Communist, Communist, and post-Communist history.

Why Insurance?

Chapter 1, "Fundamentals and Terminology," explained that all industrial societies allow insurance transactions because the benefits far outweigh the costs for individuals and society. The following list provides a review of the benefits and costs.

Benefits

- Insurance provides payment for unexpected losses for businesses and families, allowing their activities to continue despite unfavorable events.
- Insurance smooths the costs of loss, allowing the substitution of a regular predictable expense for large, irregular losses.
- Insurance allows smaller firms to pool their loss exposures and thus to compete more effectively with larger firms.

- Insurance reduces the risk to lenders and thus lowers the cost of capital.
- In the United States, insurers support loss prevention agencies and provide inducements for individuals and companies to engage in loss prevention and loss reduction activities. Premium credits often are given for smoke alarms, fire sprinklers, and drivers' training programs. Experience-rating credits are common to some lines of commercial insurance.

Costs

All enterprises, including insurance companies, use scarce resources of land, labor, and capital. In addition, insurance fraud causes losses.

Why Private Insurance?

If the reader accepts the argument that society experiences a net gain by allowing the insurance transaction, then the next logical question is, "Should insurance be transacted by private companies in a free market or by government-operated insurers?" In the United States, Japan, and in Western European democracies, the answer that has been given is "both." Generally, transactions involving personal and commercial property, liability, and life insurance occur in the free marketplace, while insurance operations involving the "social safety net" are conducted by the government. Social, economic, and political philosophies explain why and how democracies develop an economic safety net for their citizens. In fact, all industrialized societies provide economic security in varying degrees to their citizens. Generally, all countries have kept under government control the insurance aspects of this safety net, such as the provision of pensions or health insurance. In the United States, the government-provided safety net, commonly known as Social Security (which includes Medicare and Medicaid), operates in conjunction with the private insurance markets. In Western Europe, the governments have taken a larger role in providing economic security.

At this point in the review, you should remember two of the most important and distinct functions of insurance operations, public or private: (1) the pooling or insurance function, and (2) the investment function. The insurance function involves the insurance company transferring money from all the parties exposed to loss to the parties experiencing the loss. The investment function requires the insurer to hold and invest funds (reserves) collected in advance of losses. The following data provide some perspective on the investment holdings of private U.S. insurers. In a recent year, U.S. life insurers held assets of more than $2 trillion, while U.S. property insurers held assets of more than $200 billion.

No logical reason prevents a government agency from operating an insurance pool and doing so efficiently and effectively. However, a compelling argument can be made that governments should not operate insurance companies in free-market economies, except when absolutely necessary, because of the investment effect on capital markets. Using the data just presented, ask yourself how the U.S. economy might be different if $2.2 trillion were removed from the private sector and placed in the public sector? In fact, insurance companies remain one of the U.S. economy's largest financial intermediaries. Thus, it is not the pooling or insurance function but the investment function that provides the strongest argument favoring private insurance enterprise. It would seem almost a farce for former Communist countries to try to privatize their economies and yet allow government insurers to invest in private enterprise, because the result would be government ownership of the means of production, the very disease that private markets were meant to cure.

Competition and Efficiency

One of the most important contributions of insurers to a private enterprise economy is efficiency in the capital markets. Because insurers must compete for customers, they feel compelled to make efficient investment choices. If a particular insurer were to make poor investment decisions, its potential customers would find better deals with other insurers. After years of poor investment decisions, it is likely that both agents and customers would abandon this carrier. Thus, large life insurers that must invest millions of dollars each week would be very unlikely to finance steel mills in areas where there was no convenient transportation network or to finance tourist hotels located downwind of steel mills. The author's consulting and research efforts have shown repeatedly that competition forces insurers to be effective investors. Moreover, most economists believe that capital rationing by free market forces is one of the great engines driving free-enterprise economies.

By contrast, the author interviewed the head of the social insurance system of one Western

European country. When I tried to understand how the vast amount of funds the insurance program accumulated was invested, it became clear that political considerations were prominent influences in making financial decisions. In one case, a steel mill was located where unemployment was greatest, which was not where the transportation system was best. Also, hotels were placed where powerful politicians, who provided oversight to the social insurance administrators, "suggested" they might be located. The point is not to argue about the rightness or wrongness of this approach to rationing capital from a societal standpoint, but to point out that the results are probably not as efficient as they would be if the capital were rationed in the free markets.

Essential Requirements of a Free Enterprise (Capitalist) System

I assume that most readers of this text have already taken an introductory course or two in economics, and I present the following list as a reminder of the basic requirements of a free enterprise economy:

- Currency and a banking system
- Laws and a legal system
- Financial instruments and financial markets
- Cultural acceptance, including a general level of education that provides a sufficient number of capable workers, a work ethic that encourages productive workers, managerial talent to take risks and provide direction, and a minimum level of honesty and trust, so that large organizations can be formed and contracts be honored without undue agency costs

The Requirements of a Private Insurance Market

The foregoing items represent a minimum list of necessary components for a free-enterprise market to function. The next list, and this discussion is greatly simplified, represents the particular components needed for private insurance transactions:

- Special legal provisions and precedent-honoring court decisions forming a comprehensive framework in which insurance transactions can be completed in confidence
- Actuarial statistics and historical data that allow accurate loss estimates and reliable ratemaking

- A regulatory authority with the power to enforce an insurance code that protects the rights of insurance buyers and sellers
- Marketing channels capable of efficiently connecting buyers and sellers
- Managerial expertise in insurance company operations
- Investment outlets for the vast reserves needed to operate private insurance companies

Difficulties Starting a Private Insurance System in Eastern Europe

The countries of Eastern Europe have had more than fifteen years to privatize their markets, including their insurance markets. Poland, the Czech Republic, Hungary, Estonia, and Slovenia made substantial progress and have joined the European Union (EU).

No Recent History of Private Insurance In Russia, the Baltic countries, and East Germany (but not all Eastern European countries), citizens did not own private property, including the houses or apartments in which they lived; therefore, they had little need for property insurance. In countries such as Bulgaria, where private ownership of homes was allowed, property insurance was mandatory. Moreover, Eastern European countries, unlike the United States, had a comprehensive social safety net that generally provided universal access to health care, pensions, and survivor benefits. Consequently, private insurance was neither much needed nor purchased. Today, many people purchase private automobile insurance in Poland, Hungary, and the Czech Republic. Despite this coverage being mandatory, much of automobile insurance still is being provided by government-controlled insurers that formerly were state insurance monopolies. Therefore, private insurance—in automobile and all other lines—still remains in the early stages of development. Hungary, however, which gave up state ownership of its former insurance monopoly and has had a liberal view toward allowing in foreign capital, has made considerable progress in privatizing its insurance market.

No Recent History of Risk Management Government ownership of the means of production, such as factories and railroads, and centrally planned economies were the distinctive features of the Communist economic system. The failure of this system to produce a satisfactory amount of consumer goods or technological innovation is well known. In the Communist economic system, factory managers were given output quotas—for example, a specific number of automobiles, tons of steel, or pounds of sausage. The quotas did not specify that the output should minimize the number of worker injuries or the amount of environmental damage. Consequently, worker safety often was of less concern and environmental damage appears greater in Eastern Europe than in Western Europe. Moreover, if property was destroyed, it was the state's property that was lost, and the cost was not borne directly by the factory managers.

As Eastern European economies develop private markets and private ownership, it will be interesting to observe whether Western risk management practices are introduced. Private ownership would appear to provide much greater incentive for a higher level of stewardship and for the purchase of private insurance than the Communist system, but time and careful research will be needed to provide decisive evidence to support such a contention. In any case, a private insurance system would surely need to implement or encourage loss prevention activities at a much higher level than previously was the case.

Little Respect (Trust) for the Insurance Institution At its most essential level, an insurance contract represents a conditional promise to pay a future benefit. The transaction rests on a foundation of trust. With no historical experience to provide guidance, it takes great faith for an individual or a factory owner to forgo current consumption to purchase a conditional promise, but many people in Poland, Slovenia, and Hungary have purchased private automobile insurance and, when allowed, private pensions.

Currencies Not Stable—Inflation Insurance can function in an inflationary environment, but not as efficiently as when currencies provide a stable yardstick of value. If the value of property or the economic impact of a premature death cannot be measured easily, or if the measurement changes on a monthly basis, it is difficult to know how much insurance to purchase. Thus, the unstable currencies that characterized the initial phase of the privatization of many Eastern European countries represented a serious obstacle to a private insurance operation. Within the first three years of allowing private markets, Poland, the Czech Republic, Hungary, and Slovenia had stabilized their currency.

Few Places to Invest Funds Safely in Private Enterprise As has already been noted, to operate safely and to benefit a private-enterprise economy, insurance companies must invest large reserves efficiently. However, Eastern European countries still have underdeveloped financial markets. Until efficient domestic capital markets are functioning actively, a significant obstacle to private insurance operations will remain in place.

Accounting Standards Are Undeveloped The Communist economies required record keeping or accounting activities. Double-entry bookkeeping was used at some factories, but different names were used for profit and net worth. Nevertheless, the Communist accounting system was inadequate for internal management or disclosure requirements required in Western capital markets. Varying degrees of progress in standardized accounting and auditing practices are reported in Eastern Europe, but until generally accepted accounting and auditing principles and practices are used frequently, operating an insurance enterprise will remain difficult.

"Foreign" Insurance Regulations, No Local Legal Precedents Many Eastern European countries reviewed the insurance regulations of Western European countries when writing their insurance laws. Today, the insurance regulations in Poland, the Czech Republic, Hungary, Slovenia, and other former Communist countries comply with EU standards. Maintaining insurer solvency and policing market conduct remains a challenge.

Little Managerial Expertise, Especially in Insurance Western insurers rely on risk-taking entrepreneurs, on advertising and marketing skills sharpened in a competitive market, and on attracting, retaining, and motivating employees. However, countries like Poland and Hungary were able to attract emigrants or foreign firms to provide management training and skills. After fifteen years, these countries have made considerable progress in this area.

Little Actuarial Data Western insurers use databases representing life, marine, and fire insurance experience dating back more than 100 years. Data on life expectancy in countries where millions of people "disappeared," where health problems often went uncategorized, or where other data were kept secret or simply not kept would, at the least, provide an insufficient basis for calculating insurance premiums accurately. Likewise, the number of vehicles quadrupled in many of these countries in the early years of their post-Communist transition. Thus, premium calculations and reserve requirements still require substantial margins for error.

The Future

I hope just thinking about the material contained in this appendix justified the reader's effort and that predictions, accurate or otherwise, were not the reader's sought-after goal. The author has observed considerable progress, especially in Poland, Hungary, the Czech Republic, and Slovenia. Eastern European countries now have had time to develop the essential components of a market-based economy and for the "invisible hand" of self-interest to work its wonders. Many countries have developed successful economies, including a growing number of economic assets that require private insurance transactions and growing incomes that suggest more life insurance and retirement savings. Therefore, I expect to report continuing progress, including the privatization of all remaining former state insurance monopolies and an increasing amount of private insurance premiums per person.

CHAPTER 5

Insurance Occupations

After studying this chapter, you should be able to:

- Explain some fundamental principles of agency law

- Describe an insurance agent's duties

- Explain the difference between insurance agents and brokers

- Explain the insurance underwriter's functions

- Identify a loss adjuster's responsibilities

- Explain the occupation of insurance company accountant

- Describe the insurance actuary's occupation

In the preceding chapter, we described several different kinds of insurance companies. In this chapter, we examine the internal functions of insurance companies by looking at different insurance occupations. Insurance companies need the services of different professionals. This chapter explains what these specialists contribute to the overall operations of the insurance company.

In recent years, the insurance industry employed about 2 million people. Over 1 million work in home offices and about 645,000 work as agents or brokers. With the appearance of Internet sales of insurance and other direct marketing approaches, insurance marketing currently is undergoing significant change. In this chapter, we will discuss the current and anticipated effects of e-commerce on the marketing of insurance. As a result of competition from other financial service providers, direct sales methods, technological change, and a declining demand for certain types of insurance, the number of people working in the insurance industry—especially as sales agents—has declined in recent years.

As this chapter is being revised, these changes continue, and describing the future of insurance marketing is a challenge. Insurance companies currently are developing strategies for simultaneously selling products through multiple distribution channels ranging from Internet sales to the traditional channel of career agents directly tied to one company. Because the cost to the insurance company of the various channels is different, the question of pricing the product becomes an issue. Should the costs of the more expensive channel be borne by the consumer through higher prices for an almost homogeneous product but with different service levels? This strategy leads to the question of whether consumers will pay more for the same product depending on the distribution method. One alternative would be for the career sales force to accept lower commissions to compete better with other marketing channels. Another alternative would be for insurance companies to accept lower returns for sales from their career agents than from the Internet, or from producers who are independent of the company than from the company's own agents. One purpose of this chapter is to lay a solid foundation of vocabulary and legal principles to allow both the current and future marketing systems to be understood better. Figure 5–1 presents an outline of today's insurance marketing channels.

AGENTS AND BROKERS

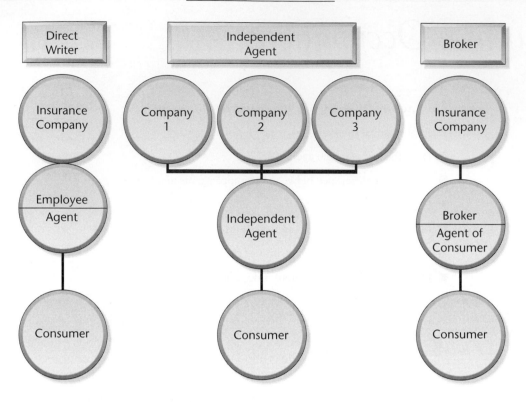

DIRECT MARKETING

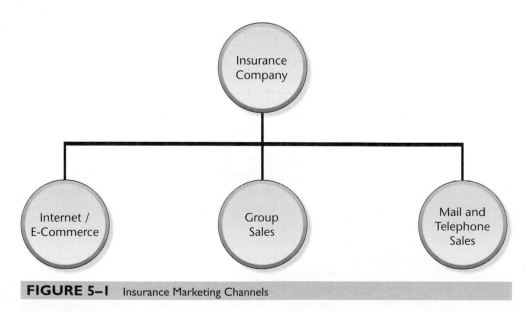

FIGURE 5–1 Insurance Marketing Channels

FIGURE 5–2   Insurance Occupations

If one mentions insurance occupations to students, the first one they usually think of is insurance agent, often with somewhat negative feelings. One purpose in presenting this material is to counteract this impression, explaining the role of the professional agent as a knowledgeable financial advisor who must acquire much expertise before being able to work with the public. Figure 5–2 presents an outline of the occupations described in this chapter.

INSURANCE MARKETING AND DISTRIBUTION

Insurance agents and brokers remain important links in the marketing chain connecting insurance companies with insurance consumers. However, in some lines of insurance, particularly personal automobile insurance and term life insurance, the marketing model is undergoing significant change from this traditional pattern. In automobile insurance, for example, it was estimated recently that direct marketing accounted for about 30 percent of the policies sold. **Direct marketing** includes mail solicitations, solicitations aimed at affinity groups (such as all the employees of a company, or the graduates of a particular university), or Internet solicitations. Term life insurance is another coverage that also has been sold successfully using direct marketing techniques.

Direct marketing

E-commerce

The term **e-commerce** describes the use of the Internet to automate insurance and other transactions. So far, most of the insurance transactions on the Internet have occurred between insurers and personal consumers. From the insurance company's standpoint, e-commerce allows cost-cutting efficiencies and direct contact with its customers. From the consumers' standpoint, e-commerce allows transaction possibilities at a location and at a time of their choosing. Moreover, if cost-cutting savings are realized and then passed forward to consumers, e-commerce will result in lower insurance costs. Because personal automobile insurance and term life insurance are either frequently purchased or relatively simple insurance products, they have been the two most popular insurance products sold on the Internet. Moreover, the Internet lends itself to price comparison shopping, and brand identification of these two types of insurance apparently has not been given much value by price-conscious consumers.[1]

There are expectations that the Internet also will modify the marketing of commercial insurance coverages. Because commercial loss exposures tend to be more complicated than personal loss exposures, the Internet has not yet had results in commercial insurance comparable to the results in personal auto or term life insurance. However, commentators expect that companies needing insurance increasingly will solicit bids for commercial coverage and those insurers willing to provide coverage will use the Internet to complete commercial insurance transactions. For example, one can imagine that a firm needing commercial coverage for a warehouse could post architectural drawings and a virtual tour of the facility, as well as other useful information relative to the risk, on a Web site and seek bids for coverage. Likewise, an insurer might post the basic underwriting parameters it uses when providing workers' compensation or some other commercial insurance coverage. The possibilities of using the Internet to purchase insurance without an initial contact by an agent or broker appear substantial.

INSURANCE AGENTS AND BROKERS

Despite the inroads made by direct marketing methods, the occupation of insurance agent remains a challenging and potentially rewarding one. This occupation allows a person to be of great service. Before describing some of the activities and qualifications needed to be an insurance agent, we present some terminology.

Agency Law

Agent

Principal

A deeper understanding of the occupation of insurance agent begins with an understanding of agency law.[2] An **agent** is a person authorized to act for another person. The agent may create, perform, or terminate a contract for another person. The person on whose behalf the agent acts is the **principal**. By law, the agent's acts become the acts of the principal. Any person who legally can enter a contract can appoint an agent. By law, an insurance company, like other companies, is considered a person. Generally, the insurance company is the principal employing or contracting the insurance agent.

The law defines several duties that agents owe their principals. Among these are the duty of loyalty (agents must not further their own interest at their principal's expense), the duty of care (that is, the duty not to be negligent), and the duty to obey instructions. If the agent has an interest in matters that are adverse to the principal's interest, the agent must inform the principal. An agent cannot serve two principals having adverse interests unless both principals consent. The agent has the duty to inform the principal of all relevant information and to keep a proper account of all money or

---

[1] The author and a colleague investigated the quality of life insurance advice given on the Internet and have found the early results were questionable. See Mark S. Dorfman and Saul W. Adelman, "An Analysis of the Quality of Internet Life Insurance Advice," *Risk Management and Insurance Review*, Vol. 5, No. 2 (Fall 2002).
[2] See Douglas R. Richmond, "Insurance Agent and Broker Liability," *Tort Trial and Insurance Practice Law Journal* (Fall 2004, pp. 1–58) for a comprehensive discussion of many of the issues summarized in this section.

other assets. The agent has a duty of reasonable care, meaning the agent should not attempt to do business he or she cannot perform properly. The principal has the duty of paying for the agent's services and honoring all other agreed-on commitments to the agent.

An agency contract between the insurance agent and the insurance company establishes the rights and duties of each party. Through the agency contract or agreement, agents receive **actual authority** from their principals. The written appointment of an agent is an example of express (written) authority. The **express authority** provides details of the agent's duties and responsibilities. **Incidental authority** to do things normally required to accomplish the specified acts accompanies express authority. That is, the express authority identifies specific acts an agent may do; incidental authority covers all the details necessary to accomplish the agent's work, which are too numerous to itemize in an agency contract.

Some insurance agents have only the authority to solicit business for their principal, the insurance company. Other agents have the authority to bind their principal to insurance contracts. The ability to bind is important because agents having this power can start insurance contracts locally before submitting them for home-office approval. Insurance companies call agents whose authority is limited to the solicitation of business *special* or *soliciting agents*. Agents with the authority to bind their principals to contracts are called *general agents*. This term is used especially in property insurance, where agents with binding authority are common.

So long as the agent acts within the scope of the express authority, the principal is bound by the agent's actions. If agents go beyond the scope of their authority, substantial legal issues may arise. For example, if an agent had **apparent (implied) authority** but lacked actual (express) authority to complete some action, the principal still may be bound by the agent's action. Apparent authority questions arise when the agent's specific actions appear to be consistent with authorized actions but the actions, in fact, are not authorized. For example, a local agent in Mobile, Alabama, may have collected premiums due at the home office in Chicago, Illinois. The local agent acted in an unauthorized manner, but a consumer probably would not be aware of the scope of the agent's authority. Thus, a court would protect the consumer if the insurer denied a claim because the premium was not submitted properly. However, not all cases are clear. Some premium notices inform the consumer that premiums may be paid only at the home office. Therefore, consumers, having been notified adequately of the required time and place of premium payment, should follow the insurer's instructions or else they risk denial of their claims.

In some cases, an insurer may **ratify** (approve) actions that are beyond the scope of the agent's authority, such as allowing local agents to collect premiums. Such ratification binds the insurer to the agent's actions and may create undesired precedents. When an insurer terminates an agency relationship, it should remove all stationery, signs, advertising brochures, underwriting manuals, or other items that might create the impression of agency when this relationship no longer exists.

Two other basic legal doctrines relating to agency are (1) knowledge given to the agent is considered to be provided to the principal as well, and (2) payment made to the agent is considered to be conveyed to the principal when the agent has actual or apparent authority to receive premium payments.

In cases where information or payment is not forwarded to the insurer's home office after an insured gives it to an agent, the insurer may deny a loss claim believing it has been misinformed or unpaid. If the agent is responsible for the problem, a court will require the insurer to pay the claim regardless of contractual language. As noted, sometimes the insured is notified clearly that payment must be made to the home

Actual authority

Express authority

Incidental authority

Apparent (implied) authority

Ratify

office to prevent payment to its agents. The factual circumstances in each case determine the insurer's responsibility for paying claims.

The relations between the agent and the insurance applicant are often at issue in court. As stated previously, the agent legally is obligated to promote the insurer's interest. However, the consumer relies on the agent for many things, including providing an appropriate contract and interpreting the contract. Because courts recognize the insurance agent as a professional, and many agents promote this image by advertising their professional and educational accomplishments, courts can protect the consumer's interest when disputes arise resulting from an agent's action or inaction.

Consider a case where an agent encouraged a person to change insurers. The consumer agreed to do so provided the coverage was "the same as before." Shortly after the new policy was in place, a loss occurred that would have been covered by the original policy but was excluded by the replacement policy. After the insurer denied the claim, the insured sued the agent for professional negligence. In this instance, the court held that the agent was responsible for uncovered losses until the insured received the newly issued policy and had the opportunity to read it. Although this was not a landmark case, it does illustrate the delicate nature of the relationship among insurer, agent, and insured. It also shows why this triangular relationship sometimes results in lawsuits, if for no other reason than substantial sums of money frequently are involved in insurance transactions.

An additional lesson may be drawn from the case above. Insurance agents need to purchase errors and omissions liability insurance. This coverage, sometimes called *malpractice insurance*, provides payment if a third party is injured by the insurance agent's mistakes. Not only does this insurance pay legal judgments against negligent insurance agents, but the insurer also provides funds for the agent's legal defense, even in cases where lawsuits are groundless.

Insurance Broker

Broker

An insurance **broker** is an agent with the limited authority to find an insurance company willing to accept a transfer of an insurance applicant's exposure to loss. The insurance applicant hires the broker to find an insurer that will accept the risk transfer. In this transaction, the insurance applicant is the principal and the broker is the agent. The insurance broker's function is similar to that of the real estate broker who is hired to find a buyer for a client's home or to the stockbroker who is hired to find a buyer for a client's stock. In all these cases, the broker helps to bring two parties together to complete a transaction.

Because of the rules of insurance law, it makes a difference if the consumer is dealing with an agent or a broker. For example, an insurance applicant must not conceal any facts or information that is relevant to the loss exposure to be transferred. If the applicant does conceal material facts, the insurer will have legal grounds to avoid paying a claim. If an applicant has given all the facts to the company's agent, then the insured has met the legal requirement concerning concealment. However, it is important to remember that the broker's principal is the insurance applicant, not the insurance company. Therefore, if an applicant tells the facts to his or her own agent, the broker, that does not necessarily inform the insurance company of the facts. If neither the applicant nor the broker passes along all the facts to the insurer, then a possibility exists that the insurer will not pay for the insured's losses.

Some courts have reached a different conclusion about the relationship between an insurance applicant and the insurance broker. In one court case involving the relationship among the insured, the insurance company, and a broker, an Illinois appellate court stated that although ordinarily the insurance broker is the insured's agent, timely notice of a claim given by the insured to the insurance broker amounted to timely notice to the insurer because of the insurer's past practices and custom. The court felt that because the insurer used the broker as an intermediary for practically all aspects of the transaction, it was unfair for the company to deny that the broker was acting as its agent for the purpose of giving notice of loss. Because of the possible confusion of insurance applicants, as illustrated in the case just described, a few states have outlawed the legal distinction of broker, designating all such relationships as agency relationships (with the insurer as the broker's principal).

Adding to the potential for confusion is the rule that brokers cannot bind insurers to contracts because they are agents of the applicant. Some brokers, however, are licensed simultaneously as agents, and in their capacity as agents, they may have binding authority from a particular insurer.

The rules governing a broker's duties to a principal are the same as those presented earlier. The possibility of breaching the duty of loyalty—no conflict of interest or no self-dealing at the principal's expense—can be a sensitive subject. The broker earns a commission as a percentage of the premium that the insurer charges the principal (insured). If the broker approached two insurers charging different prices, and if all other factors were the same, such as the services offered by the insurers, the principal's best interest would be served by the lower-cost insurer, whereas the broker's best interest would be met by the higher-cost insurer. Several different factors encourage the broker to put the client's interest first, including the broker's own integrity and desire to do a good job, the desire to maintain a good reputation, and the possibility of being sued for malpractice, fraud, or breach of duty if the truth is exposed.

In the fall of 2004, New York state attorney general Eliot Spitzer made some serious accusations of fraud and conflict of interest against some of the largest insurance brokers in the United States. The brokers were accused of bid rigging and of collecting substantial "contingent commissions." The bid rigging charges arose from the practice of submitting fraudulent or "artificial" high bids that made the bid of the insurance company that the broker selected and recommended appear to be the best choice. The contingent commissions issue arose from the volume of business the broker directed to particular insurers, thus violating their duty to their principal of not self-dealing at the buyer's expense. Volume-based commissions are found in other industries, but the size of these commissions and the fact that they were not transparent to the insurance applicants provided the basis of the legal complaint. Following the investigation and legal charges, many large insurance brokers announced they would no longer accept contingent commissions. Several of the brokers also paid large fines to settle the legal complaints.

Insurance brokers are especially useful in commercial insurance. Businesses often have unique property or liability exposures or require insurance contracts written to their specifications. In these cases, the broker can help write the specifications for the insurance or even design the insurance program and then find an insurer willing to provide the coverage. Businesses often employ brokers when insuring their employee benefit plans, such as their group life and health insurance. Most individual needs for insurance can be met with standard coverages and do not require a broker's service. In cases of people with poor driving records or substandard health, however, a broker may be required to find an insurer willing to accept the exposure. Because brokers shop for insurance on a daily basis, they have information about pricing and coverage availability unknown to businesses that shop for insurance only annually.

Licensing Requirements

All states have laws requiring people who sell insurance to have a license to engage in this activity.[3] By requiring a license, the state can help protect the public from uneducated, incompetent, and unscrupulous people. Because more than 50 insurance jurisdictions exist, it was difficult for a person to become a licensed agent in more than one or two states before the Graham-Leach-Bliley Act (GLB). The new law, however, mandates uniformity in agent licensing requirements and thus agents now will be able to operate on a national basis. The issue of nationwide producer licensing can be explored at this Web site: (*http://www.licenseregistry.com/*). Today, licensed agents are required to be at least 18 years old, to have good morals (no felony convictions), and to pass an examination demonstrating knowledge of the industry. Generally, states require people to participate in classroom instruction before taking the required insurance examination. Many states require agents to participate in continuing education classes to maintain their licenses.

Life insurance agents selling variable annuities or variable life insurance—products that have significant investment characteristics—must have a federal security dealer's license in addition to their state license. To get their federal securities license, life insurance agents must pass one or more examinations given by the National Association of Security Dealers (NASD). The NASD Web site, (*http://www.nasd.com/*), provides a good description of the association's activities, including the following quotation:

> Under federal law, virtually every securities firm doing business with the U.S. public is a member of this private, not-for-profit organization. Roughly 5,300 brokerage firms, over 92,000 branch offices and more than 664,000 registered securities representatives come under our jurisdiction.

Property and Liability Insurance Agents and Brokers

Several important differences distinguish the duties of a life insurance agent from those of a property and liability insurance agent. For this reason, we describe life insurance agents separately from property insurance agents. Although both are salespeople in the broad sense of the word, their duties and relations to their insurance companies are different.

Property and liability insurers traditionally use two main marketing channels: the independent agency system and the exclusive agent or direct writing system. Insurers call property insurance companies selling insurance through their own employee-agents **direct writers**. Experts make a technical distinction between exclusive agents and direct writing agents. *Exclusive agents* are not employees of the insurer but agree to place all their business with one insurer. Direct writing agents are employees of one insurer.

Direct writers

Independent agents represent several different insurance companies. Thus, the independent agent may place a client's homeowners insurance with one company and the same client's automobile insurance with another company. Unlike the agent working for a direct writer, the independent agent owns the business that is placed with an insurance company. That is, the agent, not the insurance company, is responsible for renewing the client's insurance policies. In current practice, even in the independent agency system, much of the billing, policy issuance, and renewal reminders actually come from the company providing the coverage. If an independent agent's relationship with a particular insurer is severed, the agent retains the right to place the affected

Independent agents

---

[3] The NAIC Web site (*http://www.naic.org/*) is a good beginning link to the Web sites of the various states.

business with a different insurer. This ownership right in the business affects how agents are compensated. Direct writers pay their employees a salary plus a commission or bonus for production. Independent agents earn only commission income. The independent agent earns the same percentage commission on both initial premiums and renewals, while direct writing companies often pay higher initial than renewal commissions.

Life Insurance Agents and Brokers

We have noted several times in this chapter that there have been significant changes in the marketing of all types of insurance in the preceding decades. The marketing of life insurance has been an area of obvious change. During the early part of the twentieth century, it was common for life insurance agents to come to an insured's home on a weekly or monthly basis to collect a small premium for "burial" insurance. This type of life insurance now has almost disappeared. From before World War II through the 1970s, it was common for life insurance agents to make sales visits to clients' homes to arrange relatively large amounts of individual life insurance coverage. Today, this type of service is increasingly rare, especially for low- and lower-middle-income people. Now, many individuals who previously identified themselves as life insurance agents call themselves "professional financial planners." These financial planners believe the new identification better reflects the fact that they can offer a broader range of services than the traditional life insurance agent.

The main function of the life insurance agent that is most familiar to the public is to motivate people to apply for life insurance. An important distinction between the life and the property insurance agent's activity is the limitation on the life insurance agent's authority. Although the property agent can, and often does, have the legal authority to bind a principal to an insurance contract, the life insurance agent never has this authority. The reason for this difference in authority is that property insurance contracts typically may be canceled by the insurer at any time after a short notice period. Life insurance companies cannot cancel contracts after a brief initial period except for nonpayment of premiums. To minimize fraud and misunderstanding, the power to bind the life insurance company remains with the home office. More information concerning the insurance agent profession can be found on the Internet at the National Association of Professional Insurance Agents (PIA) Web site (*http://www.pianet.com/*).

Brokers

The brokerage function operates in life insurance much as it does in property insurance. In the last few years, some life insurance agents have given up their exclusive arrangement with one carrier and have become full-time brokers. Like property brokers, life brokers evaluate the market for their clients and may deal with many different carriers. They may place their term life insurance business with one carrier, their pension business with another, and their universal life insurance sales with a third carrier. The appearance of widespread life insurance brokerage occurred in the rapidly changing financial environment of recent years.

Even traditional agents sometimes may act as a broker, for instance, to find an insurer willing to accept the exposure for a client with impaired health or a hazardous job. Some insurance companies specialize in substandard health coverage. If an application is turned down by the home office, then the soliciting agent may act as a broker for a client in poor health and try to find an alternate company that is willing to provide coverage.

An Insurance Agent's Duties

What are the duties of an insurance agent? To sell insurance, of course! This answer, however, is much too simple. Much more is involved. The good insurance agent must be able to inform clients, motivate them to take a specified course of action, provide service before and after losses, and exercise judgment in selecting clients for the insurance company.

Providing consumers with service and information is at the heart of the agent's job. Explaining the features of the coverage provided in the insurance contract, which can be complex and difficult for people to understand, is one of the agent's most important functions. A good agent also must provide information about related areas. For instance, the life insurance agent must know about and be able to explain certain aspects of the federal income tax and the unified transfer (gift and estate) tax laws. The life insurance agent also must be familiar with Social Security and other government benefits. The property insurance agent, like the college insurance professor, will get an unending stream of what-if questions: "What if my suitcase containing my dog's diamond-covered collar is stolen in France during a thunderstorm while I am on vacation—am I covered?" The property agent also must be familiar with certain aspects of real estate law and very familiar with property values. Again, providing consumers with factual information that they can understand is an important function of the insurance agent.

Selling or motivating consumers is another primary assignment for the insurance agent. Providing motivation is perhaps more of a task for the life insurance agent than the property insurance agent. Most Americans recognize the need for automobile and homeowners insurance in adequate amounts, but the need for life insurance in adequate amounts is not as easily seen. Thus, the agent must demonstrate to prospective consumers the financial loss the family would suffer because of premature death. The agent then should motivate these people to act to protect their families from this potential loss.

Insurance agents must use judgment in submitting applications to their companies. Insurers call this process *field underwriting*. The agent must be familiar with a company's requirements for acceptable applications. If substandard risks (for example, people who are greatly overweight or drivers with three recent accidents) are unacceptable to the insurer, the agent must not submit such applications. Nor should the agent submit applications after detecting the presence of the moral hazard.

The insurance agent should give clients continuous service. Before losses have occurred, the property agent must provide information to clients and see that their coverage is complete and accurately reflects the value of the covered property or potential liability. After a loss, the agent again must provide information and counsel. The agent should recognize that a client's need for service after a loss is usually greater than before the loss. Life insurance agents also should give clients continuous service. Births, inflation, new debts, divorces, accumulations of sizable estates, changes in the Social Security laws, and many other factors create changing needs for life insurance. The life insurance agent should provide clients with a regular review of their insurance needs and compare the amount of insurance they own with these needs.

We have just presented a rather long list of an agent's duties. Before completing this discussion, we must mention something an agent must not do: practice law. It is a crime for any person other than a licensed attorney to give legal advice. This crime is **Unauthorized practice of law** called the **unauthorized practice of law**. States have passed these laws to prevent unqualified people from giving legal advice to the public, just as they have passed laws preventing unqualified people from practicing medicine.

Life insurance agents must be familiar with this rule, especially if they sell insurance for estate planning purposes. For example, it would be permissible for an agent to point out to a client the benefits of having a valid will or the tax benefits to be gained from using a life insurance trust. However, it would be a crime for the agent to draft either the will or the trust for the client or to offer legal advice on the effect of recent court rulings on a client's existing documents.

LOSS ADJUSTER

Loss adjuster

After a loss, the insured must notify the insurance company. This notice represents a claim for payment. Before settling the claim, the insurer will conduct a claims investigation. Insurers call the person conducting the investigation a **loss adjuster**, a claims adjuster, or a claims auditor. Loss adjusting is most important in property insurance, where many losses are partial and where the extent of property damage is not always clear. Loss adjusting generally is not a problem in life insurance because insurers make no payment for partial losses and pay the full amount due after receiving proper notification of the insured's death. Life insurance companies do conduct investigations in cases involving death claims arising shortly after policies are purchased. Life insurers also use loss adjusters to investigate some claims for accidental death benefits, disability income benefits, and health insurance benefits. Nevertheless, we devote this section of the chapter to property and liability claims adjusting.

The property adjuster investigates reported losses, determines if the insurer is liable to pay the claim, or recommends that the insurer deny the claim if the facts appear to indicate denial is appropriate. Much of the loss adjuster's work is done outside the office, usually at the scene of the reported damage. In some cases, the adjuster needs only the fire marshal's report or the reports of police officials to complete an investigation. If the loss represents a substantial amount of money, the loss adjuster will form a personal opinion of the facts.

One of the first tasks the adjuster completes is to make sure the insurance company is responsible for paying for the loss. In some cases, the claimant reports the loss to the wrong company or reports property as destroyed that is different from the property covered in the insurance policy. Occasionally insureds make claims after policies expire or after the time for premium payment has elapsed. Adjusters also will reject claims when losses are caused by perils, such as floods, that are excluded specifically from coverage in the insured's policy.

In some cases, the adjuster may determine that fraud by the insured is involved in the loss, in which case the insurance company never pays for the damage. Recent years have seen widespread insurance frauds including vehicle and business arsons, faked accidents, and fictitious inventory losses. Uncovering insurance fraud makes the loss adjuster's job very important because all insureds must bear the cost of fraudulent insurance claims.

Once satisfied that the company should pay for the loss, the adjuster must form a judgment of the dollar amount of the damage. Often adjuster and insured can agree on the amount of the claim. Sometimes, however, the insured thinks the amount of loss is greater than the adjuster finds reasonable. The adjuster, who evaluates claims daily, is more familiar with the value of property and certainly does not have the personal attachment to the destroyed property that the insured does. Thus, a basis for an honest difference of opinion exists. If the insured and adjuster cannot agree on the amount of the claim, appraisal or arbitration provisions in property insurance policies provide for resolving disputes without court litigation.

Most insurers expect their loss adjusters to settle claims fairly and not reduce the payments for legitimate losses. Thus, insurers settle most valid claims without arbitration or suit. In fact, a good loss adjustment occurs when the insured receives the full amount of benefits permitted by the contract. Thus, if the adjuster feels the insured suffered a larger loss than claimed, the adjuster should recommend a larger settlement than the insured requested.

If the loss adjuster and the insured agree on the amount of the loss, the adjuster will complete the investigation by recommending the claim payment to the insurer. In the case of small losses, some adjusters can authorize or actually make the payment without further delay. If, however, adjusters feel the claim has no validity, they will recommend that the insurance company deny it. If the insured still believes the denied claim to be valid, he or she can hire a lawyer and sue the insurance company for breach of contract. Such a suit means a court decides whether the insurance company should pay the claim.

EMPLOYEES, INDEPENDENT ADJUSTMENT BUREAUS, AND PUBLIC ADJUSTERS

In the case of small claims, insurance companies often allow the selling agent to pay the claim on the spot. In large cities, many insurers operate drive-in offices to adjust automobile claims. In other cases, the company will send an employee-adjuster to the claim site to facilitate the settlement. Modern technology, including digital cameras, cell phones, and portable computers, is allowing speedier claims settlements than in the past.

Independent adjuster

Adjustment bureau

Insurance companies often use loss adjusters who are not their own employees. Instead, they hire the services of an **independent adjuster** or an independent **adjustment bureau**. This is because it would be impractical for every automobile insurance company to keep an adjuster near the scene of every possible automobile accident in the country or to send its adjusters all over the country to investigate claims. When an Indiana insurance company must pay a claim for an accident in South Carolina, it hires an adjuster near the accident to complete the investigation.

In other cases, insurers hire independent adjusters because the loss involves specialized property. For example, the author has a former student who specializes in the adjustment of heavy equipment losses. His previous experience as a mechanic provided special knowledge for determining when equipment is salvageable—that is, when it is more efficient to repair or replace damaged equipment than pay for a total loss.

Public adjuster

Independent adjusters are agents of insurers. A **public adjuster** is an agent of the insured. Although most insureds do not feel the need to hire an adjuster, in cases of complicated losses, either commercial or personal, insureds may feel a fairer settlement will be forthcoming if an adjuster is representing their interests. Public adjusters are found in larger cities.

Adjusters Are Agents

Even though the loss adjuster is employed directly by the adjustment bureau, when adjusting a loss for a particular insurance company they are agents of that insurance company. As agents, their acts or omissions may result in a company paying a claim it otherwise might deny. Therefore, the competent adjuster will take legal precautions to do only those things that promote the insurer's interest and will avoid acts that may result in litigation with insureds. To understand the adjuster's problems in this area, we must explain the legal concepts of reservation of rights, waiver, and estoppel.

Reservation of Rights

Reservation of rights

In some instances, particularly losses involving liability claims, insurers initially may not be sure if the insured's claim is covered. For example, the insured's policy may exclude losses arising from an insured's intentional acts that injure others. However, it may take a court trial to determine if a particular act was in fact intentional. In such complicated situations, insurers may assume the liability unconditionally, may deny the claim outright, or may pursue the claim but reserve the right to deny coverage at a later point when adequate information becomes available to make a correct decision. If an insurer decides to take the third route, it must give the insured adequate notice of the insurer's **reservation of rights** and carefully meet other legal formalities.

Letters informing the insured that the insurer is reserving certain rights are not denials of coverage. They represent notice from the insurer to the insured that the insurer is not certain that coverage exists, but that the insurer plans to proceed with the loss adjustment, and perhaps the legal defense, as if the coverage existed. The insurer also is putting the insured on notice that certain events may occur in the future that may cause the insurer to reevaluate its position.

Without notice that the insurer is reserving its rights, courts well might find an insurer acted in bad faith if it began paying the cost of a legal defense but later ended those payments or even sought to recoup the expenses it already paid. It also might be considered bad faith if the insurer did not inform the insured that, despite paying for a legal defense, it reserved the right not to satisfy a settlement or legal judgment.

Waiver and Estoppel

Waiver

Estoppel

A **waiver** is the intentional abandonment of a known right. **Estoppel** is a court action preventing a person from asserting his or her rights because the court found the person's conduct inconsistent with asserting the right. When either of these doctrines is applied in a particular case, an insurer may find it must pay claims it otherwise might not have had to pay. For example, an insurance policy might contain a right for the insurer to receive a complete inventory from the insured within 60 days after a loss. Such a right could be waived by an insurer. If such a right is waived, the insurer no longer can deny the claim because the insured failed to deliver the inventory when specified in the contract.

As a second example, assume that an adjuster knows that an insured's acts before the loss resulted in a breach of the contract. Assume that despite this knowledge, the adjuster continues with the investigation and claims adjustment. Then, after agreeing to the adjustment, the insurer denies the claim. It is possible in such a circumstance a court would *estop* the insurer from denying payment. Because the insurer knew about the breach of contract before agreeing to the adjustment and went ahead with the adjustment anyway, it would be unfair to allow the insurer to deny the claim later because of the breach of contract. In such cases, the court might find that the adjuster's actions caused the insured to alter behavior to his or her own detriment (for example, by not hiring an attorney early in the investigation).

The occupation of loss adjuster requires much expertise and knowledge, particularly of the law. The job also requires investigative ability and an understanding of human behavior. The adjuster must be familiar with property values when adjusting property losses. If working on liability claims (a claim made by an injured party against an insured), the adjuster must be familiar with the law relating to negligence, liability, and legal evidence. The adjuster must be able to negotiate with insureds, maintain accurate and up-to-date records, and assist home-office personnel when needed.

UNDERWRITER

Underwriter

One of the most challenging activities in an insurance company is underwriting new business. The **underwriter** reviews applications for insurance and then either accepts them at an appropriate rate or rejects them. This person makes a decision based on criteria established by the company's management (for example, no drivers accepted with three previous accidents, or no insurance provided for restaurants) and personal experience and judgment. In practice, the underwriter must be a skillful judge of people. If the applicant's morals are open to question, the underwriter probably will decline the insurance, no matter how sound the property or how healthy the life.

The goal of underwriting is to produce a pool of insureds, by categories, whose actual loss experience will approximate closely the expected loss experience of a given hypothetical pool of insureds. For example, assume that an underwriter is told that a pool of exposures with specified characteristics (e.g., a pool of brick buildings located no more than five miles from a fire station) will produce a loss rate of 1 percent of the value of the insured property. The underwriter's objective should be to place in this pool only exposures whose characteristics match the specifications. If the underwriter does the job well, the loss ratio of the insureds accepted will approximate closely the expected 1 percent figure. Of course, in any given year, deviation from the expected loss ratio is likely. In the long run, however, if the underwriter performs well, the expected and actual results should be close. Putting applicants for insurance in the classification or pool that most closely reflects the mathematically fair costs of their losses is the essence of good underwriting.

Contrary to some opinions, the underwriter is not supposed to reject so much business that the insurer experiences no losses. If the underwriter rejects all but the exceptionally safe exposures, much desirable business has been turned away. Insurance companies expect losses, and it is just as much an underwriting error to reject profitable business as it is to accept loss-prone business. The function of the underwriter is to accept applicants so that the losses paid by the insurance company closely match the losses that the company expects to pay. However, if management feels that regulators have provided inadequate rates for a class of business, the underwriter must narrow the range of acceptability to produce the expected results.

Adverse Selection

The underwriter always must be alert to the possibility of adverse selection. Adverse selection, sometimes called *antiselection*, describes the process whereby those individuals who are more than likely to experience loss try to purchase their insurance at average rates that do not truly reflect the above-average cost of their exposure. Some commentators describe adverse selection as the result of unequal (asymmetric) possession of knowledge. The underwriter who does not select applicants carefully will find actual losses well above expected losses. Recognizing that the possibility of adverse selection is always present, the underwriter must screen and rate all applications for insurance carefully. Proper classification of risks by dealing with potential adverse selection is the essence of the underwriter's assignment.

People whose property is prone to fire, those who are more than likely to have automobile accidents, and people whose health is not good need the financial security insurance can provide. In many instances, insurance companies accept such exposures. When such applicants are accepted, however, they must be charged a premium that reflects their increased costs. To accept such nonstandard risks at standard rates would mean the standard risks are subsidizing the nonstandard risks. Such a situation can result in the insurance company's collapse.

The potential for conflict between the underwriter and the insurance agent must be considered. The underwriter's performance is judged primarily on the quality rather than the quantity of successful applications produced, whereas the agent is compensated based on quantity of production. The conflict between the two parties is more apparent than real, however. The agent's responsibilities include an initial screening of applicants. If the agent knows a company will not accept a certain class of business, he or she should not submit such applications. Likewise, if the agent is aware of the moral hazard, he or she should never submit that business. Because the agent is the initial contact, in many cases the agent provides the first step in the underwriting process.

The underwriter knows that the greater amount of business accepted, the better the law of large numbers will operate. Furthermore, the agent knows that, if the applications submitted consistently result in an above-average number of claims, the company will end the agency relationship. Thus, although a potential for conflict appears because of the different objectives of the underwriter and agent, in practice they both are working toward the same goal—producing a large group of properly classified insureds. Experienced underwriters have told me that in underwriting marginally acceptable exposures, the submitting agent's historical performance often determines the application's acceptability.

Property Insurance Underwriting

Selecting insureds properly and charging them a rate that fairly reflects the expected loss is the substance of underwriting. In underwriting and rating property for fire insurance, for example, the underwriter considers such factors as:

- The type of construction, for example, brick or wood
- The occupancy or use of the building (commercial or residential)
- The nature of the surrounding property
- The fire protection provided by the community where the property is located
- Any safety features incorporated in the property, such as fire sprinklers or alarms

In underwriting and rating automobile insurance, the age of the driver, the use to which the automobile will be put, the driver's accident and moving violation record, and the driver's gender all traditionally have been used to determine an appropriate rate for an applicant.

The underwriter has several sources for obtaining underwriting information. The application supplied by the potential insured provides the usual starting point. Public records on traffic violations are available. Investigations by the insurer's employees can be used to verify facts. Also, credit-rating agencies can be used to provide important supplemental information.

Life Insurance Underwriting

The life insurance underwriter has reason to believe that if a sufficiently large number of 35-year-old healthy men are combined, the insurance pool will experience a death rate of about 2.11 deaths per 1,000 of insureds. Thus, the factors determining an insured's life insurance rate are (1) the applicant's age, (2) the applicant's gender, and (3) the status of the applicant's health—almost always established by medical examination. Life insurance companies usually have medical staff to assist in assessing an applicant's health.

In addition to the variables cited, the life insurance underwriter will be interested in such items as the insured's occupation, hobbies, total amount of life insurance owned, general financial condition, and any indications of a moral hazard. Like the property insurance underwriter, the life insurance underwriter constantly must be alert to the possibility of adverse selection.

Medical Information Bureau (MIB)

The **Medical Information Bureau (MIB)**, whose Web site is (*http://www.mib.com/*), provides assistance to the life insurance underwriter. The MIB was formed in 1902 by physicians who were medical directors of about 15 life insurance companies. Only life insurance companies may belong to the MIB. One requirement for membership is that the life insurance company has a licensed physician as its medical director.

The MIB provides a central location for storing information about life insurance applicants. Today, information about applicants is primarily medical, including blood pressure and other test results. Previously, nonmedical information relating to an applicant's moral habits was recorded. Some nonmedical information is still recorded, including bad driving records and dangerous hobbies. The information is in coded form, and the MIB protects its confidentiality. The MIB maintains records on people who have taken medical examinations in connection with the purchase of life insurance. All member companies submit reports on their applications to the MIB, and all are able to request MIB reports to assist in the underwriting process. Consumers must authorize the MIB review in writing during the application process. They also have a right to request a review of their MIB file and make corrections if needed.

Underwriting and Privacy

To do the job properly, an underwriter needs accurate information. But a question arises: "At what point does the underwriter's need for information conflict with an individual's right to privacy?" Commentators have given the conflict between these two positions much deserved attention.

The more accurate the information the insurer has, the fairer the premium charges are. Does an insurer have the right, however, to determine if an applicant uses marijuana, is an anarchist, or is an adulterer? To what length must an insurer go to protect the confidentiality of its information? Should all information be routinely passed along to the MIB or a credit reporting bureau? What rights should a consumer have to correct any mistakes or distortions of information? These are difficult questions, and class discussions with students have convinced me that each of us probably would draw a slightly different line between the insurer's need to know and an individual's right to privacy, between what is an acceptable business practice and what is unacceptable.

Federal rules governing this area are found in the Fair Credit Reporting Act (15 U.S.C. 1681) enacted in 1971. Details of this act may be found at this Web site: (*http://www.ftc.gov/os/statutes/fcra.htm/*). This act requires an insurer to notify an applicant before making an investigation. The applicant is allowed to examine any relevant records the insurer has, as well as correct or amend information or have the facts reinvestigated. Whether the Fair Credit Reporting Act is sufficient to protect privacy and produce fair results is debatable. It is a question of where to draw the line between conflicting rights in a democratic society.

ACCOUNTANT

Insurance company accounting is significantly different from manufacturing company accounting. Most of a manufacturing company's assets consist of buildings, equipment, and inventory. In contrast, the great majority of an insurance company's assets will be financial securities whose market values may change every business day. Likewise, a manufacturer's liabilities may include trade debt, as well as short- and long-term borrowing whose values can be calculated and presented in a straightforward way. The insurer's main liabilities are the expected payment for its insureds' losses, and these payments remain indefinite in amount and timing until they are actually made. Insurance contracts, especially life insurance contacts, can have very long durations, and expensing the usual and substantial initial costs of selling the insurance over the contract's life can create serious problems of income recognition. For these reasons, accountants have developed special rules called *Generally Accepted Accounting Principles* (GAAP) for insurance companies. The U.S. GAAP accounting rules are designed to present a fair representation of the condition of the firm for various stakeholders. State regulators, however, are concerned with making sure companies remain solvent and can pay claims. Therefore, regulators require very conservative statements reflecting rules governed by *Statutory Accounting Principles* (SAP). These rules, among other requirements, do not count the insurer's buildings or equipment as part of "admitted assets" because they are not available to meet policy owner claims. Thus, U.S. insurance companies keep two separate sets of accounting records.

Because many insurers operate internationally, and because investors, rating agencies, insurance supervisors, and insurance companies themselves need harmonized consolidated financial reports, the International Accounting Standards Board (IASB) developed a framework of accounting rules known as the International Financial Reporting Standards (IFRS).[4] The first phase of the IFRS became effective in the European Union (EU) in 2005, and the second phase is scheduled to be effective in 2008.

The major accounting issues addressed by the IFRS reveal the core theoretical issues insurance industry accountants must address. They include the following questions:

- Should financial assets be valued at the market rate or based on historical amortized cost?
- When should income be recognized, especially with long-duration contracts?
- How should the riskiness of assets or liabilities (including estimated losses) be measured and reported?
- Will market-value measures of assets, liabilities, and income lead to a real or a "paper" increase in an insurance company's earnings volatility?

It is beyond the scope of this text to present or even summarize the technical arguments supporting various positions on these complex issues; however, these arguments can be found with an Internet search using "IFRS" as a keyword. Readers can draw one conclusion, though: insurance industry accounting is interesting and undergoing important changes needed to present reports that accurately reflect the results of insurance transactions.

ACTUARY

Actuary

Somebody gave the life underwriter the idea that if the company insured a large enough number of healthy 35-year-old men, the death rate would be 2.11 per 1,000. Somebody gave the property underwriter the idea that if the company insured enough brick buildings located within five miles of a fire station, the loss rate would be 1 percent of the value of the insured property. That somebody is called an **actuary**. Simply put, actuaries make projections of the future based on historical results, probabilistic models, and their own judgment. Readers interested in learning more about becoming an actuary should visit the following Web site: (*http://www.beanactuary.org/*).

---

[4] Readers wanting to learn more about the IASB or the IFRS can use an Internet search engine for current information on both subjects.

Insurance companies rely on actuarial mathematicians to compile statistics of losses, to develop insurance rates, to calculate dividends, and to evaluate the financial standing of the insurance company. Actuaries develop rates by reviewing past statistics and projecting future results. In insurance, the price of the policy is determined before the loss costs are known, and it is the challenge of actuarial science to predict these costs.

Part of the difficulty of the actuary's job is developing rates that are fair to all insureds. Wooden houses are more loss-prone than brick houses, so the two must be charged different rates. Women aged 21 have lower mortality than do women aged 65, so they are charged different life insurance rates. As the actuary tries to draw finer and finer distinctions (for example, between houses 10 miles from a fire station and houses 13 miles away, or between persons 25 pounds overweight and persons 35 pounds overweight), the challenge becomes greater. Remember that the law of large numbers relies on the numbers in question being sufficiently large, and if the actuary and the underwriter try to draw distinctions that are too fine, they will lose the predictability provided by this law. Thus, the actuary's task is to develop distinctions treating all members of the insurance pool fairly, yet at the same time preserving the predictability provided by the law of large numbers. In addition to developing rates, insurance companies need actuaries to calculate and analyze operating results or profits, calculate dividends, and develop scientific loss reserves—all calculations involving estimates of unknown factors.

The actuary is a skilled mathematician who solves insurance problems. Actuaries have professional societies that award designations to members who pass a rigorous series of examinations. The Fellow of the Society of Actuaries (FSA) designation is earned by those working in the life insurance area. (The FSA Web site is *http://www.soa.org/*.) Actuaries working in the non–life insurance area pass the examinations leading to the Fellow of the Casualty Actuary Society (FCAS) designation. (The FCAS Web site is *http://www.casact.org/*.) These actuarial designations can be obtained only after earning a college degree, gaining several years of practical experience, and studying many hours of mathematics and accounting, as well as passing the examinations.

The demand for the services of actuaries is strong. Not only do insurance companies need actuaries, but so do regulating agencies and consulting companies working in the area of pension plans and other employee benefits.

ATTORNEY

Attorneys represent the insurance company's interest in lawsuits against insureds, against other insurers, and against other parties claiming that the insurer's actions injured them or their interests. Attorneys assist in developing the wording of insurance policies and deal with regulatory bodies, explaining the company's viewpoint and arguing the company's position at regulatory hearings. Life insurers rely on a legal staff to assist agents in underwriting advanced cases involving estate planning and employee benefits. Attorneys also are needed to give advice on other aspects of the insurance company's activities. No insurance company could operate without an attorney's services.

FINANCE PROFESSIONALS

Insurance companies need financial administrators to prepare budgets and coordinate the company's cash inflows and outflows. Because the inflows and outflows of insurance companies are predictable, insurers often need to and are able to commit funds months before they actually receive them. For example, if a developer of a shopping mall or large motel complex needs financing over a multiyear development period, an insurer can agree to supply funds in advance for the development period. The predictability of cash inflows is a significant difference between insurance companies and other lenders.

The investment of company funds, which is of crucial importance to an insurance company because of the millions (and sometimes billions) of dollars involved, is a major responsibility of financial managers. Many insurers have a staff of financiers who analyze investment proposals for private placements. Because of their very large cash flow, investment decisions require a staff of highly trained financial analysts.

OTHER OCCUPATIONS

Property insurers need architects and engineers to evaluate the potential for loss in various factories, apartment buildings, and shopping malls. Life insurers need physicians to assist in evaluating applicants for insurance. Most insurance companies need people skilled in management information systems to handle the large amounts of data generated by an insurance company's operations. Insurance companies need secretaries, clerks, advertising people, personnel administrators, convention and travel planners, and many other skilled persons to carry on their operations.

It should be clear that the insurance industry provides many different and challenging employment opportunities. Many insurance occupations require considerable technical expertise, especially those of accountant, actuary, attorney, underwriter, and loss adjuster. Insurance careers can provide people with the satisfaction of knowing that families and businesses are more secure and likely to endure, thanks in some part to their efforts. This significant career reward should not be overlooked.

SUMMARY

Insurance agents and brokers bring buyers and sellers of insurance together. The agent represents the insurance company. The broker represents the purchaser of insurance. Agency law governs the relations between agents and their principal, the insurance company.

In property insurance, the two basic types of agent are those who are employees of direct writers and those who work as independent agents representing several different insurance companies. The life insurance agent most familiar to the public is known as the *special* or *soliciting agent*. The agent's assignment is to secure applications for insurance. Life insurance agents do not have the power to bind their company.

The duties of an insurance agent are much broader than merely selling insurance. A good agent provides clients with information and service both before and after a loss. The agent exercises judgment about which applications for insurance to submit to the insurer. The occupation of insurance agent has provided thousands of men and women with rewarding careers.

The loss adjuster's work begins once a claim for payment reaches the insurer. The adjuster must investigate the claim, report the findings to the insurer, and sometimes negotiate a fair settlement. The adjuster must carefully avoid mistakes involving the legal doctrines of waiver and estoppel, which might force an insurer to pay claims it otherwise might deny. Many adjusters work for independent adjustment bureaus rather than directly for insurance companies.

Underwriters must select and rate applications for insurance. They must be constantly alert to the possibility of people more likely than average to experience a loss applying for insurance at standard rates. The results of such adverse selections are losses greater than the insurance company anticipated when rates were formulated. The result of good underwriting is to have the insurer's actual experience closely match the expected experience.

The insurance company accountant must consider carefully how to present financial records that satisfy insurance regulators, investors, policy owners, and other interested parties. Questions of when to recognize income and how to recognize risk present special problems to insurance industry accountants.

The actuary is the insurance company's mathematician and statistician. Actuaries develop the prices for the various kinds of insurance that the company offers. Actuaries' skills are needed to calculate the company's profits and the dividends it pays. No insurance company could operate without the services of an actuary. Many other talents are needed to make an insurance company run. Attorneys, financiers, accountants, marketing personnel, and many other skilled professionals are required to allow the insurance operation to perform its crucial tasks.

REVIEW TERMS

- Actual authority
- Actuary
- Adjustment bureau
- Adverse selection
- Agent
- Apparent (implied) authority
- Broker
- Direct marketing

- Direct writers
- E-commerce
- Estoppel
- Express authority
- Incidental authority
- Independent adjuster
- Independent agent
- Loss adjuster

- Medical Information Bureau (MIB)
- Principal
- Public adjuster
- Ratify
- Reservation of rights
- Unauthorized practice of law
- Underwriter
- Waiver

REVIEW

1. What duties do principals owe their agents? What duties do agents owe their principals?
2. What areas of the law should be familiar to property insurance agents? What areas of the law should a life insurance agent know? How does knowledge of the law assist the loss adjuster?
3. Explain the basis for conflict between the insurance agent and the home-office underwriter. In practice, why are such conflicts often not a problem?
4. Describe the differences between an insurance agent and an insurance broker. Are these differences important to the insurance consumer?
5. Why do life insurance agents and property insurance agents have different grants of authority?
6. What factors should the consumer consider in choosing a property insurance agent? A life insurance agent?
7. Explain the difference between waiver and estoppel. How can the doctrines of waiver and estoppel result

in an insurance company paying for a claim it otherwise might deny?
8. What purpose does a "reservation of rights" letter serve?
9. Should a good job of loss adjusting always involve the claims adjuster negotiating the lowest possible dollar amount of claims settlement? What rights do insureds have if they feel the proposed loss adjustment is unfair?
10. What incentive does the insurer have to settle claims fairly?
11. Why do insurance companies hire independent loss adjustment bureaus?
12. Why must the underwriter be concerned about adverse selection?
13. What kind of information could the property insurance agent or the life insurance agent get from a credit bureau that would be helpful in making insurance underwriting decisions?

OBJECTIVE QUESTIONS

1. The definition of agent is a person:
   a. Working for another person
   b. Authorized to act for another person
   c. Signing a contract for another person
   d. Substituted to another person's rights and duties

2. A broker is:
   a. The agent of the insured
   b. The agent of the insurance company
   c. Neither the agent of the insurance company nor the insured, but his or her own agent
   d. Never used in life insurance
3. Independent loss adjusters:
   a. Are technically agents of the insurance company whose loss they are adjusting
   b. Are technically agents of the insured
   c. Are neither agents of the insurance company nor of the insured, but independent of both
   d. Are independent of the insurance company, but only until the claim is settled
4. A waiver is:
   a. A condition in property insurance
   b. A condition found only in life insurance
   c. A condition found in both life and property insurance
   d. The intentional abandonment of a known right
5. If an insurer "ratifies" an agent's action it means:
   a. The agent is fired.
   b. The agent is promoted.

c. The agent acted illegally, but the insurer must pay the fine.
d. The agent acted beyond the scope of authority, but the company agreed to accept the results.

6. An insurance company whose agents are also employees of the company is called a:
   a. Direct writer
   b. Casualty underwriter
   c. Comprehensive insurer
   d. Investor-owned company
7. An organization that collects data on life insurance applicants is the:
   a. CIA
   b. CBS
   c. MIB
   d. FCAS
8. If an insurance agent were to give legal advice to a client, this would be:
   a. A required part of the job
   b. A crime
   c. Only a problem if the advice was incorrect and led to a client's loss
   d. A violation of the Fair Trade Act

DISCUSSION QUESTIONS

1. What do you think would be the most difficult aspects of the job of:
   a. Life insurance agent?
   b. Property and liability insurance agent?
   c. Loss adjuster?
   d. Actuary?
   e. Property insurance underwriter?
2. Explain why an insurer's obligation to pay may be an issue before the loss is adjusted and why this leads to the insurer having to reserve its rights before the adjustment proceeds.
3. Do you think a college education is necessary to perform the following occupations effectively?
   a. Life insurance agent
   b. Loss adjuster
   c. Property insurance underwriter
   d. Actuary

INTERNET RESEARCH ASSIGNMENTS

1. Assume that you are a licensed insurance agent in your home state and you want to sell insurance in a nearby state. What are the requirements for obtaining a non-resident license in the nearby state? Start your search at this site: (*http://www.licenseregistry.com/products_ services/non_resident_licensing.htm/*).
2. Identify one of the minimum standards of supervision under the National Association of Security Dealers

Code. Start your search at this site: (*http://www.nasd. com/*). (Hint: check the section "CONDUCT RULES (3000)" in the *NASD Manual*.)
3. What is the MIB's position on an insurance applicant's right to privacy? Start your search at this site: (*http:// www.mib.com/*). Do you agree or disagree with the MIB's position? Why?

Appendix A: Legal Issues Involving Insurance Agents and Brokers

Here are two fictional legal cases involving insurance agents and brokers. These cases are based on real incidents and are fairly typical of legal problems involving insurance agents.

Case 1

Facts

Adams purchased a boat, motor, and trailer for $8,000. He contacted Brown, an agent of Water Mutual Insurance Company, and requested full coverage for his new property. A policy was issued to Adams, who then paid the premium. In applying for the coverage, Adams indicated the boat would be operated on inland lakes and streams. He subsequently lent the boat to his brother-in-law, whose actions resulted in the boat's sinking in the Atlantic Ocean. A nearby fishing boat saved his brother-in-law.

Questions

Does an agent who has been asked to provide a policy giving the insured full coverage have to provide a policy providing coverage under any and all circumstances? Does an insured have a duty to read an insurance policy once it has been issued and be familiar with any limitations or exclusions from coverage? (The policy in question contained a clause excluding coverage when the boat was operated in salt water.)

Conclusion

In this case the court held that the agent would have an impossible burden of intuitive foresight to find a policy providing coverage against all possible losses. Moreover, the agent would have to explain to the insured the policy's provisions and exclusions applying to any and all circumstances. On the other hand, the insured did have a duty to read the policy issued to him, a duty he failed to fulfill. Had he done his duty, Adams would have been aware of the relevant exclusion. He then would have renegotiated the contract or acted within its conditions.

Case 2

Facts

Daniels owned a factory and had a fire insurance policy covering the building and its contents. The fire insurance policy expired on November 2. On October 2, True Blue Insurance Company sent Daniels a premium-due notice. On November 2, he was sent a notice informing him that his policy had been terminated. The termination notice contained a reinstatement offer with the following conditions: Payment of premium had to be received at the True Blue home office prior to a specified date (December 7). A check would be accepted as payment if honored on first presentation to a bank.

On November 30, Daniels mailed a check to the Southern Insurance Agency, but Southern Insurance never forwarded the premium to True Blue. In September of the following year, Daniels suffered a substantial loss and submitted a claim to the insurer. True Blue denied the claim for lack of an in-force contract.

Questions

Did Daniels have a valid claim against either True Blue or Southern Insurance Agency? Did the agency have actual or apparent authority to collect the overdue premium?

Conclusion

The court held that Daniels was given clear notice that payment had to be received at the home office to effect reinstatement. Furthermore, Daniels never received any evidence of an in-force policy, such as the issuance of renewal policies. Thus, adequate evidence existed to relieve True Blue of any duty to pay the claim. On the other hand, the court found that the Southern Insurance Agency did accept the $7,000 premium payment and had remitted no premium to any insurer. Thus, the jury awarded Daniels a $75,000 verdict against the Southern Insurance Agency.

Appendix B: The Ethical Choice

Introduction

This appendix provides a short survey of a critically important topic—ethics. As has been the case many times in writing this text, I am summarizing and simplifying a great body of knowledge and information. In fact, this appendix summarizes an entire library of work. The next few pages will not substitute for a course in ethics. The two purposes of this appendix are, first, to present some of the vocabulary that frames ethical problems and, second, to illustrate some of the problems facing insurance agents trying to make ethical choices.

The following five areas of ethical problems are encountered frequently by agents:

1. Making false or misleading representation of products or services
2. Failing to identify the customer's needs and to recommend products and services that meet those needs
3. Lack of knowledge or skills to perform one's duties competently
4. Conflicts of interest between personal financial gain and properly performing one's duties
5. Making disparaging remarks about competitors

One question that will occur immediately to some readers is: "Why include material on ethics, which can be the subject of one or more demanding university courses, in this textbook?" The answer is simple and straightforward. The career of insurance agent, as well as the other insurance occupations described in this chapter, cannot be understood without an appreciation of how ethical choices are made. For insurance professionals, the need to make ethical choices may be a daily event, thus making the right ethical choice is an essential ingredient of being a professional (or being a successful one, at any rate).

Vocabulary

The study of ethics is a well-recognized branch of philosophy. Philosophers and teachers of ethics disagree about many things, including the definitions of terms they use. In fact, in preparing this material, I have reviewed a dozen or more definitions of the term *ethics*. Disagreement about the meaning of words makes communications between people stimulating but difficult. The following definitions appear in a commonly available dictionary and convey the substance of the meaning of the terms, but they may not satisfy all philosophers:

- **Dilemma**: A situation that requires a choice between options that are or seem equally unfavorable or mutually exclusive.
- **Ethics**: A set of principles of right conduct.
- **Integrity**: a. Steadfast adherence to a strict moral or ethical code. b. The state of being unimpaired; soundness. c. The quality or condition of being whole or undivided, completeness.
- **Morality**: a. The quality of being in accord with standards of right or good conduct. b. A system of ideas of right and wrong conduct. c. Virtuous conduct.
- **Value**: A principle, standard, or quality considered worthwhile or desirable.
- **Vice**: a. An evil, degrading, or immoral practice or habit. b. A serious moral failing. c. Wicked or evil conduct or corrupt habits
- **Virtue**: a. Moral excellence and righteousness; goodness. b. An example or kind of moral excellence.

The foregoing definitions should prepare readers for the material to follow in this appendix. In this paragraph, the words defined in the short glossary are italicized so you can see my use of these hard-to-define terms. Our focus in this appendix is on analyzing ethical *dilemmas*, a choice between two unappealing options. Life often presents us with ethical dilemmas. For example, a man makes a promise to his spouse to be home by 6 P.M. On the way home, he witnesses a car accident and stops to help because he sees an injured person. Helping the person injured in the accident means he will not arrive home before 9 P.M. This man must make a choice between breaking a promise and not helping a person in need. To solve the problem—and quickly, in the case of an emergency—he must rank his values. In this case, while he greatly values keeping his word, he values helping an injured person more highly. Note that his choice was mutually exclusive. If he helped, he could not keep his promise to his spouse, and vice versa. The philosopher might ask if he made the *ethical* (right) choice. Were his *morals* good in this instance? (Was his actual behavior consistent with the ethics he claims?) Did he demonstrate *virtue* (habitually doing the right thing) and *integrity* (always behaving ethically)? Or is this instance of breaking a promise indicative of *vice* (behaving unethically)? To evaluate a given instance of behavior, it would be most useful to have a set of standards against which an action can be judged. We will call such a set of standards *ethical norms*.

Ethical Norms

Ethical philosophers have not produced general agreement on standards for determining whether a given choice (or action) is ethical. In fact, many standards or rules have been proposed, and each has been subjected to substantial criticism. There is no universally accepted standard of right behavior that I have been able to uncover. Instead of depending on one generally accepted criterion, I present three alternatives that appear regularly in ethical discussions.

- Consider the consequences: The ethical choice produces the most good.
- Universal principles: The ethical choice is the one everybody should follow.
- Relativism: Because there is no single fixed principle, the ethical choice must be determined by reference to what everybody in society does.

The Rule of Consequences: The Right Choice Produces the Most Good

This rule suggests that the right (good) choice produces the most good (utility). The problem is that the choice that produces the most good is a function of one's values. In the preceding example, given the choice of breaking a promise or saving a life, I suspect (and hope) that most people would find saving the life would produce the most good. But this cannot be proved. If a person were to value keeping one's promise more highly than all other values, then consequentialism would lead to a different ethical choice in our hypothetical case.

Among the objections to exclusive reliance on the rule of consequences to make the right choice is the problem with people who define the "good" as "their good." That is, such people always view the good (ethical) choice as the one that maximizes their own good. This position is called *ethical egoism*. If the argument is made that individual greed and selfishness produce the greatest good for the greatest number—which is one reading to be made of Adam Smith's

"invisible hand of self-interest" argument—then there is a platform on which the ethical egoist can stand. The general problem is, who defines "good"?

A second objection to consequentialism involves the problem of comparing good (utility) between individuals. Suppose one were presented with two mutually exclusive choices. The first alternative reduces 10 percent of the public's good (utility) while raising the good of the remaining 90 percent. The second choice is to do nothing. How is the ethical choice made? The consequentialist would opt for the first choice because it produces the most good. But suppose the reduction of the 10 percent's good meant their enslavement, and the increase in the 90 percent's good resulted from enslaving the minority? Consequentialism produces what I would call a very unappealing result in this case. Consequentialism cannot help us to solve all ethical dilemmas because we cannot always measure the consequences of a given choice in a meaningful way. While consequentialism can provide a good start toward solving ethical problems and can provide a frame of reference, many cases exist where it is not a reliable measure.

The Universal Rule: The Good Choice Is the One Everybody Should Follow

The great German philosopher Immanuel Kant wrote, "One ought only to act such that the principle of one's act could become a universal law of human action in a world in which one would hope to live." He also wrote, "One ought to treat others as having intrinsic value in themselves, and not merely as a means to achieve one's ends." To put the matter simply, Kant said that we should act only as we would want everybody to act, and we should respect other people. Those are two good benchmarks against which to judge our choices, but they are not without problems.

One problem with Kant's rule arises when we must choose between two good actions, actions we would want everybody to follow, like keeping promises and helping people in distress. If this problem is pursued to logical ends, we find ourselves having to rank what is most good, and that, as we just saw, is a subjective problem.

Even when choosing between acts that are considered universally good (telling the truth) and bad (lying), Kant's rule is not always helpful. Consider the situation where telling the truth—that a dying friend looks terrible—does much more harm than lying. Perhaps, in some cases, the good choice is determined by the situation.

The Rule of Relativism: The Good Choice Must Be Determined by Reference to What Everybody in Society Does

We just illustrated the strong argument for relativism in ethics. Simply put, we often must act in a context that defies the use of universal rules. Thus, if all ethical people lie to dying people, that is the ethical (right) thing to do in this circumstance. This rule, sometimes called *situation ethics*, provides a fair standard for making choices—that is, when not pushed too far. If all ethical people honor contracts, or refrain from killing or assaulting other people, then doing what everybody does in a given situation is a safe, ethical choice. But consider the case where even "ethical" people keep two, or even three, sets of accounting records to evade tax payments. Does the majority practice make the practice (tax evasion) ethical? Consider a cannibal society, for an extreme example of when this might not be a good thing. Ethical relativism may not be very helpful to a professional trying to make an ethical decision. For example, if most agents in an office pad their expense account with extra charges, are agents who honestly report their expenses unethical?

Consider one other problem with ethical relativism: It is nearly impossible to compare one society's actions to another's logically. For example, it is currently legal in Florida for an insurance agent to offer a client a rebate, and presumably some agents do so. However, because rebating commissions is illegal in California and almost all other states, presumably most agents do not engage in this practice. How do we compare the ethics of Florida agents to California agents? The very same activity is legal in one location and illegal in another, but is it ethical (good, right) in both locations? Either location? Neither location? This example leads to one more point.

Ethical behavior and legal behavior often are, but need not be, the same thing. For example, some laws passed in this country's history had some remarkably cruel consequences for minority citizens. Many people chose to disregard these laws and stood on firm ethical grounds despite their illegal actions.

More to the point in this discussion, legal behavior often represents the minimum responsibility a professional owes to a client. For example, the law may require disclosure of some factual material during the sales process. The legal requirement may be met by handing an explanatory pamphlet to a potential client. The ethical requirement may not be met, however, until the professional provides a meaningful explanation of the facts covered in the pamphlet using terms that the client understands.

A Concluding Comment About Ethical Rules

Reading the literature on ethics and the great debates stretching back to Aristotle may leave a reader confused and perhaps even a bit discouraged. If these great ethical philosophers cannot reach general agreement about what is the ethical choice, yet seem to be quite capable of poking holes in the arguments of others, how do we expect insurance professionals, professors, and laypersons to make the ethical choice at all times? I will not resolve this puzzle, but I will offer the following compilation of the three rules just discussed to identify a standard for making ethical choices. The ethical choice is the one that provides a positive answer to each of the following questions:

- Are the consequences of the act good for everybody affected by the decision?
- Does the act proceed from a principle that, if followed by everybody, would result in a good society?
- Was the act the best choice in the particular case in question?
- Would the person repeat this act if it were sure to be subject to public scrutiny?

Of course, this list of questions contains circular problems requiring the definition of good and is, no doubt, subject to other logical criticism. It may fall short when dealing with cases where one must choose between the lesser of two evils. Nevertheless, because it combines the ideas of some of history's greatest ethical philosophers, it has much to recommend it. Therefore, we will move on to the next section of this appendix and illustrate how this approach can be applied to some frequently encountered dilemmas faced by insurance professionals.

Three Practice Cases

We will present a set of facts and provide some ethical insights regarding the outcomes. Then we will modify the facts slightly and allow readers to develop an analysis. As we have noted several times in this appendix, no way exists to prove what *the* ethical choice is in a given circumstance. However, if one accepts the ethical tests presented previously as being a reasonable basis to judge a given set of choices (actions), then one is able to reach conclusions in some cases.

Facts: Case One

Mr. Q and Agent W have been involved in the sales process for several months, and Mr. Q finally has agreed to apply for $250,000 of whole life insurance. He has taken a medical exam and submitted a premium of $3,500 to Agent W. When the medical exam results are returned, Agent W discovers that Mr. Q has an extremely serious case of heart disease. He calls Mr. Q and tells him that the life insurance company will not insure him at standard rates and may not insure him at all. Mr. Q thanks Agent W very much and says, "Please drop this matter, and please do not discuss my health problems with anybody, especially my family, as they do not know about my problem and I do not want them to worry about me."

Question 1. Should Agent W inform Mr. Q's wife if she is (1) a personal friend, (2) Agent W's attorney, or (3) Agent W's sister?

Analysis. Insurance agents have a duty to protect the confidentiality of information that comes into their possession. Any breach of this duty would fail our ethical tests; that is, (1) Mr. Q has indicated his good would be diminished if this confidence were breached, a negative consequence of this choice; (2) society would not be a better place if all professionals breached their clients' confidential information; and (3) most ethical insurance agents will not breach the confidential information of their clients. (I base this on personal knowledge of many agent friends, not on scientifically gathered evidence. The possibility of a lawsuit would act as a constraint in this case, even if ethical concerns would not.)

Question 2. We will change the facts slightly. Instead of heart disease, assume the medical examination reveals that Mr. Q has a virulent and always fatal sexually transmitted disease. Should Agent W inform Mr. Q's wife? Does your answer change if Mrs. Q is Agent W's longtime secretary? Does your answer change if Mrs. Q is Agent W's sister?

Assignment: Carefully discuss this dilemma explaining an ethical rule that can justify not informing an endangered party and a rule that justifies informing an endangered party in this case.

Facts: Case Two

L. J. Silver, a Caribbean cruise ship captain, is 47 years old. He purchased a life insurance policy from Agent Hawkins 20 years ago when his first child, Robinson, was born. This policy was a traditional cash-value life insurance policy that was average in all respects. Last week, a cruising tourist, a life insurance agent named Peter Pott, suggested that Captain Silver replace his old policy with a new type of policy that would provide much better performance than the old policy. When he returned home, Silver called his agent, Hawkins, and said he wanted to cash in his old policy. Hawkins arranged a conference with Silver and examined Agent Pott's proposal. He discovered that Agent Pott's policy illustration was based on very "aggressive" assumptions about interest earnings, mortality charges, and other elements of life insurance policy design. The proposed policy was more risky in every respect when compared to the present policy. He also realized that Silver could be sold a new policy from his company that was similar to the one suggested by Agent Pott. However, his policy illustrations were based on even more "aggressive" assumptions than were Agent Pott's.

Question 1. Should Agent Hawkins try to persuade his client to retain his current policy by explaining the problems with Agent Pott's illustration, thereby discrediting Agent Pott and his company?

Analysis. Telling the truth is the ethical choice in this case. It has the good consequence of allowing Silver to judge for himself, based on facts, if the proposed policy change meets his needs. Telling the truth, even if it exposes another's shortcomings, is a rule that—if universally followed—benefits society. Finally, in this instance, ethical agents, who must work in a competitive environment, certainly will explain the weakness of a competitor's proposal.

Question 2. Should Agent Hawkins try to sell Silver a new policy from his company, a policy based on assumptions he knows to be very aggressive and risky? If Silver exchanges his current policy for a new policy, he incurs substantial expenses and gives up some potentially valuable contractual rights. Agent Hawkins receives no compensation if Silver retains his existing policy, but he earns a substantial commission if Silver exchanges policies. However, Agent Hawkins believes that if he does not recommend the policy exchange, Silver will make the exchange for Agent Pott's policy.

Analysis. Provide an ethical foundation for Agent Hawkins encouraging Silver to retain his current policy. Is there any ethical justification for Agent Hawkins to promote the aggressive illustration from his company? Is there any ethical justification for Agent Hawkins to discredit Agent Pott's illustration and policy?

Facts: Case Three

Ernest Money is an independent property insurance agent. His agency represents two different insurance companies, the Rockhard Insurance Company and the Smoothflow Insurance Company. Rockhard is a very highly rated insurance company that provides excellent claims adjustment service. It charges premiums and pays its agents commissions that are about 20 percent higher than Smoothflow. It also provides cruises and other expensive vacations to agents meeting or exceeding $1 million in premium volume. Smoothflow is a financially sound but less highly rated company than Rockhard. It is known for its very competitive premium charges but also for loss adjustments that tend to be "on the low side and on the slow side." Because Smoothflow's commissions are a percentage of its low premiums, Ernest earns less on business placed with Smoothflow. Therefore, as a general rule, when clients do not appear interested in the price of coverage, Ernest places their insurance with Rockhard. By contrast, when Ernest feels he is in a competitive situation, he provides quotations from Smoothflow.

Question 1. Does Agent Money's rule for placing insurance with the two carriers that he represents appear to be ethical?

Analysis. The appearance is that Agent Money is not always putting his clients' interests above his own. But the key word in the preceding sentence is "appearance." The consequences of Agent Money's actions are difficult to foresee. Some clients will spend more money than they would if the more competitive carrier was used, but they also will get a faster and more generous claim settlement if a loss occurs. The ambiguity of the consequences also makes it difficult to determine if Agent Money's actions would benefit society if universally followed. Finally, independent property insurance agents face this difficult dilemma frequently, and to be ethical, each must reach a conscientious decision that professional agents would recognize as fair. However, it is doubtful that a general consensus would be reached in this case.

A further step Agent Money could take when placing clients' insurance coverage would be to provide his potential clients with complete information on both carriers and allow them to make their own choice. Providing complete information to insurance clients meets all the ethical tests outlined in this appendix.

Question 2. April Day, who knows very little about insurance, came to Agent Money's office because her sister, May Day, recommended his agency. April needs homeowners insurance. Agent Money tries to explain the strengths and weaknesses of his two alternative carriers. Unfortunately, April does not want to be involved in the decision and instructs Agent Money to choose the carrier that "provides the best coverage for the money." What should Agent Money do? Coincidentally, selling a Rockhard policy to May Day will qualify Agent Money for a round-the-world cruise.

Analysis. A dilemma for student analysis. Present ethical arguments for and against either of Agent Money's recommendations.

Suggestions for Further Study

Aristotle. "Nicomachean Ethics," in *The Basic Works of Aristotle.* Richard McKeon, ed. (New York: Random House, 1941).

Dewey, John. *Theory of the Moral Life* (New York: Holt, Rinehart, and Winston, 1960).

Donaldson, T., and P. Werhana. *Ethical Issues in Business: A Philosophical Approach*, 5th ed. (Upper Saddle River, N.J.: Prentice Hall, 1996).

Feezell, R., and C. Hancock. *How Should I Live: Philosophical Conversations About Moral Life* (New York: Paragon House, 1991).

Fletcher, Joseph. *Situation Ethics: The New Morality* (Philadelphia: Westminster Press, 1966).

Kant, Immanuel. *Lectures on Ethics.* Louis Infield, trans. (New York: Harper and Row, 1963).

CHAPTER 6

The Insurance Market: The Economic Problem

After studying this chapter, you should be able to:

■ Describe the main participants in the insurance market

■ Explain how the economic theory of supply and demand applies to the insurance market

■ Identify some insurance markets with distribution problems

■ Describe the requirements for being an effective insurance consumer

■ Describe how the courts, the law, and the insurance commissioner provide consumer protection in the insurance market

The U.S. insurance market often receives public attention. In the aftermath of the hurricane seasons of 2004 and 2005 and the World Trade Center and Pentagon terrorist attacks of September 11, 2001, insurance experts and politicians raised serious questions about the capacity of the property insurance industry to respond to future terrorist attacks as well as natural catastrophes. The role of private health insurance remains a national concern. This chapter provides an overview of some of the economic laws and forces operating in the insurance market and provides a framework to discuss and understand these issues.

Most U.S. business schools teach microeconomic analysis because it provides special insight into problems involving the allocation of resources. This chapter uses traditional microeconomic tools to describe the insurance transaction. We explore the interface between economics and insurance. This chapter, however, does not exhaust the analytical possibilities of the subject. Rather, it provides a necessary foundation appropriate for an introductory risk management and insurance text. It is important for students of risk and insurance to integrate the core business school requirements such as economics, statistics, business law, and finance with the material covered in this introductory textbook.

Market
A **market** is a place where buyers and sellers transact business. Usually a market involves just two parties: buyers and sellers. The insurance market is unusual because it has three major players: sellers (insurance companies, their agents, and brokers); buyers (almost every adult American purchases one or more types of insurance, and so do all businesses); and regulators. Regulation affects both insurance buyers and sellers in many different ways. For example, some laws compel individuals and business firms to purchase insurance while other regulations require sellers to provide insurance to specific groups.

Figure 6–1 presents the insurance market graphically. The figure shows more than three "players" in the insurance marketplace and suggests competition between agents, brokers, and insurers to provide insurance to the public. Insurance companies compete

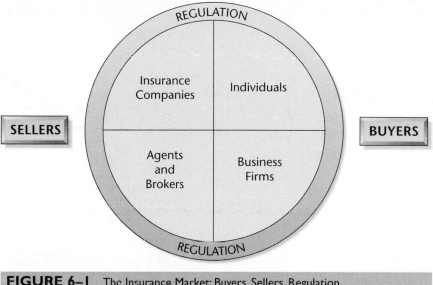

FIGURE 6–1   The Insurance Market: Buyers, Sellers, Regulation

with each other to retain existing insureds and to attract new ones. Agents compete with each other, sometimes compete against brokers, and sometimes compete directly with insurers for business. One point of this figure is that the insurance market is highly competitive. Another is that regulation is integral to this market.

ECONOMIC THEORY

To understand the insurance market and some of its problems better, we turn to the fundamental topic of the law of supply and demand.

Supply and Demand

It has long been held that the most efficient distribution of society's scarce resources would occur if prices were set in a perfectly competitive market. In this context, *efficient* means that nobody's welfare could increase without decreasing somebody else's welfare. Unfortunately, the requirements for perfect competition generally do not exist in our world. These requirements include:

- Numerous independent sellers, each holding a market share that is too small to influence price
- Numerous well-informed consumers
- A homogeneous, perfectly substitutable product
- Freedom of entry and exit

In this perfectly competitive world, one equilibrium price prevails, satisfying both producers and consumers and maximizing welfare. This point is shown as price P1 and quantity Q1 in Figure 6–2. In the diagram, the demand curve slopes backward, indicating that utility-maximizing consumers purchase less insurance as the price rises. Less insurance may be the result of lower quantity purchased, higher deductibles, or coverage of more limited perils. The supply curve, in this case a short-run curve, slopes forward, showing that insurers will provide more insurance as prices rise. If students recall

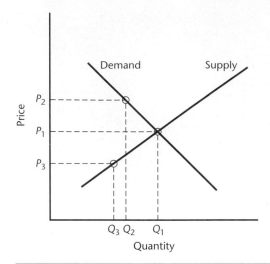

FIGURE 6–2   The Law of Supply and Demand

their lessons from microeconomics, they will realize that if any other price except the equilibrium price, P1, were tried tentatively by producers or consumers, dynamic forces would set in, readjusting the price up or down to P1. A freely competitive market, for insurance or other goods, serves as a screening device. People who are most willing and able to pay get what is sold; and firms providing insurance at the least cost supply it.

If the market price were changed from that freely determined by the forces of supply and demand, the economic model predicts lower total welfare. If, for example, a monopoly existed, or monopoly results were achieved by collusion among suppliers, the price would rise and the quantity demanded would decrease. This relationship is shown as price P2 and quantity Q2 in Figure 6–2. If transactions were made at price P2, consumers would be hurt in two ways. First, some consumers would purchase the good, but they would have to pay the higher price. Paying a higher price reduces consumers' welfare. Second, some consumers who would have purchased the good at the freely set price will not make the purchase at the higher price. Because they could not purchase the good at the lower price, the forgone consumption reduces their utility.

Consider the alternative to an artificially high price. Assume that the prevailing market price was artificially lowered from the freely determined price, perhaps by regulation. Then, just as in the preceding case, total welfare would be lowered. This point is shown in Figure 6–2 as price P3 and quantity Q3. Here, demand would increase but supply, especially in the long run, would decrease because firms will not supply as much of the good at the lower price. To make the argument clearer, assume that regulation lowered the price below the producers' costs. In the long run, producers would be bankrupt if they sold the product at that price. Even if prices were lowered from the free market price by a small amount, the sellers would attempt to cut back on services or other costs or move to more lucrative areas to maintain profits.

Turning from this economic theory to the insurance market, some of the industry's critics claim that insurance prices should be lowered by regulation to deprive the industry of its "excess" profits that result from collusion in rate making. Critics claim that collusion arises because most insurers use standard policies provided by rating bureaus. The rating bureaus also provide standardized loss data that insurers use to set their individual rates. Thus, while subscribers to ratings bureaus can and do set their own rates, they begin with the same foundation of loss data.

The industry claims that lowering prices will deprive it of its just rewards and will result in a reduced supply of insurance. In other words, in terms of Figure 6–2, industry critics claim that lowering the price of insurance represents a move from P2 to P1, depriving the industry of collusive profits while increasing society's welfare. The insurance industry argues that mandated lower prices represent a move from P1 to P3. Insurers further maintain that mandating lower prices will reduce the supply of insurance and perhaps bankrupt some insurers. This chapter's appendix provides further discussion of some advanced microeconomic theory relating to the insurance market. To continue from this point, we first describe several historical market problems and continue to expand on the description of the insurance market.

Historical Problems

The following insurance markets historically have had problems:

- The automobile insurance market for high-risk drivers has been a problem for decades.
- The property insurance market for some inner-city property has been a problem since the mid-1960s.
- Special liability insurance markets, including medical malpractice, environmental impairment liability, and municipal liability insurance markets, have been recurrent problems since the mid-1970s.
- The insurance industry generally excluded terrorism coverage after the September 11, 2001, attacks. Loss of this coverage required government intervention in the insurance market. We described the government's response to the terrorism insurance problem in Chapter 2, "Defining the Insurable Event."

Automobile Insurance

Drivers causing repeated accidents or those convicted of serious driving offenses at first will find their insurance cost increasing at renewal. If their driving problems continue, they usually find it difficult or impossible to purchase coverage in the voluntary market. That is, without government intervention, most insurers would not provide insurance to the worst drivers. The government does intervene in the market because lack of insurance probably would not keep the uninsured drivers off the road. Instead, these people would drive without insurance, would probably injure more people, and their innocent victims would be unable to recover compensation for their injuries. Currently, state governments typically require each insurer voluntarily accepting automobile insurance to also accept a proportionate number of applications from the unwanted drivers. Therefore, if an insurer voluntarily writes 10 percent of the state's automobile insurance, it also will have to accept 10 percent of the bad drivers in that state. It can charge these drivers a higher rate for coverage, but even the higher rate may not cover the anticipated costs of providing the insurance. The state rules forcing companies to insure some percentage of bad drivers are known as **automobile insurance plans** or **assigned risk plans**. Another approach to providing insurance to these drivers is the **joint underwriting association (JUA)**. In states where JUAs operate, the insurers agree to share the profits or losses of a pool of insurers providing insurance to this group. In all these cases, insurers—who presumably pass their costs forward—charge the involuntary market losses to the voluntary market.

Readers may wonder why insurers do not charge the appropriately high premium in the voluntary market. One explanation is that if they did so, many high-risk drivers

Automobile insurance plans

Assigned risk plans

Joint underwriting association (JUA)

would not or could not pay for insurance. Lack of insurance would not keep many of these drivers off the road, as stated before, and the cost of the accidents caused by these uninsured drivers likely would be borne by their victims. Thus, the state-mandated subsidy keeps the insurance for high-risk drivers "affordable." Moreover, some commentators believe that the state has an obligation to provide affordable insurance coverage for their citizens.

Fair Access to Insurance Requirements (FAIR) Plans

Fair Access to Insurance Requirements (FAIR) plans are designed to deal with the problem of unavailability of property insurance in inner-city areas. FAIR plans have operated since 1968 and now are found in about 27 states, the District of Columbia, and Puerto Rico.

Insure.com is a Web site containing a good deal of interesting insurance information (*http://info.insure.com/*). One link within that site (*http://info.insure.com/home/fairplans.html/*) lists all the FAIR plans currently operating and provides contact information for each of these plans. More information, including data, can be found using a search engine with the keywords "FAIR insurance plans."

There is some variation in rules and coverages offered among the states in the provisions of their respective FAIR plans, but the following characteristics generally apply. FAIR plans guarantee property owners an inspection of their property if they request it. If the property is insurable, an appropriate rate is charged. If the property is uninsurable, the owner must be given written notice of any improvements or loss prevention measures required to make the property insurable. Once the property is insured, the property owner must maintain it in insurable condition to keep the insurance in force. Nevertheless, owners cannot be discriminated against individually because of factors over which they have no control, such as general neighborhood deterioration.

FAIR plans have been controversial since their beginning. Underwriting losses (claims for payments that exceed premiums earned) have occurred in most states in most years with these plans. These underwriting losses have been passed forward to other property owners, causing them to subsidize inner-city property owners. Welfare economics provides little guidance in reaching conclusions when one group wins and another loses welfare because of mandated subsidization.

The success or failure of FAIR plans is hard to measure. Clearly, there are property owners with insurance who, without FAIR plans, might not have it. FAIR plans have increased the welfare of these people. Critics, however, claim that FAIR plan insurance has led to an increase in arson for profit. Perhaps the outcome of the debate depends on whether the yardstick is financial or social. The availability of property insurance at affordable rates is important to every property owner, and FAIR plans have helped many people purchase affordable insurance. The social question involves who is to bear the costs for this affordable coverage and how the costs are to be transferred. Is society a better place if most property owners are forced to provide a subsidy to inner-city property owners? Like other questions of mandated subsidization, the answer requires a value judgment.

Special Liability Insurance

Since the mid-1980s, several lines of liability insurance have been either unavailable or unaffordable at times for certain groups. Included in the list of insurance applicants that have had problems buying insurance are the following:

- Cities (which face lawsuits because of the actions or inaction of their police, fire, or street repair departments)

- Day care centers (after several widely reported cases of alleged child molestation)
- Directors and officers of corporations (who have been sued in cases of mergers, failed mergers, disappointing earnings, "cooked books," and bankruptcies)
- Health care providers, especially physicians and hospitals (whose errors and omissions can result in large damage awards)
- Manufacturers (whose operations could result in environmental impairment liability)

Insurers in these cases behaved as if one or more of the criteria for the ideally insurable exposure were missing. As we described them in Chapter 2, these criteria include predictable losses, economically feasible premiums, and no catastrophic loss potential.

THE INSURANCE CONSUMER

The author's research suggests that one missing ingredient in the insurance market may be a well-informed consumer. This contention raises another interesting question: "Why isn't the insurance consumer well informed?" Perhaps it is not clear that the rewards of making informed decisions are worth the cost of getting the needed information. Although this argument does hold some amount of truth, it leaves unanswered the question of whether the present cost of getting information is unnecessarily high. The cost of obtaining information involves time, effort, and sometimes money—usually in that order. The Internet has lowered some of the cost barriers to obtaining insurance information. Using a search engine, the author typed "Insurance information" and got millions of hits. The first ten appeared to be useful to consumers shopping for coverage, but some of the other sites uncovered were less helpful. Unfortunately, the author's research suggests that getting information about insurance on the Internet is not a good substitute for expert advice.[1]

The cost of getting information needed to make effective purchase decisions may be examined in terms of the problems encountered in obtaining this knowledge. Perhaps the main problem in making an informed decision is the insurance contract itself. The typical insurance contract is a complex legal document that is difficult for most consumers to understand. Few people have enough legal knowledge to comprehend the meaning of the wording in a property insurance contract, and a life insurance contract can be even more difficult to grasp. Besides the legal knowledge needed to understand a contract, knowledge of finance is needed to evaluate an insurance policy's cost.

The industry explains the legal complexity of insurance contracts as necessary to reduce misunderstanding or litigation. For more than three decades, the industry has made significant efforts to write personal insurance policies in simpler language. State insurance commissioners who have the power to keep undesirable insurance products from being sold provide some aid to consumers. The term *undesirable* can be used to describe policies that are unduly complex, as well as those offering worthless protection.

It is a generally accepted tenet of industrial organization theory that the more informed the consumer is, the more likely the producer is to add to the consumer's

---

[1] Mark S. Dorfman and Saul W. Adelman, "An Analysis of the Quality of Internet Life Insurance Advice," *Risk Management and Insurance Review*, Vol. 5, No. 2 (Fall 2002), pp. 135–154.

information. Conversely, the more uninformed the consumer appears, the more likely the producer is to withhold information. That is, the well-informed consumer usually is provided facts during a sales presentation, while the uninformed consumer often gets just razzle-dazzle or even worse.

Informed consumers are more likely to receive not only informative advertising but also genuine product improvements. Why should a producer spend time and money improving a product when the customer cannot tell the difference between the improved and unimproved version? Many researchers think the responsibility for problems existing in markets in which the consumer remains uninformed lies with both the producer and the consumer. If producers viewed consumers as being well informed, the nature and content of their advertising efforts probably would become more informative. Product innovation would be truly that, not just new coverings on old products. So the price of remaining uninformed includes not only wasted dollars in some cases but also many other side effects that, in the long run, can prove even more expensive.

An additional problem that comes with uninformed consumers is that they rarely know the right questions to ask. Even if a consumer asks a good question, the answer might be so technical that he or she would find it difficult to understand. Therefore, the most important of all decisions the insurance consumer must make is the decision to become informed about an admittedly difficult subject.

The Consumer's Choices: Company, Agent or Broker, Policy, Amount, and Price

An economist analyzing the consumer's problem in the insurance market would conclude that this purchase is difficult to make knowledgeably. The informed consumer must make five separate choices: company, agent (or broker), policy, amount, and price. We will discuss each of these choices now. One reason this material is presented so extensively is to alert the reader to how difficult it is to be an informed insurance purchaser. In addition, it provides some insight into why many people buy insurance without adequate information or sufficient shopping. Finally, it may help readers to be better-informed insurance consumers themselves. The impact of the Internet on the insurance purchase must again be noted. Not only does the Internet allow comparison shopping for some personal lines of coverage, but some Internet sites also provide a considerable amount of useful information on how to purchase insurance.

Selection of a Good Insurance Company

Consumers should consider three criteria when choosing an insurance company:

- Financial strength
- Fairness and promptness in processing claims
- The ability and willingness to provide service before and after a loss

An insurance policy is a promise. Like all promises, it is worth no more than the word and the financial strength of the person or company making it. Therefore, the first priority in choosing an insurance company is to find a financially strong company.

Financial Ratings Firms Consumers can get a professional opinion of the financial strength of many insurance companies by reviewing the ratings provided by an independent financial ratings firm. The following firms provide financial ratings of insurance companies: A.M. Best Company (*http://www.ambest.com/*), Standard & Poors (*http://www.standardandpoors.com/*), Moody's Investor's Services (*http://www.moodys. com/*), and Weiss Research (*http://www.weissratings.com/*).

The following points list some critics' concerns about relying too heavily on an insurer's financial rating when making a purchase decision:

- The ratings firms often do not agree among themselves on a specific insurance company's merits.[2]
- All ratings firms can and have made mistakes.
- One letter grade cannot sum up an insurance company's operations accurately.
- Slight differences in letter grades probably do not make a sound basis for choosing one insurer over another.
- Companies with high ratings can sell policies that are not the most efficient choices.
- Ratings are estimates; they are no guarantee of the future.

Other Information. Other sources of information about specific insurance companies include insurance agents, state insurance regulators, and satisfied or dissatisfied customers. All these sources may be subject to biases. Agents may have a monetary interest in recommending a company. Dissatisfied customers may be victims of their own misunderstanding. Moreover, stories about a few unhappy customers are more likely to receive public attention than the successful handling of thousands of claims in which customers were satisfied by their insurer's efforts. State insurance regulators may be forced to limit their comments because of the sensitive and potentially influential nature of their statements.

Once a financially sound company is identified, the consumer should determine the company's reputation for fairness and promptness in settling claims and its reputation for providing service. An agent's motivation to provide good service comes from the company. If the home office stresses good service, the agent is more likely to provide it than if the company appears indifferent.

Selection of a Good Insurance Agent or Broker

A good insurance agent has considerable knowledge of the protection being offered and also understands related areas of personal finance. A good agent is a person of integrity who puts a client's interest first, before his or her own. Good agents communicate clearly, so the insured understands the needs that the insurance fulfills and the rights and duties that the contract creates.

Evidence of an agent's knowledge is found in the ability to answer questions clearly. If the agent cannot answer a question immediately, he or she knows where to get the answer. Some agents have earned professional designations. Traditional professional designations include the **Chartered Life Underwriter (CLU)** and **Chartered Property Casualty Underwriter (CPCU)**. Some life insurance agents who have expanded their practice into professional financial planning also can earn the **Certified Financial Planner (CFP)** designation.[3]

It is often difficult for a consumer to form an opinion about an agent's trustworthiness. A recent resource is found on the Web sites of various state insurance departments that lists the names of agents who have been disciplined or have had their license revoked for unethical or illegal behavior. The following hyperlink provides links to all state insurance departments: (*http://www.naic.org/*).

Chartered Life Underwriter (CLU)

Chartered Property Casualty Underwriter (CPCU)

Certified Financial Planner (CFP)

---

[2] Steven W. Pottier and David W. Sommer, "Property-Liability Insurer Financial Strength Ratings: Differences Across Rating Agencies," *The Journal of Risk and Insurance* (December 1999; Vol. 66, No. 4), pp. 621–642.
[3] The respective Web sites for the organizations sponsoring these designations are as follows: CFP (*http://www.cfp.net/become/*); CLU (*http://www.amercoll.edu/*); CPCU (*http://www.cpcusociety.org/*).

E-Commerce and Direct Marketing   We have noted previously that more and more consumers purchase insurance products through a direct marketing channel such as the Internet rather than use a local insurance agent. However, just as in any purchase, the insurance buyer using the Internet should take steps to ensure that the seller is reputable and meets all the criteria—especially that of financial strength—for selling a high-quality product.

Selection of a Good Insurance Policy

To choose a good insurance policy, the consumer must understand the need for insurance. Only then can it be determined whether a particular policy meets this need. By definition, a good insurance policy is one that meets the consumer's needs without providing more insurance than is required. In choosing a good property and liability insurance policy, the consumer's selections are standardized. The two largest non–life exposures are the home and automobile. The consumer's role is easier today, when one or two packaged plans of insurance can cover most property needs. Before 1950, it was necessary to buy several different policies and riders, and even then the consumer could not always be sure there were no gaps or overlaps in insurance coverage. Today, insureds with money-making hobbies or unusual property (such as expensive artwork, extensive gun or coin collections, or a large greenhouse) may need to amend the standard policy to tailor the coverage to their needs.

Choosing a good life insurance policy is more difficult than choosing a good non–life insurance policy because life insurance policies are not standardized. Some policies combine savings with protection; some policies are purely protection. Some companies' policies are combined with desirable riders, while others are combined with less desirable ones. Some companies provide for a substantial surrender charge, while others do not. Recognizing purchase substitutes in the life insurance market is not an easy task. The informed consumer knows the correct questions to ask and can understand the answers.

Selection of the Proper Amount of Insurance

Choosing the proper amount of insurance, like choosing the proper policy, begins with knowledge of the consumer's individual need for insurance. The need for insurance is related to the severity and the frequency of a potential loss. In property insurance, the need for protection usually is based on either the acquisition cost or the replacement value of a physical asset. This need can be calculated. In cases of business income insurance or liability claims, estimates of potential losses are needed. It has been suggested that people tend to buy too much insurance for low-severity, high-frequency losses but tend to purchase inadequate coverage for high-severity, low-frequency exposures. An example of such a mistake would be to purchase a service contract on a new car extending the warranty several years while simultaneously driving with the minimum amount of liability coverage. The most one could lose in terms of a car repair bill is far less than the most one could lose in a liability suit.

In choosing the proper amount of life or disability insurance, the starting point is the consumer's financial goals. How much money would this person need to solve financial problems if death or disability were to occur immediately? The second step involves determining the amount of available assets to meet these needs. Available assets include existing life insurance policies, individual savings, Social Security benefits, and group life insurance provided by employers. If a gap exists between financial needs and available assets, this gap is the appropriate amount of life insurance to purchase. For the purposes of this chapter, it suffices to note that making an informed purchase of the proper amount of life insurance often is a complicated procedure.[4] Despite the difficulty in choosing the proper amount of insurance, some commonsense rules apply:

- Insure first those exposures to loss that are most likely to cause the greatest amount of damage.
- Never expose more to loss than you can afford to lose.
- Never risk a great loss (a high percentage of your assets) in exchange for a small gain (saving the insurance premium).

Paying the Right Price

Useful hints for consumers will help them to pay the right price, but few absolute rules exist. The right price is the one that provides the consumer with the greatest amount of insurance after considering the other four criteria just described. That is, the right price for insurance is not necessarily the lowest price. The lowest price may come from a company whose financial strength is questionable. It may come from a company that too frequently resists or denies its insureds' legitimate claims. It may come from an insurer whose agents are not trained adequately or from a company whose policies do not offer coverage as valuable as that offered by other companies. For these and other reasons, the consumer first should consider all the other criteria mentioned and then search for the right price.

One rule in finding the right price is to engage in comparison shopping. Researchers have found considerable price variation for comparable insurance policies offered by similar insurers. The need for shopping is true in both life and property insurance.

Conclusion

Being an informed insurance consumer is not easy. However, shopping for insurance on the Internet has become a productive source of information on price and other aspects of insurance in recent years. The author is not recommending any particular Web sites, but entering the keywords "XYZ automobile insurance company," "homeowners insurance costs," "XYZ life insurance company," or "health insurance premium comparisons" into an Internet search engine should produce the desired Web sites for a particular company or an insurance price-comparison Web site. As of this writing, several Web sites have side-by-side comparisons of many insurance companies and the insurance premiums they charge. Initial research suggests that price shopping on the Internet is proving to be an effective way to lower a consumer's insurance costs. However, as we have just suggested, the insurance with the lowest cost may not be the best "bargain."

It is worthwhile for the consumer to make informed purchase decisions. If you consider the imperfections in the insurance market caused by uninformed consumers, or if you consider that each year, many Americans might spend more than $1,200 on homeowners insurance, $1,500 to insure one automobile, and $1,600 on life insurance, you can understand that being an informed consumer does not cost—it pays. Moreover, the dividends earned by the informed consumer continue for years.

CONSUMER PROTECTION: THE ROLE OF THE COURTS, THE LAW, AND INSURANCE COMMISSIONERS

We have examined two of the three sides of the insurance market: sellers and buyers. The third side is regulation. Regulation can come from one of three sources: the courts, state insurance law (and, to limited extent, federal law), and state insurance

---

[4] Chapter 12, "Professional Financial Planning," describes the "needs-based purchase" of life insurance in detail.

commissioners. Transactions in the insurance market cannot be understood without appreciating the role of regulation. This chapter provides an overview of regulation that is just sufficient to see the interface between regulation, buyers, and sellers. We present the specific details of insurance regulation, its history, and current policy in Chapter 7, "Insurance Regulation."

The Courts

If an insured believes that he or she has not received what the insurance contract promised, the insured has the opportunity to bring a case to court. If the court is convinced the insured has not been dealt with fairly, it can force the insurance company to correct the situation. The usual reason for litigation is the insurer's denial of the insured's claim for payment. That is, after a claim is denied, the insured sues the insurer for breach of contract.

An insurer may deny claims for many legitimate reasons, including the following:

- The insured may have attempted to defraud the insurer.
- The contract might not be in force because the insured did not pay premiums.
- The coverage may have been suspended because an insured violated a contract condition.
- The loss may have been caused by an excluded peril.

Most of these grounds for claims denial raise questions of fact. Were the premiums paid promptly? When was the notice of cancellation mailed? What, in fact, was the proximate peril causing the loss? A jury in court often must resolve questions such as these. It is the function of the court to protect the legitimate rights of both insured and insurer. On the one hand, if an insurer were to pay claims that should be denied, it would hurt the interest of all members of the insurance pool by increasing costs. On the other hand, the denial of valid claims is intolerable, and courts can prevent such an injustice. Thus, the role of the court is to protect the legitimate rights of both parties to an insurance contract.

Stare decisis

The doctrine of ***stare decisis*** gives court decisions in a particular case added weight if the decision is considered to set a precedent. The literal translation of the term *stare decisis* is "to stand by decisions." In practice, the doctrine means current court decisions will be consistent with previous decisions involving the same, or essentially similar, facts. For example, if a state court sets a precedent and decides that the term *animal* includes birds and fish, the next time the issue arises in litigation, that precedent will be followed in that state. If a court in another state (jurisdiction) decides a contract meaning to exclude bird damage must specify birds and animals, that decision will be precedent-setting in that state. *Stare decisis* adds certainty to the outcome of litigation. It also greatly enhances the role and power of the court in the area of consumer protection.

The Law

The insurance laws (codes) of the various states provide consumers with essential protection. They establish rules of conduct, requiring some behaviors and forbidding others. For instance, Article 24 of New York State's revised insurance code (*http://assembly.state.ny.us/leg/*) is titled "Unfair Methods of Competition and Unfair and Deceptive Acts and Practices." One part of this article states, "No person shall engage in this state in any trade practice which is defined . . . to be an unfair or deceptive act or practice." The article goes on to define several prohibited unfair or deceptive acts or practices. The list includes (1) issuing or circulating false literature, (2) making false statements or rumors about insurance institutions, and (3) making incomplete comparisons between insurance contracts.

New York's Article 24 is an example of a law that prohibits direct abuse of consumers. In some broad sense, all insurance law is designed to protect the consumer's interest. Rules and regulations governing company solvency, licensing of agents, approval of policy forms, licensing of insurance companies, and rate regulation all promote and protect consumer rights. The law, however, is fairly rigid. It can deal only with issues in general. It can mark out boundaries between acceptable and unacceptable behavior. For dealing with particular problems on a daily basis, however, a more flexible institution is needed. The state insurance commissioner is this flexible institution. The combination of state insurance law and the actions of the state's insurance commissioner provide a state with insurance regulation.

The Insurance Commissioner

Every state has an insurance commissioner, an administrator in charge of insurance regulation. This person's responsibilities include interpreting and enforcing the state's insurance code. In most states the governor appoints an insurance commissioner; in a few states, the commissioner is elected.

Two selections from New York's insurance law read as follows:

- The superintendent shall possess the rights, powers, and duties, in connection with the business of insurance in this state, expressed or reasonably implied by this chapter or any other applicable law of this state.
- The superintendent and the department have broad authority under this chapter to investigate activities which may be fraudulent and to develop evidence thereon. This article is intended to permit the full utilization of the expertise of the superintendent and the department so that they may more effectively investigate and discover insurance frauds, halt fraudulent activities, and assist and receive assistance from federal and state law enforcement agencies in the prosecution of persons who are parties to insurance frauds.

Two important differences exist between the role of the courts and the role of the insurance commissioner. First, unlike courts, the commissioner can initiate action even before a complaint is brought by an insured. Second, a court will decide if the Very Mean Insurance Company has been unfair in denying the claim of John Consumer. If the insurance commissioner becomes convinced that the Very Mean Insurance Company is denying many insureds' claims unfairly, however, the commissioner has the duty to correct this situation or withdraw this company's license to conduct business. The courts protect individual consumers from injustice. The commissioner protects all the state's insureds from injustice.

SUMMARY

When the insurance market shows signs of disruption for some kinds of insurance in some geographic areas, industry critics blame collusive price setting and poor business judgment for the problems. The insurance industry blames cost factors beyond its control.

Neither the supply of nor the demand for insurance is elastic. That is, price changes do not produce proportionate effects on the quantity sold. The result of such price inelasticity is a less-than-optimal welfare distribution when prices are arbitrarily changed up or down.

Historically, availability and affordability problems have occurred when providing insurance to poor drivers, inner-city property owners, and individuals and businesses needing some specific types of liability insurance. In the first two areas, which have been long-standing problems, measures have been enacted to create an involuntary market. In these cases, insurers voluntarily writing the good risks have been forced to accept some percentage of the less desirable exposures. In automobile insurance, such plans are called automobile insurance plans or assigned risk plans; in property insurance, these plans are called FAIR plans.

The insurance consumer generally is not well informed when making this purchase. Acquiring the needed information takes time and effort. Costs of making uninformed purchases include wasting money on the wrong policy, buying from the wrong company, and paying the wrong price. An uninformed consumer causes other market imperfections. The industry has no incentive to improve products or even to provide educational information to uninformed consumers. Thus, the consumer must accept some responsibility for the insurance industry's performance. To make an informed choice, the consumer must choose all the following:

1. A good insurance company
2. A good insurance agent or broker
3. A good insurance policy
4. The right amount of insurance
5. The right price

The courts, the law, and the insurance commissioner protect the insurance consumer. The courts protect insureds or insurers from particular injustices. The law determines the boundary between acceptable and unacceptable behavior. The insurance commissioner interprets and enforces the law for the benefit of all consumers.

REVIEW TERMS

- Assigned risk plan
- Automobile insurance plan
- Certified Financial Planner (CFP)
- Chartered Life Underwriter (CLU)
- Chartered Property Casualty Underwriter (CPCU)

- Fair Access to Insurance Requirements (FAIR) plan
- Financial ratings firm
- Insurance commissioner

- Joint underwriting association (JUA)
- Market
- *Stare decisis*

REVIEW

1. Most markets have two participants. The chapter suggests that the insurance market has three participants. Who is the third participant in the insurance market? Can you think of other markets where buyers are forced to purchase a product and sellers are forced to sell it?
2. What are the requirements for a perfectly competitive market? What is one of the main benefits of perfect competition?
3. Some critics claim the industry charges high prices because insurers collude when setting rates. Explain the basis for this criticism.
4. If insurers colluded and raised the price of insurance, what would you predict would be the effect on the quantity sold? Explain your answer.
5. If the government made insurers lower the price of insurance 25 percent, what would you predict would be the effect on the quantity sold? Explain your answer.

6. What is a FAIR plan? How does it work? If underwriting losses of FAIR plans are passed on to other insureds, is this mandated subsidization?
7. Explain the purpose of assigned risk plans and JUAs in automobile insurance.
8. Describe the problems caused by uninformed consumers in the insurance market.
9. How does the role of the courts differ from the role of the insurance commissioner in protecting the consumer?
10. Describe the important factors to consider when choosing an insurance company.
11. Why is the lowest-priced insurance not necessarily the best buy?
12. What information do financial ratings firms provide? What are some potential problems with their ratings?
13. Explain three commonsense rules for choosing the proper amount of insurance.

OBJECTIVE QUESTIONS

1. All the following criteria are specified in the model for perfect competition except:
   a. Government regulation
   b. Numerous independent sellers
   c. Numerous well-informed buyers
   d. Freedom of entry and exit

2. To make automobile insurance available to high-risk drivers, various states have used each of the following approaches except:
   a. JUAs
   b. Federal mandatory plans
   c. Assigned risk plans
   d. Auto insurance plans

3. The most important choice a consumer must make when purchasing insurance is:
   a. The lowest price
   b. The most coverage available
   c. Coverage from a company of unquestioned solvency
   d. Coverage from a company with the widest array of policy alternatives

4. *Stare decisis* means:
   a. All things considered.
   b. To stand by decisions.
   c. Innocent parties prevail.
   d. It is impolite to stare.

5. All the following parties are participants in the insurance market except:
   a. Insurance buyers

b. Insurance companies
c. Government regulators
d. The Federal Reserve

6. Insurance consumers can get information about the financial strength of insurance companies from:
   a. The Federal Reserve
   b. Financial ratings firms
   c. Credit information bureaus
   d. Public policy organizations (PPOs)

7. Which of the following designations cannot be earned by insurance agents?
   a. HMO
   b. CLU
   c. CPCU
   d. CFP

8. In most states, the insurance commissioner is:
   a. Elected
   b. Impeached
   c. Appointed by the governor
   d. Appointed by the president

DISCUSSION QUESTIONS

1. Why is the role of regulation in the insurance market so extensive?

2. Do you think FAIR plans or automobile insurance plans represent legitimate government intervention in the insurance market? Explain your position.

3. Do you think consumers should assume much of the responsibility for promoting their own welfare in the insurance market or do you think the government should do more?

INTERNET RESEARCH ASSIGNMENTS

1. Identify the current top five strongest life insurance companies as rated by Weiss Ratings. Start your search at this site: (*http://www.weissratings.com/*).

2. What is the subject of Article 28 of the New York Insurance Code? Start your search at (*http://assembly. state.ny.us/*) or (*http://public.leginfo.state.ny.us/menugetf. cgi?COMMONQUERY=LAWS/*).

3. Find the consumer-based insurance Web site of your state's insurance commissioner's office. What does the

Web site recommend to consumers who believe their insurer is treating them unfairly?

4. Find a Web site for one specific life insurance company and one specific property and casualty insurance company. In your opinion, does each of these Web sites provide information allowing a consumer to make an informed choice about the products for sale?

Appendix: Further Consideration of Supply and Demand

Elasticity of Supply and Demand for Insurance

Neither the supply nor the demand for insurance is perfectly elastic. That is, a change in price will not have proportionate effects on either the supply of or the demand for insurance.

The supply of insurance is inelastic, in part, because it is limited by regulatory and self-imposed solvency rules. One such rule limits net new premiums to some multiple of the insurer's surplus (typically between two and four), which is similar to the net worth account of conventional corporations. Such a limit on premiums also places a direct limit on the supply of insurance. As an insurer gets closer to selling out of insurance, it must seek new capital, purchase reinsurance, or become more restrictive in its underwriting standards. Thus, increasing the price of insurance will not necessarily draw an increased supply of insurance into the market, especially if insurers' surplus accounts have been depleted by years of underwriting or investment losses or if reinsurance is unattractively priced or unavailable.

Here is an example of how the premium-surplus ratio might work. Assume a beginning surplus of $1 million. Assume that net premiums of $4 million are written and that the acceptable premium-surplus ratio is 4. If the insurer loses $500,000 each year on its underwriting and investments, it will be bankrupt in about two years because the losses will equal its beginning surplus. Moreover, after the first year's loss, it will be able to write only $2 million in new business because its surplus is reduced by half because of the first year's loss.

Oddly, raising the price of insurance could decrease the supply of insurance. This peculiar result occurs because for a given quantity of insurance, higher prices increase the numerator of the premium-surplus ratio but not the denominator. For example, if the premium-surplus ratio equaled 2 and an insurer had only $1 million in surplus, it could write only $2 million in new premiums. Assume that the $2 million in premiums represented a given quantity of insurance. Then, if prices doubled, the quantity of insurance sold must be halved to keep the ratio constant. Depending on where the industry is on the supply curve, a rise in price can cause the supply curve to bend backward in the short run (segment C–D in Figure 6–3), a most unusual result. Although price increases might lower insurance supply, regulations lowering the price of insurance also would be expected to reduce supply, because providing insurance is a function of available capital, and capital can be moved easily from state to state or from an unprofitable line of insurance (for example, automobile insurance) to a profitable line (for example, commercial property insurance). For this reason, states that created conditions that insurers find intolerable also find many insurers trying to withdraw from their jurisdictions.

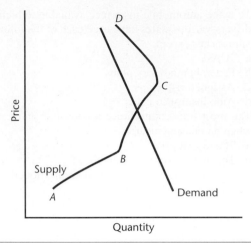

FIGURE 6–3   Hypothetical Supply and Demand for Insurance

Like supply, the demand for insurance also is inelastic. Thus, even if the price increases, demand does not go down proportionately. Some insurance is required by law (on vehicles) or by lenders (on mortgaged property). In other cases, consumers see insurance as a necessity to be purchased (though perhaps in smaller quantities) regardless of increased price. Unfortunately for consumers, in most cases no purchase substitute exists for insurance, though quantity and quality (deductibles and exclusions) can be adjusted. Inelastic demand results in higher collusive or monopoly profits than elastic demand. Hypothetical supply and demand curves in the insurance market are shown in Figure 6–3. These curves do not represent any particular type of insurance or geographic area. Realistic curves would require empirical investigation. The supply curve has three segments. Segment A–B is price-elastic; in this area, higher prices increase supply proportionately. Segment B–C shows relative inelasticity; thus, price increases do not increase supply as insurers reach their maximum output limit based on the premium-surplus solvency test. Segment C–D shows that increasing price can actually reduce supply.

Shifting Supply and Demand Curves

Sometimes people conducting economic analysis or teaching economics behave as if demand and supply curves actually existed in consumers' and suppliers' minds and actually could be measured by observers. Actually, supply and demand curves only represent a useful theoretical approach for explaining how

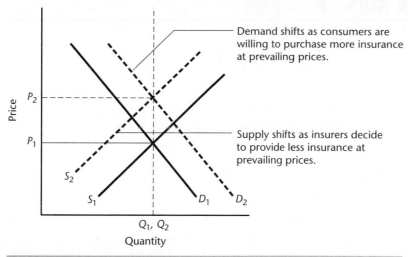

Demand shifts as consumers are
willing to purchase more insurance
at prevailing prices.

Supply shifts as insurers decide
to provide less insurance at
prevailing prices.

FIGURE 6–4   Shifting Supply and Demand

free markets determine prices. These theoretical curves can provide useful insight into such questions as what would happen if, in the aftermath of a widely reported loss (for example, a terrible earthquake, fire, or very expensive legal judgment against a well-known insured), people and businesses demanded significantly more insurance coverage. That is, if existing prices did not change, people made newly aware of some increased loss potential now want to increase their insurance purchases. Such a change would be shown by a move from demand curve D1 to D2 in Figure 6–4. Economists like to answer such questions by "holding other factors constant." In this case, other factors will not remain constant. The same factors that cause insureds to want to purchase more coverage are likely to cause insurers to offer less coverage at existing prices. That is, with an increased awareness of loss potential, insurers/suppliers will require a higher insurance rate for the same

supply of coverage. This change is shown in Figure 6–4 by a shift from supply curve S1 to S2. These two reactions, insureds wanting to purchase more coverage at existing prices and suppliers wanting to supply less coverage at prevailing prices, represent shifts of the supply and demand curves. The intersection of the new curves (D2 and S2) determines prices after the shift. In this example, given the hypothetical slopes of the old and new supply and demand curves, prices will rise from P1 (the intersection of D1 and S1) to P2 (the intersection of D2 and S2), and the quantity of insurance exchanged will be about the same. This particular result may not be a realistic representation of what would happen in an actual time period, but such an analysis provides economists and students of insurance a framework to study such a change in attitudes of buyers and sellers of insurance.

CHAPTER 7

Insurance Regulation

After studying this chapter, you should be able to:

■ Define the term *regulation*

■ Give four reasons why the insurance industry and the insurance transaction are comprehensively regulated

■ Identify the important landmarks in the history of insurance regulation

■ Identify the National Association of Insurance Commissioners (NAIC) and the role it plays in insurance regulation

■ Describe the main regulatory activities of state insurance departments, including the following:
  - Solvency regulation
  - Rate regulation
  - Investment regulation
  - Regulation of agents and company officers

Chapter 6, "The Insurance Market—The Economic Problem," implied that if the insurance market were not regulated, consumer welfare would not be maximized. We suggested several reasons for this outcome. For example, if weak or devious insurers freely set inadequate prices, some consumers would pay too little for their coverage, and ultimately their insurer would become insolvent. Other consumers, lacking good information or failing to shop for coverage, would pay too much, and their welfare would be diminished by this decision. In general, consumers do not shop efficiently for insurance because making the right choices is difficult and time-consuming. Therefore, the government supervises the market to protect consumers. Depending on one's perspective, insurance *regulation* (or insurance *supervision*, as it is known in Europe) may be viewed either as a form of governmental consumer protection or as government interference with transactions between insurance buyers and sellers. Today, some people favor more governmental regulation of insurance and others favor less. In this chapter, we describe insurance regulation in the United States and provide historical background explaining its development.

INSURANCE REGULATION

A dictionary defines *regulation* as "a rule or order prescribed by authority; . . . a governing direction or law." Insurance regulation provides the insurance market with direction, management, control, and correction. In this introductory text, a simple definition of the word *regulation* helps the reader understand a complicated subject: Regulation represents the rules by which the game is played.

The rules for a game, such as football, result in two things that on the surface appear contradictory but in reality are not—a loss of freedom and the creation of freedom.

For example, in football, a rule against illegitimate blocking means a player loses the freedom to block another whose back is turned. It also means all players have gained some freedom from being hit while their backs are turned. If the rule is broken, as is often the case, the offending team incurs a penalty. Insurance regulations have their parallels to this situation. They restrict some freedoms to create others. The freedom to market any insurance policy, for example, is restricted. Policy forms must be approved before they are sold to the public. At the same time, this restriction of freedom creates a freedom for the consumer—to remain unhindered by undesirable policy forms when making a purchase decision.

Insurance regulation arises from two separate sources, both working together: the law and the administration of the law. A third important participant in the provision of insurance regulation is the courts: state and federal, original jurisdiction, and appellate. Courts apply regulation to both the insurance regulators and the industry. A court interprets the law and it interprets the administration of the law. By interpreting the law, a court validates the rules of the game and the application of the rules. Courts, however, never initiate regulation. They react only when matters are brought to their attention.

McCarran-Ferguson Act (Public Law-15)

The governing federal insurance law is the **McCarran-Ferguson Act (Public Law-15)**. In a most unusual outcome for a federal law, the McCarran-Ferguson Act turns over the regulation of the insurance industry to the states. We present the history and reasons for the McCarran-Ferguson Act later in this chapter. Each of the fifty states, Washington, D.C., Puerto Rico, American Samoa, Guam, and the U.S. Virgin Islands has its own insurance code. An official, usually known as the insurance commissioner, whose job is to apply state insurance laws to specific cases, conducts the administration of a state's insurance laws. A more recent federal law, the **Gramm-Leach-Bliley Act (GLB)**, passed in November 1999, provides a framework for regulating all financial services providers, including insurance companies. This law, which we discuss in this chapter, leaves insurance regulation primarily where it has historically been, in the hands of the states.

Gramm-Leach-Bliley Act (GLB)

Insurance regulation

We now have developed the basis for a more thorough definition of **insurance regulation**: the rules of the insurance market, as established by law, administered by public officials, and interpreted by the courts, all for the purpose of promoting and protecting the public interest.

THE REASONS FOR INSURANCE REGULATION

We all know football would not be enjoyable for spectators or participants if there were no rules. Football and other sports have rules for the benefit of all. Similarly, many rules govern the insurance transaction. The insurance transaction between consumer and insurer is made in a comprehensively regulated market. Insurers generally are not free to write any contract they choose, are not free to charge any price they choose, and, for some types of personal insurance, must accept insureds they did not freely choose. The following four reasons explain why the insurance market is regulated so extensively:

- The potentially severe impact of an insurer's insolvency
- The unequal knowledge and bargaining power of the buyer and seller
- The problem of insurance pricing
- The promotion of social goals

Solvency

Promoting insurer solvency is the most important goal of insurance regulation. **Solvency** makes the result of the insurance transaction certain and predictable. One explanation for extensive regulation to promote insurer solvency is that individual insureds are not capable of self-protection in this transaction. Insurance is nothing more than a contingent promise to be delivered in the future. The promise is worth no more than the company standing behind it. Consumers cannot evaluate or monitor insurance company solvency because insurance accounting and actuarial procedures are too technical and complicated. Therefore, the government monitors insurer solvency on the public's behalf.

A second reason for the importance of solvency regulation is that if an insurer becomes insolvent, the problems for insureds can be very serious. The potential results of insurer insolvency include houses destroyed with no funds to rebuild, liability suits with only personal assets available to satisfy judgments, or widows left with dependent children and unfulfilled financial plans. The scope and severity of problems arising from an insurer's bankruptcy explain why an insurer's solvency is of utmost concern to the public, and hence to the regulators.

A third explanation for solvency regulation is that life insurance companies (and, to a much smaller extent, property insurance companies) are responsible for sizable amounts of consumer savings. Legally, the relationship between insurer and insured is comparable to that of debtor and creditor, but the relationship bears a close resemblance to the fiduciary arrangement found between a bank and its depositor. Fiduciaries are held to strict requirements for their actions because they require public confidence. Because insurers' operations parallel those of fiduciaries, the insurer's solvency is a subject for public regulation.

Unequal Knowledge and Bargaining Power

An insurer has enormous advantages in technical expertise compared to the typical consumer. For example, most insureds do not understand the insurance policy as well as the insurer who sold the policy. Also, many insureds feel unequal to the insurer when loss adjustment disputes arise. Therefore, one purpose of insurance regulation is to compensate for this imbalance.

The model for perfect competition calls for both well-informed buyers and well-informed sellers. As the market moves away from this ideal, competition deteriorates and problems arise. One sign of the deterioration of competition is the existence of different prices for identical goods. Informed purchasers also do not pay more for goods of inferior quality than for goods of superior quality. Unfortunately, both situations occur today in the insurance market despite regulation. We can only imagine how much worse the situation would be for the consumer if there were no regulation.

Part of the imbalance in knowledge between insurer and insured is explained by the complexity of the insurance contract. Most contracts are long and contain words that are meaningful to lawyers but often not to the public. Regulation is needed to prevent dishonest insurers from taking advantage of the consumer's relatively uninformed position by eliminating inherently unfair contracts from the marketplace.

Part of the imbalance in knowledge between insurer and insured is explained by the fact that insurance is an intangible good. As such, it is difficult for a consumer to evaluate the product's performance until it may be too late to argue about it. For example, if a consumer purchases an inferior television set is purchased, he or she usually discovers the problem shortly afterward and begins to insist that the set be repaired or replaced, or else they demand a refund. The problems created by an inferior insurance policy ordinarily are not readily apparent to the consumer. The insured usually does not find out the policy is problematic until he or she has made a claim for payment—a poor time to learn one's insurance policy is inferior. Because the insurer's performance is difficult for the consumer to evaluate properly before a loss, regulators must help.

Prices

In the market for most consumer goods and services, we assume the law of supply and demand, operating through competition, determines the price. Although the ideal of perfect competition is rarely realized, we often achieve a satisfactory level, or workable competition, in our economy. Competition, however, does not necessarily work to the consumer's advantage in the insurance market.

Part of the problem with competition in insurance is that insurers must set prices before costs are fully known. Although lacking the complete details of cost is not unusual in manufacturing, the life insurer or liability insurer might have to wait fifty or more years to learn them. If an insurer overestimates its costs when setting its premiums, the company makes money. If the insurer underestimates its costs, ultimately the company becomes insolvent. Consumers would be worse off if they purchased insurance from a company that underpriced its insurance and became insolvent than if they paid too much for protection. In neither case, however, would consumers' welfare be maximized. Unfortunately, consumers unaided by expert opinion are not good judges of the fairness or adequacy of an insurance company's rates.

Because free price competition cannot be relied on to promote consumers' welfare in the insurance market, solvency regulation substitutes for uncontrolled competition. The issue confronting regulators is how much pricing freedom to allow the industry. There are two main regulatory responses to this question: (1) **prior approval**, which requires insurers to get approval from the regulator before using a rate, and (2) **open rating**, which allows an insurer to use whatever rate it chooses after filing the rate and the supporting statistics with the regulator. Open rating, the more popular scheme in the United States, allows the regulator to reject any rates in use. Such regulatory disapproval means the insurer must stop using the rates. This approach allows more freedom for insurers to compete on prices, with some regulatory control retained. The current directives controlling insurer pricing in the European Union also follows the open rating model.

Prior approval

Open rating

Promotion of Social Goals

Some insurance regulation is designed to promote social objectives such as making insurance more widely available (affordable) or ending objectionable discrimination. For example, some people believe the public should have the right to purchase insurance at affordable rates. This belief has led many states to pass laws forcing insurers to accept applicants they would have rejected otherwise. Moreover, in some cases, regulation has forced insurers to use lower rates than they would have chosen otherwise.

Blanket rejection by insurers of certain exposures, such as inner-city property or drivers with bad driving records, means some people find private insurance unavailable or unaffordable. Presumably the social goal of making insurance widely available takes precedence over other goals, such as freedom of the insurer to contract with whom it prefers. The goal of making insurance widely available, however, may conflict with the goal of insurer solvency if an insurer is forced to accept too many poor risks at inadequate rates. Likewise, if regulation forces insurers to overlook valid underwriting criteria to promote social goals, such as making society more equitable, the resulting mandated subsidization conflicts with the goal of mathematical fairness to all insureds.

THE HISTORY OF INSURANCE REGULATION

Many insurance students are surprised to learn that individual states, not the federal government, regulate the insurance market. Insurance regulation is an exception to the rule that the federal government regulates industries whose business involves interstate commerce. This result occurred when Congress passed a law in 1945 giving the states the power to regulate the insurance market. The history of insurance regulation provides the background needed to understand the ongoing debate concerning the desirability of state insurance regulation.

Before 1850, Americans did not purchase insurance as frequently as today, and the insurance market was not regulated extensively. The states issued charters for incorporation and the federal government provided some regulation through postal laws.

Paul v. Virginia

In *Paul* v. *Virginia* (1869), the U.S. Supreme Court addressed the question of whether the state or federal government should regulate the insurance market. The question before the court was: "Is insurance a transaction in interstate commerce?" If the answer was "yes," the Constitution of the United States gave the federal government the power to provide regulation. If the answer was "no," the states would provide the regulation.

In this case, Mr. Paul, an agent of a New York insurer, was convicted of violating a Virginia law prohibiting solicitation of business without a state-issued license. Mr. Paul argued that he did not need a license from Virginia because his activities involved interstate commerce. The state, which stood to lose substantial tax revenue on insurance transactions, opposed this argument. It maintained Paul was a citizen of the state, conducting business in the state and therefore was subject to state regulation. The Supreme Court agreed with the state's interpretation. Thus, for about the next seventy-five years, the insurance transaction was not considered interstate commerce. It was a transaction to be regulated and taxed by the various states.

Armstrong and Merritt Investigations

How effective was the regulation provided by the states? Based on subsequent revelation, one must conclude the states were probably much better at taxation than they were at regulation. For example, in 1905 New York State made an extensive investigation, known as the **Armstrong Investigation**, into the life insurance industry. The revelations were scandalous. The investigation revealed abuses such as unethical business acquisition methods, unjustifiable home-office expenses, and unethical political influence. Five years later, New York investigated its fire insurers in the **Merritt Committee Investigation**. The results again revealed many unethical and undesirable occurrences.

These investigations resulted in a new insurance code for New York State.[1] The quality of the regulation provided by the states was not uniform, however. Some states were more effective than others were, and for the next fifty years, few states were as actively involved in insurance regulation as was New York State.

Armstrong Investigation

Merritt Committee Investigation

South-Eastern Underwriters Association (SEUA)

South-Eastern Underwriters Association (SEUA)

In 1944, in the **South-Eastern Underwriters Association (SEUA)** case, the Supreme Court reversed the decision it rendered in *Paul* v. *Virginia*. It concluded that insurance was indeed interstate commerce. In this 4-to-3 decision, the Court declared that the federal antitrust laws could be applied to insurance company operations.

---

[1] Readers can find New York's insurance code at this Web site: (*http://assembly.state.ny.us/leg/?cl=52/*).

The facts in this case were as follows. The SEUA had a near-monopoly on the property insurance business in the southeastern United States. To promote and extend its power, the association engaged in boycotts, rate-making conspiracies, tie-in contracts, and other abuses outlawed by federal antitrust legislation. Unfortunately for the consumer, the federal antitrust statutes apparently did not apply to these offenses because of the *Paul* v. *Virginia* decision. In reversing *Paul* v. *Virginia*, the Supreme Court concluded that the insurance transaction was in fact interstate commerce and therefore was subject to federal regulation including the antitrust laws.

The SEUA decision did not upset the regulatory picture for long. First, there was no existing federal insurance code, so the SEUA decision left the industry virtually unregulated. Second, both the industry and the state regulators expressed strong opposition to federal regulation. As a result, in 1945 Congress passed the McCarran-Ferguson **McCarran Act** Act, also known as the **McCarran Act**. The appendix to this chapter reproduces the entire act, which is brief.

The McCarran Act

The McCarran Act expressed the intent of Congress to allow the states to continue to regulate and tax the business of insurance. The law provides an exemption for the insurance industry applying to the activities that:

- Constitute the "business of insurance"
- Are regulated by state law
- Do not constitute an agreement or act "to boycott, coerce, or intimidate."

Sections 2 and 3 of the law declare, however, that if state law does not provide consumers with the type of protection found in the federal antitrust laws and the Federal Trade Commission Act, then federal laws will be applied.

Among the most important issues that courts have decided regarding the McCarran Act is that joint rate-making by property insurers is the "business of insurance" and therefore is exempt from federal antitrust laws.

One Supreme Court case involving the "business of insurance" question occurred in the late 1950s. In the Variable Annuity Life Insurance Co. of America (VALIC) case (*SEC* v. *Variable Annuity Life Insurance Co. of America*, 1959), the question arose whether the Securities and Exchange Commission (SEC) had the right and duty to regulate various aspects of a new insurance product, the variable annuity. Until an annuitant receives regular payments from the insurer, the variable annuity is similar to a **Investment** mutual fund. Under the **Investment Company Act of 1940**, the SEC was given the re-**Company Act** sponsibility for regulating mutual funds. Thus, the SEC thought it had the responsibility **of 1940** for regulating the variable annuity. The insurance companies selling variable annuities felt they were exempt from SEC regulation under the provisions of the McCarran Act.

In a 5-to-4 decision, the Supreme Court supported the SEC's position. It decided that the SEC should regulate variable annuity sales. The majority of the Court ruled that during the accumulation period, the variable annuity was not an insurance transaction to any significant extent. The real meaning of the decision was that if insurers engage in transactions that are not "the business of insurance," they lose the McCarran Act exemption from federal regulations.

Gramm-Leach-Bliley Act of 1999 (GLB)

Simply put, the main purposes of GLB were to modernize the U.S. financial services markets, to formalize the regulation of these markets, and to make the markets more competitive, thereby providing benefits to consumers. As discussed in Chapter 4, "Insurance Companies," GLB allows the combination of banks, insurance companies, and security dealers into financial service holding companies. Regulation of each component part of such a holding company follows the historic pattern. So the Federal Reserve and the Treasury Department continue to supervise banks, the SEC continues to supervise security dealers, and state insurance commissioners continue to supervise insurance companies.

The forces underlying the passage of GLB included the following:

- Consumer needs
- Banks wanting to expand the scope of the financial services they could offer
- International/global competition
- Technology

Consumer Needs

Before GLB, U.S. consumers of financial services faced a large number of complex transaction alternatives offered by various types of financial services firms. In many cases, these alternatives provided similar benefits but had different costs and different risk potential. In many cases, the consumer could neither calculate the costs nor correctly evaluate the risk. Presumably, one benefit of GLB is to make the market(s) for financial services more transparent to more consumers, allowing them to better pursue their own self-interest. Commentators believe that those larger firms enjoying *economies of scale* and *economies of scope* will be able to pass cost savings on to their customers. **Economies of scale** imply lower costs per unit produced as firms become larger. **Economies of scope** imply that it is more efficient for one firm to offer several different types of financial transactions than for separate firms each to offer only one type of financial service. For example, economies of scale arise if a large firm could afford more efficient computer and communications networks or could spread its marketing costs over a larger number of units sold. Economies of scope arise if one visit could result in a mortgage loan, homeowners insurance, and perhaps insurance on the homeowner's life. If nothing else, it would be more convenient for consumers to fill out one form to complete these transactions than to complete three forms and have three different financial service providers process these transactions.

Economies of scale

Economies of scope

Banks

Most large U.S. banks were among the strongest supporters of GLB. During the decade preceding GLB's passage, banks had gone through a period of rapid consolidation. Many banks became national in scope and hence became very profitable. Driven by the potential for economies of scale and scope offered by new computer and communications technology, many bank leaders became convinced that they could serve the market better as broad-based financial service providers.

International/Global Competition

European Union (EU) banks had been allowed to combine all financial service functions well before the passage of GLB in the United States. The potential for global competition provided an incentive for U.S. banks to want a level playing field with their international competitors. That is, U.S. banks believed that if they had to compete with other nations' banks for business, they wanted to be of comparable size and offer comparable services to their clients. In fact, EU banks have more flexibility than U.S. banks even with GLB, because EU banks can take equity positions in nonfinancial firms while U.S. banks currently cannot.

Technology

One of the major forces behind the passage of GLB was technology. Personal computers, faxes, e-mail, pagers, digital cameras, personal digital assistants (PDAs), mobile phones, scanners, and the Internet have changed the way many people solve problems and conduct business transactions. Moreover, change appears to feed on itself: each new development seems to come more quickly and be accepted more rapidly than the preceding one. For the financial services industry, this technology means that people who operate these tools may make better, smarter, and quicker decisions. Computer and communication technology will give people more information, including expert advice, and will facilitate communications between customers and service providers twenty-four hours a day, seven days a week. Because banks and other financial services providers believed that GLB offered them the potential for adapting all these technological possibilities to handle financial service transactions and better serve their clients, they promoted the new legislation.

Important Provisions of GLB

The following list presents a few of the major sections of GLB.[2]

- Title 1 allows the creation of financial service holding companies and repeals the Glass-Steagall Act.
- Title 2 contains regulations affecting the securities industry.
- Title 3 contains regulations affecting the insurance industry.
- Title 5 deals with privacy issues.

Financial services

Among the more important definitions in GLB is the definition of financial services. GLB defines **financial services** to include (1) lending, investing, or safeguarding money or securities; (2) underwriting or selling insurance or annuities; (3) giving financial advice; (4) underwriting, dealing in, or making a market in securities; and (5) engaging in other activities that previously had been permitted by the Federal Reserve Bank.

The following are examples of the GLB provisions that affect insurance transactions:

- Tying the purchase of insurance to other transactions—specifically loan acceptance or denial—is forbidden.
- Misrepresenting any aspects of insurance products is forbidden.
- Disclosures that insurance is not a bank deposit, not guaranteed, and not insured by the federal government are required.
- Commissions for insurance sales are limited to licensed agents.
- Referral fees paid to bank employees cannot be based on sales.
- Health information collected for insurance purposes cannot be released.
- Insurance records must be maintained separately from other financial records.

GLB requires the states to develop standards for uniformity in the licensing of insurance agents. As of this writing, full implementation of a uniform licensing requirement has not occurred at the state level, nor has a federal licensing law been implemented along the lines of GLB requirements. Various reasons for this have been suggested, including the lack of need for such a law and the ongoing issue of states' rights versus federal rights.

STATE OR FEDERAL REGULATION?

Because the McCarran Act is now more than sixty years old, readers might think it has become accepted by the insurance industry, state and federal regulators, and the public. However, the act remains controversial. As we shall see shortly, forces advocating

---

[2] This Web site reproduces the complete act and the legislative analysis: (*http://www.senate.gov/ ~banking/conf/*).

federal regulation and those opposing it continue to argue about the desirability of continued state regulation.

State Insurance Regulation

At present, each state has its own insurance laws and its own administrator responsible for regulating the insurance market within the boundaries of the respective laws. One result of regulation by the various states and U.S. territories is that companies operating on a national basis must comply with more than fifty potentially different sets of rules and regulations. Even when regulations are similar, insurers with national operations must get more than fifty different approvals for rates and policy forms.

Appleton rule

Within this framework of insurance regulation by the states, the extraterritorial rule of New York State must be given special consideration. In 1939, New York made the **Appleton rule** part of its insurance code. Put simply, the rule states that insurance companies doing any business in New York State must be in substantial compliance with all New York's rules in whatever state they do business. (See: Article 11, Section 1106.) Because most of the largest life and non–life insurers transact business in New York, the New York insurance code has an impact well beyond the state borders. Thus, consumers who are not New York residents get the benefit of New York legislation if they deal with an insurer that does business in New York.

The National Association of Insurance Commissioners (NAIC)

The National Association of Insurance Commissioners (NAIC; *http://www.naic.org/*) is a private, nonprofit association of state insurance commissioners that furnishes some uniformity to state insurance regulation. The organization meets formally twice a year to consider matters of common concern. Between scheduled meetings, its subcommittees consider special problems. A key function of the NAIC is to develop model bills for the various states to introduce in their own legislatures. Because many states often adopt such model legislation, some uniformity exists in the insurance codes of the different states. Readers can visit the NAIC Web site cited above for current information about its activities and publications.

Repeal of the McCarran Act: Both Sides of the Argument

Since the McCarran Act was passed in 1945, many critics have called for its modification or repeal.

The following arguments support continuing state insurance regulation:

- State regulation is a known quantity. In most jurisdictions, it has worked reasonably well. Moreover, in recent years, the states have engaged in a substantial effort to rebuild their regulatory ability. Solvency regulations have been strengthened, financial reporting requirements have been increased, and new computer-based monitoring programs have been installed.
- If federal insurance law were in place, state regulation still would be needed to cover intrastate insurers.
- State insurance regulation allows for experimentation. If regulatory mistakes are made, they will not have national impact. If new regulations prove successful, on the other hand, other states can copy them. For example, both Wisconsin and New York implemented risk-based capital early warning systems before the NAIC suggested them.
- State insurance regulation is closer to the public and its problems and can respond to local conditions. For example, the automobile insurance problems confronting California may not be comparable to the problems faced in Iowa, and different

regulatory approaches may be appropriate. Removing regulation to Washington would only result in Washington establishing regional or state administrative offices. Thus, little would be gained from such a move.

- The NAIC began an accreditation program in the early 1990s that gives recognition to those state insurance departments meeting specified standards. Presumably, the new standards result in the various states providing more financial resources to their insurance departments and in more uniformity in regulatory ability among the states.

The following arguments favor changing to federal insurance regulation:

- There likely will be substantial improvements in the efficiency and uniformity of regulation. Instead of having to comply with the rules of more than fifty different jurisdictions to operate nationally, an insurance company would have to comply with the rules of only one jurisdiction.

- Insurance companies exercise more influence over state regulators and legislators than they could at the national level. One fact is clear in this regard: although an insurer presently may withdraw from a state whose regulation it finds displeasing, it could not withdraw from federal jurisdiction without going out of business.

- Despite the new NAIC accreditation program, some states still do not have sufficient numbers of expertly trained personnel. Some commentators believe that not all the states have adequate budgets to regulate the insurance market as thoroughly as this important market warrants. A federal regulatory agency is more likely to be adequately staffed with experts, and better funded as well, than are the regulatory departments of some states.

- The federal government is better able to fund for insurance company insolvencies. Using a pattern similar to the Federal Deposit Insurance Corporation (which protects bank depositors), the Security Protection Insurance Corporation (which protects investors), and the Pension Benefit Guarantee Corporation (which protects workers with pension plans), the federal government could provide a national financial cushion backed by the taxing power of the federal government to protect victims of insurance company insolvencies. Critics note that some of these federal programs have flirted with insolvency. However, the savings and loan bailout showed the federal government can print enough money to cover the losses resulting from catastrophic problems.

- The current system creates a substantial barrier to foreign insurance companies that want to enter the U.S. market, thereby creating an international trade issue.

The Optional Federal Charter (OFC)[3]

Optional Federal Charter (OFC)

The most commonly advocated solution for dealing with the uniformity and efficiency problems of state insurance regulation involves the creation by Congress of an **Optional Federal Charter (OFC)**. Under typical OFC proposals, none of which have been enacted into law as this chapter is being written, insurers would have the option of either continuing to be regulated under the state-based system or choosing to be regulated by the federal government. Insurers choosing to be federally chartered would be subject to regulation by a federal insurance office in the Treasury department. In exchange for being allowed to operate in a competitive environment free of

---

[3] Readers interested in this topic will find an extended discussion in this article: Robert Cooper and Mark Dorfman, "Modernizing U. S. Insurance Regulation: What Can Be Learned from the European Union," *Journal of Insurance Regulation*, Summer 2004, Vol. 22. No. 4, pp. 3–34.

rate regulation and prior approval of policy forms, federally chartered entities would be subject to regular Sherman Act restrictions. Current OFC proposals rely primarily on the continued operation of the state guaranty funds, require companies choosing the federal option to shoulder the costs of the federal charter, and provide for federally chartered insurers to be subject to all taxes imposed under the authority of state law.

Opposition to the OFC is summarized in the testimony of Alessandro Iuppa, Maine Superintendent of Insurance and President of the NAIC.[4] Superintendent Iuppa made the following three points in his testimony before the Committee on Banking, Housing, and Urban Affairs of the U.S. Senate on July 11, 2006:

- First, state insurance officials strongly believe that a coordinated, national system of state-based insurance supervision has met and will continue to meet the needs of the modern financial marketplace while effectively protecting individual and commercial policyholders. State insurance supervision is dynamic, and state officials work continuously to retool and upgrade supervision to keep pace with the evolving business of insurance that we oversee. The perfect example of our success is the Interstate Compact for life insurance and other asset-preservation insurance products. Twenty-seven states have joined the Compact in twenty-seven months—with more on the way—and we plan for this state-based national system with its single point of entry and national review standards to become fully operational in early 2007.

- Second, insurance is a unique and complex product that is fundamentally different from other financial services, such as banking and securities. Consequently, the state-based system has evolved over the years to address these fundamental differences.

- Third, despite states' long history of success protecting consumers and modernizing insurance supervision, some propose to radically restructure the current system by installing a new federal insurance regulator, developing a new federal bureaucracy from scratch, and allowing insurance companies to "opt out" of comprehensive state oversight and policyholder protection. Risk and insurance touch the lives of every citizen and the fortunes of every business, and the nation's insurance officials welcome congressional interest in these issues. However, a bifurcated regulatory regime with redundant and overlapping responsibilities will result in policyholder confusion, market uncertainty, and other unintended consequences that will harm individuals, families and businesses that rely on insurance for financial protection against the risks of everyday life. For these reasons, the Senate Banking Committee and Congress should reject the notion of a federal insurance regime.

REGULATED ACTIVITIES

We defined *regulation* earlier in this chapter as "the rules of the insurance market." We now describe some of the more important insurer activities to which the rules apply. Because more than fifty different sets of rules exist, the description is general. If readers need specific information about a particular state's laws, they must refer to the insurance code of that state. Many states now post their important insurance information, including some regulatory policies, on their Web sites. For example, if "North Carolina Insurance Department" is typed into a search engine, the reader will arrive at

---

[4] (*http://www.naic.org/Releases/2006_docs/iuppa_senate_banking_testimony.pdf/*). Readers interested in the NAIC state insurance compact should consult this Web site: (*http://www.insurancecompact.org/*).

(*http://www.ncdoi.com/*). Other useful Web sites for legal information and searches are (*http://www.nolo.com/* and *http://www.law.cornell.edu/*).

Please recall that the main purposes of regulation are to maintain the solvency of the insurer, to equalize the imbalance of knowledge and bargaining power between the insurer and insured, to deal with a unique pricing problem that does not allow for free competition, and to promote specific social goals. In general, these regulatory aims can be placed into two categories: (1) to promote insurer solvency and (2) to maintain order in the insurance market. The following regulatory rules should be considered in light of these objectives.

Legal Reserves and Surplus

From the instant of its formation and all through its existence, an insurer must comply with the reserve and surplus requirements of the state in which it is domiciled. Reserve and surplus accounts are a cushion, beyond current operating income, available to meet an insurer's financial obligations. If an insurer fails to maintain the minimum amount of specified capital, it is placed under the commissioner's supervision until it can be determined whether rehabilitation or liquidation best serves the public interest. If an insurer's capital and surplus fall below the minimum standard, it is considered **impaired**. If an insurer's liabilities exceed the value of its assets, it is **insolvent**.

Impaired

Insolvent

Surplus

An insurer needs **surplus**—an excess of assets over liabilities—as a cushion against bad underwriting results (more losses than predicted) and poor investment results (lower earnings than projected). It is probable every insurer will experience less-than-desirable underwriting or investment results at some time, and an adequate surplus allows an insurer to ride through such a period without injury to its insureds.

The law requires an insurer to maintain minimum reserves on the liability side of its balance sheet. The insurer must maintain offsetting assets on the other side of the statement. Therefore, the purpose of reserve requirements is to force the insurer to maintain a certain minimum amount of assets. The investment requirements determine the quality of these assets. Working together, the reserve and the investment requirements are important tools in promoting insurer solvency.

Before an insurer is granted a license to operate in a state, it must establish that it has satisfied the state's minimum capital and surplus requirements. These requirements vary from state to state. The fact that many insurance companies have begun operations in recent decades proves these requirements are not significant barriers to entering the industry.

Admitted Assets

Admitted assets

Nonadmitted assets

State regulation requires insurers to categorize their assets as *admitted assets* or *nonadmitted assets*. This accounting procedure is different from Generally Accepted Accounting Principles (GAAP) and represents an attempt to evaluate insurers' assets in the most conservative manner. **Admitted assets** are assets that are readily available to pay claims, such as negotiable securities and real estate holdings. State law allows only admitted assets to offset an insurer's liabilities. **Nonadmitted assets** are not available to meet the company's liability to its insureds. Examples of nonadmitted assets include such things as office furniture, supplies, and equipment. (Some states allow home-office buildings to be calculated as part of the insurer's admitted assets.)

Property Insurance Reserve Accounts

Unearned premium reserve

Property insurers need an **unearned premium reserve** because insureds pay for their insurance in advance, typically one year at a time. For example, when homeowners pay annual premiums, during the first month the insurer earns one-twelfth of the premium and must show eleven-twelfths of the premium in its reserve account. The unearned fraction represents eleven of the twelve months of the year that have not passed and for which the premium was paid. Theoretically, if all insureds terminate their contracts at any point, the amount in the unearned premium reserve will be sufficient to return the unearned premium amounts.

Loss reserve

The **loss reserve** is set up to account for unpaid losses. The loss reserve is especially important for insurers writing liability insurance, but it also applies to other lines of insurance. The claims covered by this reserve account may be losses that have been reported, but the claim has not yet been paid or losses not yet reported to the insurer. For both unreported and reported-but-unsettled losses, the insurer makes actuarial estimates of expected loss payments. Actuaries call the estimate of unreported losses the **incurred but not reported (IBNR) reserve**. Unreported losses represent unpaid liabilities. In addition to unreported losses, unpaid claims may be the result of an unsettled lawsuit or a claim on which the insurer and insured cannot agree.

Incurred but not reported (IBNR) reserve

By observing years of data, actuaries can estimate what percentage of the losses from a given year have been settled and what percentage remain to be settled. For example, perhaps after one year, 80 percent of a given year's automobile physical damage claims have been settled, leaving 20 percent of the claims unsettled and requiring a reserve. After two years, perhaps the percentages are 90 and 10 percent, respectively. By the third year, all the automobile physical damage claims are settled. In comparison, after one year, perhaps only 60 percent of automobile liability claims are settled, with a reserve needed for the 40 percent remaining to be settled. Perhaps after three years, because of litigation or other problems, 20 percent of the automobile liability claims remain outstanding and still require an estimate of their outcome to be held in a reserve.

In liability insurance, many years may pass between the time an insurer is notified an insured is suing them and the time the case is closed. In some lines of liability insurance, twenty or more years may elapse between the time an incident occurs and the time a lawsuit is brought. Another ten or more years might pass before such a claim results in a payment from the insurer to an injured victim. Because the losses they represent can be unresolved for such long periods and may involve large amounts of money, loss reserves are essential to present fairly the accounting statements of liability insurers.

Life Insurers Reserve Accounts

Policy reserve

Life insurers maintain a **policy reserve** that represents the difference between the mathematical liability of a future death claim and the value of future premiums the insured will pay the insurer. The policy reserve is best illustrated by reference to a level-premium whole life policy. With this contract, the insurer is obligated to pay a death claim whenever death occurs and the insured is scheduled to pay regular level premiums for life. Each year, the present value of the death claim increases as the insured ages and the probability of death increases. At the same time, the present value of future premiums decreases as more of the premiums are collected. As the value of the death benefit increases while the present value of future premiums decreases, the policy reserve must increase to keep the equation in balance. This relationship is illustrated in Figure 7–1. Because the insurer must keep investment assets to offset the policy reserve liability, the insureds have financial protection in the event of an insurer's financial weakness.

FIGURE 7–1 Life Insurance Reserves

| Legal Reserve | = | Present Value of Future Death Claims | − | Present Value of Future Net Premiums |

While our level-premium whole life example focused on one policy, in practice, life insurers do not calculate their policy reserves on an individual policy basis. Instead, they consider blocks of similar policies and calculate the reserve for the whole block of business. Likewise, while the example dealt with one policy type, insurers must keep policy reserves for all types of policies sold. The relationship between the time and probability of the death benefit and the value of future premiums (if any) determines the amount of policy reserve for each policy type.

Asset valuation reserve (AVR)

Interest maintenance reserve (IMR)

Since 1992, the NAIC has required life insurers to keep two different reserve accounts to protect insureds from financial weakness caused by poor investment results. The **asset valuation reserve (AVR)** is supposed to act as a buffer that allows insurers to absorb losses arising from sales of assets for less than their cost (capital losses). These losses arise from what financiers call "business risk." The **interest maintenance reserve (IMR)** is designed to allow insurers to absorb losses caused by changes (increases) in interest rates on government securities.

The AVR requires the insurer to consider the riskiness of its holdings of the following asset categories: corporate and municipal bonds, common and preferred stocks, mortgages, real estate, and joint ventures. This reserve does not apply to cash, U.S. government securities, or policyholder loans. The company, based on maximum guidelines developed by the NAIC, must keep a percentage of each category of assets in the AVR. For example, the maximum guideline for the safest bonds is 1 percent of face value, while the formula for the lowest safety category calls for 20 percent of value. For mortgages, the percentage required in the AVR varies from 3.5 percent to 10.5 percent depending on the delinquency rate of the mortgage class. In all cases, the amount an insurer has in its AVR is a function of both the NAIC maximum guidelines and its own investment results.

If an insurer's investment results are poor in a particular year, the AVR will increase, but if previous years' results were good, the balance in the AVR may be sufficient to absorb actual realized losses. In fact, one purpose of the AVR is to act as a buffer, so investment declines in a particular year can be dampened. For example, assume that a company began the year with a $10 million balance in the AVR. During the year, the insurer had $1 million in realized capital losses and another $1 million in unrealized losses. The AVR formula might call for a transfer to the reserve of only $800,000 this year, with the balance of the losses to be amortized in future years. Thus, despite $2 million in losses this year, only $800,000 will be charged to operating results.

The IMR applies only to U.S. government securities and guaranteed securities of agencies backed by the credit of the U.S. government. The IMR accumulates interest-related realized gains and losses and amortizes them into an insurer's income over the remaining life of the investments sold. Like the AVR, the IMR acts as a buffer, dampening the effect of a single year's gains or losses on an insurer's operating income.

Investment reserve requirements or any other type of reserve requirement cannot provide an absolute guarantee of insurer solvency, as history has shown. Reserve requirements, however, should allow an insurer to be rehabilitated or liquidated with much less injury to its insureds than otherwise would be the case.

Regular Audits and Solvency Testing

Every insurance company is required to file an annual statement with the insurance department in each state in which it transacts business, as well as with the NAIC. The various state insurance departments verify these reports by an audit about once every three years. The audit is conducted by the state insurance department of the state in which the insurer is domiciled, joined by representatives of insurance departments of other states. The NAIC audit procedure divides the country into six zones, with one representative from each zone participating in each audit.

In addition to on-site inspection and audit, the NAIC Insurance Regulatory Information System (IRIS) monitors insurer solvency annually. IRIS is a computer-based testing system designed to spot solvency problems before they result in losses to insureds. Using IRIS, the NAIC calculates twelve ratios based on data submitted by each insurer to be audited. Companies not submitting to this audit are reported to the licensing states.[5]

The main outcome of IRIS occurs when the computer analysis flags any ratios outside a normal range of expected results. Companies with the highest number of abnormal results receive the highest priority for examination by state examiners. After the first-phase computer analysis of IRIS results, a second-phase analysis of companies with four or more ratios outside the normal range occurs. Logical explanations for abnormal ratios may exist, such as solid but rapid growth, a merger of two companies, or unusual investment results. Alternatively, firms with many abnormal ratios also may be in weak financial condition, but if caught promptly, insurance departments may be able to take action protecting policyowners' interests.

Regulators also use other sources of information when evaluating insurers, including SEC filings, financial ratings companies' reports, complaint ratios, news articles, and letters from competitors and agents.

Risk-Based Capital (RBC)[6]

Risk-based capital (RBC)

In 1992, after the well-publicized failure of three large life insurance companies and the financial weakening of others, the NAIC developed a new **risk-based capital (RBC)** requirement for life insurance companies. The difference between the fixed minimum amount of capital standard and the RBC standard is that the RBC standard takes into account differences in an insurer's underwriting and investment practices in developing a capital and surplus requirement for that specific company. For example, consider two insurers similar in size. One company operates very conservatively, whereas the other operates very aggressively. Under the previous rules, both insurers might have the same minimum capital requirement. Under the RBC rules, the aggressive insurer might have to maintain 150 percent more capital and surplus than the conservative insurer. RBC is the estimated amount of capital needed to cushion the risks of operating an insurance company based on the risks inherent in a particular insurer's operations.

Guaranty Funds[7]

All states have solvency laws and guaranty funds to protect insureds from losses caused by insolvent insurers. State regulators are likely to intervene in an insurer's independent operations when the company's surplus accounts reach an unacceptably low level or if the company's conduct appears to be jeopardizing the policyowner's interests. Regulators call the first phase of intervention conservatorship, rehabilitation, or receivership. If this phase fails to correct the problems, regulators can order the next level of intervention, which is liquidation. In the case of small insurers, the state might try to rehabilitate the company, find a solvent insurer to assume the business, or liquidate the company using the guaranty fund. The failure of both large and small insurers can require policyowners to give up some contractual rights, including access to their

---

[5] Readers can find more information about the IRIS system at this Web site: (*http://www.naic.org/*). Use "IRIS ratios" as keywords in a search at this site.

[6] Readers can find more information about risk-based capital requirements at this Web site: (*http://www. naic.org/*).

[7] Readers can find more information about guaranty funds at this Web site: (*http://www.naic.org/*).

funds for stated periods. In some cases involving life insurance companies, policyowners received lower investment returns than called for in contracts issued by failed insurers.

The various state funds have different limits on the amount of benefits available to injured insureds. Differences also appear in eligibility for compensation. The policyowner's residency at the time the policy was purchased or the insolvency declared may result in different treatment in different states. Some states treat individual policyowners differently from large corporate policyowners. The 1989 NAIC Guaranty Fund Model Act provides some national uniformity among the various state regulations.

The money to finance a state's guaranty fund comes from assessments on all insurers doing business in that state. Thus, there is a transfer of funds from solvent insurers to support the insureds of insolvent insurers. The fairness and logic of such a transfer are subject to criticism because the most likely transfer is from insureds purchasing coverage from insurers charging adequate (higher) premiums to insureds of companies charging inadequate (lower) premiums. Critics note that insureds who already paid a higher price for their insurance now must pay even more to support insureds who voluntarily chose to purchase insurance at a lower price.

Rate Regulations

As mentioned previously, open and unrestrained price competition generally does not work in the insurance market because prices must be set long before the final costs are known. Inadequate prices, which may not be determined until years after they have been used, may result in insurer insolvency. Unnecessarily high prices result in a clear loss of consumer welfare. Thus, rate regulation has been substituted for unrestrained price competition in the insurance market.

Fair

Adequate

Not unfairly discriminatory

The overall regulatory objective is to produce insurance rates that are *fair, adequate, and not unfairly discriminatory*. These words all have latitudes of meaning. That is, they may mean different things to different regulators. In general, **fair** means rates that are not too high compared with the underlying risk. **Adequate** means rates that are not too low, based on actuarial statistics. **Not unfairly discriminatory** means similar exposures are charged similar prices and dissimilar exposures are not charged the same price.

Rate regulation, however it is approached in a given state, is at the heart of the effort to promote insurer solvency. Rate regulation also protects the consumer from the disadvantage of unequal knowledge relative to the insurer. Many parties believe the inequality of knowledge is not as great in commercial insurance as it is in personal insurance. Therefore, these parties argue, rate and perhaps other regulations designed for the personal market are not required in areas where buyer and seller are on more equal terms. Thus, more flexibility is given insurers in setting commercial property insurance and reinsurance rates than in setting personal insurance rates.

Antitrust Concerns and Rate-Making

Rating bureau

A particular concern about federal regulation if the McCarran Act were repealed would be the applicability of the federal antitrust statutes to insurance company rate-making. In many different lines of insurance, such as automobile liability and fire insurance, companies pool their data using an intermediary called a **rating bureau**. Rating bureaus develop advisory rates for use by its members or provide raw data to its members. This practice clearly involves collusion leading up to setting a price and thus would be illegal under federal antitrust law. If federal regulations, including the antitrust laws, were imposed, it would have the effect of causing every company to duplicate the rate-making and data collection efforts of the others. Federal regulation also would give large companies, with their larger databases, a competitive advantage over smaller companies. Thus, federal regulation, without an antitrust exemption, potentially could rearrange the competitive structure of the industry. As the matter now stands, the largest property insurance rating bureau, the Insurance Services Office, supplies its members and regulatory agencies with loss data but not actual rates. Each company is free to use this loss data combined with its own expense structure to develop its rates.

Investment Activities

Insurance companies are not free to invest funds in all available alternatives. Because inferior investments may jeopardize insurer solvency, states have limited the types of investments insurers may make. State regulation specifies the classes of acceptable and unacceptable investments and the method used to value assets.

Because life insurance companies hold vast amounts of the public's savings and because life insurance contracts may extend over long periods of time—neither of which generally occurs in non–life insurance—life insurers generally are not allowed to make risky investments. Typical restrictions on life insurers include a limitation on the total amount of common stock a company may own. In New York, for example, the limit is about 10 percent of the insurer's admitted assets. Property insurers are less severely restricted from purchasing common stock and have done so to a considerable extent. Life insurers offering newer products based on the performance of a portfolio of equity investments may do so within the framework of special rules for these products.

Policy Form Approval and Expense Limitations

State regulation requires insurers to get a policy form approved before selling it to the public. Many states have regulations that apply to policy forms used to sell life, health, property, and other personal insurance coverages. For example, states require cash-value life insurance policy forms to have certain minimum guarantees, require property insurance forms to contain specified provisions, and require health insurance to provide minimum cancellation rights. Many states have laws specifying the minimum type size that can be used in insurance policies, and some states have laws requiring explicit labeling for clauses restricting insurance coverage. The purpose of policy form approval is to keep unfair and gimmicky policy forms out of the market. It is regulation designed to deal with the unequal knowledge and bargaining power of insured and insurer.

Qualifications or Licenses for Companies, Agents, Brokers, Loss Adjusters, and Company Officers

Each state applies its own regulations before granting people a license to begin operating an insurance company. The most important of these regulations specify a required minimum amount of capital and surplus to form a new insurer. Additional rules often require a minimum number of potential policyholders and qualified members of the board of directors. It is beyond the scope of this introductory text to describe the steps needed to form and begin to operate an insurance company in a particular state, but this information is available at the insurance department of each state. Many states now have their requirements on their Web sites. Before an insurance company domiciled in one state can transact business in another state, it must secure a license to operate from the state in which it wants to do business. This requirement allows a state to regulate and control *foreign* insurers to protect its citizens.

Admitted and Nonadmitted Insurers

The term *foreign* was italicized in the preceding sentence to alert readers to a rather peculiar use of this word. Foreign insurance does not refer to insurance provided from outside the United States; that is called *alien* insurance. The following short glossary should help keep matters straight:

- **Admitted insurance:** Insurance obtained from insurers licensed by the state in which the insurance is purchased. This term covers both foreign and domestic insurance.
- **Alien insurance:** Insurance provided by a non-U.S. insurer.
- **Domestic insurance:** Insurance provided by a licensed insurer within the state providing the license.
- **Foreign insurance:** Insurance provided by an insurer licensed by a state other than the one in which the insurance applies.
- **Nonadmitted insurance:** Insurance obtained from insurers who are not licensed in the jurisdiction where the policy is purchased or the exposure is located.
- **Surplus-lines insurance:** Insurance purchased through a specially licensed broker from a nonadmitted insurer.

In some instances, a citizen may require insurance of a type or in an amount not available from insurers doing business in the state. Only when insurance is unavailable domestically (within the insured's state) may it be placed with a nonadmitted insurer. States control such business by requiring domestic agents to secure a surplus-lines license before placing business with nonadmitted insurers. Surplus-lines agents or brokers generally may not place business with a nonadmitted insurer unless they can establish domestic insurance is unavailable. By controlling insurance agents, the state can monitor the amount of insurance placed with nonadmitted insurers. The justification for surplus-lines regulation is that the state can exercise no control over nonadmitted insurers but can control legally the excess and surplus-lines agent.

Some large insurance brokers and their large clients argue that surplus-lines regulations add an unnecessary level of regulation and expense to consumers. They argue that the only potential insureds who use the nonadmitted market are large industrial companies that have risk management and legal staffs to protect them from undesirable insurers.

Countersignature Laws

Countersignature laws

A more obvious attempt to promote domestic insurance transactions comes from **countersignature laws**. These laws require all non–life insurance contracts to be signed by a domestic agent, even if the agent did not solicit the business. A domestic agent receives a commission for merely signing his or her name to the policy. Countersignature laws have been criticized because they add to the insured's cost but do not provide corresponding benefits.

Agents and Brokers Licenses

All states require insurance agents and brokers to secure a license before transacting business. One of the mandates of the GLB caused the states to standardize their approach to licensing agents so that agents can operate across state lines.

Some states also require licenses for loss adjusters. All have rules governing who may be an insurance company officer. Many states require an applicant for a license to pass an examination that evaluates his or her knowledge of the insurance business. Many states now require agents to earn continuing education credits to maintain their licenses. Rules promoting more knowledgeable agents and brokers benefit consumers but may prove to be a hardship on companies relying on untrained or part-time agents.

Twisting

State insurance codes establish rules outlining unacceptable conduct by an agent or broker. Misrepresentation, including any incomplete comparisons causing an insured to exchange one insurance policy for another (a practice called **twisting**), is forbidden.

Anti-rebating laws prevent agents from sharing their commissions with an insured. Critics claim that rather than directly protecting the consumer, anti-rebating laws protect insurance agents from having to share their income with the customer. Those in favor of changing the law argue that change will benefit consumers by lowering prices. Those opposed to the change argue that only consumers who are successful bargainers will benefit, causing others to bear the burden of the higher prices. Those opposed to a change also question whether insurance agents would be able to earn adequate incomes.

Consumer Complaints

The insurance commissioner's office generally has a staff available to deal with consumer complaints against insurers or agents. Today, many state insurance departments maintain Web sites that often allow consumers to check on agents and insurance companies and provide a path for lodging complaints. These sites also may contain other useful consumer information about policy forms and special advice for older consumers. This NAIC Web site provides a link to the various state Web sites: (*http://www.naic.org/*).

Many complaints are the result of consumer misunderstanding, and it is the regulator's job to treat both insurer and insured fairly. Typically, the regulator forwards a complaint to the insurer and asks for a response within a limited period of time. If an insurer's response is not satisfactory, the regulator can direct a course of action. The insurer is most likely to comply with the regulator's directive, however, because its license to operate is jeopardized by noncompliance.

Taxation

Taxation is a form of regulation that both the states and the federal government have adopted. Taxation of insurance companies is not without problems, however. Some problems arise because the industry is composed of for-profit (stock) and nonprofit (mutual) competitors. This situation has led to complex income tax formulas, especially at the federal level. A much simpler tax is the state premium tax, which is typically a flat percentage, such as 2 percent, of the premium a consumer pays. The amount of the tax varies from state to state and is often different among the various lines of insurance within a given state. The premium tax, like a tax on salt, is a tax on a necessity; thus, it is a valuable source of income in most states.

The tax on the insurance transaction was justified originally as a source of revenue to supply the funds the states needed to provide regulation. Today, though, the states collect much more money in tax revenue than they spend on insurance regulation. The consumer's interest probably would be better served if the taxes were lower or the money spent on regulation increased. The consumer, however, does not see the premium tax directly because the insurer builds it into the insurance rates.

SUMMARY

Insurance regulation determines how and by whom insurance transactions may be made. Regulation is established by law, administered by public officials, and interpreted by courts when disputes arise.

The purposes of insurance regulation are to promote insurer solvency, balance the inequality of knowledge between the insurance companies and consumers, deal with a unique pricing problem requiring some limits on free and unrestrained competition, and promote certain social goals.

In 1869, the states were given the authority to provide insurance regulation by the *Paul v. Virginia* decision of the Supreme Court. In 1944, the Supreme Court reversed itself in the *South-Eastern Underwriters Association (SEUA)* case, holding that insurance transactions were subject to federal regulation, including the antitrust laws. In 1945, Congress passed the McCarran Act, which allowed the states to continue to provide insurance regulation, because it found state insurance regulation to be in the public interest.

The question of continued state insurance regulation versus federal insurance regulation is of current concern. Good arguments exist to support both sides of the question. Continued strengthening and improving of state regulation would be the best argument for continuing the current regulatory situation. Although the various states have their own rules, all the states regulate the same activities. Among the areas and activities regulated are the following:

- Legal reserves and surplus requirements
- Investment decisions
- Rates
- Policy form approval and expense limitation
- Licensing of companies, agents, and brokers
- Taxation

All insurance regulation can be judged in the context of how well it promotes and protects the consumer's interest.

REVIEW TERMS

- Admitted assets
- Admitted insurance
- Alien insurance
- Anti-rebating laws
- Appleton rule
- Armstrong Investigation
- Asset valuation reserve (AVR)
- Countersignature laws
- Domestic insurance
- Economies of scale
- Economies of scope
- Financial services
- Foreign insurance
- Gramm-Leach-Bliley Act (GLB)

- Impaired
- Insolvent
- Insurance regulation
- Insurance Regulatory Information System (IRIS)
- Interest maintenance reserve (IMR)
- Loss reserve
- McCarran Act
- McCarran-Ferguson Act (Public Law-15)
- Merritt Committee Investigation
- Nonadmitted assets
- Nonadmitted insurance

- Open rating
- Optional Federal Charter (OFC)
- Policy reserve
- Prior approval
- Rating bureau
- Risk-based capital (RBC)
- Solvency
- South-Eastern Underwriters Association (SEUA) case
- Surplus-lines insurance
- Twisting
- Unearned premium reserve

REVIEW

1. What does the term *insurance regulation* mean?
2. Why is the solvency of insurers so important to regulators? How do the regulators try to establish and maintain insurers' solvency?
3. What is meant by unequal knowledge and bargaining powers? Why do regulators have to protect the purchasers of homeowners insurance more than the purchasers of large commercial insurance policies?

4. How does the pricing of an insurance policy for the insurer differ from a bologna manufacturer's pricing its product? Why does the difference in pricing problems require that insurance pricing be subject to regulation?
5. Why might the lowest-priced insurance policy be undesirable from the consumer's standpoint?

6. Describe the two approaches to rate regulation in insurance.
7. What was the outcome of the *Paul* v. *Virginia* case?
8. What effect did the McCarran Act have on insurance regulation? Why was it passed?
9. List the arguments favoring continued state regulation of insurance. What arguments favor federal insurance regulation?
10. What is the role of the NAIC? What are its main functions?
11. What are insurance company reserve requirements? How do they work to protect the consumer?
12. Explain the nature of the risk-based capital ratio.
13. Describe the main methods for regulating the investment activities of insurers.

OBJECTIVE QUESTIONS

1. All the following are reasons to explain why the insurance transaction is so carefully regulated except:
   a. Insolvent insurers can create serious social-economic problems.
   b. Insurance buyers and sellers have unequal knowledge.
   c. Insurance prices must be set before costs are known.
   d. Insurance company failures were a significant contributing factor to the Great Depression of the 1930s.
2. The first insurance case dealing with the question of state versus federal insurance regulations to reach the Supreme Court was:
   a. The South-Eastern Underwriters Association (SEUA) case
   b. The Gramm-Leach-Bliley Act (GLB)
   c. *Paul* v. *Virginia*
   d. *Merritt* v. *New York*
3. The two main regulatory approaches to supervising insurers' prices are called:
   a. Controlled and uncontrolled competition
   b. Free competition and restrained competition
   c. Prior approval and open rating
   d. Level loss and expected loss competition
4. All the following arguments have been used to support state insurance regulation except:
   a. State regulation is known to be effective.
   b. State regulation is cheaper to administer.
   c. State regulation allows experimentation.
   d. State regulation is more responsive to local conditions.
5. The federal law that allows the combination of banks and insurance companies is:
   a. The Federal Insurance Act of 1984
   b. The Gramm-Leach-Bliley Act (GLB)
   c. The McCarran-Ferguson Act
   d. The Federal Banking-Insurance Act of 1984
6. If an insurer's liabilities exceed the value of its assets, it is:
   a. Delisted
   b. Demutualized
   c. Impaired
   d. Insolvent
7. Assets that are readily available to pay claims are called:
   a. Admitted assets
   b. Real assets
   c. Accepted assets
   d. Standard operating assets
8. "Insurance provided by a licensed insurer within the state providing the license" is the definition of:
   a. Foreign insurance
   b. State insurance
   c. Local insurance
   d. Domestic insurance

DISCUSSION QUESTIONS

1. Which level of government do you think should regulate the insurance industry, the various states, or the federal government? Explain your reasoning.
2. What arguments would you make for allowing insurers to set their own rates and be regulated by market or competitive forces? What arguments would you make for continuing regulatory approval of insurance rates?
3. What arrangements do you think would best protect the interests of both insureds and insurers with respect to handling consumers' complaints?

1. Describe the two most recent new releases on the NAIC Web site: (*http://www.naic.org/*).
2. Find the link to your state's department of insurance from this Web site: (*http://www.naic.org/*). Who is your state's insurance commissioner?
3. After finding your state's department of insurance Web site (see #2 above), explore the information provided for insurance consumers. Briefly list and describe some of the information provided for consumers to help them purchase insurance. Briefly describe the information provided for consumers who believe they have had an unsatisfactory claims experience.

Appendix: The McCarran-Ferguson Act (P.L.–15)

To express the intent of the Congress with reference to the regulation of the business of insurance:

Be it enacted by the Senate and House of Representatives of the United States of America in Congress assembled, that the Congress hereby declares that the continued regulation and taxation by the several States of the business of insurance is in the public interest, and that silence on the part of the Congress shall not be construed to impose any barrier to the regulation or taxation of such business by the several States.

Sec. 2. (a) The business of insurance, and every person engaged therein, shall be subject to the laws of the several States which relate to the regulation or taxation of such business.

(b) No Act of Congress shall be construed to invalidate, impair, or supersede any law enacted by any State for the purpose of regulating the business of insurance, or which imposes a fee or tax upon such business, unless such Act specifically relates to the business of insurance: Provided, that after January 1, 1948, the Act of July 2, 1890, as amended, known as the Sherman Act, and the Act of October 15, 1914, as amended, known as the Clayton Act, and the Act of September 26, 1914, known as the Federal Trade Commission Act, as amended, shall be applicable to the business of insurance to the extent that such business is not regulated by State law.

Sec. 3. (a) Until January 1, 1948, the Act of July 2, 1890, as amended, known as the Sherman Act, and the Act of October 15, 1914, as amended, known as the Clayton Act, and the Act of September 26, 1914, known as the Federal Trade Commission Act, as amended, and the Act of June 19, 1936, known as the Robinson-Patman Anti-Discrimination Act, shall not apply to the business of insurance or to acts in the conduct thereof.

(b) Nothing contained in this Act shall render the said Sherman Act inapplicable to any agreement to boycott, coerce, or intimidate, or act of boycott, coercion, or intimidation.

Sec. 4. Nothing contained in this Act shall be construed to affect in any manner the application to the business of insurance of the Act of July 5, 1935, as amended, known as the National Labor Relations Act, or the Act of June 25, 1938, as amended, known as the Fair Labor Standards Act of 1938, or the Act of June 5, 1920, known as the Merchant Marine Act, 1920.

Sec. 5. As used in this Act, the term "State" includes the several States, Alaska, Hawaii, Puerto Rico, and the District of Columbia.

Sec. 6. If any provision of this Act, or the application of such provision to any person or circumstances, shall be held invalid, the remainder of the Act, and the application of such provision to persons or circumstances other than those as to which it is held invalid, shall not be affected.

Approved March 9, 1945

CHAPTER 8

Insurance Contracts

After studying this chapter, you should be able to:

■ Identify some basic vocabulary used in contract law

■ List the four essential elements of a valid contract

■ Describe several features that distinguish insurance contracts from other contracts

■ Explain the principle of indemnity and the most important ways insurance companies maintain this principle

■ Discuss the implications of insurance contracts being made in utmost good faith

■ Identify the ways an insurance contract may be ended

Chapter 6, "The Insurance Market: The Economic Problem," described the various players in the insurance market—the sellers, the buyers, and the regulators. Now we come to a turn in the road and move from the insurance market to the subject of insurance contracts. We illustrate the discussion using the two most widely purchased personal insurance contracts, the homeowners and the personal auto policy. Most students in an introductory insurance course can learn the principles of insurance contract construction adequately by focusing on personal insurance contracts, which coincidentally they, like most Americans, almost certainly will purchase.

All insurance purchases involve contracts. In fact, insurance is a distinct branch of contract law, and a general knowledge of contract law is essential to understanding insurance. The first part of the chapter presents some basic vocabulary and rules of contract law. Next, we explain the special characteristics distinguishing insurance contracts from other contracts.

Figure 8–1 presents an outline of the material covered in this chapter.

CONTRACT TERMINOLOGY

Contract

A **contract** is a legally binding agreement that creates rights and duties for those who are parties to it. If one party to the contract fails to perform its duties without a legal excuse, attorneys say that the contract is *breached*. If a contract is breached or if disputes arise between the parties about the interpretation of the contract, the issues may be settled by a court. Courts can enforce their judgments and settle contractual disputes using a variety of remedies. For example, a court can require performance of the original contract by the breaching party, or it can direct that the injured party be compensated for damages caused by the breach.

Valid contract

A **valid contract** is one that a court will enforce. We describe the elements of a valid contract shortly. Two other categories of contracts are voidable and void contracts. A **voidable contract** allows one party the option of breaking the agreement because of an act or omission of an act (a breach) by the other party. The party with the

Voidable contract

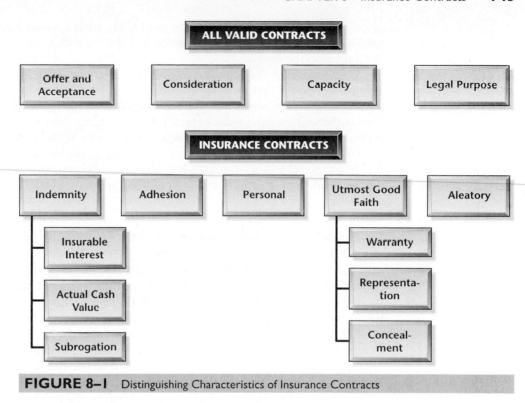

FIGURE 8–1   Distinguishing Characteristics of Insurance Contracts

right to void the contract instead may choose to have the contract enforced. A good example of a voidable contract in insurance is one in which the insured has attempted to defraud the insurer. After the insurer establishes the insured's fraud, it will be released from its contractual obligations. At the insurer's option, the contract can be set aside, or voided.

If, however, an insurer breaches the contract by refusing to pay a valid claim, its insured can go to court to force the insurer to perform. If a court believes an insurer denied the claim in bad faith, it may penalize the insurer for amounts substantially greater than the original amount of damages sustained by the insured.

Void contract

A **void contract** is one a court will not enforce because it lacks one or more features of a valid contract. For example, assume that an insurance contract is purchased for an illegal purpose, such as insuring property with the intent of committing the fraud of arson. A court would not enforce such a contract's provisions after discovering the illegal purpose. Likewise, if an incompetent person (such as a person declared legally insane) were to enter into an insurance contract, this contract would be considered, in legal Latin, *void ab initio,* void from the beginning. In legal terms, the court is saying that a contract never existed.

Binder

Binder

In property insurance, a temporary contract called a **binder** often is used before the formal insurance policy is issued. The binder must meet all the requirements for a legal contract. It is distinguished by its temporary nature (often 30 days or less). The purpose of the binder is to provide coverage during the time it takes to process an application. A binder may be oral or written. An oral binder, such as one that an agent may give over the telephone, should be followed by a written document to reduce the likelihood of disputes and to protect the positions of both parties. Normally, written binders will specify the amount of insurance, the period during which the binder is effective, and the parties to the binder.

Parol evidence rule

With respect to oral binders, or contracts, we must define the **parol evidence rule**. This rule provides that after an oral agreement is put in writing, no evidence of additions or conflicts between the oral and written agreements can be introduced in court. That is, the written agreement's terms take precedence over the oral agreement's terms if there is a conflict between the two. For example, if the oral agreement called for $185,000 of insurance and the written agreement provided for $180,000, and assuming the difference resulted from an ambiguity rather than from a clerical error, the parol evidence rule would support the $180,000 figure.

Conditional Receipt

Conditional receipt

Binders are not used in life insurance because life insurance agents lack the authority to bind their companies. Temporary coverage, however, that is contingent on an applicant's ability to present evidence of insurability can be provided by a **conditional receipt**. Life insurance agents give an applicant a conditional receipt when the applicant submits a premium payment with the application. With one common type of conditional receipt, if evidence of insurability exists, coverage begins from the date of the receipt. Evidence of insurability always includes, but is not limited to, good health. Occupation would be another factor. As an example, assume that Francis Drake submits a $400 premium with his application for $180,000 of life insurance. The following day, he takes and passes a medical examination. The next day, he drowns in a fishing accident. Despite the fact that death occurred before the policy was issued, there would be a $180,000 payment by the insurer because there was a conditional receipt and evidence of insurability.

The main difference between the property insurance binder and the life insurance conditional receipt is the contingent nature of the conditional receipt. The life insurer is not bound to honor claims if the terms of the conditional receipt are not met. The conditional receipt also implies that a premium payment accompanied the application, while property insurers generally do not require an advance premium payment when they issue a binder. In fact, a binder often is required to give the insurer time to calculate the appropriate charge for the insurance.

ELEMENTS OF A VALID CONTRACT

All valid contracts must have the following four elements: offer and acceptance, consideration, capacity, and legal purpose.

Offer and Acceptance

Offer

Acceptance

Transactions begin when one person proposes to exchange something of value with another person. The **offer** is the proposal to make an exchange. If the second person agrees to the exchange, this is **acceptance**. The offer must be reasonably definite and communicated clearly. The acceptance must be unconditional, unequivocal, and communicated clearly.

All parties to a contract must agree to exactly the same terms. There must be a *meeting of the minds*. To create a contract, one party makes an offer to another party to do something or not to do something. The second party may accept or reject this offer or may make a *counteroffer*. When one party makes an offer and the second party accepts it without qualifications, a necessary requirement for a contract is met.

The offer and acceptance may be oral or in writing. The law recognizes both forms of communication. In property insurance, as noted, most states allow oral insurance binders and contracts, but they are usually put in writing as soon as possible to provide protection for both the insured and insurer.

When purchasing insurance, an individual ordinarily completes an application and in doing so makes an offer to purchase insurance. If the insurer accepts the offer, it agrees to insure the applicant. Note that insurance agents, though soliciting new business, legally are not offering to sell insurance. Technically, we say they are inviting the insured to make an offer. If the insurer issues a policy, that indicates acceptance.

Consideration

Consideration

The value exchanged between the parties to the contract, that is, what each party gives to the other, is the **consideration**. Consideration may take a tangible form such as money, or it may take the form of a promise to do something or not to do it. There must be an exchange of consideration to have a valid contract.

In an insurance contract, the consideration that the insurer gives is a contingent promise to pay the insured. That is, the insurer agrees to make payment only if a covered loss occurs. If such an event does not occur, the insurer need not make payment. In return for the insurer's promise, the insured gives two things—money (premiums) and a promise to follow the provisions and stipulations in the insurance contract.

Unilateral contracts

Most insurance contracts are **unilateral contracts**. That is, only the insurer makes an enforceable promise. The insured does not promise to pay the premiums and cannot be sued for failure to do so. Insureds, however, cannot collect for losses if they do not pay premiums because timely payment of the premium is a condition of the contract. Contracts in which both parties make enforceable promises are called **bilateral contracts**.

Bilateral contracts

Capacity

Capacity

Not every person has the legal **capacity** to enter into a contract. As a rule, for reasons of social welfare, minors, the insane, and the intoxicated cannot enter into a binding agreement. The purpose of this rule is to keep people from taking advantage of parties who presumably do not have the capacity to understand the agreement they are making.

State law defines the period of minority as ending at age 18. If a 13-year-old were to enter into a contract, it would be voidable at the youngster's option. If a minor chose not to void the contract, the youngster could *ratify* or *affirm* it when reaching age 18.

Although as a rule minors can disaffirm contracts, they cannot do so when contracting for a necessary good or service. In most instances, courts have held that insurance contracts are not necessities. However, when minors own and operate motor vehicles, own property, or have dependents, the court may consider insurance a necessary purchase that cannot be disaffirmed. Many state laws allow older minors to make binding agreements for insurance.

Insurance companies also must be qualified to enter into contracts. They must have a license to operate in each state where they do business. If an insured were injured because he or she dealt unknowingly with an unqualified insurer, the insured could look to the court for a remedy. The unauthorized insurer would be subject to fines and penalties.

Legal Purpose

Legal purpose

A contract must have a **legal purpose**, a function or intention permitted by law. Contracts having an antisocial purpose are legally unenforceable. No court will aid the parties to such a contract. An insurance policy purchased as a gamble on a famous person's life or on any life in which the contract owner has no legal interest is an example of an unenforceable contract. If a person attempted to collect proceeds from contracts where an insurable interest was lacking, a court would hold the contract void, as we explain later when describing the doctrine of *insurable interest*.

DISTINGUISHING CHARACTERISTICS OF INSURANCE CONTRACTS

All valid contracts must have the four essential features just presented if a court is to enforce their provisions. Insurance contracts are distinctive. They have some unique elements (centering on the contingent promise to pay for covered losses) but share other characteristics (such as subrogation and arbitration conditions) with other business contracts. We now will describe in detail the following distinctive characteristics and legal doctrines applying to insurance contracts:

- Principle of indemnity
- Rules of insurable interest
- Limiting recovery to actual cash value (ACV)
- Subrogation in insurance
- Doctrine of adhesion
- Personal contract
- Doctrine of utmost good faith
- Aleatory contract concept

Principle of Indemnity

Indemnity

Insurance contracts provide compensation for an insured's losses. The insured, however, should not profit from an insurance transaction, or else the insurance will provide an incentive to cause fraudulent losses or to overstate claims. **Indemnity** means that the insured should be placed in the same financial position after the insured loss as before it. Any departure from this rule should be on the side of undercompensation. Insurers enforce the principle of indemnity through the insurable interest requirement, ACV settlements, and the operation of subrogation. We will discuss each of these topics separately.

Three Exceptions to the Rule

We can note the following three exceptions to the rule that insurance contracts are contracts of indemnity: life insurance, replacement-cost insurance, and valued insurance.

Life Insurance   Because the economic value of a human life cannot be measured precisely before death, life insurance cannot be a contract of indemnity. A person could not be put in exactly the same financial position occupied before death because that position includes unknown future income. Nevertheless, life insurance underwriters are careful not to overinsure by allowing insureds to acquire more life insurance than their financial position justifies. Overinsurance creates an unacceptable moral hazard for life insurers, who do not want their insureds worth more dead than alive. Thus, in practice, life insurance honors the principle of indemnity, but it does not do so legally.

Replacement-cost insurance

Replacement-Cost Insurance   **Replacement-cost insurance** is written when the insurer promises to pay an amount equal to the full cost of repairing or replacing the property without deduction for depreciation. If an insured loses an old, run-down building and it is replaced by a new building, the insured obviously is better off after the loss. Replacement-cost coverage is a typical feature of homeowners insurance policies and also is found in other property contracts. Because insurance companies are well aware of the potential moral hazard created by writing this coverage, they place conditions and restrictions in replacement-cost contracts to reduce this problem. One typical restriction is a requirement that the insured rebuild, usually at the same location. If no rebuilding is done, the insurer pays the actual cash value of the loss, which can be substantially less than the replacement cost. (We define the term *actual cash value,* or *ACV,* shortly.)

Valued insurance policy

Valued Insurance Policies   A **valued insurance policy** is another exception to the rule of indemnity. Valued policies pay the limit of liability whenever an insured total loss occurs. The value of the insured property is agreed to before the policy is written. If a total loss occurs, it may cause more or less damage than the stated amount. Nevertheless, the stated amount will be paid. Insurers write some ocean and inland marine insurance contracts on a valued basis. The use of valued policies generally is limited to objects for which market value may fluctuate or be difficult to determine accurately after a loss, such as art objects and other collector's items. Underwriters respect the principle of indemnity when writing valued policies and generally require insureds to get appraisals of their property to establish its insurable value.

Insurable Interest

If people could insure property or a life in which they had no financial interest, insurance would become gambling. An insured would be enriched if these losses occurred. Such contracts of insurance were written for a time in England, but the fraud and murder associated with them caused laws to be passed prohibiting the issuance of insurance policies in which the insured lacked interest in the loss.

Property Insurance

This statement is the essence of our insurance laws today: No one may collect insurance proceeds without demonstrating a personal loss from the insured event. In property insurance, one must show a legally recognized form of ownership such as a title, deed, or another demonstrable financial interest. Insurable financial interests not involving property ownership include bailments, mortgage loans, or other transactions where someone pledges property to secure a loan. In some cases, courts have allowed recovery where the insured had a contract to purchase a structure (or the expectation of inheritance), but the transaction was not complete at the time of an insured loss. This description should make it clear that more than one party may have an insurable interest in the same property. For example, both the owner and the mortgage loan holder may have insurance on the same building.

In property insurance, this interest must be shown to exist when the loss occurs. As noted, a person may purchase insurance on property not yet owned. To collect the insurance proceeds, however, the person must demonstrate a financial loss from the insured event.

For example, assume Bud and Miller each owns one-half interest in a bar and both are insureds under the same contract. If a loss occurs, each could collect only half the proceeds. Now assume that on October 14, Bud sells his interest to Miller. If a loss occurs on October 15, Bud cannot collect from his insurance policy because at the time of the loss, he had no insurable interest in the property. In other words, he already was entitled to the sale proceeds at the time of the fire. If he were able to receive the insurance proceeds and the sale proceeds, he would be enriched by collecting twice for the same property.

Life Insurance

In life insurance, the policyowner must show a recognized interest in having the insured's life continue. This interest must be shown when the policy is purchased. People are presumed to have an unlimited insurable interest in their own lives and may purchase any amount of insurance on their own lives that an insurer will issue. Furthermore, the law presumes that a husband and wife have an unlimited interest in each other's lives. Beyond close family relationships, an insurable interest must be demonstrated; it will not be presumed to exist. Interests that generally can be demonstrated include creditors in the lives of their debtors (but the amount of insurance must bear a reasonable relationship to the debt), partners in each other's lives, and employers in the lives of their key employees.

Unlike the case of property insurance, the insurable interest must be demonstrated at the time the life insurance is purchased. It need not be shown when the loss occurs. This rule is a choice of the lesser of two evils. On the one hand, divorce removes a spouse's insurable interest. If a policy were to be canceled at this point for lack of insurable interest, the insureds would stand to lose some money. If, for example, the husband were terminally ill, the loss could be substantial. On the other hand, allowing the wife to collect when she no longer has an insurable interest may create a moral hazard. It is somewhat reassuring to know that the law will not allow murderers to benefit from their misdeeds. In the event of a murder, the life insurer, at a court's direction, usually will pay the proceeds to a trust to be distributed to the victim's rightful heirs, excluding the murderer.

Owner

Beneficiary

In life insurance, another distinction must be made. The owner of the insurance policy, not the beneficiary, must demonstrate the insurable interest. The **owner** of the policy is the party who can enforce the contractual rights, such as naming the beneficiary, assigning the policy, or taking out loans from the insurer. The **beneficiary** is the party who receives the funds at the insured's death. The beneficiary need not have an insurable interest in the insured's life. The owner, however, also may be the beneficiary of the policy.

Insured

For example, Father may be the **insured** (the person whose death will cause the policy to mature as a death claim). Mother may be the owner, and Child the beneficiary. In this case, the beneficiary well may have an insurable interest. It is possible, however, to name as the beneficiary of a life insurance policy a charity or the U.S. government, neither of which would be expected to have an insurable interest in the insured's life.

Actual Cash Value

Actual cash value (ACV)

Replacement cost

Actual cash value (ACV) generally means replacement cost at the time of loss less depreciation. Equation 8–1 shows this definition mathematically. **Replacement cost** means the dollar amount required to rebuild a similar structure (or part of a structure if the loss is partial) meeting the building code requirements in effect at the time of original construction. Replacement cost of the building does not equal fair market value of the property because market value would include the value of the land and its location. Location can be an important factor in property value but not in replacement cost. For example, it might cost the same amount to build a beautiful home in location A or location B. However, if location B were downwind of an unpleasant-smelling agricultural plant, the home's market value would be less at location B.

$$\text{ACV} = \text{Replacement cost} - \text{Depreciation} \qquad \textbf{(8.1)}$$

Depreciation is expressed as a fraction. The numerator is the number of years the structure was in use. The denominator is an estimate of the useful life of the structure. For example, a building used for 15 years having an expected useful life of 60 years would be one-quarter depreciated (15/60) and three-quarters undepreciated (45/60). This depreciation calculation is not the equivalent of the accounting concept because the accounting concept is based on purchase price, while depreciation for ACV calculations is based on replacement cost and an estimate of the asset's useful life.

Consider a home that has been occupied one-quarter of its useful life. It has a replacement cost of $150,000. (Assume that its historical cost was $100,000, producing an accounting book value of $75,000 on a straight-line basis. The historical cost and accounting book value are irrelevant to the ACV calculation.) Its ACV is $150,000 × 3/4 (the undepreciated amount) = $112,500. As a second example, assume that this building sustains a $50,000 (replacement-cost value) loss. The ACV of this *partial loss* is $50,000 × 3/4 = $37,500.

Sometimes insurers do not use an ACV provision in their policies. In cases where the replacement cost of a building is greater than its market value, as is often the case with older buildings, insurers provide coverage based on replacement cost with modern construction techniques. Insurers call this provision **functional replacement**. For example, functional replacement allows wallboard to be substituted for plaster walls and plastic pipes for copper pipes.

Subrogation

Subrogation is the legal substitution of one person in another's place. Subrogation is supported by the theory that, if a person must pay a debt for which another is liable, such payment should give the person a right to collect the debt from the liable party.

In insurance, subrogation gives the insurer the right to collect from a third party after paying its insured's claim. A typical case of subrogation arises in automobile insurance collision claims. Suppose Lois Steam, the psychologist, is responsible for a collision with Eileen Dover, the architect. Eileen may sue Lois for damages or she may collect from her own automobile collision insurance. If she chooses to collect from her own insurance, her insurance company will be subrogated to her right to sue Lois. Eileen cannot collect for her loss both from her insurer and from Lois. Thus, subrogation prevents insureds from profiting on their insurance by collecting twice for the same loss. Subrogation also prevents negligent parties from escaping payment for their acts because the injured party has insurance. Figure 8–2 presents the operation of subrogation in automobile insurance.

A typical automobile insurance policy provides the following:

> In the event of any payment under this policy, the company shall be subrogated to all the insured's right of recovery. . . . The insured shall do nothing after the loss to prejudice such rights.

If Eileen were to waive her right to sue Lois, she in essence would waive her insurer's right as well. Because the insurer's position would be prejudiced by Eileen's action, it need not pay Eileen's claim. However, many insurance contracts allow the insured to waive subrogation rights in advance of a loss, as would happen if a hold-harmless agreement were in effect and as is common in property owner and tenant leases in which property owners agree in advance not to sue negligent tenants for fire losses.

If an insurer were to receive more compensation than it paid its insured from a subrogation lawsuit, the difference generally belongs to the insured. For example, assume that Eileen collected $4,500 from her insurer because of her collision with Lois.

Functional replacement

Subrogation

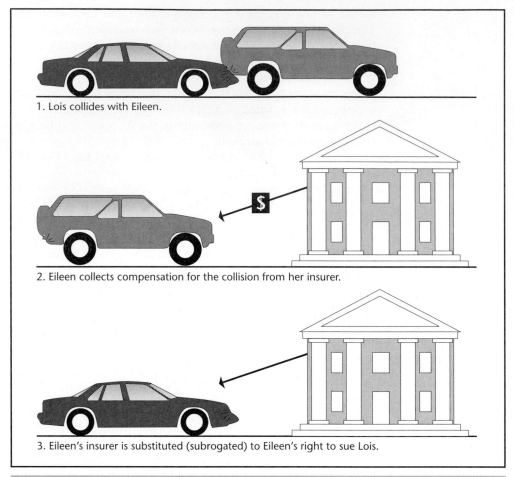

1. Lois collides with Eileen.

2. Eileen collects compensation for the collision from her insurer.

3. Eileen's insurer is substituted (subrogated) to Eileen's right to sue Lois.

FIGURE 8–2 Subrogation—Automobile Insurance

Her insurer reduced the $5,000 damage claim to $4,500 because of a $500 deductible in her collision coverage. The insurer sued for and collected $5,000 from Lois. The insurer then must reimburse Eileen for the $500 deductible. Insurers must compensate their insureds fully for their losses before the insurers can keep any proceeds from subrogation litigation.

Subrogation does not exist in life insurance because life insurance is not a contract of indemnity. Thus, if Karl Marx is killed by his neighbor's negligence, Mrs. Marx may collect whatever damages a court will award for her husband's wrongful death. She also may collect any life insurance proceeds. The life insurer is not subrogated to the liability claim and cannot sue the negligent party.

Generally, an insurer has no right to subrogate against its own insured if an insured's negligence results in the insurer paying a claim. First, because insureds have no right to sue themselves, the insurer has no right that could be substituted. Second, the value of the insurance contract would be greatly diminished if an insurer could sue negligent insureds. Such a provision would make most liability insurance valueless. When the insured's negligence causes the destruction of his or her insured property, as is often the case, property insurance also would be useless.

Consider the following facts. An insurance company issued a property insurance policy to Fishy Corporation and paid the corporation after a fire loss. It then tried to collect for its payment by suing a corporate officer, Captain Dan, whose negligence caused the loss. Technically, Captain Dan was not an insured under the policy issued to Fishy Corporation, so the insurer asserted that he could be sued as a negligent third party. The court, using the following words, stated the insurer had no right to recover its payment from Captain Dan:

> A person not named in an insurance policy is considered an insured for purposes of preventing subrogation, when the insurer seeks subrogation in attempting to recover from the insured on the risk the insurer agreed to take upon payment of the premium.[1]

Contract of Adhesion

Skilled lawyers working for insurance companies or insurance rating bureaus such as the Insurance Services Organization draft insurance contracts. These attorneys understand the meaning of the words used in insurance contracts and of the drafting and legal history of these contracts. Consumers do not have this specialized knowledge. Risk managers of larger organizations and their brokers may have comparable knowledge and information, and in some cases, they may draft their own contracts. However, individuals and small firms cannot bargain with the insurer about the wording of the contract. They may accept the contract unaltered or they may reject it.

Contracts of adhesion

Because this unequal knowledge and unequal bargaining power are perceived to give the insurer a significant advantage over the insured, most states classify insurance contracts as **contracts of adhesion**. The general rule covering contracts of adhesion is this: any language that a court determines is *ambiguous* (open to more than one reasonable interpretation) will be construed against the drafter of the contract. Legal scholars use the Latin phrase, *contra proferentum*, "an ambiguous provision is construed most strongly against the person who selected the language," to describe this outcome.[2]

Perhaps my favorite case involving the question of an ambiguity in an insurance contract is the case of *Holiday Inns Incorporated* v. *Aetna Insurance Company*.[3] In March 1975, Aetna issued a policy insuring the Beirut Holiday Inn for:

> all risks . . . of direct physical loss or damage . . . except . . . *Loss by war, invasion, act of foreign enemy, hostilities or warlike operations (whether war be declared or not), civil war, mutiny, insurrection, revolution, conspiracy, military or usurped power* [emphasis added].

After the policy was issued, the property was damaged extensively by rockets, grenades, and ensuing fires in heavy fighting between rival ethnic, political, and religious groups. The hotel was closed to guests and Holiday Inns filed a claim for loss with the insurer. Aetna denied the claim, citing the italicized exclusion. The case then went to court.

The court made the following points:

1. Under an all-risk policy, the burden is on the insurer to prove that the proximate cause of the loss was excluded.

---

[1] *Fireman's Insurance Company* v. *Wheeler* [New York Supreme Court] *1991 CCH Fire Cases*, p. 8539.
[2] *Black's Law Dictionary*, 6th ed. (St. Paul, Minn.: West Publishing Company, 1990.)
[3] *1984 CCH Fire and Casualty Cases*, pp. 430–69. Despite being more than 20 years old, this case remains my favorite illustration of the doctrine of *contra proferentum*.

2. Exclusions are given the interpretation most favorable to the insured.

3. The insurer must demonstrate that the interpretation favoring it is the only reasonable reading of the policy language.

The court defined *war* as "a course of hostility engaged in by entities having at least significant attributes of sovereignty." Because none of the warring factions in Lebanon had sovereignty, the court held that the damage did not arise from war, as strictly defined. After lengthy argument, the court concluded that Aetna had to pay Holiday Inns for the damage.

In the Holiday Inns case, the court's reasoning shows the strictness of the application of the doctrine of *contra proferentum* in insurance contracts. It is an excellent demonstration of how costly it can be to use the English language (or any language) imprecisely. How often do we believe our communications are clear, when, in fact, they are subject to more than one interpretation? Any professor constructing multiple-choice test questions is in a good position to answer this query with humility. The *Holiday Inns* v. *Aetna* case holds a valuable lesson for all business students. Aetna's lawyers were neither unskilled nor unmindful of their objective, yet they still failed to communicate precisely. Precise use of the English language is a challenging task.

Another interesting case provides a second example of a court's ability to find language ambiguous. In this case, a health insurance policy excluded payment for "experimental treatment." It then defined the term to mean "treatment not approved or accepted as essential by any of the following four named entities: (1) the American Medical Association; (2) the U.S. Surgeon General; (3) the U.S. Department of Public Health; or (4) the National Institute of Health." The court found this standard to be ambiguous because of the inability of the insured or the insurer to know from reading the policy what procedures were covered and which were excluded. The court noted that exclusions must be clear and unmistakable, and ambiguities must be construed against the insurer.

As we noted when discussing arson claims in Chapter 1, "Fundamentals and Terminology," the costs of the pro-insured bias associated with the contract of adhesion rule most likely are borne by the pool of insureds—not the insurance company or its owners. U.S. courts have placed a significant burden on insurance companies. They must write unambiguous contracts, clearly communicating coverages and exclusions of coverage, using a relatively imprecise tool, English.

Reasonable Expectations

Reasonable expectations

Closely related to the rule governing contracts of adhesion is the evolving doctrine of **reasonable expectations**, which various state courts have been applying since the 1960s. In general, the courts of at least ten states have created coverage when the reasonable expectations of insureds would result in a claim payment, despite a lack of either contractual language creating the coverage or ambiguities allowing the application of the doctrine applying to contracts of adhesion.

The courts have applied the reasonable expectations doctrine in cases in which they determined that insurers misled the insured into expecting coverage. In one such case, a travel-insurance vending machine was placed in front of a nonscheduled (charter) airline's departure gate. The policy sold by the machine excluded coverage for nonscheduled flights. The court ruled that the placement of the machine created the expectation of coverage and, therefore, it directed the insurer to pay the resulting claim.[4] The point of this case, and the court's purpose in all cases in which a court creates coverage, is to produce equity, or fairness, in the insurance market.

---

[4] *Lacks* v. *Fidelity & Casualty Co.*, 306 N.Y. 357, 118 N.E. 2d 555 (1954).

In an Iowa case, an insured's policy required evidence of forced entry on the exterior of the building before the insured could collect on a burglary policy. The burglars entered the building without leaving evidence of forced entry on the building's exterior but left such evidence on the interior doors. The insurer denied coverage. The court directed the insurer to pay, disregarding the unambiguous exclusion stating:

> . . . nothing . . . would have led (the insured) to reasonably anticipate (the insurer) would bury within the definition of "burglary" another exclusion denying coverage when, no matter how extensive the proof of a third-party burglary, no marks were left on the exterior of the premises.[5]

The reasonable expectations doctrine has been accepted by some courts and rejected by others. Even among those courts that reject this line of argument, some have noted that their rejection applied to specific factual circumstances and not to the broad argument of providing a remedy when an insurer's actions produce unfairness. The reasonable expectations argument is more likely to succeed when courts find bizarre or unusual policy definitions or when exclusions eliminate the "dominant" purpose of the contract.

The Personal Feature

Insurance policies are personal contracts, and thus insurance contracts cannot be freely transferred to other parties. When the parties to an insurance contract reach agreement, one of the points they agreed to is to do business with each other. Each has considered the other's character and conduct. For good reasons, neither wants the other party to find a substitute party to the agreement. From the insurer's standpoint, it tries carefully to minimize the moral hazard. Allowing an insured to transfer an insurance policy freely could negate the underwriting efforts. For example, when Mrs. Sand purchased her auto insurance, her insurer considered the fact that she had no previous accidents or speeding tickets. If Mrs. Sand sells her auto to Fred Chopin, she may not transfer her insurance coverage to Fred along with the auto. The insurer wants the right to choose with whom it will do business. Likewise, when Mrs. Sand chose to purchase insurance from the Big Insurance Company, she considered its reputation and its excellent services. She did not choose to deal with the Little Insurance Company, and she may not want her contract transferred to that company.

Assignment

Assignment

The term **assignment** describes the situation in which one party transfers its rights and duties under a contract to another party. In many contractual situations, assignment of a contract is allowed. The insuring agreement of the homeowners policy, which is typical of many non–life insurance contracts, contains the following statement:

> Assignment of this policy shall not be valid except with the written consent of this company.

This sentence means that the policy can be assigned to another person *only* if the insurer agrees.

Unlike property insurance policies, life insurance policies can be assigned freely if the insurer is notified properly. A valid assignment of a life insurance policy does not change the life covered by the insurance, but it does change the party who may exercise the benefits of ownership, such as naming a beneficiary.

---

[5] *C&J Fertilizer v. Allied Mutual Insurance Co.*, 227 N.W. 2d 169 (1975).

Utmost Good Faith (Latin: *Uberrimae Fidei*)

A person buying insurance is held to the highest standard of honesty in dealing with the insurer. The penalty for a lesser level of truthfulness is the insurer's right to void the contract. Consider the words of one court in describing this doctrine:

> It is well established under the doctrine of *uberrimae fidei* that the parties to a marine insurance policy must accord each other the highest degree of good faith. This stringent doctrine requires the assured to disclose to the insurer all known circumstances that materially affect the risk being insured. Since the assured is in the best position to know of any circumstances material to the risk, he must reveal those facts to the underwriter, rather than wait for the underwriter to inquire. . . . The assured's failure to meet this standard entitles the underwriter to void the policy *ab initio*.[6]

This high level of good faith that an insured owes an insurer is reflected in the legal doctrines of warranty, representation, and concealment.

Warranty

Warranty

Affirmative warranty

Promissory warranty

Expressed warranties

Implied warranties

In insurance terminology, a **warranty** is a statement that something has happened or exists (**affirmative warranty**) or something will happen (**promissory warranty**). Another distinction sometimes arises between written warranties (known as **expressed warranties**) and commonly understood warranties (known as **implied warranties**).

The traditional doctrine of warranty, which has its origin in ocean marine insurance, is very strict: Any breach of a warranty by an insured allows the insurer to void the contract. For example, a shipowner must warrant that his ship is in seaworthy condition when it leaves the harbor (affirmative warranty), and that it will sail from New York to Amsterdam carrying a cargo of glassware (promissory warranty). If the ship were seriously leaking, if the destination were Japan, or if the cargo were liquor, any one of these deviations would constitute a breach of warranty. Regardless of whether the breach contributed to a loss, the insurer could void the contract under the strict doctrine of warranty.

Because the doctrine of warranty is so strict, it has potential for injuring insureds and working against the ideal to honor reasonable expectations of insureds. Thus, state laws and court decisions have mitigated the harsh effects of this doctrine. Perhaps the simplest method of achieving fairer results is to hold certain policy provisions to be representations rather than warranties, for the rules relating to representation are not so strict.

The following case illustrates the interpretation that a court can make of a statement held to be a warranty. Jones, a jeweler, purchased an insurance policy covering his inventory. In completing the application, Jones warranted that 100 percent of the inventory would be kept in a safe or vault when the premises were closed. After the policy was issued, burglars entered the firm when it was closed and removed more than $75,000 in jewelry that was not put in the safe. No jewelry in the safe was stolen. Jones filed a claim with the insurer. The insurer denied the claim based on breach of warranty. The court held the policy language was clear and unambiguous, and the insured was bound by the policy provisions. It held the insured breached a warranty, and it therefore granted summary judgment to the insurer, relieving it of any obligation to pay the claim.[7]

---

[6] *Knight v. United States Fire Ins. Co.*, 804 F. 2d. 9 (2d Cir. 1986).
[7] *1983 CCH Fire and Casualty Cases*, pp. 156–158.

Representations

Representations

Before entering an insurance contract, insurers usually ask applicants several questions about the loss exposure. Courts call the applicant's answers, usually found in a formal application for insurance, **representations**. These statements are made to induce the insurer to enter the contract. The general rule with respect to representations is that, if the consumer gives false answers and the answers are material to the risk, the insurer can void the contract. The test of **materiality** is a negative answer to the question: Would the insurer have written the same policy at the same price if it had known the truth? For example, when applying for automobile insurance, Denton Fender is asked if he has had any accidents in the past three years or any health problems. He answers "no" to both questions. In fact, he was responsible for two serious traffic accidents and has athlete's foot. The first false response is undoubtedly material; the second is not. If the question is raised in court, all the insurer must do to make its point is to show that it has declined to accept at standard rates any insureds with two previous accidents. If the company consistently charges extra for people with athlete's foot, this representation also would be considered material.

Materiality

Another example of a material misrepresentation involves an insured who made false statements after a loss. The insured's property was destroyed in a fire that the insurance loss adjuster believed was suspicious. On the insurance application, the insured denied making other insurance applications. This statement was false. The insured denied, after the loss, knowing two people previously convicted of insurance fraud. This statement was false. The court record states:

> We hold when an insurance policy clearly states that material misrepresentations will void the policy, the insurer need not pay for an alleged loss if the insured makes a material misrepresentation to the insurer while it is investigating the claim. The (misrepresentation) clause applies before and after the loss. . . . False statements after a loss are material if they might have affected the attitude or action of the insurer, or if they are calculated to discourage, mislead, or deflect the company's investigation. The right rule of law, we believe, is one that provides insureds with an incentive to tell the truth.[8]

Statements of opinion, however, are insufficient to allow the insurer to void the contract. For example, if a person with undiagnosed cancer states on a health application that he does not have cancer, and that person had no reason to believe he had cancer, then a subsequent diagnosis would not be sufficient to void the contract even though the statement was technically false.

Concealment

Concealment

Concealment is silence when obligated to speak or a failure to disclose material information. Because the insurance contract is one of utmost good faith, the applicant for insurance must reveal all material facts. The best test of the materiality of a concealment is the same as it is for a misrepresentation. Would the insurer write the same contract at the same rate if it knew all the facts? For example, when applying for life insurance, Mary Stuart is asked if she has gone to the doctor in the past three years. She truthfully answers "no." She fails to add that she has had severe chest pains and has collapsed on several occasions but has not sought medical treatment. Under these circumstances, the insurer well may prove a case of concealment and thereby be able to void the insurance policy.

---

[8] *Longobardi* v. *Chubb Insurance Company* (New Jersey Supreme Court). *1991 CCH Fire Cases*, p. 8257. Also see *Roth* v. *Chubb* (New Jersey Superior Court). *1993–94 CCH Fire and Casualty Cases*, p. 14,645.

Voiding a contract based on concealment is more difficult for the insurer than voidance for a misrepresentation. In general, the insurer must prove to a jury's satisfaction that the applicant certainly knew he or she was concealing a material fact from the insurer to deceive the insurer. This strict requirement works to the insured's benefit.

In a Minnesota case, an employee applied for life insurance for himself and his wife, as he was allowed to do under his employer's group life insurance plan. The applicant omitted mentioning that his wife had diabetes, hypertension, and other health problems. After her death, the insured submitted a claim, which the insurer denied. The insured sued the insurer and the trial court upheld the insured's claim. The appellate court reversed the lower court's judgment, stating:

> In situations such as this one, where the questions are more specific, the court concludes that the "willfully false or intentionally misleading" standard does not require an intent to deceive. All that is required is that the insured have full knowledge of the facts concealed and that these facts probably would have precluded issuance of the policy if known to the insurance company. This is an objective standard; the facts must be revealed; and the insurance company, not the insured, assesses their significance. Thus, widower's statements were willfully false and intentionally misleading under state law.[9]

In summary, the rules of warranty, representation, and concealment distinguish insurance contracts from other transactions. If an insured deals with an insurer in less than an honorable way, the insured's actions may relieve the insurer of the duty to indemnify the insured if a loss occurs. However, the law and the courts are modifying the strict doctrines and legal technicalities continually so reasonable expectations of reasonable people are honored.

The Entire Contract and Incontestability Clauses

Entire contract

Two important clauses found in life insurance (and sometimes health insurance) policies are related to the question of warranty, representation, and concealment. **Entire contract** statutes require that any statements made by an applicant for life insurance be attached physically to the policy. The policy, with the application attached, constitutes the entire contract between the two parties. One purpose of this provision is to prevent the insured from claiming that the insurance agent or medical examiner recorded information incorrectly. After the contract is signed, the insured is bound by the responses as they are recorded. A second reason for this provision is to prevent insurers from attaching wording to the contract that the insured has not seen, such as the corporate bylaws. This provision is called **incorporation by reference**.

Incorporation by reference

Incontestable clause

The **incontestable clause** of life insurance policies states that after a given period, usually one or two years, the insurer no longer can contest a policy to void the contract. Thus, if an insured makes a material misrepresentation in applying for life insurance, the insurer must discover the false statement within a limited period of time, or the policy provides coverage despite the material misrepresentation in the application. In practice, life insurers review death claims that occur within the contestable period very carefully. If the insurer discovers a material misrepresentation while the policy is contestable, it will void the policy.

The purpose of this clause is to protect the beneficiary from stale claims of fraud. It would be especially difficult for the beneficiary to defend a claim of fraud forty years after the alleged fraud occurred. The defense would be especially difficult when the

---

[9] *Ellis v. Great-West Life Assurance Co.*, Nos. 93-1973 and 93-1975 (8th Cir. December 23, 1994).

insured is dead. The incontestable clause is not designed to encourage fraud or cheat life insurance companies; rather, it is an instance of choosing between two undesirable alternatives: allowing collection on an insurance policy even when fraud exists versus depriving some insureds of expected benefits. The law has chosen the first alternative.

The Aleatory Feature

Aleatory

Insurance contracts are **aleatory**; so is gambling. This term means that the parties to the contract know in advance that the dollars they will exchange will be unequal. The insured pays the premium and collects a large sum if a large loss occurs or collects nothing if no loss occurs. The opposite is true for the insurer. In most instances, it collects a premium and pays nothing. In a few cases, it collects a relatively small premium and pays a large amount. The aleatory feature of insurance policies differs from other business contracts, where consideration of equal value is exchanged. We call equal exchange contracts *commutative contracts*.

DISCHARGE OF INSURANCE CONTRACTS

Performance

We have explained how insurance contracts are created and what distinguishes them from other contracts. Now we will explain how insurance contracts are terminated. In the normal course of events, insurance contracts end by **performance**. That is, each party does what it has agreed to do. The insurer renders payment if a loss occurs or stands ready to do so if none occurs. In most cases, no loss occurs. The insurer still performed as required by standing ready to pay legitimate claims. Insureds discharge their duties by paying premiums and abiding by the conditions of the contract.

Condition precedent

Courts categorize the conditions of an insurance policy as either conditions precedent or conditions subsequent. A **condition precedent** is something that must be done by one party to activate the other party's duty to perform. For example, a homeowners insurance policy imposes the duty on an insured to give "prompt notice" of loss to the insurer and to supply an inventory of the damage within sixty days of the loss. The insured must satisfy both conditions precedent before the insurer is obligated to pay the claim.

Condition subsequent

A **condition subsequent** ends an existing duty of immediate performance. For example, the homeowners insurance contract also requires that insureds who begin a lawsuit to contest a claim denial begin the suit within one year of the date of the loss. If the insured does not bring a suit in a timely fashion, the insurer is relieved of its duty to pay the claim.

Insurance contracts may be terminated if either party fails to perform its duties. Thus, if an insured fails to comply with the conditions of the policy, the contract is breached. This breach allows the insurer to avoid its contractual liability. Sometimes the issue of the materiality of a breach is open to question or litigation. Courts generally will not allow insurers to avoid payment when the insured's breach of contract is slight. A material breach of contract by the insured, however, is an excuse for nonperformance by the insurer.

In those cases where a court decides that an insurer has acted in bad faith when denying a legitimate claim, the consequences for the insurer can be severe. In such cases, courts have ordered claims payment, plus recovery of pretrial interest, legal fees, and, in cases of outrageous conduct, punitive damages.

Recision

Insurance contracts also may be ended by recision. **Recision** is an agreement (contract) by both parties to end a contract. All the requisites of a contract are required. If recision is mutual, both parties voluntarily relinquish their rights and duties under contract. If one party feels it was the victim of fraud, it may ask the court to rescind the contract. Recision is a well-recognized equitable remedy from English common law.

Reformed

If mistakes have been made in a policy—for example, if $100,000 is typed in place of the correct amount, $10,000—the policy may be **reformed**. That is, the policy may be corrected so one party cannot take advantage of the other party's mistake. Reformation of errors in contracts is another common-law doctrine designed to produce fair, equitable results.

The legal doctrines of waiver and estoppel, defined earlier with respect to loss adjusting, also have application to contracts. That is, either party to an insurance contract may give up a known right voluntarily. This instance is a waiver of rights. For example, the insurance company may give up its right to a complete inventory within 60 days of a loss and grant the insured an extended period to file the necessary information.

If an insurer's behavior is inconsistent with claiming its rights, it may be *estopped* from such an assertion. For example, a Maine court decided that an insurer's failure to warn its insureds that occupancy of their home was a condition precedent was behavior inconsistent with asserting its rights. Therefore, it *estopped* the insurer from denying a claim because the contract's conditions were breached. The insured established that the insurer's agent had reason to know or suspect the condition was not being met when the policy was issued. This court stated that, because the insurer issued the policy requiring occupancy while it was aware (through the knowledge of its agent) that this condition was not met, it was only fair that the company be *estopped* from denying a claim.[10]

SUMMARY

Insurance contracts must meet these four criteria: offer and acceptance, consideration, capacity, and legal purpose. The following characteristics also distinguish insurance contracts from all others. Insurance contracts are contracts of indemnity, contracts of adhesion, personal contracts, contracts of utmost good faith, and aleatory contracts.

Insurance contracts may be discharged by performance, breach of contract conditions, and recision. Contracts are also subject to reformation, waiver, and estoppel.

REVIEW TERMS

- Acceptance
- Actual cash value (ACV)
- Affirmative warranty
- Aleatory
- Assignment
- Beneficiary
- Bilateral contracts
- Binder
- Capacity
- Concealment
- Condition precedent
- Condition subsequent
- Conditional receipt
- Consideration
- Contract
- Contract of adhesion

- Depreciation
- Entire contract
- Expressed warranties
- Functional replacement
- Implied warranties
- Incontestable clause
- Incorporations by reference
- Indemnity
- Insured
- Legal purpose
- Materiality
- Offer
- Owner
- Parol evidence rule
- Performance

- Promissory warranty
- Reasonable expectations
- Recision
- Reformed
- Replacement cost
- Replacement-cost insurance
- Representation
- Subrogation
- Unilateral contracts
- Valid contract
- Valued insurance policy
- Void contract
- Voidable contract
- War
- Warranty

---

[10] *Roberts et al.* v. *Maine Bonding and Casualty Company, 1979 CCH Fire and Casualty Cases*, pp. 555–558.

REVIEW

1. How do binders differ from conditional receipts?
2. What are the important differences between a valid contract, an invalid contract, and a voidable contract?
3. List the four elements of a valid contract. What is the legal result if only three of the four elements are present?
4. Why is legal capacity required to enter into a valid contract?
5. What is indemnity? Identify three ways that the principle of indemnity is enforced in property insurance contracts.
6. Are there any exceptions to the rule that insurance contracts are contracts of indemnity, defined strictly?
7. Describe one difference between life insurance and property insurance in the requirement for insurable interest.
8. Does actual cash value always mean fair market value?
9. How does subrogation prevent a person from collecting twice for the same debt or from the same insured injury?
10. Why are the rules on the right to assign a property insurance contract different from the rules on the right to assign a life insurance contract?
11. Give two examples of promissory and affirmative warranties.
12. What difference does it make to an insured if a false statement made by the insured is considered a warranty or a representation?
13. Explain the advantages of the incontestable clause in life insurance from society's standpoint.
14. How are insurance contracts usually ended? List other methods by which insurance contracts may be terminated.

OBJECTIVE QUESTIONS

1. Choose the one true statement about conditional receipts:
   a. Used only in property insurance
   b. Provides permanent coverage when accompanied by first premium payment
   c. Used only in life insurance
   d. Used mainly when insuring minors
2. Each of the following coverages is an exception to the rule of indemnity except:
   a. Actual cash value property insurance
   b. Life insurance
   c. Replacement cost insurance
   d. Valued insurance policies
3. Subrogation in insurance means:
   a. Losses must be reported in a timely way to the insurance company.
   b. Losses must be considered legally binding.
   c. The insured must pay premiums before losses can be paid.
   d. One party is being substituted for another in terms of legal rights.
4. Because insurance contracts are considered contracts of adhesion, which of the following is true?
   a. Ambiguities are construed against the writer of the contract.
   b. Larger losses attach before smaller losses.
   c. The courts will adhere to precedents set in previous cases.
   d. Each party is responsible for providing its own attorney if a breach of contract occurs.
5. What is the impact of the parol evidence rule?
   a. People on parole cannot make valid insurance contracts.
   b. Written evidence takes precedence over oral evidence.
   c. Oral evidence takes precedence over written evidence.
   d. Whichever party speaks first presents the evidence.
6. A temporary property insurance contract is called:
   a. A binder
   b. A parol contract
   c. A rescinded contract
   d. A hypothetical contract
7. What type of insurance policy often is used for artwork and collector's items?
   a. Liability policy
   b. The standard art insurance policy
   c. A valued insurance policy
   d. The commercial marine insurance policy
8. "Replacement cost at the time of loss less depreciation" is the definition of:
   a. The maximum covered loss
   b. Actual cash value
   c. Fair market value
   d. The maximum replacement of loss

INTERNET RESEARCH ASSIGNMENTS

1. Use the Internet to look up definitions of the following two legal terms: "Res judicata" and "Emancipation of minors." Start your search at this site: (*http://www.law.cornell.edu/wex/index.php/Category: Definition/*).
2. Follow a hyperlink from each definition found in the preceding assignment and describe the material presented.
3. Search for a firm that allows property insurance applications and one that allows life insurance applications on the Internet. Consider the requirements for entering a binding contract and describe how each step is met in an Internet insurance transaction.

Appendix: Cases for Discussion

Material Misrepresentation

Facts

The insured, Mrs. M, suffered a $100,000 fire loss in 1990. After the fire, her then-current homeowner's insurer, Insurer 1, informed Mrs. M that her coverage would not be renewed. When the policy expired, Mrs. M applied for coverage with a second insurer—the present defendant, Insurer 2.

When it issued the policy, Insurer 2 gave Mrs. M a copy of her application, which she signed but claimed not to have read. The application for the second policy did not contain truthful information about the 1990 fire and the nonrenewal of coverage by Insurer 1.

After the policy had been in force for about six months, Mrs. M filed a claim for theft coverage with Insurer 2. At the time of the claim, Mrs. M's misrepresentations were discovered, and the claim was denied. Mrs. M disputed that she made misrepresentations and took Insurer 2 to court to affirm her claim, saying that the insurer's agent had been informed of the truth, and knowledge conveyed to the agent must be imputed to the insurer. The agent emphatically denied being informed of prior losses or of notice of nonrenewal by Insurer 1, and it is undisputed that such information was not on the application.

The application for the coverage with Insurer 2 had the following provision immediately above the signature: "I have read this application before signing. . . . To the best of my knowledge, the statements made by me on this application are true. I request the Company, in reliance thereon, to issue the insurance applied for."

Conclusion

In giving its verdict in favor of the defendant, Insurer 2, the court stated, "If a person fails to read the [insurance contract application], he signs the same at his peril and is *estopped* to deny his obligation. He will be conclusively presumed to know the contents of the contract and must suffer the consequences of his negligence."

Questions

1. Do you think most insureds you know read either their insurance policies or the application forms they fill out? Explain your answer.
2. Do you think insureds like Mrs. M should be bound by the written applications they have signed? Should they be bound even if, hypothetically, they told the truth to the agent and the agent filled out the form incorrectly? Explain your answer.
3. Do you think the burden should be on the insurer to investigate the information on an application thoroughly before a loss, rather than waiting to investigate applications only after a loss occurs? Explain your answer.

Contract of Adhesion: The Metpath Case[11]

Background

Metpath, Inc. was a company that provided clinical analysis of medical specimens on a national basis. It depended on air transportation for delivery of specimens to its main laboratory in New Jersey. Threatened with the strike of air traffic controllers in 1981, Metpath hired an insurance broker to secure an extra-expense insurance policy to cover it in the event of such an occurrence. The relevant language of the policy included the following:

---

[11] *1982 CCH Fire and Casualty Cases*, pp. 1186–1190.

> This policy covers the necessary Extra Expense . . . incurred by the Assured . . . to continue . . . the normal operation of the Assured's business caused by or resulting from a strike or slowdown of Air Traffic Controllers. . . .
>
> There shall be no liability under this policy until seven days from the commencement of a strike or slowdown.

On August 3, 1981, the air traffic controllers began a strike. On August 6, President Reagan fired all the striking air controllers. Subsequently, Metpath filed a claim for payment under the policy, which the insurer denied. The reasons for allowing the denial of coverage to stand in the court decision (New York Supreme Court, Appellate Division, May 13, 1982) provide several important highlights to the material covered in this and earlier chapters.

Contract of Adhesion

Because the policy in question was drafted by the broker hired by Metpath to secure coverage, and because the question of coverage centered on the meaning of the word *strike,* the court held that any ambiguities in the policy wording must be interpreted strictly against Metpath. Thus, the court held that a strike existed for only three days (a period shorter than the deductible period), after which time there was no longer a strike because all the employees had been fired. The court noted the contract coverage was "during a period of a strike or slowdown," whereas Metpath did not request coverage specifying "labor interruption, business interruption, or transportation interruption." Thus, Metpath was held to the strict meaning of the words used in the contract, because the insurer (presumably) contemplated these words in constructing its premium rate.

Agents-Brokers

The insured's broker, who had been instructed in June 1981 to secure coverage against extra expenses caused by the impending strike, supplied the policy in question. This decision highlights the fact that the broker was held to be the insured's agent and the broker's acts (and omission) in drafting a policy were attributed to its principal, Metpath.

Reasonable Expectations

In a minority dissenting opinion, two justices thought that Metpath had a valid claim for insurance coverage. These justices believed that the damage (i.e., extra expenses incurred) that Metpath suffered was, in fact, "caused by or resulting from a strike." They thought that the proper outcome of the case could occur only by considering the intentions of both parties respecting the insured peril and the reasonable expectations of both parties with respect to coverage provided. Because the policy-provided coverage would cease after a new contract was ratified, it appeared to these justices that there should be some coverage afforded Metpath because the fired controllers never ratified a new contract. As noted, however, the majority of the judges thought that the strict meaning of the insured's (agent's) written word superseded the insured's "reasonable expectations" of coverage.

Questions

1. Do you support the majority or the minority opinion of the court in this case? Explain your answer.
2. Do you think Metpath's broker was negligent?
3. Do you think there would have been a different outcome if the insurance company, rather than Metpath, had supplied the policy?

Breach of Warranty: General Chicken Case

The General Chicken restaurant purchased business interruption insurance using Justin Case Company as insurance brokers. The brokers placed the business, as requested, with a property insurance company. The policy, when issued, contained an automatic sprinkler warranty requiring the insured to use due diligence in maintaining the sprinklers in working condition. When a fire loss occurred, the sprinkler system did not operate and the restaurant was a total loss. In the trial, it came out that the brokers apparently knew the sprinkler system had been shut off.

Questions

1. Do you think the insured breached a warranty? Was the warranty in question promissory or affirmative? Does this make a difference?
2. Did the broker's knowledge make a difference in your answer? Why or why not?
3. If the system were inoperable because of scheduled maintenance (which was not the case here), would you still allow the insurer to avoid payment?

CHAPTER 9

Basic Property and Liability Insurance Contracts

After studying this chapter, you should be able to:

- Explain why insurers often use standard forms in property insurance

- Identify five common elements of property insurance policies

- Explain several purposes of exclusions

- Identify eight common conditions found in property insurance policies

- Describe the insured's duties after a loss

Chapter 8, "Insurance Contracts," presented the principles of contract law and the characteristics that distinguish insurance contracts from other contracts. Now we turn our attention to the construction of actual insurance contracts. Our background reference in Chapters 9 through 12 is U.S. or English common law and U.S. insurance policies. My experience teaching in Austria, Germany, and France leads me to believe that much of this material has international relevance. That is, while Austria traces its legal background to Roman law and not to English common law, there are many similarities between Austrian and U.S. personal insurance policies. There are also many similarities between Austrian and American squirrels. The explanation of both these similarities lies in the fact that the problems to be solved are similar. That is, to climb oak trees and eat acorns, squirrels in Austria and the United States need claws and a bushy tail. Likewise, insurers in Austria and the United States must have contract language to create a binding agreement, to define important terms, to exclude uninsurable perils, and so forth. Without having ever seen a Japanese, Mexican, or Italian insurance policy, the author would guess that similarities exist between them and their U.S. counterparts as well, because the problems that insurance policies must solve are similar around the globe.

There has been considerable evolution from the early Lloyd's of London ocean marine contract to the most recent version of the Insurance Services Office (ISO) home-owners contract. Insurers have learned many expensive lessons about human nature (morale and moral hazards) and court interpretations of ambiguities. Think of the problems you would face if asked to write a property insurance contract from scratch, in light of all the court cases presented thus far in the text. Creating an unambiguous insurance contract that encompasses all the principles of insurance presented in Chapter 2, "Defining the Insurable Event," and achieving the aims of the insurer and insured is a challenging assignment. This chapter explains how insurers accomplish this ongoing task.

One purpose of this and the following two chapters is to make reading insurance policies more meaningful. Another purpose is to demonstrate technical English in action. A third purpose is to integrate the material many readers covered in a business

Declarations	Establish "named insured" Provides rating information
Insuring Agreements	Create binding agreement between insurer and insured Subagreements provide specific coverage
Deductibles	Cause insured to bear first dollars of covered losses Control insurance costs and morale hazard
Definitions	Establish meaning of important words found in the policy, thereby reducing room for ambiguity
Exclusions	Limit insurance coverage by specifically identifying perils, people, property, or time period not covered
Conditions	Specify the rights and duties of the insurer and insured under the contract
Endorsements and Riders	Amend contracts to create more coverage

FIGURE 9–1   Building Blocks of Insurance Policy

- Is the property covered?
- Is the person covered?
- Is the loss caused by a covered peril?
- Do any deductibles or exclusions apply to the loss?
- Do policy conditions limit the amount of coverage?
- Is the location of the loss covered?
- Did the loss occur during a covered time period?

FIGURE 9–2   Can I collect on my claim?

law course with the study of insurance. A fourth purpose is to help students think logically and constructively about problem solving. Writing a clearly understood and legally binding insurance policy presents many difficult problems.

Commercial and personal property insurance policies have the following common elements: declarations, insuring agreement(s), deductibles, definitions, exclusions, endorsements or riders, and conditions.

We define and explain each of these elements in this chapter. Figure 9–1 shows these basic building blocks graphically.

When reading an insurance policy, the insured likely is most concerned about collecting payment from the insurer. Unfortunately, he or she often does not read the policy for the first time until after a loss has occurred. To answer the question, "Can I collect on my claim?" the questions appearing in Figure 9–2 must be answered first.

I recommend using this checklist when answering the review questions at the end of Chapter 10 and Chapter 11 and in other situations in which the problem is to determine whether an insurer is obligated to pay a claim.

STANDARD POLICIES

Insurance rating organizations prepare standard versions of the most widely used property and liability insurance contracts. Most U.S. insurers use forms prepared by the ISO (*http://www.iso.com/*) or the American Association of Insurance Services (*http://www.aais.org/*).

Why were property insurance policies standardized? What advantages do consumers derive from standardized policies? The following is a partial list of reasons:

- Standardized policies are more economical for the insurer to print and use. These savings should be reflected in lower insurance rates.
- It is more economical to calculate one insurance rate for a standardized policy than many different rates for numerous insurance policies.
- The standardized policy has the large statistical base needed for rate-making accuracy. That is, because many insurers use the same policy format, their loss and claims expense data can be combined. Combining data would not be logical if each company covered different perils or had different conditions in their individual contracts.
- The meaning of standardized policies becomes widely known by attorneys, courts, insurers' employees, and by some consumers, resulting in less insurance litigation.
- If the standardized policy is a good one, it tends to remove less desirable policies from the market.
- Standardized packaged policies may reduce adverse selection if insureds must purchase a predetermined bundle of coverage and not just coverage for the exposure most likely to cause a loss.

One drawback of standardized policies is the possibility that some needs for insurance may go unmet. Because the standardized policy can be modified by endorsements, the needs of consumers with unusual loss exposures often can be satisfied. By endorsing standardized policies, only the consumers who require the particular coverage are charged for it. If an infrequently needed coverage were included in a standardized policy, all consumers, most of whom would not need the protection, would have to share the cost of coverage.

BASIC PARTS OF AN INSURANCE POLICY

Declarations

Declarations

The first element of a property and liability insurance contract usually is the declarations. The **declarations** present the important facts about the coverage provided and personalize the coverage to a particular insured. For example, they specify which house (located at 123 Main Street), which car (VIN 123456789), and which person (John James Audubon) are covered. The declarations also specify the insurer's limits of liability ($350,000 for the house, $1 million for liability), the annual premium, and payments due for shorter (quarterly, semiannual) periods. The declarations are prepared from information that the insured provided in the insurance application.

Insuring Agreement

Insuring agreement

The **insuring agreement** is the specific language creating the contract. In broad terms, it describes the insurer's and the insured's rights and duties. Often, subagreements are used to identify specific perils covered by the policy or to indicate coverage is provided on an open-perils basis. In the insuring agreement, the insurer states that it provides the insurance described in the policy and the insured agrees to comply with the conditions of the policy.

The main homeowners (HO) insuring agreement is the following:

HOMEOWNERS 2—BROAD FORM AGREEMENT

We will provide the insurance described in this policy in return for the premium and compliance with all applicable provisions of this policy.

The ISO personal auto policy (PAP) follows a slightly different pattern. The policy master agreement is followed by subagreements for any coverage the insured purchases. The master agreement reads as follows:

PERSONAL AUTO POLICY AGREEMENT

In return for payment of the premium and subject to all the terms of this policy, we agree with you as follows:

The subagreement for the liability coverage follows with:

PART A—LIABILITY COVERAGE INSURING AGREEMENT

A. We will pay damages for "bodily injury" or "property damage" for which any "insured" becomes legally responsible because of an auto accident. Damages include prejudgment interest awarded against the "insured." We will settle or defend, as we consider appropriate, any claim or suit asking for these damages. In addition to our limit of liability, we will pay all defense costs we incur. Our duty to settle or defend ends when our limit of liability for this coverage has been exhausted by payment of judgments or settlements. We have no duty to defend any suit or settle any claim for "bodily injury" or "property damage" not covered under this policy.

The subagreement for medical payments coverage reads as follows:

PART B—MEDICAL PAYMENTS COVERAGE INSURING AGREEMENT

A. We will pay reasonable expenses incurred for necessary medical and funeral services because of "bodily injury":

  1. Caused by accident; and

  2. Sustained by an "insured."

With the automobile policy, the insured may choose not to purchase all parts of the package. However, the only effective insuring agreements are those for which the declarations show that a premium was paid.

Deductibles

Deductible

Straight deductible

Percentage deductible

Property insurance policies require the insured to pay the first dollars of an insured loss. Insurers call this amount the **deductible**. Several variations of deductible provisions exist.

Policies using a **straight deductible** require the insurer to pay only for the amount of loss in excess of the deductible. For example, if there was a $100,000 loss and a $200 straight deductible, the insured would pay $200 and the insurer would pay the remaining $99,800.

After Hurricane Andrew in 1992, many insurers in Florida and other states began to use percentage deductibles. A **percentage deductible** requires the policyowner to pay the first percentage of a loss, for example, 2 percent, with the insurer paying the amount in excess of the deductible. For example, a 2 percent deductible on a $200,000 home destroyed by hurricane wind damage would require the insured to pay $4,000 ($.02 \times \$200,000$) and the insurer to pay $196,000 ($.98 \times \$200,000$). Insurance companies can combine the straight and percentage deductibles; for example, they can apply the percentage deductible to hurricane damage but the straight deductible to non-hurricane losses.

Some policies state that the deductible is taken from the loss. Other policies state that the deductible is taken from the claims payment. The difference in wording can produce a different claims payment. For example, an insured may lose $50,000 in property but have only $30,000 in insurance. If a $200 deductible is taken from the loss, the insured files a claim for $49,800, and receives a payment for $30,000, the policy limit. If the $200 reduces the claims payment, the insured receives $29,800.

Deductible provisions serve several purposes. First, they reduce the morale hazard because the insured must pay a small part of every loss. Most insureds presumably do not like to lose the deductible amount, say $500, so they also are not indifferent to insured losses. Second, deductibles eliminate the expenses involved in settling small claims. It is illogical for the insurer to incur $1,000 of expenses to settle a $500 claim. The savings from reduced expenses and payments for small losses are reflected in lower premiums. Therefore, the larger the deductible an insured chooses, the lower the insurance premium. Third, deductibles cause the policyowner to finance some of the loss. In the case of percentage deductibles, for example, the amount of a loss shifted to policyowners can be a significant financial contribution to overall loss costs.

Some insurers encourage insureds to use premium dollars more efficiently by choosing larger deductibles and using the savings to lower premiums or increase policy limits. In personal and commercial insurance purchases, it is wise to consider several combinations of deductible, premium, and policy limit before choosing one.

Definitions

Definitions

A definition of *war* never appeared in the insurance policy in the *Holiday Inns* v. *Aetna* case discussed in Chapter 8. The court defined the word. Perhaps if the definition had appeared in the policy, the litigation would have been avoided. Insurers often provide **definitions** of words they consider important or subject to misinterpretation. The definitions may appear as a glossary found at the beginning of the policy or elsewhere in the body of the contract.

Of the many definitions provided, none is more important than the definition of *insured*. Here are some important definitions from the homeowners (HO) policy:

DEFINITIONS

In this policy, "you" and "your" refer to the "named insured" shown in the Declarations and the spouse if a resident of the same household. "We," "us," and "our" refer to the Company providing this insurance. In addition, certain words and phrases are defined as follows:

1. "Bodily injury" means bodily harm, sickness, or disease, including required care, loss of services, and death that results.

2. "Business" means trade, profession, or occupation.

3. "Insured" means:
   a. You and residents of your household who are:
      (1) Your relatives; or
      (2) Other persons under the age 21 and in the care of any person named above.

The definition of *occupying* in the PAP is also interesting because the term has a broader meaning than "being in a car." The definitions section of the PAP states: " 'Occupying' means in, upon, getting in, on, out, or off." For example, if Mike Angelo, the artist, injures himself when painting the roof of his car, he may be able to claim he was occupying (*upon*) his vehicle. Or, if Shirley U. Jest, the comedian, injures her back while trying to adjust her child's car seat, she may be able to collect for medical expenses resulting from an injury sustained while *in* an auto.

Exclusions

Exclusions

Exclusions identify losses not covered. If an insurer denies a claim based on an exclusion and the insured then contests the denial, the insurer has the legal burden of proving that it applied the exclusion correctly.

Property insurance exclusions serve the following purposes:

- *To Eliminate Losses Arising from Catastrophic Events.* For example, insurers exclude damage from nuclear radiation.

- *To Eliminate Losses Associated with the Moral or Morale Hazard.* For example, the HO policy excludes theft committed by an insured.

- *To Eliminate Coverage Not Needed by the Typical Insured.* In these cases, insurers allow those insureds who need special coverage to pay an extra charge to remove the exclusion. For example, the HO policy excludes liability losses arising from business pursuits, but the policy can be endorsed to cover specified business pursuits (such as baby-sitting).

- *To Eliminate Coverage Where Another Policy Is Specifically Designed to Provide Coverage.* For example, the HO policy excludes coverage from liability claims arising from the ownership, maintenance, or use of most motor vehicles, most watercraft, and aircraft.

- *To Exclude Noninsured Parties from Benefiting from Coverage.* For example, the HO policy excludes coverage from benefiting bailees. A **bailment** implies possession of property by a party other than the owner, with the intent of returning the property to the owner. Examples of bailments include property left with dry cleaners or stored in warehouses. The party owning the property is the **bailor**. The party in temporary possession of the property is the **bailee**. The intent

Bailment

Bailor

Bailee

of this exclusion is to cause the bailee to bear the cost of loss to the goods in its care (for example, the homeowner's fur coat).

- *To Control Costs and Keep Premiums Affordable.* This category of exclusions explains why wear-and-tear "losses" are not covered.

Endorsements

Endorsements modify standard insurance contracts. They can add coverage directly or they can add coverage by deleting an exclusion in the standard policy. Sometimes an endorsement can eliminate coverage (for a reduction in premium) or exclude an insured (for example, a teenage driver). Thus, endorsements can be used to achieve a variety of coverage goals.

CONDITIONS

Conditions

165 lines

1943 New York Standard Fire Insurance Policy (SFP)

Insurance policies contain many important **conditions**. The conditions provide a framework for the insurance policy, explaining many of the important relationships, rights, and duties of the insurer and insured. The **165 lines** of the **1943 New York Standard Fire Insurance Policy (SFP)** contain most of the conditions frequently found in current policy forms. Figure 9–3 presents the traditional 165 lines.

The SFP served as the mandatory foundation of all property insurance forms for about three decades. Since 1976, the ISO has replaced the traditional wording with more modern, simplified English. Because much of the court-interpreted meaning of the modern forms results from litigation arising from the 165 lines, we refer to the traditional wording for illustrations.

Fraud

The first six lines of the 165 lines explain the results of fraud committed by an insured. The following case illustrates the results of insurance fraud.

Facts: Liam insured his house with the ABC Insurance Company. The policy was for $5,000 coverage on the house and $3,000 on the contents. After a fire destroyed the house, Liam filed a sworn proof of loss that included a claim for a number of nonexistent items. Later, Liam dropped the claim for the contents, but the claim for the dwelling continued. The court denied Liam any recovery. The court stated its reasons for denying Liam recovery for either the contents or the house as follows:

> We conclude that the provisions of the insurance policy as to concealment and fraud are applicable here and that a sworn proof of loss which includes numerous nonexistent items voids the entire policy as a matter of law.[1]

The provisions of the current homeowners contract are typical of modern language fraud provisions: [Section 1—Conditions . . . (Q.)]

---

[1] Ky. C.A. W-58-71, June 20, 1975.

1 **Concealment,** This entire policy shall be void if, whether
2 **fraud.** before or after a loss, the insured has wil-
3 fully concealed or misrepresented any ma-
4 terial fact or circumstance concerning this insurance or the
5 subject thereof, or the interest of the insured therein, or in case
6 of any fraud or false swearing by the insured relating thereto.
7 **Uninsurable** This policy shall not cover accounts, bills,
8 **and** currency, deeds, evidences of debt, money or
9 **excepted property.** securities; nor, unless specifically named
10 hereon in writing, bullion or manuscripts.
11 **Perils not** This Company shall not be liable for loss by
12 **included.** fire or other perils insured against in this
13 policy caused, directly or indirectly, by: (a)
14 enemy attack by armed forces, including action taken by mili-
15 tary, naval or air forces in resisting an actual or an immediately
16 impending enemy attack; (b) invasion; (c) insurrection; (d)
17 rebellion; (e) revolution; (f) civil war; (g) usurped power; (h)
18 order of any civil authority except acts of destruction at the time
19 of and for the purpose of preventing the spread of fire, provided
20 that such fire did not originate from any of the perils excluded
21 by this policy; (i) neglect of the insured to use all reasonable
22 means to save and preserve the property at and after a loss, or
23 when the property is endangered by fire in neighboring prem-
24 ises; (j) nor shall this Company be liable for loss by theft.
25 **Other Insurance.** Other insurance may be prohibited or the
26 amount of insurance may be limited by en-
27 dorsement attached hereto.
28 **Conditions suspending or restricting insurance. Unless other-**
29 **wise provided in writing added hereto this Company shall not**
30 **be liable for loss occurring**
31 (a) while the hazard is increased by any means within the con-
32 trol or knowledge of the insured; or
33 (b) while a described building, whether intended for occupancy
34 by owner or tenant, is vacant or unoccupied beyond a period of
35 sixty consecutive days; or
36 (c) as a result of explosion or riot, unless fire ensue, and in
37 that event for loss by fire only.
38 **Other perils** Any other peril to be insured against or sub-
39 **or subjects.** ject of insurance to be covered in this policy
40 shall be by endorsement in writing hereon or
41 added hereto.
42 **Added provisions.** The extent of the application of insurance
43 under this policy and of the contribution to
44 be made by this Company in case of loss, and any other pro-
45 vision or agreement not inconsistent with the provisions of this
46 policy, may be provided for in writing added hereto, but no pro-
47 vision may be waived except such as by the terms of this policy
48 is subject to change.
49 **Waiver** No permission affecting this insurance shall
50 **provisions.** exist, or waiver of any provision be valid,
51 unless granted herein or expressed in writing
52 added hereto. No provision, stipulation or forfeiture shall be
53 held to be waived by any requirement or proceeding on the part
54 of this Company relating to appraisal or to any examination
55 provided for herein.
56 **Cancellation** This policy shall be cancelled at any time
57 **of policy.** at the request of the insured, in which case
58 this Company shall, upon demand and sur-
59 render of this policy, refund the excess of paid premium above
60 the customary short rates for the expired time. This pol-
61 icy may be cancelled at any time by this Company by giving
62 to the insured a five days' written notice of cancellation with
63 or without tender of the excess of paid premium above the pro
64 rata premium for the expired time, which excess, if not ten-
65 dered, shall be refunded on demand. Notice of cancellation shall
66 state that said excess premium (if not tendered) will be re-
67 funded on demand.
68 **Mortgage** If loss hereunder is made payable, in whole
69 **interests and** or in part, to a designated mortgagee not
70 **obligations.** named herein as the insured, such interest in
71 this policy may be cancelled by giving to such
72 mortgagee a ten days' written notice of can-
73 cellation.
74 If the insured fails to render proof of loss such mortgagee, upon
75 notice, shall render proof of loss in the form herein specified
76 within sixty (60) days thereafter and shall be subject to the pro-
77 visions hereof relating to appraisal and time of payment and of
78 bringing suit. If this Company shall claim that no liability ex-
79 isted as to the mortgagor or owner, it shall, to the extent of pay-
80 ment of loss to the mortgagee, be subrogated to all the mort-
81 gagee's rights of recovery, but without impairing mortgagee's
82 right to sue; or it may pay off the mortgage debt and require
83 an assignment thereof and of the mortgage. Other provisions

84 relating to the interests and obligations of such mortgagee may
85 be added hereto by agreement in writing.
86 **Pro rata liability.** This Company shall not be liable for a greater
87 proportion of any loss than the amount
88 hereby insured shall bear to the whole insurance covering the
89 property against the peril involved, whether collectible or not.
90 **Requirements in** The insured shall give immediate written
91 **case loss occurs.** notice to this Company of any loss, protect
92 the property from further damage, forthwith
93 separate the damaged and undamaged personal property, put
94 it in the best possible order, furnish a complete inventory of
95 the destroyed, damaged and undamaged property, showing in
96 detail quantities, costs, actual cash value and amount of loss
97 claimed; **and within sixty days after the loss, unless such time**
98 **is extended in writing by this Company, the insured shall render**
99 **to this Company a proof of loss,** signed and sworn to by the
100 insured, stating the knowledge and belief of the insured as to
101 the following: the time and origin of the loss, the interest of the
102 insured and of all others in the property, the actual cash value of
103 each item thereof and the amount of loss thereto, all encum-
104 brances thereon, all other contracts of insurance, whether valid
105 or not, covering any of said property, any changes in the title,
106 use, occupation, location, possession or exposures of said prop-
107 erty since the issuing of this policy, by whom and for what
108 purpose any building herein described and the several parts
109 thereof were occupied at the time of loss and whether or not it
110 then stood on leased ground, and shall furnish a copy of all the
111 descriptions and schedules in all policies and, if required, verified
112 plans and specifications of any building, fixtures or machinery
113 destroyed or damaged. The insured, as often as may be reason-
114 ably required, shall exhibit to any person designated by this
115 Company all that remains of any property herein described, and
116 submit to examinations under oath by any person named by this
117 Company, and subscribe the same; and, as often as may be
118 reasonably required, shall produce for examination all books of
119 account, bills, invoices and other vouchers, or certified copies
120 thereof if originals be lost, at such reasonable time and place as
121 may be designated by this Company or its representative, and
122 shall permit extracts and copies thereof to be made.
123 **Appraisal.** In case the insured and this Company shall
124 fail to agree as to the actual cash value or
125 the amount of loss, then, on the written demand of either, each
126 shall select a competent and disinterested appraiser and notify
127 the other of the appraiser selected within twenty days of such
128 demand. The appraisers shall first select a competent and dis-
129 interested umpire; and failing for fifteen days to agree upon
130 such umpire, then, on request of the insured or this Company,
131 such umpire shall be selected by a judge of a court of record in
132 the state in which the property covered is located. The ap-
133 praisers shall then appraise the loss, stating separately actual
134 cash value and loss to each item; and, failing to agree, shall
135 submit their differences, only, to the umpire. An award in writ-
136 ing, so itemized, of any two when filed with this Company shall
137 determine the amount of actual cash value and loss. Each
138 appraiser shall be paid by the party selecting him and the ex-
139 penses of appraisal and umpire shall be paid by the parties
140 equally.
141 **Company's** It shall be optional with this Company to
142 **options.** take all, or any part, of the property at the
143 agreed or appraised value, and also to re-
144 pair, rebuild or replace the property destroyed or damaged with
145 other of like kind and quality within a reasonable time, on giv-
146 ing notice of its intention so to do within thirty days after the
147 receipt of the proof of loss herein required.
148 **Abandonment.** There can be no abandonment to this Com-
149 pany of any property.
150 **When loss** The amount of loss for which this Company
151 **payable.** may be liable shall be payable sixty days
152 after proof of loss, as herein provided, is
153 received by this Company and ascertainment of the loss is made
154 either by agreement between the insured and this Company ex-
155 pressed in writing or by the filing with this Company of an
156 award as herein provided.
157 **Suit.** No suit or action on this policy for the recov-
158 ery of any claim shall be sustainable in any
159 court of law or equity unless all the requirements of this policy
160 shall have been complied with, and unless commenced within
161 twelve months next after inception of the loss.
162 **Subrogation.** This Company may require from the insured
163 an assignment of all right of recovery against
164 any party for loss to the extent that payment therefor is made
165 by this Company.

In Witness Whereof, this Company has executed and attested these presents; but this policy shall not be valid unless countersigned by the duly authorized Agent of this Company at the agency hereinbefore mentioned.

FIGURE 9–3   165 Lines of the Standard Fire Insurance Policy

> We provide coverage to no "insureds" under this policy if, whether before or after a loss, an "insured" has:
>
> a. Intentionally concealed or misrepresented any material fact or circumstances;
> b. Engaged in fraudulent conduct; or
> c. Made false statements; relating to this insurance.

Suspension of Coverage

Some insurance policies specify circumstances that suspend coverage. Often the word *while* precedes these conditions, implying that while the specified condition is present, coverage is suspended, but if the condition ends, coverage is reinstated. Conditions suspending coverage in the 165 lines include:

Vacant

Unoccupied

- Increase in hazard within the knowledge of the insured.
- Vacant or unoccupied for more than sixty consecutive days. (**Vacant** means that both the insureds and their possessions are absent from the house. **Unoccupied** means the people have left, but their possessions remain.)

Increase in hazard

The following case illustrates the **increase in hazard** provision. The Saggy Company purchased a fire insurance policy on its warehouse. In fact, the building was not being used as a warehouse but as a mattress factory. It contained flammable material such as cotton and cotton dust. When the "warehouse" burned, the insurer denied the claim because the hazard was increased within the control or knowledge of the insured. The court ruled in favor of the insurer, finding the increase of hazard was "substantial" when the warehouse was used for making mattresses.

If a case is litigated, a court must decide whether the hazard was increased "substantially." In this case, a court ruled that the increase was substantial. In other cases, the opposite conclusion may be reached. The issue of substantiality is a question of fact. Likewise, if questions of fact arise about whether a building was vacant or unoccupied, this issue also will have to be litigated.

Cancellation

Short-rate cancellation schedule

The insured may cancel the HO contract at any time and receive a refund for any unearned portion of the premium. When insureds cancel their policy, the **short-rate cancellation schedule** allows the insurer to recover the expenses of issuing the policy if this extra reduction is allowed by state law.

Pro rata cancellation

Insurers also may cancel property insurance policies while they are in force or decline to renew them at the end of the policy period. The contract explains the insurer's rights of cancellation in detail. For reasons of social policy, many states restrict insurers' rights to cancel personal insurance policies. Many commercial policies may be canceled at any time, but insureds must be given notice to allow time to find new coverage. If the insurer rather than the insured cancels the policy, the refund will be larger because the insurer bears the costs of issuing the policy. When the insurer cancels the policy, the refund is *pro rata*, or proportional to the number of days the policy was in force. That is, with a **pro rata cancellation**, if a policy was in force 60 days out of the 360-day business year, the insured would be entitled to a 5/6 [(360 − 60) / 360 = 83 percent] refund. If the insured were to cancel, the short-rate calculation would be used, resulting in a 73 percent refund. Refunding a lesser amount than the pro-rata result enables the insurer to recover some costs of issuing the policy and the cancellation.

Not all insurance policies may be canceled by the insurer. After a limited period of one to two years, life insurance policies cannot be canceled. The same rule applies to many health insurance policy forms. Some insurers, in both instances, may want to cancel the policy if the insured's health deteriorates, but society and socially responsible insurers would be worse off if such cancellations were allowed.

Other Insurance

Other-insurance clause

In some cases, insureds may have more than one insurance policy on the same property. If more than one policy is in force, the **other-insurance clause** applies. The following HO policy clause states:

> Other Insurance. If a loss covered by this policy is also covered by other insurance we will pay only the proportion of the loss that the limit of liability that applies under this policy bears to the total amount of insurance covering the loss.

For example, assume that Bertha Dablues, a well-known nightclub singer, has a $150,000 home and two $150,000 insurance policies. Assume that she has two policies because she made an honest mistake about the expiration date of her first policy and purchased a second policy with a different insurer. She has a total of $300,000 in insurance, so each insurer will pay only ($150,000 / $300,000 = 1/2) one-half of a loss if her house is destroyed in a fire. This scenario presents an example of a pro rata other-insurance clause. Other-insurance clauses prevent an insured from profiting from buying several insurance contracts either deliberately or by mistake. They enforce the principle of indemnity by keeping insureds from profiting from losses.

Duties After Loss or Occurrence

The insured's duties after a loss (the term *occurrence* has been substituted for the term *loss* in the liability section of the homeowners policy) are usually extensive. Prompt notice of loss must be given. In the event of a theft, the insured must notify the police. Inventories must be completed. The HO-2 policy requirements are typical (Section II—Conditions):

> ## C. DUTIES AFTER "OCCURRENCE"
>
> In case of an "occurrence," you or another "insured" will perform the following duties that apply. We have no duty to provide coverage under this policy if your failure to comply with the following duties is prejudicial to us. You will help us by seeing that these duties are performed.
>
> 1. Give written notice to us or our agent as soon as is practical, which sets forth:
>   a. The identity of the policy and the "named insured" shown in the Declarations;
>   b. Reasonably available information on the time, place and circumstances of the "occurrence"; and
>   c. Names and addresses of any claimants and witnesses;
> 2. Cooperate with us in the investigation, settlement or defense of any claim or suit;

3. Promptly forward to us every notice, demand, summons or other process relating to the "occurrence";
4. At our request, help us:
   a. To make settlement;
   b. To enforce any right of contribution or indemnity against any person or organization who may be liable to an "insured";
   c. With the conduct of suits and attend hearings and trials; and
   d. To secure and give evidence and obtain the attendance of witnesses;

Immediate notice

The question of what constitutes "prompt," "as soon as practicable," or "immediate" notice is one of fact. The insured must act reasonably. Waiting two weeks to report a fire loss probably would not be considered "immediate" by a jury; but calling the insurance agent right after calling the fire department probably would not be necessary. The purpose for the **immediate notice** provision is to allow the insurer to investigate the claim promptly. If the insurer can investigate promptly, as is the insurer's right under the policy, the insured has fulfilled the requirement of the contract.

In practice, problems arise regarding the immediate notice provision. For example, in some environmental impairment cases, insureds who originally thought they had minor problems failed to report them immediately to their insurers. Subsequently, when these problems proved to be very substantial, the insureds reported them, but the insurers then denied the claims based on the late notice. Courts have been divided on the question of whether the insurer should have to prove that the insured's delay in reporting claims caused damages, but the majority have held that insurers need only prove lack of immediate notice before allowing them to avoid the entire contract.

All duties required of the insured after a loss must be performed, or the insurer may void the entire policy. In other cases when an insured fails to perform as required by the policy, the insurer may withhold payment for part of the loss. Because the policy requires that undamaged property must be protected, if a fire on the roof exposes furniture to damage from the weather, the furniture should be removed to a warehouse. If property is not protected and suffers damage because of the lack of care, the insurer need not pay for the subsequent damage. Requiring protection of undamaged property reduces the morale hazard.

Insurers have a right to a complete inventory, signed and sworn to by the insured. We have already presented the effect of falsely reporting the loss: allowing the insurer to void the entire contract.

The insurer has a right to the cooperation of the insured after a loss has taken place. This cooperation may take more than one form, and any substantial concealment or misrepresentation at this stage allows the insurer to void the contract.

Consider the outcome of the following case involving the cooperation clause. The insured's property burned, and she filed a claim with her insurer. During an examination under oath, the insured's attorney objected to some of the insurer's questions. The attorney refused to allow his client (the insured) to answer any further questions. The insurer's lawyer, who was conducting the investigation, informed the insured and her attorney before they left the conference that the refusal to answer the questions could result in the insured's loss of contract rights.

The court granted summary judgment for the insurance company. The reasoning was explicit:

> We find that the defendant's motion for summary judgment should (be) granted unconditionally. The plaintiff's obligation of cooperation was not met by her extremely limited testimony at the examination nor was there any indication that she would cooperate as required in the near future. . . . The plaintiff's willful refusal to answer material and relevant questions constituted a material breach of substantial conditions of the insurance policy.[2]

Appraisal

Appraisal procedure

Unsettled disagreements about the value of property losses are handled by an **appraisal procedure**. The procedure requires each party to select its own "competent and disinterested" appraiser. The two appraisers in turn select an umpire. The umpire only considers items on which the appraisers cannot agree. The purpose of this procedure is to avoid litigation when only the amount of damage is at issue. Note the following description of the appraisal procedure:

> Appraisal. If you and we fail to agree on the amount of loss, either may demand an appraisal of the loss. In this event, each party will choose a competent appraiser within 20 days after receiving a written request from the other. The two appraisers will choose an umpire. If they cannot agree upon an umpire within 15 days, you or we may request that the choice be made by a judge of a court of record in the state where the "residence premises" is located. The appraisers will separately set the amount of loss. If the appraisers submit a written report of an agreement to us, the amount agreed upon will be the amount of loss. If they fail to agree, they will submit their differences to the umpire. A decision agreed to by any two will set the amount of loss.
>   Each party will:
>
> 1. Pay its own appraiser; and
> 2. Bear the other expenses of the appraisal and umpire equally.

The contract makes the appraisal procedure binding on both parties, and courts have enforced this procedure, as the following case illustrates. A hailstorm damaged the insured's roof. The insurance company estimated that the roof sustained $528 in damage. The insured claimed $5,000 in damage. Because the parties were unable to agree, the insurer invoked the appraisal provision. The insured refused to participate in the appraisal process as called for in the contract. Instead, the insured sued the insurer for breach of contract. The trial court jury found for the insurer, upholding the contractual language. The appellate court sustained the trial court's verdict.[3]

---

[2] *Pizzirusso* v. *Allstate Insurance Company*, reported in *1989 CCH Insurance Law Reports—Fire and Casualty*, pp. 2739–40.
[3] *Pyles* v. *United Services Automobile Association* (Texas Court of Appeals), *1991 CCH Fire Cases*, p. 8553.

Salvage

> *Recovered Property.* If you or we recover any property for which we have made payment under this policy, you or we will notify the other of the recovery. At your option the property will be returned to or retained by you or it will become our property. If the recovered property is returned to or retained by you, the loss payment will be adjusted based on the amount you received for the recovered property.

The HO contract gives the insurer the option of taking the insured's damaged property once the company pays the insured's claim. The insured, however, has the option of keeping the damaged property and accepting a smaller insurance settlement. Moreover, the insured cannot abandon property on the front lawn of the insurance company. Once it pays a claim for a total loss, the option to take the property belongs to the insurer. The insured does not have the option to force the insurer to take it.

Claims Payment

The loss payment provision establishes the insured's legal right to a claim payment in a relatively short time after the loss has been adjusted, as described below:

> *Loss Payment.* We will adjust all losses with you. We will pay you unless some other person is named in the policy or is legally entitled to receive payment. Loss will be payable sixty days after we receive your proof of loss and:
>
> 1. Reach an agreement with you;
> 2. There is an entry of a final judgment; or
> 3. There is a filing of an appraisal award with us.

Property insurance policies must state a period within which the insurer should pay claims. The period must be long enough for the insurer to investigate and process the claim payment, but it should not be so long as to frustrate the rights of the insured. The HO policy allows the insurer sixty days to pay claims after receipt of proof of loss and the insured agrees to the settlement offer. If the claim is denied, the insured has twelve months from the date of the loss to sue the insurer.

SUMMARY

Property and liability insurance policies generally have the following seven common elements:

1. *Declarations*: Personalize the contract and contain information used to determine the insurance premium
2. *Insuring Agreement(s)*: Make(s) the contractual promises
3. *Deductibles*: Cause the insured to pay the first dollars of a loss
4. *Definitions*: Make the meaning of important terms clearer
5. *Exclusions*: Eliminate the insurers' liability from undesired perils or hazards
6. *Endorsements*: Allow the coverage to be tailored to individual situations
7. *Conditions*: Provide the framework for implementing contractual agreements

The typical insurance policy conditions explained in this chapter were the following:

- Concealment and fraud
- Excluded losses
- Increase in hazard

- Vacancy or unoccupancy
- Cancellation rights
- Other insurance provisions
- Insured's duties after a loss
- Appraisal procedure

REVIEW TERMS

- 165 lines
- 1943 New York Standard Fire Insurance Policy (SFP)
- Appraisal procedure
- Bailee
- Bailment
- Bailor

- Conditions
- Declarations
- Deductible
- Definitions
- Exclusions
- Immediate notice
- Increase in hazard

- Insuring agreement
- Other-insurance clause
- Pro rata cancellation
- Short-rate cancellation schedule
- Straight deductible
- Unoccupied
- Vacant

REVIEW

1. What are the advantages of standardized property insurance contracts? What are the disadvantages?
2. What information is found in the declarations?
3. Explain the purpose of the insuring agreement.
4. What purposes do deductible provisions serve for insurers?
5. List several reasons why insurance contracts contain exclusions.
6. Identify two conditions that suspend a fire insurance policy. What reasons explain the suspension of coverage in each case?
7. Why are the insurer's rights to cancel a fire insurance policy different from the insured's rights to cancel the policy?
8. Explain the purpose of the immediate-notice provision.
9. Explain the purpose of an other-insurance clause. How does it relate to the principle of indemnity?
10. List some of the duties of the insured after a loss occurs. What can happen if the insured fails to perform these duties?
11. When is the appraisal procedure used?

OBJECTIVE QUESTIONS

1. Deductibles:
   a. Cause the insured to pay the first dollars of a loss
   b. Cause the insurance company to pay the first dollars of a loss
   c. Cause the loss to be deducted from the policy face
   d. Cause the policy face limit to be deducted from the loss
2. If an insured cancels her insurance policy:
   a. The short-rate cancellation table is used to calculate the refund.
   b. The Greenwich mean cancellation table is used to calculate the refund.
   c. The pro rata cancellation calculation is used to calculate the refund.
   d. The mensa table is used to calculate the refund.
3. The insurer agrees to make loss payments under the HO policy:
   a. Generally, within sixty days of a claim being filed by an insured
   b. As soon as practicable
   c. Before the policy expires
   d. Within sixty days of a claim being filed if an agreement is reached with the insured
4. The purpose of the declarations section of an insurance policy is to:
   a. Declare the insurance company's intention to provide coverage
   b. Declare the insured's intention to purchase insurance
   c. State the important facts about the coverage provided and personalize the coverage to a particular insured
   d. Declare the policy to be canceled by mutual agreement
5. The clause that creates a binding agreement between the insurer and insured is called the:
   a. Binding clause
   b. Mutual agreement
   c. Ratification clause
   d. Insuring agreement

6. Assume that the insured has a $10,000 loss and a $250 straight deductible taken from the loss. The insured has $8,000 of insurance. How much will the insurer pay for this loss?
   a. $10,000
   b. $8,000
   c. $9,750
   d. $7,750

7. If an insured files a fraudulent claim after a loss occurs, the most likely result will be:
   a. The insured will go to jail.
   b. The insurer will not pay the claim after the fraud is discovered.

c. The insurer will pay the claim but try to recover the insurance proceeds by way of subrogation against the insured.
d. The insured will collect, but only for half the amount claimed, with half the loss being considered a "fraud" penalty.

8. To settle disagreements over the amount of property losses, the _____ procedure is used:
   a. Appraisal
   b. Settlement/pro rata
   c. Disagreement
   d. Salvage

INTERNET RESEARCH ASSIGNMENTS

1. Follow this link, (*http://www.iso.com/links/*), to a second link, (*http://www.insurancejournal.com/*), and describe an insurance-related story from your geographic area.

2. Follow this link, (*http://www.aais.org/*), and summarize a report or an article on personal lines insurance.

VACANCY CLAUSE

The Roberts family owned a house in Alabama. It was insured with a fire insurance policy issued by the Sparkler Mutual Insurance Company. On April 1, the Roberts moved to Tennessee. Their son, Bob, remained in the Alabama home for an additional month. Thereafter, the home was rented to a tenant who lived in the home for the month of May. Mr. Roberts returned to the home irregularly, remaining overnight on July 4 and on a few other occasions. A few pieces of furniture remained in the home until August. On or about August 4, the home and its contents were destroyed by fire.

1. Do you think that Sparkler Mutual should pay for the loss? Explain your reasons.
2. What does the word *occupancy* mean? (You may want to refer to a law dictionary.)
3. Did the family's absence affect the chance of loss in this case?

CHAPTER 10

Homeowners Insurance (HO)

After studying this chapter, you should be able to:

■ Describe the basic coverages provided by the HO insurance forms

■ Explain the meanings of words defined in the HO definitions section

■ Identify the 16 specific property perils covered by the HO-2 contract

■ Identify the categories of covered persons under the liability section of the HO

■ Identify the main property and liability exclusions found in the HO insurance policies

■ Describe the effect of underinsurance on HO loss settlements

People purchase homeowners insurance (HO) to protect some of their most important assets: their home and its contents, assets they almost certainly could not afford to lose. Moreover, when people borrow money to purchase their home, lenders require insurance to protect their financial interest in the property. Thus, HO is an essential purchase for most of us.

The Insurance Services Office (ISO) (*http://www.iso.com/*) HO policy combines property insurance, comprehensive personal liability insurance, additional living expense coverage, replacement-cost coverage, and medical-expense-coverage-for-others in one convenient package. We use the HO-2 as sample material in this chapter. Appendix A, "Homeowners Insurance Policies HO-2 and HO-3," at the end of the book, reproduces the complete policy.

The ISO has revised the HO policy many times. Policy revisions accomplish several purposes. In some instances, court decisions were inconsistent with the drafter's intent and the ISO modified the wording to achieve the insurer's aims. In other instances, societal changes required adding contract language, including the exclusion that eliminates coverage for liability arising from the use of controlled substances.

While we use the ISO forms for sample material in this book, other rating agencies use different forms with different provisions. Also, some insurance companies use their own forms. Our purpose definitely is not to promote memorizing one rating agency's policy forms. Rather, the educational purposes of presenting this material include:

• Explaining one widely used method of providing an important element of economic security to U.S. society.

• Demonstrating the drafter's precise use of English to form a complex contract.[1]

---

[1] My point regarding English is too narrow; I could have used the term *language* to make my meaning universal. One of my more enjoyable teaching experiences occurred in a class at the Wirtschaftsuniversität in Vienna, where the students and I compared U.S. HO contracts to their Austrian counterparts. Many of the insurance policy construction problems each society had to solve were similar, even if the language was not. However, this chapter obviously deals with the use of English in such contracts, which is why I continue to use the term *English* here.

- Illustrating the impact of court interpretations on contract language.
- Illustrating the application of contract provisions commonly found in many U.S. insurance policies in addition to the HO.
- Explaining a critical risk management function. For risk managers to fulfill their responsibilities competently, they must be able to interpret insurance contract language.
- Illustrating some of the principles of insurance discussed in Chapter 2, "Defining the Insurable Event," by showing how they are incorporated in an actual insurance policy.

Students have told me that learning the meaning of the HO is a desirable and important result of examining the HO because they expect to purchase this insurance at some point in their lives. This chapter does not provide exhaustive coverage of the HO because that is not necessary to achieve the educational goals just listed. We cover only the main features of the policy.

The ISO HO program uses the following six forms:

1. HO-1: Basic[2]
2. HO-2: Broad
3. HO-3: Special
4. HO-4: Contents Broad (coverage for renters)
5. HO-6: Unit Owners (condominium-type coverage)
6. HO-8: Modified

ISO forms HO-1, HO-2, HO-3, and HO-8 are used to insure an owner's interest in a home and its contents and provide personal liability coverage. The scope of the coverage is broader in HO-3 than in HO-2, which in turn provides more coverage than HO-1. Because of its narrow scope, insurers no longer sell the HO-1 form very often. The HO-8 form covers houses having a replacement cost greater than market value. This result is most likely to occur in older homes that have plaster walls and hardwood floors. Such homes usually are found in older neighborhoods. If these homes were destroyed, they could be replaced more economically using modern construction techniques (such as drywall and plywood) without loss in usefulness. HO-8 provides for functional replacement rather than replacement with material of "like kind."

Personal property

The HO-4 form covers the contents and personal liability of renters. Apartment renters need coverage for their **personal property** and need the liability coverage provided by the HO-4 form. The HO-6 form covers the property interest, contents, and personal liability of people owning a unit in a condominium or a cooperative building. The HO forms cannot be used to cover mobile homes or house trailers. The ISO makes available other, more limited forms for this property.

POLICY LAYOUT

Figure 10–1 shows an outline of the HO-2 policy used as sample material throughout this chapter.

Declarations

The HO's front page displays descriptive material insurers call the *declarations* (Figure 10–2). The information provided in the insurance application allows the insurer

---

[2] The ISO currently designates these forms HO 00 01, HO 00 02, and so forth.

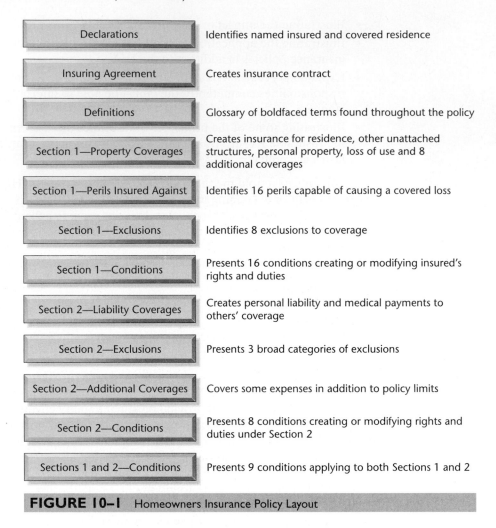

Declarations	Identifies named insured and covered residence
Insuring Agreement	Creates insurance contract
Definitions	Glossary of boldfaced terms found throughout the policy
Section 1—Property Coverages	Creates insurance for residence, other unattached structures, personal property, loss of use and 8 additional coverages
Section 1—Perils Insured Against	Identifies 16 perils capable of causing a covered loss
Section 1—Exclusions	Identifies 8 exclusions to coverage
Section 1—Conditions	Presents 16 conditions creating or modifying insured's rights and duties
Section 2—Liability Coverages	Creates personal liability and medical payments to others' coverage
Section 2—Exclusions	Presents 3 broad categories of exclusions
Section 2—Additional Coverages	Covers some expenses in addition to policy limits
Section 2—Conditions	Presents 8 conditions creating or modifying rights and duties under Section 2
Sections 1 and 2—Conditions	Presents 9 conditions applying to both Sections 1 and 2

FIGURE 10–1   Homeowners Insurance Policy Layout

to complete the blanks shown in Figure 10–2. The declarations contain the rating information that the insurer uses to calculate the premium, including the following:

- The name and address of the (named) insured
- The time when the policy begins and ends
- The maximum limits of the insurance company's liability for the different coverages
- Any applicable deductible provisions

The insurer's limit of liability is divided into two sections. Section 1 provides property insurance protection and is divided into four coverages (or insuring agreements), each with a separate limit of liability. Section 2 provides liability coverage and is divided into two coverages.

Divided coverage   The HO package is **divided coverage**. Each coverage (A through F) is treated separately. Dollars may not be transferred among the various coverages. The maximum amount the insured could collect is the sum of all the coverages. That is, if a property loss is total, an insured theoretically could collect the total amount of Section 1, Coverages A through D. If a liability loss occurred in addition to a property loss, the

NAME OF COMPANY

**HOMEOWNERS POLICY
DECLARATIONS**

RENEWAL OF NUMBER

No. H
Named Insured and Mailing Address (No., Street, Apt., Town or City, County, State, Zip Code)

Policy Period: Years   From: To: 12:01 A.M. Standard Time at the **residence premises.**

The **residence premises** covered by this policy is located at the above address unless otherwise stated: (No., Street, Apt., Town or City, County, State, Zip Code)

Coverage is provided where a premium or limit of liability is shown for the coverage.

Coverages and Limit of Liability	Section I Coverages				Section II Coverages	
	A. Dwelling	B. Other Structures	C. Personal Property	D. Loss of Use	E. Personal Liability Each occurrence	F. Medical Payments to Others Each person
	$	$	$	$	$	$

Premium	Basic Policy Premium	Additional Premiums			Total Prepaid Premium	Premium if paid in installments	Payable: At each At subsequent Inception (and) anniversary
	$	$	$	$	$	$	$ $

Premium for Scheduled Personal Property $ $ $ $

Form and Endorsements made part of this Policy at time of issue: Combined Premium $ $ $ $
Insert Number(s) and Edition Date(s)   Form HO-   Endorsement(s) HO-

DEDUCT-IBLE	SECTION I	OTHER	In case of a loss under Section I, we cover only that part of the loss over the deductible stated.
	$	$	

Section II   Other **insured locations:** (No., Street, Apt., Town or City, County, State, Zip Code)

Special State Provisions	South Carolina: Valuation Clause (Cov. A) $	Minnesota: Insurable Value (Cov. A) $	New York: Coinsurance Clause Applies ☐ Yes ☐ No

Mortgagee (Name and address)

Countersigned:

By_____   Authorized Representative

RATING INFORMATION								

NUMBER OF FAMILIES: Not Town/rowhouse—Number of Families 1 2 3 4 | Town/rowhouse—Family units in Fire Div. 3-4 5-8 9over | HO-4 HO-6 Self-Rating Code No Yes | HO-4 and HO-6 Not rented to others | If YES Number of Families— 1-4 5-10 11-40 over40 | HO-6 Rented to others 1-4 5-10 11-40 over40 | If NO Number of Families | Annual Fire E.C. Rate | Year of Constr. Year Code

Code (1) (3) (6) (8)   (2) (4) (9)   (9)   (1) (2)   (3) (4)   (5) (6) (7) (8)

CONSTRUCTION: Frame (1) | Brick, Stone or Masonry (2) | Brick, Stone or (3) Veneer | Approved Masonry Roof | Frame with Aluminum or (5) Plastic Siding | Fire (4) Resistive | Mobile Homes enclosed (6) Foundation | Mobile Homes Not enclosed (7) Foundation | Modular Homes rated (9) as Frame | Specifically Rated—Not (8) Fire Resistive | Unapproved Roof

PROTECTION: Code | Not more than   feet from hydrant | Not more than   miles from Fire Dept. | Southern: Inside City limits | Inside Protected Suburb | Inside Fire District | Fire District or Town (   )

ZONE Code | PREMIUM GR. NO. | DEDUCTIBLE: Type Code   Size Code   Section I $ Other $

STATISTICAL REPORTING INFORMATION Codes: No. Type Classif. Cov. E Cov. F | Premium: Prepaid; | If paid in Installments; | Payable at: Inception | Each Anniversary

Snowmobiles $ $ $ $
Watercraft   (2) $ $ $ $
Outboard Motor   (1) $ $ $ $
ALL OTHER PREMIUMS (except Scheduled Personal Property) $ $ $ $

(a) The **residence premises** is not seasonal; (b) no **business** pursuits are conducted on the **residence premises**; (c) the **residence premises** is the only premises where the Named Insured or spouse maintains a residence other than business or farm properties; (d) the **insured** has no full time **residence employee(s)**; (e) the **insured** has no outboard motor(s) or watercraft otherwise excluded under this policy for which coverage is desired. Exception, if any, to (a), (b), (c), (d) or (e)*.

*Absence of an entry means "no exceptions".

THIS DECLARATIONS PAGE, WITH POLICY JACKET, HOMEOWNERS POLICY FORM, AND ENDORSEMENTS IF ANY, ISSUED TO FORM A PART THEREOF, COMPLETES THE ABOVE NUMBERED HOMEOWNERS POLICY.

FIGURE 10–2   Declarations Page—Homeowners Insurance Policy

Dwelling

Other structures

Unscheduled personal property

Section 2 coverages, E and F, would add to the amount the insured could collect under the policy.

Coverage A, **dwelling**, covers the insured's home. Coverage B applies to **other structures**, such as an unattached garage or shed. If the garage is attached to the house, it is covered under Coverage A. Coverage C, **unscheduled personal property**, applies to

Loss of use

property usually found in homes, such as furniture, clothes, appliances, and other personal property.[3] Coverage D, **loss of use**, pays for extra expenses if a covered loss prevents the insured from living in the home.

The limits of liability for the various insuring agreements found in Section 1 are determined as a percentage of Coverage A. That is, once the insured chooses an amount for Coverage A, Coverage B automatically equals 10 percent of this amount. Coverage C equals 50 percent of Coverage A. Coverage D equals 20 percent of Coverage A. If an insured needs additional protection, Coverages B, C, or D may be increased. Coverage may not be reduced below the specified percentages. The insured must pay an additional charge for increased coverage.

As an example of the coverage percentages, assume that a homeowner, Phil Harmonic, the orchestra director, purchases $100,000 of insurance on his dwelling (Coverage A). Coverage B (other structures) automatically equals $10,000. If Phil had an elaborate (unattached) enclosed swimming pool worth $25,000 on his property, Coverage B would have to be increased. Coverage C automatically equals $50,000 (50 percent of $100,000). Again, if the homeowner had more than $50,000 in personal property, this coverage would have to be increased. Coverage D automatically equals $20,000 (20 percent of Coverage A), and it also can be increased if needed.

Section 2 provides liability protection and is divided into two coverages. Coverage E provides protection from adverse legal judgments. Coverage F provides for medical payments to those injured by accident occurring at the insured's premises or resulting from the insured's activities. The medical payments coverage (Coverage F) is available without establishing the homeowner's legal liability.

DEFINITIONS

Named insured

Insured

Immediately following the insuring agreement is a short glossary that determines the meaning of eight important terms. Each of the eight definitions in the glossary is important, but the definitions of **named insured** and **insured** are especially important because they determine who is entitled to coverage.[4]

DEFINITIONS

A. In this policy, "you" and "your" refer to the "named insured" shown in the Declarations and the spouse if a resident of the same household. "We," "us" and "our" refer to the Company providing this insurance.

B. In addition, certain words and phrases are defined as follows:
   5. "Insured" means:
   a. You and residents of your household who are:
      (1) Your relatives; or
      (2) Other persons under the age of 21 and in the care of any person named above;
   b. A student enrolled in school full time, as defined by the school, who was a resident of your household before moving out to attend school, provided the student is under the age of:
      (1) 24 and your relative; or
      (2) 21 and in your care or the care of a person described in a. (1) above;

---

[3] Scheduled personal property is covered by an inland marine insurance endorsement, not by Coverage C.
[4] This section is abbreviated for simplicity, as are many of the quoted selections in this chapter.

Note carefully that insured status requires residence in the household. The question of residence raises issues of fact to be determined by a court in some cases. For example, is a divorced or separated adult child living in his or her parents' home for an indefinite period a resident of the parents' household? Is an adult child (under age 24) who is pursuing graduate study or a military career and who continues to use the parents' address considered a resident of the parent's household despite not having lived at home for years? Is a minor child in the regular weekend custody of a divorced parent a resident of that parent's household for the weekend? These issues have been litigated many times. In general, courts have held that no single fact determines residence, but the intent of the individual weighs strongly in the determination of the issue.

Note also that being classified as an insured can be advantageous in some instances and disadvantageous in others. For example, being an insured under a parent's HO is helpful when a college student has property stolen while away at school. On the other hand, if a parent has property stolen by an insured, such as an adult child, the loss is excluded from coverage.

SECTION I—PROPERTY COVERAGES

Section 1 of the HO consists of the following five parts:

1. Coverage A: Dwelling
2. Coverage B: Other Structures
3. Coverage C: Personal Property
4. Coverage D: Loss of Use
5. Additional Coverages

Section 1 establishes categories of insured property and identifies the losses that are covered and those that are excluded. This section of the policy also identifies several kinds of property subject to maximum limits of recovery.

SECTION I—PROPERTY COVERAGES

A. COVERAGE A—DWELLING

1. We cover:
   a. The dwelling on the "residence premises" shown in the Declarations, including structures attached to the dwelling; and
   b. Materials and supplies located on or next to the "residence premises" used to construct, alter or repair the dwelling or other structures on the "residence premises."
2. We do not cover land, including land on which the dwelling is located.

Coverage A applies to the insured's residence premises shown on the declarations page. A second home or summer cottage, which might be considered a temporary residence, is not covered because it does not appear in the declarations.

B. COVERAGE B—OTHER STRUCTURES

1. We cover other structures on the "residence premises" set apart from the dwelling by clear space. This includes structures connected to the dwelling by only a fence, utility line, or similar connection.

2. We do not cover:
   a. Land, including land on which the other structures are located;
   b. Other structures rented or held for rental to any person not a tenant of the dwelling, unless used solely as a private garage;
   c. Other structures from which any "business" is conducted; or
   d. Other structures used to store "business" property. However, we do cover a structure that contains "business" property solely owned by an "insured" or a tenant of the dwelling provided that "business" property does not include gaseous or liquid fuel, other than fuel in a permanently installed fuel tank of a vehicle or craft parked or stored in the structure.
3. The limit of liability for this coverage will not be more than 10% of the limit of liability that applies to Coverage A. Use of this coverage does not reduce the Coverage A limit of liability.

Coverage B applies to other structures on the residence premises separated from the home by a clear space. An unattached garage, swimming pool, or tool shed are examples of property covered in this section. The policy also makes clear that a claim for loss under Coverage B does not reduce the amount available for losses to the dwelling.

C. COVERAGE C—PERSONAL PROPERTY

1. Covered Property
We cover personal property owned or used by an "insured" while it is anywhere in the world. After a loss and at your request, we will cover personal property owned by:
a. Others while the property is on the part of the "residence premises" occupied by an "insured"; or
b. A guest or a "residence employee," while the property is in any residence occupied by an "insured."

Real property

Sometimes the question is raised whether a specific item is real or personal property. If it is real property, it is covered under Coverage A. If it is personal, it is covered under Coverage C. The English common-law rule is that land and anything permanently attached to land is **real property**. Thus, built-in appliances are real property. Wall-to-wall carpeting often presents a problem in this context. In general, insurers consider wall-to-wall carpeting as real property if it lies over an unfinished floor and consider it personal property if it is placed over a finished floor.

Special limits of liability

The **special limits of liability** section establishes maximum dollar amounts that an insured can recover when the specifically identified property is damaged. For some property (jewelry, for example), the special limits apply only to loss by the peril of theft. Losses from other perils are covered without the special limit applying. With other property (for example, money, bank notes, and coins), any loss is subject to the specified limits.

3. Special Limits of Liability
The special limit for each category shown below is the total limit for each loss for all property in that category. These special limits do not increase the Coverage C limit of liability.

a. $200 on money, bank notes, bullion, gold other than goldware, silver other than silverware, platinum other than platinumware, coins, medals, scrip, stored value cards, and smart cards.

b. $1,500 on securities, accounts, deeds, evidences of debt, letters of credit, notes other than bank notes, manuscripts, personal records, passports, tickets, and stamps. This dollar limit applies to these categories regardless of the medium (such as paper or computer software) on which the material exists.

   This limit includes the cost to research, replace, or restore the information from the lost or damaged material.

c. $1,500 on watercraft of all types, including their trailers, furnishings, equipment, and outboard engines or motors.

d. $1,500 on trailers or semitrailers not used with watercraft of all types.

e. $1,500 for loss by theft of jewelry, watches, furs, precious and semiprecious stones.

f. $2,500 for loss by theft of firearms and related equipment.

g. $2,500 for loss by theft of silverware, silver-plated ware, goldware, gold-plated ware, platinumware, platinum-plated ware, and pewterware. This includes flatware, hollowware, tea sets, trays, and trophies made of or including silver, gold, or pewter.

h. $2,500 on property, on the "residence premises," used primarily for "business" purposes.

i. $500 on property, away from the "residence premises," used primarily for "business" purposes. However, this limit does not apply to loss to electronic apparatus and other property described in Categories j. and k. below.

j. $1,500 on electronic apparatus and accessories, while in or upon a "motor vehicle," but only if the apparatus is equipped to be operated by power from the "motor vehicle's" electrical system while still capable of being operated by other power sources.

   Accessories include antennas, tapes, wires, records, discs, or other media that can be used with any apparatus described in this Category j.

k. $1,500 on electronic apparatus and accessories used primarily for "business" while away from the "residence premises" and not in or upon a "motor vehicle." The apparatus must be equipped to be operated by power from the "motor vehicle's" electrical system while still capable of being operated by other power sources.

   Accessories include antennas, tapes, wires, records, discs, or other media that can be used with any apparatus described in this Category k.

Section 1 specifically excludes some property from coverage, including the following:

- Personal property insured elsewhere, such as in a personal property floater
- Animals, birds, or fish
- Motor vehicles and equipment
- Property associated with renting of an apartment
- Business data stored in computers

D. COVERAGE D—LOSS OF USE

The limit of liability for Coverage D is the total limit for the coverages in 1. Additional Living Expense, 2. Fair Rental Value, and 3. Civil Authority Prohibits Use below.

1. Additional Living Expense

If a loss covered under Section I makes that part of the "residence premises" where you reside not fit to live in, we cover any necessary increase in living

> expenses incurred by you so that your household can maintain its normal standard of living.
>
> Payment will be for the shortest time required to repair or replace the damage or, if you permanently relocate, the shortest time required for your household to settle elsewhere.

Coverage D—Loss of Use covers only the "necessary increase in living expenses . . . for the shortest time required to repair or replace the damage."

As an example of this coverage, assume that Jack and Jane Rabbit lose their house in a fire. They subsequently move to the Hutch Motel while their home is being rebuilt. Their increase in expenses includes the motel bill ($3,500), the increase in their food cost (prefire food cost = $800, postfire restaurant food cost = $2,000, increase = $1,200), and miscellaneous increase in expenses = $1,000. Coverage D would pay the total increase in expenses of $5,700 ($3,500 + $1,200 + $1,000).

Additional Coverage

1. Debris removal costs are covered within specified limits.
2. Expenses incurred to protect property from further damage are covered.
3. A limited amount of coverage is available for damage to trees and shrubs.
4. Fire department service charges will be reimbursed.
5. Property removed from the residence because it was endangered by an insured peril and subsequently damaged or stolen at the removal site is covered. This clause expands the coverage already available for coverage of property off the premises.
6. Credit card fraud and similar frauds are covered for a limited amount.
7. Certain loss assessments in cooperative-type buildings are paid up to a $1,000 limit.
8. Loss due to collapse is covered.
9. Glass or safety glazing material is covered.
10. Coverage of the landlord's furnishings, which is limited to $2,500, is useful for homeowners renting an apartment on the residence premises.

Collapse

Collapse

Concurrent causation

Collapse (number 8 in the preceding list) had been a specifically named peril in prior versions of the HO insurance policy. Now it is given special treatment. **Collapse** is difficult to define because it can be the result of many different causes. Some courts require that a structure actually must fall into rubble before declaring the peril to have occurred. Other courts have declared buildings collapsed that have suffered significant structural weakness but have not actually fallen down. Moreover, some courts have introduced the doctrine of **concurrent causation**. This rule states that the HO provides coverage when a loss arises from two separately identifiable perils, one covered (for example, negligence or collapse) and one excluded (for example, underground water pressure). These concurrent-causation-theory decisions led to deliberate treatment of losses associated with collapse as an additional coverage instead of as a named peril.[5]

---

[5] See *Safeco Insurance Company of America* v. *Guyton*, 692 Fed. (2nd.) 551 (1982), and *Premier Insurance Company* v. *Welch*, 140 Cal. App. (3rd.) 720 (1983).

The HO only covers collapsed structures (fallen down as opposed to settling, cracking, etc.) if the insured can prove that one of the listed causes was the exclusive cause of the collapse. For students interested in contract construction, precise use of English, and court interpretation modifying drafters' intentions, the evolution of the treatment of collapse provides an excellent case study.

SECTION I—PERILS INSURED AGAINST IN THE BROAD FORM, HO-2

Property insurance policies take one of two basic formats: (1) They may specify the perils that can produce an insured loss, or (2) they may omit identifying covered perils and specify the exclusions that apply.[6] Section 1, the Property Insurance Section of HO-2, is an example of the first approach. It states the following:

HO-2
SECTION I—PERILS INSURED AGAINST

We insure for direct physical loss to the property described in Coverages A, B, and C caused by any of the following perils unless the loss is excluded under Section I—Exclusions.

A list of 16 specific perils follows this clause. Compare the *specified-perils* language to the *open-perils* language of HO-3, the Special Form.[7]

HO-3
SECTION I—PERILS INSURED AGAINST

A. COVERAGE A—DWELLING AND COVERAGE B—OTHER STRUCTURES

1. We insure against risk of direct physical loss to property described in Coverages A and B.

2. We do not insure, however, for loss:
   a. Excluded under Section I—Exclusions;
   b. Involving collapse, except as provided in E.8. Collapse under Section 1—Property Coverages; or
   c. Caused by:
      (1) Freezing of a plumbing, heating, air conditioning, or automatic fire protective sprinkler system or of a household appliance, or by discharge, leakage, or overflow from within the system or appliance caused by freezing. This provision does not apply if you have used reasonable care to:
         (a) Maintain heat in the building; or
         (b) Shut off the water supply and drain all systems and appliances of water.

---

[6] Insurers now are avoiding a previously used term, *all risks coverage*, because no insurance policy covers all possible losses. Insurers also are avoiding the term *comprehensive coverage* for the same reason.
[7] Several reviewers of this chapter pointed out that the HO-3 is the more frequently purchased and desirable HO form.

Open-perils policy format

Specified-perils policy format

Both formats can produce about the same result. A policy may be written specifying 16 perils that can produce an insured loss, or on an open-perils basis but containing a list of exclusions so only 16 perils remain that can result in a covered loss. The **open-perils policy format** still provides broader coverage because it would pay for a claim in those cases where a peril goes unspecified in **specified-perils policy format** but is not excluded in an open-perils contract. For example, if a deer were to crash through a picture window and cause $5,000 worth of property damage within the home, HO-2 would not cover the loss because the peril is not specified, but HO-3 would cover this claim because this peril is not excluded.

If legal disputes arise about whether or not a loss is covered by the policy, established principles of insurance law puts the initial burden on the insured to demonstrate which covered peril caused the loss. Assuming that the insured has met this burden, the insurer then can demonstrate whether any exclusions apply. However, with the open-perils contract, the initial legal burden shifts to the insurer to prove that an exclusion applies.

Specified Perils

If any property loss (dwelling or contents) is covered under HO-2, the loss must have a specified peril as its proximate cause. The property section of HO-2 provides coverage only if a loss is caused by one of the following perils:

1. Fire or Lightning

Fire

Fire means a *hostile* fire—that is, one not contained in its proper place. The word *fire* is ordinarily used and commonly understood by people. Yet when found in an insurance policy, it takes on a specific and restricted meaning.

Lightning

Lightning is a powerful discharge of natural electricity. Direct losses from lightning sometimes are hard to prove, especially when the only damage that occurs is to television sets and other appliances.

2. Windstorm or Hail

HO-2 provides protection against tornadoes and all other sources of violent wind damage. The coverage excludes damage to the interior of the buildings or contents if no damage is first sustained by the exterior of the building. Thus, damage sustained because a window is left open is excluded.

3. Explosion

Explosion is a difficult term to define, and the policy does not define it. There may be fire or loud noise and violent expansion of gases accompanying an explosion. When a combination of some or all these events causes damage (for instance, when a water heater explodes), HO-2 covers the damage.

4. Riot or Civil Commotion

War, civil war, and insurrection are not covered, but lesser hostilities are covered.

5, 6. Aircraft and Vehicles

Aircraft damage includes damage caused by spacecraft falling on a house and damage done by sonic booms or model planes.

HO-2 (but not HO-3) excludes losses to fences, driveways, and walks caused by vehicles operated by an occupant of the house.

7. Sudden and Accidental Smoke Damage

The definition of *sudden* has been interpreted differently by various courts. In some cases, it has meant an unforeseen event of short duration. Other courts have omitted reference to the duration of the event. Thus, the smoke damage caused by a smoldering electric blanket may be covered under this provision, as may damage resulting from faulty cooking appliances. If firefighters cause water damage as they put out the smoldering blanket, this too would be covered because the proximate cause of the loss would be the smoldering blanket or stove.

8. Vandalism or Malicious Mischief

Vandalism

If others willfully and intentionally damage the homeowner's property, there is coverage for **vandalism**. In the HO-2 contract, the coverage for these two perils is suspended if the house has been vacant for 60 consecutive days before the loss. *Vacant* means the insureds and their possessions are absent from the house. When an insured takes a vacation with plans to return home, the house is unoccupied rather than vacant, and the coverage remains in effect.

In an interesting case touching on this point, a court found the damage caused to the interior of a house when a deer crashed through windows both on entering and leaving was not covered under this section of the policy. In reaching its decision, the court stated: "The animal was incapable of forming the requisite intent of committing a wrongful act that would result in senseless damage."[8]

9. Theft

Theft

Theft means the crime of removing property without the owner's permission. Theft generally does not include losses by fraud or mysterious disappearance of property. Three exclusions to theft coverage are in the HO, including theft committed by an insured. Additional restrictions apply if the theft occurs off the residence premises, including in a college dorm or apartment.

10. Falling Objects

The building must sustain exterior damage before interior damage is covered. If a tree limb were to fall and break through the roof, the policy would cover the roof and damaged contents. If the homeowner drops a television set, destroying the set and a chair, no coverage is provided.

11. Weight of Ice, Snow, or Sleet

This provision is more useful in Minnesota than in Florida. Yet if four feet of snow were to fall on an insured house in Florida and cause damage, HO-2 would cover the loss.

12. Accidental Discharge or Overflow of Water or Steam

Loss caused by accidental discharge from plumbing, appliances, sprinkler systems, or air conditioners is covered. Damage to these items is insured if the damage is caused by an insured peril as described in the next paragraph. Damage sustained if the building is vacant for more than 60 consecutive days before a loss is excluded, as is mold damage and damage attributed to the malfunction of a sump pump.

13. Sudden and Accidental Tearing Apart, Cracking, Burning, or Bulging

The provision covers the explosion of water heaters, heating systems, air conditioners, or sprinklers, but losses resulting from freezing are covered separately.

14. Freezing

If the building is occupied, or even if the building is unoccupied—so long as a serious attempt is made to heat it while it is unoccupied—and damage is caused by frozen pipes that burst, HO-2 provides coverage.

---

[8] *Stack v. The Hanover Ins. Co.*, Ala., C.A., 1975.

Mold

In recent years, litigation relating to loss caused by mold has received media attention. Some of these cases have involved claims of millions of dollars of damages, but it is too early to assess their impact on the insurance market.[10] Among the questions being raised in courts is whether mold damage resulted from insurers' improper claims settlement practices (undue delay in paying for covered losses), construction defects, or neglect of insureds to protect property.

Mold is a type of fungi. About 100,000 different kinds of mold exist. Some molds produce mycotoxins that can kill humans, and many people also experience allergic reactions to molds. Indoors, mold is likely to grow where there is moisture and warmth such as in basements and bathrooms. Mold can grow in drywall, carpets, or furniture upholstery.

Considering the mold exclusion found in HO-3 is instructive.

A. COVERAGE A—DWELLING AND COVERAGE B—OTHER STRUCTURES

1. We insure against risk of direct physical loss to property described in Coverages A and B.
2. We do not insure, however, for loss:
   (Caused by)

   (1–4)

   (5) Mold, fungus, or wet rot. However, we do insure for loss caused by mold, fungus, or wet rot that is hidden within the walls or ceilings or beneath the floors or above the ceilings of a structure if such loss results from the accidental discharge or overflow of water or steam from within:
   (a) A plumbing, heating, air conditioning, or automatic fire protective sprinkler system, or a household appliance, on the "residence premises";
   (b) A storm drain, or water, steam or sewer pipes, off the "residence premises."

   For purposes of this provision, a plumbing system or household appliance does not include a sump, sump pump, or related equipment or a roof drain, gutter, downspout, or similar fixtures or equipment;

The wording in the foregoing box suggests the following sequence:

1. The insurer grants coverage for direct physical loss to the property.
2. The insurer then excludes coverage for several specified losses.
3. The (5th) exclusion eliminates coverage for mold. However, the policy then modifies this exclusion to grant coverage for mold under specified conditions.

Discussing this topic illustrates the old saying "The big hand gives it to you, the little hand takes it away." It might be added, "Another little hand gives it back, sometimes." This discussion also suggests why insurance policies have become so complex. The interplay between insurers, insureds, and plaintiffs' attorneys makes great demands on the courts to interpret policy language.

Other Exclusions

The earth-movement exclusion and the water-damage exclusion eliminate coverage for catastrophic perils. The neglect exclusion provides an incentive to protect undamaged

---

[10] An Internet search with the keyword "insurance mold litigation" will provide current information about this issue.

property from loss. It is designed to minimize the morale hazard. The war exclusion relieves the insurer from another catastrophic loss exposure. The intentional-loss exclusion relieves the insurer of liability if a loss is caused intentionally by an insured. Even "innocent" insureds are excluded from coverage. In some jurisdictions, courts provided protection for innocent co-insureds when one spouse deliberately burned a house covered in a divorce settlement.

SECTION I—CONDITIONS

C. LOSS SETTLEMENT

In this Condition C, the terms "cost to repair or replace" and "replacement cost" do not include the increased costs incurred to comply with the enforcement of any ordinance or law, except to the extent that coverage for these increased costs is provided in E.11. Ordinance or Law under Section I—Property Coverages. Covered property losses are settled as follows:

1. Property of the following types:
    a. Personal property;
    b. Awnings, carpeting, household appliances, outdoor antennas, and outdoor equipment, whether or not attached to buildings;
    c. Structures that are not buildings; and
    d. Grave markers, including mausoleums; at actual cash value at the time of loss but not more than the amount required to repair or replace.

2. Buildings covered under Coverage A or B at replacement cost without deduction for depreciation, subject to the following:
    a. If, at the time of loss, the amount of insurance in this policy on the damaged building is 80% or more of the full replacement cost of the building immediately before the loss, we will pay the cost to repair or replace, after application of any deductible and without deduction for depreciation, but not more than the least of the following amounts:
       (1) The limit of liability under this policy that applies to the building;
       (2) The replacement cost of that part of the building damaged with material of like kind and quality and for like use; or
       (3) The necessary amount actually spent to repair or replace the damaged building. If the building is rebuilt at a new premises, the cost described in (2) above is limited to the cost which would have been incurred if the building had been built at the original premises.
    b. If, at the time of loss, the amount of insurance in this policy on the damaged building is less than 80% of the full replacement cost of the building immediately before the loss, we will pay the greater of the following amounts, but not more than the limit of liability under this policy that applies to the building:
       (1) The actual cash value of that part of the building damaged; or
       (2) That proportion of the cost to repair or replace, after application of any deductible and without deduction for depreciation, that part of the building damaged, which the total amount of insurance in this policy on the damaged building bears to 80% of the replacement cost of the building. . . .
    d. We will pay no more than the actual cash value of the damage until actual repair or replacement is complete. Once actual repair or replacement is complete, we will settle the loss as noted in 2.a. and b. above.

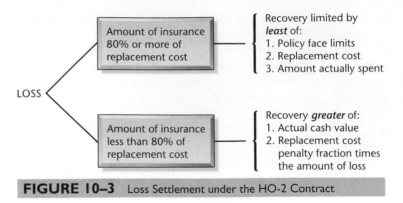

FIGURE 10–3 Loss Settlement under the HO-2 Contract

Loss Settlement

Loss settlement

The **loss settlement** provision requires careful study because it presents several alternative paths to determine the amount of payment made to the insured in the event of loss. These paths are shown in Figure 10–3, in which the language of the policy with respect to recovery for buildings (Coverage A) and other structures (Coverage B) is illustrated.

Replacement Cost and Coinsurance

Coinsurance clause

The loss settlement provision of HO-2 contains a penalty provision that applies if the insured has purchased less insurance than 80 percent of replacement cost. The HO penalty provision is similar to the coinsurance provision commonly found in commercial property insurance policies. The purpose of both the **coinsurance clause** and the HO loss settlement clause is to make underinsurance unattractive to the insured. Both clauses provide for the insured to pay a penalty based on the amount of underinsurance. The mathematics of this penalty follows shortly.

Many property policies contain a clause requiring the insured to purchase some minimum amount of insurance if the insured wants full coverage on all losses. If the insured purchases less than the minimum amount, there will be only partial recovery for losses. In the HO policy, the minimum amount of insurance is stated as a percentage of the replacement cost of the insured property.

To determine whether the insured has met the coinsurance requirement on the dwelling, insurers use the following rules:

- If the amount of insurance purchased, divided by 80 percent of the replacement cost of the building, is equal to or greater than 1, then the insurance company will pay the replacement cost of the loss minus the deductible. The maximum amount paid will be the policy limit of coverage.
- If the amount of insurance purchased, divided by 80 percent of the replacement cost of the building, is less than 1, the larger of the following two is paid but no more than the policy limit of coverage.
- The actual cash value of the loss less the deductible.
- The result of

$$\frac{\text{Amount of insurance}}{80\% \times \text{Replacement cost of building}} \times (\text{replacement cost of loss} - \text{the deductible})$$

If the first term in the equation is less than 1, the insured will bear a portion of the loss. The insured is said to be a "coinsurer of the loss." If the fraction is equal to or greater than 1, the insurer will pay the full amount of loss, limited to the amount of insurance purchased.

Mathematical Examples of HO Loss Settlement

Assume that Queen Victoria owns a $1 million castlelike house, and it would take $1 million to replace the house with a comparable one. The market value of the palace may be more or less than the replacement cost depending on many facts, including its location. Assume that her insurance policy has an 80 percent replacement-cost clause, and that Queen Victoria purchases $600,000 of insurance. Ignoring the deductible provision for the sake of simplicity, if there is a $200,000 loss, the insurer will pay the following:

$$\frac{\$600,000}{80\%\,(\$1,000,000)} \times \$200,000 = \$150,000$$

In the case of this partial loss, Queen Victoria will pay $50,000 and the insurer will pay $150,000 of the $200,000 loss.

If a total loss occurs, the formula produces the following $750,000 result:

$$\frac{\$600,000}{80\%\,(\$1,000,000)} \times \$1,000,000 = \$750,000$$

However, Queen Victoria has only $600,000 of insurance, so $600,000 is the maximum amount she can collect for this loss. In all property insurance policies, the insurance proceeds are restricted to the policy limits.

Reconsider this example, but assume that Queen Victoria purchases $800,000 of insurance. All other facts remain unchanged. In the case of a $200,000 loss, she now collects $200,000 because the fraction $800,000/$800,000 equals 1. In the case of a total loss, she will collect $800,000 because the $800,000 insurance policy is less than the $1 million loss.

Assuming she was underinsured, and the actual cash value of Queen Victoria's home produced a larger loss payment than the coinsurance formula, she would receive an actual cash value settlement. For example, assume that the home was 95 percent undepreciated, and that there was a 50 percent coinsurance deficiency. The actual cash value settlement would be greater than the coinsurance penalty and Queen Victoria is entitled to the greater of the two settlements. Never forget, however, that the policy's limit of liability is the maximum an insured can recover. Also, the deductible provision applies to all loss settlements even though it was not illustrated in the foregoing examples.

Reasons for the Coinsurance Requirement

What is the reason for the coinsurance requirement? It exists to keep insurance rates fair. Property insurance rates are expressed as an amount per $100 of value, such as $0.30 per $100. Most property losses are partial losses. The coinsurance requirement is the connection between these two apparently unrelated facts, as further explanations will show.

The actual cost of insuring any $100 segment of property value is found by multiplying the probability of loss for this particular $100 of value by $100 (see Figure 10–4). Because the probability of a loss to the first $100 of a house's value is greater than the probability of a loss to the last $100 of value, the cost of insurance for these two different $100 segments should be different. In practice, they are not. The rate is $0.30 per $100 for

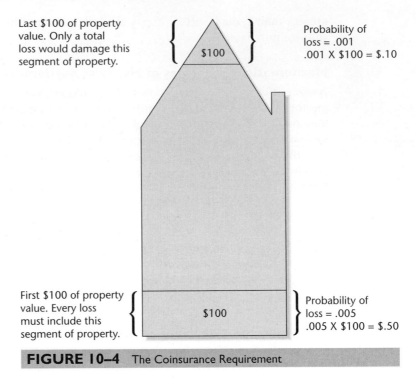

Last $100 of property value. Only a total loss would damage this segment of property.

$100

Probability of loss = .001
.001 X $100 = $.10

First $100 of property value. Every loss must include this segment of property.

$100

Probability of loss = .005
.005 X $100 = $.50

FIGURE 10–4 The Coinsurance Requirement

all $100 segments. The $0.30 per $100 figure is the average cost and results in a fair price only when the insured purchases an amount of insurance equal to the full property value.

If property owners, recognizing most losses are partial, purchased insurance equal to only 50 percent of the value of the covered property, they may think that they transferred the most significant part of the risk. Without the coinsurance penalty, they would have an advantageous deal. If the average rate ($0.30 per $100) was paid, the insured would be paying a rate below the rate mathematically appropriate to the amount of risk transferred. The coinsurance requirement of property insurance policies prevents insureds from taking advantage of the insurer's average rate structure. If someone purchases insurance equal to 50 percent of the value of the property when the insurer requires 80 percent coverage, that insured will receive only partial recovery for a loss.

Students often ask why the HO requires coverage equaling only 80 percent and not 100 percent of replacement cost. The answer involves the effects of inflation on construction costs. If 100 percent coverage was required (and some reporting forms used in commercial insurance do require this amount of coverage) and inflation equaled 1 percent a month (or any other amount), insureds initially purchasing adequate coverage would face a coinsurance penalty after the first month. After a year, they would face a 12 percent penalty. Thus, to avoid the coinsurance penalty, the HO requires coverage that at least equals 80 percent of replacement cost, but careful insureds will purchase 100 percent coverage with an "inflation guard" endorsement that increases coverage on a regular basis to offset the effects of inflation. Insureds who initially purchase only 80 percent coverage will be penalized after a short period of rapid inflation. As our example pointed out, even without inflation, an insured with only 80 percent coverage will be assuming 20 percent of all total losses.

Mortgage Clause

Mortgage clause

The HO **mortgage clause** protects creditors making loans secured by the insured property. A mortgage is evidence of a debt. It is the security agreement when a loan is made on real estate. A mortgage gives the lender (mortgagee) a legal interest in the mortgaged property. If the borrower (mortgagor) defaults on the loan agreement, the mortgagee may foreclose on the mortgage and sell the property to satisfy the debt. Both the mortgagor and mortgagee, therefore, have an insurable interest in the property.

To illustrate the mortgage clause, consider the case of Genghis O. Kahn. Genghis recently purchased a $250,000 house in Ephraim, Wisconsin. He used $50,000 of his own money for a down payment and borrowed $200,000 from the Eighteenth National Bank of Ephraim. To secure the loan, he mortgaged his new home to the bank. If an uninsured loss occurred, Genghis not only would lose his $50,000 down payment, but also he still would owe the bank $200,000. The bank would have some land and a pile of ashes as security for a $200,000 loan. Considering the nomadic ways of Genghis, these ashes would not be great security.

To protect the bank's interest, the bank could require Genghis to purchase insurance and add the Eighteenth National Bank as an additional insured. If, however, any action on the part of Genghis (such as an attempt to defraud the insurer) were to result in suspension of the coverage, the bank could lose its insurance protection. As a second alternative, the bank could purchase its own insurance, but there are many problems when the lender insures mortgaged property separately. Rather than probe these complex issues, consider the solution: the standard mortgage clause. The HO contract solves this issue as follows:

K. MORTGAGE CLAUSE

1. If a mortgagee is named in this policy, any loss payable under Coverage A or B will be paid to the mortgagee and you, as interests appear. If more than one mortgagee is named, the order of payment will be the same as the order of precedence of the mortgages.

2. If we deny your claim, that denial will not apply to a valid claim of the mortgagee, if the mortgagee:
   a. Notifies us of any change in ownership, occupancy, or substantial change in risk of which the mortgagee is aware;
   b. Pays any premium due under this policy on demand if you have neglected to pay the premium; and
   c. Submits a signed, sworn statement of loss within 60 days after receiving notice from us of your failure to do so. Paragraphs E. Appraisal, G. Suit Against Us, and I. Loss Payment under Section I—Conditions also apply to the mortgagee.

3. If we decide to cancel or not to renew this policy, the mortgagee will be notified at least 10 days before the date cancellation or nonrenewal takes effect.

4. If we pay the mortgagee for any loss and deny payment to you:
   a. We are subrogated to all the rights of the mortgagee granted under the mortgage on the property; or
   b. At our option, we may pay to the mortgagee the whole principal on the mortgage plus any accrued interest. In this event, we will receive a full assignment and transfer of the mortgage and all securities held as collateral to the mortgage debt.

5. Subrogation will not impair the right of the mortgagee to recover the full amount of the mortgagee's claim.

SECTION 2—LIABILITY COVERAGES[11]

SECTION II—LIABILITY COVERAGES

A. COVERAGE E—PERSONAL LIABILITY

If a claim is made or a suit is brought against an "insured" for damages because of "bodily injury" or "property damage" caused by an "occurrence" to which this coverage applies, we will:

1. Pay up to our limit of liability for the damages for which an "insured" is legally liable; and

2. Provide a defense at our expense by counsel of our choice, even if the suit is groundless, false, or fraudulent. We may investigate and settle any claim or suit that we decide is appropriate. Our duty to settle or defend ends when our limit of liability for the "occurrence" has been exhausted by payment of a judgment or settlement.

B. COVERAGE F—MEDICAL PAYMENTS TO OTHERS

We will pay the necessary medical expenses that are incurred or medically ascertained within three years from the date of an accident causing "bodily injury." Medical expenses means reasonable charges for medical, surgical, x-ray, dental, ambulance, hospital, professional nursing, and prosthetic devices. Medical expenses do not include expenses for funeral services. This coverage does not apply to you or regular residents of your household except "residence employees." As to others, this coverage applies only:

1. To a person on the "insured location" with the permission of an "insured"; or
2. To a person off the "insured location," if the "bodily injury":
   a. Arises out of a condition on the "insured location" or the ways immediately adjoining;
   b. Is caused by the activities of an "insured";
   c. Is caused by a "residence employee" in the course of the "residence employee's" employment by an "insured"; or
   d. Is caused by an animal owned by or in the care of an "insured."

In general, Coverage E commits the insurer to pay for successful judgments against its insured resulting from the nonbusiness activities of the named insured and household residents. It agrees to provide the insured with an attorney to defend lawsuits. The insurer retains the right to make a settlement with a claimant if the insurer concludes a settlement is appropriate. Under Coverage F, the insurer agrees to pay for medical expenses to persons other than the insured.

As an example of the protection provided by Coverage E, assume that an insured homeowner named Rimski, while unloading his shotgun, accidentally blows a hole in a car belonging to Korsakov. Whether the accident happens at home or away from the resident premises is not a question because coverage applies anywhere in the world.

Korsakov could sue Rimski to collect for the damage negligently done to his automobile. In this example, where the damage is definitely the insured's (Rimski's)

---

[11] I remind readers that the basic description of legal liability is presented in Chapter 2.

sponsibility, the insurer usually will try to settle with the injured third party (Korsakov), thereby avoiding litigation. In other cases, in which an insured's responsibility for injuring another is not clearly established, the insurer may choose to defend the insured in court. The decision to try to settle a claim or to defend an insured rests with the insurer in the HO contract. By contrast, in many professional liability insurance policies such as medical liability insurance, the insured (whose professional reputation may be at issue) can prevent an insurer from trying to settle a claim without litigation.

The insurer's duty to make payment on its insured's behalf is not exactly coincident with its duty to defend its insureds. Payment is required only for covered acts. A legal defense is required even for false, fraudulent, or groundless lawsuits.

SECTION 2—EXCLUSIONS

Because Coverages E and F are open perils coverages, several important exclusions limit the insurer's liability.

Claims Not Covered

A. "MOTOR VEHICLE LIABILITY"

1. Coverages E and F do not apply to any "motor vehicle liability" if, at the time and place of an "occurrence," the involved "motor vehicle":
   a. Is registered for use on public roads or property; . . .

B. "WATERCRAFT LIABILITY"

1. Coverages E and F do not apply to any "watercraft liability" if, at the time of an "occurrence," the involved watercraft is being:
   a. Operated in, or practicing for, any prearranged or organized race, speed contest or other competition. This exclusion does not apply to a sailing vessel or a predicted log cruise; . . .

C. "AIRCRAFT LIABILITY"

This policy does not cover "aircraft liability."

---

1. Expected or Intended Injury

This exclusion has been the subject of much litigation. One Minnesota case involved an injury caused in a fight when one 16-year-old struck another youth after wrapping a belt around his hand. The 16-year-old causing the injury was an insured under his parents' HO. When the injured youth sued for more than $50,000 in damages, the insureds looked to their HO policy for coverage. The insurer denied the coverage because it resulted from an intentional injury and thus was excluded specifically by the policy. The insureds claimed that there was no intent to cause such extensive damage. The court upheld the insurer's position, stating the following:

> The "intent" required to exclude coverage is neither the "intent to act" nor the "intent to cause the specific injury complained of." Rather it is the "intent to cause bodily injury."

Because it was clear to this court that the insured intended to injure the other youth, as a matter of law, the insurer properly denied coverage.[12]

In a 1991 decision, the Ohio Supreme Court reached the opposite conclusion.[13] In this case, after an exchange of insults, a teenager shot one member of a group of youths in the eye with a BB gun. Afterwards, the defendant stated his intention was to scare the other youths, not to harm them. The court felt that only the act of shooting the gun was intended, not the subsequent injury. The court stated, "The plain language of the policy is in terms of an intentional or expected injury, not an intentional or expected act." Therefore, because the injury was unintended, the insurer had to provide coverage.

E. COVERAGE E—PERSONAL LIABILITY AND COVERAGE F—MEDICAL PAYMENTS TO OTHERS

Coverages **E** and **F** do not apply to the following:

1. **Expected Or Intended Injury**
   "Bodily injury" or "property damage" which is expected or intended by an "insured" even if the resulting "bodily injury" or "property damage":
   a. Is of a different kind, quality or degree than initially expected or intended; or
   b. Is sustained by a different person, entity, real or personal property, than initially expected or intended.
   However, this Exclusion **E.1** does not apply to "bodily injury" resulting from the use of reasonable force by an "insured" to protect persons or property;

---

2. Business

---

2. **"Business"**
   a. "Bodily injury" or "property damage" arising out of or in connection with a "business" conducted from an "insured location" or engaged in by an "insured," whether or not the "business" is owned or operated by an "insured" or employs an "insured."
   This Exclusion **E.2.** applies but is not limited to an act or omission, regardless of its nature or circumstances, involving a service or duty rendered, promised, owed, or implied to be provided because of the nature of the "business."
   b. This Exclusion **E.2.** does not apply to:
   (2) An "insured" under the age of 21 years involved in a part-time or occasional, self-employed "business" with no employees;

Historically, much litigation has arisen involving the interpretation of the business-pursuits exclusion because people mix their personal lives, hobbies, and business activities. The personal liability coverage provided by the HO policy is designed to cover liability arising from personal activities. But courts frequently were asked to address the following types of questions: Does regular child care for a fee in the insured's home

---

[12] *Iowa Kemper Insurance Company* v. *Stone et al.*, reported in *1978 CCH Fire and Casualty Cases*, p. 1035.
[13] *Physicians Insurance Co. of Ohio* v. *Swanson* (1991).

cause the exclusion to be effective? Is an injury caused by a child while delivering newspapers excluded as a "business pursuit"? Is a teenager who occasionally baby-sits engaged in business? Because different courts in different jurisdictions reached different conclusions given similar circumstances, the HO now addresses some of these questions.

Perhaps the safest point to note is that if an insured injures somebody while engaged in an activity having some continuity and done for monetary gain, a strong possibility exists that the HO will not provide liability coverage. Therefore, insureds engaging in business activities should purchase an appropriate endorsement for their HO policies to cover these activities or should purchase an appropriate business liability policy.

3. Professional Services

This clause reinforces the preceding clause, making it clear that if an insured is sued for actions as an accountant, attorney, or physician, etc., the HO will not provide coverage.

6., 7., 8.: Communicable Diseases, Sexual Molestation, Controlled Substance

Before adding specifically worded exclusions, insurers relied on the intentional injury exclusion to preclude covering damage claims arising from injuries caused by sexually transmitted diseases, sexual molestation, or the use of controlled substances. The newer explicit wording is designed to address any ambiguities courts have found with the intentional injury line of defense, including the mental incapacity of the molester.

The controlled substance exclusion precludes liability coverage for activities that law-abiding homeowners and their insurers do not want to subsidize. The purpose of all these exclusions is to relieve the insurer of responsibility for paying such claims.

SECTIONS 1 AND 2—CONDITIONS

The final section of HO-2 contains conditions applicable to both Sections 1 and 2. Most of these items deal with subjects discussed in Chapters 8 and 9:

- Concealment and fraud.
- Waiver provisions.
- Cancellation by insurer and insured.
- Assignment (not valid unless insurer has given written consent).
- Subrogation.
- Death of an insured. (The legal representatives of the insured continue to receive coverage after the insured's death.)

ENDORSEMENTS

Insureds can add about 100 different endorsements to the HO contract. These include the following:

- HO-46, Theft Coverage Extension (broadens the definition of the peril)
- HO-61, Scheduled Personal Property Endorsement (adds inland marine coverage for valuable furs, jewelry, and similar items)
- HO-71, Business Pursuits (modifies standard policy exclusion and provides liability coverage for a few business pursuits, including sales and instructional occupations)

- HO-75, Watercraft (removes the standard policy exclusion that restricts liability coverage for watercraft)
- HO-323, Home Day Care Coverage Endorsement (extends coverage for home day care business conducted on the premises)

Adding coverage by endorsement quite naturally increases the insured's premium.

REDUCTION OF INSURANCE RESULTING FROM PREVIOUS LOSSES

Does a payment by an insurer reduce the amount of protection available for subsequent losses? If the policy is silent on this question, one may assume that the full limit of liability is available for each separate loss, without reduction for previous occurrences. Liability insurance policies generally provide for the full limit of liability for each occurrence. In addition, there usually is no additional premium to be paid. It is important to read all insurance policies carefully, however, to determine how the payment of a claim affects the policy limits for subsequent losses.

SUMMARY

The ISO HO series provides a combination of fire, personal liability, and additional living expense protection. We used the HO-2 to illustrate the principles of insurance policy construction and to achieve several other important educational objectives. As Table 10–1 shows, HO-2 is divided into six coverages.

Insurance policies are constructed in the following manner:

1. Declarations: Personalize the insurance contract to the insured by identifying the insured, the insurance company, the coverage amounts, and deductibles, among other particulars.
2. Definitions: A glossary defines important terms that appear throughout the policy.
3. Section 1—Property Coverages (A, B, C, and D): Describes the property covered, sets forth

special limits on certain property, and provides some additional coverages beyond those shown on the declarations page.

4. Section 1—Perils Insured Against: The HO-2 specifically identifies 16 perils as being a potential source of a covered loss. The HO-3, by contrast, provides open-perils coverage but relies on exclusions to limit the insurer's liability.
5. Section 1—Exclusions: HO-2 lists several sources of loss for which the insurer is not liable. In general these exclusions do one or more of the following things:

- Eliminate coverage for catastrophic perils
- Control the moral and morale hazard
- Control costs

TABLE 10–1	Protection Provided by Homeowners Insurance
	Protects Insured if Loss Is
Coverage A* Dwelling	Damage to insured's house.
Coverage B* Other structures	Damage to insured's nonattached garage, sheds, etc.
Coverage C Personal Property	Damage to contents of home; contents need not be on premises, but some policies limit coverage on property away from home.
Coverage D Loss of use	Extra expense of renting quarters after an insured peril.
Coverage E Personal Liability	Liability for bodily injury to property damage to another person, or the person's property.
Coverage F Medical payments to others	Medical expenses incurred by others, for which homeowner is reponsible.

*May be written on a specified-perils basis as in HO-2, or on an open-perils basis, as in HO-3.

- Exclude coverages that can benefit only a few insureds who can purchase such coverage for an additional premium if it is needed

6. Section 1—Conditions: The loss settlement provision determines the amount of proceeds an insured will receive in the event of a covered loss. The mortgage clause describes the rights and duties of the insurer, mortgagor (insured), and mortgagee (lender). Several of the other clauses in this section were described in Chapters 8 and 9.

7. Section 2—Liability Coverages (E and F): Provide the insured with protection in the event of an unfavorable judgment in a negligence lawsuit. Coverage F provides medical payments to others regardless of the insured's provable negligence.

8. Section 2—Exclusions: Several exclusions limit the insurer's liability for claims under Section 2. Among these are exclusions for claims:

- Arising from the ownership, maintenance, or use of motor vehicles, watercraft, or aircraft
- Stemming from intentionally caused injuries
- Arising from a business activity
- Arising from the transmission of a communicable disease, sexual molestation, or the use, sale, or manufacture of a controlled substance

---

REVIEW TERMS

- Additional living expense
- Coinsurance
- Collapse
- Concurrent causation
- Divided coverage
- Dwelling
- Explosion
- Fire
- Insured

- Intentional injury
- Lightning
- Loss of use
- Loss settlement
- Mortgage clause
- Named insured
- Ordinance-or-law exclusion
- Open-perils policy format

- Other structures
- Personal property
- Real property
- Special limits of liability
- Specified-perils policy format
- Theft
- Unscheduled personal property
- Vandalism

REVIEW

1. Describe some individuals who are protected by the HO who are parties to the contract. Distinguish the named insured from other insureds. Describe some covered people who are not parties to the contract.

2. List the four coverages found in Section 1 of the HO. Give an example of a loss covered by each section.

3. List the two coverages found in Section 2 of the HO. Give an example of a loss covered by each section.

4. What is the relationship between the ordinance-or-law exclusion and building codes?

5. Why is the mortgage clause of the HO desirable from a lender's viewpoint?

6. What is the difference between a specified-perils policy and an open-perils policy? Is one format always to be preferred to the other?

7. In the case of the deer that crashed into a home, why did the court decide the damage was not vandalism?

8. Why do property insurance policies contain exclusions? Illustrate your answer with examples from the HO.

9. Will an exclusion result in partial recovery?

10. Why are limits placed on coin, stamp, and gun collections in the HO? Can this kind of property be insured?

11. (Questions 11–15 are related.) Assume that John Marshall owns a $150,000 (replacement cost of the structure) home. (Ignore the deductible clause and consider just the coinsurance requirement.) If John purchased $120,000 of insurance, how much would he collect for a partial loss of $40,000? For a total loss of $150,000?

12. If John purchased $100,000 of insurance, how much would he collect for a $40,000 loss? How much would he collect for a total loss? (Ignore the deductible clause.)

13. Next, assume that John Marshall purchased $50,000 of insurance on his $150,000 home. How much would he collect for a partial loss of $40,000? How much would he collect for a total loss? (Ignore the deductible clause.)

14. Now assume that all the conditions of the loss settlement clause of the HO apply to the case. Assume that

John has $100,000 coverage on his $150,000 house, which has been used for only one-eighth of its estimated useful life. How much would John collect for a $40,000 partial loss? How much would be collected for a total loss?

15. Finally, given the same amount of coverage as in the preceding question, if John's home had been used for seven-eighths of its estimated useful life, how much would John collect for a $40,000 partial loss?

16. Under the HO, will a theft loss in April mean less coverage available for a fire in July?

OBJECTIVE QUESTIONS

Assume that Bill Clanton owns the ISO HO-2 policy described in this chapter and reproduced in Appendix A. The limits are as follows:

> A = $120,000
> B = $12,000
> C = $60,000
> D = $24,000
> E = $100,000
> F = $5,000

A $250 deductible applies to Section 1, Coverages A through D. The replacement cost of Bill's home is $130,000, the contents are valued at $70,000, and depreciation on the home is set at 30 percent.

Your assignment is to compute the amount that Bill will collect in each of the following circumstances. (Assume each event occurs separately.)

1. Bill's house and all its contents are destroyed by a tornado. It takes six months to rebuild the home, and Bill's additional living expenses amount to $12,000.

2. A neighbor's eight-year-old child accidentally releases the brakes on his family's pickup truck, sending it crashing into Bill's home. Damage to the home amounts to $15,000. The truck is destroyed. Its actual cash value before the loss was $22,000. The child and Bill both suffer broken arms. Medical expenses amount to $5,000 for each person.

3. Bill's unattached tool shed burns, destroying the shed (damage = $7,000) and the lawn care equipment inside (damage = $3,000).

4. Bill negligently starts a fire while cooking. His home and all the contents are a total loss. It costs Bill an additional $14,000 to live in a rental home while his house is being rebuilt.

5. Bill negligently burns some leaves and causes his neighbor's house to burn (damage = $170,000).

6. While playing golf, Bill's sliced drive hits another golfer, knocking him out. Bill yelled a warning before the victim, Bob, was hit. Bob claims not to have heard the warning and sues Bill for $60,000 in medical expenses, $6,000 in lost wages because he couldn't perform his clerical work for the local government for three months, and $100,000 for pain and suffering. Assume that Bob wins the case and it costs an additional $20,000 to provide Bill with a legal defense.

7. While his daughter is away at college, her stereo is stolen from her dorm room (damage = $1,500).

8. While carrying his portable color television set to the basement, Bill drops it. It is a total loss (damage = $850).

9. Bill is a certified public accountant working from his office at home. He is sued for negligence in preparing Al's income tax. The suit is successful and Al wins a $40,000 judgment.

Answers to Odd-Numbered Questions

The first step I recommend is to check the recovery ratio. Bill is required to have Coverage A equal to or greater than 80 percent of $130,000 ($104,000). Because he has $120,000 in Coverage A, he will collect in full on all losses, up to the face amount of his coverage, $120,000. If he has a total loss, he will pay the difference between the $130,000 in damage and the $120,000 limit of liability.

1. The Coverage A loss is total, so Bill receives the limit of coverage, $120,000, not the replacement cost of the damage, $130,000. The contents, Coverage C, limit is $60,000, so Bill again cannot fully replace the damaged property (of $70,000). Bill can collect the $12,000 in additional living expenses under Coverage D, which has a $24,000 limit. The Section 1 deductible, $250, would come from the $130,000 Coverage A claim (making the claim equal to $129,750). Because the limit of Coverage A is less than the amount claimed, Bill receives $120,000 without reduction for the deductible. Bill's total recovery is $120,000 + $60,000 + $12,000 = $192,000.

3. Tool shed = $7,000 destroyed; equipment = $3,000 also destroyed. Answer: Tool shed is covered under Coverage B. Limit = $12,000; deductible = $250; $7,000 damage − $250 deductible = $6,750 damage. Recovery = $6,750.

   Lawn care equipment is covered under Coverage C, personal property. Recovery = $3,000 (deductible does not apply twice).

5. The fire caused to the neighbor's home will result in a property damage liability claim of $170,000. Coverage E has a $100,000 limit, so this is the maximum recovery.
7. Assuming dependency and residency of the daughter, recovery under Coverage C = $1,500 − $250 deductible = $1,250.

9. The business exclusion applies to Bill's accounting activities; thus, there will be no recovery in this instance.

INTERNET RESEARCH ASSIGNMENTS

1. Choose a well-known property insurer that operates in your state and determine if your state insurance commissioner has had complaints about this company in recent years. Start your search at this site: (*http://www.naic.org/*).
2. Determine if your state's insurance department publishes consumer information (guides to purchasing insurance) specifically relating to homeowners insurance. Start your search at this site: (*http://www.naic.org/*). If your state does not publish such information online, use the consumer publications of North Carolina found at this site: (*http://www.ncdoi.com/*). (*Hint: use the "Consumer" pull-down tab or the "Search" box.*) Describe three specific recommendations given to consumers in the homeowners publication.
3. The unendorsed HO contract does not cover the peril of flood. Start at this site, (*http://www.floodsmart. gov/*), and explore the relative flood risk of your home (or an "average" home in the city where you or your parents reside) and estimate the premium for the dwelling and contents. You can view flood maps at (*http://hazards.fema.gov/*) by clicking "map viewer."
4. Estimate the square-foot cost of replacing a relatively low-quality home versus a relatively high-quality home in the city where you reside or where your college or university is located. Start your search at this site: (*http://www.building-cost.net/*).

BUYING HOMEOWNERS INSURANCE

This chapter provided considerable technical detail about homeowners insurance. In previous editions, this chapter concluded with some suggestions for people interested in purchasing homeowners insurance. In this edition, readers interested in consumer guidance are directed to the Web site (*http://www.iii.org/individuals/homei/*) for more information on various forms of individual coverage, including homeowners insurance.

CHAPTER 11

The Personal Auto Policy

After studying this chapter, you should be able to:

- Explain how the tort liability system applies to automobile accidents

- Describe the classes of people covered under the Personal Auto Policy (PAP)

- Explain the four main coverages provided by the PAP

- Identify the important exclusions in the PAP

- Describe the purpose of uninsured motorist insurance

- Distinguish between collision and "other than collision" damage coverage

- Explain how insurers settle losses under the PAP

This is the final chapter devoted to insurance policy construction. We presented the basic rules of contract law in Chapter 8, "Insurance Contracts." Chapter 9, "Basic Property and Liability Insurance Contracts," presented the basic principles of insurance policy construction. We analyzed the homeowners insurance policy (HO) in Chapter 10, "Homeowners Insurance (HO)." Now we analyze the Insurance Services Office (ISO) (*http://www.iso.com/*) Personal Auto Policy (PAP), a form written in simplified English to cover the family automobile. This chapter's appendix describes the no-fault automobile insurance approach to compensating injured people. The no-fault system is much less common today than is the tort-liability alternative and the insurance policy described in this chapter.

Several characteristics distinguish the PAP from the HO. The PAP emphasizes liability protection, making it the first coverage in the policy, rather than the last as the HO does. The potential for nonfamily members to use the family automobile is greater than nonfamily members living in the family home. The possibility that an insured may drive nonowned automobiles also makes the PAP a complex policy. Finally, the PAP presents consumers with more choice of coverage and policy limits than the HO. Where the HO Sections 1 and 2 coverages are packaged together and policy limits are determined by a formula based on the value of the residence, in the PAP the insured may decline to purchase Coverages B through D and the extra-expense options, such as towing coverage. The PAP policy limits for liability (Coverage A) range from the minimum required by state law (for example, $25,000) to more than $1,000,000. No formula determines the relationship between the various section limits as was the case with the homeowners policy.

THE TORT LIABILITY SYSTEM AND AUTOMOBILE INSURANCE: A REVIEW CASE[1]

To review the tort liability system as it relates to automobile insurance, consider the following case. Assume that Rita Book, a librarian, uses her car to commute to work in

---

[1] For interesting stories and loss data, see this Web site: (*http://www.hwysafety.org/*).

the library. As she enters the intersection of Dickens Street and Hugo Way, her car is struck broadside by another car driven by Rex Cars. Rita's car is "totaled" (damage equals $25,000) and, in addition to other injuries, Rita's arm is broken (damage equals $90,000 in medical expenses and $15,000 in lost income). Rex's auto is damaged ($15,000 to the front end), and his skull is cracked. In addition, Rex expects to lose $15,000 of income he would have earned as a driving instructor.

A driver has a duty of care to act as a reasonable person when operating an automobile. On this basis, Rita (plaintiff) goes to court and sues Rex (defendant) for negligently injuring her. She sues for $230,000 in damages. This amount includes $100,000 for pain and suffering.

Rex could defend himself in court by trying to establish contributory negligence by Rita. He could try to prove that Rita ran a stop sign before entering the intersection. (If such were the case, Rex would have a valid defense and could countersue Rita for the cost of his damages.) Rex could try to establish that he was trying to escape some great danger to himself and, in the process of the escape, injured Rita. This line might provide a valid defense. Or Rex may try to establish any other ground to justify his actions or to discredit Rita's actions.

Despite a vigorous defense, assume that a jury finds Rex negligent in the operation of his car. The trial results in a $230,000 judgment in favor of Rita. Because Rex has a PAP, the insurance company will pay for the attorney to defend Rex. The insurer also will pay the judgment on Rex's behalf, up to the policy limits.

Note the different types of damages done by Rex in this case:

- Bodily injury to Rita, including medical expenses, lost wages, and compensation for pain and suffering
- Physical damage to Rita's car
- Physical damage to Rex's car

Although I am generally opposed to an endless string of what-if questions in class, several are suggested in this case, and I cannot pass up the opportunity to share them:

1. What if the car Rita was driving was not her own? What if it belonged to her son, a neighbor, her employer, an auto rental company, or a car dealership?
2. What if Rita was on an errand for her employer when the accident happened?
3. What if Rex had no valid insurance? What if Rex was taking people on a tour of the city for a fee, or if he was delivering pizzas on his part-time job?

These questions raise a few of the issues dealt with in the PAP. We will cover many of the answers in this chapter, but our treatment of the PAP is not meant to be exhaustive. Moreover, the answers may change as new policy provisions are introduced and as courts provide new interpretations of policy language. For these reasons, it is important not only to learn the policy language, but also to learn the reasons for the various policy provisions.

THE PERSONAL AUTO POLICY LAYOUT

The PAP begins with a declarations page, insuring agreement, and definitions as shown in Figure 11–1. The coverage sections follow, and the policy ends with a section covering the insured's duties after a loss and one containing general policy provisions.

Declarations   A typical declarations page appears in Figure 11–2. The **declarations** identify the named insured, the vehicles covered, and the premium charged for the coverage. The insuring agreement describes the insurance in broad terms.

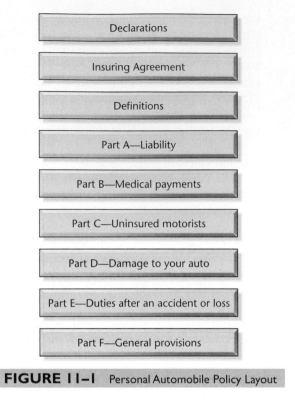

FIGURE 11–1   Personal Automobile Policy Layout

Definitions[2]

The PAP begins with definitions that apply throughout the policy. Two of these terms, *you* and *your covered auto*, merit special attention:

DEFINITIONS

A. Throughout this policy, "you" and "your" refer to:
　　1. The "named insured" shown in the Declarations; and
　　2. The spouse if a resident of the same household.

　　. . .

B. "We", "us," and "our" refer to the Company providing this insurance.

C. For purposes of this policy, a private passenger type auto, pickup or van shall be deemed to be owned by a person if leased:
　　1. Under a written agreement to that person; and
　　2. For a continuous period of at least 6 months. Other words and phrases are defined. They are in quotation marks when used.

D. "Bodily injury" means bodily harm, sickness or disease, including death that results.

---

[2] This chapter contains several quotations from the 2005 ISO PAP, the version currently in use as this material is being prepared. I have abbreviated selections like this one for simplicity. The full text is reproduced in Appendix B. I am most grateful to the ISO for its permission to use its copyrighted material in this text.

E.   "Business" includes trade, profession or occupation.

F.   "Family member" means a person related to you by blood, marriage or adoption who is a resident of your household. This includes a ward or fosterchild.

G.   "Occupying" means:
1.   In;
2.   Upon; or
3.   Getting in, on, out or off.

H.   "Property damage" means physical injury to, destruction of or loss of use of tangible property.

J.   "Your covered auto" means:
1.   Any vehicle shown in the Declarations.
2.   A "newly acquired auto".

FIGURE 11–2   Sample Declarations Page: Personal Auto Policy

Name of Insurer

Named Insured and Mailing Address (No., Street, Apt., Town or City, County, State, Zip Code)

Policy Period:
From: To: 12:01 A.M. Standard Time

Description of Auto(s) or Trailer(s)

AUTO	Year	Trade Name—Model	VIN	Symbol	Age
1					
2					
3					
4					

The Auto(s) or Trailer(s) described in this policy is principally garaged at the above address unless otherwise stated: (No., Street, Apt., Town or City, County, State, Zip Code)

Coverage is provided where a premium and a limit of liability are shown on the coverage.

Coverages	Limit of Liability		Premium			
			Auto 1	Auto 2	Auto 3	Auto 4
A. Liability	$ each accident		$	$	$	$
A. Liability						
Bodily Injury	$ each person $ each accident		$	$	$	$
Property Damage	$ each accident		$	$	$	$
B. Medical Payments	$ each person		$	$	$	$
C. Uninsured Motorists	$ each accident		$	$	$	$
C. Uninsured Motorists	$ each person $ each accident		$	$	$	$
D. Damage to your Auto 1. Collision Loss	Actual Cash Value minus $ Deductible		$	$	$	$
2. Other than Collision Loss	$ Deductible		$	$	$	$
Towing and Labor Costs	$ each disablement		$	$	$	$
			$	$	$	$

Endorsements made part of this Policy at time of issue:

Endorsement Premium $

| Total Premium Per Auto | $ | $ | $ | $ |

Total Premium $

Loss Payee (Name and address)	

Countersigned:

By _____

Authorized Representative

THIS DECLARATIONS PAGE WITH PERSONAL AUTO POLICY PROVISIONS OR POLICY JACKET AND PERSONAL AUTO POLICY FORM, TOGETHER WITH ENDORSEMENTS, IF ANY, ISSUED TO FORM A PART THEREOF, COMPLETES THE ABOVE NUMBERED POLICY.

Note that the definitions of *spouse* and *family member* refer to resident status. In Chapter 10, we explained that the term *resident* could constitute a question of fact that required a court decision. Note also that the term *occupying* is defined more broadly than *driving*. The "covered autos" phrase requires specific listing, including the vehicle identification number, in the declarations. In addition, careful wording in the contract provides for situations involving replacement autos as well as newly purchased additional autos.

Part A—Liability

In our review case, a court holds Rex responsible for injuring Rita to the extent of $230,000. The court awards Rita a judgment, and Rex then looks to his insurer to pay the claim. Rex finds coverage in Part A of his PAP. The key words in the insuring agreement for Part A of the PAP are the following:

PART A—LIABILITY COVERAGE INSURING AGREEMENT

A. We will pay damages for "bodily injury" or "property damage" for which any "insured" becomes legally responsible because of an auto accident. Damages include prejudgment interest awarded against the "insured." We will settle or defend, as we consider appropriate, any claim or suit asking for these damages. In addition to our limit of liability, we will pay all defense costs we incur. Our duty to settle or defend ends when our limit of liability for this coverage has been exhausted by payment of judgments or settlements. We have no duty to defend any suit or settle any claim for "bodily injury" or "property damage" not covered under this policy.

Automobile liability insurance

The insurer agrees to defend its insured in court, as well as to pay legal judgments on behalf of its insureds, as a part of **automobile liability insurance**. As a result, the insured does not have to pay for an attorney if sued. Thus, if Rex's defense costs $30,000, the insurer would pay this cost in addition to the $230,000 judgment. In the PAP, the cost to defend an insured does not reduce the money available to pay claims. The policy states: "In addition to our limit of liability, we will pay all defense costs we incur."

The PAP makes explicit that the insurer need not provide a defense if litigation arises from an event not covered by the policy. For example, if an injury results while an insured uses a covered auto as a taxi, the insurer is not obligated to pay liability claims or provide a defense because the policy excludes liability coverage for insureds using their autos as public livery vehicles.

Insurers reserve the right to investigate all claims made against insureds and to settle any claims or suits that they deem appropriate. So if the insured clearly was negligent in causing the loss, the insurer can offer the victim a settlement without the insured's consent. The insurer avoids litigation and the defense costs if the victim accepts the settlement. The insurer's duty to defend its insured ends after a claimant has accepted a settlement offer or if an actual payment is made to settle a legal judgment.

Limit of Liability

Single limit of liability

The declarations page provides a **single limit of liability**, such as $500,000. This amount is the limit for all types of damage that an insured may cause in one occurrence. If judgments exceed this limit, the insured, not the insurer, is responsible for the excess.

Split limits

The PAP may be written with **split limits** by using an endorsement. When Coverage A is written with split limits, three separate numbers are indicated in this fashion: ###/###/###. (Insurers typically omit the last three zeros and the dollar signs when referring to the split limits.) The first number is the maximum that the insured will pay for one injured person. The second number is the maximum that the insurer will pay for the injuries sustained by all the people injured in a single accident. The third number is the maximum that the insurer will pay for property damage. For example, consider the split limits of 100/300/50. Under these limits, the insurer pays a maximum of $100,000 to any one injured person and a maximum of $300,000 for any one accident regardless of the number of injured people. The third number indicates that the insurer will pay up to $50,000 for property damage liability for each accident.

In some cases, the single-limit policy will provide more compensation to the insured's injured victims than the split-limits policy. For example, consider a single limit of $500,000 versus split limits of 100/300/50. If the insured's victim, Paul Barer, the mortician, sustained $300,000 in damages, he would receive this amount if the insured had a single limit policy because it is less than the limit of $500,000. However, he would receive only $100,000 if the insured had 100/300/50 split limits because this contract limits recovery for one individual to $100,000.

As a second example, consider the split limits of 250/500/5. Assume that Hannibal Moe, the elephant trainer, causes a collision injuring four people and they file suit in the following order (the insurer pays claims in the order in which the suits are settled): A's injuries total $400,000, B's equal $100,000, C's amount to $250,000, and D's are $500,000. With split limits, A can collect $250,000, the maximum the insurer will pay for any one person. B will collect $100,000, bringing the total paid by the insurer to $350,000. The remaining $150,000 ($500,000 − $350,000) will go to C. In all, $150,000 of A's claim, $100,000 of C's claim, and D's entire claim will not be satisfied by Hannibal's insurance contract. Not only will Hannibal be liable for the unsatisfied claims, but also he will pay for any additional defense costs because the company's obligation to defend ends after it pays the limit of liability.

It is very important to have adequate limits. What is an adequate limit? An adequate limit is one large enough to cover any damage you may cause with an auto. If one is responsible for killing a doctor earning $4 million a year, forcing a school bus carrying 30 children off the road (all of whom are injured), or causing a truck loaded with 100 flat-panel color television sets to overturn (or even perhaps doing all this damage as a result of a single negligent act), one may be faced with $10 million or more in claims. Because it is rather easy to conceive of situations involving large amounts of damage, experts generally recommend high limits of liability coverage. Moreover, increasing the limit from some minimum specified by the state financial responsibility laws (which can be wholly inadequate) does not increase the insured's overall premium by nearly as much as the percentage increase in coverage.

Some commentators believe the amount of liability insurance people purchase should be a function of the amount of their wealth; meaning that a wealthy person should purchase more liability insurance than a poor person. However, all socially responsible drivers want to compensate their potential victims adequately, and this attitude requires a sufficiently large amount of liability insurance.

Insureds

B. "Insured" as used in this Part means:
1. You or any "family member" for the ownership, maintenance, or use of any auto or "trailer."
2. Any person using "your covered auto."

3. For "your covered auto," any person or organization but only with respect to legal responsibility for acts or omissions of a person for whom coverage is afforded under this Part.
4. For any auto or "trailer," other than "your covered auto," any other person or organization but only with respect to legal responsibility for acts or omissions of you or any "family member" for whom coverage is afforded under this Part. This Provision (B.4.) applies only if the person or organization does not own or hire the auto or "trailer."

The PAP provides coverage for four categories of insureds that have potential liability arising from the use of an auto:

- *Category 1*: The named insured and resident family members are covered for the ownership, maintenance, or use of any auto, whether it is owned or borrowed, unless an exclusion applies.

- *Category 2*: Covers any person using the named insured's covered auto. That is, the car owner's insurance, not the driver's insurance, would pay a claim if the owner let somebody borrow his or her auto. For example, assume that Daniel Boone lets his neighbor, Andy Jackson, borrow his car. As a general rule, coverage on the car involved in the accident is considered **primary coverage**. Primary coverage pays first. If Boone's insurance was exhausted by a claim (Jackson was sued for $150,000 and Boone's insurance had a limit of $100,000), then Jackson could turn to his own insurer to pay the remainder of the claim until his own insurance was exhausted. We call Jackson's insurance **excess coverage**. Excess coverage pays after the limits of the primary coverage have been exhausted.

Primary coverage

Excess coverage

- *Categories 3 and 4*: In some situations, people or organizations other than a driver can be sued due to a driver's negligence. In some of these instances, the PAP will cover the liability of these people. For example, assume that the Alpha Beta Gamma Omega fraternity sends a brother, Bozo, to get some liquid refreshments for a "blast." Assume that Bozo uses his own car to do this. If Bozo causes an automobile accident while returning with the drinks, Bozo's PAP would cover the fraternity's liability. The fraternity's liability arises because Bozo was technically an agent of the fraternity while on this mission. The difference between Categories 3 and 4 is between the insured driving an owned or a nonowned vehicle.

Exclusions

Coverage A has several important exclusions relieving the insurer of liability. The PAP divides these exclusions into two sections labeled Part A and Part B.

The exclusions in Part A state that, "we do not provide Liability Coverage for any 'insured'":

1. "who intentionally causes 'bodily injury' or 'property damage'." Because intentional injuries are not accidental losses, they are not insurable.

2, 3. There is no liability coverage for property owned, transported by, rented to, used by, or in the care of a covered person. Two considerations are working here: First, Coverage A provides liability protection, not property protection, and people logically cannot be liable to themselves. That is, if we cause an auto accident, we cannot turn around and sue ourselves because we destroyed our own property. Second, the HO policy provides insurance for the insured's personal property.

For example, assume that Teddy Roosevelt uses his car to deliver his television set for repair. While driving to the repair shop, Teddy runs a stop sign and destroys both the television set and his car. There is no coverage for the television set under the PAP because of these exclusions. Damage to Teddy's automobile, however, is covered by Teddy's PAP under Coverage D, collision damage. If Teddy had an HO insurance policy, presumably he could collect for damage to his personal property, the television set (as damage caused by the peril of "vehicles"), for the amount in excess of the deductible.

4. There is generally no coverage if an employee of the insured sustains injury because it is expected that workers' compensation insurance will cover this event.
5. There is no coverage if the auto can be hired by the public to carry persons or property for a fee, but car pooling is permissible.
6, 7. Excludes coverage for some circumstances involving the automobile and other nonfarming businesses.
8. There is no coverage when a person uses an auto without a reasonable belief that he or she is entitled to do so. The issue of what is a "reasonable belief" can be a question of fact to be tried in court.

Part B of the liability coverage exclusions states, "We do not provide Liability Coverage for the . . . use of":

1. Vehicles with fewer than four wheels (meaning motorcycles, mopeds, and so forth).
2. Vehicles, other than the covered auto, owned by the insured or furnished for regular use, such as leased cars, or cars furnished by a business, or cars owned but not listed on the declarations page. This exclusion causes insureds having vehicles in the excluded categories to declare them and pay a premium for them if they want insurance on these vehicles.
3. Any vehicle located inside a facility designed for racing. This exclusion removes coverage from insureds engaging in automobile racing. Race car drivers need to purchase separate insurance policies and should not rely on the PAP for coverage of their racing activities.

In summary, the PAP provides the insured with financial protection from lawsuits of people claiming they were injured by an insured. Under the tort liability system, injured parties either must sue the insured or be offered a settlement of the claim before collecting for their injuries. Several exclusions apply to restrict the scope of the liability coverage.

PART B—MEDICAL PAYMENTS

Automobile medical payments coverage

The purpose of the **automobile medical payments coverage** is to pay for relatively small amounts of medical expenses on a no-fault basis. This coverage eliminates the need of eligible people to sue to recover for their injuries, thus reducing the likelihood of litigation under Part A.

The insuring agreement for Part B reads as follows:

> ### PART B—MEDICAL PAYMENTS COVERAGE
> ### INSURING AGREEMENT
>
> A. We will pay reasonable expenses incurred for necessary medical and funeral services because of "bodily injury":
>   1. Caused by accident; and

2. Sustained by an "insured."
   We will pay only those expenses incurred for services rendered within 3 years from the date of the accident.

Covered persons include the named insured and family members when they are in a motor vehicle or struck by a motor vehicle designed for use on public roads. Thus, if Rita Book or her family members are injured when riding in an auto or bus, or as pedestrians, if an auto, bus, or motorcycle strikes them, they could look to their insurer for indemnity for medical or funeral expenses up to the policy's limit of liability. There is a three-year time limit from the date of the accident for this coverage. Alternatively, if Rita is squashed by a bulldozer, plowed under by a farm tractor, or hit by a freight train, there would be no coverage because these vehicles are not designed for the road. Likewise, there is an exclusion if she sustains injury while driving or riding a motorcycle. The additional exclusions to the medical payments coverage, including one applying to automobile racing, are similar to those discussed in Part A, Liability Coverage. The "Limit of Liability" section makes it clear that a single limit of liability, stated in the declarations, applies to each insured involved in an accident.

PART C—UNINSURED MOTORIST COVERAGE

Purpose

The purpose of uninsured motorist (UM) insurance is to protect people from financially irresponsible drivers who neither purchase liability insurance nor have adequate financial resources to compensate people they injure with their automobiles. It is important to recognize that UM coverage is fault-based. Insureds must show they are *legally entitled to recover damages* from a negligent uninsured motorist to receive UM benefits.

Coverage Under the PAP

The insuring agreement for Part C reads as follows:

INSURING AGREEMENT

A. We will pay compensatory damages which an "insured" is legally entitled to recover from the owner or operator of an "uninsured motor vehicle" because of "bodily injury":
   1. Sustained by an "insured"; and
   2. Caused by an accident.
      The owner's or operator's liability for these damages must arise out of the ownership, maintenance, or use of the "uninsured motor vehicle."
      Any judgment for damages arising out of a suit brought without our written consent is not binding on us.

These words create a legal right for insureds to collect compensatory (but not punitive) damages from their own insurer if the insured is injured by an uninsured motorist, but only for bodily injury. The intention of the insurer not to pay punitive or exemplary damages is repeated in the exclusions section of this coverage.

Uninsured motorist

The term **uninsured motorist** includes the following categories:

- Drivers without insurance
- Drivers with less insurance than the minimum required by state law
- Hit-and-run drivers
- Drivers with coverage provided by insolvent insurers

In general, suing uninsured motorists, especially hit-and-run drivers, is not a promising source of recovery. Because UM coverage is fault-based, insureds must convince their own insurer that the driver of the uninsured automobile caused the accident. Only when the other driver is negligent is the insured legally entitled to recovery.

If the insured cannot establish the uninsured driver's negligence, or if the extent of the damages is subject to dispute, then an awkward situation is created under this coverage. The insured must confront his or her own insurer to resolve the dispute. In such circumstances, the policy provides for an *arbitration* process to determine if the insured actually is entitled to recover damages, and, if so, in what amount.

The limit of liability for this coverage is found on the policy's declarations page, subject to reduction for any recovery from the negligent driver or from a workers' compensation claim. The exclusions to this coverage are similar to those already discussed and appear in the PAP reproduced at the end of this book.

The State's Response to Uninsured Motorists

The various states generally have approached the problem of accidents caused by financially irresponsible drivers in four ways:

- Some states have made uninsured motorists' protection (such as Coverage C of the PAP) virtually mandatory. In some states, motorists can decline UM coverage but must sign a waiver to do so.
- Most states have passed financial responsibility laws.
- Some states have passed compulsory automobile insurance laws.
- A few states maintain unsatisfied judgment funds.

Financial responsibility laws

Financial responsibility laws require drivers to furnish evidence of financial responsibility to retain their driver's license or their auto registration. Most drivers purchase liability insurance (such as Coverage A of the PAP), which is acceptable evidence of financial responsibility. Alternative evidence would be a surety bond or a deposit of assets. Drivers must establish their financial responsibility after they have been involved in an automobile accident or after they have been arrested for a serious traffic violation.

Compulsory insurance laws

Among the states that have passed **compulsory insurance laws** are Arkansas, Indiana, Massachusetts, New York, Louisiana, and North Carolina. In these states, drivers must show evidence of purchasing at least the minimum required amount of insurance before the state issues automobile license plates.

Unsatisfied judgment funds

A few states operate **unsatisfied judgment funds**. These states use revenue collected from license plate sales or from insurance premium taxes to make payments to injured victims of uninsured motorists.

Underinsured Motorists

A situation similar to being injured by an uninsured motorist would arise if an underinsured motorist injured the insured. Assume, for example, that Robert F. Lee is

Underinsured motorists insurance

injured in an auto accident caused by a driver having the minimum legal amount of insurance, $25,000, and that Robert incurs $600,000 in medical expenses and lost wages. After winning a legal judgment, he collects $25,000 from the negligent driver's insurer. If the negligent driver had no other financial resources, Robert would bear $575,000 of his loss. Now, assume that Robert has $1,000,000 of **underinsured motorists insurance**. In this case, Robert could collect the remaining amount of damages from his own insurer because it defines an *underinsured motor vehicle* as any vehicle that is insured for less than the amount of Robert's Coverage C, uninsured motorist limits. In the more complex language of the policy, an underinsured motor vehicle is "a land motor vehicle . . . to which a bodily injury liability . . . policy applies at the time of the accident but its limit for bodily injury liability is less than the limit of liability for this coverage." Underinsured motorist coverage is not part of the basic coverage provided by the PAP and is added to the contract by endorsement.

PART D—DAMAGE TO YOUR AUTO

The PAP agreement for auto property damage, including an extensive definition of collision, reads as follows:

PART D—COVERAGE FOR DAMAGE TO YOUR AUTO INSURING AGREEMENT

A. We will pay for direct and accidental loss to "your covered auto" or any "non-owned auto," including their equipment, minus any applicable deductible shown in the Declarations. If loss to more than one "your covered auto" or "non-owned auto" results from the same "collision," only the highest applicable deductible will apply. We will pay for loss to "your covered auto" caused by:
   1. Other than "collision" only if the Declarations indicate that Other Than Collision Coverage is provided for that auto.
   2. "Collision" only if the Declarations indicate that Collision Coverage is provided for that auto.
   If there is a loss to a "non-owned auto," we will provide the broadest coverage applicable to any "your covered auto" shown in the Declarations.

B. "Collision" means the upset of "your covered auto" or a "non-owned auto" or their impact with another vehicle or object.
   Loss caused by the following is considered other than "collision":
   1. Missiles or falling objects;
   2. Fire;
   3. Theft or larceny;
   4. Explosion or earthquake;
   5. Windstorm;
   6. Hail, water or flood;
   7. Malicious mischief or vandalism;
   8. Riot or civil commotion;
   9. Contact with bird or animal; or
   10. Breakage of glass.

These words give the insured coverage for damage to a covered auto. Insurers historically called this combination of coverage *comprehensive* and collision. Today these are referred to as *collision* and *other-than-collision* coverages. A deductible usually applies to the collision coverage and a deductible also may apply to the other-than-collision section. Any deductible appears on the declarations page.

Twelve exclusions apply to this coverage, including damage resulting from wear and tear, war, or radioactive contamination. Many of the other exclusions are by now familiar to readers. However, the exclusion relating to electronic equipment has been changed since the previous version of the PAP. In recent years, equipment such as navigational systems and Internet access systems has become more common as standard or optional equipment. Consumers purchasing automobile insurance have a reasonable expectation of coverage when the manufacturer permanently installs this equipment. Therefore, with a limit of $1,000, Part D covers electronic equipment that reproduces, receives, or transmits audio, visual, or data signals and is permanently installed, including both manufacturer installed and after-market equipment.

Collision

The extended definition of **collision** states: If a collision follows from one of the other perils listed, the damage is *not* considered to be collision. For example, if a bird were to hit the windshield, and in so doing, cause the driver to lose control of the auto and collide with a tree, the proximate cause of the loss would be hitting the bird. Even if insureds did not purchase collision coverage under Part D, recovery would still be possible if they purchased **other-than-collision coverage**. The coverage for damage to your auto is open-perils coverage. The meaning of the insuring clause is quite clear: If there is a loss and the cause is not excluded, the insurance company pays.

Other-than-collision coverage

Loss Settlement

Insurers adjust losses under Coverage D on an actual cash value (ACV) basis—that is, replacement cost minus depreciation. In cases where the cost of repair exceeds the market value of the auto, the loss is declared "total" and insurers pay the actual cash value for the vehicle. One source used to determine an auto's ACV is a monthly publication available to auto dealers and others in financing automobile transactions.

The PAP limits the insured's recovery to "the amount necessary to repair or replace the property with other property of like kind and quality." This wording allows insurers to use after-market repair parts instead of repair parts made by the car's manufacturer.

LIMIT OF LIABILITY

A. Our limit of liability for loss will be the lesser of the:
1. Actual cash value of the stolen or damaged property; or
2. Amount necessary to repair or replace the property with other property of like kind and quality.

   However, the most we will pay for loss to:
1. Any "non-owned auto" which is a trailer is $1500.
2. Electronic equipment that reproduces, receives or transmits audio, visual or data signals, which is permanently installed in the auto in locations not used by the auto manufacturer for installation of such equipment, is $1,000.

B. An adjustment for depreciation and physical condition will be made in determining actual cash value in the event of a total loss.

C. If a repair or replacement results in better than like kind or quality, we will not pay for the amount of the betterment.

The interpretation of item C reproduced in the preceding box describing a "betterment" associated with repair has been subject to discussion. One interpretation of this clause suggests that if an after-market repair part costs half of an original equipment manufacturer's part, the insured who insists on using original manufacturer parts must bear the additional cost. (An *after-market repair part* is a part made by a manufacturer other than the original equipment manufacturer; for example, a hood made by Generic Hoods, Inc. instead of by Ford.) A second interpretation of this clause suggests that if an insured runs over an object in the road and ruins an engine that already has been operated for 40,000 miles, the insurer could deduct some amount for the betterment when a rebuilt engine replaces a used engine.

PART E—DUTIES AFTER AN ACCIDENT OR LOSS

PART E – DUTIES AFTER AN ACCIDENT OR LOSS

We have no duty to provide coverage under this policy if the failure to comply with the following duties is prejudicial to us:

A. We must be notified promptly of how, when and where the accident or loss happened. Notice should also include the names and addresses of any injured persons and of any witnesses.

B. A person seeking any coverage must:
1. Cooperate with us in the investigation, settlement or defense of any claim or suit.
2. Promptly send us copies of any notices or legal papers received in connection with the accident or loss.
3. Submit, as often as we reasonably require:
    (a) To physical exams by physicians we select. We will pay for these exams.
    (b) To examination under oath and subscribe the same.
4. Authorize us to obtain:
    (a) Medical reports; and
    (b) Other pertinent records.
5. Submit a proof of loss when required by us.

C. A person seeking Uninsured Motorists Coverage must also:
1. Promptly notify the police if a hit-and-run driver is involved.
2. Promptly send us copies of the legal papers if a suit is brought.

D. A person seeking Coverage For Damage To Your Auto must also:
1. Take reasonable steps after loss to protect "your covered auto" or any "non-owned auto" and their equipment from further loss. We will pay reasonable expenses incurred to do this.
2. Promptly notify the police if "your covered auto" or any "non-owned auto" is stolen.
3. Permit us to inspect and appraise the damaged property before its repair or disposal.

The conditions of the PAP, like the conditions of all property and liability insurance contracts, are important and the insured must comply with them to collect insurance proceeds. The policy states that if the insured fails to comply with the listed duties and the results are prejudicial (harmful) to the insurer, then "We have no duty to provide coverage under this policy."

The policy's language states that in the event of loss, the insured must notify the insurer promptly of how, when, and where the loss occurred. This notice of loss requirement allows the company to investigate the loss while the evidence is still fresh.

The insured must protect the damaged property from further loss. The insurer agrees to pay for reasonable expenses incurred to protect the property. Thus, if an auto went into a ditch, the insurance company generally would pay to have it towed to a garage and stored until it could be repaired.

The insured must cooperate with the insurer in settling the loss. That is, the insured must supply evidence, testify at trials or hearings as needed, and help to obtain the attendance of witnesses.

An insured making a claim under Coverage C, Uninsured Motorist Coverage, for damage attributed to a hit-and-run driver has a duty to notify the police promptly after the incident.

PART F—GENERAL PROVISIONS

The general provisions are similar to those found in the HO policy. Therefore, we provide only a quick review here.

Bankruptcy of the insured does not relieve the insurer from paying injured third parties. Without this statement, a legal judgment that bankrupted the insured could relieve the insurer from making a liability payment because a bankrupt insured may no longer be legally obligated to the injured person.

Fraud by the insured against the insurer voids the policy. The PAP makes this point explicitly.

The insured cannot sue the company for payment until all the terms of the policy have been complied with; under Coverage A, the insurer agrees in writing that the insured is obligated to pay a claim; or a court delivers a judgment favoring an injured person.

An important provision covers the insurer's right to subrogation ("Our Right to Recover Payment"). *Subrogation* means the insurer receives the insured's right to sue a negligent party once the insurer has paid for a loss. If the insured does something *after* a loss (such as signing a waiver releasing a negligent party for his or her actions) to impair the insurer's subrogation rights, the insured has breached the contract, and thus the insurer may not pay for the loss.

Territory covered   Other conditions of the PAP relate to the **territory covered**. (Canada, Puerto Rico, and the United States are covered territories, but Mexico and other foreign countries are not covered. Therefore, U.S. drivers should purchase appropriate insurance before driving in Mexico or other foreign countries.) Assignment of the PAP is invalid without the written consent of insurer. State law often affects cancellation of the contract rights of each party, but the PAP presents the details of each party's termination rights.

The final two sections of the PAP cover *assignment* (transfer of your interest in this policy) and a provision covering the possibility of an insured having more than one policy that applies to the same accident (that is, two or more auto policies). The policy states that the PAP may not be assigned without the insurer's written consent, and if more than one policy applies to the same accident, the insurer's liability will not exceed the highest applicable limit of liability under any one policy. This latter provision is often called an "anti-stacking" provision, and its purpose is to limit an insured's ability to increase coverage by claiming payment for the same loss from more than one policy.

SUMMARY

Automobile accidents cause billions of dollars in annual damage, including destroyed property, medical and funeral expenses, and lost income. Under the tort liability system, if one person injures another, the injured party (plaintiff) must sue the negligent party (defendant) to collect for the injuries caused by the negligence. Motorists can purchase a package of insurance protection to cover losses related to the ownership and use of an auto. We examined one such policy, the ISO PAP.

Part A of the PAP provides coverage for an insured (a term much broader than *named insured*) who is legally liable for injuring another or another's property. Several important definitions and exclusions—such as intentionally caused injury—apply to this coverage.

Part B of the PAP provides medical expense coverage for the insureds—again subject to limits of liability and relevant exclusions—such as injuries resulting from using vehicles having fewer than four wheels.

Part C protects insureds if uninsured motorists injure them. The various states have passed different types of laws to manage the problem of uninsured motorists. Some states have allowed motorists to collect for damages under this coverage under unusual circumstances even when there was no direct contact with an uninsured vehicle.

Part D provides property protection for the insured's auto. This coverage makes an important distinction between collision and other types of damage.

Parts E and F are general conditions with which insureds must comply to get the benefit of the policy.

REVIEW TERMS

- Automobile liability insurance
- Automobile medical payments coverage
- Collision
- Compulsory insurance laws
- Declarations
- Excess coverage
- Financial responsibility laws
- Other-than-collision coverage
- Primary coverage
- Single limit of liability
- Split limits of liability
- Territory covered
- Underinsured motorists insurance
- Uninsured motorist
- Unsatisfied judgment funds

REVIEW

1. Briefly, how does the tort liability system apply to automobile accidents?
2. Explain the difference between primary and excess coverage in automobile insurance.
3. Several distinct categories of drivers are insured under the terms of the PAP. Identify three categories of drivers covered by the PAP and give examples of each category.
4. Explain whether each of the following people described here has coverage under Part A of the PAP and say why or why not. Bob, the named insured, is an auto mechanic. Bob and his wife, Belle, own and drive a Ford. They have two children, Ben and Bill. Ben, age 26, is in the U.S. Army and comes home to visit about twice a year. Bill is 16, lives at home, and has a learner's permit but no permanent driver's license. Ben often rents cars on weekends and drives battle tanks as his military assignments. Bob drives the church van to pick up nondriving members each Sunday. Bob also test-drives vehicles after he has repaired them at his place of employment, Barney's Garage. Bill has been known to lend the family car to his teenage pal, Bubba. Once, Bubba actually lent the auto to his girlfriend, Brenda.
5. Does the PAP provide coverage if a named insured drives a nonowned auto? What is the definition of a nonowned auto?
6. What are the four general areas of protection provided by Coverages A through D of the PAP?
7. Assume that an insured causes an automobile accident that injures five people and damages one auto. Assume that each of the injured parties successfully sues for $20,000. The damaged auto was worth $10,000. How much would the insurer pay if:
   a. the insured carried 10/20/5 limits?
   b. the insured carried 50/100/5 limits?
   c. the insured carried 100/300/50 limits?
8. Why is damage to an insured's own property excluded under Part A?
9. Identify other major categories of exclusions under Part A.

10. What situations are covered by the medical expense protection part of the PAP? If an insured were struck by a car while walking, would there be coverage under this provision?
11. Why do drivers need uninsured motorists insurance if they have purchased liability and property damage insurance?
12. How have the various states responded to the problem of uninsured motorists?
13. Explain the difference between an uninsured and an underinsured motorist.
14. What are the insured's major duties after a loss?
15. Do insureds have a right to demand replacement of parts damaged in a collision with parts from the original equipment manufacturer?
16. How does the legal doctrine of subrogation apply under the PAP?

OBJECTIVE QUESTIONS

Assume that Herb Avon, the vegetarian, owns the PAP discussed in this chapter and reproduced as Appendix B. His policy has the following limits:

> A = $100,000
> B = $3,000
> C = $100,000
> D = $250 deductible—collision; $250 deductible—other than collision

Assume that each of the events described in the following situations occurs separately. The actual cash value of Herb's car is $14,500. You are to calculate the amount Herb's insurer will pay.

1. Herb negligently collides with a farm tractor. The tractor is on the highway to get from one farm to another. Herb was at fault. The farmer successfully sues for $80,000 in bodily injury damages and $21,000 in property damage to his tractor. The lawyers charge $10,000 to defend Herb in court.
2. Herb's daughter, Peggy Sue, strikes their home and their second car while learning how to drive. She is 16 years old and has a learner's permit. Damage to Herb's home is $30,000 and to the second car (both vehicles are insured with the same policy) is $15,000.
3. Herb runs a stop sign and collides with a parked car, causing $4,000 of damage to each vehicle.
4. While using his car as a delivery vehicle for a local florist, Herb is struck by an uninsured motorist. He has $15,000 in medical expenses and lost wages. His car is destroyed (replacement value is $16,000).
5. Herb lends his auto to Emmy Lou. Emmy Lou has her own PAP with coverage identical to Herb's. Emmy Lou runs over and injures a famous baseball player who recently signed a three-year, $27 million contract. Emmy Lou is sued for $32 million. (Answer with respect to Herb's PAP.)
6. Herb borrows his neighbor's car for a week while the neighbor is on vacation. Unfortunately, Herb did $4,000 damage to the neighbor's car while he was driving it.
7. Herb hits a deer on Door County Highway A. His car is destroyed.

Answers to Odd-Numbered Questions

1. Insurer will pay the limit of Coverage A, which is $100,000 plus $10,000 in legal costs (damage = $101,000, leaving $1,000 uncovered).
3. As a property liability claim, $4,000 damage to the other car is covered; $4,000 damage to Herb's car is covered as a collision claim; $250 deductible applies to the claim for Herb's car. The total paid by the PAP = $4,000 + $3,750.
5. Herb's PAP provides $100,000 coverage for Emmy Lou, who is an insured under Coverage A. When the limit is exhausted, Emmy Lou may look to her own insurer for excess coverage. If the claim is still not satisfied, Emmy Lou's assets (and perhaps Herb's, if it is asserted Herb was negligent in lending the car to a reckless driver) will have to be used to pay the claim. Bankruptcy may follow this chain of events.
7. The deer damage is considered other-than-collision damage and Herb receives the actual cash value, which is $14,500 less the $250 deductible.

INTERNET RESEARCH ASSIGNMENTS

1. How many people were killed in automobile accidents in your state in the most recent year for which data is available at this site: (*http://www.iihs.org/*). Describe one of the leading causes of fatal automobile accidents.
2. Determine if your state's insurance department publishes consumer information (guides to purchasing insurance) specifically relating to automobile insurance. Start your search at this site: (*http://www.naic.org/*). If your state does not publish such information

online, use the consumer publications of North Carolina found at this site: (*http://www.ncdoi.com/*) (*Hint: use the "Consumer" pull-down tab or the "Search" box.*) Describe three specific recommendations given to consumers in the automobile insurance publication.

3. Determine if your state has a financial responsibility law, a compulsory insurance law, or an unsatisfied judgment fund. What are the general requirements in your state?

4. In some states, property damage coverage is available under uninsured motorist coverage. Find out if your state allows purchase of this coverage.

5. Determine if your state has a version of automobile no-fault legislation. If so, under what circumstances can a person still sue for bodily injuries caused by a negligent driver?

Appendix – No-Fault Automobile Insurance

Under the tort liability system, the injured party either must sue the person causing the injury or be offered a settlement of the claim by the defendant's insurer to be compensated for the loss. **No-fault automobile insurance** is an alternative procedure for compensating injured victims of automobile accidents. A central feature of all true no-fault proposals is that people injured in automobile accidents will collect for their injuries from their own insurers. Injuries for which no-fault insurance arrangements provide compensation include lost income, medical expenses, and burial expenses. No compensation is paid for pain and suffering. Nothing is novel in collecting from one's own insurer. Most insurance is based on the idea that insureds will collect compensation from their own insurer. Thus, if Dangerous Dan McGrew negligently burns down his house, he collects from his own HO insurance. If he negligently wraps his car around a tree, he collects from his own automobile insurer.

The novel feature of no-fault automobile liability insurance proposals is that Dan McGrew will collect from his own insurer even if Calamity Jane negligently caused his injury. No-fault insurance proposals create the right to collect from one's own insurer. At the same time, these proposals remove the right and need to sue the negligent party. Thus, pure no-fault insurance would eliminate the need for liability insurance because nobody would have to (or be able to) sue a negligent party to collect for damages.

No-fault insurance does not mean no one is at fault in causing automobile accidents. The name comes from the fact that no necessity exists to prove who is at fault in causing an accident to collect for damages. Under a pure no-fault compensation system, all parties involved in an automobile accident

receive compensation for their injuries from their own insurer, regardless of who caused the accident. The difference in the approach to victim compensation between the no-fault and the tort liability system is illustrated in Figure 11–3. Under the tort liability system, the injured party must sue the negligent party to collect for damages. Such suits to establish the defendant's negligence can be long and complex. Furthermore, in states where contributory negligence rules prevent the plaintiff from recovering anything, both plaintiff and defendant could bear the cost of their own injuries. No-fault insurance laws are designed to reduce or eliminate negligence lawsuits, facilitate loss payments, and help control the problem of uncompensated victims.

Since the 1970s, when the first no-fault automobile insurance laws were enacted, 16 states enacted some form of these rules. Subsequently five states allowed their no-fault laws to expire. After several decades, it remains unclear if no-fault automobile insurance has produced the cost savings and other benefits that its proponents claimed. Among the problems that have been detected in those states that adopted no-fault automobile insurance laws are fraud, overuse of medical services, and increased involvement of attorneys and other professionals.

None of the current state no-fault plans involves pure no-fault laws. They are best described as *modified no-fault laws*. That is, under the current arrangements, after some threshold of damage has been reached, the injured party may revert to the liability system to seek compensation. The threshold may be either a dollar amount such as $2,500 or a **verbal threshold**, such as one eliminating lawsuits unless "injury results in death, serious impairment of bodily function, or permanent and serious disfigurement."

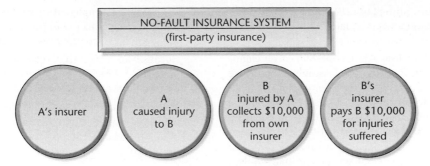

1. A negligently injures B causing $10,000 damage.
2. B collects $10,000 from his own insurer.

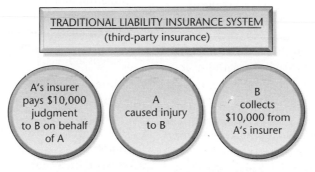

1. A negligently injures B causing $10,000 damage.
2. B sues A and wins a $10,000 judgment.
3. A's insurer pays B $10,000 on A's behalf.

FIGURE 11–3 No-Fault Insurance Compared with Tort Liability Insurance

To protect residents in a no-fault state from liability suits of nonresidents, the various state laws provide for property damage and bodily injury liability insurance. That is, if a resident of a no-fault state injures an out-of-state resident, the tort liability system provides compensation to the victim. Generally, no-fault insurance is designed to speed the compensation of victims of less-serious traffic accidents by eliminating delays caused by courts and insurance companies in transferring compensation to injured parties.

No-Fault Versus Tort Liability

Both no-fault insurance plans and the tort liability system are designed to compensate the victims of automobile accidents. Under no-fault, injured parties collect from their own insurer for their injuries. Under the tort liability system, the injured party sues the negligent party and collects from the negli-gent party's insurer. Critics have made the following four criticisms of the tort liability system:

1. Not enough of the dollars put into the traditional tort liability system are finding their way to automobile accident victims. Only about one-sixth of the economic damage caused by automobiles is being compensated for by the tort liability system. More specifically, fees for a plaintiff's lawyers may run from 25 to 33 percent of the plaintiff's recovery amount. Defendant's attorney's fees, court costs, and insurance company expenses also represent dollars that do not go to victims. The substantial legal fees earned in automobile litigation make supporters of the no-fault system suspicious of lawyers' motives in providing a vigorous defense of the tort liability system.

2. Claimants are not always indemnified fairly. That is, critics of the tort liability system maintain that small claims (sometimes called nuisance claims) often are overcompensated while large claims are undercompensated. Critics complain the dramatic presentations

of some lawyers and plaintiffs result in extraordinarily large judgments virtually unrelated to the damage sustained.

3. Recovery is often slow. About one-half of all claims are not settled after two years. In some areas, where courts are backlogged with cases, some claims remain unsettled after four years. Critics charge this situation works against poorer victims because their financial assets may not permit them to wait this long for payment. In such circumstances, a poor person would be more apt to accept a smaller settlement than would a wealthy person who could wait for a larger settlement offer or wait and take the case to court. Supporters of no-fault insurance claim that their system reduces court congestion and speeds recovery to victims.

4. Proving negligence is often difficult, especially years after an accident occurs. In some cases, the circumstances of the accident are such that negligence cannot be determined or established. (For instance, it is often difficult to establish who is at fault in accidents occurring during rush hour on expressways.) After a period, witnesses die, move, or their memories fade.

In defense of the tort liability system, supporters use the following arguments:

1. It may encourage good driving because drivers who cause accidents find their insurance premiums increased.

In some cases, negligent drivers cause more damage than their insurance will pay for and they must pay unmet claims from their own assets.

2. Because an adversarial relationship exists between plaintiff and defendant, damages and all other facts have to be proved. Thus, fraud is reduced.

3. In many cases, claims are settled in less than six months without litigation. Only a relatively small number of claims actually proceed through the litigation stage.

4. Payments for pain and suffering involve claims for real injuries, and generally they are not compensated by a no-fault system.

5. The tradition in the United States is for responsible parties to bear the costs of their negligent actions. (Critics have countered that the costs are borne by the insurance companies directly, and all their insureds indirectly, not by negligent drivers.)

After more than three decades of experience, there has been considerable analysis of these claims and counterclaims. Readers interested in learning more about the arguments surrounding "no-fault automobile insurance" should type in this phrase as a keyword on a search engine.

CHAPTER 12

Professional Financial Planning

After studying this chapter, you should be able to:

■ Understand the financial planning process

■ Understand the role that life insurance products play in a comprehensive financial plan

■ Describe a needs-based purchase of life insurance

■ Describe estate planning

■ Explain how life insurance can be used to fund business continuation agreements

■ Describe some aspects of the taxation of life insurance benefits

Personal financial planning for Americans can be difficult because they may not have the background or the time to put the needed plans into operation. Among the typical questions they face are the following:

• How much money will my family need in the event of a premature death?

• How much money should I save to finance a child's college education? In addition, how should the savings be held?

• How much money do I need to save for retirement? What is the most tax-efficient way to hold these savings?

Increasingly, Americans have been turning to financial planning professionals to provide needed advice and help to complete their personal financial plans. This chapter centers on a description of the financial planning process. The chapter also gives special attention to the role insurance products play in the solution to personal financial problems. The description of the financial planning process will be of interest to people considering pursuing a career as a professional financial planner and for people who want to complete their personal financial planning in an organized way.

The knowledge needed by professional financial planners is very broad and includes the following subjects:

• Taxes: federal and state income and estate tax laws

• Social Security rules and benefits

• Investment alternatives

• Life insurance, property insurance, and annuity arrangements

• Employee benefits, especially retirement and health insurance plans

This textbook introduces these subjects. Mastering each of these topics, however, requires much study, and in far greater depth than can be presented in an introductory textbook. This chapter includes sections on the taxation of life insurance and on the use of life insurance to solve business continuation problems. Professional financial planners must have a far broader understanding of taxes than solely those issues involving life insurance contracts. However, we present just this area of taxation because of the insurance focus of this introductory textbook. The chapter introduces the complex subject of business life insurance because financial planners often recommend the use of life insurance to preserve the value of business interests. As in the taxation section, the scope of this introductory textbook allows us to present only a summary of this interesting topic.

The chapter divides the financial life cycle into three segments: the early adult years, the middle years, and the later years. We then illustrate the financial planning process by describing the crucial financial problems that planners and their clients must solve during these periods. During the early adult years, the two main objectives of many financial plans are to provide adequate funds for families should wage earners die prematurely and to provide adequate funds for a child's college education. During the middle adult years, people typically direct their financial plans toward saving for retirement. During the later adult years, financial plans must allow for the most efficient transfer of property and wealth from the owner to survivors. Overall, professional financial planning is about problem solving, setting financial goals, and executing strategies to achieve them.

PROFESSIONAL FINANCIAL PLANNERS

Before developing a financial plan, the planner must establish a relationship with a client. Early in the process, planners should make clear how they charge for their services and make any other disclosures needed to keep the relationship on the highest ethical level. Several professional associations offer degrees or certificates recognizing educational achievements of financial planners. The following list includes some of the more widely recognized financial planning credentials:

- **Certified Financial Planner (CFP)**. The CFP Board of Standards awards this designation after candidates have completed a five-course education program and passed the CFP Certification Examination. It takes about two years to complete the five courses. The CFP Web site provides information about this program: (*http://www.cfp.net/*). The CFP exam topic list provides an excellent review of the scope of professional financial planning. Readers can find this list at (*http://www.cfp.net/become/topiclist.asp/*).
- **Chartered Financial Consultant (ChFC)**. The American College of Financial Planning awards this designation. Candidates complete the five-course CFP program and then take three more courses in the ChFC curriculum. The ChFC program Web site is (*http://www.amercoll.edu/courses/Curriculum/Designations/chfc.asp/*).
- **Personal Financial Specialist (PFS)**. The American Institute of Certified Public Accountants awards this designation to candidates who pass an examination and provide references from satisfied clients. Its Web site is (*http://www.aicpa.org/index.htm/*). Information about its financial planning activities can be found at (*http://www.aicpa.org/members/div/pfp/index.htm/*).

THE PROFESSIONAL FINANCIAL PLANNING PROCESS

The financial planning process may be outlined by the following five steps:

- Step 1: Motivate and educate clients
- Step 2: Collect data

- Step 3: Develop goals
- Step 4: Implement plans
- Step 5: Review and update plans

Step 1: Motivate and Educate Clients

Overcoming the public's tendency to avoid completing a financial plan is a difficult problem. Reasons why people avoid planning include not knowing where to start and not understanding the importance of getting an early start on their financial plans. Therefore, people need education and motivation to overcome inaction and begin to solve their financial problems.

Step 2: Collect Data

People need to collect relevant data and records to complete useful financial plans. Typically, planning begins with a statement of net worth and a cash flow statement or budget. One use of a cash budget is to control spending and increase savings. The cash budget is the heart of the financial plan and can be developed from tax returns and checkbook records. Cash budgets also provide the foundation for estimating future needs.

Adjusted cost basis

Planners need to know how property was acquired (for example, by purchase or by gift), when it was acquired, who the legal owners are, and the owner's adjusted cost basis in the property. The **adjusted cost basis**, simply put, is the net cash outflow for purchased property; usually this figure includes the purchase price and any expenses incurred to acquire the property. Determining the cost basis can be complicated in some cases, especially for gifted or inherited property.

Acceptance of Risk

Planners need to know their client's attitude toward accepting financial risk because financial planning requires a trade-off between risk-and-return alternatives. Planners need a careful assessment of the client's attitude toward risk to make recommendations that are well suited to a particular client. High-risk plans for risk-averse people or low-risk plans for aggressive investors are not likely to be followed. Unfortunately for planners, people's reaction to risk is difficult to measure, probably changes over time, and depends on the situation faced.

Before developing financial strategies, planners should place clients in one of three groups. The following three categories are roughly drawn:

- *Risk-tolerant* people are aware of the chance of loss and willingly bear significantly increased chances of loss in expectation of greater investment returns. These people are aggressive investors but not gamblers. Gamblers create risk for thrills, and financial plans should not be looked at as gambles.
- *Risk-averse* people are made uncomfortable by substantial loss potential and forgo significantly increased chances of gains to reduce their chances of loss.
- *Risk-neutral* people engage in mathematically fair trade-offs between the potential for loss and the chance of gain.

As noted, a careful evaluation of a client's risk tolerance is an essential but difficult process. Some planners use a questionnaire to help them assess their client's risk tolerance. Other planners look for clues in their client's existing investment, insurance, and other real-life choices and also interview the client directly about his or her preferences. Many planners combine both of these approaches. Unfortunately, each of these alternatives has shortcomings, and planners must recognize that identifying a client's risk tolerance requires art as well as science.

Step 3: Develop Goals

With the statement of net worth and cash budget in hand, a family can develop its financial goals. It is important to be thorough, considering all sources of wealth, income, and estimated expenditures. People and families must consider and rank their needs and desires. Most people find their assets and income inadequate to satisfy all their needs and wants. Developing a financial plan forces people to identify the goals they value most and allows them to set a course to achieve their goals. Often financial planners recommend separating goals into short-, intermediate-, and long-term goals. Goal setting allows people to compare actual results with expected results and to keep goals from conflicting with each other. For example, some people might have short-term goals (buying a house, sending children to private schools, taking vacations) that cannot be reached with current income and may jeopardize intermediate goals (such as financing college educations) and long-term goals (saving for retirement). Good communication between planners and clients, and among family members, is needed to set realistic goals.

Asset allocation plan

Many people need to begin a savings plan. People need savings to fund such things as college educations, their retirement, large purchases (including down payments on real estate), and the costs of emergencies. A savings plan also implies the presence of an investment plan to hold the savings. An investment plan requires an **asset allocation plan**. Using an asset allocation plan, a person identifies what percentages of assets will be held in low-risk investments, such as money market funds and certificates of deposits (CDs); what percentage will be held in average-risk investments such as *growth* or *indexed mutual funds* (or their close counterparts, *exchange traded funds*, ETFs); and what percentage will be held in higher-risk investments.[1] The asset allocation will reflect a person's attitude towards risk, and regular reallocation is required because market fluctuations will shift the actual proportions in an investment portfolio away from the desired target ranges.

Step 4: Implement Plans

Financial planning often results in the need to make changes. In some cases, people need legal documents such as a will. Many people also will need to purchase more life insurance. Data on the average amount of life insurance Americans own reveal many people have relatively low amounts of coverage.[2] The next section of this chapter describes a model for calculating the amount of life insurance needed in a personal financial plan.

Step 5: Review and Update Plans

Plans change. People get raises, have more children, assume responsibility for their parents, get divorced, and inherit wealth. Intelligent planning requires accommodating all such changes into the financial plan, which means regular and frequent plan reviews.

---

[1] These investment topics go beyond the scope of this textbook but are critically important. Our focus remains on the role of insurance products in comprehensive financial plans. For readers unfamiliar with the concepts of asset allocation strategies, ETFs, or indexed mutual funds, an investment course or a search of the Internet will provide more detailed information.

[2] Readers can find life insurance data at (*http://www.acli.com/*). For an international perspective on the "protection gap," readers can use the Internet to review a study on this subject published by the Swiss Re, "Mortality Protection: The Core of Life." SIGMA No. 4/2004. The Swiss Re Web site is (*http://www.swissre.com/*).

THE EARLY ADULT YEARS: CALCULATING THE LIFE INSURANCE NEED AND FUNDING COLLEGE EDUCATIONS

There are no set boundaries for the "early adult years." The characteristics of this period include first jobs, first marriages, children, and an accumulation of debt, including mortgage loans on first houses. In cases where families have formed, especially families with young children, life insurance becomes a key ingredient of a sound financial plan. There is no substitute for life insurance. It is a guarantee of future purchasing power if people die prematurely. That is, life insurance allows children to be educated and mortgage loans to be repaid even if a wage earner dies during the early adult years. Many families with children want to provide them with a college education. Financing a college education can be a significant expense for most families, one that they should address in the early adult years. The best financial plan for financing a college education requires both a savings plan and a plan for premature death protection.

The Needs-Based Purchase of Life Insurance

A needs analysis can identify the financial problems caused by a premature death. Many financial planners believe people should purchase life insurance on a needs basis rather than as an attempt to replace lost earnings. A **needs-based purchase** means that people purchase life insurance in an amount equal to the difference between the assets required to complete a financial plan and the assets available to meet the needs.

Life insurance policies that have a savings feature that can be used to keep premiums affordable in later years are called **permanent policies**, or **cash value life insurance**. **Term insurance** has no savings element and provides coverage for only a limited number of years. **Permanent needs** for life insurance are not a function of time; these needs exist at all ages. **Temporary need** life insurance comes to a projected end and is designed to meet needs that exist for only a portion of a person's life.

Here is a typical list of needs for postdeath resources. Those needs marked with a (**P**) are permanent needs; those with a (**T**) are temporary needs:

- *A burial fund* (**P**): Funeral and final illness expenses may amount to more than $15,000. This need is present at any age, so it is permanent.
- *An education fund* (**T**): At present, four years of undergraduate education may cost from $25,000 to more than $125,000. College costs have risen almost twice as fast as other items in recent years. This need no longer exists after the education is complete, so it is temporary.
- *An income fund* (**T**): In families, the greatest need ordinarily would be for regular income to meet daily expenses during the dependency period. The need is greatest if the wage earner's death leaves a dependent spouse and children. If either the children or the spouse would work after the wage earner's death, the income need is reduced. This need does not exist after children become financially independent or surviving spouses receive retirement income, so this need is temporary.
- *A debt-retirement fund* (**T**): If they are homeowners, most young families have a large mortgage debt. Other large debts arise from unpaid credit card balances and purchases of vehicles on credit. Frequently, people purchase life insurance to repay these debts if the breadwinner dies prematurely. Not all loans and debts legally are payable when a person dies. Many people, however, do not want their survivors to face regular debt installment payments after the family's main source of income disappears. After people repay their debts, this need does not exist, so it is temporary.

Needs-based purchase

Permanent policies

Cash value life insurance

Term insurance

Permanent needs

Temporary need

FIGURE 12–1 An Equation for the Needs-Based Purchase of Life Insurance

- *An estate preservation fund* (**P**): The costs of settling an estate (burial costs, court costs, attorney fees, federal transfer taxes, and state death taxes) reduce the funds available for heirs. Life insurance can replace the shrinkage caused by these expenses. For people with large amounts of assets, the goal of estate preservation often creates a need for life insurance because large estates might be subject to the federal unified transfer tax. This tax, which currently is set to expire in 2010 and then possibly may be reinstated, is explained in the estate planning section of this chapter. This need exists throughout life, so it is permanent.

After financial planners calculate the total need for postdeath funds, they then calculate the total assets available to meet these needs. Available assets often include the following items:

- Social Security benefits
- Death benefits from employment, such as group life insurance
- Savings accounts, investments, and other liquid assets
- Proceeds from life insurance policies already owned
- Business interests, home equity, and other nonliquid assets

The need for new life insurance equals the difference between the assets required to complete the life insurance plan and the assets available to meet these needs.

Figure 12–1 presents the needs-based equation for life insurance purchases.

We now present a personal life insurance model or plan that shows how to determine the amount of life insurance to purchase in a specific, theoretical case. In developing a plan to deal with premature death, planners must assume that the death is immediate because any other assumption would leave the financial problems of a premature death unsolved for an unspecified time. That is, if the plan assumed that death would not occur for five years, and if a client died during the first five years, then the likelihood of unmet financial needs would arise.

Life Insurance Planning: A Case Study

Louis and Marie Burton are each 26 years old. They had their first child, Pete, when they were 24 years old. Louis sells men's clothes in a department store. Marie works in a franchise doughnut shop. Their stated goal in the event of Louis's premature death is to have adequate resources to allow Marie to remain at home and raise Pete.

Their statement of net worth appears in Table 12–1 and their cash flow statement for 2008 appears in Table 12–2.

Table 12–3 shows the first few years of a simplified life insurance plan for the Burtons. This output reflects estimated results if the current family situation continues until Pete is age 10. (This example is simplified. In practice, many financial planners recommend funding the period until the child graduates college.) Our example assumes both parents live, continue to work, save, and spend in the same percentages as they did in 2008. If this estimate is accurate, the Burtons will accumulate savings of $62,166.

TABLE 12–1   Statement of Net Worth

Assets	
Bank account	$ 2,300
House	175,000
2 cars	14,000
400 shares of common stock	24,500
Total	$215,800
Liabilities	
Home mortgage	$160,000
Car loan	7,500
Charge card debt	1,750
Total	$169,250
Net Worth	$ 46,550

TABLE 12–2   Cash Flow Statement for 2008

Income	
Louis	$40,000
Marie	35,000
Investments	1,200
Total	$76,200
Taxes	
Social Security	$ 5,738
Federal income	17,526
State income	3,048
Real estate	1,100
Total	27,412
Disposable Income	$48,789
Expenses	
Food	$ 3,903
Shelter	12,197
Autos	4,879
All other	21,955
Total	$42,934
Savings	$ 5,855

Table 12–4 is based on the assumption that Louis dies on January 1, 2009. At this time, Marie stops working to stay at home to raise Pete. Both Marie and Pete are eligible for Social Security survivor benefits. Social Security benefits automatically increase with inflation. (See Chapter 22, "Social Security," or the Social Security Web site, (*http://www.ssa.gov/*), for a description of this program's benefits.) The survivors' benefits are shown as income in Table 12–4. With Louis deceased, the family's expenses drop by one-third. Under these assumptions, savings become negative, indicating expenses in excess of income. The present value of the deficit totals $197,056, using a 4 percent assumed discount factor. This amount, $197,056, is the exact amount needed on January 1, 2009, to fund all the deficits projected through 2016, before Pete is age 11. That is, if withdrawals equal the projected deficits between income and expenses each

TABLE 12–3 Burton Life Insurance Plan

Inflation Rate = 0.04

Year	2008	2009	2010	2011	2012	2013	2014	2015	2016
Pete's age	2	3	4	5	6	7	8	9	10
Income (in dollars)									
Louis	40,000	41,600	43,264	44,995	46,794	48,666	50,613	52,637	54,743
Marie	35,000	36,400	37,856	39,370	40,945	42,583	44,286	46,058	47,900
Investments	1,200	1,248	1,298	1,350	1,404	1,460	1,518	1,579	1,642
Total	76,200	79,248	82,418	85,715	89,143	92,709	96,417	100,274	104,285
Taxes (in dollars)									
Social Security	5,738	5,967	6,206	6,454	6,712	6,981	7,260	7,550	7,852
Federal income	17,526	18,227	18,956	19,714	20,503	21,323	22,176	23,063	23,986
State income	3,048	3,170	3,297	3,429	3,566	3,708	3,857	4,011	4,171
Real estate	1,100	1,100	1,100	1,100	1,100	1,100	1,100	1,100	1,100
Total	27,412	28,464	29,559	30,697	31,881	33,112	34,393	35,724	37,109
Disposable income (in dollars)	48,788	50,784	52,859	55,018	57,262	59,597	62,024	64,550	67,176
Expenses (in dollars)									
Food	3,903	4,063	4,229	4,401	4,581	4,768	4,962	5,164	5,374
Shelter	2,197	12,696	13,215	13,754	14,316	14,899	15,506	16,137	16,794
Autos	4,879	5,078	5,286	5,502	5,726	5,960	6,202	6,455	6,718
All other	21,955	22,853	23,787	24,758	25,768	26,819	27,911	29,047	30,229
Total	42,934	44,690	46,517	48,415	50,391	52,446	54,581	56,803	59,115
Savings (in dollars)	5,855	6,094	6,342	6,602	6,871	7,151	7,443	7,747	8,061
Total savings	5,855	11,949	18,291	24,893	31,764	38,915	46,358	54,105	62,166

year and if the balance of the fund earns 4 percent interest (after taxes), the final withdrawal will exhaust the fund.

Using the equation for a needs-based life insurance purchase shown in Figure 12–1, if Louis and Marie currently own no individual life insurance, they should purchase $197,056 to meet the goal of allowing Marie to stay at home and raise Pete until he is age 10. Assuming that Louis already owns $100,000 of individual life insurance, then he should purchase $97,056 ($197,056 − $100,000) of new life insurance. Assuming that Louis also qualifies for $25,000 of group life insurance and that the Burtons are convinced this insurance will be available during the period of Pete's dependency, $25,000 could be subtracted from $97,056, leaving $72,056 ($97,056 − $25,000) as the amount of new life insurance to be purchased.

This example greatly simplified the life insurance planning approach used to calculate the funds needed to support Marie and Pete. In the real world, things rarely move in a straight line, and estimates and reality rarely coincide. For example, it would be unusual for inflation to equal 4 percent annually for an eight-year planning period. (Table 12–4 shows nine years, but the data for the first year are known.) Once a spreadsheet is constructed on the computer, however, all assumptions can be modified easily. What if Marie works after Louis's death? What if she works part time? What if "all other" expenses were broken down into greater detail? A good financial plan must be flexible, and a professional financial planner must be able to incorporate changes and alternatives into financial plans.

TABLE 12–4   The Burton Life Insurance Plan After Louis's Death

Year	2008	2009	2010	2011	2012	2013	2014	2015	2016
Pete's age	2	3	4	5	6	7	8	9	10
Income (in dollars)									
Louis	40,000	0	0	0	0	0	0	0	0
Marie	35,000	0	0	0	0	0	0	0	0
Social Security		7,500	7,800	8,112	8,436	8,774	9,125	9,490	9,869
Investments	1,200	1,248	1,298	1,350	1,404	1,460	1,518	1,579	1,642
TOTAL	76,200	8,748	9,098	9,462	9,840	10,234	10,643	11,069	11,511
Taxes (in dollars)									
Social Security	5,738	0	0	0	0	0	0	0	0
Federal income	17,526	0	0	0	0	0	0	0	0
State income	3,048	0	0	0	0	0	0	0	0
Real estate	1,100	1,144	1,190	1,237	1,287	1,338	1,392	1,448	1,505
TOTAL	27,412	1,144	1,190	1,237	1,287	1,338	1,392	1,448	1,505
Disposable income (in dollars)	48,788	7,604	7,908	8,225	8,553	8,896	9,251	9,621	10,006
Expenses (in dollars)									
Food	3,903	2,576	2,679	2,786	2,898	3,014	3,134	3,260	3,390
Shelter	12,197	12,696	13,215	13,754	14,316	14,899	15,506	16,137	16,794
Autos	4,879	2,439	2,537	2,638	2,744	2,854	2,968	3,087	3,210
All other	21,955	14,490	15,070	15,673	16,299	16,951	17,630	18,335	19,068
TOTAL	42,934	32,201	33,501	34,851	36,257	37,718	39,238	40,819	42,462
Savings (in dollars)	5,854	(24,597)	(25,593)	(26,626)	(27,704)	(28,822)	(29,987)	(31,198)	(32,456)
Present value of the deficit		**197,056**							

TECHNICAL NOTE ON THE SPREADSHEET

The $197,056 is the present value of an "annuity due." That is, the payments are assumed to occur at the *beginning* of the year rather than at the end of the year. The payments from an *ordinary annuity* occur at the end of the year. The reason we assume that the stream is an annuity due is that payments for various items in the Burtons' standard of living will occur during the year. In other words, we conservatively assume all deficits occur at the beginning of the year. The effect of this assumption is to reduce by one year the interest that can be earned on the balance.

The formula used in my Excel spreadsheet to calculate the present value of the future deficits at the beginning of the second year is: 5ABS(NPV(0.04,D22: J22) + C22), where row 22 looks like this:

	A	B	C	D	E	F	G	H	I	J
22	Savings	5,854	(24,597)	(25,593)	(26,626)	(27,704)	(28,822)	(29,987)	(31,198)	(32,456)
			197,056							

Insurance for Wives, Children, and College Students

In the Burton case study, the wife's income provides a significant portion of the family's resources. Therefore, the Burtons cannot complete their life insurance plans until they consider the effect of Marie's premature death, in addition to Louis's. Using a spreadsheet similar to the one in Table 12–4, showing Marie's income and expenses eliminated, the impact of Marie's premature death could be estimated.

Since the 1980s, more than one-half of all American married women work outside the home. Planners should consider the income earned by these women when developing family life insurance plans. In family situations, it is often asked, "Should the wife's or the children's lives also be insured?" As a rule, the family's insurance priorities must be ranked, insuring the most serious exposure to loss first. The most serious exposure to loss for most families is the premature death of the main source(s) of the family's income. Only after the primary wage earner's life has been insured adequately should the lives of the other members of the family be considered for insurance.

Insurance for Homemakers

Even if one member of a couple does not work outside the home, he or she still makes a contribution to the household that needs to be considered when purchasing life insurance. A homemaker supplies valuable economic services in the work he or she does within the home. If the homemaker dies prematurely, the need for services in the home continues. Someone would have to raise the children and help with the household chores. Insurance proceeds can be used to purchase many of the replacement services, such as day care and housekeeping, that would be needed to keep the family unit operating without a homemaker. The amount of insurance purchased should be related to the financial need created by the absence of the homemaker.

Each family faces different circumstances. In some cases, grandparents or other family members can supply needed services and help. In other cases, there may be no dependent children. Often, if the source of secondary income dies, the primary income continues. Thus, with a needs-based approach, the amount of life insurance appropriate for the secondary wage earner usually is less than the amount required for the primary wage earner. If insurance dollars are limited, they should be spent to insure the family's main source of income, whether provided by the wife or the husband. In many cases, life insurance on a secondary wage earner meets a definite economic need and is a logical purchase.

Insurance for Children

Because they do not produce current income for the family, there is much less economic reason for insuring children than there is for insuring either husband or wife. The premature death of a child means funeral expenses, but beyond that, only seldom are there unfavorable economic consequences from a child's death. Only after the wage earner and spouse have been insured adequately should life insurance on children be considered. Many financial planners believe that life insurance proceeds should fund economic needs. If such needs are not present, the purchase of life insurance cannot be justified logically.

Insurance for College Students

Students in college are sometimes sold "college special" policies designed for seniors. If life insurance is purchased only to meet specific and current economic needs, however, then life insurance for college students often makes little or no sense.

Life insurance salespeople operating near college campuses suggest three potential needs to college students: (1) a general need for life insurance protection, (2) a general need for savings, and (3) a need to obtain the future right to purchase life insurance. Under careful examination, these arguments have little validity for most students.

Most college students have no dependents, no large debts, and no business obligations. In such circumstances, it is hard to demonstrate an immediate need for life insurance protection. Most college students do not have regular salaries. If such is the case, starting a regular savings program using a life insurance product seems premature. Using strained logic—some commentators might say "deception"—college students are encouraged to borrow money to begin their savings program. Because most college students have no regular income, the loan of the first premium is at the heart of many college life insurance sales schemes. What businessperson ever would borrow money at an 8 or 9 percent interest rate to start a savings plan earning 3 or 4 percent interest income? To borrow money to pay the first premium on a whole life insurance policy is, in this case, ridiculous.

In examining the third part of the typical argument made to college students, statistics reveal that few healthy 21-year-olds become uninsurable by the time they reach age 25, or even age 30. If a college student desires protection against becoming uninsurable, a convertible-term insurance policy can provide such protection at a fraction of the premium of the policies usually sold to college students. Most college students do not need to begin a life insurance program before they have a regular salary or dependents. Therefore, they should carefully analyze the arguments of anyone suggesting such a purchase.

Financing A College Education[3]

Financing college tuition is one of the three largest financial problems facing many middle-income Americans. The other two are financing a residence and financing retirement. The federal government accords each of these financial problems special tax advantages. Developing a financial plan to finance a college education requires current knowledge of state and federal tax provisions; therefore, people often consult with professional financial planners to develop appropriate funding strategies. College funding plans often require life insurance because it provides certainty that money will be available even if a wage earner dies prematurely.

Tax-Advantaged Funding Strategies

One point that most financial planners make regarding funding college tuition is that tax-advantaged strategies usually are more efficient (produce more funds) than non-tax-advantaged strategies. One explanation for this dominance is that most tax-advantaged strategies let investors earn income on funds that they otherwise would use to pay taxes. A second generally accepted rule is that the earlier a family starts saving for college, the better the results, giving tax-advantaged compound interest the chance to work over a longer period.

Section 529 **Section 529 Plans (State Tuition Assistance Plans)**   The **Section 529** plan is a state-sponsored education savings program that allows parents, other relatives, and friends to contribute to a child's college education. The 529 plan allows for significantly higher contributions than other tax-advantaged options. The contribution limit was $127,000 for each beneficiary in a recent year. Contributions to the 529 plan are not tax-deductible,

---

[3] The keywords "saving for college" produced more than 32 million hits on a popular Internet search engine. Many Web sites have "calculators" that allow users to estimate the costs of a college education. These calculators produce estimates, and some estimates will prove to be more accurate than others.

but investment income may escape both state and federal tax income taxation at withdrawal if used for qualified education expenses. Readers can find much relevant information, including specific details of various state plans, at (*http://www.savingfor college.com/*).

The general features of 529 plans include the following points:

- The contributor owns the account.
- The account owner selects the investment strategy when making the initial contribution. The owner can make changes in the initial investment strategy once a year under current rules. If investments perform poorly, of course, college funding goals may not be achieved, and 529 plan investments must be reviewed regularly for both risk and return results.
- The account owner is entitled to select or change the designated beneficiary (to a member of the student's family) or even take funds back if that beneficiary elects not to attend college or receives a full or partial scholarship.
- Withdrawals of earnings for nonqualified educational expenses are taxed as ordinary income and may be subject to a 10% penalty.

In addition to the 529 plan, the government has encouraged saving for college with two other tax advantaged programs, the *Hope Credit* and the *Lifetime Learning Credit*.[4] These plans have lower limits and appear less useful for middle income families than does the 529 plan.

Three Important Questions   The following three questions are among the most important ones that parents and planners must consider when analyzing the college funding decision:

1. If a college education costs ($10,000 each year) when the child is age (5?), what will be the estimated total cost of tuition if costs inflate at an annual rate of (8?) percent? The numbers in the parenthesis are just examples, but using spreadsheets or financial calculators can provide the needed savings goal.
2. If a parent dies prematurely, what amount of death benefits is needed to fund the college tuition? In most cases, family wage earners survive to see their children finish college, but in some cases, they do not. Therefore, every college savings plan should include an adequate amount of life insurance protection so that the college education will be funded in the event of a premature death.
3. What amount of annual savings is needed to fund the tuition payments fully if the parent survives? Once the cost of a college education has been estimated, it usually is wise to begin to save to accumulate the needed funds. As noted, the federal (and state) governments provide tax-advantaged savings alternatives that produce the best results when savings begin before the student needs the tuition payments.

THE MIDDLE YEARS: FINANCING RETIREMENT

At some point in the financial life cycle, children become independent, mortgages are repaid, and families accumulate savings. The family's main financial concern shifts from the problems presented by the premature death of the wage earner to financing the retirement years. This change is likely to occur between ages 40 and 60. We call this period the *middle years*. Some aspects of retirement funding occur long before middle

[4] Readers can find detailed information about these two credits at the Internal Revenue Service (IRS) Web site: (*http://www.irs.gov/*). Use the two credits as keywords in the IRS Web site search engine.

age. Participation in Social Security and employer-sponsored pension plans begins in the early stages of employment. However, sometime during middle age, the financial planning focus changes from the concerns of early adult life to the concerns of middle life, with an emphasis on saving for retirement.

The evolution is gradual and arises from a series of modifications to existing financial plans. The availability of savings and the proximity of retirement are key factors. Generally, each person surviving to mid-life faces the problem of planning to finance a retirement period. In recent years, this problem has become more severe for many Americans for the following reasons:

- Many employers have reduced their commitment to funding retirement programs.
- Social Security has increased the normal retirement age and lowered benefit targets.
- Retirees have become responsible for a greater portion of their health care expenses.
- Increases in longevity have placed greater burdens on retirement savings.

People can use computers and spreadsheets to estimate the need for retirement income in the same fashion presented in the Burton case study. Various Web sites also have retirement income needs calculators. In any case, the logical solution involves estimating the assets available at retirement, subtracting the cost of living for the longest period of expected life, and funding the difference between available assets and need for income with some form of preretirement savings. To complete the solution to the problem, estimates must be made of the following variables: inflation rates, investment returns, tax rates before and after retirement, spending needs in retirement, and the length of life. The reader now will understand that any preretirement financial plan will need many reviews and modifications before retirement begins. The potential for outliving one's wealth or spending down one's assets too quickly in retirement is a serious issue with unpleasant consequences if mistakes are made.

Planners follow the same general sequence of steps for middle years as for the early years:

1. Collect and analyze data and other relevant information.
2. Specify the financial goals.
3. Implement the strategy.
4. Monitor and modify the plan to meet changing circumstances and goals.

Financial plans requiring early and regular savings will be the most likely to allow people to maintain their standard of living during retirement. Table 12–5 presents some estimates of expected retirement periods by the Bureau of the Census (*http://www.census.gov/*).

Table 12–5 shows that for any year observed, women are expected to outlive men. This statistical fact has serious implications for women's financial plans. Experts have paid special attention to women's financial planning problems, and the Web site of the Women's Institute for a Secure Retirement (*http://www.wiser.heinz.org/*) provides access to some of this literature.

In summary, a person planning for retirement must solve the following problems:

- Estimating the length of his or her life and future health status (and for a spouse, where applicable)
- Forecasting the amount and sources of preretirement and postretirement income
- Predicting the amount and type of retirement expenses

TABLE 12–5 Life Expectancy		
Life Expectancy at Age 65 (Middle Mortality Assumption)		
Year of 65th Birthday	*Male*	*Female*
2004	16.3	19.7
2005	16.4	19.7
2010	16.8	20.0
2015	17.2	20.3
2020	17.6	20.6
2025	18.0	20.9
2030	18.5	21.2
2035	18.9	21.5
2040	19.3	21.8
2045	19.8	22.1
2050	20.3	22.4

SOURCE: U.S. Department of Commerce, Economics, and Statistics Administration, Bureau of Census: *Current Population Reports—Population Projections of the United States . . . 1995–2050*, p. 1130.

- Estimating the age of retirement
- Gauging the impact of inflation on preretirement and postretirement finances
- Anticipating the possibility of dependent children, parents, or both

The Role of Life Insurance and Annuities in the Middle Years

People can use life insurance products to fund both premature death and retirement financial needs.

Premature Death Protection

While planning retirement finances should receive priority attention during middle age, plans for premature death or disability remain important in many cases. Usually people need a final expense fund to pay the expenses of a last illness and all other final expenses. Survivors typically require emergency funds. Sometimes a debt retirement fund may be required to repay outstanding business debts. In other cases, the financial future of children, parents, or a spouse with physical or mental problems is a concern. Such needs should be met by a dependent support fund backed by adequate life insurance.

Individual savings are likely to be greater in middle age than during the young adult period. Available savings reduce the need for life insurance. Social Security survivor benefits also meet a portion of the need for postdeath resources.

The most logical way to determine the amount of life or disability insurance needed during middle age is to construct a financial model similar to the models presented in the preceding section of this chapter. As always, immediate death or disability is the basic premise. Spreadsheet models of postdeath financial requirements can accommodate changes in both financial circumstances and inflation estimates.

Retirement Funding

Annuity

The insurance contract designed to provide retirement funds that a person cannot outlive is called an **annuity**. By pooling the mortality exposures of many people, called *annuitants*, insurers are able to guarantee each annuitant a stream of income that will last until death. Annuities also earn investment income that accumulates on a tax-advantaged basis. Chapter 14, "Standard Life Insurance Contract Provisions and Options," provides a complete discussion of annuities. At this point, we note that people have been purchasing large amounts of annuities in the past two decades.

THE LATER YEARS

Estate planning

At some point, people must transfer their wealth from one generation to another. We call the process of planning the transfer of wealth **estate planning**. The purpose of estate planning is to produce a logical and economic transfer of assets consistent with the owner's desires and lifetime needs.

Wills

Will

Probate

Every estate plan requires a will. A **will** is a legal document in which a person directs the disposal of his or her assets at death. **Probate** is the name for the legal (court-supervised) process of transferring property at a person's death. Only an attorney can write wills and provide legal advice on alternative courses of action. Even people with few assets need a will if they want those assets distributed according to their wishes. Families with children can use their will to appoint guardians for their children, and a carefully drafted will can minimize probate problems.

Intestate

The will must be made while the person is competent, "of a sound mind." It must be properly witnessed, and it must be in a form acceptable to the court. Some states accept handwritten wills; others do not. If a person dies without a will, the state determines who receives the decedent's property. A person dying without a will is said to have died **intestate**, and some studies have shown that about 40 percent of all people die without wills. All states have laws prescribing the intestate distribution of property.

Federal Estate Tax[5]

Federal estate tax

Federal gift tax

Uniform transfer tax

Gross estate

The federal government taxes property transferred at death. This tax is called the **federal estate tax**. The government also taxes lifetime gifts. This tax is called the **federal gift tax**. Together, both taxes are known as the **uniform transfer tax**. Some states also impose a death tax, while others impose an inheritance tax.[6]

The government calls all the property a person owns at death the **gross estate**. The gross estate includes a person's house and other real property, personal property, trust property, tax-advantaged retirement plans, and the face amount of life insurance policies in which they have an ownership interest. Given the wide scope of the property included in the gross estate, it is quite possible for many middle-income people to acquire taxable estates. The fair market value of the gross estate at the time of death, plus certain gifts made during the decedent's lifetime, is subject to the estate tax. Funeral, administrative, and other expenses, as well as outstanding debts, may be deducted from the gross estate.

Marital deduction

Annual gift tax exclusion

Two of the most important estate tax deductions are the unlimited marital deduction and the annual gift tax exclusion. The **marital deduction** allows the first spouse to die to give all his or her property to the surviving spouse without any estate or gift tax liability. Because of the progressive nature of the federal estate tax, however, at the second spouse's death, even greater estate taxes may be payable than if some other arrangement were made at the first spouse's death. The **annual gift tax exclusion** in a recent year allowed $12,000 per donee to be given free of the gift tax. If both husband and wife make the gift, $24,000 may be given. These gifts need not be added back to the taxable estate.

Before the year 2001, the federal estate taxes were calculated as shown in Table 12–6. The Tax Reform Act of 2001 modified the rates and exempt estate sizes as shown in the

The Tax Relief Act of 2001

---

[5] **The Tax Relief Act of 2001** schedules the federal estate tax to end in the year 2010; however, there is a "sunset" provision in this act, the effect of which is to reintroduce the federal estate tax in 2011.

[6] Readers wanting a comprehensive description of the "federal estate tax" can type in those keywords in an Internet search engine. A good place to start learning more about this tax is at the IRS Web site, (*http://www.irs.gov/*). Form 706 and Publication 950 provide a detailed description of this tax.

TABLE 12–6 Federal Unified Estate and Gift Tax Rates in Effect before Tax Reform Act of 2001

A	B	C	D
More Than (in dollars)	*But Not More Than (in dollars)*	*Tax on A (in dollars)*	*Rate on Excess (%)*
0	10,000	—	18
10,000	20,000	1,800	20
20,000	40,000	3,800	22
40,000	60,000	8,200	24
60,000	80,000	13,000	26
80,000	100,000	18,200	28
100,000	150,000	23,800	30
150,000	250,000	38,800	32
250,000	500,000	70,800	34
500,000	750,000	155,800	37
750,000	1,000,000	248,300	39
1,000,000	1,250,000	345,800	41
1,250,000	1,500,000	448,300	43
1,500,000	2,000,000	555,800	45
2,000,000	2,500,000	780,800	49
2,500,000	3,000,000	1,025,800	53
3,000,000	NA	1,290,800	55

Unified Credit by Year, Tax Credit, and Exclusion Amount before TRA 2001

Year	*Tax Credit (in dollars)*	*Exclusion Amount (in dollars)*
1997	192,800	600,000
1998	202,050	625,000
1999	211,300	650,000
2000	220,550	675,000
2001	220,550	675,000
2002	229,800	700,000
2003	229,800	700,000
2004	287,300	850,000
2005	326,300	950,000
2006	345,800	1,000,000

Changes in Rate Schedule for Estate and Gift Taxes under Tax Relief Act of 2001

Calendar Year	*Estate and GST Tax Death—Time Transfer Exemptions (in dollars)*	*Highest Transfer Rates*	*Life Time Gift Tax Exemption (in dollars)*	*Unified Tax Credit (in dollars)*
1997	600,000	55%	600,000	192,800
1998	625,000	55%	625,000	202,050
1999	650,000	55%	650,000	211,300
2000	675,000	55%	675,000	220,550
2001	675,000	55%	675,000	220,550
2002	1,000,000	50%	1,000,000	345,800
2003	1,000,000	49%	1,000,000	345,800
2004	1,500,000	48%	1,000,000	555,800
2005	1,500,000	47%	1,000,000	555,800
2006	2,000,000	46%	1,000,000	780,800
2007	2,000,000	45%	1,000,000	780,800
2008	2,000,000	45%	1,000,000	780,800
2009	3,500,000	45%	1,000,000	1,565,800
2010	Repealed	35% gift tax only		
2011	Sunset provision	Sunset provision	Back to 2001 law	Back to 2001 law

bottom part of the table, but unless the law is specifically extended, the tax rates will revert to the 2001 rates, which is why both parts of the table are shown. An increasing credit against the federal estate tax allows estates worth less than the amount specified each year to pass free of the federal estate tax. Because large estates often need cash to pay the estate taxes, life insurance is often purchased to supply the cash needed.

Life Insurance and Estate Planning

The need to pay the federal estate tax in cash within nine months of a person's death, the desire to make cash bequests, and the general need for liquidity (cash) all can be met with life insurance. Life insurance supplies the cash just when it is needed. Available cash can be important because much of the wealth in large estates will be in land, buildings, artwork, closely held business investments, or other illiquid assets not easily or quickly turned into the cash needed to pay bills.

Trust

Life insurance trust

A frequent arrangement is for the life insurance proceeds to be paid into a trust for the benefit of the heirs. A **trust** is a legal arrangement allowing one person, called a *trustee*, to manage property for the benefit of another person, called the *beneficiary*. Attorneys call a trust funded with life insurance proceeds a **life insurance trust**. Typically, the cash in the life insurance trust is used to purchase the assets from the estate at set prices. The effect of such an arrangement is to leave the productive assets in the trust and the cash in the estate. The cash in the estate then is available to pay taxes and meet other cash needs. Questions of who is to own the policy and who is to be the beneficiary have significant tax implications.

Survivor life insurance

Another policy type especially useful in estate planning is **survivor life insurance**, which is also called *second-to-die* life insurance. These policies insure two lives under one contract. The beneficiary is paid only after the second death. The estate plan involves passing the estate of the first spouse to die to the surviving spouse. The unlimited marital deduction eliminates the federal estate tax on this transfer. At the second death, assuming no remarriage or other significant change in factors, the federal estate tax will apply. At this point, the survivorship life insurance policy matures, producing the cash needed to pay the taxes. After the first death, these policies often have large increases in cash values.

Readers should realize that this introductory text has given a very complex subject simplified treatment. Estate planning is a subject for advanced texts and courses in universities and law schools. After reading this material, you should understand that life insurance is a useful tool in solving estate planning problems.

Liquidating Retirement Savings[7]

One of the most challenging problems facing professional financial planners is advising clients on how to liquidate the savings that have accumulated for retirement. Where possible, planners recommend using one or more of the following alternatives to save for retirement: qualified pension plans, Individual Retirement Accounts (IRAs), Keogh plans, 401 (k) plans, or 403 (b) plans. These plans are described in Chapter 21, "Employee Benefits." For now, a few financial planning points can be noted. The government encourages people to save for retirement by providing tax incentives that defer taxes, but at some point, presumably in retirement, people must

---

[7] Readers wanting comprehensive information about "liquidating retirement savings" should type these keywords into an Internet search engine. Several financial services providers offer current discussions of this topic, accompanied by a prioritized order of assets to liquidate.

withdraw the funds and pay the taxes. To discourage the preretirement withdrawal of tax-advantaged retirement savings, the government applies a 10 percent early withdrawal penalty on most withdrawals made before age 59½. If a participant dies or becomes disabled before this age, the penalty does not apply, but ordinary income taxes may apply. If a participant tries to avoid taxes by keeping funds in a tax-advantaged retirement plan after age 70½, another penalty—50 percent of the required minimum distribution—applies. Describing the Internal Revenue Code minimum distribution rules is beyond the scope of this text. However, we can note that much financial planning is required between the ages of 59½ and 70½ to allow people to enjoy their retirement savings, achieve their other financial planning goals, and minimize their tax burden.

BUSINESS USES OF LIFE INSURANCE

Businesses often purchase life insurance for the following reasons:

- To provide benefits for employees
- To protect the firm against the financial problems caused by the loss of a key person
- To aid in transferring business ownership

Group life insurance

Businesses purchase **group life insurance** as an employee benefit. Many employers, including the federal government, provide group life insurance as a benefit. The purpose of this life insurance is to help attract, motivate, and retain employees. We describe employee benefits funded by insurance, including group life insurance, in Chapter 21.

Key employee life insurance

In Chapter 3, "Risk Management," we noted that if a business were to lose a key person, its earning power could be harmed, perhaps seriously. **Key employee life insurance** can protect firms from financial problems caused by such losses. The first step in the risk management process is to identify the key person. It may be the president, the chief researcher, a top salesperson, or an engineer. The next step is to measure the financial loss the key person's death would cause. Such a measure will usually involve estimating the cost of replacing the key employee. To measure the loss, firms also need to estimate the effect on profits while a replacement is hired and trained and has achieved the same level of productivity as the original employee. After identifying and measuring the potential loss, the business purchases a life insurance policy on the key employee's life. The business is the *owner* and the *beneficiary* of the policy and the key employee is the *insured*. The business pays the premiums. For this arrangement to work, the key person must be insurable and must give permission for the purchase.

Split-dollar life insurance

Another business use of life insurance is to provide a means of rewarding and retaining valuable personnel. The **split-dollar life insurance** plan allows firms to achieve this end. With this approach, both employer and employee pay a part of the premium for an insurance policy with a savings feature. The employer's share typically equals the annual increase in savings. As the savings increase each year, so does the employer's premium payment. When the annual increase in savings equals or exceeds the level premium, the employee contributes nothing for the insurance. Employees who terminate employment at this point (several years after the policy had been in force) give up an important fringe benefit.

In a split-dollar plan, the employer receives an amount equal to the savings value at the employee's death. The employee's beneficiary receives an amount equal to the face value minus the savings value. For example, assume that after 15 years, the split-dollar life insurance policy has a face value of $100,000 and a cash value of $25,000. The total employer-paid premiums over the 15 years equal $25,000. At the employee's death, the employer receives $25,000 of the death proceeds, and the employee's beneficiary receives $75,000. From the employer's standpoint, the cost of the policy becomes the forgone interest on the premium payments because the absolute amount of premiums is returned at the employee's death.

Funding Business Continuation Agreements with Life Insurance

Partnerships, sole proprietorships, and closely held corporations often need to purchase life insurance to facilitate the transfer of ownership when a proprietor dies. If a proprietorship is sold at a predetermined price at the owner's death, the arrangement relieves the spouse of having to worry about operating the business. Because the buyout allows the continuation of the business, and because most firms are worth more as going concerns than they would be in liquidation, the heirs benefit from the higher value. Often the business can be sold to a key employee. In any event, a life insurance policy on the owner provides the cash needed to complete the purchase. The money will be there when it is needed. In general, the person who buys the business will be the beneficiary who also pays the premiums. A legal agreement for the purchase between the buyer and seller, called a **buy-and-sell agreement**, also must be arranged before the plan becomes effective. Thus, people need the services of both an attorney and a life insurance agent to arrange and fund the business continuation plan (a buy-and-sell agreement properly funded by life insurance).

Buy-and-sell agreement

Calculating the appropriate value of the business interest is an important part of the process. The Internal Revenue Service (IRS) requires the value determined in the buy-and-sell agreement to be a fair price because the purchase price ordinarily will be a part of the decedent's estate and subject to the estate tax. This price also sets the purchaser's cost basis in the business. As a business grows and prospers, the amount of life insurance needed for purchasing the owner's interest increases. Thus, buy-and-sell life insurance plans should be flexible and be reevaluated regularly.

Partnerships and closely held corporations also present the need for business continuation life insurance. Often the surviving partners or shareholders want to purchase the interest of the member who dies. Life insurance policies can be used to fund the purchase.

Cross-purchase plan

Entity plan

The buy-and-sell plans can be arranged in either of two ways. Each partner (shareholder) can purchase life insurance on every other partner (shareholder); this plan is called the **cross-purchase plan**. The partnership (corporation) can purchase the insurance on each partner (shareholder); this plan is called the **entity plan**. The second alternative involves a much smaller number of policies. If there were eight partners involved in a cross-purchase plan, each partner would have to purchase seven policies, and a total of 56 policies would be purchased. Under the entity plan, only eight policies would be needed. Tax consequences, however, may favor the cross-purchase arrangement in some cases.

Although our discussion of business life insurance is in terms of dealing with financial problems associated with the death of a business owner, the disability of the owner creates similar challenges, and in some cases even more severe difficulties. Long-term disability income policies, therefore, are a logical part of the risk management approach to solving business continuation problems of closely held businesses.

THE TAXATION OF LIFE INSURANCE

Death Proceeds

On the one hand, premium payments for individually purchased life insurance are not deductible from a person's federal income tax. On the other hand, when the beneficiary receives the proceeds of a life insurance policy, no federal income tax applies to this amount. If the beneficiary does not take the proceeds as a lump sum of cash (which is one of several *settlement options* described in Chapter 14, "Standard Life Insurance Contract Provisions and Options") and instead takes a series of payments that includes interest earnings, federal income tax is paid on the interest portion. Another exception to the general rule is the **transfer for value rule**. In this case, if a life insurance contract is sold or transferred for value, the difference between the death benefit paid and the purchaser's cost is ordinary taxable income.

Transfer for value rule

If the insured has any legal rights (called *incidents of ownership*) in a life insurance policy, or if the proceeds are payable to the insured's estate, the proceeds of the life insurance policy are included in the gross estate and may be subject to the estate tax. Incidents of ownership include the right to change the beneficiary, the right to take a loan, or the right to any dividends. However, if the gross estate is less than the exempt amount, no federal estate tax will be paid. Thus, for small estates, neither the federal income nor the estate tax applies to life insurance proceeds.

Living Benefits: Dividends, Savings, and Accelerated Death Benefits

The policy owner has three ways to receive cash from a life insurance policy while the insured is living:

1. If the policy is participating, the contract entitles the owner to a share of the profits. Insurers call this share a "dividend." Dividend options are described in Chapter 14.
2. If a life insurance policy has a savings value, the policy owner has a legal right to withdraw this value.
3. If the insured is terminally ill, many policies give the owner the right to receive a lump sum settlement based on the policy's death benefit.

Even if the policy owner takes the dividends in cash, which is one of several alternatives that most insurers provide, the dividends received from a participating life insurance policy are not subject to federal income tax because the IRS views these dividends as a return of part of the premium and not as earned income.

Several types of life insurance policies have a savings feature, which Chapter 13, "Life Insurance Policies," describes. The general rule is, if the insured withdraws the savings value and if this value exceeds the insured's adjusted cost basis (premiums paid minus dividends received), the excess is subject to federal income tax in the year of the withdrawal. For example, Bill Shakespeare purchased a whole life insurance policy 35 years ago when he was 25 years old. He decides to retire at age 60 and he withdraws the cash value of his life insurance to buy a recreational motor home. Assume Bill's total premiums ($50,000) minus dividends he received ($21,000) equal $29,000. If Bill withdraws $35,000 in cash value, $6,000 ($35,000 − $29,000) is subject to tax. For the past 35 years, Bill has not had to report the interest income on the savings value of the policy. When he makes the withdrawal, however, the excess of the cash value over his adjusted cost basis is subject to the income tax at ordinary rates.

Accelerated death benefit

Many insurers allow an **accelerated death benefit**, which permits the early withdrawal of death benefits in cases where insureds are terminally ill. The IRS issued a regulation in June 1993 applying to the taxation of these early payments. These regulations provide that payments meeting a three-part test will be identified as a qualified accelerated death benefit, in which case the benefits may be received on the same tax-free basis applying to conventional death benefits. Summarizing the test: (1) the insured must be terminally ill; (2) the reduction of the remaining face value of coverage is limited; and (3) the cash value of the remaining death benefit may not be reduced.

SUMMARY

Professional financial planning is a five-step process: (1) motivate people, (2) collect data, (3) develop goals, (4) implement goals, and (5) review and update plans. The financial planning process has a different focus throughout the financial life cycle. In the early years, the focus is on premature death. Life insurance also can be used to guarantee funding for college tuition if a parent or parents were to die prematurely. In the middle years, life insurance and annuities can be used to provide funds for the retirement period, often on a tax-advantaged basis. In the later years, the focus of financial plans is on estate planning, or the efficient passing of property from wealth-owners to successors. Life insurance often is used to provide needed cash in estate plans.

People should purchase life insurance to meet specific needs that could not be met by other assets if death were to occur immediately. Needs common to most families include (1) a burial fund, (2) an education fund, (3) an income fund, and (4) a debt-retirement fund.

Spouses working at home provide valuable economic services to the family. Often it is desirable to purchase life insurance on a homemaker to permit the family to withstand the financial burdens caused by his or her premature death. Much less of a case can be made for insuring the lives of most children or college students. Only after the main wage earner's life has been insured adequately should insurance be considered for other family members.

A business purchases life insurance for three reasons: (1) to provide employee benefits (group life insurance); (2) to indemnify the firm for the financial loss suffered if a key employee dies prematurely (or is disabled); and (3) to finance the transfer of ownership rights from current to future owners.

Generalizations about the taxation of life insurance transactions are not easily made. The chapter described some basic points on taxation of the life insurance transaction.

REVIEW TERMS

- Accelerated death benefit
- Adjusted cost basis
- Annuity
- Buy-and-sell agreement
- Cash value life insurance
- Cross-purchase plan
- Entity plan
- Estate planning
- Federal estate tax
- Federal gift tax
- Gift tax exclusion
- Gross estate
- Group life insurance
- Incidents of ownership
- Intestate
- Key employee life insurance
- Life insurance
- Life insurance trust
- Marital deduction
- Needs-based purchase
- Permanent needs
- Permanent policies
- Probate
- Section 529
- Split-dollar life insurance
- Survivor life insurance
- Temporary need
- Term insurance
- Trust
- Uniform transfer tax
- Will

REVIEW

1. List and explain the different categories of need that life insurance can fill in the event of a premature death. Separate your list into permanent and temporary needs.
2. Other than life insurance, what assets are available to most American families at death?
3. Identify the five steps in the life insurance planning process.
4. Explain how the use of computers and spreadsheets makes the needs-based calculation of life insurance requirements more realistic.
5. Is it wise for college students to buy life insurance while they are still in college? What are some arguments on both sides of this issue?
6. What purposes are served when businesses purchase life insurance?
7. Describe key employee life insurance.
8. What is a buy-and-sell agreement, and what role does life insurance play in such a plan?
9. What is the purpose of a will? What happens if a person dies without a valid will?
10. Define the term *gross estate*.
11. How large is the annual gift tax exclusion? How can it be doubled?
12. Describe a second-to-die life insurance policy. What purpose does it serve?
13. Explain the purpose of life insurance in an estate plan.
14. Define the term *split-dollar life insurance*.
15. Explain the difference between the cross-purchase plan and the entity plan.
16. Does the federal income tax apply to life insurance death proceeds? Are there exceptions to the general rule?
17. When does the federal estate tax apply to life insurance proceeds?
18. Describe the likely tax consequences of cashing in a life insurance policy after 20 years.

OBJECTIVE QUESTIONS

1. This text states that the first step in the financial planning process is:
   a. To recommend the right amount of life insurance for a particular client
   b. To recommend the right life insurance policy for a particular client
   c. To motivate and educate clients
   d. To reduce the amount of taxes a client must pay
2. The need for postdeath financial resources includes all the following categories except:
   a. A wealth accumulation fund
   b. An income fund to support dependents
   c. An education fund
   d. A burial fund
3. The text identifies all the following categories of assets as often available to meet postdeath financial needs except:
   a. Social Security benefits
   b. Group life insurance
   c. Tax refunds
   d. Savings accounts and other liquid assets
4. The process of planning the transfer of wealth from one generation to another generally is called:
   a. Wealth transfer planning
   b. Wealth accumulation planning
   c. Estate planning
   d. Continuation planning
5. The "net cash outflow" for purchased property is called:
   a. Net cost basis
   b. Adjusted cash basis
   c. Accounting cost basis
   d. Present value basis
6. The needs-based purchase of life insurance is based on which equation?
   a. Life insurance purchased = financial needs − available assets.
   b. Life insurance needs = Social Security benefits − available assets.
   c. Financial needs = available assets − life insurance.
   d. Life insurance needs = Social Security benefits + burial fund.
7. Which of the following cases would make the best subject for the purchase of life insurance (assuming none of them currently own it)?
   a. Healthy college senior, no debts, but plans to go to graduate school
   b. Single woman, no debts, good job
   c. Baseball player, large salary, no dependents, no debt
   d. Single mother, two children, good salary, some debts
8. The court-supervised process for transferring property at death is called:
   a. Probate
   b. Estate planning
   c. Will oversight process
   d. Adjunct administration

DISCUSSION QUESTION

Using an electronic spreadsheet, prepare a life insurance plan for the Chestnut family. (Do not consider any other aspects of a complete financial plan.) Pattern your response on Tables 12–1 to 12–4. Your final report should explain your conclusion about how much life insurance the Chestnuts need to purchase.

Facts and Data

Bill and Hope Chestnut are 34 years old. They live in Terre Haute, Indiana. Their one child, Cindy, is 12. Bill works as an engineer for the local telephone company. Hope is a research chemist with a steel company. Hope's parents are deceased. Bill's parents are alive, and his father works for the U.S. Postal Service. Bill's parents live in Washington, D.C.

Two years ago, using money that Hope inherited from her parents' estate, the Chestnut family made a down payment on a new house. What current assets they now have also can be traced to this inheritance. Bill and Hope each have two sisters. Only Hope's older sister lives near the Chestnuts.

The Chestnuts' statement of net worth and most recent cash flow statement appear as Table 12–7 and Table 12–8, respectively. The Chestnuts have no individually purchased life insurance.

Both Chestnuts are optimistic about their financial future. Both have made progress in their careers and feel future advancement should follow. When confronted with the question, "What are your plans if either or both spouses were to die prematurely?" the Chestnuts admitted giving the matter little thought. They lacked formal plans but assumed one of their sisters would raise Cindy if they both died prematurely. They also felt that if one parent died prematurely, the surviving spouse would raise Cindy while continuing to work. They thought the surviving parent's earnings would provide adequate income for the family. The Chestnuts have no will and no written financial plans.

TABLE 12–7   Chestnut Family Statement of Net Worth: December 31, Last Year

Assets

Cash and checking	$ 1,500
Money market fund	3,000
100 shares common stock (market value)	5,500
Car	6,500
House	100,000
Total assets	$116,500

Liabilities

Credit card	$ 1,200
Car loan	3,500
Home mortgage loan	78,292
Total	$ 82,992
Net worth	33,508
Total liabilities and net worth	$116,500

TABLE 12–8   Chestnut Family Cash Flow Statement: January 1 to December 31, This Year

Income

Bill's salary	$28,000
Hope's salary	28,000
Investment income	680
Total income	$56,680
Income taxes (federal, state, local)	$15,870
Real estate tax	1,200
Social Security (FICA)	4,284
Total taxes	$21,354
Disposable income ($56,680 − $21,354)	$35,326

Expenses

Housing (mortgage payment $8,813)	$12,484
Transportation	5,899
Food	5,334
Vacation/entertainment	4,239
All other	7,000
Total expenses	$34,957
Net cash flow ($35,326 − $34,957)	$ 369

INTERNET RESEARCH ASSIGNMENT

1. Find one or more "life insurance needs calculators" on the Internet and see what answers they provide for the life insurance needs of Sara and Tom in the following problems:
   a. Sara is employed as a certified public accountant (CPA); there are no children in the family. Her husband, Tom, is employed as an architect. Tom and Sara each make $75,000 a year. Both are age 25 and are healthy. How much insurance does the family need on Sara's life?
   b. Now assume that the family has four-year-old twins. Sara plans to remain at home to raise the children until they reach age 12. Assuming that Sara earns no employment income, calculate the

family's need for life insurance on Sara's life. (Hint: make any reasonable estimates needed to keep this problem simple.) How much insurance is needed on Tom's life?

2. List the special circumstances found under the "Financial Planning for Special Circumstances" heading of the first section of the most recent topic list for the cfp® certification examination. Use this site: (*http://www.cfp.net/become/topiclist.asp/*).

3. Determine the following information for your state: (a) does the state have an estate tax; if so, describe its general characteristics? (b) Does your state have an inheritance tax; if so describe its general characteristics? (c) Find a description of the intestate law in your state and describe its general characteristics?

4. Determine the current state of the unified transfer tax. Has the tax been eliminated? Modified? Reverted back to the 2001 law?

CHAPTER 13

Life Insurance Policies

After studying this chapter, you should be able to:

■ Identify the markets for group, industrial, and individual life insurance

■ Describe different types of term insurance and explain their uses

■ Describe whole life insurance and explain its uses

■ Explain how whole life insurance policies build cash value

■ Explain the advantages and disadvantages of combining saving with life insurance

■ Explain how universal life insurance differs from traditional forms of life insurance

■ Describe the flexible investment options available with variable life insurance policies

One purpose of Chapter 12, "Professional Financial Planning," was to provide a basis for understanding how much life insurance a person or family would need to provide adequate coverage. One purpose of this chapter and the following four chapters is to describe several different types of insurance that people can use in their financial plans. Life insurance policies protect against the financial problems associated with premature death. Some life insurance policies also provide a savings fund for retirement or other purposes. Medical expense insurance and disability insurance pay for medical expenses or replace income lost because of disability. Annuities provide a guaranteed income that annuitants cannot outlive.

We begin this chapter by examining three ways that consumers acquire life insurance. Then we describe different types of term, whole life, universal, variable, and other life insurance policies. Next, we examine the advantages and disadvantages of saving with life insurance. Overall, this chapter deals with the question of identifying the appropriate life insurance policy for the needs and goals of different people. The chapter's appendix briefly describes life insurance mathematics. Interested readers will find that understanding life insurance mathematics brings into clearer focus many of the ideas presented in the chapter.

THREE WAYS LIFE INSURANCE IS DISTRIBUTED

Insurance companies distribute life insurance in three different ways:

- Group life insurance
- Industrial or debit life insurance
- Individual life insurance

Group Life Insurance

Group life insurance

Group life insurance is provided to a well-defined group of people who are associated for some purpose other than purchasing life insurance. Most commonly covered by group life insurance are employee groups, such as all the employees of the local school system or of the General Electric Corporation. Professional associations, such as the American Medical Association and the American Accounting Association, also can obtain group insurance for their members. We explain group life insurance more completely in Chapter 21, "Employee Benefits."

Credit life insurance

Credit life insurance is a special type of group life insurance purchased by a lender for its group of debtors. Banks, credit unions, and retail stores that sell merchandise on credit often offer credit life insurance to their customers. If the debtor dies with the loan outstanding, the life insurance proceeds repay the debt.

Group life insurance is term coverage and does not provide a savings value. Financial planners generally do not recommend relying on group life insurance as the exclusive source of postdeath funds in a financial plan because it is unlikely to match individual needs, may be unavailable after a job loss, and has no savings value.

Industrial Life Insurance

Industrial life insurance

Debit life insurance

Burial insurance

Currently, industrial life insurance is such a small fraction of the total life insurance market that we include it mostly as a matter of historical interest. People purchase **industrial life insurance** in small amounts, usually $2,000 or less. Typically, the premiums are collected at the insured's home on a regular (generally weekly or monthly) basis. Industrial life insurance is also called **debit life insurance** or **burial insurance**, and the agents selling it are called *debit agents*. Industrial life insurance was designed to meet the needs of low-income workers. The weekly visit of the debit agent coincided with the weekly paycheck, and the purpose of the insurance was to provide a burial fund.

The cost of industrial life insurance is high for two reasons. The health, and thus the life expectancy, of low-income workers is not as good as the average member of society. Second, it is a significant administrative expense for an agent to collect and account for numerous small premium payments. Because the cost of this coverage is relatively expensive compared to other individual coverage, and because there has been some alleged abuse of this product in the form of encouraging low-income people to purchase multiple policies rather than purchase a lower-cost individual policy, some critics have suggested banning the product. The sellers of industrial life have countered that, if the product were banned, the people they now cover would have no life insurance. From the standpoint of most U.S. consumers, industrial life insurance has little appeal. The benefits are small; the cost is high.

Individual Life Insurance

Ordinary life insurance

Most consumers purchase *individual life insurance*, which also is called **ordinary life insurance**. Unlike industrial life insurance, consumers may purchase $100,000 (and larger) individual life policies.

Table 13–1 provides a comparison of annual purchases and the amount of life insurance in force for selected years.

TERM INSURANCE

Term life insurance policy

When a life insurer sells a **term life insurance policy**, it promises to pay the beneficiary if the insured dies within a specified period. If the insured outlives the period, the insurer makes no payment. Term life insurance is similar to property insurance in this respect. If there is no loss to a home or automobile while such a policy is in force, the insurer makes no payment. Moreover, like property insurance policies, term insurance does not build savings or cash value, as do other types of life insurance. Thus, term insurance is often spoken of as providing "pure death protection." Term life insurance is

TABLE 13–1   Life Insurance Statistics Selected Years 1980–2004 (Millions of dollars)

Life Insurance Purchases[a] in the United States

Year	Individual	Group	Industrial
1980	385,575	183,418	3,609
1990	1,069,660	459,271	220[c]
1997	1,203,681	688,589	
1998	1,324,671	739,508	
1999	1,399,848	966,858	
2000	1,593,907	921,001	
2001	1,600,471	1,172,080	
2002	1,752,941	1,013,728	
2003	1,772,673	1,050,318	
2004	1,846,384	3,099,415	

Life Insurance in Force[b] in the United States (Millions of dollars)

Year	Individual	Group	Industrial	Credit
1980	1,760,474	1,579,355	35,994	165,215
1990	5,391,053	3,753,506	24,071	248,038
1997	7,854,570	5,279,042	17,991	212,255
1998	8,505,894	5,735,273	17,365	212,917
1999	9,172,397	6,110,218		213,453
2000	9,376,370	6,376,127		200,770
2001	9,345,723	6,765,074		178,851
2002	9,311,729	6,876,075		158,534
2003	9,654,731	7,236,191		152,739
2004	9,717,377	7,630,503		160,371

[a]*Purchases means new insurance purchased in a given year.*
[b]*In force is the current total face amount of potential life insurance claims.*
[c]*Included with individual starting in 1994.*
SOURCE: *Life Insurance Fact Book* (Washington, D.C.: American Council of Life Insurers, annual).

a relatively simple type of insurance, and partly for this reason, it has been among the first insurance products successfully sold on the Internet. (Readers can use the keywords "life insurance rates" or "life insurance costs" in a search engine to discover various Web sites selling life insurance on the Internet.)

Unlike the risk of losing a home or automobile, death is a certainty. The time of death, however, is not. Most term insurance is purchased by people between the ages of 25 and 65. Most insureds do not die before age 65. Thus, many people pay term life insurance premiums but their policies never result in a death claim. However, a few term life insurance policies result in claims far larger than the premiums paid. Most people would much rather be among those who pay term insurance premiums but receive no death proceeds. Yet to say such people have received nothing for their money is a serious error. Who can measure or ignore the precious peace of mind that term life insurance has provided such people and their families?

Types of Term Life Insurance

Insurers sell several types of term life insurance policies, including the following categories:

Yearly renewable term

Annually renewable term

- Single-year term policies promise to pay if the insured dies within the one-year policy term. If they have the renewability feature, described shortly, insurers call these single-year policies **yearly renewable term** or **annually renewable term** policies.

- Five-year term policies pay if death occurs within five years of the policy's purchase.
- Longer-term policies may last for 10, 15, or 20 years, for example.
- Term to a specified age (such as 60 or 65) policies pay if death occurs before the designated age.

Decreasing term life insurance

Multiyear term policies may have benefits that decrease, increase, or remain level. A **decreasing term life insurance** policy provides the beneficiary with less proceeds each year the policy is in force. That is, if death occurs in the first policy year, the beneficiary receives the face amount, for example, $100,000. If death occurs in a succeeding year, the proceeds will be less. For example, in year 21, the proceeds may equal only $38,100. In a decreasing term policy, the premiums remain the same each year but purchase less insurance. That is, the death benefit decreases because the chance of death increases with age. Decreasing term insurance is useful, for example, to provide funds to repay a mortgage or provide support for a dependent child until the child reaches age 21. Over time, the funds needed to accomplish each of these goals decreases, and so do the insurance proceeds.

Increasing term life insurance

An **increasing term life insurance** policy provides proceeds that increase each year. If death occurs in the first year, the insurer pays the face amount of the policy—for example, $100,000. In the 20th year, perhaps $145,000 would be paid to the beneficiary. Such policies are useful in an inflationary economy. For example, as the price of a college education increases, so do the insurance proceeds. Premiums for these policies increase at each renewal.

Level term life insurance

A **level term life insurance** policy pays the same amount of benefits if death occurs at any point while the policy is in force. Table 13–2 presents a sales illustration for a 20-year level term policy prepared for Richard L. Heart. The insurance company guarantees the premium and death benefit for 20 years. At the end of the 20th year, Richard may keep the policy but the premiums may rise steeply to reflect his age at that time. In this illustration, the nonguaranteed premium does not rise in the 20th year assuming the insurer's current experience with mortality and investment results remain favorable. As the column heading indicates, the nonguaranteed premium is subject to change.

Figure 13–1 illustrates increasing term, decreasing term, and level term insurance death benefits. Many families purchase level term policies for the period of child dependency. Even though this approach may provide "extra" coverage as each year of dependency disappears as the child grows older, the potential for inflation and unanticipated needs makes a margin of safety desirable.

Renewable term

Renewable term policies allow the insured to continue the coverage up to a specified age regardless of the status of the insured's health or other relevant factors

TABLE 13–2 Sales Illustration for 20-Year Level Term Insurance Policy

Hypothetical Life Insurance Company
Illustration for Richard L. Heart
Age 35, Nonsmoking

Year	Age	Guaranteed Premium	Death Benefit	Nonguaranteed Current Premium	Death Benefit
0	35	$ 450	$250,000	$450	$250,000
5	40	$ 450	$250,000	$450	$250,000
10	45	$ 450	$250,000	$450	$250,000
20	55	$2,700	$250,000	$450	$250,000

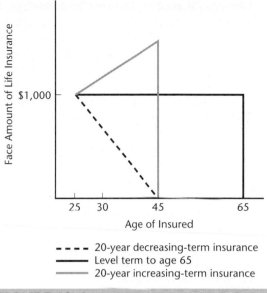

FIGURE 13–1   Three Term Life Insurance Policies

including occupation. If, for example, a five-year term policy is not renewable, an insurer could end the insurance at the end of any five-year period. The insurer could not end coverage if the policy was renewable. Although renewable term policies cost more, the guaranteed renewal feature is worthwhile for many people because it transfers the risk of becoming uninsurable to the insurance company.

Each time a term insurance policy is renewed, the premium increases because the insured is older. Thus, the premiums for yearly renewable term insurance increase each year at renewal. With a five-year term policy, the premiums increase at each fifth anniversary. For example, assume a 28-year-old insured pays $2 each year for $1,000 of five-year renewable term insurance. At age 33, on renewal of the policy, his premiums increase to $2.50 a year for the next five years. At age 38, the premiums will increase again to $3.50 a year, and an increase will follow at each renewal, until he no longer can renew the policy.

Convertible term   **Convertible term** policies allow the insured the option of converting the policy to a whole life policy. This privilege can be valuable if the term insurance is about to expire and the insured wants to continue the coverage on a permanent basis. Some insureds want to begin a savings program when their income increases. When the insured makes the conversion, the premium increases.

Combinations of term insurance features may be purchased. Thus, Thomas Paine may purchase a ten-year, renewable, convertible, level term policy. Such a policy would provide level benefits for ten years, allow him to renew the policy at the end of year 10 (if he was younger than the maximum age for renewability), or allow him to convert to a whole life policy of the same face amount of insurance.

Uses of Term Life Insurance

Term life insurance can prove useful in solving many financial problems. It can be used when the need for life insurance is temporary. It is also useful when people need the maximum coverage and have limited financial resources. Because of competition for large-sized policies, the price of term insurance decreased significantly during the late

1990s both on the Internet and through the traditional marketing channels using agents and brokers. The price of term insurance is attractive to many people.

In the event of a premature death, the education fund need can be met by a level term policy. Assume King George has a son, Prince George. Assume the son is now six years old and shows promise of becoming a scholar. King George thinks that, if he should die prematurely, he would like a fund of $80,000 available for his son's college education. Prince George will enter college in 11 years and remain there for 4 years. Thus, because the need for an education fund exists for only 15 years, it could be met with a 15-year level term policy.

People often use term life insurance to repay debts. The need for life insurance is temporary because most debts are temporary. For example, many home mortgages last from 15 to 30 years. When homeowners use installment payments to retire the mortgage, the amount of debt decreases each year. Thus, a $230,000 mortgage requires only $230,000 of life insurance proceeds before the homeowner makes the first loan repayment. Afterwards, less insurance is needed. A decreasing term policy can be coordinated to cover the loan balance outstanding. Many homeowners purchase a decreasing term policy to retire the mortgage if the family wage earner dies. Mortgages generally do not become payable at the homeowner's death. However, the proceeds of the life insurance can relieve the survivors of having to make monthly mortgage payments.

Some of or all the need for the income to support dependents can be met by term insurance. The need for funds to support dependent children is temporary. Once the children become financially independent, the need for funds to support them ends. However, if a child, or a spouse, is likely to be a permanent dependent, perhaps because of a permanent disability, then term life insurance is unlikely to be the best choice to fund problems caused by a premature death.

At any age, term insurance premiums are lower than whole life insurance premiums. Therefore, term insurance should be used when the need is for maximum life insurance protection—especially if a consumer's life insurance dollars are limited. An example of this situation would be a young family with two or more dependent children and limited disposable income.

Term life insurance can be a valuable part of an individual's life insurance plans. Term policies are flexible and initially have lower premiums than other forms of life insurance. Term insurance cannot solve all life insurance problems, however. Generally, it should not be used when the need for life insurance is permanent rather than temporary, as would be the case with a burial fund. Nor can term insurance by itself provide a regular forced savings plan. Insuring permanent needs while accumulating savings requires a whole life plan.

Whole Life Insurance

Whole life insurance

Whole life insurance policies promise to pay the beneficiary whenever death occurs. "Till death do us part," is the insurer's promise. Whole life policies also promise payment if the insured reaches a specified age such as 100 or 120.[1] When insurers make a claim payment, they say the policy has *matured*. The insurer knows for a certainty it eventually must pay a claim on every whole life policy remaining in force. This circumstance is different from both property insurance and term life insurance policies. Because claims are a certainty with whole life policies, the insurer must collect enough premiums to pay them. This fact is one reason why whole life insurance premiums initially are larger than term life insurance premiums.

---

[1] New whole life insurance polices based on the 2001 CSO mature at age 120.

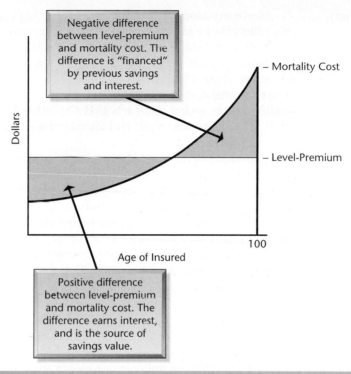

Negative difference between level-premium and mortality cost. The difference is "financed" by previous savings and interest.

– Mortality Cost

– Level-Premium

Dollars

100

Age of Insured

Positive difference between level-premium and mortality cost. The difference earns interest, and is the source of savings value.

FIGURE 13–2   The Origin of Savings Value in Level-Premium Whole Life Insurance

Cash Values

Cash value

The level-premium method of paying for whole life insurance produces a savings value, called the **cash value**, in permanent life insurance policies such as whole life insurance. The insurer initially charges a larger premium than is necessary to pay the early death claims. This additional charge continues during the first portion of the policy's duration. Figure 13–2 illustrates this concept. After a period, these additional charges and the compound interest on them generate a significant savings value. Life insurers invest their insureds' cash value in relatively safe investments such as federal government debt issues or mortgage loans. These safe investments allow the insurer to guarantee an increase in cash values, and traditional whole life policies always contain a table presenting these guaranteed values.

One purpose for building the savings value is to finance the large premiums needed to keep the policy in force in the years when the probability of death is high. In addition to keeping premiums level, the savings in the whole life policy are the basis of several important contractual rights. Policyowners can withdraw all their cash value at once if they want to end the policy. People can use the cash value to purchase an annuity at older ages when they need retirement income. Some or all of the cash value can be borrowed from the insurer at any time. Borrowing is limited to the amount of cash value available, and insurers charge interest on the loan. Because a whole life policy combines savings and life insurance protection, it can play many roles in life insurance plans.

Types of Whole Life Policies

Insurers classify whole life insurance policies in the following categories based on the method of premium payment: single premium, continuous premium, and limited payment.

Single-premium whole life insurance

Modified endowment contracts (MECs)

Continuous-premium whole life insurance

Level-premium whole life insurance

Straight-premium whole life insurance

Single-premium whole life insurance policies are those for which, in exchange for one relatively large premium, the insurer promises to pay the claim whenever death occurs. Because the one premium is large, consumers needing a great deal of life insurance generally cannot use the single-premium method. For example, if the single premium for $1,000 of whole life insurance was $350 for a male age 20, then $100,000 of insurance will cost $35,000. In 1988, Congress classified single-premium policies as **modified endowment contracts (MECs)**.[2] It then eliminated the tax advantages for modified endowments while still allowing tax advantages for more traditional forms of cash value insurance.

Continuous-premium whole life insurance policies require insureds to pay the same premium as long as they live or until they reach the specified maturity age. Insurers also call these policies **level-premium whole life insurance** and **straight-premium whole life insurance**. The premiums take into account, mathematically, both compound interest and the probability of the insured's death. An insured's death means that the insurer must make a claims payment. It also means an insured no longer will make premium payments to the insurer.

The premium schedule of limited-payment whole life insurance policies falls somewhere between that of single-premium and continuous-premium policies. In each case, the protection continues until the insured dies. Insureds with limited-payment policies pay premiums for only a limited number of years. Examples include 10-payment and 20-payment whole life policies and policies paid up at age 60 or 65.

The size of each premium payment is a function of the number of times it will be paid. The fewer the number of payments, the larger each payment will be. Thus, for a man age 35, payments for a 10-payment whole life policy will be larger than the payments required for a whole life policy paid up at 65, where 30 payments are due.

People wanting long-term death protection but who do not want to continue paying life insurance premiums, especially during retirement, might choose limited-payment policies. These policies are also useful to people wanting to combine more savings with their life insurance purchase. The "secret" of the limited-payment whole life policy is that the insurer is willing to accept a smaller number of larger payments, and, as a result, greater compound interest is earned compared to the continuous premium plan.

Insurers continue to develop new combinations of coverage and payment plans. It is unnecessary to describe these different types of coverage in an introductory textbook. However, two other types of payment plans for whole life insurance deserve brief mention. **Modified whole life insurance** policies have level premiums rising in stair steps. The first step is below that of straight life, while the last step is above the comparable straight life premium. Typical modified whole life policies have three or fewer steps.

Modified whole life insurance

Combination whole life insurance

Combination whole life insurance policies combine decreasing term insurance with a whole life policy. The scheduled decreases in the term insurance portion, however, are exactly offset by additions to the whole life portion. The additions arise from the reinvestment of dividends paid on the cash value of the whole life portion. Over time, the policy replaces term insurance with whole life insurance. That is, while the policy face remains constant, the underlying term or whole life proportion changes until the term insurance finally disappears. The sales appeal of this policy type arises because after the term insurance has been replaced with whole life insurance, the insured has a

---

[2] Any life insurance policy failing a "seven-pay" test is considered a modified endowment contract (MEC). To avoid being labeled an MEC and losing the advantage of tax-free policy loans, premiums cannot be paid more rapidly than necessary to provide the paid-up death benefits that seven level annual payments can purchase. This is not a simple concept; nevertheless, it is what the Internal Revenue Service (IRS) rule states.

whole life policy purchased at a lower cost than a traditional whole life policy. The cost may be lowered significantly if a large proportion of term insurance is chosen initially.

The Uses of Whole Life Insurance

Whole life insurance policies meet people's needs for permanent protection combined with savings. Permanent protection needs include a burial fund and an income fund in cases in which a spouse, child, or parent depends permanently on the insured for financial support. Life insurance used in estate plans and in business continuation arrangements often are cash value insurance. Such permanent needs generally cannot be met by term insurance because term insurance becomes unaffordable or is often unavailable after age 65, while these needs may continue after that age.

A Whole Life Ledger Sheet

Excess interest provision

Table 13–3 is a summary ledger sheet prepared for Vince Vango. It is for an *excess interest whole life policy*. The **excess interest provision** means the cash values will increase faster than the guaranteed rate if the insurer earns rates of return greater than the guaranteed rate, as it is currently doing. The insurer guarantees the maximum annual premium and a minimum cash surrender value. The nonguaranteed death benefits in this illustration show the effect of nonguaranteed dividends, which are used to purchase paid-up additional death benefits. The company notes that this column is based on its current dividend scale and that actual dividends may be more or less than those illustrated.

Whole life insurance as a percentage of all policies sold in the United States has fallen by a large percentage in the past three decades. Several reasons explain this declining market share, including the following:

- Term insurance has increased significantly in popularity. The decline in term life insurance rates reflects the steadily improving longevity of the past 30 years. Moreover, term life insurance premiums have been the subject of intense price competition, including competition arising from sales on the Internet.

- Variable-universal policies increased in popularity in the latter half of the 1990s, but the sales of these policies have grown more slowly in recent years.

- Inflation causes erosion of the purchasing power of both the face amount and the savings value of traditional whole life insurance policies. Many people became displeased with the performance of their cash value whole life policies and began a program combining term life insurance with equity investments as a substitute.

TABLE 13–3   Whole Life Insurance Sales Illustration

Illustration for Vince Vango
Age 35, Nonsmoking
Annual Premium = $3,000
Face Amount = $250,000

Year	Age	Guaranteed Premium	Guaranteed Cash Surrender Value	Death Benefit	Nonguaranteed Cash Surrender Value (current)	Nonguaranteed Death Benefit (current)
0	35	$3,000	$ 0	$250,000	$ 0	$250,000
5	40	$3,000	$ 9,000	$250,000	$ 9,300	$252,000
10	45	$3,000	$27,500	$250,000	$29,000	$254,000
20	55	$3,000	$65,000	$250,000	$86,000	$287,000

- The easy availability of tax-advantaged savings in Individual Retirement Accounts (IRAs) created a substitute savings alternative for some people.
- Whole life insurance involves relatively high transaction costs, and the expenses of the policy are not as transparent to consumers as are the charges for newer policy types.

UNIVERSAL LIFE INSURANCE

As we just noted, beginning in the late 1970s, the traditional whole life policies found increasingly less acceptance by consumers as many consumers of financial services became more sophisticated and focused on investment yields. In this environment, two new life insurance products emerged, universal life insurance and variable-universal life insurance.

Universal life insurance

Universal life insurance allows the insured to buy term insurance and invest an additional amount with the insurance company. The insurer's investments supporting universal life insurance are typically in short-term (six months or less) federal government debt issues. In other words, the underlying investments supporting universal life insurance are similar to a money market mutual fund. The policy allows the insured to determine both the amount and the frequency of the premium payments within limits. The minimum premium is the amount needed to keep a term insurance policy in force. An Internal Revenue Service (IRS) formula determines the maximum premium.

Typically, the insurer subtracts a monthly mortality (term insurance) charge and an expense charge from the insured's accumulated premium fund. Neither the mortality charge nor the expense charge is guaranteed; they may fluctuate based on the insurer's experience. The accumulated premium deposits, minus expense and mortality charges, produce a cash value. This cash value then earns two types of interest.

Guaranteed interest rate

Excess interest rate

The contract specifies a **guaranteed interest rate**. The guaranteed rate produces a guaranteed minimum cash value. The insurer also credits an **excess interest rate** if policy conditions are met. The excess interest rate is determined by a formula or by company declaration. When a formula is used, the formula is usually tied to the interest rate on short-term U.S. Treasury securities.

Universal Life Insurance Death Benefits

Universal life insurance death benefits follow one of two patterns, usually identified as Plan A or Plan B. Figure 13–3 shows these plans graphically.

Plan B is easier to describe because the death benefit is equal to the initial amount of insurance plus any accumulated cash value at death. Insurers base the term insurance charge on the death benefit, which they call the **amount at risk**. The insurance company guarantees the initial death benefit regardless of operating results.

Amount at risk

Under the more complicated Plan A, the death benefit remains level until the cash value exceeds a specified amount. If the cash value exceeds the specified amount, insurers add only the increase above this amount to the death benefit. The result is a minimum amount of insurance included in the death proceeds. As in Plan B, the insurer bases the mortality charge on the amount at risk to the insurer. This amount decreases at first and then remains constant once the cash value exceeds the threshold.

Uses of Universal Life Insurance

Universal life insurance can be used as a substitute for traditional whole life insurance in most cases. The following features distinguish universal life insurance from traditional whole life policies:

- *Flexibility of Premium Payments*: Within the minimum and maximum limits, the insured can choose the frequency and amount of premium payments. Most

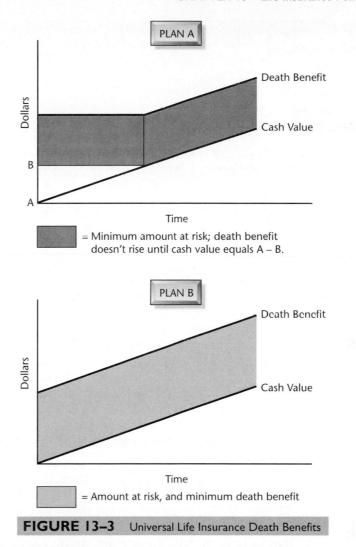

FIGURE 13-3 Universal Life Insurance Death Benefits

insurers use a suggested premium payment to produce the results illustrated when the policy is purchased. The insured need not make the suggested payment. If the policy has sufficient cash value to cover the mortality and expense charges, a premium is not required.

- *Ability to Earn a Greater Return When Interest Rates Rise*: During periods of inflation, short-term interest rates change regularly. In general, short-term interest rates increase when prices rise because the federal government attempts to control inflation using interest rates to restrain the economy.

- *Flexibility of Death Benefits*: As we just explained, by controlling the premium payments or by switching between Plan A and Plan B, the insured can exercise considerable control over the universal life insurance death benefit.

- *Breakdown of Component Costs and Returns*: The annual statement accompanying a universal life insurance policy identifies the mortality costs, expense loadings, and investment earnings. This breakdown is not provided in traditional whole life policies. Even calculating the rate of return on the savings portion of traditional policies is subject to considerable dispute. However, universal life insurance policies with surrender charges (rear-end loads) or with formulas linking the excess interest credits with policyholder loans also may obscure the policy's real rate of return.

TABLE 13–4 Universal Life Insurance Sales Illustration

Illustration for W. A. Mozart
Age 35, Nonsmoker
Initial Death Benefit = $250,000
Planned Premium = $2,400
Guaranteed Interest Rate = 4%
Nonguaranteed Current Charges/Current Interest Rate = 5.25%

Age	Year	Premium	Guaranteed Cash Value	Cash Surrender Value	Death Benefit	Nonguaranteed Cash Value	Nonguaranteed Cash Surrender Value	Nonguaranteed Death Benefit
0	35	$2,400	$ 0	$ 0	$250,000	$ 0	$ 0	$250,000
5	40	$2,400	$ 8,800	$ 5,000	$260,000	$ 9,350	$ 5,600	$260,000
10	45	$2,400	$18,000	$17,000	$268,000	$20,000	$18,500	$272,000
20	55	$2,400	$36,000	$36,000	$286,000	$46,000	$46,000	$307,000
30	65	$2,400	$34,000	$34,000	$284,000	$65,000	$65,000	$354,000

In terms of legal rights and tax treatment, universal life insurance and whole life insurance policies are similar. Both allow full or partial withdrawals of cash value and both allow the beneficiary to receive the death proceeds free of federal income tax. Many traditional options and riders also are available with the universal life contract. Because it duplicates most of the advantages of traditional whole life contracts and offers the opportunity for greater investment gain and a rising death benefit, universal life insurance is an attractive substitute for the traditional whole life policy in periods of rapid inflation.

Ledger Sheet for Universal Life Insurance

W. A. Mozart asked his life insurance agent for an illustration of a universal life insurance policy. The result appears in Table 13–4. The face amount of insurance remains $250,000. The illustration assumes that Mozart continues paying an annual premium of $2,400 and the insurer credits the policy with 4 percent interest. Neither of these assumptions is likely to hold over the projected life of the policy, however. If the premiums increase or decrease or if investment results increase or decrease, the cash values will be different from those illustrated. Currently, the insurer is earning 5.25 percent on these policies, and this nonguaranteed result is illustrated alongside the guaranteed results. This illustration also assumes the policy operates under Plan B, with all increases in investment results increasing the death benefit. This policy has a surrender charge, which explains the difference between the cash value and the surrender value. The surrender charge disappears after the 20th year.

VARIABLE LIFE INSURANCE, VARIABLE-UNIVERSAL LIFE INSURANCE

Variable life insurance

Variable life insurance is a nontraditional cash value life insurance policy introduced in the late 1970s. Initially, this policy did not enjoy much popularity. Commentators give several reasons for the lack of acceptance of variable life insurance: It is more difficult to understand, may entail more risk, and is subject to both state and federal regulation. Because the underlying investments are securities and the policyowner has some investment choice, the federal government regulates variable life insurance under the provisions of the Investment Company Act of 1940. Agents selling variable life insurance must be federally registered representatives with the Securities and Exchange

Commission (SEC; *http://www.sec.gov/*) as well as insurance agents licensed by the various states. Passing the National Association of Security Dealers (NASD; *http://www.nasd.com/*) Series 6 examination permits the sale of variable life insurance products and mutual funds. Passing the Series 7 exam allows the sale of listed stocks, bonds, and option contracts.

Variable-universal life insurance (VUL)

Separate accounts

Since 1986, variable life policies have allowed flexible premium payments and the modern version of the policy is called **variable-universal life insurance (VUL)**. Today almost all variable life insurance sales are of the VUL type. Many provisions of the variable life policy follow the traditional whole life level-premium plan. That is, a cash value develops when premiums exceed mortality charges and expenses. When the cash value develops, the insured can choose one or more underlying investment funds, called **separate accounts**. The typical choices available in the separate accounts include money market, common stock, and bond funds. These separate accounts are comparable to the mutual funds available to all investors. The cash value earns a return (positive or negative) based on the performance of an underlying separate account. Insurers do not guarantee a minimum cash value; however, they do guarantee a minimum death benefit.

Variable life insurance, depending on the investment account(s) chosen, can duplicate either universal life insurance or traditional whole life insurance. For example, it could resemble universal life if the underlying investment is a money market fund. If the underlying investment vehicle is a long-term bond fund, the policy would operate more like traditional whole life insurance.

Table 13–5 shows a sales illustration for a variable-universal life insurance policy for Frank Joseph, a conservative investor who is willing to assume some risk in exchange for a higher return with his purchase of life insurance.

In practice, because this policy is so complicated, several pages of definitions, warnings, and explanations such as the following precede the numerical illustration:

- The life insurance policy illustrated on the following pages is a flexible premium variable life insurance policy, which is commonly called "Variable-Universal Life."

- Subject to minimum and maximum premium requirements explained below, premium payments may be made at any time and in any amount.

- This illustration is a hypothetical example to assist you in understanding the way a variable life insurance policy operates by showing how the performance of the

TABLE 13–5   Variable-Universal Life Insurance Sales Illustration

Illustration for Frank Joseph
Age 35, Nonsmoking
Initial Death Benefit = $100,000
Planned Premium = $1,307 annually

| | *Guaranteed Basis @ 4%* | | | *Nonguaranteed Basis @ 6.25%* | | |
Year	*Premium*	*Net Cash Value*	*Death Benefit*	*Premium*	*Net Cash Value*	*Death Benefit*
1	$1,307	$ 0	$100,000	$1,307	$ 0	$100,000
2	$1,307	$ 0	$100,000	$1,307	$ 136	$100,000
3	$1,307	$ 1,015	$100,000	$1,307	$ 1,527	$100,000
7	$1,307	$ 7,556	$100,000	$1,307	$ 7,957	$100,000
8	$1,307	$ 8,982	$100,000	$1,307	$ 9,799	$100,000
9	$1,307	$10,448	$100,000	$1,307	$11,745	$100,000
20	$1,307	$27,471	$100,000	$ 0	$41,787	$104,546
21	$1,307	$29,214	$100,000	$ 0	$46,593	$107,528

underlying investment accounts could affect the policy account value and death benefits. Actual results are likely to be different from and may be more or less favorable than those shown in this illustration.

ENDOWMENT LIFE INSURANCE

In the United States, endowment life insurance is mainly of historical interest. However, this policy type still is sold in other countries. Insurers no longer sell this policy type in the United States because the Deficit Reduction Act of 1984 eliminated most of its tax advantages.[3] Because some U.S. endowment policies remain in force, we continue to describe this policy type.

Endowment life insurance

An **endowment life insurance** policy creates two rights for the insured. The first is to have the beneficiary paid if the insured dies before the policy matures or "endows." The second is for the insured to collect the endowment if he or she is alive when the policy matures. Figure 13–4 presents this concept graphically. With endowment life insurance, either the insured or the beneficiary will collect the face amount of the policy.

The insured-owner may choose an endowment period as a specific number of years or may choose to have the policy endow at a specified age. Thus, Ben Dreenken, the bartender, may purchase a 10-year, 15-year, or 20-year endowment. Alternatively, he may purchase an endowment to age 60 or 65. The general rule is that the shorter the endowment period, the higher the premium for a given amount of insurance.

The two promises made in an endowment life insurance policy may sound attractive. If the insured dies, the beneficiary collects the proceeds. If the insured lives, the insured collects the endowment. Although the promises represent a sure thing, this policy type is expensive. Because the insurer pays a claim on all endowment policies, it includes charges in the premium for both living and dying.

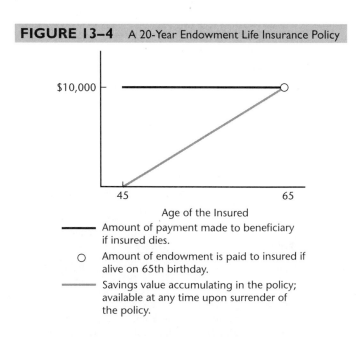

FIGURE 13–4   A 20-Year Endowment Life Insurance Policy

$10,000

45   65

Age of the Insured

——— Amount of payment made to beneficiary if insured dies.

○   Amount of endowment is paid to insured if alive on 65th birthday.

——— Savings value accumulating in the policy; available at any time upon surrender of the policy.

---

[3] The Internal Revenue Code classifies endowments as an MEC in its regulations.

REASONS FOR SAVING WITH LIFE INSURANCE

Many consumers choose a life policy with a savings value, including whole life, universal, or VUL policies. Here are some good reasons for this choice:

- Many consumers do not save money unless forced to do so by a regular savings plan, such as the one incorporated in these policies. Even people who save sometimes spend their savings once they reach a significant amount. Such spending defeats the purposes of a savings program.

- Experts invest savings in these life insurance policies.

- People saving with life insurance receive federal income tax advantages. The interest on the savings is not tax free, but it is tax deferred. No federal income tax need be paid on the interest earned on the savings element of a life insurance policy unless the policy is surrendered and the owner withdraws the cash value.[4] If the savings are not withdrawn and the policy matures as a death benefit, then no federal income tax applies.

- The savings element of a whole life policy provides some protection from creditors' claims in the event of an insured's bankruptcy. Depending on the beneficiary designation and relevant state and federal bankruptcy laws, the savings in a life insurance policy may not be subject to seizure by creditors of a bankrupt insured. Protection from creditors' claims is a technical and complex issue.

BUY TERM AND INVEST THE DIFFERENCE

Carefully examine the annual premiums for term and whole life presented in Table 13–6. At every age listed, term insurance requires a considerably smaller initial premium outlay than whole life insurance.

Some financial planners suggest that consumers "buy term insurance and invest the difference." The "difference" is the difference in premium between term insurance and some form of permanent insurance. Table 13–6 shows that at age 20, this difference is $9.28 ($11.34 − $2.06) for each $1,000 of life insurance. At age 40, the difference is $17.34 ($20.90 − $3.56). Advocates of term insurance stress the following three points:

- The consumer who buys term and invests the difference not only leaves the insurance death benefits to the beneficiary but also leaves the amount of savings

TABLE 13–6   Representative Annual Life Insurance Premiums for $1,000 of Insurance

Age	Single-Year Term[a]	Whole Life[b]
20	$2.06	$11.34
25	$2.16	$12.95
30	$2.29	$15.10
35	$2.62	$17.51
40	$3.56	$20.90
45	$5.33	$25.56

[a]The term policy is renewable and convertible. Premiums increase each year.
[b]The whole life policy pays nonguaranteed dividends that reduce the premium outlay.

---

[4] Chapter 12 covered the taxation of life insurance policies.

accumulated outside the policy. These savings can reach significant amounts when compound interest is earned. In later years, the outside savings can exceed the original amount of insurance.

- Many needs for life insurance present in the early family years no longer exist at age 65. If a need for life insurance continues, savings will be available to meet it.
- The investment return and accumulated savings outside the life insurance policy each may be significantly greater than returns and accumulations inside the policy.

Commentators favoring whole life insurance offer the following counterarguments:

- If consumers invest the difference outside the policy, they forgo the advantages of safety and guaranteed earnings the insurance provides. In other words, one reason the investment returns and accumulations are greater outside the policy is because there is more risk.
- Many people cannot save regularly and leave their savings accounts undisturbed. If people cannot do these two things, the advice to buy term and invest the difference will leave them worse off.
- Many people are not skilled enough to invest wisely at rates significantly higher than those earned by a cash value life insurance policy.
- If the need for life insurance should continue beyond the original plans, the advice could prove costly. If the term policies were not convertible, the advice could produce unmet needs. The savings fund built up outside the policy, however, would prevent a totally unmet need.
- If the savings are outside the policy, insureds may give up tax advantages and protection from creditors' claims.

A modern variation of the buy-term-invest-the-difference strategy involves investing the difference in an IRA. (Chapter 21 describes both traditional and Roth IRAs.) This strategy allows the owner to retain the tax-advantaged investment earnings of cash value life insurance. It also allows the owner to keep the IRA investment plus the term life death benefits if the owner dies. Moreover, the transaction costs of this approach potentially are less than a comparable life insurance purchase. Among the potential disadvantages of this strategy, it must be noted that an IRA has limitations on the amount that can be deposited and high-income earners are subject to an eligibility phase-out. The tax consequences of the IRA strategy involve a potential penalty if the IRA is withdrawn before age 59½, but generalizations are not appropriate on overall tax consequences. In conclusion, for investors who are willing to accept more risk, buying term insurance and investing the difference in an IRA is an alternative that they should consider.

SUMMARY

Table 13–7 provides a comparison of three of the policy types described in this chapter.

People may acquire life insurance in three ways. Many employees are covered by group life insurance, which is a frequent benefit provided to workers. Industrial life insurance, which is available in relatively small amounts, can be used to provide a burial fund. Most consumers purchase their life insurance on an individual basis from life insurance agents.

Term insurance, which provides protection for a limited period, involves the lowest premium outlay. Term insurance generally should not be used when the need for protection is permanent or when the insured wants savings benefits. Whole life insurance policies, which have no time limit for the payment of death proceeds, combine a savings element with life insurance protection. Many consumers want to combine these savings features with life insurance protection.

TABLE 13–7 Policy Comparison Chart

	Level Term	*Ordinary Whole Life*	*Variable-Universal*
Death Benefit	Level	Level	Level or increasing
Cash Value Savings	None	Minimum schedule—guaranteed	Depends on investments—not guaranteed
Premiums	Increase with age	Level for lifetime	Flexible premiums, within limits
Uses	• Temporary needs • Maximum coverage	• Combines savings and protection • Permanent needs	• Combines insurance with investment • Policy may adjust favorably in mild inflation
Disadvantages	• No savings value • Premiums may become unaffordable • Insurance may be required when insured is too old to purchase term insurance	• Policy hurt by inflation • High acquisition costs	• Risk of investment decline borne by insured

Because term insurance premiums are lower than whole life insurance premiums, consumers have been advised to save the difference in premiums outside the insurance policy. On the one hand, following this advice allows the possibility of leaving more proceeds to survivors. On the other hand, people should be confident of their ability to save regularly, invest wisely, and leave the savings untouched before they consider or follow this advice.

Life insurers sell many policies other than term and whole life insurance. Universal life insurance combines flexibility in premium payments with the opportunity for increased interest earnings. Variable-universal life insurance allows the insured an opportunity to invest cash values in one or more separate investment accounts maintained by the insurer.

REVIEW TERMS

- Amount at risk
- Annually renewable term
- Burial insurance
- Cash value
- Combination whole life insurance
- Continuous-premium whole life insurance
- Convertible term
- Credit life insurance
- Debit life insurance
- Decreasing term life insurance
- Endowment life insurance
- Excess interest provision

- Excess interest rate
- Group life insurance
- Guaranteed interest rate
- Increasing term life insurance
- Industrial life insurance
- Level-premium whole life insurance
- Level term life insurance
- Limited-payment whole life insurance
- Modified endowment contracts (MECs)
- Modified whole life insurance
- Ordinary life insurance

- Renewable term
- Separate accounts
- Single-premium whole life insurance
- Straight-premium whole life insurance
- Term life insurance
- Universal life insurance
- Variable life insurance
- Variable-universal life insurance (VUL)
- Whole life insurance
- Yearly renewable term

REVIEW

1. Identify four different types of groups that may purchase group life insurance.
2. Has group insurance always been purchased in greater amounts than individual or industrial insurance?

3. Describe the conversion privilege found in group life insurance. Under what circumstances is it especially useful? Why is this privilege rarely used?
4. What is the function of credit life insurance?

5. List some of the differences between industrial and individual life insurance.
6. Explain why the cost of industrial life insurance is higher than group or individual life insurance.
7. Identify the contractual rights that the owner of a life insurance policy may exercise.
8. Describe four different types of term insurance policies based on their potential time span.
9. Why are decreasing term policies frequently used to repay mortgage loans?
10. Explain why the renewability feature makes term insurance more attractive to some buyers.
11. How does convertible term life insurance differ from renewable term life insurance?
12. Develop a set of family circumstances in which term insurance is the most appropriate type of policy to meet the consumer's needs.
13. Develop a set of family circumstances in which traditional cash value, whole life insurance is the most appropriate type of policy to meet the consumer's needs.

14. Why have many consumers found the savings aspect of whole life insurance policies useful?
15. For a healthy man aged 27, rank the following policies in order of their premium size, from largest to smallest.
   a. Continuous-premium whole life
   b. Ten-payment whole life
   c. Single-premium whole life
   d. Whole life paid up at age 65
16. Describe some family circumstances in which a consumer logically might choose a universal or variable life insurance policy.
17. Describe the advantages and disadvantages of buying term insurance and investing the difference.
18. Why does a whole life insurance policy require a larger premium than a term insurance policy?
19. What are the main differences between universal life insurance and traditional whole life insurance?
20. Explain the two different types of death benefit plans offered with universal life insurance.
21. How can a variable life insurance policy be operated like a universal or whole life insurance policy?

OBJECTIVE QUESTIONS

1. The simplest form of life insurance is:
   a. Single premium whole life
   b. Term life insurance
   c. Universal life insurance
   d. Variable life insurance
2. Choose the true statement about whole life insurance:
   a. Builds a guaranteed savings (cash) value
   b. Must be purchased in amounts greater than $100,000
   c. Is usually the insurance with the lowest premium for a given age
   d. Provides temporary protection
3. Each of the following features distinguishes universal life insurance from traditional whole life insurance except:
   a. Universal life allows consumers to see the component costs and returns.
   b. Universal life allows flexibility of premium payments.
   c. Universal life allows borrowing the face amount after the first five years.
   d. Universal life provides some flexibility in death benefits.
4. Choose the true statement about variable life insurance:
   a. Savings values are guaranteed.
   b. Cost is usually lower than term insurance.
   c. The policy owner has flexibility in investment choice.
   d. Investment risk borne by the insurance company.

5. The investments supporting the cash values of traditional whole life insurance policies are:
   a. Common stock/equity investments
   b. Short-term government debt issues
   c. Municipal debt
   d. Federal government debt issues and real estate mortgages
6. Choose the true statement about industrial life insurance.
   a. It also is called discount life insurance.
   b. It is more expensive than ordinary life insurance.
   c. It is less expensive than ordinary life insurance.
   d. It is widely used in estate plans.
7. Choose the true statement about convertible term life insurance.
   a. It is cheaper to convert the older the insured gets.
   b. It allows conversion from individual to group insurance.
   c. It allows the insured to convert to whole life insurance within five years of a spouse's death.
   d. It allows conversion from term to cash value life insurance.
8. Selling which of the following types of life insurance policies requires registering with the NASD?
   a. Variable life insurance
   b. Term life insurance
   c. Whole life insurance
   d. Limited-pay whole life insurance

DISCUSSION QUESTIONS

1. Why are variable-universal life insurance (VUL) policies especially useful in times of inflation?
2. Some critics have argued that industrial life insurance is an undesirable product, no longer justified or nec-

essary, and thus should be eliminated from the market. What do you think of this suggestion?

3. What is your position on the buy-term-and-invest-the-difference argument? Explain your conclusions.

INTERNET ASSIGNMENTS

1. The NASD Investment Company Products/Variable Contracts Limited Representative Qualification Examination (Test Series 6) has six topical sections. What are they? Start your search at this site: (*http://www.nasd.com/*).
2. Get five price (premium) quotations for $500,000 of term life insurance. Assume that the subject is a

21 year old male, 6 feet tall, weighing 180 pounds, and in good health. Fill in any other information needed for a healthy, normal person (without dangerous hobbies, etc.) to obtain the quotations. Start by entering the keywords "cost of term life insurance" into a search engine.

Appendix: Simplified Life Insurance Mathematics

Many of my students have indicated that they find basic life insurance calculations interesting. As has been the case several times before in this text, the following material simplifies a complex subject. Readers wanting information that is more detailed should consult a textbook on actuarial mathematics.

We begin this appendix by describing the **mortality table**, the basis of all life insurance premium calculations. Premium calculations for term life insurance and whole life insurance follow. We describe only briefly the calculation of level premiums for term and whole life insurance policies. The concepts are what is important, not the calculations, and certainly not the numbers.

Mortality Tables

Insurance companies have kept statistics on births and deaths for more than 200 years. Readers interested in the most recent U.S. birth, death, and other demographic data can find it at this Web site: (*http://www.cdc.gov/nchs/*). Actuaries build mortality tables based on observations of the number of deaths in a population. Mortality tables indicate the probability of death in a pool of insured lives.

The **2001 Commissioners Standard Ordinary Mortality Table** is the current mortality table that the various states have adopted for many regulatory purposes, including the minimum valuation standards

for life insurance products.[5] Table 13–8 presents a section of the 2001 Commissioners Standard Ordinary Mortality Table. The second and fourth columns are the annual expected number of deaths per thousand lives for males and females, respectively. The data show that if a company were to insure 10,000 lives of men age 35, it should expect 1.24 deaths per thousand men insured. That means it should expect 12.4 deaths in a group of 10,000 insureds.

Some Simplifying Assumptions

Before we begin to explore the mathematics of life insurance, we must make some simplifying assumptions:

1. The actual number of deaths will equal the mortality table estimates.
2. There are no transaction costs; the insurer makes only death benefit payments.
3. Insureds pay all premiums on the first day of the year. Insurers pay all death claims on the last day of the year. The effect of this assumption is to allow the insurer to earn a full year's interest on the death claims.

These assumptions are not realistic; actuaries make them to simplify initial premium calculations.

---

[5] Use the search engine at the following Web site to learn more about the actuarial details of this table's construction: (*http://www.actuary.org/search.asp/*).

TABLE 13–8 A Section of Commissioners 2001 Standard Ordinary Mortality Table

Commissioners 2001 Standard Ordinary Mortality Table
Male and Female
Age Last Birthday

Age Last Birthday	Male 1000qx	Male Life Expectation	Female 1000qx	Female Life Expectation
0	0.72	75.67	0.42	79.87
1	0.46	74.73	0.31	78.90
2	0.33	73.76	0.23	77.93
3	0.24	72.79	0.20	76.95
4	0.21	71.81	0.19	75.96
5	0.22	70.82	0.18	74.98
6	0.22	69.84	0.19	73.99
7	0.22	68.85	0.21	73.00
8	0.22	67.87	0.21	72.02
9	0.23	66.88	0.21	71.03
10	0.24	65.90	0.22	70.05
11	0.28	64.91	0.25	69.06
12	0.34	63.93	0.27	68.08
13	0.40	62.95	0.31	67.10
14	0.52	61.98	0.34	66.12
15	0.66	61.01	0.36	65.14
16	0.78	60.05	0.39	64.17
17	0.89	59.10	0.41	63.19
18	0.95	58.15	0.44	62.22
19	0.98	57.21	0.46	61.25
20	1.00	56.26	0.47	60.27
21	1.01	55.32	0.49	59.30
22	1.02	54.37	0.50	58.33
23	1.04	53.43	0.51	57.36
24	1.06	52.48	0.53	56.39
25	1.09	51.54	0.55	55.42
26	1.14	50.60	0.58	54.45
27	1.17	49.65	0.61	53.48
28	1.16	48.71	0.64	52.51
29	1.15	47.77	0.67	51.55
30	1.14	46.82	0.70	50.58
31	1.13	45.88	0.75	49.62
32	1.14	44.93	0.79	48.65
33	1.16	43.98	0.85	47.69
34	1.19	43.03	0.92	46.73
35	**1.24**	**42.08**	**1.00**	**45.78**
36	**1.31**	**41.14**	**1.07**	**44.82**
37	**1.39**	**40.19**	**1.14**	**43.87**
38	**1.49**	**39.25**	**1.20**	**42.92**
39	**1.59**	**38.30**	**1.26**	**41.97**

In a following stage, the actuaries "load" premiums for transaction costs, unexpected deaths, and lower interest expectations. We call the simplified, unrealistic premiums *net premiums*. They are always less than the actual premium charged by life insurers, which is called the *gross premium*.

Single-Premium, One-Year Term Insurance

When a consumer purchases a single-premium, one-year term insurance policy, the insurer promises to pay the beneficiary only if the insured dies in the next 365 days. If the insured lives, the insurer makes no payment.

Assume that 10,000 healthy males, age 35, purchase a $1,000 single-year, term life insurance policy. The mortality table reveals a death rate of 1.24 for each 1,000 lives insured. Thus, if 10,000 lives are insured, there will be 12.4 (10 × 1.24) death claims. A $1,000 payment is required for each claim. Thus, the insurer pays a total of $12,400 ($1,000 × 12.4 claims).

Does the insurer need to collect $12,400 in premiums at the beginning of the year? Not quite. It will earn interest for one year on the money it collects. We assume that interest is earned at a rate of 3 percent.

In our example, the insurer expects to pay benefits of $12,400 at the end of the year. How much money should it have on hand at the beginning of the year to fund the claims? Financiers use present value calculations to answer this question. **Present value calculations** combine interest rates, time periods, and an ending balance of $1 to calculate a beginning amount, the present value of the $1. A present value calculation tells us that if we invest $0.97 at the beginning of the year, we will have $1 at the end of the year, assuming that we earn 3 percent interest.

Returning to the $12,400 claims payment, we find the insurer needs about $0.97 for each dollar it must pay at the end of the year, so the insurer must have $12,028 (0.97 × $12,400) on hand at the beginning of the year to meet its obligations. The insurance pool began with 10,000 premium-paying members. Each member will have to pay $12,028/10,000 or $1.20 as a premium for the one-year term insurance promise of a $1,000 death benefit.

Single-Premium, Five-Year Term Insurance[6]

Assume that a consumer wants to purchase a single-premium, five-year term insurance policy from the insurer. What will the net premium be? The insurer promises to pay a beneficiary $1,000 if death occurs in the five years following the purchase of the policy.

Assume that 10,000 men buy our five-year term insurance policy beginning at age 35. In the first year, 12.4 (10,000 × 1.24) insureds die. The insurance company will need $12,400 at the end of the first year to pay these claims. It needs only $12,028 (0.97 × $12,400) at the beginning of the first year.

In the second year, 13.084 of the original 10,000 insureds die. (This calculation results from the death rate at age 36, multiplied by the 9,988 survivors from the original group of 10,000.) The insurance company needs $13,084 at the end of the second year to pay each $1,000 claim. It needs $12,333 (0.94 × $13,084) on hand at the beginning of the first year to meet these claims. Note that two years of interest is earned on this money, and the present value of $1 for two years at 3 percent interest is $0.94.

In the third year, all the living insureds are age 37, and 13.865 of them die. The insurance company pays $13,865 in benefits at the end of the third year. It needs $12,688 (0.91 × $13,865) at the beginning of the first year to meet these claims.

Following the same mathematical procedure, the company needs $14,841 at the end of the fourth year, or $13,186.37 at the beginning of the first year, to meet fourth-year death claims. The mortality table predicts 14.841 of the original 10,000 insureds die in the fourth year. The present value table shows $0.88 is the present value of $1 due in four years. In the fifth year of the insurance, 15.814 insureds die, and the insurer needs $13,641 (0.86 × $15,814) at the beginning of the first year to pay these claims.

Therefore, at the beginning of the first year, the insurer will need to have on hand the present value of all the money that it must pay as death claims. This sum equals $63,876.

$12,028	for first-year claims
$12,333	for second-year claims
$12,688	for third-year claims
$13,186	for fourth-year claims
$13,641	for fifth-year claims
$63,876	for all claims

When the total present value of the claims is divided by the 10,000 people purchasing the insurance, it produces a premium of $6.38. Thus, in exchange for a net single premium of $6.38, a 35-year-old male could purchase a promise from the insurer to pay a beneficiary $1,000 if he should die within the next five years.

As a general formula, the calculation for the premium took the following format:

(Number of deaths in a given year/Number of insureds at the beginning of the plan) × ($1,000 death benefit) × Present value in a given year (discount at specified rate, 3% in this example)

Thus, for the first year of the five-year term plan, the formula calls for the following:

$$12.4/10,000 \times \$1000 \times 0.97 = \$1.20$$

In the fifth year, the formula calls for the following:

$$15.814/10,000 \times \$1000 \times 0.86 = \$1.36$$

The sum of the five annual premiums equals $6.38.

[6] Readers should note that these calculations were made with six-decimal precision on a computer spreadsheet, and the result produced slight rounding errors in the following data.

Single-Premium, Whole Life Insurance

Assume that our 35-year-old male consumer wants to purchase a single-premium, whole life insurance policy from the insurer. What is the net single premium? The insurer promises to pay the beneficiary $1,000 whenever death occurs. Furthermore, if the insured is alive at age 120, he collects the policy's maturity value.

To calculate the premium, we must make 85 calculations—one for each year in which the insured may die between ages 35 and 120. The first five calculations are identical to the ones just completed for the five-year term policy. Another 80 calculations in the same format would follow. Each year the probability of death and the present value amount would change. When we calculate the total amount of premiums for 65 years, it equals $291.

In exchange for $291, the insurer agrees to pay a beneficiary $1,000 whenever death occurs. Once you understand the mathematical concept resulting in the $291 net single premium, we can explore several other interesting concepts.

One conclusion is the high net single premium for whole life insurance keeps this method of payment from being useful to most consumers. If a 35-year-old male consumer needed $500,000 of life insurance, the net single premium would be $145,500.00 (500 × $291). This large outlay is the reason insurers developed the level-premium method of payment for whole life insurance.

Leveling the Whole Life Premium

Because the single premium required to purchase whole life insurance is impractical for most people to pay, life insurers developed a different system of premium payment: the level-premium (or continuous-premium) plan. The level-premium plan begins with the net single premium. I will abandon mathematical calculations at this point and simply present the concepts. The interested reader should refer to an actuarial textbook.

Two factors are considered when leveling the premium—interest and mortality, the same two factors

we used to calculate the net single premium. In arriving at a net single premium of $291 for a 35-year-old man, the insurer assumed that it would have the entire premium on hand at the beginning of the policy period. It assumed it would earn 3 percent interest on this sum to pay its death claims. If the insured pays level premiums rather than the lump sum of $291, however, not all the interest that would have been earned is available. The missing interest must be included in the level premium.

To be more specific, a man at age 35 could be expected to pay a maximum of 65 continuous premiums. The size of these level premiums cannot be found by dividing $291 by 65, however. A good deal of interest that the insurer would earn on the $291 must be included in the level premiums.

A second factor is even more obvious than the missing interest. Not all insureds who begin to pay a series of 65 level payments live to complete all the payments. In fact, only a few people live to age 120. Thus, a charge must be added to the level premiums for those insureds that do not live to age 119 to pay their premium. These missing premiums, like the missing interest, raise the level premium well beyond the result of $291 divided by 65 ($4.48).

For the purpose of illustration, we assume the annual net level premium for a whole life policy issued to a 35-year-old man is $12.50. That is, the life insurance company is willing to accept from the insured the promise to pay $12.50 so long as he remains alive, in exchange for the promise to pay a beneficiary $1,000 whenever the insured dies.

Some students rather easily understand the actuarial concepts just described. Other students find these ideas challenging. Either way, once readers understand the mathematics of life insurance, it becomes easier to see the differences between the policy types described in this chapter. The main distinction between the various policies centers on whether savings accumulate, and if they do, how insurers invest these savings. The mortality table and compound interest remain the essential building blocks of all the different kinds of life insurance policies.

CHAPTER 14

Standard Life Insurance Contract Provisions and Options

After studying this chapter, you should be able to:

■ Identify and explain the purpose of the basic features of a life insurance contract

■ Distinguish between the insured, the owner, and the beneficiary of a life insurance policy

■ Describe the insured's rights when ending a cash value life insurance policy

■ Explain the effect of an insured's suicide on the insurer's duty to pay proceeds on life insurance

■ Describe an insured's right to borrow against a life insurance policy's cash value

■ Identify five different ways a beneficiary may take proceeds after the insured's death

■ Explain why some extra-cost options are more valuable than others

No standardized life insurance policies exist; however, life insurance policies must have provisions required by state law. For example, New York's insurance law states:

All life insurance policies, except as otherwise stated herein, delivered or issued for delivery in this state, shall contain in substance the following provisions, or provisions which the superintendent deems to be more favorable to policyholders.[1]

INSURED, OWNER, AND BENEFICIARY—WHO'S WHO?

Insured

Owner

A life insurance policy creates three distinct classifications of interest: insured, owner, and beneficiary. The **insured** is the person whose death causes the insurer to pay the claim. The **owner** is the person who may exercise the rights created by the contract. Ownership rights in life insurance policies may include the following:

• The right to change ownership
• The right to assign the policy as security for a loan
• The right to name a beneficiary
• The right to participating dividends
• The right to take any surrender value

---

[1] Readers interested in specific issues can use legal research Internet sites such as (*http://www.law.cornell.edu/*), (*http://www.findlaw.com/*), or a search engine such as (*http://lawcrawler.findlaw.com/*).

Beneficiary

The **beneficiary** is the person receiving the proceeds when the insured dies. A person, a trust, an estate, or a business may be a beneficiary. One person may be both insured and owner, or owner and beneficiary. A person cannot be both insured and beneficiary.

The owner of the life insurance policy has the right to name a beneficiary. If the owner has the right to change beneficiaries after the initial choice, the beneficiary is called a **revocable beneficiary**. The owner cannot change an **irrevocable beneficiary**. Generally, the revocable beneficiary has no rights in the policy while the insured is alive. An irrevocable beneficiary has a vested interest in the death benefit and can prevent the owner from taking any action—such as assigning the policy or borrowing from it—reducing the beneficiary's interest.

Revocable beneficiary

Irrevocable beneficiary

Beneficiary Designation

Policyowners should identify the beneficiary clearly. A designation such as "my wife" or "my children" can lead to litigation in cases of multiple marriages, children born of different marriages, or illegitimate children. To prevent confusion, the owner may designate "my wife, Marie Antoinette," or, "all the children born of my marriage to Marie Antoinette, share and share alike." Usually, policyowners name *primary* (first) and *contingent* (second, third, etc.) *beneficiaries* to deal with the problems arising if the primary beneficiary predeceases the insured. An example of a successive beneficiary designation is: "Proceeds to my wife (Cathy T. Grate). If my wife predeceases me, then to my children (Tom, Dick, and Harry Grate)—share and share alike. If both my wife and my children predecease me, then to the American Red Cross."

In cases involving frequent beneficiary changes or unclear beneficiary designations, the insurer can transfer the policy proceeds to the court and let the court decide who is rightfully entitled to the money. In other cases of ambiguity, such as the aftermath of catastrophes such as the terrorist attacks of September 11, 2001, or Hurricane Katrina, where the order of deaths, or even the fact of death of a missing person, might arise, insurers can use the court system to resolve legal issues.[2] Attorneys call this process **interpleader**. Interpleader relieves the insurer from having to make restitution to an injured party if the "wrong" person is paid the policy benefits.

Interpleader

In a New York court case, the Metropolitan Life Insurance Company used the interpleader process to deal with the distribution of death benefits under the following circumstances. As part of a divorce proceeding, the husband entered into a court-sanctioned divorce agreement naming his then-living children as the irrevocable beneficiaries of his life insurance policy. Some years after the divorce, he began living with another woman and, subsequently, named her the beneficiary of the disputed life insurance. At his death, the insurer was confronted by a claim from the children of the first marriage, as well as the named beneficiary. The insurer turned the proceeds over to the court, which awarded the proceeds to the children for the following reason:

> Under New York law, the designation of children of a marriage as the irrevocable beneficiaries of a life insurance policy, when made pursuant to a divorce decree, vests with the children the right to the proceeds . . . even if the decedent has changed the beneficiary under the policy.[3]

---

[2] State law determines the death of missing people. Many states amended these laws after the terrorist attacks of September 11, 2001. Here is the pertinent law of New Jersey: "Currently, *N.J.S.A.* 3B:27-1 provides that a resident or nonresident of this State who is absent for a continuous period of five years, during which that person has not been heard from, and which absence is not satisfactorily explained after diligent search or inquiry, is presumed to be dead. Chapter 247 amends that statute by adding a new subsection b. to provide that a person who is exposed to a specific catastrophic event that has resulted in a great loss of life to persons known and unknown and whose absence following that event is not satisfactorily explained after diligent search or inquiry is presumed to be dead."

[3] *Metropolitan Life Insurance Company (plaintiff)* v. *Benevant et al.*, U.S. District Ct. NY (October 22, 1993). Cited in *CCH Life Cases 1993*, p. 4953.

GENERAL LIFE INSURANCE POLICY PROVISIONS[4]

New York law does not require all life insurance policies to have identical or standard wording. The law requires that approved policies satisfy at least the minimum provisions of the law. Thus, the wording and the format of life insurance policies sold in New York by different insurers may differ from one another. However worded, the following provisions appear in life insurance contracts issued in New York:

- Grace period
- Reinstatement
- Incontestable clause
- Entire-contract provision
- Misstatement-of-age provision
- Annual apportionment of surplus

In addition to the mandatory provisions, many companies include optional clauses and features.

Grace Period

Grace period

If the insured neglects to pay a premium when it is due, the policy does not end immediately. Before the due date, the insurer will send the insured a notice of when the premium is due. If the insured forgets to pay the premium or decides to end the contract, the **grace period** provides him or her a period of 31 days to pay the premium without forfeiting any contractual rights. If the policyholder dies during the grace period, the insurer will pay the proceeds, minus the overdue premium, to the beneficiary. If the policyholder does not pay the premium before the end of the 31 days provided by the grace period, however, the policy is said to have lapsed.

Lapsed policy

A **lapsed policy** means that the insured voluntarily has given up the life insurance contract. Letting a life insurance policy lapse usually is expensive to the insured and to the insurer. Because most of the expenses of acquiring the life insurance policy and putting it in force occur in the first year of the policy, these expenses must be recovered in the early years of the contract or the insurer loses money. These acquisition costs include the salesperson's commission, the cost of a medical examination, and home-office administration costs.

When insureds let a policy lapse, it means they have become displeased with their purchase or perhaps cannot afford to pay the premiums. Perhaps the insured purchased the wrong type of policy, found a better offer from another insurer, or no longer needs (or never did need) the insurance. Whatever the reason, a lapsed life insurance policy represents a mistake—often an expensive one.

If an insured allows a policy that has accumulated a cash value to lapse, the policy provides the owner several choices with respect to having the cash value returned. We describe these nonforfeiture options later in this chapter.

The Reinstatement Provision

Reinstatement provision

After a policy lapses, the insured has an opportunity to reinstate (renew) it if specified conditions are met. The opportunity to renew a lapsed policy is called the **reinstatement provision**.

---

[4] A sample whole life insurance policy and an accompanying application for life insurance can be found in Appendix C. The sample policy was provided by the American Council of Life Insurance and is used with permission.

New York has a limit of three years from the date of default in which the owner may reinstate the policy. Furthermore, the insured must not have withdrawn the cash surrender value but must have chosen a nonforfeiture option that allows the policy to continue. Other conditions that must be met to reinstate a policy are the following:

- Evidence of insurability, including good health
- Payment of all premiums in default, with interest
- Repayment or reinstatement of any policy loans, with interest

Evidence of insurability

Evidence of insurability, beyond the good health of the insured, means that among other things, the insured must not be engaged in any dangerous occupations or hobbies or be awaiting execution for a crime. Insurers require payment of all defaulted premiums with compound interest. Likewise, the owner must repay any outstanding policy loans with interest.

You may ask why a consumer would want to reinstate a policy rather than purchase a new one because the requirements for reinstatement are the same with respect to insurability. Furthermore, reinstatement usually involves a larger outlay of cash than starting a new policy because all past unpaid premiums must be repaid with interest. The answer is that by reinstating a lapsed policy, the consumer avoids being charged a second time for the large initial expenses of a new policy. Also, after a policy has been reinstated, the cash value is restored immediately. The premium will be lower on the reinstated policy because it was issued at an earlier age. An additional consideration may be a change in policy terms from one series of policies to the next, with the original policy having more favorable terms. An example would be a maximum interest charge on loans of 5 percent in the reinstated policy versus 8 percent in a new policy, or less favorable settlement options on a new policy compared with the old one. Two other factors need to be cited. First, when the policy is reinstated, the suicide clause time period does not restart and only statements made for the purpose of reinstatement are contestable until a new time period expires. The incontestable clause is discussed just below; the suicide clause (an optional provision) will be discussed shortly.

The Incontestable Clause

Incontestable clause

Insurance contracts are contracts made in utmost good faith, which means that an applicant may not answer questions untruthfully or conceal information that an honest person would reveal. If an insured (or owner) lies or conceals material facts, the insurer may go to court and contest the policy for the purpose of voiding the policy. The **incontestable clause** states that if there is a valid contract between the insurer and insured, the insurer may not contest the policy to void it after the policy has been in force for a one-year or two-year period. Thus, a life insurer has only a relatively short period of time in which to uncover any fraud. Generally, after the specified time has elapsed, even if a notorious fraud is uncovered, the insurer cannot void the policy. This solution balances the right of the insurer to know the truth when entering the contract with the innocent beneficiary's right of recovery.

A life insurance policy may be ended if the premiums are not paid. Also, suspected fraudulent claims for accidental death benefits or disability income benefits can be contested. Likewise, an insurer may go to court and try to establish that a valid contract never existed between the two parties. But in general, the incontestable clause prevents an insurer from avoiding claims payments. It is interesting to note that this clause was included voluntarily in the contracts of some life insurers after 1850. The motive was to establish public confidence. Such a public relations effort was required because a few disreputable life insurers were voiding contracts on the slightest technical grounds.

The Entire-Contract Provision

Entire-contract provision

New York law requires that the written policy, including the application for the insurance when attached to the policy, constitute the entire contract between the parties. The **entire-contract provision** serves two purposes. It allows the insured a chance to review the answers as they are recorded in the application, and it prevents the insurer from making any hidden document or undisclosed restrictions a part of the contract. Historically, some companies incorporated their bylaws in their contracts by reference only, thus frustrating beneficiaries seeking death proceeds.

The entire-contract clause explains one reason that the handwritten application is attached to each contract. Including the application provides a chance for policyowners to review the statements made in the application, which is now a part of the contract. Only information based upon the attached statements can be contested within the contestable period. With the widespread use of copying equipment, it is a simple matter to attach a copy of the application to the policy. An insured should review the application carefully to see that all oral responses were recorded accurately.

The Misstatement-of-Age Provision

Misstatement-of-age provision

The incontestable clause prevents an insurer from voiding a policy because of an insured's misrepresentations. Because the applicant's age is a key factor in underwriting and pricing the insurance, a misstatement of age, either intentionally or by mistake, causes rating errors. The **misstatement-of-age provision** allows the insurer to adjust the face amount of insurance to reflect the insured's true age, rather than allowing the insurer to void a policy if a misstatement is discovered. For example, if the insured, Ann Alitic, reported her age to be three years less than it actually was, the benefits, $100,000, would have to be reduced to $92,000, or whatever amount of insurance the premiums would purchase at the insured's true age.

Annual Apportionment of Divisible Surplus

Participating policies

New York law requires that once a year, the life insurance company must determine whether any dividends are payable to its policyholders. If there is a divisible surplus, the insurer must pay dividends. The rule applies to **participating policies**.

Insurers use two different methods to price their policies. The participating plan involves a relatively large initial premium followed at the end of the year by a dividend. The participating premium is relatively large because insurers use conservative estimates of mortality, administrative expenses, and interest earnings to determine the figure. For instance, assumed mortality losses may be 20 percent higher than actuarial estimates. When the bad results do not occur, the excess premium is returned to the policyholder as a dividend. The return of the overcharge is not comparable to the payment of common stock cash dividends, and it is not treated as a dividend for tax purposes.

Nonparticipating (nonpar) policies

Nonparticipating (nonpar) policies use more realistic projections of operating results and require a lower initial premium. Nonpar policies do not pay dividends to policyholders at the end of the year, but modern forms credit excess interest payments if the insurer earns investment returns beyond the guaranteed rate.

Participating dividends or excess interest payments are not guaranteed. Many consumers have not understood this point very well. When presented computer-generated *policy illustrations* showing what would happen if specified conditions were realized, they assumed that these results would be achieved. Regulation requires insurance companies to make policy illustrations based on their current experience. If conditions improve, as would be the case if years were added to our life expectancy, dividends would increase. If conditions get worse (say, if life expectancy decreases), dividends would decrease accordingly. Similarly, if investment earnings rise or fall substantially, dividends or excess interest payments are affected.

New York law requires insurers to calculate and pay dividends annually on participating policies. This requirement prevents insurance companies from retaining the dividends and not paying them to policyholders who die or let their policies lapse. **Tontine** Some insurers used this plan, called the **tontine** system, before 1900. Under this plan, insurers made dividend payments only to the longest-living member of an "insurance pool." The tontine led to serious consumer abuses and therefore is forbidden by the divisible surplus requirement. The abuses stemmed from the potentially long time period before the insurer had to pay the accumulated dividends. Under the now-outlawed tontine arrangement, the insurer could control the money and the compound interest thereon for 80 or more years with no legal responsibility to pay anybody.

The Suicide Clause and Other Restrictive Clauses

Suicide clause New York law allows a life insurer to exclude payment for death by suicide if the suicide occurs within two years from the policy issue date. The purpose of the **suicide clause** is to control the moral hazard. (Many insurance companies have a one-year restriction that is more favorable to the policyholder and permissible under law.) After the two-year restriction, the company will pay for suicide deaths. One explanation of the two-year restriction is, after the waiting period, the suicide presumably has been caused by mental illness. Because the policy will pay for death caused by other illnesses, it must cover deaths caused by mental illness as well.

An interesting court case illustrates the simultaneous operation of the accidental death and suicide clauses.[5] The insured died of fatal burns suffered in the bathroom of a psychiatric hospital. Circumstantial evidence suggested that only the insured could have started the fire. In general, beneficiaries claiming accidental death benefits have the legal burden of proving that death was in fact accidental, while insurers claiming that death was caused by suicide have the burden of proving this assertion. In this case, the judge gave the jury the following instructions: "If you are unable to decide whether the death was accident or suicide, your verdict must be that the cause of death was by accident." The jury found in favor of the beneficiary.

New York law allows, but does not require, the following restrictive clauses:

- *War restrictions.* This clause may exclude death while in the military or death caused by military action.
- *Aviation restrictions.* This clause may restrict payments for noncommercial flights.
- *Hazardous occupation restrictions.* This clause may reduce or eliminate payment if the insured changes to a more hazardous occupation.

FOUR OPTIONS THAT PROVIDE THE INSURED WITH CHOICES

The following four general requirements provide the insured with choices:

- Dividend options
- Nonforfeiture options
- Policyholder loans
- Settlement options

---

[5] *Evans v. Provident Life and Accident Insurance Company* (Kansas Supreme Court), *1991 CCH Life, Health and Accident Cases*, p. 3467.

Dividend Options

Participating life insurance policies pay dividends to the policyowner. Owners may choose what form the dividends take. The following are four standard dividend options:

- Dividends may be taken in cash.
- Dividends may be used to pay a portion of the next premium.
- Dividends may be left in an account with the insurer to accumulate at interest.
- Dividends may be used to purchase single-premium, paid-up insurance. For example, a $50 dividend may purchase $123 of paid-up whole life insurance at age 40. At the insured's death, the beneficiary receives the sum of the paid-up additions, plus the face amount of the policy. Even if the insured has become uninsurable, the owner still may acquire more life insurance using this dividend option.

Some companies offer other dividend options in addition to these four, including allowing owners to use the dividend to purchase one-year term insurance. This dividend option often limits the additional term insurance the owner can purchase to the amount of the policy's cash value. Some companies allow the purchase of a combination of term and paid-up whole life with dividends. Using dividend options allows insureds to increase coverage without incurring acquisition costs and without having to provide evidence of insurability. Thus, dividend options create flexibility in a consumer's life insurance plan.

Nonforfeiture Options

In general business, if one party fails to complete contractual arrangements as called for, the other party may void the contract and perhaps confiscate property to satisfy a debt. If a life insurance company were allowed to cancel a life insurance policy for nonpayment of premiums, the consumer would be seriously disadvantaged. Insureds in poor health and unable to make payments would be clear losers, as would insureds with large savings accumulated in the life insurance policy. To prevent such injustices, the law provides that life insurance policies that have a savings value are not forfeited if the policies are lapsed. The development of the **nonforfeiture option** is associated with one of the first insurance commissioners of Massachusetts, **Elizur Wright**. Wright was a champion of the insurance consumer. In addition to the nonforfeiture requirement, he promoted more complete disclosure of life insurance company financial information and the legal reserve basis of accounting for the liabilities of life insurance companies.

When an insured stops paying premiums on a continuous-premium whole life policy or other policy that requires more payments, the insurer grants three options: cash, term insurance, and whole life insurance that is fully paid up, but for an amount less than the original policy.

Assume that 60-year-old Johann S. Bach has a continuous-premium whole life insurance policy on which he has paid premiums for 20 years. The contract requires payments until age 100, but Johann decides to stop premium payments. The face amount of his insurance is $400,000 and the cash value is $166,800. When he stops his premium payments, Johann may ask for the $166,800 in a lump sum from the insurer. This situation illustrates the first option, taking the **cash surrender value**. If the cash is withdrawn in this manner, the policy may not be reinstated and ordinary income taxes may be incurred.[6]

Nonforfeiture option

Elizur Wright

Cash surrender value

---

[6] Chapter 12, "Professional Financial Planning," describes the taxation of life insurance policies.

Extended-term option

As a second option, Johann may choose to convert to a term insurance policy that provides the same face amount as his whole life policy, $400,000. The insurer will determine how long the $400,000 of term insurance will continue if a $166,800 premium were paid. Assume that the answer is 14 years and 4 months. Thus, without paying another premium, Johann could continue with $400,000 of life insurance protection. However, at age 74 and 4 months, the insurance protection and the cash value would be gone, and the term insurance has no cash value. Insurers call this option the **extended-term option**. A policy lapsed under this option may be reinstated under the reinstatement provision.

Reduced paid-up insurance option

As a third nonforfeiture option, Johann may choose a reduced amount of paid-up life insurance. That is, he currently has a $400,000 whole life policy with $166,800 cash value. If he stops paying premiums, he may choose a fully paid-up policy with a face amount of $212,500. This option is called the **reduced paid-up insurance option**. A policy lapsed under this option also is subject to the reinstatement provisions.

In our example, Johann S. Bach had a whole life policy; any policy with a cash surrender value would have the three standard nonforfeiture options available. Policies such as ten-payment whole life and life paid up at 65 show cash values after the first few years. All these policies have a nonforfeiture value. If an owner does not choose a nonforfeiture option after lapsing a policy, the insurer automatically chooses one. Frequently, the extended-term option is the automatic choice.

Conversion to an Annuity

Insurance companies generally allow owners to convert cash value life insurance to annuities. For example, Hunter Fischer, the famous outdoorsman, buys a $150,000 whole life insurance policy when he is 30 years old. He pays a level premium every year. Assume that Hunter lives to be age 65, he no longer has dependent children, his mortgage is paid, and his need for life insurance no longer exists. He now needs a regular stream of income in retirement. Thus, he converts his life insurance policy to an annuity.

Assume that Hunter Fischer's $150,000 whole life policy has a cash value of $130,000 when he reaches age 65. As we noted, he uses the cash value to purchase a single-premium immediate pure annuity. The annuity guarantees payment of about $1,000 a month for the rest of his life. It generally is more efficient to convert the cash value contract than to purchase a new annuity contract for the following two reasons: (1) no new acquisitions charges and commissions occur, and (2) the cash value life insurance contract may have more favorable annuity assumptions than the new updated annuity contract that will predict that people live longer lives.

Policyholder Loans

Loan provision

Life insurance policies with cash surrender values have a **loan provision**. This provision gives the policyowner the right to borrow an amount of money less than or equal to the cash value of the policy. The company generally has the right to delay making the loan for up to six months.

The interest rate charged for the loan is stated in the policy. Unless the policy provides for variable rates, it remains unchanged even though general interest rates fluctuate. Interest rates typically range from 6 to 8 percent. Since 1980, life insurers typically have used variable rates that change with general interest rates.

Policyholder loan

The **policyholder loan** is secured by the cash surrender value of the life insurance policy. The insured is not legally required to repay the loan. If the loan is outstanding when the insured dies, however, the insurer deducts the amount of the loan and accrued interest from the insurance proceeds. If the loan and the accumulated interest exceed the accumulated cash value, then the policy lapses.

Taking a loan against a life insurance policy is one alternative to surrendering the policy for its cash value. Taking a loan leaves the policy and some of the life insurance protection in force.

Some insureds may wonder why they must pay interest to the insurer when they are borrowing their own savings. The answer is fairly simple. When the premiums were calculated, the insurance company assumed it would earn compound interest on the money. If this interest is not earned, the premium calculation becomes inaccurate. Thus, if Johann S. Bach borrows the $166,800 cash value of his policy, interest is charged. Yet he still may not have to pay the interest out of his own pocket. If the policy is a participating policy, the dividends may more than cover the interest charges. However, some insurers calculate differing levels of dividends for borrowed and unborrowed portions of the cash value. That is, if Johann Bach borrows only half of his cash value, he may earn 3 percent interest on the borrowed half and a 6 percent return on the unborrowed half. In either case, the cash value on policies, including those having outstanding loans, continues to increase. However, compound interest on the unpaid loan requires ever-increasing dividends to prevent the policy from lapsing.

Automatic premium loan (APL)

The **automatic premium loan (APL)** provision, which typically is found in policies that have a cash surrender value, requires the insurer to advance a loan to the insured for the purpose of paying the premium. Thus, if an insured does not pay the premium when due and the grace period expires (and there is sufficient cash value), the insurer makes an automatic loan to the insured to pay the overdue premium.

Settlement Options

The financial flexibility that a whole life insurance contract offers the insured should be apparent. Through various provisions, such as the dividend options, the nonforfeiture options, and the loan provision, as well as some provisions yet to be described, insureds can fashion a life insurance contract to suit their needs. Even in cases in which needs change dramatically years after the policy was written, the policy often can be changed to meet these new circumstances. Settlement options provide additional flexibility.

Settlement options

Settlement options determine how the death proceeds are paid to the beneficiary. The following are five basic options:

- Cash
- Fixed amount
- Fixed period
- Interest only
- Life income

Beneficiaries take more than 95 percent of all life insurance proceeds in cash. If no other settlement option is chosen, insurers pay the proceeds in cash.

Fixed-amount option

The **fixed-amount option** provides the beneficiary with regular, fixed-income payments. Interest income is earned on balances that remain with the insurer. Federal income tax applies to the interest portion of these payments. The payments continue until the death proceeds and the interest thereon are exhausted. This option is logical when people need income for a limited period, such as while Social Security benefits are unavailable or when they want to create and contribute to an education fund. Using this option, the beneficiary can receive an insurance payment before each tuition bill.

Fixed-period option

The **fixed-period option** is similar to the fixed-amount option. With the fixed-amount option, the choice of the amount of each payment determines how long the payments will last. With the fixed-period option, the choice of the length of the period

DIVIDEND OPTIONS	NONFORFEITURE OPTIONS	SETTLEMENT OPTIONS
• Cash • Premium Payments • Paid-up Additions • Accumulation at Interest • Term Insurance	• Cash • Paid-up Whole Life Insurance • Extended Term Insurance	• Cash • Fixed-amount Payment • Fixed-period Payment • Interest Only • Life Income

FIGURE 14–1 Typical Life Insurance Policy Options

determines the size of each payment. This option might be used to fund four (or ten?) years of a college education.

Interest-only option

Under the **interest-only option**, the proceeds are left with the insured. The insurer pays the first beneficiary (for example, the widow) regular payments composed entirely of interest earnings. After the first beneficiary's death, the insurer pays the death proceeds to a second beneficiary—for example, a child. The interest-only arrangement can be useful, for example, if the beneficiary has substantial investment, wage, or social security income.

Life-income option

The **life-income option** guarantees for a lifetime a series of regular payments to the beneficiary. (This choice is the *annuity* option; the details of annuities are presented in Chapter 15, "Annuities.") In its simplest form, the insurer makes payments under this option only if the beneficiary is alive. Assume that Mrs. Johann S. Bach receives the proceeds of a $400,000 policy under the life-income option, getting $50,000-a-year payments, and that she lives only three years beyond old Johann (after all, they had 20 children). So she received only $150,000 of the benefits. The remainder of the money that she did not receive is pooled to pay benefits to other annuitants.

Despite the potential for "losing" some of the death proceeds, the life-income settlement option can be quite practical. A beneficiary's need for income ends when the beneficiary dies. In some cases, there may be no dependent beneficiaries other than a surviving spouse. The life-income option, because the payments are guaranteed for life, can provide a sure source of income to the surviving spouse. Because the payments include a portion of principal, they will significantly exceed interest-only payments at later ages. This settlement option makes good sense if the surviving spouse is inexperienced in investing money. It is also useful if the surviving spouse has an unscrupulous relative or friend who may talk the beneficiary out of the money if a large lump sum of cash were paid.

Figure 14–1 provides a review of the dividend, nonforfeiture, and settlement options found in life insurance policies.

AVAILABLE RIDERS AND OPTIONS

Like automobiles, which can be purchased with such extra-cost options as a sunroof, global positioning system, and remote-control engine starter, life insurance policies also can be purchased with extra-cost options. Like the automobile options, many people find some life insurance policy options useful. Consumers frequently purchase the following three options:

- Guaranteed insurability
- Waiver of premium
- Double indemnity

The Guaranteed-Insurability Option

Guaranteed-insurability option

If insureds purchase the **guaranteed-insurability option**, they obtain the legal right to purchase more insurance at predetermined intervals and at standard rates, regardless of changes in insurability. For example, this option may provide the right to purchase an additional $20,000 of insurance on every third anniversary of the policy issue date until the insured reaches the age of 38. If the policy was issued at age 20, the insured could purchase an additional $120,000 of life insurance. An option that is not used is forfeited, but any future options remain available. Some companies allow an additional purchase at marriage or at the birth of children.

This option can prove valuable to insureds whose health declines significantly after purchasing the life insurance. The cost of including this option in the policy is relatively modest. With one well-known company, the cost is about $2 for every $1,000 of insurance that can be purchased under the option. This company limits the total amount of insurance available for purchase under the option to twice the face amount of the original policy. With a $50,000 original policy, an additional $100,000 could be purchased, for a maximum total of $150,000 of life insurance. Naturally, each time more insurance is purchased, the premium increases. The increased premium is based on the insured's age at the time he or she exercises the option.

The Waiver-of-Premium Option

Waiver-of-premium option

The **waiver-of-premium option** provides a valuable right for the insured. If the insured becomes totally disabled, the insurer forgives any premium due during the period of disability, and the life insurance policy remains in force. Usually a six-month waiting period applies to the benefit. Moreover, even though the insured pays no premiums while disabled, participating dividends are paid and cash values continue to increase according to schedule.

The cost for the waiver-of-premium option usually is modest. For a whole life policy on a male age 25, the cost is about $0.30 a year for each $1,000 of insurance with one well-known company. Some companies include the waiver-of-premium provision as a part of their whole life contracts rather than as an extra-cost option.

The Double-Indemnity Option

Double-indemnity option

The **double-indemnity option** provides that, if the insured's death is a result of a specified peril, essentially some form of accident, twice the face of the policy will be paid. Some companies take this idea one step further and pay higher multiples of the policy face if death occurs from an accident on a common carrier or in some other specific type of accident or circumstance.

Critics object to this option, claiming it is inconsistent with the needs-based life insurance purchase. If a family needs $260,000 of insurance proceeds if the wage earner dies prematurely, it needs this amount whether the death results from a heart attack or a plane accident.

Other objections to multiple-indemnity provisions include the misdirection of consumer dollars spent for the option. A typical cost is $0.75 a year per $1,000 of insurance. This money may be better spent on increasing the face amount of protection.

In defense of the option, some people believe it makes the life insurance policy easier to sell to individuals who otherwise would not make the purchase. Also, between the ages of 20 and 40, death by accident occurs at a relatively significant rate compared with other causes of death during that period. These arguments, however, do not refute the opinion that informed consumers should not base the amount of life insurance they purchase on the chance that they will die in an accident.

SUMMARY

Life insurance policies do not have the standardized format of homeowners insurance or the personal automobile policy. However, they do have several general provisions required by state law. New York State requires the following provisions:

- A 31-day grace period in which past-due premiums are accepted without penalty
- A three-year reinstatement privilege in which the insured may reinstate a lapsed policy provided evidence of insurability is presented, all past-due premiums are paid with interest, and the cash value of the policy has not been withdrawn
- An incontestable clause that prevents a legal challenge of the contract by the insurer after the first year or two of the policy
- An entire-contract provision that makes the written policy and application, if attached, the entire contract between the parties
- A requirement that any divisible surplus will be apportioned annually—thus, dividends on participating life insurance policies must be declared and paid each year if they are earned

With participating life insurance policies, insurers charge a relatively large premium at the beginning of the policy year and pay a dividend at the end of the year. Nonparticipating policies require a relatively low initial premium and do not pay dividends, but some modern policies credit excess interest if it is earned.

The following are five ways in which consumers may choose to receive life insurance dividends:

- Cash
- A reduction of the next premium payment
- Accumulations at interest
- Purchase of paid-up whole life insurance
- Purchase of one-year term insurance

If an insured (owner) allows a policy with cash value to lapse, a nonforfeiture option applies. This option allows the insured three choices: (1) receive the cash surrender value, (2) receive a reduced amount of paid-up whole life insurance, or (3) receive term insurance in an amount equal to the face of the lapsed policy. The length of the term is determined by the cash value of the policy before it was lapsed.

Policyholders have the legal right to borrow their policy's cash values. They are charged interest on such policyholder loans, but the loans (and, in some cases, the interest) need not be repaid in cash. Insurers subtract unpaid loan balances from death proceeds.

After an insured dies, the beneficiary may receive the proceeds in one of five ways. About 95 percent of beneficiaries take a lump sum of cash. Other choices include regular payments of a fixed amount or regular payments for a limited period of time. Some beneficiaries take just the interest earned on the proceeds and have the principal go to a second beneficiary. The life-income option promises payments as long as the beneficiary lives. The age and gender of the beneficiary determine the amount of each payment taken under the life-income option.

Life insurers sell extra-cost options. The guaranteed-insurability option gives an insured the right to purchase additional amounts of insurance regardless of changes in health. The waiver-of-premium option allows insureds to omit premium payments due while the insured is totally disabled. Even though insureds do not pay premiums, dividends and scheduled increases in cash value continue to be earned. A questionable option is one providing for multiples of the face amount of insurance if an insured dies from accidental causes. Insurers call this option the double-indemnity option.

REVIEW TERMS

- Automatic premium loan (APL)
- Beneficiary
- Cash surrender value
- Double-indemnity option
- Entire-contract provision
- Evidence of insurability

- Extended-term option
- Fixed-amount option
- Fixed-period option
- Grace period
- Guaranteed-insurability option
- Illustrations

- Incontestable clause
- Insured
- Interest-only option
- Interpleader
- Irrevocable beneficiary
- Lapsed policy

- Life-income option
- Loan provision
- Misstatement-of-age provision
- Nonforfeiture option
- Nonparticipating (nonpar) policies

- Owner
- Participating policies
- Policyholder loan
- Reduced paid-up insurance option
- Reinstatement provision

- Revocable beneficiary
- Settlement options
- Suicide clause
- Tontine
- Waiver-of-premium option

REVIEW

1. Define the terms *insured*, *owner*, and *beneficiary*.
2. Give the reasons for a life insurance policy containing each of the following provisions:
   a. Grace period
   b. Reinstatement
   c. Incontestable clause
   d. Entire-contract clause
   e. Misstatement-of-age clause
   f. Annual apportionment of divisible surplus
   g. Loan
3. What is a lapsed life insurance policy? What are some possible causes of lapsation? Is a lapsed policy a problem or a benefit to the insured? To the insurer?
4. Give some reasons why an insured might prefer to reinstate an existing policy that has lapsed rather than begin a new one.
5. Does the incontestable clause mean that an insured always "gets away with" fraud against the insurer? Is the purpose of the incontestable clause to protect the insured from fraud? Does the incontestable clause encourage fraud?
6. What will an insurer do if it learns that an applicant misstated his or her age on a life insurance application? Buster Brown knowingly tells the insurer that

his age is 28 when he is actually 38. What effect will this lie have on his insurance contract?
7. Describe some of the differences between participating and nonparticipating life insurance. Which plan should a consumer purchase?
8. Are participating dividends guaranteed?
9. Identify four dividend options.
10. Describe the three typical nonforfeiture options. Why do insurers offer nonforfeiture options? Illustrate the three nonforfeiture options in the case of John Brahms, who currently has a policy with $24,000 of cash value. John is 38 years old.
11. Do insureds have a legal right to a loan secured by their cash value? Describe some circumstances when a policyholder loan provision is an advantage to the insured but a disadvantage to the insurer.
12. What is an automatic premium loan?
13. Explain five different settlement options. Give an example where each alternative might be useful.
14. Describe the benefits provided by the guaranteed-insurability and waiver-of-premium options.
15. What are some objections to the double-indemnity option? What is the justification for this option?

OBJECTIVE QUESTIONS

1. In a life insurance policy, the owner is the party:
   a. Who receives the death benefits
   b. Who can exercise the contractual rights, such as naming the beneficiary
   c. Whose death causes the policy to pay death benefits
   d. Who pays the premiums
2. The policy provision that allows premiums to be paid after the due date is called:
   a. The lapse provision
   b. The past-due premium provision
   c. The redemption provision
   d. The grace period provision
3. The effect of the incontestable clause is:
   a. To prevent insurers from contesting policies after a year or two from the policy's beginning
   b. To prevent insureds from suing the life insurer after a year or two from the policy's beginning

   c. To prevent insurers from changing policy provisions after a year or two from the policy's beginning
   d. To allow insurers to change policy provisions after a year or two from the policy's beginning
4. Which of the following alternatives is not a typical dividend option?
   a. A lifetime income annuity
   b. Cash
   c. Accumulation at interest
   d. Reduction of the next premium
5. The settlement option that pays a monthly amount until death is an annuity called:
   a. The fixed period option
   b. The fixed amount option
   c. The life income option
   d. The fixed death option

6. The person who receives the proceeds of a life insurance policy is called:
   a. The beneficiary
   b. The receiver in due course
   c. The policyowner
   d. The insured
7. If an insured voluntarily gives up the life insurance contract, the policy is:
   a. Reinstated
   b. On extended warranty
   c. Foreclosed
   d. Lapsed
8. If an insured misstates her age, the insurer:
   a. Recalculates the amount of insurance based on the insured's true age
   b. Cancels the policy as soon as the misstatement is discovered
   c. Sues the insured for breach of contract
   d. Withholds payment if the misstatement is discovered after the insured's death, or rescinds the policy if the misstatement is discovered during the insured's lifetime

DISCUSSION QUESTIONS

1. If tontines were legal, would they serve any economic purpose for the individual? For society? Because many states have legal lotteries, do you think that states ought to be allowed to operate tontines?
2. Ed Jenner purchased a $400,000 continuous-premium whole life policy 15 years ago. Today, the policy has a cash value of $230,000. If Ed were to die tomorrow and his beneficiary were to take the policy proceeds as a cash settlement, list several different reasons why the amount of cash could be more or less than $400,000.
3. Do you think that dividends should be paid to policyholders who have borrowed all their cash value? If you believe that dividends should be paid to these borrowers, do you think that the rate on dividends should be the same for nonborrowers if the insurer can earn substantially more income on the money it invests than on the policyholder-loan charge?

INTERNET RESEARCH ASSIGNMENTS

1. Answer this legal question: I purchased a life insurance policy to be used for my childrens' college education. I don't know how to designate safely how the money should be given out. Can I just name an executor? Start your search at this site: (*http://law.freeadvice.com/insurance_law/life_insurance_law/*).
2. Answer this legal question: Can a life insurance company deny a claim on a valid policy if the insured dies? Start your search at this site: (*http://law.freeadvice.com/insurance_law/life_insurance_law/*).

CHAPTER 15

Annuities

After studying this chapter, you should be able to:

- Explain the purpose of an annuity

- Identify five different ways that annuities can be classified or described

- Explain why some annuities come with guarantees

- Identify the special features of a variable annuity

- Explain the income tax treatment of annuities

An annuity contract makes the accumulation and liquidation of wealth possible. Many people purchase annuities to finance their retirement because insurance companies can guarantee that the annuitant cannot outlive the stream of income. That is, the insurer can guarantee payments to the annuitant until the annuitant dies. The insurer makes this guarantee based on the insurance principles presented in Chapter 1, "Fundamentals and Terminology": pooling of many similar exposures to loss, premiums paid in advance, and predictability based on the law of large numbers. If someone purchases an annuity, the insured "loss" is living a long time. This sounds like a loss many people may like. However, old age without money can be a calamity.

Many people acquire annuity protection by participating in a pension plan. When the employer agrees to provide retirement income, the income is an annuity promise to the retiree. Because of tax advantages, the public's awareness of increasing life spans, and the work of professional financial planners and financial services companies, individually purchased annuities have become increasingly popular. This chapter's appendix describes some of the innovations and product developments that are appear in the annuity marketplace.

DEFINITIONS

Annuity

Annuitant

Successor beneficiary

Financiers describe any regular series of periodic payments, such as $1,000 each year for ten years, as an **annuity**. An *annuity insurance policy* (from here on referred to simply as an "annuity") is a contract in which the insurer promises the insured, called the **annuitant**, a series of periodic payments, often for a lifetime. If, after the death of the annuitant(s), guaranteed payments continue to a second beneficiary, this person is a **successor beneficiary**. The insurance company uses the law of large numbers to predict the amount of payments it must make, and then it charges each annuitant a fair share for these predicted payments.

An annuity insurance operation transfers funds from those who die at a relatively early age to those who live to relatively old ages. That is, some annuitants will live to take out much more than they paid in premiums. (Annuity premiums technically are called *considerations*. For simplicity, we will continue to call them *premiums*.) Other

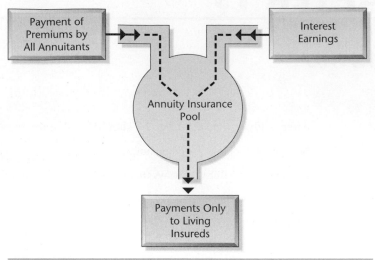

FIGURE 15–1 The Annuity Insurance Operation

annuitants will not live long enough to take out as much as they paid in premiums. An insurance company earns interest on all the money in the pool. Therefore, the annuitant's payments come from three sources:

- Liquidation of the original premium payment, or *principal*
- Interest earned on the principal
- Funds made available by the relatively early death of other annuitants

Figure 15–1 illustrates this concept.

It is interesting to note that the mortality table used to predict annuity payments is not the same one used to calculate life insurance. People who purchase annuities generally live longer than people who do not. The explanation of this curious fact is adverse selection.

Adverse selection in life insurance means that those people with a greater-than-average likelihood of premature death try to purchase life insurance at regular rates. Life insurers try to prevent adverse selection by requiring medical examinations and other underwriting precautions. It is more difficult to prevent adverse selection by people purchasing annuities. Theoretically, an insurer could require a medical examination and then reject the super-healthy as poor risks.[1] However, rejecting healthy people probably is not a sound approach to take with the public. Therefore, the insurer recognizes that people who purchase annuities are probably in above-average health, which explains why they use a mortality table reflecting better-than-average mortality. Thus, annuity mortality tables project longer survivorship than life insurance mortality tables.

Uses of Annuities and Suitability Issues

Because an annuity guarantees a steady stream of income that the recipient cannot outlive, most people use them to finance their retirement cash flow needs. An annuity maximizes annual cash flow for people who are willing to liquidate their assets.

Annuities are especially useful to people in good health when they begin to receive annuity payments from the insurer. Generally, people using annuities do not give the highest priority to maximizing the amount of their wealth left to survivors. That is,

---

[1] Theoretically, insurers also could lower payments for people in above-average health or increase payments for people with substandard health.

annuities are used to liquidate wealth, and if the annuitant dies soon after beginning to receive annuity payments, a substantial amount of wealth may be lost. Therefore, annuities generally would not be suitable for people in poor health or who have limited life expectancies.

Structured settlements

Courts often approve the use of annuities in **structured settlements** in negligence cases. In these instances, instead of the defendant paying a lump sum to a plaintiff, the defendant (using the services of an insurer) promises a series of payments to the injured party. One benefit to the injured party is the professional money management skills that the insurer provides—skills that the injured party may not possess or as easily obtain. A second benefit is that, whereas a large lump sum of money could be dissipated by bad decisions, the structured settlement produces guaranteed cash inflow.

CLASSIFICATION OF ANNUITIES

Insurers classify annuities using the following five criteria:

- Method of premium payment
- Time when benefits begin
- Promises purchased
- Number of annuitants covered
- Type of benefits

Thus, a consumer may purchase an annual-premium, cash-refund, fixed-benefit, joint-and-survivor, and deferred-benefit annuity. One purpose of this section is to clarify this complicated sentence by explaining the various types of annuity contracts.

Method of Premium Payment

Single-premium annuity

Annual-premium annuity

If an annuity is purchased with a single-premium payment, it is a **single-premium annuity**. An annuity also may be purchased by a series of annual (or more frequent) payments. Insurers call this method of premium payment an **annual-premium annuity**.

Assume that Charles Lemain, now age 39, wants to purchase an annuity that will pay him $500 a month when he retires in 25 years, at age 65. He has four payment options:

Single-premium immediate annuity

Level-premium deferred annuity

Flexible-premium deferred annuity

Single-premium deferred annuity

1. One payment of $70,000 on his 65th birthday (**single-premium immediate annuity**)
2. A series of 25 $1,600 payments, beginning on his 40th birthday (**level-premium deferred annuity**)
3. A series of 25 unequal payments, beginning on his 40th birthday (**flexible-premium deferred annuity**)
4. One payment of $16,000 on his 40th birthday (**single-premium deferred annuity**)

With the second method, 25 payments of $1,600 equal $40,000. Where does the difference between the $70,000 for the single-premium immediate annuity and the total of $40,000 in level premiums come from? It results from the compound interest the insurer earns on the advance payments. Compound interest also explains the difference between the one-time payment of $16,000 at age 40 and the $70,000 payment required at age 65 to receive $500 a month.

Beginning of Benefits

Immediate annuity

Deferred annuity

If a person pays for an annuity and the benefits begin after a relatively short delay, that is an **immediate annuity**. If a person pays for an annuity and benefits do not begin at once, that is a **deferred annuity**.

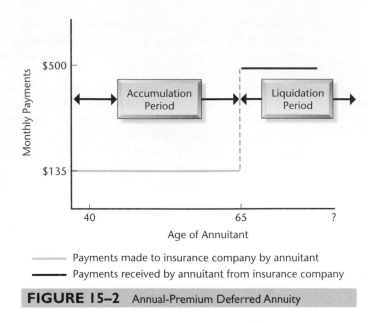

FIGURE 15–2 Annual-Premium Deferred Annuity

Readers might get confused when they consider both the method of premium payment and the time that benefits begin. It is possible to purchase a single-premium *immediate* annuity. For example, Charles Lemain pays $70,000 for benefits of $500 a month beginning immediately, or he may pay a $16,000 premium, wait 25 years, and then collect benefits of $500 a month, illustrating a single-premium deferred annuity. Figure 15–2 illustrates the annual-premium deferred annuity. Insurers call the period during which the annuitant is paying premiums to the insurer the **accumulation period**. Insurers call the period during which the insurer makes payments to the annuitant the **liquidation period**. With most deferred annuities, if an annuitant dies during the accumulation period, a beneficiary is entitled to the return of the premiums, often with interest.

Accumulation period

Liquidation period

Single-Premium Deferred Annuity

Single-premium deferred annuity (SPDA)

If the owner paid a single premium more than one period before the initial receipt of benefits, the contract is called a **single-premium deferred annuity (SPDA)** contract. The deposit earns compound interest at a minimum guaranteed rate, and this interest accrues on a tax-deferred basis until liquidation. In liquidation, only the interest portion of each annuity payment is taxed.

Excess interest

In some cases, if the insurer earns interest on its investment portfolio in excess of the minimum rate guaranteed in the contract, the insurance company credits the **excess interest** (the difference between the actual investment earnings and the minimum guaranteed earnings) to the account. However, even if the insurer's investment earnings decline below the guaranteed amount, the annuitant's earnings credit will not be less than the minimum rate guaranteed.

Typically, insurers guarantee SPDA current interest rates for one year. However, some carriers offer lower current rates but guarantee this rate for up to five years. (Currently available annuity rates and information can be found using the keyword "annuity rates" in an Internet search engine.) SPDAs usually are a no-load[2] contract with back-end surrender charges that typically decline and finally disappear over a six- to

---

[2] A no-load contract is one in which no explicit expense charge, known as a "load," is assessed against the first (or only) premium. Such a charge would reduce the net amount that is invested in the annuity. Instead, with a no-load annuity, issuers would recover acquisition expenses over time from the difference between the income they earn on investments and the rate they credit on the annuity.

ten-year period. The surrender charge allows the carrier to recover its acquisition costs if policyholders cancel the contract in its early years.

Flexible-Premium Deferred Annuity

Flexible-premium deferred annuity (FPDA)

Often people plan to accumulate the sum needed to purchase an annuity at retirement by purchasing a series of single-premium deferred annuities. Because insurance companies have minimum deposit requirements of about $5,000 for SPDAs, another contract, the **flexible-premium deferred annuity (FPDA)**, must be used for deposits of smaller amounts. The FPDA does not require the annuitant to make an even series of level payments. The annuitant determines the contributions within minimum-amount (typically $25) and maximum-frequency (typically monthly) limits established by the insurer. Because of this flexibility, insurers have higher administrative charges for these contracts than SPDAs. Some FPDA contracts provide for the deduction of an expense charge from each premium payment (a **front-end load**). Other contracts provide for surrender charges (a **back-end load**). And some insurers impose both front-end and back-end loads. Insurers often reduce surrender charges on a straight-line basis over time. For example, a company may assess an 8 percent charge for surrender within the first year and reduce this charge by 1 percent each year until it disappears by the ninth year.

Front-end load

Back-end load

Like the SPDA, FPDA contracts have minimum guaranteed interest rates that are well under current market rates. They also have a provision for crediting excess earnings when available. For example, the guaranteed accumulation rate may be 3.5 percent, but the carrier actually may declare a rate of 5 percent for the first year. On each policy anniversary, the insurer declares an excess interest rate for the upcoming period in keeping with the current investment climate.

Table 15–1 illustrates a ledger for an FPDA contract. In Table 15–1, we assume the annuitant makes annual deposits of $1,000. Level annual deposits are not necessary. In some years, no deposit may be made; in others, a sum much greater than $1,000 may be deposited. The table also shows the difference between the current rate the insurer is illustrating, about 8 percent, and the rate the insurer guarantees, which is 3.5 percent. This insurer imposes a 16 percent surrender charge on withdrawals during the first year. The insurer then reduces the surrender charge 3 percent each year until no surrender charge remains after the fifth year.

Promises Purchased

Pure annuity

Straight-life annuity

The basic annuity promise is for the insurer to agree to continue payments only for as long as the annuitant is alive—"Till death do us part." Insurers call this most simple of annuity contracts a **pure annuity** or **straight-life annuity**. There is no guarantee of the total amount of money the annuitant will receive with such a contract.

TABLE 15–1 Flexible Premium Deferred Annuity (FPDA) Ledger

Year	Annual Premium	8% Current Rate Cash Value	Surrender Value	3.5% Guaranteed Rate Cash Value	Surrender Value
1	$1,000	$ 1,083	$ 909	$ 1,035	$ 869
2	$1,000	$ 2,255	$ 1,962	$ 2,106	$ 1,832
3	$1,000	$ 3,523	$ 3,171	$ 3,215	$ 2,893
4	$1,000	$ 4,897	$ 4,554	$ 4,362	$ 4,057
5	$1,000	$ 6,384	$ 6,129	$ 5,550	$ 5,328
...					
10	$1,000	$ 15,878	$ 15,878	$12,142	$12,142
...					
30	$1,000	$128,645	$128,645	$53,429	$53,429

For example, if Charles Lemain purchases a pure annuity for $70,000 and dies after receiving only one payment of $500, the insurer is not obligated to make any more payments. Even though Charles's estate suffers a large financial loss in our example, there is much logic behind this arrangement.[3] Charles purchased the annuity to provide retirement income, and with the pure annuity, income payments end when the need ends. Moreover, for a given amount of premium dollars, the pure annuity provides the largest monthly payments. Some financial planners suggest that if Charles were concerned about leaving funds for his survivors, he could purchase a life insurance policy in any amount, including the $70,000 amount of the annuity premium. In cases where there were no survivors (or no survivors with financial needs), or if the life insurance premiums were not affordable, then Charles would be unlikely to purchase life insurance to compliment the annuity purchase. However, in other cases where survivors' needs for funds were unmet, purchasing life insurance to compliment the annuity purchase could be a logical option.

Many people who purchase annuities are not happy with the thought of "losing" most of their premium payment should they die after receiving just a few annuity payments. Therefore, insurance companies allow annuitants to purchase guarantees specifying a maximum amount of dollars going to a successor beneficiary. These guarantees come with a price. The stronger (more valuable) the guarantee purchased, the greater the premium for a given annuity liquidation payment.

If a person wants to specify a minimum total payment to be received from the insurer, two choices are available. The individual may specify a minimum number of years in which the insurer must make a payment or choose either of two refund options.

Five-years-certain

For example, an annuity, **five-years-certain**, calls for payments for five years or until the annuitant dies, whichever event occurs last. For example, if Charles purchases such a contract and lives only one month after receiving the first payment, a successor beneficiary will receive payments for an additional four years and 11 months. Alternatively, if Charles lives for 32 years after the first payment, payments continue for the 32-year period. Insurers call these contracts **period-certain life-income annuities**.

Period-certain life-income annuities

Most companies limit the maximum number of years certain to 20. The longer the period certain the annuitant chooses, the smaller installment payment each $1,000 of premium will purchase. With one large company, a $1,000 premium for a man age 65 provides a monthly benefit of $7.03 with a pure annuity. If the ten-years-certain option is purchased, the insurer reduces the monthly benefit to $6.45. If the 20-years-certain option is purchased, the insurer reduces the monthly benefit to $5.22. Thus, when the annuitant chooses a 20-year guarantee option at age 65, monthly benefits are about 26 percent less than the benefits provided by a pure annuity.

Cash-refund annuity

A second method of guaranteeing a minimum return from an annuity is to purchase a refund option. A **cash-refund annuity** specifies that if an annuitant dies before having received a total amount of annuity payments equal to the premium paid, a second beneficiary will receive the difference in cash at the time of the annuitant's death. An **installment-refund annuity** guarantees that if an annuitant dies before having received annuity payments equal to the premium paid, the annuity payments will continue to a successor beneficiary until the insurer pays out a total amount of dollars equal to the premium.

Installment-refund annuity

---

[3] In principle, the $70,000 "loss" suffered by Charles's estate is no different from Charles buying a $70,000 life insurance policy and dying after making only one premium payment, thereby receiving a "windfall gain." In the life insurance case, the life insurance company suffers a large financial "loss." In each case, the transaction is entered knowing that the exchange of dollars will be unequal, but each side receives fair value based on the contingent promises exchanged.

Assume that Charles paid $70,000 for a $500-a-month refund annuity. If he dies after receiving payments for four years, he will have received $24,000 in annuity payments [$500 × 12 months × 4 years]. If he had purchased a cash-refund annuity, a successor beneficiary will receive a $46,000 cash payment ($70,000 minus $24,000) at his death. If he had purchased an installment-refund annuity, a successor beneficiary will continue to receive the monthly payments of $500 for seven years and nine months until the sum of both streams of payments equal $70,000. Alternatively, if Charles lives 11.6 years or longer, he will receive at least $70,000 in annuity payments. If he lives beyond this point, he will continue to receive monthly payments, but no refund will be paid at his death.

If you are wondering how an insurer can guarantee to return at a minimum all an annuitant's premium and also guarantee payments so long as the annuitant is alive, the answer is compound interest. With all annuities for which a minimum return is guaranteed, monthly payments are less than with a pure annuity for each $1,000 of premium paid. The smaller the monthly payment, the greater the interest earned on the remaining principal.

Again, assume that Charles Lemain pays a $70,000 premium for a *pure* annuity. First-year benefits amount to $6,000 ($7.03 × 70 × 12 or [monthly rate per $1,000 × number of $1,000s purchased × 12 months]). Thus, $64,000 is left to earn interest the second year. If an annuity, *20-years-certain*, had been purchased, first-year benefits would have been about $4,400 ($5.22 × 70 × 12). Under this plan, $65,600 would have been left to earn interest the second year. Therefore, the longer the minimum guarantee, the larger part interest earnings play in each annuity payment.

Number of Annuitants

Single-life annuity

Joint-life annuity

Joint-and-survivor annuity

Joint-and-one-half survivor annuity

An annuity may be purchased to cover one or more lives. A **single-life annuity** covers one life. A **joint-life annuity** covers two lives. With this contract, payments end at the death of either annuitant. A **joint-and-survivor annuity** provides payment to two annuitants, with the payments continuing for as long as either annuitant is alive. If the payments are reduced by one-half (or two-thirds) after the death of one annuitant, the contract is called a **joint-and-one-half survivor annuity** (or *joint-and-two-thirds survivor annuity*).

Types of Benefits

Fixed-dollar benefits

An annuity may provide two types of benefits: (1) fixed-dollar benefits or (2) variable-dollar benefits. **Fixed-dollar benefits** mean each regular monthly benefit is the same. Thus, a $500-a-month benefit remains $500 a month for the contract period. In some cases, insurers allow annuitants to participate in excess earnings, which can increase annuity benefits if the insurer earns investment income beyond that guaranteed. In no event do solvent insurers lower annuity benefits.

Variable annuity

Insurers call an annuity in which the amounts of regular payments are not fixed a **variable annuity**. The variable annuity is designed to overcome the problems that inflation causes people with fixed-dollar incomes. Consider the problem an annuitant would have with a fixed $250-a-month annuity income that began in 1965. In 1965, the annuity income probably provided for an adequate standard of living. After all, a first-class postage stamp cost 5 cents, gasoline cost 35 cents a gallon, and a big Chevrolet cost about $4,000. By 2007, a $250-a-month income would not provide for anywhere near the same standard of living. As of this writing, a first-class postage stamp costs 39 cents, gasoline costs about $2.50 a gallon, and a big Chevy is no longer made but a comparable Suburban costs more than $40,000. Inflation is a great enemy of fixed-dollar income.

The variable annuity was developed in the 1950s to provide constant purchasing power rather than a constant number of dollars. With one common approach to the liquidation of variable annuities, the dollar amount of the payments may increase or decrease from year to year. Thus, the annuitant may receive $500 a month for the first year and $560 a month for the second year. If prices of consumer goods have risen from the first to the second year, the $60 increase in the annuity payment allows the annuitant to maintain the same standard of living.

A portfolio of common stock is used to provide the varying amount of dollars. In theory, in the long run, the same forces that drive up consumer prices during an inflationary period also drive up the earnings of corporations. The increase in earnings such companies report theoretically causes their market values to increase. Another way of stating this point, albeit far too simply, is that the economic forces that inflated the price of a Chevrolet from $4,000 to $40,000 would also inflate General Motors earnings and stock value. If an insurer were to own a portfolio of many companies with increasing earnings, dividends, and market prices, it could pay an increasing number of dollars to its annuitants.

In the nearly 60-year period during which variable annuities have been available, the theory underlying the variable annuity has proved to be mostly correct. In the short run, the theory need not hold true. Thus, in the period from 1973 to 1975, the prices of most consumer goods rose at about a 12 percent rate. The stock market, on the contrary, sustained a severe setback. This result was exactly the opposite of the theory supporting the variable annuity.

The appendix to this chapter describes some of the recent and interesting guarantees that insurers have developed for the variable annuity. The appendix will demonstrate the creative talents of actuaries and financial engineers and will be of interest to readers wanting to know about some current developments in variable annuity design.

Figure 15–3 provides a review of annuity classifications.

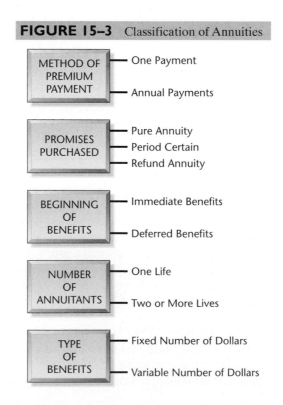

FIGURE 15–3 Classification of Annuities

METHOD OF PREMIUM PAYMENT
— One Payment
— Annual Payments

PROMISES PURCHASED
— Pure Annuity
— Period Certain
— Refund Annuity

BEGINNING OF BENEFITS
— Immediate Benefits
— Deferred Benefits

NUMBER OF ANNUITANTS
— One Life
— Two or More Lives

TYPE OF BENEFITS
— Fixed Number of Dollars
— Variable Number of Dollars

THE EFFECT OF AGE AND GENDER ON ANNUITY BENEFITS

Annuity benefits are determined through the use of a mortality table. The age at which an annuitant begins to receive benefits is an important determinant of the size of each monthly installment. The annuity mortality table shows that men age 65 have a longer life expectancy than do men age 70. The longer the life expectancy of an annuitant, the greater the number of benefit payments the insurer likely will have to make. Thus, a man age 65 receives $7.03 a month in benefits for each $1,000 premium with one large company. A man age 70 receives $8.45, and a man age 75 receives $10.41. The older the annuitant is when the annuity begins, the shorter is the average period in which the insurer expects to pay benefits, and thus each benefit payment may be larger.

Women have a longer life expectancy than men. Thus, if a man and a woman of the same age pay a $1,000 premium for an annuity, the male annuitant will receive a greater monthly payment. Because the insurer expects to pay benefits over a shorter period of time to a male annuitant, the size of each payment will be larger. As a practical matter, rather than have separate male and female mortality tables, some insurers treat women the same as men who are four or five years younger. Such treatment reduces their monthly benefits. For example, for a $1,000 premium, one company pays men age 65 $7.03 of monthly benefits with a pure annuity. A 65-year-old woman will be treated like a 60-year-old man and will receive $5.98 of monthly benefits. The 65-year-old woman, however, is likely to receive her benefits for several more years than the 65-year-old man, so this procedure produces actuarially fair results.

TAXATION OF ANNUITIES

Withdrawals from deferred annuities may be made during the accumulation period or during the liquidation period. The tax consequences of a withdrawal during the *accumulation* period generally are not favorable and may incur a significant tax penalty that we describe shortly. The tax consequences of withdrawal during the *liquidation* period can be favorable because tax deferral continues for the duration of the liquidation.

Withdrawal Before Annuitization

If the annuitant funds a deferred annuity with a series of deposits, there will be a growing accumulation of funds prior to liquidation. No federal income tax is paid on the investment income earned on this accumulation unless funds are withdrawn before age 59½. If an annuity owner withdraws funds during the accumulation period, the first withdrawal is treated as if it is interest income and it is subject to taxation as ordinary income. If the withdrawal is greater than all the investment income earned, however, the difference is treated as a return of principal. For example, assume that Jane Austen deposited $5,000 in annuity premiums and that investment income increased the value of her account by $2,000, so its total current value is $7,000. Now assume that she withdraws $2,500. In the year of withdrawal, she must report $2,000 as ordinary income. The $500 is considered a return of capital. Moreover, after 1986, a 10 percent penalty tax is applied to the $2,000 taxable withdrawal. Thus, if Jane Austen makes a withdrawal prior to age 59½, she will pay the 10 percent penalty tax ($200) plus any additional ordinary income tax applicable.

Annuity Liquidation Distributions

When the annuitant receives liquidation payments, part of the payment is a return of principal. This part of the return is exempt from federal income tax. The amount of the payment attributed to the return of principal is determined by an exclusion ratio. Most

Exclusion ratio simply, the **exclusion ratio** is the amount paid for an annuity divided by the expected return from the annuity. The mathematics of the exclusion ratio is not important here but is covered in texts describing the federal income tax.

As an example of the favorable tax treatment of annuity withdrawals, assume that Jean Valjean paid $70,000 for an annuity. During his expected lifetime, he will receive $100,000 in annuity benefit payments from the insurer. This figure would be calculated using Internal Revenue Service (IRS) annuity tables. In this case, Jean Valjean may exclude 70 percent [70,000 (premium)/100,000 (expected return)] of each payment, paying taxes only on the remaining 30 percent. Thus, if Jean receives $6,000 from his annuity in 2007, he reports only (0.3 × $6,000) or $1,800 as taxable income. If he is in the 28 percent marginal rate bracket, he pays only (0.28 × $1,800) or $504 in taxes on $6,000 in cash flow.

The IRS Web site (*http://www.irs.gov/*) provides detailed information, examples, and worksheets describing annuity taxation. As this chapter is being written, this information is found in *Publication 939 (04/2003), General Rule for Pensions and Annuities*.

SUMMARY

Life annuities provide a steady stream of income that an annuitant cannot outlive. The payment received by each annuitant comes from three sources: (1) liquidation of the principal, (2) interest, and (3) survivorship benefits.

Annuities are used to provide regular income in retirement years. Individually purchased annuities may be used to supplement the income provided by Social Security and company pension plans.

Annuities are categorized by the following five criteria:

1. Method of premium payment—one or more frequent (e.g., annual or monthly) payments
2. Promises purchased—pure, period-certain, or refund annuity
3. Beginning of benefits—immediate or deferred
4. Number of annuitants—one or more lives
5. Type of benefits—fixed or variable

The size of each annuity benefit payment is a function of the premium payment(s), the age and gender of the annuitant, and interest earnings.

REVIEW TERMS

- Accumulation period
- Annual-premium annuity
- Annuitant
- Annuity
- Annuity, five-years-certain
- Cash-refund annuity
- Deferred annuity
- Excess interest
- Exclusion ratio
- Fixed-dollar benefits
- Flexible-premium deferred annuity (FPDA)
- Immediate annuity
- Installment-refund annuity
- Joint-and-one-half-survivor annuity
- Joint-and-survivor annuity
- Joint-life annuity
- Level-premium deferred annuity
- Liquidation period
- Period-certain life-income annuities
- Pure annuity
- Single-life annuity
- Single-premium annuity
- Single-premium deferred annuity (SPDA)
- Single-premium immediate annuity
- Straight-life annuity
- Structured settlements
- Variable annuity

REVIEW

1. How do most Americans qualify for annuity payments?
2. Identify the three sources of funds used to pay annuity benefits.
3. Describe adverse selection with respect to an annuity. How is adverse selection related to the fact that the annuity mortality tables show lower mortality at any specified age than do life insurance tables?

4. Define the following terms:
   a. Single-premium immediate annuity
   b. Single-premium deferred annuity
   c. Annual-premium deferred annuity
5. Give some reasons for and against purchasing a refund annuity.
6. How does a cash-refund annuity differ from an installment-refund annuity?
7. Which will provide a larger monthly payment to a male annuitant age 65: an annuity, five-years-certain, or an installment-refund annuity? Assume that the same amount of money is available for each purchase.
8. Why do some insurers treat female annuitants as if they were male annuitants of a younger age?
9. Describe a structured settlement. What is its purpose?

10. What circumstances favor the purchase of a pure annuity over an annuity 20-years-certain? What circumstances favor an annuity 20-years-certain over a pure annuity?
11. Illustrate the difference between a joint-life annuity and a joint-and-survivor annuity.
12. Briefly explain the purpose of a variable annuity and the financial theory that underlies it.
13. Has the theory underlying variable annuities been proved right or wrong during the last several decades?
14. Describe a financial circumstance in which owning a variable annuity would not be a good idea.
15. What are the consequences of Stevie Ray withdrawing all his funds from an annuity as a lump sum of cash before liquidation? Steve is 42 years old.
16. Describe the exclusion ratio and its purpose.

OBJECTIVE QUESTIONS

1. The definition of an annuity insurance policy is:
   a. A promise of a series of payments by insurer to an annuitant, often for a lifetime
   b. A contingent promise to make payments to a beneficiary at the annuitant's death
   c. A series of payments from an insurer used to repay a mortgage loan
   d. A contract made to provide indemnity payments for long-term care
2. An annuitant makes one payment to the insurer 15 years before he retires. At retirement, the insurer pays the annuitant a lifetime income on a monthly basis. This transaction is an example of a:
   a. Flexible premium annuity
   b. Variable annuity
   c. Single-premium deferred annuity
   d. Single-premium immediate annuity
3. If an annuitant withdraws funds from an annuity during the early years of the accumulation period and receives less than the contract's prewithdrawal value, this result is likely due to a(n):
   a. Accumulation penalty
   b. Discount on deposit
   c. Surrender charge
   d. Lost interest penalty
4. If an annuity contract contains a promise to continue payments until the second of two deaths, it is called a:
   a. Double indemnity annuity
   b. Joint-and-survivor annuity
   c. Joint death annuity
   d. Double life annuity

5. The period when the insurer makes payments to the annuitant is called:
   a. The retirement period
   b. The deferral period
   c. The accumulation period
   d. The liquidation period
6. Which of the following annuities would pay the highest monthly income for a $1,000 premium, holding all other factors constant?
   a. Straight-life annuity
   b. Annuity five-years-certain
   c. Annuity ten-years-certain
   d. Cash refund annuity
7. An annuity that does not have fixed payments during liquidation is the:
   a. Refund annuity
   b. Variable annuity
   c. Immediate annuity
   d. Vested annuity
8. Choose the true statement.
   a. If funds are withdrawn from an annuity during the accumulation period, no federal income tax is paid.
   b. If funds are withdrawn from an annuity during liquidation, no federal income tax is paid.
   c. If funds are withdrawn from an annuity before age 59½, there is a federal income tax penalty in addition to the ordinary income tax.
   d. If funds are withdrawn from an annuity, and the annuitant is older than age 75, no federal income tax is paid.

DISCUSSION QUESTIONS

Harry Ito is about to retire. He plans to sell his business sometime in the next five years and is considering using the $100,000 proceeds from the sale to purchase an annuity.

1. Under what set of circumstances would the annuity be desirable?

2. If an annuity is purchased, what features should it have with respect to guarantees?

3. If Mr. Ito doesn't purchase an annuity, what alternative uses of the $100,000 could provide him with a life income in retirement?

INTERNET RESEARCH ASSIGNMENTS

1. Calculate the monthly lifetime income a male age 65 living in your state can receive for a deposit of $500,000. What is the effect of a five-year certain guarantee? A ten-year certain guarantee? Start your search by entering the keyword "annuity rates" in a search engine.

2. Now assume that the subject in the preceding problem is married to a female aged 65. What monthly income will the couple receive on a joint-and-last-survivor basis? Guaranteed for ten-years certain?

3. Search the Internet for inflation data for the past 30 years. Assuming an income of $75,000 today, what would be the equivalent purchasing power 10 years ago, 20 years ago, and 30 years ago? What can you conclude about inflation and purchasing power?

4. Search the Internet for short-term treasury interest rates and compare these rates to annuity liquidation rates found in this chapter. At what age does it make sense to use an annuity distribution versus merely investing in U.S. Treasuries? How does the preservation of capital come into play when considering these two alternatives?

Appendix: Recent Developments in Variable Annuity Guarantees

The variable annuity in its accumulation phase is directly comparable to a mutual fund. In both cases, a customer deposits money (mutual fund purchase = annuity premium payment) which results in an accumulation credit (mutual fund shares = annuity accumulation units). The number of (shares = accumulation units) credited is determined by the value of an underlying portfolio of assets on the day the deposit is made. One significant difference between the mutual fund and the variable annuity, however, is their tax treatment during the accumulation period. The mutual fund can produce annual taxable income, while taxation of investment gains from the annuity is postponed until the annuitant receives liquidation payments, as we explained in the taxation section of this chapter. Offsetting the tax advantages in many cases are the higher expense loadings of annuities compared to mutual funds and the loss of capital gain treatment on distributions.

The variable annuity's tax advantages during the accumulation period, the public's increasing awareness of the problems associated with underfunded retirement periods, and the rising stock market of the late 1990s led to increasingly large amounts of variable annuity sales. The declining stock market results between 2000 and 2003 dampened variable annuity sales and led financial service firms to offer various guarantees designed to increase the contract's appeal.

The following four categories of guarantees are typical of recent developments in the variable annuity market:

- Guaranteed minimum death benefit (GMDB)
- Guaranteed minimum income benefit (GMIB)
- Guaranteed minimum accumulation benefit (GMAB)
- Guaranteed minimum withdrawal benefit (GMWB)

Guaranteed Minimum Death Benefit (GMDB)

Without the GMDB, the policyholder would receive a death benefit equal to the current fund value. If the GMDB were in force, however, the policyholder would be entitled to a refund equal to *at least* the premiums paid or some other amount determined by a contractual formula. Thus, the GMDB can be seen as a "put option" available if the actual fund value is below the guaranteed amount. One formula used when calculating the GMDB makes the death benefit equal to the premiums paid growing at some rate of interest. Some providers have a formula with a "ratchet" provision. These companies use an initial GMDB equal to the premium paid, but the GMDB is reset on each policy anniversary to the current account value if it is higher than the original GMDB. Some companies have capped their GMDB to some percentage, for example 200 percent, of the premiums paid.

An Example of the GMDB

Hunter Fischer, the outdoorsman, paid a total of $100,000 in annuity premium deposits for a variable annuity between ages 50 and 60, when he died unexpectedly. He had planned to continue making $10,000 annual annuity deposits until he retired at age 65, at which time he would have begun to receive liquidation payments. At the date of his death, the total value in his accumulation account was $75,000. The accumulation account was impacted adversely by a stock market decline the year before Hunter died. The GMDB would add back the $25,000 negative difference between the actual fund value and the sum of Hunter's premiums, providing a $100,000 payment to Hunter's survivors. If the actual fund value in Hunter's account were greater than $100,000 (say, $180,000) then the larger amount would be paid to Hunter's survivors.

If Hunter's GMDB had a more generous formula than just a return of premiums, then Hunter's survivors would be entitled to receive the guaranteed amount at a minimum. For example, assume the premium deposits growing at some interest rate equaled $118,000 when Hunter died, while the actual accumulation equaled $75,000 on this date. Then the survivors would receive the $118,000.

Guaranteed Minimum Income Benefit (GMIB)

Without a GMIB, the annuitant's liquidation income would be calculated by a simultaneous consideration of the account value when the liquidation begins and the then-current mortality table factors. With the GMIB in effect, interest and mortality table factors can be guaranteed at the date of issue. The GMIB is a put option that can be used if the account value declines or if mortality factors less favorable to the annuitant develop during the accumulation period. Thus, the GMIB can guarantee a minimum amount of income regardless of fortuitous events. Many companies providing this guarantee require a waiting period, often ten years after the GMIB is issued. The waiting period protects the insurer from the adverse selection arising from a precipitous drop in the stock market shortly after the annuity and guarantee is purchased.

An Example of the GMIB

Assume that Hunter Fischer lives to age 65 and has made a total $150,000 in annual variable annuity premium deposits between ages 50 and 65. Hunter retired at age 65 and requested his annuity income payments from the insurer. Unfortunately, the year before he retired, the stock market portfolio in which his accumulations were invested declined significantly and his actual account value equaled only $75,000. Because he purchased the GMIB, Hunter's insurer made liquidation payments based on the $150,000 total premiums paid, and not on the actual account value of $75,000. Of course, if Hunter's accumulation account is worth $200,000 when he reaches age 65, his liquidation payments would be calculated using this larger amount.

Guaranteed Minimum Accumulation Benefit (GMAB)

If policyholders surrender the annuity after some period, for example, ten years, they are entitled to the then-current value of the contract. If they had purchased the GMAB, however, they would be entitled to a guaranteed minimum value, typically equal to the premiums paid, but some issuers also guarantee a minimum interest rate on the premiums. The GMAB is a put option that can be exercised if the fund value is below the guaranteed value at the option date.

An Example of the GMAB

Assume that Hunter Fischer pays a total of $100,000 in annuity deposits between ages 50 and 60. Originally he planned to continue making premium deposits until age 65, but he changes his mind and decides to end his annuity by withdrawing all his funds at age 60. On the day he terminates his contract, the actual value of his accumulation fund in $80,000. If he had purchased the GMAB, though, the insurer will allow him to withdraw the full $100,000.

Some insurers allow sequential renewals of the guarantee with a "ratchet" provision. That is, if the first option date (for example, the annuity's tenth anniversary) expires and the GMAB is valuable because the actual account value (for example, $50,000) is below the guaranteed amount ($100,000), then the GMAB amount remains the same ($100,000) for the next guarantee period. But if the GMAB is not valuable because the actual amount in the account (for example, $200,000) is more than the guaranteed amount ($100,000), then the GMAB ratchets up to the actual account value on the tenth anniversary date.

Guaranteed Minimum Withdrawal Benefit (GMWB)

In a standard variable annuity contract, the policyholder may withdraw some percentage (for example, 6 percent) of the current account value each year. If the account has had a poor year, the amount available under this formula will decline. The GMWB allows the policyholder to make a minimum withdrawal equal to a percentage of the GMWB balance (which is usually the amount of premiums paid). Of course, if the actual account value is greater than the GMWB balance, the policyholder will withdraw a percentage of the larger amount.

An Example of the GMWB

Assume that Hunter Fischer makes a total of $150,000 in annuity premium deposits between his 50th and 65th birthdays and that Hunter plans to withdraw 6 percent of his account value each year after his 65th birthday. If the account is worth $150,000 when the withdrawals begin, Hunter receives $9,000 (.06 × $150,000 = $9,000). Assume that in the year of withdrawal, Hunter's actual account value is less than $150,000 (for example, $100,000); then Hunter will receive $9,000 rather than the $6,000 (.06 × $100,000 = $6,000) that he would have received if the guarantee were not purchased.

The Cost of Purchasing the Guarantees

As was the case with the mortality guarantees offered with fixed benefit annuities (recall the cash refund and installment refund guarantees described earlier in this chapter), the guaranteed minimum benefits now being offered with variable annuities have a cost. Issuers have been charging from 15 to as much as 75 basis points of the account balance each year, depending on the guarantee chosen. (A "basis point" equals 1/100 of 1 percent.) Whether these charges are fair and adequate is an actuarial issue beyond the scope of this text. To protect themselves against portfolio declines, insurers offering these guarantees have engaged in sophisticated financial hedges that transfer to the capital markets some of the risk of annuitants exercising their options.

Equity-Indexed Annuities

Recent years have seen many new products developed in the annuity market. The equity-indexed annuity (EIA) is one of these developments. Currently there is no standard EIA; each company's contract is likely to have unique features. This brief description is largely drawn from a more detailed description of these products found at the U.S. Securities and Exchange Commission (SEC) Web site, (*http://www.sec. gov/investor/pubs/ equityidxannuity.htm/*).

During the accumulation period, EIAs offer policyowners two rates of return: (1) a minimum interest rate (for example, 3 percent) or (2) a return based on a stock market index such as the Standard and Poors 500 index. The credit for the indexed return usually is limited to some percentage gain in the index, such as 80 percent. This percentage is called the *participation rate*. For example, if the participation rate is 80 percent and the index rises 9 percent, the EIA account would earn only 7.2 percent (0.80 × 0.09 = 0.072). Product designers have included interest rate caps that limit the amount of interest credited. For example, if there were a 7 percent cap in the previous example, the gain credited would be 7 percent, not the 7.2 percent produced by the formula. Thus, there is a definite upside limit on the amount of gain an EIA purchaser can receive.

Product designers also have been creative in the indexing method contained in these contracts, but describing these different methods is beyond the scope of this text, and the reader interested in this matter should consult the previously cited SEC Web site or other Web sites produced by entering the keyword "equity-indexed annuity" into a search engine. The SEC site makes two additional points about EIAs: (1) purchasers can lose money with these products if issuers provide for significant surrender charges or if tax penalties apply when contracts are not held to maturity; and (2) most EIAs are not registered with the SEC, unlike variable annuities, which require SEC registration.

CHAPTER 16

Medical Expense and Disability Income Insurance

After studying this chapter, you should be able to:

■ Explain why health insurance costs have been increasing in the United States

■ Describe five different types of private health insurance coverage

■ Identify common health insurance contract provisions

■ Describe some of the important exclusions often found in health insurance policies

This chapter describes individually purchased medical expense insurance. This type of insurance plays an important role in financing health care in the United States. Financing health care is one of the most controversial topics in this text. However, financing health care is only one aspect of a problem with medical, legal, tax, ethical, economic, and other dimensions.

We begin the chapter by providing a summary of the arguments made by critics and defenders of the current U.S. health care system. These arguments provide background needed to understand individual medical expense insurance coverages. The next section of the chapter describes the following five different types of coverage:

1. Basic medical insurance
2. Major medical insurance
3. Disability income insurance
4. Medicare supplement insurance
5. Long-term care insurance

The next section after that describes several types of health insurance providers. The chapter concludes with a description of common contract provisions found in health insurance contracts.

FINANCING HEALTH CARE IN THE UNITED STATES

Providing and financing health care are very serious problems. The politics of these problems have proved controversial for decades. The three central concerns the United States (and other societies) must confront when providing health care to its citizens are affordability, access to care, and quality of care.

Criticisms of the Current System

Many experts have prepared comprehensive criticisms of the U.S. health care system, and some have proposed solutions they think will improve the system. Insurance companies and their customers are not disinterested parties in this debate; they have a great stake in providing affordable, safe, and effective health care to our society. The following material summarizes a large body of literature.

TABLE 16–1 Organization for Economic Cooperation and Development (OECD) Health Statistics for Year 2003

	Canada	France	Germany	Japan	United Kingdom	United States
Health care spending per capita (USD)	3,003	2,903	2,996	2,139	2,231	5,635
Health care spending, percent of gross domestic product (GDP)	9.9	9.4	9.9	6.5	7.7	15
Life expectancy at birth, males (years)	77.2	75.8	75.5	78.4	76.2	74.5
Infant mortality/1,000 live births	5.4	6.5	5.8	4.3	6.3	8.4

SOURCE: (*http://www.OECD.org*).

Americans Pay Too Much for Health Care

Some commentators state that Americans pay too much for health care relative to other industrialized countries. Moreover, despite spending about twice as much as other countries, the United States does not rank highly in quality of health care as measured by life expectancy or infant mortality. Consider the data in Table 16–1.

Some of the high cost of U.S. health care and some of the quality problems can be attributed to sociocultural factors that include AIDS, violence, substance abuse (including alcohol), and sexually transmitted diseases. In addition, the United States pays a significant cost for medical research and makes the most recent developments in medical technology available to many of its citizens. The critics note that all the countries in this sample except the United States provide medical care to their citizens mostly outside the private market, and many believe nonmarket solutions are appropriate when dealing with health care.

Increasing Health Care Costs

The following excerpt from a report found on the Centers for Medicare and Medicaid Services (CMS) Web site (*http://cms.hhs.gov/*) provides relevant data on health care spending in the United States:

> The CMS Office of the Actuary determines the amount of money used for the purchase of health care goods and services on an annual basis. These estimates include expenditures as well as the source of financing for these purchases.
>
> Major findings are as follows: The U.S. spent $1.9 trillion on health care, or $6,280 per person, in 2004. Health spending rose 7.9 percent in 2004, slower than the 8.2 percent growth in 2003 and 9.1 percent growth in 2002.
>
> The health spending share of GDP grew 0.1 percentage point to 16.0 percent in 2004. This was a smaller increase in share than experienced in recent years as economic growth in 2004 grew at its fastest rate since 1989.
>
> The share of personal health care spending growth associated with prescription drugs has declined since 2000, coincident with a higher share of spending growth for hospital services. Prescription drug spending had accounted for a 23 percent share of personal health spending growth between 1997 and 2000, but by 2002–2004 it accounted for only 14 percent. Conversely, hospital spending accounted for 28 percent of personal health spending growth between 1997 and 2000, and 38 percent by 2002–2004.
>
> Spending for physician services accelerated from 6.9 percent in 2000 to 8.6 percent in 2001.

TABLE 16–2   U.S. Consumer Price Index and Medical Expenses (1982–1984 = 100)

Year	All Items	Medical Care
1970	38.8	34.0
1975	53.8	47.5
1980	82.4	74.9
1985	107.6	113.5
1990	130.7	162.8
1995	152.4	224.2
2000	172.2	266.0
2001	177.1	278.8
2002	179.9	292.9
2003	184.0	306.0
2004	188.9	321.3
2005	195.3	336.7

SOURCE: Bureau of Labor Statistics Web site (*http://bls.gov/data/*).

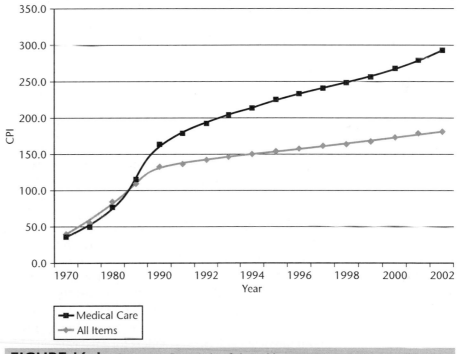

FIGURE 16–1   Consumer Price Index, Selected Items

SOURCE: Bureau of Labor Statistics Web site (*http://bls.gov/data/*).

For more than two decades, medical care costs in the United States have risen more rapidly than the general category of expenses measured by the consumer price index (CPI). Table 16–2 and Figure 16–1 present data documenting this increase.

Reasons for Medical Inflation   Table 16–2 and Figure 16–1 show that in recent years, medical costs, including physicians, nurses, medicine, medical equipment, and buildings, rose at rates more than twice that of the general CPI. The reasons behind the increase include the following:

- Technological improvements in health care have proved to be expensive. The costs of medical research, development of new equipment and pharmaceuticals, and certifying this technology for government approval costs billions of dollars each year, and health care consumers bear a large part of these costs. On the other hand, it is likely that technological improvements, such as new drugs or new surgical techniques, result in more rapid cures, thus helping to control health care costs.

- Medical malpractice insurance costs have increased over the past two decades, with million- and multimillion-dollar claims recorded. Whether such claims are frequent or uncommon remains a point of dispute. As commentators note, one reason for the increase in malpractice insurance costs is the increase in medical malpractice claims made by patients. In addition to the direct costs of insurance, **Defensive** the practice of defensive medicine adds to medical costs. **Defensive medicine** **medicine** means physicians and hospitals conduct more tests, take more X-ray films, magnetic resonance imaging (MRIs) or computerized axial tomography (CAT) scans and keep patients hospitalized longer than they might otherwise think necessary in the absence of potential legal liability.[1]

- Hospital labor costs, energy costs, and other costs have increased substantially, and hospitals have passed these costs along to the public.

- Increasing use of outpatient care may have increased costs. Many procedures that formerly required hospitalization now are routinely done in outpatient clinics. Some authorities believe such outpatient care actually may be more expensive than care in the hospital.

- Catastrophic cases involving AIDS, drug abuse, victims of violence, and premature infants have proved costly to some hospitals. Hospitals shift the cost of providing care for these people to users "better able" to pay for health care.

- The economics of the health care system are not configured to limit the costs of health care. The economics of the health care delivery system are rather complex. **Fee-for-service** In a **fee-for-service** system, physicians and hospitals earn more money as they deliver more health care, and in many respects, they control the demand for health care. They do not earn as much for practicing preventive care. In many cases, including workers' compensation claims, the patient does not pay the bill, or even a portion of the bill, so the consumer (patient) is indifferent to the costs involved. This indifference was true for many group health insurance plans until employer-provided group insurance plans began cost-shifting efforts that resulted in placing **Employer-** more of the cost on employees. **Employer-to-employee cost shifting** involves larger **to-employee** deductibles, larger participation percentages, and other changes that increase the **cost shifting** employee's costs. If employer efforts at cost shifting succeed, then the patient may exercise more responsibility in choosing the amount of health care consumed.

- In an effort to control its costs, the federal government changed its method of reimbursing health care providers for Medicare and Medicaid patients. Because of this government-to-private sector cost shifting, private patients and their insurers now pay many of the expenses formerly borne by the federal government. Cost shifting does not reduce health care costs; it redistributes these costs.

The Aging of the U.S. Population   Time will make the twin problems of cost control and universal access worse, especially as the large number of Americans born after 1946 begin to retire in the next decade. A search of the Internet on the keyword "elderly population in the United States" will produce a great deal of information and data on this subject. Figures 16–2 and 16–3 come from the Social Security Administration (SSA) Web site (*http://www.ssa.gov/*).

Figure 16–2 reveals the intermediate estimates of life expectancy, and it shows a steady increase for both males and females. Figure 16–3 shows three separate estimates

---

[1] We discuss medical malpractice issues more completely in a section on professional liability insurance in Chapter 20, "Special Liability Insurance."

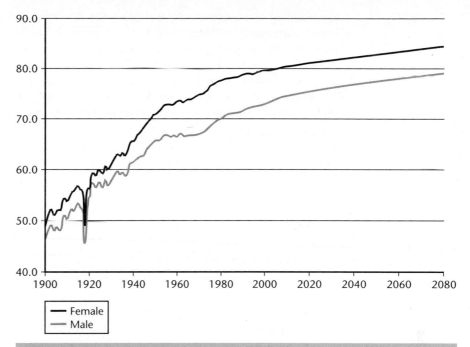

FIGURE 16–2   Male and Female Life Expectancy (in years) 1900–2080 Actual and Projected Intermediate Alternative

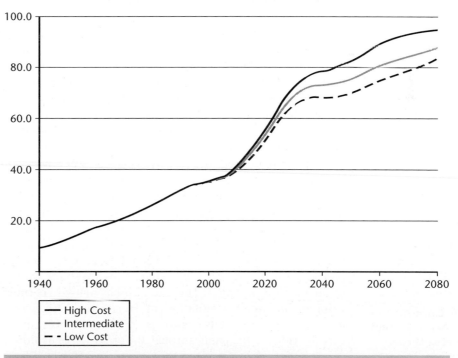

FIGURE 16–3   Social Security Area Population Aged 65 and Older (in millions), 1940–2080 Actual and Projected by Alternative

of the number of people age 65 and older for the coming decades, and the important difference among the estimates is the rate of increase. The increase in elderly people appears inevitable. Evidence suggests that as people get older, their medical expenditures increase. In a recent year, people 65 and older were about 12 percent of the population, but they consumed about one-third of all medical resources. Complex predictions of supply and demand for health care services are beyond the scope of this textbook, but an increase in demand as our society ages seems a safe prediction.

Inadequate Access

Some commentators believe that too many Americans have inadequate access to the health care delivery system. The following quotation came from the U.S. Census Bureau Web site (*http://www.census.gov/*) in January 2007:[2]

> In 2005, 46.6 million people were without health insurance coverage, up from 45.3 million in 2004. The percentage of people without health insurance coverage increased from 15.6 percent in 2004 to 15.9 percent in 2005. The number of people with health insurance coverage increased from 245.9 million to 247.3 million in 2005.

Uninsured people have no health insurance coverage because they are not aged, not poor, not currently employed, declined their employer's health care coverage, or worked for employers not providing health insurance. We also note that federal law (the Consolidated Omnibus Budget Reconciliation Act of 1985, better known as COBRA) requires hospital emergency rooms to treat any person that needs medical attention regardless of his or her ability to pay. Therefore, even uninsured Americans have access to emergency health care. However, access to emergency health care does not provide access to ongoing therapy required to cure many diseases.

Quality Issues and Rationing Health Care

Quality of health care is a challenge to measure or discuss. Health care is a scarce resource; no society can provide every person with all the health care services he or she wants or needs. In the United States, health care is rationed, in large part, by price. People with insurance, or people with sufficient assets, can consume more health care services than can people without insurance or sufficient assets. In countries not using market approaches to providing health care, services may be rationed by queuing, by withholding services, or by some form of cost-benefit approach. No matter how they do it, all societies ration health care, and one result is that the quality of some people's health care is lower than others.

The rationing of health care by managed care providers in the United States is a quality issue that receives continuing attention. In one case, after reports that providers sent some new mothers home just hours after giving birth, Congress passed a law forcing caregivers to keep new mothers and their newborn babies in the hospital for a minimum amount of time. Because of the public's concern about quality issues, some managed care providers have joined quality assurance associations to accredit their members and encourage quality care. The **National Committee for Quality Assurance** (NCQA; *http://www.ncqa.org/index.htm/*) maintains a Web site with report cards for various types of health care providers. This site also has many hyperlinks to related sites. The **Joint Commission on Accreditation of Healthcare Organizations** (JCAHO; (*http://www. jcaho.org/*) states that its mission is "[t]o continuously improve the safety and quality of care provided to the public through the provision of health care accreditation and related services that support performance improvement in health care organizations."

National Committee for Quality Assurance

Joint Commission on Accreditation of Healthcare Organizations

---

[2] (*http://www.census.gov/Press-Release/www/releases/archives/income_wealth/005647.html*).

Defending the Current System

Many experts and commentators defend the current U.S. health care system. While they admit some weaknesses exist, these people believe they can be addressed by moderate changes as opposed to radical overhaul. Some evidence suggests that cost containment strategies used for years by employers have met with some degree of success. A second line of defense of the current system is that, as a matter of philosophy and ethics, the current market-based system is more compatible with the U.S. social philosophy than is a government-based health care delivery system.

Cost Containment

Unlike cost shifting, employers use cost containment measures to retard the growth rate in their health insurance costs. Because most Americans receive their access to health care through employer-provided group plans, these efforts directly affect both workers and employers. Employers have tried the following techniques to control their costs:

- *Preadmission Testing and Case Management.* Before employees enter the hospital, they must call a designated authority (often a registered nurse) who authorizes admission for a specified number of days for a given diagnosis. One purpose of this approach is to shorten hospital stays by having patients complete required tests before entering the hospital. Case management has its greatest potential for savings in the expensive claims that affect a relatively small number of employees.

- *Utilization Review.* Some employers hire medical auditors to monitor the appropriateness and quality of care, to identify unfavorable trends, problem areas, and problem doctors. Such audits may result in denying payment for unnecessary care or billing errors.

- *Second Opinions.* Some employers require or allow employees to get a second opinion for some procedures. The second opinion is supposed to validate the original diagnosis and eliminate unnecessary procedures. Experience with this approach has been mixed. Most often, the second opinion confirms the first, and in cases where there is a difference, the first opinion proves correct. Thus, some employers who tried this technique have not continued it.

- *Home Health Care, Hospice Care, Skilled Nursing Care.* Some employers' health insurance plans cover alternatives to hospitalization. These plans cover home care, hospice care (a facility for the terminally ill), or care in a skilled nursing home.

- *Generic Drugs.* To control the cost of prescription medicines, some plans reimburse a higher percentage for the costs of generic drugs than for branded drugs.

Politics and Philosophy

At this point, we remind the reader that this is an introductory risk management and insurance textbook, and our focus in this chapter is on the role that individual insurance plays in health care financing in the United States. We presented the preceding material to place individual health insurance policies in perspective. At the core of all the arguments about the provision of health care to our citizens lie the issues of universal access, quality of care, control of costs, methods of rationing scarce supply, and market-based or government-provided benefits. The following Web sites present a sample of organizations providing differing positions on this critical subject:

- *The Cato Institute* (*http://www.cato.org/*): The Cato Institute seeks to broaden the parameters of public policy debate to allow consideration of the traditional American principles of limited government, individual liberty, free markets and peace. Toward that goal, the institute strives to achieve greater involvement of the lay public in questions of policy and the proper role of government.

- *The Congressional Budget Office (CBO)* (*http://www.cbo.gov/*): The CBO aims to provide Congress with the objective, timely, nonpartisan analyses needed for economic and budget decisions and with the information and estimates required for the Congressional budget process. Compared with the missions of Congress's other support agencies—the Congressional Research Service and the General Accounting Office (GAO)—the CBO's mandate is relatively narrow. But its subject matter gives it a broad reach, reflecting the wide array of activities that the federal budget covers and the major role the budget plays in the U.S. economy.

- *Rand Institution* (*http://www.rand.org/health_area/pubs.html/*): The Rand Institution's stated mission is to help improve policy and decision making through research and analysis. They do that in many ways, by developing new knowledge to inform decision makers without suggesting any specific course of action; by spelling out the range of available options and analyzing their relative advantages and disadvantages; and sometimes by making specific policy recommendations.

- *Upjohn Institute* (*http://www.upjohninst.org/*): The W.E. Upjohn Institute is an independent, nonprofit research organization devoted to finding, evaluating, and promoting solutions to employment-related problems.

We now make a transition from providing background information to the chapter's main topic: individually purchased medical expense and disability income insurance. The first point to note is that most working people do not acquire their medical expense insurance on an individual basis; they receive this coverage as a benefit provided by their employer. The same holds true for the source of disability income insurance; it is mainly provided by employers. In contrast, individuals do purchase the majority of Medicare supplement insurance and long-term care insurance, though as we shall point out, long-term care insurance is not a widely purchased contract.

FIVE KINDS OF HEALTH INSURANCE COVERAGE

Insurers sell the following five types of health insurance policies to individuals:

- Basic medical expense insurance
- Major medical insurance
- Disability income insurance
- Medicare supplement insurance
- Long-term care insurance

Figure 16–4 provides an outline of the five types of health insurance policies described in this section.

Basic Medical Expense Insurance

Medical expense insurance policies historically provided coverage only when the insured was hospitalized. Now most policies cover outpatient treatment as well. **Blue Cross** and **Blue Shield** insurance policies pay benefits directly to the service provider after the medical bills are submitted to the insurer by the hospital or physician. Other insurance companies pay the insured or allow the insured to assign benefits to the provider.

Medical expense insurance policies

Blue Cross

Blue Shield

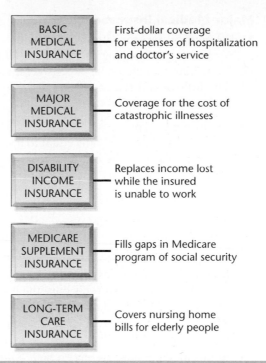

FIGURE 16–4   Five Types of Medical Expense and Disability Insurance Policies

Basic medical insurance

First-dollar coverage

Basic medical insurance policies often have no deductible provision; salespeople call this type of insurance **first-dollar coverage** because the insurer pays covered losses from the first dollar onward. For example, if Florence Nightingale incurs $1,700 in expenses having an arm set in the emergency room, basic medical insurance would cover the entire bill.

Insurance companies other than Blue Cross typically provide "reasonable and customary" payments for the care provided; however, dollar limitations may apply. Some contracts provide benefits paying a specific dollar amount (for example, $150 per day) which can be substantially less than the amount the hospital charges. If an insured wants a contract specifying larger benefit payments, he or she can buy that coverage for higher premiums. Contracts can provide various benefit periods, including 60-day, 90-day, and 120-day periods, with the premiums increased accordingly.

Surgical Contracts

Surgical contracts provide coverage for the costs of surgical procedures. Some specify a maximum amount of coverage for a representative group of surgical procedures. The stated amount is the most that the insurer will pay for one procedure. If a patient needs two procedures during one hospitalization, the more expensive treatment determines the payment. **Surgical schedules** identify a maximum dollar amount for the most difficult procedure and provide a representative list of other procedures and their reimbursement rates. For example, a $1,000 surgical schedule pays $1,000 for the most difficult operation and all other procedures are proportionately less. Modern surgical contracts offer coverage on a reasonable and customary basis. In this case, there is no need to schedule representative procedures or maintain different maximum levels of reimbursement.

Surgical schedules

Major Medical Insurance

Major medical insurance

Major medical insurance policies provide coverage for potentially large medical expenses rather than paying for the first dollar of loss. This coverage provides valuable family protection but can be expensive, costing families more than $800 a month.

The following three characteristics distinguish major medical coverage from basic medical plans:

- Major medical policies have a *deductible provision*. They cause insureds to pay an amount of medical bills equal to a substantial deductible, perhaps $500. This deductible lowers the insurer's costs because the first dollars of all losses are not covered, and these are the most likely to be incurred. Second, in marginal cases where treatment may not be necessary, the insured has a strong incentive to avoid overusing medical care. Some policies apply the deductible to each illness or accident but limit the total amount deducted to some annual maximum. If Florence Nightingale had a $1,700 medical bill with a $500 deductible, the insurer would pay only $1,200 ($1,700 − $500).

Participation provision

- Major medical policies include an agreement where the insurer pays only a percentage of the insured's bills; the insured must pay the difference. This sharing of costs is called the **participation provision**. Typically the insurer pays 75 to 80 percent of the bills after the deductible requirement is met. The insured pays the remaining 20 to 25 percent.

- Major medical policies have a *high limit of liability*, such as $100,000, $500,000, or even larger.

As an example of a major medical plan, assume that Nick Romanoff incurs $28,000 in medical expenses while being treated in a hospital and that he has a $100,000 major medical policy with a $500 deductible and an 80 percent participation provision. Under these circumstances, Nick collects $22,000 from his major medical insurance, calculated as follows:

Insurance payment

$28,000	Medical expense
(−)$500	Deductible
$27,500	Covered expense
$22,000	Covered expense × covered percentage (80%) equals the **insurance payment** (0.8 × 27,500) = $22,000
$ 5,500	Covered expense × patient's copayment percentage equals the patient's responsibility (0.2 × 27,500) = $5,500

Some major medical policies place a cap on the insured's payments. In the preceding example, Nick collected $22,000 from the insurer, but he also paid $6,000 (the $500 deductible plus $5,500 in participation payments). If his major medical policy capped the insured's payments at $3,000, for example, his participation payment responsibility would have ended after he paid $2,500 because at this point the deductible ($500) plus his participation payment equaled the cap ($3,000).

Disability Income Insurance

Disability income insurance

Disability resulting from illness or accident may be an even greater peril to a family than premature death because disability not only cuts off income but also may create large medical expenses. Moreover, a six-month or longer period of disability is a more likely cause of loss to people in their working years than is premature death. **Disability income insurance** replaces income not earned because of illness or accident. Disability

Elimination period

income insurance policies are designated as either short or long term, depending on the period for which coverage is provided. Short-term policies provide a specific number of weeks of coverage (perhaps 30 weeks) after a brief (for example, one-week) elimination period. An **elimination period**, also called a *waiting period*, is a period that must pass before an insured is eligible to receive insurance payments. The purpose of the elimination period is to exclude payments for minor illness. The elimination period is consistent with the purpose of insurance to cover severe losses but not expenses. This provision also helps keep premiums affordable.

Long-term disability income insurance policies provide a number of years of protection after a substantial elimination period (for example, six months of continuous disability) has elapsed. Coverage typically ends at age 65, the age when many people retire.

Disability income insurance is a logical complement to life insurance, although people do not purchase it as often. One explanation for the less frequent individual purchase of disability insurance is that benefits from workers' compensation, Social Security, and successful negligence lawsuits (if a person is disabled by another's negligence) may provide disability income. Nevertheless, individually purchased disability income insurance can be important in cases where other sources of funds are inadequate or unavailable.

Definition of Disability

The definition of the term *disability* is one of the most important contractual features. Some contracts have an "own profession" clause while others have an "any profession" clause. Even among these categories, different insurers can vary contractual language. Consider the following clause defining the term "totally disabled":

> The insured is totally disabled when he is unable to perform the principal duties of his occupation. After the initial period, the insured is totally disabled when he is unable to perform the principal duties of his occupation and is not gainfully employed in any occupation.

The previous definition states that after the initial period defined by the contract, the insured remains disabled if he or she still cannot perform the principal duties of his or her occupation and is not employed. Under this definition, the insured can choose not to work in another occupation. Contrast this definition with "the inability to perform any occupation that the insured is reasonably fitted for by education, training, and experience." Under this definition, if the insured is able to work in any reasonable profession, the insurer makes no disability payments.

Insurers can use a combination of definitions. For example, insurers may define disability as "the inability to engage in (all or principal) duties of one's own occupation," and then after a period of years, redefine disability as "the inability to engage in an occupation that the insured is reasonably fit for by training, education, and experience."

Benefit Period and Amount

Insurers generally state disability benefits as a dollar amount per week or month, for a stated number of weeks, months, or years. Disability contracts also vary according to the length of each benefit period and the amount of each monthly benefit. Benefits may be paid for any practical length of time, including for life. However, insurers often terminate or modify benefits at age 65 to integrate the plan with Social Security and private retirement benefits. In general, the longer the potential benefits for a covered disability, the more expensive the contract is.

Insurers restrict the amount of the benefit to 60 or 70 percent of the insured's gross wage (earned income) for total disability benefits. The percentage set by underwriters is typically a function of the absolute level of wage income and the taxation of the benefits. The reduced benefit is necessary to encourage rehabilitation and reduce malingering. The wage-replacement percentage typically declines for higher wage earners. For example, a professional earning $300,000 per year may be allowed only a 50 percent replacement rate by the underwriters. The $150,000 (50% × $300,000) earned income replacement is considered sufficient income to cover expenses but also encourages rehabilitation.

Partial disability

Residual disability benefit

Some disability income policies include a definition of **partial disability**. The term **residual disability benefit** is commonly used to describe a partial disability payment. A residual disability benefit allows payments to be made to a person working only part time while recovering from an illness. The insurer uses a formula comparing pre-disability and post-disability income to calculate insurance payments making up the difference between the two. Insurers call this provision a **rehabilitation benefit**.

Rehabilitation benefit

Disability income riders

In addition to purchasing a separate disability income policy, a second way to acquire disability income protection is in the form of an extra-cost rider attached to a life insurance policy. **Disability income riders** on life insurance policies provide for payments, such as $10 a month for each $1,000 of life insurance, if an insured becomes totally disabled. Insurers may apply an upper limit such as $500 a month.

Medicare Supplement Insurance

Medicare supplement insurance

Medicare supplement insurance, also known as *Medigap* insurance, is designed specifically to supplement benefits provided under the Medicare program. This coverage typically pays for such things as the various Medicare deductibles, additional expenses when Medicare coverage ends, and the difference, if any, between the "reasonable payment" provided by Medicare for a physician's services and the amount actually charged by the physician.

The patient's share of Medicare cost is subject to change each year. Readers can find current information at this Web site: (*http://www.medicare.gov/*). To illustrate just one gap in Medicare coverage, consider inpatient hospital care. In 2006, the patient is responsible for a *one-time* deductible of $952 for hospital stays of 60 days or less. For longer hospital stays, the patient is responsible for a copayment of $238 *each day* for stays between 61 and 90 days. Finally, in 2006 Medicare requires a copayment of $476 each day for additional days taken from the 60-day reserve that patients can use only once in their lifetimes. You can calculate that in the event of a hospital stay of 150 days in 2006, the patient would be responsible for $36,652 [$952 + (30 × $238) + (60 × $476)] in Medicare copayment and deductible charges. Moreover, other copayments apply to such things as short-term stays in nursing homes and to certain charges by physicians and other service providers. Therefore, the great majority of Medicare beneficiaries also have purchased Medigap coverage. In a recent year, more than 70 percent of people enrolled under Medicare purchased some form of Medicare gap-filling coverage.

In November 1990, the Omnibus Budget Reconciliation Act authorized the National Association of Insurance Commissioners (NAIC)[3] to develop ten standard Medigap policies, with each covering a core group of minimum benefits. The law imposes a $25,000 fine for insurers selling contracts that do not meet the following standards:

- *Open Enrollment.* Insurers must accept individuals age 65 or older who buy Medigap policies within six months of enrolling in Medicare, regardless of their health status, claims experience, or medical condition.

---

[3] The National Association of Insurance Commissioners (NAIC) Web address is (*http://www.naic.org/*).

- *Preexisting Conditions*. Insurers can exclude benefits for conditions diagnosed or being treated for within the six months before the policy was issued.
- *Duplicate Coverage*. Insurers cannot sell a Medigap policy to a person who already has a Medigap policy unless it is a replacement policy.
- *Loss Ratios*. Medigap policies must return in benefits at least 60 percent of the premium earned on individually purchased Medigap policies and at least 75 percent of the earned premium on group policies.
- *Guaranteed Renewable*. Insurers cannot cancel or refuse to renew Medigap policies solely because of the insured's health condition. Policies can be canceled only for nonpayment of premiums or material misrepresentation.

Insurers base the premiums for Medigap coverage on the insured's age when the policy is issued and the amount of coverage provided. Like Medicare, Medigap policies typically do not cover expenses for intermediate or long-term custodial care. (Further information on Medicare itself is found in Chapter 22, "Social Security.")

Long-Term Care Insurance

Demographics

Long-term care   Many Americans could benefit from insurance policies covering lengthy stays in **long-term care** facilities. Among the different types of conditions that can create a need for long-term care are paraplegia, arthritis, mental illness, mental retardation, and respiratory disorders. These conditions affect both young and old people, arguing against the common misconception that only older people require long-term care. Moreover, many modern long-term care insurance policies provide coverage for insureds who want to receive care in their own homes rather than go to a nursing home.

As our society ages and health care costs increase, long-term care facilities will become more necessary. Within the next two decades, the United States will experience the demographic effect of the retirement of about 50 million people born between 1946 and 1964. Demographers predict over 10 million people within this group will be disabled, and about 4 million of these will need care in nursing homes or in their own residences. This estimate cannot be exact, as medical and technological advances could extend the life expectancies of disabled people.

Other demographic factors also point to a greater need for long-term care facilities and for innovative methods to finance people's stays in such facilities. The following demographic factors lead to the conclusion that the need for nursing homes will increase in the next few decades:

- Many women now work outside the home and cannot provide care for elderly relatives as often happened in the past.
- Many families have fewer children than preceding generations, making care of elderly parents by family members more difficult.
- The mobility of American families means many children no longer live close enough to their parents to provide care if it is needed.

The Financial Problem

While the problem of financing long-term care for an ever-growing population of aging Americans is apparent to gerontologists and demographers, the solution remains subject to considerable debate. Some people recommend an enlarged role for private insurance, despite limited success in marketing long-term care products to date. Other people recommend a much greater emphasis on public financing of long-term care costs.

Few experts, however, support the prevailing system, in which about one-third of all long-term care expenses are financed by families and about two-thirds are financed by the federal and state governments, primarily as part of the **Medicaid** program. Currently, private long-term care insurance finances less than 1 percent of all long-term care expenses.

A stay of two years in a nursing home, which is about the average length of stay, may cost more than $120,000. This sum is greater than many families' total assets. Thus, the need for long-term care can eliminate the savings of many Americans. Unfortunately, most health insurance policies, including Medicare and Medicare supplemental insurance, currently do not cover long-term nursing home expenses.

Objections to the prevailing system arise for the following reasons:

- It causes many people to "spend down" (exhaust) their financial assets to qualify for Medicaid. Preplanning this "spend-down" raises a serious ethical issue, while forcing a spend-down may involve the loss of dignity.

- It leaves many people exposed to loss of their savings because most Americans have no financial strategy for dealing with this loss exposure. Included in the group of people exposed to this loss are children whose parents need long-term care.

- It worsens the financial problems experienced by both state and federal governments.

Long-Term Care Policy Development

Despite the fact that this peril lacks some qualities of an ideally insurable exposure, some insurers developed long-term care policies in the 1970s, but these initial policies drew criticism for their high cost and narrow scope of benefits. Recent policies have improved, but marketing has been difficult. Long-term care insurance policies are not standardized. However, the NAIC has developed (and regularly modified) model legislation specifying minimum standards and other guidelines for long-term care policies. The 2000 NAIC model act recommended that carriers price their products with sufficiently large initial premiums to prevent the need for future rate increases. Earlier NAIC model regulations provided such consumer protections as requiring insurers to offer inflation protections and preventing insurers from (1) not renewing policies because of age or deteriorating health; or (2) increasing premiums because of a person's age or having filed a claim.

Several reasons might explain why long-term care insurance has not been widely purchased including the following:

- People do not correctly understand the likelihood or the cost of the peril.
- People mistakenly believe their individual health insurance, group health insurance, Medigap, or Medicare covers this potential loss.
- People plan to spend down or give away their assets and rely on Medicaid to finance their long-term care needs. The government has tightened restrictions on this strategy, but some planners still promote this ethically questionable plan.
- People believe that currently available long-term care insurance policies are too expensive or too restrictive in their terms.
- On the one hand, it would be favorable to purchase and pay for a long-term care policy 10 to 15 years before retirement. On the other hand, such premium payments may reduce the amount saved for retirement income. Delaying the purchase of long-term care insurance until retirement places the cost beyond many people's ability to pay the premiums.

Long-Term Care Policy Provisions   Among the many issues that long-term care insurance policy designers must address, three are especially important: the trigger of coverage, the benefits provided, and the limitations of coverage. A fourth concern is premiums. The general pattern for U.S. insurers is to require level premiums payable for life using merged-gender (unisex) rates that increase rapidly with age. Premiums also are based on the applicant's health when the policy is purchased, with discounts offered for people in above-average health, and surcharges applied for people in substandard health. Some carriers offer discounts to married couples when both spouses purchase coverage.

Some policies specify medical certification of need as the trigger of coverage. More modern policies specify the insured event as an inability to perform a specified number of *activities of daily living (ADL),* which are listed below. A few policies mention the loss of cognitive capability, thus covering mental impairment.

Two types of benefits are most common. One type of long-term care policy provides a specified daily dollar limit of coverage ($100, $200, or more) that is paid regardless of the expenses incurred. Another type of policy provides a percentage reimbursement of the costs incurred (limited to 100 percent). Naturally, the higher the percentage covered, the higher the premium. Modern policies allow insureds to purchase inflation protection for an extra premium.

Most policies specify a waiting period (such as 20 or 90 days), and most specify a maximum amount of coverage, typically ranging from $100,000 to $1 million. Some policies specify the coverage maximum as a number of years (or months) in a long-term care facility.

The Continuing Debate

To date, the issue of whether a practical long-term care insurance policy can be marketed broadly remains a question.[4]

Because the vocabulary of the long-term care debate is not familiar to the public, the following short glossary provides definitions of several terms often heard in debates concerning long-term care insurance:

Activity of daily living (ADL)

- **Activity of daily living (ADL).** Most long-term care insurance policies define the peril insured against as the inability to perform one or more ADLs, which include the following:
  - Shopping
  - Doing light housework
  - Preparing meals
  - Bathing
  - Dressing
  - Getting in and out of bed or chair
  - Getting outside and walking

Adult day care

- **Adult day care**. Includes personal care and supervision.

Continuing-care retirement community

- **Continuing-care retirement community**. A group living arrangement for elderly people with independent living units and a nursing facility. Admission usually involves a large front-end fee.

---

[4] An interesting analysis describing the results of marketing long-term care insurance to federal employees was prepared by the U.S. Government Accountability Office: "Long-term Care Insurance: Federal Program Compared Favorably with Other Products, and Analysis of Claims Trend Could Inform Future Decisions" (March 2006). (GAO-06-401)

Custodial care

- **Custodial care**. Care for the activities of daily living (bathing, dressing, and toileting, for example). There is no expectation this care will improve the person's health. The goal is to maintain people at their current level. Providing this care requires no medical training. To be covered by insurance, it requires a physician's orders.

Hospice

- **Hospice**. A facility caring for the terminally ill. A life expectancy of six months or less certified by a physician is the basic criterion for entry into a hospice. To receive Medicare certification, a hospice must have 24-hour staffing by medical and nursing personnel; counseling, including bereavement counseling; and physical therapy facilities.

Intermediate care

- **Intermediate care**. Occasional nursing and rehabilitative care, ordered by a physician. This level of care is performed under the supervision of skilled medical personnel.

Respite care

- **Respite care**. Provides relief for the primary caregiver of an ill or disabled person. Provides services in either the provider's or the disabled person's home, allowing the primary caregiver to be absent for a time.

Skilled nursing care

- **Skilled nursing care**. Daily nursing and rehabilitative care ordered by a physician. This level of care is performed under the supervision of skilled medical personnel.

Skilled nursing facility

- **Skilled nursing facility**. A state-licensed facility providing skilled nursing services.

HEALTH INSURANCE PROVIDERS

Blue Cross and Blue Shield insurance organizations provided health insurance to more than 94 million Americans in 2006. Blue Cross provides direct payments to health care providers on behalf of their insureds. Typically, Blue Cross policies cover charges for semiprivate rooms, other hospital charges such as use of the operating room, and charges for some types of outpatient care. The typical Blue Cross benefit provides coverage for a specified number of days in a hospital, such as 120 days. With hospital costs averaging more than $1,000 a day, this is no small benefit.

Blue Shield provides payments for physicians' services, including dental and vision services in some cases. Blue Shield benefits often provide coverage based on usual, reasonable, and customary (URC) charges. In some cases, Blue Shield payments may be less than the patient has been billed, leaving the patient with a portion of the bill to pay. In other cases, physicians accept Blue Shield payments as full payment regardless of the amount billed.

Blue Cross and Blue Shield began as two separate organizations. Blue Cross plans began operations in the early 1930s, while Blue Shield plans began in the late 1930s. In 1982, the operations of both organizations were combined into the Blue Cross and Blue Shield Association. The association's Web site, (*http://www.bcbs.com/*), contains hyperlinks to its local affiliates, a frequently-asked-questions (FAQ) section, and a good deal of other information.

Health Maintenance Organizations (HMOs) and Preferred Provider Organizations (PPOs)

Traditionally, Americans received health care from doctors and hospitals of their choice. When insured, their expenses were reimbursed by insurance companies or covered on a service basis by Blue Cross and Blue Shield plans. In 1982, traditional insurers provided about 95 percent of all health insurance. In a recent year, it was estimated they provided less than 10 percent of this coverage. Two other kinds of health care providers, health maintenance organizations (HMOs) and preferred provider organizations (PPOs), now cover more than half the health insurance market.

Health Maintenance Organizations (HMOs)

Health maintenance organizations (HMOs) operate in limited geographic areas, providing members with broad health care coverage in exchange for a set fee called a **capitation payment**. HMOs typically cover physicians' charges, hospital costs, X-ray films, and emergency care. The capitation payment does not change with usage, but often the HMO applies a small fee or copayment, such as $15, to each physician visit or prescription to discourage overuse. Because it receives a set fee, the HMO has a profit incentive to keep members healthy. Therefore, HMOs provide regular physical examinations.

The Health Maintenance Act of 1973 (as amended) dramatically increased use of HMOs. This federal law required certain employers to offer an HMO option in addition to their regular health insurance plan. Because they stress prevention, provide broad coverage, and do not require long claims forms to be filed, HMOs have proved popular, especially with younger people, who usually require less care for chronic illness.

HMOs are organized in two different ways. *Individual practice HMOs* contract with specific physicians and hospitals. These doctors and hospitals may provide service to the public in addition to members of other HMOs. Participants in the individual practice HMOs can choose a physician from among those participating in the plan. The physician then charges the HMO a fee for each patient seen. *Group practice HMOs* have a limited number of medical providers that a member may use. These doctors and medical professionals often work exclusively for the HMO.

Many employers have found HMOs to be a cost-effective choice in providing health insurance to their employees. However, some employers have found that when younger employees choose HMO coverage and older employees remain in traditional plans, any savings realized from the HMO are spent on the increased cost of the traditional plans.

As noted, when given the option, younger people often choose the HMO because of the emphasis on prevention and the minimum of paperwork. Other people have objected to joining an HMO after identifying the following shortcomings:

- Members must choose from a limited number of physicians and hospitals. Members with a long-standing relationship with their non-HMO physician often do not want to change to the HMO physician.
- Members sometimes have long waits for service.
- Members have complained they were given indifferent treatment by HMO personnel.
- Some members express concern about early release from care facilities because longer stays increase the HMO's costs but do not increase revenue. For the same reason, much public concern has also been expressed about HMOs unfairly denying patients' needs for expensive treatments.
- Some HMOs have experienced financial difficulties.

Many HMOs participate in an accreditation program. The JCAHO (*http://www.jcaho.org/*) and the NCQA (*http://www.ncqa.org/*) provide accreditation programs for HMOs and other health care entities. Accreditation by these organizations is a signal of an HMO's commitment to quality. These organizations' Web sites provide explanations of their programs and recent news of their activities.

Health maintenance organizations (HMOs)

Capitation payment

Preferred provider organizations (PPOs)

Preferred Provider Organizations (PPOs)

Preferred provider organizations (PPOs) are another alternative to traditional health care providers. PPOs, usually associations of cooperating physicians and hospitals, agree to provide employers with health care services for their employees at discount prices.

PPOs differ from HMOs in several ways. First, the employer's cost with PPOs is determined by use. A fee is charged for each use, but the fee is lower than the provider's usual charge for the service provided. Second, covered employees do not have to use the personnel or facilities of the PPO. If employees use non-PPO providers, however, the employees pay higher costs. For example, physicians may agree to charge PPO members less than their customary fee for a particular service. In addition, the employer's health care plan may provide reimbursement for 80 percent of the cost if a PPO provider is used and only 60 percent if the employee uses a non-PPO physician. Third, the PPO arrangement may not provide coverage for annual physical examinations as do HMOs.

Managed Care

Managed care

Both HMOs and PPOs provide managed care. Insurers define the term **managed care** as any plan that actively integrates the financing of health-related services and the delivery of health care. By definition, managed care plans actively influence the doctor-patient relationship, the type of care provided, the amount paid for the care, and where the care is delivered. Typically, managed care plans exhibit one or more of the following characteristics that differentiate them from traditional health insurance plans:

- Managed care plans use financial incentives that encourage members to use health care providers identified by the plan. By negotiating reduced charges with preferred providers or fixing capitation payments for a period, health care costs can be controlled more effectively than in traditional indemnity plans.
- Managed care plans involve contractual arrangements with selected health care providers, or the hiring of employees to provide a comprehensive set of benefits to members.

Managed care plans often have a quality assurance plan to monitor the appropriateness of health care provided, which in turn controls health care provider costs.

COMMON CONTRACT PROVISIONS

Unlike property insurance, standard health insurance policies do not exist. Rather, all states have passed, with some variation, model health insurance legislation that specifies both mandatory and optional provisions applying to individual accident and sickness policies. Many of these provisions are comparable to those in life insurance policies (described in Chapter 13, "Life Insurance Policies") and the following discussion is simplified to avoid repetition.

Entire Contract

This provision states that the written policy, its application, and endorsements constitute the entire agreement. No other documents or unattached applications may be incorporated by reference to modify the contract's terms. In addition, if there are any changes, they must be written and are valid only if the company agrees to them. Agents may not waive or modify the terms of the written contract.

Grace Period

The grace period allows the policy to remain in force for a short period while the premium is past due, typically 31 days for annual premium policies. If the premium remains unpaid after the grace period expires (and proper notification has occurred), the policy terminates.

Reinstatement

If the policy lapses after the grace period, the insured may reinstate the contract under certain conditions. Typically, the insured must submit an application with the past-due premium. The insurer then issues a conditional receipt pending a reinstatement decision by the company's underwriters. Under the uniform provisions, reinstatement is assumed automatically if the insurer fails to respond within 45 days.

Incontestable Clause

Health insurance contracts contain either a time limit on certain defenses or an incontestable clause limiting an insurer's right to contest the claim. A time-limit-on-certain-defenses clause provides a two-year or three-year period after the contract starts for the insurance company to contest the contract. After the stipulated period, the contract cannot be contested except for fraudulent misstatements. Insurers must pay even if there were fraudulent misstatements at the time of the application if a policy contains an incontestable clause.

Claims

The insured must file a claim notice and submit a proof of loss within specified time limits. The insurer has specified time limits to supply claim forms and pay the claim. The time limits allow insurers a period to investigate and validate the claim.

Physical Exam and Autopsy

Insurers retain the right to examine an insured as often as necessary to determine claim legitimacy; however, insurers cannot harass the insured by unreasonable requirements. If insureds die, insurers may require an autopsy to settle cause-of-loss disputes.

Legal Action

Legal action against the insurer cannot begin until 60 days after the insured submits the proof of loss, and such legal action must be filed within three years of submitting the proof of loss. This provision provides sufficient time for the insurer to process and investigate the claim and a sufficient time for the insured to begin legal action if the claim is denied.

Change of Beneficiary

The insured must notify the insurer in writing to change a beneficiary. Typically, the beneficiary is the person responsible for paying medical expenses incurred. Thus, the insured and the beneficiary are often, but not always, the same individual.

Optional Contract Provisions

Health insurance contracts may contain the following optional provisions:

- *Change in Occupation and Illegal Occupation.* Some policies allow the insurer to reduce benefits if the insured is injured or becomes sick after assuming a more hazardous occupation than declared on the application. Some policies allow the insurer to deny payment if an insured is injured while engaged in an illegal occupation or while committing a felony.

- *Misstatement of Age.* If insureds misstate their age, this provision allows the insurer to change benefit amounts to reflect the insured's true age. Insurers increase benefits if the true age is overstated or decrease them if it is understated. The time limit on certain defenses and the incontestable clause do not bar this benefit adjustment.
- *Intoxication and Narcotics.* This provision allows insurers to deny claims resulting from the use of narcotics or intoxicants. This provision does not apply if the insured is taking prescription medicines at the direction of a physician.
- *Unpaid Premiums.* This provision allows insurers to withhold from claims payments a sum equal to any unpaid premiums.
- *Cancellation.* The insured can purchase policies that restrict the insurer's right to cancel the policy. In the absence of such restrictions, the insurer still must give five days' notice before canceling a policy. An insurer returns a larger percentage of the premium if it cancels the policy than if the insured initiates the cancellation.

Definitions and Exclusions

One of the most important parts of a health insurance policy is the definitions. Because the existence of coverage may be determined by a definition, consumers should read the definitions carefully and compare definitions of different policies.

Guaranteed renewable

An important health insurance policy provision relates to renewability. The uniform provisions of the model health insurance statute restrict insurers' rights to cancel health insurance policies. Some contracts, including those identified as **guaranteed renewable**, however, allow the insurer to raise premium charges. Generally, premium increases must affect a whole class of business rather than an individual policy. Nevertheless, the best guarantee that a consumer can purchase with a health insurance policy

Noncancellable

is a **noncancellable** policy. With such a policy, the insurer cannot increase the premium during the life of the policy.

Preexisting conditions

The exclusions in health insurance policies are important, but they are not numerous. The major exclusion pertains to preexisting conditions. To prevent people who are about to enter the hospital from collecting benefits from insurance purchased shortly before hospitalization, most health insurance policies exclude payment for preexisting conditions. The definition of **preexisting conditions** describes an excluded period, typically ranging from six months to two years before the policy was purchased. The insurer then states that no payment will be made for losses arising from health problems the insured was treated for or knew (or had reason to know) about during the excluded period. The longer the specified period, the less desirable the coverage is. Another way of viewing this exclusion is to note that the health insurer intends to cover losses resulting from illness or accident arising after the effective date of the policy.

For example, a person may have recovered fully from the effects of an ear operation occurring six months before the purchase of insurance. If an ear problem again is manifested a week after the policy's effective date and the policy specified a one-year preexisting condition exclusion, the cost of treating the illness would not be covered. Thus, it is more desirable to have a relatively short preexisting coverage period so an illness can be labeled a new problem rather than a preexisting condition.

Other items often excluded in health insurance policies include outpatient treatment of mental illness, alcoholism, or drug abuse. Elective cosmetic surgery, such as face lifts and breast augmentations, often is excluded as well. Insurers exclude coverage for experimental treatments. This definition is problematic because at some point, some experiments become generally accepted practice.

Coordination-of-benefits

A policy with a **coordination-of-benefits** provision is one that may not pay or will pay only a portion of its benefits if another policy is available to cover the loss. The coordination-of-benefits clause prevents an insured from collecting more than needed to provide indemnity. This clause also determines the order in which insurers are responsible for payment in cases involving multiple policies. Because it is possible for the same period of hospitalization to be covered by automobile medical insurance, group medical insurance, workers' compensation, and individually purchased coverage, the coordination-of-benefits clause provides for each insurer to pay a portion of the total expenses. Some coordination-of-benefit clauses determine whether the policy provides primary or excess coverage. Coordination-of-benefits clauses prevent the insured from profiting from multiple insurance policies covering the same loss.

SUMMARY

The three major concerns about the U.S. health care system involve questions of affordability, access to care, and quality of care. Among major industrial countries, Americans spend the most for health care, both per capita and as a percent of GDP. Moreover, health care costs have increased much more rapidly than other categories of expenses measured by the CPI. Many reasons explain the increase in health care costs, including the cost of technological improvements and medical malpractice costs. The aging of U.S. society is likely to further increase health care costs. Defenders of the U.S. health care system believe that cost containment approaches used by some employers, including case management and utilization reviews, can be used to improve the current system so that radical change is not needed.

People purchase health insurance to protect against the potentially high cost of paying for health care services and the potentially large loss of income while they are unable to work. Basic medical expense insurance pays for the first-dollar costs of hospitalization and associated expenses. Major medical insurance pays for the costs of catastrophic illness. These policies have high maximum limits and a deductible provision. Major medical policies also have a participation provision that requires the insured to pay a portion of the covered loss.

Disability income insurance is purchased to replace income lost while people are unable to work. This coverage may be purchased separately or as a rider attached to a life insurance policy. Medicare supplement policies are designed to fill in gaps in Medicare benefits such as deductible amounts and participation percentages. Neither the Medicare coverage nor the supplemental policies provide long-term care coverage.

Long-term care insurance will be needed by an increasing number of Americans in the next few decades as our society ages. Before more private long-term care insurance is sold, many underwriting and educational problems must be addressed.

Private life insurance companies and non–life insurance companies, HMOs, PPOs, and Blue Cross/Blue Shield plans are the major providers of health insurance in the United States. Providers of managed care include HMOs and PPOs.

Common medical expense insurance policy provisions include a grace period, an entire contract clause, and an incontestable clause. Definitions are an extremely important feature of a health insurance policy. Terms such as *disability*, *renewable*, and *preexisting condition* take on specific meanings that may vary from company to company.

REVIEW TERMS

- Activity of daily living (ADL)
- Adult day care
- Basic medical insurance
- Blue Cross
- Blue Shield
- Capitation payments
- Continuing-care retirement community
- Coordination-of-benefits
- Custodial care
- Defensive medicine
- Disability

- Disability income insurance
- Disability income rider
- Elimination period
- Employer-to-employee cost shifting
- Fee-for-service system
- First-dollar coverage
- Guaranteed renewable
- Health maintenance organization (HMO)
- Hospice
- Insurance payment

- Intermediate care
- Long-term care
- Major medical insurance
- Managed care
- Medicaid
- Medical expense insurance policies
- Medicare supplement insurance
- Noncancellable
- Partial disability
- Participation provision

- Preexisting conditions
- Preferred provider organization (PPO)
- Rehabilitation benefit
- Residual disability benefit
- Respite care
- Skilled nursing care
- Skilled nursing facility
- Surgical contracts
- Surgical schedules

REVIEW

1. Identify critics' main complaints about the U.S. health care delivery system.
2. Permanent disability can be a more expensive peril than death. Explain why this is so.
3. List five activities of daily living (ADL).
4. Why are there more problems underwriting health insurance than accident insurance?
5. Identify seven reasons health care costs have been increasing in the United States.
6. Is cost shifting the same thing as cost containment? Explain your answer.
7. Identify six methods of cost containment.
8. Describe five standard clauses found in health insurance contracts.
9. What are the differences and the similarities between the participation provision of a major medical policy and the coinsurance provision of a fire insurance policy?
10. Describe the differences in renewability provisions of health insurance contracts.
11. Illness may cause two different types of monetary loss. What are they?
12. Define the term *preexisting conditions*. How does time enter into this definition?
13. Describe the purpose of the coordination-of-benefits clause.
14. How would a $3,000 surgical schedule calculate benefits? Would this approach be better than a reasonable and customary payment basis?
15. What is the main benefit of Blue Cross insurance?
16. What are the distinctive features of a major medical plan? What is the purpose of the participation provision?
17. What difference does it make how disability is defined in a health insurance policy? Give an example of a "good" definition and of a "strict" definition (from the consumer's viewpoint).
18. In a recent year, more than 70 percent of the people enrolled under Medicare purchased some form of Medicare gap-filling coverage. Why is the coverage necessary?
19. Describe the more important exclusions often found in health insurance policies.
20. Define the terms *custodial care*, *intermediate care*, *hospice*, and *skilled nursing facility*.
21. Explain the purpose of long-term care insurance.
22. Identify the problems with the current U.S. system for delivering long-term care.

OBJECTIVE QUESTIONS

1. Which of the following is not a major type of individually purchased medical expense or disability income policy?
   a. Major medical insurance
   b. Basic medical insurance
   c. Medicare
   d. Long-term care insurance
2. All the following are reasons given for increasing medical costs except:
   a. Technological improvements
   b. State and federal taxation of health insurance providers
   c. Medical malpractice insurance costs
   d. Hospital labor costs
3. Cost containment measures include all the following except:
   a. Preadmission testing
   b. Utilization review
   c. Second opinions
   d. Catastrophic care

4. The main purpose of the coordination-of-benefits clause is:
   a. To prevent overpayment of medical expense claims
   b. To coordinate benefits between life and health insurers
   c. To cause group health insurance plans to pay all claims when there is a doubt about who is responsible for payment
   d. To prevent people from suing their health insurance company
5. The country that spent the most (per capita) on health care in 2003 was which of the following?
   a. Japan
   b. Germany
   c. The United States
   d. The United Kingdom
6. A fee-for-service health care system is one that:
   a. Pays health care providers only when they provide a service

b. Pays health care providers a regular monthly salary based on seniority
c. Pays health care providers a capitation payment
d. Pays health care providers providing service to HMOs
7. The percent of uninsured Americans in 2005 was about:
   a. 2 percent
   b. 4 percent
   c. 10 percent
   d. 15 percent
8. "A facility caring for the terminally ill" is the definition of:
   a. A continuing-care retirement community
   b. A hospice
   c. A respite care center
   d. A custodial care facility

DISCUSSION QUESTIONS

1. From an underwriting standpoint, is health insurance more or less difficult to write than life insurance? What information might the underwriter need for writing health insurance that would not be needed for life insurance?
2. What methods do you think are desirable to reduce the morale and moral hazards when a health insurance policy is written?

3. What do you think should be done for the many Americans not covered by private health insurance?
4. Should private or government insurers provide long-term care insurance? Explain your answer.

INTERNET RESEARCH ASSIGNMENTS

1. Collect some recent data on health care spending in the US. Start your search at this site: (*http://cms.hhs. gov/*). (*Hint: use the search box at this site and type in the keyword "National Health Expenditure."*)
2. Update Table 16–2 to include the most recent data available. Start your search at this site: (*http://www. bls.gov/data/*). (*Hint: look for this option: "CPI-All Urban Consumers (Current Series)."*)

3. Explore the concept of universal health care by reviewing the Oregon plan. Start your search at this site: (*http://www.healthcareforalloregon.org/index.html/*). What are the economic and social arguments for and against a universal health care system? Do you think it will work? (Explain your answer.) How would you vote for such a system? (Explain why.)

CHAPTER 17

Advanced Topics in Risk Management

After studying this chapter, you should be able to:

■ Define some of the terminology of financial risk management

■ Identify some of the variables that affect the retention-insurance decision

■ Describe the special responsibilities of risk managers of international firms

■ Describe a risk management information system (RMIS)

■ Solve a complex risk management case study

Alternative risk transfer (ART) market

Modern risk management jointly considers losses that arise from both pure and speculative risks. This approach is based on the logic that a $1 million loss from currency fluctuations is as destructive to a firm's value as a $1 million fire loss. Moreover, considering all sources of loss together may produce more efficient results than the traditional separation of risk categories. Modern risk managers also recognize that a corporation's financial structure has a direct bearing on its risk management program. For example, firms financed with a large percentage of borrowed capital might have fewer good choices when making postloss financial arrangements than unleveraged firms. Today, the line drawn between insurance and other risk transfer techniques is becoming less distinct as insurance companies and other financial services firms begin to offer innovative combination products. Many formerly uninsurable exposures are finding an **alternative risk transfer (ART) market**. The ART market combines capital markets, reinsurance agreements, and investment banking arrangements to allow the transfer of risk that the ordinary insurance market cannot accommodate. This chapter introduces several innovative financial solutions to evolving risk management problems.

Among the topics covered in this chapter are the following:

- Enterprise and financial risk management
- Determining the appropriate amount of loss exposure to retain
- Risk management information systems (RMISs)
- Risk management for international loss exposures

ENTERPRISE AND FINANCIAL RISK MANAGEMENT

Traditional risk management

Traditional risk management has been devoted to solving management problems associated with pure risks—the exposures that can only produce a loss or no change. We presented the process and vocabulary of traditional risk management in Chapter 3, "Risk Management." **Financial risk management** describes a program to manage

Financial risk management

efficiently potential losses arising from such things as interest rate changes, currency

Enterprise risk management (ERM)

fluctuations, credit risks or commodity price changes. **Enterprise risk management (ERM)** implies a program that simultaneously considers all sources of loss. In other words, an ERM program combines traditional and financial risk management programs.

Some firms take a broader view of risk management. They see that the cost of capital issues and cash flow management issues are common threads connected to an ERM program. At some point in an undergraduate business education, students cover core financial issues that include calculating the weighted average cost of capital, analyzing the effect of borrowing on capital costs, and studying the impact of financial structure decisions on firm value. Describing these issues is beyond the scope of this text. However, suffice it to note that risk managers and financiers can make a strong case tying together financial and risk management decisions. This chapter will highlight some of these connections.

Chief risk officers

Beginning in the early 1990s, many large firms began designating the person in charge of their ERM program as "**chief risk officers** (CROs)". The CRO, in additional to carrying out the traditional risk manager's duties, must understand and implement financial alternatives to traditional insurance arrangements, assess the impact of merger and acquisition activity on the risk management program, and tie the risk management program to the firm's overall financial decision making.

The description of financial risk management in this chapter is relatively simple compared to the complexity of this topic. Evolution of the instruments of financial risk management occurs frequently. Today's newest concept may not even be used next year because it has been replaced by an even cleverer bit of financial engineering. Therefore, our purpose, consistent with the overall objective of this textbook, is to introduce the basic elements and vocabulary of financial risk management.[1] As the first step in our description, we provide some useful vocabulary and then follow with two examples that illustrate financial risk management problems and solutions.

The Vocabulary of Financial Risk Management

Financial Perils

Credit risk

Credit risk refers to loss potential caused by a borrower defaulting on a loan. Chapter 2, "Defining the Insurable Event," describes credit risk and credit insurance.

Currency risk

Currency risk refers to loss potential caused by unfavorable fluctuations in the value of domestic currency relative to foreign currencies. An extended example of this exposure follows shortly, but here is a simple example. Assume that in January, $1 purchases 3 euros (€; the currency used by most of the European community), and in October, $1 purchases only 2€. During this period, the dollar has lost one-third of its value against the euro. If a U.S. importer needed to deliver 6€ million to obtain some inventory from a European exporter, it would pay $2 million in January (6€ million/3) but $3 million in October (6€ million/2). In this example, currency fluctuation caused a $1 million additional payment or, viewed alternatively, a $1 million loss.

Interest rate risk

Interest rate risk refers to loss potential caused by increasing interest rates reducing market value of fixed-income securities, such as bonds. The general rule is that when interest rates rise, the value of fixed-income securities falls. Falling interest rates produce gains in fixed-income security prices. The longer the maturity, the more volatile is the market price for fixed income securities.

Liquidity risk

Market risk

Liquidity risk refers to loss potential caused by having to take a substantial discount to liquidate an investment quickly. **Market risk** refers to loss potential caused by

---

[1] For a comprehensive and mathematically interesting discussion of this topic, see Neil A. Doherty, *Integrated Risk Management: Techniques and Strategies for Reducing Risk* (New York: McGraw-Hill, 2000).

having to liquidate an investment at an unfavorable price, perhaps during a downturn of the business cycle.

Hedging Revisited

Chapter 3 defined hedging as "taking two simultaneous positions that offset each other so that no matter what the outcome of some event based on chance, the hedger neither wins nor loses."[2] In this chapter, we will modify this definition slightly to the following: **Hedging** is taking two positions whose gains and losses will offset each other for the purpose of limiting risk. The difference between the two definitions emphasizes that not all hedges provide an exact offset of gains and losses. Note also how broad the second definition is; it can encompass many different transactions, including *insurance*. When an insured firm has a loss, it gains the right to collect insurance proceeds. The firm has hedged its loss exposure because the event that gives rise to the damage (loss) also gives rise to an offsetting gain (the claim against the insurance company). Modern financial arrangements allow risk managers to construct hedges against many different types of losses. Frequently these hedges involve derivative securities.

Derivative Securities and Other Financial Transactions

Derivative security refers to a financial instrument whose value is based on the value of an underlying financial asset or commodity. **Futures contracts** are orders placed by traders in advance to buy or sell a commodity or financial asset at a specified price. These contracts are traded in organized commodities or securities markets. Risk managers use futures to provide a hedge when an increase or decrease in a commodity's price can reduce profits.

Consider an airline that must purchase jet fuel in large amounts each month. Likewise, consider the position of the oil refiner that will sell the fuel. Assume that it is March and oil sells for $50 a barrel. Both the airline and the refiner are profitable at this price. If the price rises to $60 a barrel, the refiner's profits increase while the airline's profits decrease. An opposite result occurs if the price of oil drops below $50 a barrel: the airline's profits increase while the refiner's profits decrease. Assume that the risk managers of the refiner and the airlines want to hedge their positions. The airline can buy a futures contract that gives it the right to purchase oil at $50 a barrel in November. To buy this futures contract, assume that the airline must pay $1 a barrel for each of the 10,000 barrels it plans to purchase in November. To hedge its position, the refiner can sell a contract that forces it to sell a barrel of oil at $50 a barrel in November. Assume that the refiner earns $2 a barrel from selling this contract for each barrel it commits to sell. Traders or speculators would be the other party to the contract in both cases.

If price of oil rises to $60 a barrel in November, the right to purchase oil at $50 a barrel is worth $10 a barrel. Relative to its position in March, the airline loses money when it buys 10,000 gallons of fuel at $60 a barrel. Its loss, however, is reduced by the increase in value of the futures contract. The airline's $10-a-barrel gain on the futures contract is reduced by the $1 a barrel it paid for the contract in March. Nevertheless, the risk manager has hedged the potential loss from the adverse price change of oil.

At $60 a barrel, the refiner will be forced to honor its commitment to sell oil at $50 a barrel. The refiner's loss is reduced by the $2 a barrel price it received from selling the contract in March.

If the price of oil falls to $40 a barrel in November, the airline profits from the lower price of oil, but it loses the money it paid to guarantee the purchase of oil at $50 a barrel. The refiner loses profits if it sells oil at $40 a barrel, but it gains when the option that it sold for $2 a barrel expires worthless. Interested readers can see both

Hedging

Derivative security

Futures contracts

---

[2] Chapter 3, page 58.

graphical and mathematical explanations of the hedging process in the Doherty text cited in footnote 1. The point of this explanation of futures contracts is to show how risk managers of a firm dealing in commodities can hedge the firm's exposures to losses caused by adverse commodity price fluctuations.[3]

Forward contracts are similar to futures contracts, but forward contracts are not traded on organized exchanges. **Swaps** occur when two companies lend each other currencies (**currency swaps**) or one currency at different interest rates, one fixed, one floating (**interest rate swaps**).

Traded options create a legal right to buy or sell a commodity or a financial asset at an agreed-upon price for a specific period. The **option holder**, also known as the party with the *long position*, has the right to buy or sell under the agreed terms. The option writer, also known as the party with the *short position*, is obligated to buy or sell based on the choice of the option holder. A **call option** is an option to buy an underlying asset. A **put option** is an option to sell an underlying asset. A call option would have value if the holder could buy the asset (say, 100 shares of stock) for below the prevailing market price. A put option would have value if the holder could sell the stock at above the prevailing market price.[4] For the holder of the long position, puts acquire value when the price of the underlying asset falls. Thus, buying a put is a hedge against falling asset prices.

In the following section, we give two more examples of how risk managers can use options and other derivative securities as a substitute or supplement for traditional insurance contracts. Following those examples, we describe how some insurance companies have used options to hedge their loss exposures.

Two Examples of Financial Risk Management

An Interest Rate Risk Example

Six months ago, Acme Bank aggressively sought and attracted new deposits by offering one-year certificate of deposit (CD) rates that were slightly higher than the competition. Acme invested the deposits in fixed-rate loans with an average maturity of five years. The CDs, on the other hand, will mature in six months. Acme is concerned that interest rates will rise, forcing the bank to pay higher rates to retain the deposits. Because the five-year loans have a fixed interest rate, raising the rate it must pay on the CDs will reduce profitability. Management decides to hedge against the risk of rising interest rates by selling U.S. Treasury futures contracts. If interest rates rise, the value of the futures contracts will fall, enabling the bank to repurchase the contracts below the selling price. The profit on the futures transaction will help to offset, or hedge, the higher interest rates that will have to be paid to depositors. If interest rates fall, the benefit of paying lower interest rates to depositors will be reduced by a loss on the futures transaction.

A Currency Risk Example

Global, Inc. is a large manufacturer of computerized industrial equipment. A total of 40 percent of Global's sales are made to European steel mills. Ordinarily, the steel mills place advance orders with Global. These contracts specify the types and dimensions of the equipment to be produced. The contracts also specify the price to be paid in euros

---

Forward contracts

Swaps

Currency swaps

Interest rate swaps

Traded options

Option holder

Call option

Put option

---

[3] Readers interested in this subject can conduct a Web search using the keywords "commodities futures contracts."

[4] An insurance policy has some characteristics of a put option, in that property suffering a loss can be "put" to the insurance company at an amount based on the insurance contract language, which after a loss makes the put valuable. If there is no loss, the insurance company gets to keep the premium, which is comparable to a put expiring worthless.

and stipulate that the mills place a 10 percent deposit with each order. Production time usually varies between four and nine months. Global's corporate treasurer is concerned that the euro might depreciate against the dollar before delivery is made. In other words, when the equipment is delivered and payment is received in euros, those euros may convert into fewer dollars than expected when the contract was signed. Because Global's production costs are paid in dollars, the foreign exchange loss would result in lower profits. Management decides to hedge the risk by selling a forward contract in euros for roughly the amount of euros it has contracted to receive. The forward contract effectively fixes the dollar value of the euro and hence of the equipment contract. Although Global would not benefit if the euro appreciated against the dollar, neither does it lose if the euro depreciates against the dollar because the risk manager has taken a position in financial markets that is opposite to Global's manufacturing contract. If the manufacturing position loses, the financial position gains, and vice versa.

In the case of both Acme Bank and Global, Inc., financial risk managers effectively can hedge their financial risk to speculators in the financial markets.

CATASTROPHE RISK TRANSFER

Recall from Chapter 2 the principle that an ideally insurable loss exposure is unlikely to produce a catastrophic loss—that is, a loss relatively large compared to the size of the insurance pool. Nevertheless, even though insuring potentially catastrophic losses is not ideal, financiers have developed arrangements that provide protection to insurance companies faced with catastrophic exposures. Using financial engineering techniques, insurance companies can use the resources of the financial markets to broaden the scope of the coverage they can offer. These techniques are relatively recent innovations and are alternatives or supplements to traditional reinsurance arrangements. While this section applies to the financial management of insurance companies, non-insurers, especially firms with self-insurance programs, also could use these financial arrangements.

Insurance companies have used the following three financial arrangements to lessen catastrophic loss potential:

- Contingent surplus notes
- Catastrophe bonds
- Exchange traded options

Contingent Surplus Notes

Contingent surplus notes allow an insurance company to protect itself from paying a "catastrophic amount" of claims when its own finances may be weakened. The arrangement works as follows:

1. Investors put funds in a trust account, and the trustees then purchase U.S. Treasury securities.
2. Investors receive all the interest from the Treasury securities. In addition, the investors receive interest from the insurer. This additional interest is a function of the competitive capital market rates prevailing when the transaction is made. Therefore, the inducement to the investor is a higher rate of return than would be available from investing in Treasury securities.
3. In the event of a specified catastrophe, the insurer has the legal right to replace the U.S. Treasury securities in the trust account with its own "surplus notes" or, in

Contingent surplus notes

some cases, with its own preferred stock. These notes (or preferred stock) pay more interest than the Treasury securities, but there is also more risk of default because now the insurer is making the interest payments rather than the U.S. Treasury.

4. After replacing the Treasury securities with its own notes, the insurer can liquidate the Treasury securities that it acquired from the trust account and use the proceeds to pay claims.

Thus, this arrangement provides the insurer with needed liquidity when otherwise it might have to make financial arrangements at a time when the capital markets might charge punitive interest rates. Note that the insurer still must pay interest on the newly issued securities, so it has not transferred its loss exposure. However, in a sense, it has made a forward contract for liquidity at a price it could negotiate under "ordinary" circumstances; that is, in the absence of a catastrophe.

Catastrophe Bonds

Catastrophe bonds (cat bonds) allow an insurance company actually to transfer some of or all its catastrophe exposure to a trust account, as follows:

1. Investors put funds in a trust account, and the trustees then purchase U.S. Treasury securities.
2. If a specified catastrophe occurs, the insurer gets some of or all the securities in the account. Unless other arrangements are made, no repayment is made to the original investors. The trigger(s) for these bonds may be a specified amount of claims suffered by an insurer or a natural catastrophe that reaches a specified magnitude as measured by wind speed or earthquake force.
3. In one recent year, these "cat bonds" paid three to five percentage points above the **London interbank offered rate (LIBOR)**, providing the lenders with enhanced interest as an inducement to accept more risk. The buyers of the cat bonds are hedge funds, pension funds and banks, sophisticated investors who use these bonds to diversify their investment portfolios.
4. The securities offered to investors can be of two types. One guarantees repayment of principal, but it has relatively low interest. These securities are backed by zero-coupon Treasury securities of long duration. If an investor chose this option, its principal, without interest, would be returned after a length of time, such as 20 years. The foregone interest would represent an opportunity cost. The other investment would have relatively high interest so long as no catastrophe occurs, but there is no guarantee of principal.

From 1997 to 2004, the amount of catastrophe bonds outstanding rose from about $700 million to over $4.4 billion. Note that even in 2004 the outstanding amount of catastrophe bonds was relatively small compared to the hurricane damage occurring in the United States that year. One reason for the limited growth of cat bonds might be their relatively high cost compared to traditional reinsurance. Another reason might be the problem of **basis risk**, the risk that the bond proceeds will not be correlated exactly to the loss sustained by an insurer.

Exchange Traded Options

Exchange traded options are standardized contracts that give the purchaser (an insurance company) the right to a cash payment from a seller-speculator if a specified index of catastrophic losses reaches a specified level during a specified period. The incentive

Catastrophe bonds (cat bonds)

London interbank offered rate (LIBOR)

Basis risk

received by the seller is the amount it receives from the purchaser, which it can keep whether or not a catastrophe occurs. The insurer is buying a claim to liquidity in the event of a catastrophic loss, but its claim is unrelated to any particular loss it might suffer. The exchange where these options are traded guarantees the performance of the seller (speculator), and the exchange requires the sellers of these contracts to meet financial responsibility requirements. For example, the seller might be required to keep on hand in liquid form at the end of each day 20 percent of the amount it is obligated to pay in the event of the specified event. Readers can find more information about exchange traded options at the Web site of the Chicago Board Options Exchange (CBOE; *http://www.cboe.com/*). Readers can also enter the keywords "catastrophe insurance" into a search engine.

DEDUCTIBLES AND POLICY LIMITS

Deductibles

Retentions

Policy limits

One common risk management problem requires determining how much loss exposure to retain and how much to transfer. This decision often involves consideration of two topics: deductible size and policy limits. **Deductibles**, or **retentions**, cause the insured to bear the first dollars of a loss. **Policy limits**, on the other hand, determine the maximum insurance recovery. If a loss is equal to or less than the deductible, the insured bears the cost. If a loss is greater than the policy limits, the insured bears the cost of any applicable deductible plus the amount of loss above the policy limit.

When choosing a deductible and a policy limit, a trade-off between the certain payment (loss) of an insurance premium must be weighed against the possibility of uninsured losses. Some rules apply to these decisions. In general, increasing policy limits increases premium costs, but the increase is not proportional. That is, increasing policy limits often will not increase premiums by the same percentage. For example, the Red Ox Bar and Grill can increase the limit of its liability insurance from $1 million to $2 million (a 100 percent increase) for a 40 percent increase in premium.

Increasing the deductible generally reduces the premium for a given amount of coverage. The reduction in premium typically is not proportional relative to the increase in deductible. That is, the first dollars of a deductible may reduce the premium more than additional increases in the deductible. If the Red Ox increases the deductible on its fire insurance from $5,000 to $10,000, it can reduce its annual premium by 10 percent. If it raises the deductible from $5,000 to $15,000, it reduces its premium by 12 percent. In this case, the first $5,000 increase in the deductible causes a larger reduction in premium (10 percent) than the second $5,000 increase (the additional 2 percent). In practice, the increased-deductible/premium-reduction figures are subject to negotiation in commercial insurance.

Different Types of Retentions

- *Each Occurrence Retention.* This is the most common deductible formula found in property and liability contracts. The retention (or deductible) applies once for each loss, and there is no annual limit on the number of times the deductible applies or the dollar amount that the insured will bear under this clause.
- *Each Occurrence—Aggregate Retention.* This formula calls for the retention to disappear after a specified number of losses. In some cases, instead of disappearing, the size of the retention is reduced after the insured has borne a specified amount of loss.
- *Multiline Aggregate Retention.* This approach allows the insured to combine many different types of insurance (for example, auto liability, workers' compensation,

and general liability) for the purpose of calculating a maximum amount that the insured must pay before the retention disappears and the insurer begins to make payments.

The amount of these retentions could be relatively large compared with the coverage limits, and creative insureds could use self-insurance arrangements, including finite risk arrangements, to fund the retentions.[5] Several mathematical techniques have been employed to help provide insight concerning these trade-offs. In practice, no mathematical technique can "solve" these problems because no perfect method exists to add the subjective risk component to the equation. We can describe a worry factor or draw isometric curves of indifference worry factors, but the worry factor still only exists in business managers' minds. That is, two managers may perceive the first position to be more risky than the second. Because the perception of risk is subjective, all they can agree on is that the risk is greater; they cannot measure their difference in perception. In practice, risk management often is as much art as science, and two risk managers may solve the same problem efficiently but differently. Thus, mathematical generalizations about efficient risk management portfolios may be appropriate in a theoretical construct but may not be useful in practice.

Rather than present a mathematical model to solve the lower premium–higher retention trade-off, we present a description of the relevant financial factors that a risk manager must consider when making these decisions. Not all decisions are equally efficient: We can identify the extremes.

Overinsurance

We define one extreme as **overinsurance**: (1) a point at which deductibles are so small that the company is insuring expenses (predictable losses), or (2) the point at which the firm purchases so much insurance that its profitability is adversely affected.

Underinsurance

We define the other extreme as **underinsurance**: (1) the point at which a firm could not afford to pay for retentions from "normal" cash flow, or (2) the point at which a probable loss could result in the firm's insolvency (when the firm is unable to pay currently due sums) or bankruptcy (when the firm's debts exceed its available assets). Between the extremes of overinsurance and underinsurance, considerable latitude exists for an efficient risk management program.

Financial and Other Considerations

In making the trade-off between lower premiums and lower policy limits or between lower premiums and higher deductibles, the risk manager should consider the following factors: tax implications, ability to pay for losses, psychological factors, and social and ethical concerns.

Tax Implications

In general, commercial insurance premiums are a tax-deductible expense, as are uninsured losses. The main difference between the two is the timing of the expense. Insurance premiums are deductible when paid; losses are deductible when incurred. The Internal Revenue Service (IRS) consistently has opposed allowing tax deductions for advance funding of expected losses, even if firms claim to be engaging in self-insurance. Setting aside other arguments in the self-insurance decision, increasing deductibles or reducing the policy limits shifts the tax burden from the present to the future, assuming variable losses over the years but the same total loss for the period under analysis. Thus, this decision becomes, in part, a present-value financial decision, raising the necessary issue of identifying the appropriate discount rate. Put in more simple terms, paying insurance premiums implies a cost in forgone interest for the time between the premium

---

[5] Finite risk programs are described in Chapter 3.

payment and the loss. If losses are incurred during a period when a firm is unprofitable, a new issue enters the equation because tax deductions may not be as valuable. To make the mathematics of the trade-off simple, we would like to hold all other factors constant, but this is an inappropriate assumption here. At this point, the reader should see why we avoid producing a generalized mathematical model. Such an approach creates the impression of a precisely engineered solution to a problem requiring educated guesses about essential variables (i.e., the pattern of the losses and the appropriate discount rate). In addition, while many risk managers may compare their risk financing program to an industry benchmark, this approach must be used with caution because even firms in the same industry may have different capital structures and costs.

If a firm experiences an uninsured loss of property, it may deduct only the book value (undepreciated value) of the loss, which may be less than the replacement cost of the loss. For example, a firm may be using a fully depreciated but very functional printing press. Because the press is fully depreciated, the firm would not be allowed a tax deduction if it were destroyed in a fire. In contrast, the firm may be able to purchase replacement cost insurance coverage for this equipment and get a tax deduction for the insurance premium. (In this example, a taxable gain occurs if the amount paid for the loss is more than the book value of the loss.) One point of this discussion is to demonstrate to the reader the complicated interface between the risk assumption decision and tax law.

Ability to Pay for Losses

Risk managers considering a large deductible or lower policy limits to reduce insurance costs must evaluate the firm's ability to absorb uninsured losses. In Chapter 3, the risk management statement of principles and procedures established the rule that the company would assume losses to buildings and contents equal to or less than $1 million. To set an efficient retention limit, the firm must consider the following factors:

Liquidity

- *The Liquidity of Assets.* In assessing the **liquidity** of a firm's assets, risk managers must ask if sufficient cash or near-cash assets are on hand at all times to cover the retention. Do regular operations generate sufficient cash to supplement available cash assets to cover the retention? Can borrowing supplement cash on hand and regular cash flow to cover the retention at all times? If the risk manager chooses a high retention, there must be funds available to cover multiple uninsured incidents or the firm's survival is jeopardized.

- *The Stability of Net Income.* If the risk manager is considering a course that exposes the firm to uninsured losses, he or she should consider the variability of the firm's income. What if a substantial uninsured loss occurs at the bottom of the business cycle in a cyclical industry? The result would be more harmful than if the loss occurred during the peak of the cycle. Examples of cyclical industries include steel, auto, or timber industries. During the peak of the cycle, a firm likely would have more cash on hand, its borrowing power would be greater, and additional cash inflow would be more available than during a recession. However, business interruption losses would be greater during the peak of a business cycle. For these reasons, risk managers of firms with steady profits (for example, utilities or food processors) presumably could assume a greater degree of risk than firms with cyclical or seasonal profits.

- *The Amount of Net Worth.* A firm's ability to absorb uninsured losses is a function of its net worth. Net worth measures the undistributed operating profits of preceding periods; it is not a measure of available cash. If a large uninsured loss occurs, the accounting result will be a reduction of net worth (reduced profits for the current period) from what otherwise would have been reported.

- *The Increased Cost of Capital.* Significant reductions in net worth can raise a firm's cost of capital by making the firm appear riskier to lenders or investors. The cost of capital penalty is felt in a reduced common stock price and in increased borrowing costs. A sufficiently large loss—for example, one equaling the entire amount of net worth—may preclude borrowing at any price. Thus, an important constraint in making the retention choice is the effect of uninsured losses on net worth. Risk managers, working together with corporate financiers, may want to review several hypothetical possibilities to estimate the relationship between uninsured losses and cost of capital. Resulting estimates can provide useful insight but will not provide definitive answers because, once again, the postloss cost of capital calculations requires the "other factors held constant" assumption.

Psychological Factors

This discussion has avoided mathematically engineered solutions and general models because mathematical precision obscures the fact that, in practice, judgment or psychological factors play a significant—and in some cases indispensable—role in choosing deductibles and policy limits. Exxon Corporation does not make decisions; people employed as risk managers and corporate directors make corporate decisions. These people reach conclusions based on their experience, habit, intuition, attitudes toward risk, and ability to explain and sell their ideas to other managers. Professional risk managers often employ mathematics to quantify certain aspects of retention decisions. Estimates of potential losses can prove accurate and useful. Tax effects of different scenarios can be calculated. Financial ratios assuming different postloss consequences can be developed. Nevertheless, when final decisions are made regarding the right retention or the best policy limit, human beings with various tolerances for risk make it, not risk-neutral corporations.

Social and Ethical Concerns

Uninsured losses can have significant nonfinancial effects. In the absence of adequate funding, uninsured losses could bankrupt organizations and produce socially or ethically undesirable consequences, including undercompensated, dead, or injured employees, a polluted environment, or unemployed workers. These considerations cannot be factored into the deductible and policy limit decisions. For many businesspeople, social and ethical concerns will be the deciding factors in solving all business decisions, including those we have been describing.

British Petrolcum: A Case Study[6]

In an interesting case study, Neil Doherty and Clifford Smith, Jr., analyzed the insurance purchasing and risk management practices of British Petroleum (BP). In their article, the authors discovered that BP "now insures against most smaller losses while self-insuring against the larger ones." "Smaller" losses were less than $10 million, while "larger" losses were greater than $10 million.

The article begins with an extended discussion of the notion that corporations may not be efficient when they purchase insurance to transfer their loss exposures. The conventional explanation for corporate insurance fails to recognize that the company's stockholders and bondholders generally diversify their own portfolio of corporate securities. In so doing, they effectively diversify away the kinds of risks insurable through insurance companies. This contention is based on some abstract assumptions, and this

---

[6] Abstracted from Neil A. Doherty and Clifford Smith, Jr., "Corporate Insurance Strategy: The Case of British Petroleum," *Journal of Applied Corporate Finance* (Fall 1993), pp. 4–15. This article is now dated, but the points the authors make remain of current interest to risk managers, especially those of larger firms.

argument, which, as Doherty and Smith note, is at odds with generally accepted practice, is beyond the scope of this introductory text.

What BP discovered was that over a ten-year period when it self-insured relatively small losses and bought catastrophe coverage for large losses, it paid $1.15 billion in premiums and recovered $250 million in claims. Moreover, when BP had one very large loss, its insurer resisted the claim. After spending $1 million on legal fees to fight its insurer, BP recovered only 70 percent of its loss.

After reviewing its loss data, estimating future loss probabilities, and considering past experience with its insurance program, BP decided to insure its smaller losses (with either a BP captive or from a commercial insurer if it received a lower competitive bid) and assume its larger exposures. Because the insurance market for the smaller losses was more competitive than the market for very large exposures, the insurers' profits were smaller. For the large exposures, only a few underwriters at Lloyd's of London could provide the needed coverage, and they were able to extract considerable profits. In addition, its evaluation of the insurance market led BP to believe its financial capacity to absorb losses was equal to or greater than the insurance underwriters. One additional calculation also made the self-insurance of large exposures appear desirable: BP's marginal tax rate on income from oil produced in the North Sea was 87 percent. Thus, a $2 billion loss would lower firm value by only $260 million after tax deductions for the loss.

Doherty and Smith concluded by noting that economists generally focus attention on the demand for insurance coverage, while BP's risk management decisions were driven in large part by supply considerations.

INTERNATIONAL RISK MANAGEMENT

A number of large firms, sometimes called *multinational* or *international* firms, operate on a worldwide basis. Their headquarters may be in the United States, Europe, or Japan, but they have branches, subsidiaries, employees, and business dealings in dozens of different countries. Regardless of whether their headquarters is in London, Tokyo, or Peoria, Illinois, risk managers of these firms must develop comprehensive, coordinated risk management programs that are applied on a worldwide basis. This section of the chapter applies this concept to U.S. firms, but the general rules apply to firms of all nations doing business on a worldwide basis.

Many U.S. businesses participate in the international economy. Some firms are exporters, selling goods in foreign countries. Some are importers, selling goods made in foreign countries. Many U.S. firms have invested overseas in manufacturing plants, foreign distribution networks, and other assets. These investments often take the form of joint ventures with foreign partners. Some U.S. firms assemble their products in the United States using foreign-made components. Other U.S. firms do the opposite, making parts in the United States but assembling their products in foreign countries. The possibilities for U.S. firms participating in international trade are numerous and not limited to manufacturing firms. Many U.S. service firms, such as banks, insurance companies, and hotel chains, have foreign operations. Firms that engage in international trade require an international risk management program.

The steps in the risk management process (described in detail in Chapter 3) apply to international operations:

1. Identify and measure all exposures to loss.
2. Evaluate risk control and financing alternatives.
3. Implement a cost-effective program.
4. Regularly reevaluate the program to see if objectives are being met.

Although the risk management process remains the same for domestic and international loss exposures, differences in emphasis will be apparent. Some reasons for these differences include the following:

- Foreign currency considerations enter into measurement and financing problems.
- Political risks arise from unexpected interventions by foreign governments. Included in this category are trade embargoes, cancellation of export licenses, contract frustration, confiscation, expropriation, and nationalization of foreign-owned property. Risk managers also must consider war risk, international terrorism, and cultural differences (including differences in legal codes) when developing and implementing an international risk management program.
- Risk financing arrangements and practices, including insurance, vary widely throughout the world.

Because international trade involves movements of goods, marine insurance—both inland and ocean marine—takes on great importance[7]. In addition, because many manufacturing operations depend on timely delivery of goods, including those arriving from overseas, business income insurance becomes a regular consideration. This insurance pays for losses caused by delays in receiving shipments.

Identification and Measurement of Exposures

U.S.-owned property in foreign countries is valued in U.S. dollars for domestic accounting purposes. Valuing property in dollars presents two measurement problems for the U.S. risk manager. If property in foreign countries is lost, foreign currency is needed to rebuild it. If U.S. machinery is lost, however, it may take dollars to replace the equipment, and foreign insurance denominated in foreign currency may be inadequate because of currency fluctuations. The value of foreign currency in terms of the U.S. dollar changes almost every business day. Thus, the foreign currency exchange rate problem complicates the risk manager's identification and measurement assignment.

A determination of responsibility for loss of goods being shipped internationally can be made only after examination of the terms of sale specified in the contract between the importer and the exporter. *Free on board (FOB)* means the exporter is not responsible after the goods are transferred to the foreign (importer's) dock. *Free alongside ship (FAS)* means the exporter's responsibility ends at the domestic (exporter's) dock. Other terms of trade may identify specifically the party responsible for insuring the goods on the various legs traveled from the exporter's warehouse to the importer's warehouse.

Open cargo marine insurance policies

Most goods in transit can be insured by **open cargo marine insurance policies**. These policies provide automatic coverage for all shipments reported to the insurer. Policies used by high-volume shippers require monthly declarations. Shippers making only occasional shipments use policies requiring an initial premium deposit followed by a premium adjustment at year-end based on the actual volume of goods shipped.

The U.S. Export-Import Bank (*http://www.exim.gov/*) makes some political risk coverage available to U.S. firms doing business in less-developed countries. The Export-Import Bank established the Foreign Credit Insurance Association (FCIA) in 1961. The FCIA (*http://www.fcia.com/*) is an important source of export credit insurance for small U.S. exporters. FCIA policies cover many political risks, but rates are based on the countries covered, which must be scheduled on a *Country Limitation Schedule*. Private insurance, often written on a tailor-made basis, also can be used to cover exposures in

---

[7] Note that ocean marine insurance, inland marine insurance, and business income insurance are all covered in detail in Chapter 18, "Commercial Property Insurance."

developed countries. Generally, smaller firms obtain FCIA coverage, while larger firms use private insurers. Risk avoidance, rather than insurance, often is the logical solution when trading with countries in turmoil or with hostile governments.

Physical perils may affect foreign operations more than they would if similar facilities were located in the United States. Some perils, such as cyclones, typhoons, tidal waves, and earthquakes, occur with greater frequency in some foreign locations than in the United States. Some perils produce more severe losses overseas because firefighting capability is generally less effective than that found in the United States.

Danger to personnel overseas deserves special attention in international operations. Firms depending on one person or a few people to manage their foreign operations must engage in both loss prevention and loss reduction. Whenever expertise is concentrated in a few people, trained replacements become a logical part of the risk management program.

Liability losses in foreign countries are possible. Most experts would agree, however, that the United States presents the most hostile environment in the world with respect to liability losses. Thus, most successful U.S. risk managers will be well aware of the problems and possibilities presented by liability litigation. Complicating an American risk manager's job is the fact that not all countries operate with a legal system based on English common law. If a U.S. firm considers operating in a country without a familiar legal system, local legal expertise is a prerequisite to beginning operations.

Development and Implementation of Plans

The general rules of risk management apply to both domestic and international operations. The risk management tools and the rules of when to use them remain the same:

1. Avoid exposures when both the chance of loss and the severity of loss are high.
2. Engage in loss prevention and loss reduction activities until the gains realized from a program are less than the cost of the activities. Segregation of assets assumes considerable importance in international risk management, so that a peril or occurrence in one country (for example, expropriation of property) cannot jeopardize operations in other countries.
3. Insure risks when the chance of loss is low and the severity of loss is high.
4. Regularly review and evaluate the program.

The risk management process never ends. This conclusion is appropriate to domestic and international risk management problems. Strong currencies can become weak in a relatively short time. Countries considered friendly and reliable trading partners may change governments, renounce foreign debt, or become hostile to U.S. interests. Our international adversaries during the post–World War II years, the Soviet Union and its satellite countries, are now Russia and almost two dozen independent countries. All these new countries are changing their economic and political policies, and most are trying to integrate into the world economy. Each change in the world political or economic order presents the risk manager of an international firm with problems. The successful risk manager must monitor relevant financial and political change and develop a flexible, comprehensive risk management program designed to minimize loss arising from unexpected change.

Risk managers of international firms, whether based in the United States, Europe, or Asia, must be aware of the increasing availability of information on a global basis. CNN, one of the best-known U.S. cable news networks, is available almost everywhere in the world. Therefore, ideas that originate in the United States, such as environmental impairment liability or employment practices liability, can be discussed and adopted in other countries relatively quickly. The European and U.S. emphasis on worker safety, health standards, and general working conditions has not been as high a priority in some Asian countries, but after exposure to the more humane practices of other countries, workers and their governments may demand comparable treatment. Given the potential for global communications, the spread of ideas will be more rapid in the future, and this speed of change has clear implications for risk managers of international firms.

Foreign Insurance

Generalizations about foreign insurance arrangements are difficult to make. Some countries allow U.S. firms to insure U.S.-owned property with U.S. brokers and insurers. Other countries insist that all property in their territory be insured with domestic brokers and insurers (that is, those based in the foreign countries in question). We call insurers that are authorized to do business in a country **admitted insurers**. Some U.S. insurers have invested in local insurance operations overseas and are locally admitted insurers in these markets. Risk managers often do business with admitted insurers because they are legally required to do so. Some foreign countries levy fines and other penalties on companies that use **nonadmitted insurers**. Even if not required, admitted insurers can be desirable because both premiums and losses are denominated in local currencies. Alternatively, U.S. risk managers may prefer to arrange coverage with a nonadmitted insurer because it uses familiar policies written in English, because its contractual obligations are based on well-established English or U.S. law, or because it is providing international coverage for a large number of foreign operations.

U.S. firms with property located in many different countries often try to develop a global insurance program using one of two methods. One approach is to use an international insurer (or broker) having an international network of associations with local insurance companies. A second approach is to use admitted insurers in each country or region where the U.S. firm operates, but purchase a **difference-in-conditions (DIC)** insurance policy from a U.S. insurer. Insurance companies write the DIC policy on a manuscript, tailor-made basis. The DIC policy supplements the local (foreign) property coverages by broadening the covered perils, increasing policy limits, or doing both. DIC policies allow the U.S. firm to pay premiums to a U.S. insurer and collect losses in dollars if foreign insurers do not provide all the coverage that the risk manager specifies. In one sense, the DIC policy fills the gaps in coverage caused by purchasing insurance in several different countries, each having different rules, policy limits, and other peculiarities. With the DIC policy, the U.S. firm can approach global uniformity in coverage because the DIC supplement brings all policies up to its limits. Entering the keywords "difference in conditions insurance" into a search engine produces current information about this coverage.

Admitted insurers

Nonadmitted insurers

Difference-in-conditions (DIC)

RISK MANAGEMENT INFORMATION SYSTEMS (RMISs)

Risk management information systems (RMISs)

Many risk managers now use **risk management information systems (RMISs)** to record, track, and analyze losses. RMISs also are used to maintain records of plant, property, and equipment and record how they are protected from loss. Another use of RMISs is to perform statistical analysis of past losses and to forecast losses. Some firms have their RMISs tied to national networks that track such things as Occupational Safety and Health Act of 1970 (OSHA) bulletins, relevant court decisions, and proposed state and federal legislation. To achieve maximum effectiveness, RMISs must be tailored to the needs of individual organizations. Because each organization faces different physical hazards, liability exposures, and property value fluctuations, a standard

RMIS cannot be as useful as a system that has been designed carefully to solve a particular organization's specific problems.

Traditionally, many of these activities have been performed without the speed and integration that a computer allows. With RMISs, more timely, accurate, and comprehensive output permits more precise and efficient risk management decisions.

Loss Data

Loss records, including injuries to workers, liability claims, or asset losses, are the foundation of an RMIS. Federal law (OSHA) mandates complete records of employee injuries, and businesses and their insurers often require relevant data before and after losses. Computerized databases record information on the frequency, severity, causes, and outcome of losses. After the information is entered, it can be analyzed by date, location, individuals involved, or in some other meaningful way. If patterns emerge—perhaps too many injuries arise on weekends, or after considerable overtime, or in passenger cars—then the risk manager can be alerted to take corrective measures. Sometimes simple analysis reveals these loss patterns. In other cases, risk managers use more sophisticated statistical techniques, such as regression analysis, to identify a problem. All accredited U.S. business schools must incorporate statistics in their curriculums. It would not be in keeping with the purpose of this introductory risk management and insurance textbook to review all the appropriate material provided in statistics courses. One educational purpose of this book is to show the interrelationship between the study of risk management and insurance and other business and liberal arts courses. Readers interested in loss forecasting, loss modeling, confidence intervals, and other interesting statistical methods should refer to a textbook devoted to this topic.

Table 17–1 presents some hypothetical data for Big Bob's On-Time Trucking Company. The data are of the type that is easily generated by a computer database. Assume that the firm's risk manager is analyzing the annual results of vehicle collisions. She is looking for statistical patterns that may yield effective ways to lower the number of accidents and their costs.

Risk managers must employ statistical techniques to identify specific problems. This example is a classic case where statistical analysis provides fruitful insight. The first concern of the risk manager is to draw logical conclusions from the data by making intelligent comparisons. In this case, the risk manager makes two comparisons. First, she compares this year's data to historical data from her own company; second, she compares Big Bob's data to national averages. Average loss data may be provided by a trade association or from a company's insurer.

TABLE 17–1 Hypothetical Loss Data for Big Bob's On-Time Trucking Company

Drivers' Training	Past Year	1 to 5 Years	5+ Years	Total
Number of accidents	2	5	14	21
Cost of accidents	$250,000	$150,000	$350,000	$750,000
Geography	**East**	**Midwest**	**West**	**Total**
Number of accidents	10	4	7	21
Cost of accidents	$500,000	$ 85,000	$165,000	$750,000
Truck Color	**Bright**	**White**	**Metallic**	**Total**
Number of accidents	2	12	7	21
Cost of accidents	$400,000	$100,000	$250,000	$750,000

A strong RMIS can be used to evaluate the effectiveness of the risk management program, especially the loss prevention program. Finally, because the data presented in Table 17–1 apply to the core business of the firm, the risk manager will develop a comprehensive report for senior management to review. In this case, Big Bob's risk manager recommended requiring that all drivers participate annually in the company-sponsored drivers' training program. She also recommended further analysis to determine why loss costs in the East were higher than in the other regions and why white trucks were involved in more accidents than trucks of other colors. Another important point was that the white trucks were involved in twelve accidents, but in seven of those cases, they were "victims" and thus produced no (unrecovered) accident costs to the company.

Because computers can store and produce masses of data, the risk management department can be overburdened with reports and statistical analysis. Big Bob's risk manager may consider many other variables when conducting the annual loss analysis. She may consider such loss factors as weather conditions, time of day, or the driver's age and experience with the company. In many cases, large numbers of relevant independent variables exist. In practice, risk managers will want to limit their investigations and focus on those variables most subject to change and improvement.

Operating a RMIS is not without problems. If loss data are inaccurate, subsequent analysis or forecasts will be misleading. Data integrity should be checked periodically by random audit or another procedure to ensure accuracy. While each generation of computers has become progressively more reliable, backup data storage still remains necessary. For example, a firm needing to know immediately what broker arranged its inventory coverage in Austria or Brazil, and in what amount, must have access to the information even if a computer system is temporarily inoperable.

Other Information

Most large firms will keep accurate records of their acquisition and disposal of property for accounting purposes. The risk manager needs access to this information to be sure all the firm's assets have been protected, including assets that no longer show value on the balance sheet. A good RMIS tracks all the firm's property, its cost, its replacement value, preferred vendors, and how this property will be replaced if lost. Accurate inventory records, including location, amounts, and turnover, are especially useful because insurance companies frequently base loss payment and premium costs on this information.

Firms that face frequent liability claims or incidents need to track this information. If some products, people, or locations produce an extraordinary number of lawsuits, a database analysis can identify these problem areas. It may take years to settle liability claims, and RMISs can be helpful in tracking claims after the company is given notice of suit. RMISs may even be used to assess the effectiveness of counsel in representing the company's interests in lawsuits.

Firms having multiple locations, including international operations, may deal annually with several different insurance agents or brokers and have many insurance policies in force. Great accuracy is needed in maintaining insurance policy records. Some liability policies promise to provide coverage for events that happen decades after the policy was purchased. In some pollution or products liability lawsuits, determining the appropriate insurer has proven difficult for some companies. Recording insurer information is a primary use of RMISs.

In summary, an RMIS can be used for analyzing losses, evaluating loss prevention activities, controlling insurance claims, and maintaining insurance records.

SUMMARY

Enterprise risk management (ERM) is a combination of traditional and financial risk management. Financial risk management applies especially to firms in the financial or commodities industries. These firms can enter into hedging arrangements to manage the loss exposures presented by currency fluctuations, interest rate changes, and crop price changes. The tools of financial risk management include traded options, futures contracts, currency swaps, and interest rate swaps. Insurance companies also have been able to use financial transactions to hedge their exposure to catastrophic losses.

Choosing the amount of loss exposure to retain and the amount to transfer in practice often involves choosing the appropriate deductible and policy limits. Choosing a relatively high deductible or relatively low policy limit can lower premium costs, yet both actions expose the firm to the possibility of uninsured losses. Instead of a single solution, a range of solutions exists between overinsurance and underinsurance. Overinsurance involves insuring expenses or insuring against the maximum possible loss. Underinsurance involves leaving the firm exposed to probable losses that could produce insolvency or bankruptcy. Risk managers and businesses must consider the following factors to identify an efficient choice within the range of possible solutions:

- *Tax Effects.* In general, commercial insurance premiums are a tax-deductible expense, as are uninsured losses. The main difference between the two is the timing of the expense. Insurance premiums are deductible when paid; losses are deductible when incurred.

- *Ability to Pay for Losses.* To set an efficient retention limit, the firm must consider the liquidity of assets, the stability of net income, and the amount of net worth.

- *Psychological Factors.* People make decisions based on their experience, attitudes toward risk, ability to explain and sell their ideas to other managers, habits, and intuition.

- *Social and Ethical Concerns.* In the absence of adequate funding, uninsured losses could bankrupt organizations and produce socially or ethically undesirable consequences, including undercompensated, dead, or injured employees, a polluted environment, or unemployed workers.

Many U.S. firms engage in importing and exporting. These firms must apply all the rules for managing domestic loss exposures and consider the special loss potential that applies to international trade, including foreign currency valuations, political risks, and variations in international insurance arrangements.

Businesses require risk management information systems (RMISs) to record loss data, maintain records of property acquisition and disposal, and record information about insurance transactions. Risk managers use their RMISs to develop statistical analysis needed for loss prevention initiatives and to prepare required government and insurance company reports.

REVIEW TERMS

- Admitted insurers
- Alternative risk transfer (ART) market
- Call option
- Catastrophe bonds (cat bonds)
- Contingent surplus notes
- Credit risk
- Currency risk
- Currency swaps
- Deductibles
- Derivative security
- Difference-in-conditions (DIC) insurance policy
- Enterprise risk management (ERM)
- Financial risk management
- Forward contracts
- Futures contracts
- Hard market
- Hedging
- Interest rate risk
- Interest rate swaps
- Liquidity
- Liquidity risk
- London interbank offered rate (LIBOR)
- Market risk
- Nonadmitted insurers
- Open cargo marine insurance policies
- Option holder
- Option writer
- Overinsurance
- Policy limits
- Pure risks
- Put option
- Retentions
- Risk management information systems (RMISs)
- Speculative risks
- Swaps
- Traded options
- Traditional risk management
- Underinsurance

REVIEW

1. What are the types of loss dealt with by financial risk management? Describe some of the tools that are available to managers dealing with financial risks.
2. What is an RMIS? Describe some uses that risk managers can have for their RMISs.
3. Describe the relationship between deductible size and premium payments. Describe the relationship between premium size and policy limits.
4. Define the terms *overinsurance* and *underinsurance*.
5. Describe the tax considerations involved in choosing relatively high deductibles or relatively low policy limits.
6. What are some of the variables determining a firm's ability to pay for losses?
7. What role do psychological factors play in determining a firm's retention limits?
8. What role do social and ethical concerns play in determining a firm's retention limits?
9. Describe the additional concerns that distinguish international risk management from domestic risk management.
10. What are political risks?
11. Distinguish between admitted and nonadmitted insurers with respect to a given country.

OBJECTIVE QUESTIONS

1. Currency risk is defined as:
   a. The loss of value when a domestic currency can purchase less in terms of a foreign currency
   b. The loss in value of a currency due to changes in domestic interest rates
   c. The loss in the future value of a currency due to random fluctuations in gross domestic product (GDP)
   d. Loss of currency caused by theft
2. A contract to buy or sell a commodity that is traded on securities markets in advance is called:
   a. An option
   b. A forward contract
   c. A futures contract
   d. A swap
3. When choosing an appropriate deductible, a risk manager should consider each of the following except:
   a. Tax implications
   b. Investors' preferences
   c. Stability of cash flow
   d. Liquidity of assets
4. DIC policies:
   a. Are used to insure domestic insurance companies
   b. Are used to insure the difference between an international company's foreign insurance coverage and its desired level of coverage throughout the world
   c. Are used mainly during periods of political unrest or when U.S. property is threatened by terrorists or unstable foreign governments
   d. Are used mainly when the U.S. government tries to promote trade with developing economies
5. Choose the true statement:
   a. ERM is a combination of pure and financial risk management.
   b. ERM also is called "financial" risk management.
   c. ERM also is called "econometric" risk management.
   d. ERM also is called "derivative" risk management.
6. Hedging a loss exposure means:
   a. Gains outnumber losses in most cases.
   b. Underlying losses are no longer predictable.
   c. A transaction is made so that gains and losses will offset each other.
   d. No insurance is purchased because losses will be covered by cash flow.
7. If you own (hold) a put option:
   a. You have the right to sell something at a specified price.
   b. You have the right to buy something at a specified price.
   c. You have a legal liability.
   d. You have a guarantee from an insurance company to issue insurance coverage at a reduced price.
8. U.S. firms doing business in less-developed countries can get some political risk coverage from:
   a. The World Insurance Bank
   b. The U.S. Treasury
   c. The U.S. Shipping Authority
   d. The U.S. Export-Import Bank

DISCUSSION QUESTIONS

1. What effect do you think a firm's size has on its RMIS? Do you think that the increased power and lower cost of personal computers make RMIS possible (necessary) for smaller firms?
2. What arguments can be made for and against relying exclusively on quantitative analysis to make risk retention decisions?
3. Do you think financial risk management is a distinct field of risk management, or is it just another part of a complete traditional risk management program?

INTERNET RESEARCH ASSIGNMENTS

1. Go to this Web site: (*http://www.fcia.com/*). Click on the "FCIA Country Update" tab at this site and prepare a short report on the first country discussed.

2. Go to this Web site: (*http://www.exim.gov/*). Read a report on one of the U.S. Export-Import Bank "Key Markets," such as China. Briefly summarize this report, and compare it with a report on a country such as Lebanon, Syria, or Iran.

3. Investigate insurance index options. Describe the various indexes found. Start your search at this site: (*http://www.cboe.com/*).

Blue Star Airlines[8]

INTRODUCTION

Working on this case study allows students to integrate much of the material covered in this chapter, and their efforts can be measured by how well they achieve the following goals:

- Identify the facts of the case, distinguishing the important from the less-important facts.
- Recognize the existence of all types of risk.
- Recognize the existence of more than one possible acceptable outcome and be able to make a logical argument favoring the chosen solution.
- Use quantitative data to support the recommended solution.
- Organize the solution in a logical way.
- Recognize weaknesses of the recommended solution and identify needs for future revision.
- Present a plan for implementation.

A great number of relevant changes in the airline industry have occurred in the years during which this case study has been used. Among the more important details are the following. (Students should verify these facts using information available on the Internet, and they may want to add their own list of important issues relevant to the case.)[9]

1. The price of oil (and therefore jet fuel) has fluctuated widely.
2. The U.S. and European airline industries have seen the beginning of several new discount carriers, such as the one described in this case.
3. Several of the largest U.S., Canadian, and European air carriers have experienced significant financial difficulties, which in several cases have led to bankruptcy.
4. The potential for international terrorism has created significant problems for airline risk

managers, airport risk managers, and all other parties responsible for commercial airline travel.

The case begins with a purely fictional story that includes some of—but not all—the basic details needed to work on the case. Next, there is a step-by-step outline of the risk management process that provides more details and information. The author has omitted some information deliberately. When students realize details are missing, they are to provide the needed details and assumptions. Because each solution should have some unique assumptions, student results should not be the same.

The Story

Blue Star Airlines is a new venture. Presently, the company exists only as a business plan in the minds of three founding partners: Maria H., an Austrian; Louis B., a Frenchman; and, Harry T., an Englishman. Each partner is 45 years old, and each has at least 15 years of experience managing an airline. The partners have access to adequate capital to finance the venture. The business plan calls for financing the firm with 50 percent owner's equity (half of this 50 percent comes from the three founding partners, and half from offering stock to the public) and the remaining 50 percent from borrowing (half of this 50 percent comes from bank borrowing, and half from long-term debt.) Specifically, the partners plan to have beginning capital of $100 million: $25 million from the partners; $25 million from selling stock; $25 million from a bank loan; and $25 million from long-term bonds. The average cost of equity capital is 16 percent. The average before-tax cost of debt is 10 percent.

You (or your team) have been hired as risk management consultants by the founding partners to develop a risk management plan for Blue Star.

The business plan, in brief, proposes to begin service in Europe, providing frequent, low-cost service to a limited number of cities from a hub in Vienna, Austria. Vienna was chosen as the hub because of its geographic relationship to central Europe. The founders envision an increased amount of air traffic as former Communist countries become more integrated into the Western European economies. The partners

---

[8] I have been using this case study in Europe since 1993. Students can change the names of the cities if the case is assigned in the United States. For example, a U.S. replacement for Vienna, Austria, might be Indianapolis, Indiana.

[9] Among useful Web sites are the following: (*http://www.delta. com/*; *http://www.boeing.com/*); and (*http://www.faa.gov/*).

have agreed that at first the hub in Vienna will serve only ten European cities. They have not developed the final list of cities yet, and you are to participate in this process, providing a risk assessment of each destination you recommend. (Hint: Students should consider marketing factors, including avoiding major European capital cities where landing rights might be expensive or unavailable and where direct competition from national air carriers might make profitable operations difficult.) Your risk assessment should cover exposure to weather-related problems, political problems, and other relevant information. In general, the service will be used by businesspeople during the week and by vacationers on weekends. The company's marketing plan calls for awarding a free weekend round-trip after every ten business round-trips.

Facts and Assumptions

1. The firm will employ 600 people in addition to the three top managers. Occupations include pilots, flight attendants, phone reservations personnel, baggage handlers, and office personnel. The average monthly payroll, excluding the three managers, is estimated to be $2.5 million but will be paid in local currency or euros.

2. The firm plans to begin service with ten planes. Each plane will seat 130 people. It is assumed that the planes will average 80 percent of their capacity on each flight. Each of the ten cities selected for service will be served with four round trips a day from the Vienna hub. The longest flight lasts 2½ hours. The cost of a one-way ticket from Vienna to any destination city will be $250. (European students solving this case can convert all the data to euros if instructed to do so, for a European airline based in Austria obviously would use euro-based data.)

3. The company must use 10 million gallons of jet fuel each month, regardless of the cost. The ticket price of $250 for a one-way trip was set when jet fuel cost $0.50 per gallon, but in 2006, jet fuel costs have been more than $2 per gallon. Raising the ticket price is a possibility, but the business plan is to have one price for tickets to all destinations. The managers estimate that if the price were raised by 100 percent (to $500 for each round trip), volume will fall by 30 percent. That is, instead of flying on average at 80 percent capacity, if the price were raised to $500, the planes will fly at $(100 - 30\%) \times 80$ percent, or 56 percent capacity.

The fuel will be purchased on a cost-plus basis from a large international petroleum company. The fuel contract means that fluctuations in oil prices will be borne by Blue Star. One of the questions the founders have asked you to address is whether or not a hedging strategy for changes in fuel prices should be employed. As Blue Star is a young and relatively small airline without great financial reserves, the managers were concerned that an oil shock price rise could be a financial disaster. (Step 13 addresses this question.)

4. The company plans to lease its ten planes and to lease its 11 airport locations. The lease of the planes and the airport space requires that Blue Star pay for any damage to the airplanes or the airport property. A large international airline will provide the required maintenance of Blue Star's equipment. If Blue Star needs to lease another plane because one of its ten leased planes is unavailable, this airline will provide the equipment with three days' notice. The cost of such a lease is $100,000 each day. During the first three days, Blue Star must cancel all flights involving the unavailable plane. It would take six months to replace a plane permanently lost in a crash. Major mechanical difficulties would require leasing a plane for an additional seven days after the lease begins (or a total of ten days if the first three days before the replacement plane is available are counted). The business plan calls for anticipating one major mechanical breakdown each year.

   The company will own about 40 vehicles, including automobiles, trucks, and baggage-handling equipment. Food service will be contracted to a catering company with operations in each of the airport locations. The plane leases, airport leases and landing fees, and other business arrangements are estimated at about 50 percent of estimated income. These costs are fixed. Leasehold improvements at each of the 11 airport locations will average about $1 million and will be owned by Blue Star. Leasehold improvements include all assets, such as ticket counters, seats, and other property found at the airport locations.

5. Insurance costs are not fixed. Blue Star plans to combine aircraft hull and liability insurance coverage in one package. The cost of this package

has averaged $40 (U.S.) per departure over the past five years. The cost of this coverage in a given year is a function of losses paid in the past year, investment earnings potential, and competition (available capacity) in the international aviation insurance market. (Students can find recent cost trends in the aviation insurance market on the Internet. Details are reported in both insurance trade journals, such as *Business Insurance* and the *National Underwriter— Property and Casualty Edition*, and aviation journals, such as *Aviation Week & Space Technology* and *Air Transport World*. The author discovered that both airport insurance and airline insurance costs doubled after the September 11, 2001, terrorist attacks, and aviation insurance capacity and rates have been volatile since that time. Students can look up current data by entering the keywords "aviation insurance" and "aviation insurance rates" in an Internet search engine; or, if they cannot find current data, they can use $40 for each take-off in their solution.)

6. The company plans to use the most modern computer and communications equipment. The purchase cost is $30 million plus $1 million in annual maintenance. The lease cost is $8 million each year and no annual maintenance. The lease or purchase decision has not been made yet, and you have been asked to make a recommendation on this issue. Computer and communications security is a great concern to the company founders.

7. Revenue is a function of the gross national products of the European Union countries. It is estimated that revenues either will rise or fall at a rate equal to 80 percent of the change in the economy. That is, if the European economies increase or decrease by 1 percent, Blue Star's revenues will increase or decrease by 0.8 of 1 percent. The increase or decrease will be caused by changes in capacity usage, not by changes in average ticket prices.

8. Part of the initial risk management assessment is to develop a cash flow analysis assuming average (expected 80 percent capacity), above-average (90 percent capacity), and below-average (70 percent capacity) results. These spreadsheet data should be used to consider the size of an appropriate deductible for commercial insurance policies and limits on risk assumption.

The Risk Management Problem

To keep the case timely, students should do an Internet search using keywords such as "aviation," "risk management," "loss control," and "airplane catastrophes," to allow them access to current literature. Part of the assignment is to have a solution that reflects current and estimated outcomes for the airline industry, with specific reference to recent trends in the industry.

Step 1: Present a review of the important facts of the case.

(*Hint: list only five of the most important facts.*)

Step 2: Make a recommendation for the ten cities chosen for the first destinations.

(*Hint: explain such risk management concerns for international operations as the following: weather, airport security, and political stability.*)

Step 3: Using a computer spreadsheet, develop a cash flow model for the first year of operation.

(*Hint: you might need to make some assumptions.* Ignore all tax considerations. *Good solutions will consider average, above-average, and below-average revenue as described in the case. Based on this analysis, what is the largest insurance deductible you recommend for Blue Star? What ticket price do you recommend?*)

Step 4: Develop a Policy Statement

(*Hint: These are the broad-based risk management strategies. Two examples are given below. You are to recommend several additional points.*)

- Eliminate or reduce conditions and practices that cause loss.
- Purchase commercial insurance for catastrophic loss exposures.

Step 5: Outline the Risk Management Department's Responsibility

(*Hint: These are specific risk management tactics. Two examples are given below. You are to suggest several additional duties, including areas where loss prevention programs will be needed.*)

- Design and operate loss prevention programs.
- Develop insurance coverage programs and keep them current.

Step 6: Identify and Measure Direct Property Loss Potential

(*Hint: Students should identify both the* property *and the* perils *to which they are exposed. Only one example is given.*)

Property	Perils
Airplanes	Windstorm, fire, terrorism, crash on ground, destruction in air.

Step 7: Identify and Measure Business Income Loss Potential

(*Hint: Assume that a plane will be needed under the terms of the interruption agreement mentioned in the case for at least one week each year. That is, there will be three days without revenue and seven days with the borrowed plane each year.*)

Step 8: Identify and Measure Liability Loss Potential

(*Hint: Students should use the Internet to review any recent losses in these categories for airlines or other industries. Attach any articles or information to your report. The answer to this question is unknown and will always be an estimate. This exposure will always be insured.*)

- Catastrophes
- Ordinary passenger claims

Step 9: Identify and Measure Key People Loss Exposure

(*Hint: Students are to identify key people and estimate their replacement cost.*)

Step 10: Outline a Crisis Management Program

(*Students are to identify one major and one minor crisis faced by an airline company and outline steps to deal with potential catastrophes.*)

Step 11: Evaluate the Relationship between Blue Star's Financial Structure and Their Risk Management Program

(*Hint: This is a difficult question; only a short statement comparing the risk of Blue Star's financial structure and the risk of the airline industry is required.*)

Step 12: Summary

(*Hint: conclude your case study with a summary of the most important steps recommended in your solution, with a timetable if possible. For example: purchase insurance on aircraft as soon as the company is legally responsible for them. Be sure to identify any major areas of weakness in your solution and indicate any needed future work.*)

(Optional) Step 13: Describe a Hedging or Advanced Risk Transfer Program

(*These concerns involve more sophisticated items and may be omitted. Students who are interested might consider whether Blue Star should hedge currency fluctuations or interest rates, assuming that expenses are paid in euros (or dollars) and some income will be in the form of foreign currency from Eastern European countries. The following section is directed at the possibility of hedging petroleum purchases.*)

Commodities Contracts The company must use ten million gallons of jet fuel each month, regardless of the cost. A five-cent increase in the price of fuel would therefore cost the company $500,000 each month. Management believes that this kind of impact is too large to bear. (The price of jet fuel was $0.50 per gallon when the business plan was made, but the price recently has increased to more than $2.)

At issue is whether and how to hedge against the risk of a fuel price increase. If ticket prices could be changed concurrently with fuel price changes, then there would be no change in margins and no effect on income. This occurrence is not likely for two reasons. First, many of the passengers have purchased their tickets in advance, so the revenue is already fixed. Second, competition may prevent Blue Star from instantaneously raising prices in reaction to a fuel price change. For purposes of this decision, assume that there is a 30-day lag between fuel price changes and ticket price changes, so the airline is exposed for a minimum of 30 days at a time.

Hedging Alternatives

1. The airline could purchase and hold inventory in jet fuel. This alternative is probably the most costly, and it exposes the airline to the risk of price decreases and to the physical hazards of storing fuel.

2. The airline could forward-contract with the petroleum company and effectively lock in a price in advance. This action would transfer the price risk to the petroleum company. The petroleum company will charge a higher price for fuel to compensate for this risk.

3. The airline could use the futures market. Assume that the futures market represents the most cost-effective approach to the problem. This strategy involves the following considerations:
   - Having and using expertise in futures contracts, hedging, margins, and marking to market
   - Determining the quantity (number of gallons) to hedge and the specific contract to use
   - Continual monitoring of fuel costs and the hedge

Step 1 is identifying the risk. Clearly, the risk for Blue Star is that fuel prices increase; so Blue Star will want to take a position in the futures market that benefits it if prices increase. A long position (buying futures) will benefit from a price increase. The general idea is that you do in the futures market today what you are going to do in the spot market in the future. Since you are going to be buying fuel in a future spot market, you buy futures today. If prices increase, you pay more for the spot fuel in the future, but you sell your futures at a profit and, hence, your net purchase price is lower.

Step 2 involves which contract to use. Jet fuel prices are correlated most highly with the heating oil #2 futures contract. (There is not a futures contract for jet fuel specifically.) Since the exposure is for a 30-day period at a time, the contract with an expiration date greater than but closest to 30 days should be used. (Volatility tends to be higher in expiration months, so you do not want to be trading the futures contract in its expiration month.)

Step 3 involves determining the number of contracts to buy. A heating oil contract is for 42,000 gallons. If heating oil were correlated perfectly with jet fuel prices, then you simply would divide the number of gallons of jet fuel (approximately ten million gallons) by 42,000. This circumstance implies that 238 contracts should be bought. Because heating oil is not correlated perfectly with jet fuel prices, however, the hedge will be less than perfect.

CHAPTER 18

Commercial Property Insurance

After studying this chapter, you should be able to:

■ Explain how businesses can use a package insurance policy to protect themselves against direct and indirect losses

■ Identify the need for business income insurance

■ Explain the use of reporting forms in fire insurance policies

■ Define the term *fire* for insurance purposes

■ Explain how property insurance rates are developed

■ Distinguish between ocean marine insurance and inland marine insurance

■ Describe the different categories of property covered by inland marine insurance

■ List the major kinds of property insurance needed by owners of cars and planes

Starting with this chapter on commercial property insurance, we shift our emphasis from personal insurance coverage to commercial coverage. The risk manager's perspective should be kept in mind as you cover this material. Like all management functions, risk management is a means to an end, requiring tools and a strategy to be successful. Remember the goals of risk management: to keep a firm secure, to moderate great swings in cash flow or profitability caused by accidental losses, and to be efficient in putting the firm in the same financial position after a loss as before. Without insurance, most of these goals could not be accomplished efficiently. Therefore, the risk manager must be thoroughly versed in specific information about the main tool and strategy available, the commercial insurance transaction. To make the reading more interesting, I have included some insurance history lessons.

COMMERCIAL INSURANCE

Commercial and Personal Property Insurance

Commercial insurance

Personal insurance

Both businesses and homeowners need property insurance. When businesses purchase insurance, we call it **commercial insurance**. When individuals purchase insurance, we call it **personal insurance**. While the focus in this section of the text is on commercial insurance, we omit detailed analysis of commercial insurance contracts because this material is comparable to the material we described in the personal insurance contract chapters. Commercial contract provisions can be covered better in an advanced risk management or property insurance course. Instead, we describe the essential elements of the most useful property and liability insurance package.

Property and Marine (Transportation) Insurance

For insurance purposes, a broad division is made when describing physical property. Property is either permanently attached to land or it is not. We call property permanently

Real property

Personal property

Transportation insurance

Marine insurance

attached to land, such as buildings and fixtures, **real property**. **Personal property**, on the other hand, can be moved. This dichotomy in the nature of property has led to a division in property insurance. Real property historically has been covered by some type of property insurance, such as a fire insurance policy, specifying the location of the covered property. Mobile property, such as property to be exported, is generally covered by **transportation insurance**, historically called **marine insurance**.

Focusing attention on the mobility of property leads to an understanding of how these two basic property coverages have evolved. The perils facing mobile property are broader in scope than the perils facing real property. In addition to perils such as fire, lightning, and windstorm, mobile property may be sunk, confiscated, and hijacked; also, it can be collided with and stolen more easily than property attached to land. The broader scope of the perils, the difference in ability to investigate losses, and the differing potential for salvage operations have resulted in marine insurance practices that are quite distinct from comparable property insurance practices.

In this chapter, we describe both the property and transportation sections of the most frequently used package insurance policy. We also cover aviation and automobile property exposures. In the following two chapters, we cover the liability exposures of business organizations.

COMMERCIAL PACKAGE POLICY

Insurance Services Office (ISO)

Commercial package policy (CPP)

Historically, businesses had to purchase several different insurance policies when weaving together a "complete" insurance program. A small- or medium-sized manufacturing or retail firm might have needed five separate policies to achieve its insurance objectives: property insurance, liability insurance, crime insurance, automobile insurance, and transportation insurance. Specialized companies, such as building contractors, jewelry firms, and firms operating aircraft, needed even more policies. Since 1987, a package or combination of policies has allowed many firms to make one insurance purchase providing all generally needed coverages. The **Insurance Services Office (ISO)** designed the **commercial package policy (CPP)** to provide insurance coverage to a broad range of profit and nonprofit organizations, including manufacturing firms, schools, retailers, and apartment building owners. In practice, most property owners except private homeowners can use this policy.

Figure 18–1 shows the main insuring agreements of the CPP. Insureds must purchase at least two of the package's components, but they may purchase as many additional parts as they need. A reduced-size logo of Figure 18–1 appears in several of the following chapters to give you notice when we are describing each part of the package.

FIGURE 18–1   Commercial Package Policy

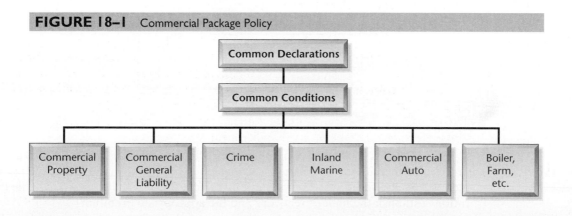

Declarations

Conditions

The CPP is preceded by declarations and conditions that apply to the entire package. The declarations usually are the first page of most insurance policies. The **declarations** establish the insured's identity and the location of the business. This section also shows the different component coverages purchased and the premium charged. The common **conditions** cover policy cancellation, assignment of the policy, and other legal rights and duties. In addition to the common declarations and conditions, each component part has its own specific declarations page and conditions.

The Insurance Services Office (ISO; *http://www.iso.com/*)

In the late 1990s, the ISO became a for-profit company providing many services for clients. Besides providing standard policy forms such as the CPP, the ISO traditionally has collected loss data and provided advisory rates to subscribers. In 1989, because of antitrust concerns, the ISO announced that it would no longer issue advisory rates, but it would continue to collect and process loss and expense data. The new procedure forces insurers to make their own rates when determining the expense and profit components of the premium. Other rating bureaus also provide commercial insurance data and some companies develop their rates and policies independently. Because of its importance, we describe commercial property insurance by focusing on the ISO commercial package policy.

BUILDING AND PERSONAL PROPERTY FORM

Building and personal property coverage form

The CPP provides property insurance in the **building and personal property coverage form**.

Property Covered

The form for building and personal property coverage identifies the building(s) covered as those listed on the declarations page. Insurers insist on careful identification of the property covered to respect the principle of definite losses. Can you imagine the legal problems arising if an owner could insure "my building"? Would this policy cover all buildings owned? All the property contained in these buildings? All the buildings at one address? Leased buildings? New additions to existing buildings? Each of these questions must be addressed to avoid misunderstanding and litigation.

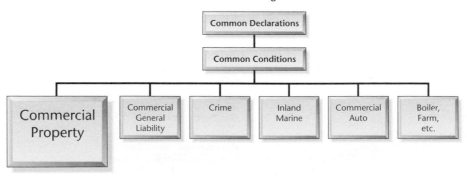

Commercial Package Insurance

Business personal property

In addition to covering the building, the CPP covers the insured's **business personal property**, which includes such items as machinery, furniture, and inventory. Inventory includes raw material, work in process, and finished goods available for sale. The declarations establish the limit of recovery and the appropriate premium.

Personal property

The third category of covered property is **personal property** not owned by the business but in its care, custody, or control. This category would be especially important to firms holding or using borrowed property, such as on-site displays or special tools.

Property Excluded from Coverage

The form for building and personal property coverage also specifies property that is not covered. Sometimes property is excluded because providing insurance would violate one of the ideals for coverage. (For example, losses of accounts, currency, and securities are not definite. "How much cash was destroyed in the fire?") Cash and near-cash items can be insured using policies having special conditions and exclusions to deal with the moral hazard. Sometimes property is excluded because the insurer wants to charge an additional premium for insureds having this type of property. (While the basic form excludes personal property while airborne or waterborne, this coverage can be added with an inland marine form for an additional premium.) Other property (vehicles, for example) is excluded because a separate policy is designed for this property.

Tangible property

Intangible property

Earlier in the chapter we noted the distinction between *real* and *personal property*. The law makes another important distinction between **tangible property** (which includes physical assets such as buildings and machinery) and **intangible property** (non-physical assets). Intangible property includes intellectual property (for example, chemical formulas and computer software), brand value, and proprietary business methods. In some cases, the value of intangible property can exceed the value of tangible property. The risks faced by intangible property, especially the perils associated with computers and communication facilities, are of considerable concern to property owners and insurers. In recent years, there have been many expensive varieties of "cybercrime," including the spread of destructive viruses and theft of intellectual property. A recent version of the Building and Personal Property Coverage Form states:

> Covered Property does not include . . . Electronic data, except as provided under Additional Coverage—Electronic Data. *The policy then defines electronic data* as information, facts, or computer programs stored as or on, created or used on, or transmitted to or from computer software . . .

The intent of this policy language is to remove coverage for damage done to electronic data. Cybercrime insurance is an evolving area. It will take time for insurers to develop appropriate policy language and premium rates before this coverage is commonly available. In the meantime, risk managers of companies with significant amounts of intangible property must review carefully their security procedures and their property and liability insurance policies.

Perils Covered

Causes-of-loss form

The property component requires a **causes-of-loss form** to complete the contract. There are three main alternatives:

1. The basic form
2. The broad form
3. The special form

The basic form covers the following perils:

1. Fire
2. Lightning
3. Explosion

4. Windstorm or hail
5. Smoke
6. Aircraft or vehicles (striking the property)
7. Riot or civil commotion
8. Vandalism
9. Sprinkler leakage
10. Sinkhole collapse
11. Volcanic action

Open-perils coverage

The *broad form* extends the coverage by adding more perils, including falling objects and water damage. This form also covers collapse, subject to the concurrent causation exclusion. The *special form* provides **open-perils coverage**. With this form, the insured is covered unless the peril causing the loss is specifically excluded. With the open-perils form, the legal burden is on the insurer to show that an exclusion applies. With the specified-perils form, the insured has the burden of showing the proximate cause of the loss was covered.

Fire Insurance History

Because fire insurance is the cornerstone of property insurance, we will examine this peril in some detail. Fire is a mixed blessing. It is useful for generating electricity and cooking, but it also causes billions of dollars in direct property damage, kills about 4,000 Americans, and injures another 25,000 annually. The Web site of the U.S. Fire Administration (*http://www.usfa.fema.gov/*) presents facts about U.S. fires as well as fire safety information.

Fire insurance has more than 200 years of history in the United States. There were the famous Chicago and San Francisco fires that destroyed almost entire cities, and less well known fires on ships and in factories that took hundreds of lives. We do not have the space or time to tell the interesting stories of famous fires nor even to devote to the parallel story of fire insurance history. Perhaps a few highlights will suffice.

Fire mark

The early fire marks of Benjamin Franklin's era still can be seen on some Philadelphia buildings as well as those of other older U.S. cities. Subscribers (insureds) would pay firefighting companies in advance. In return they would receive a **fire mark** (a metallic logo) to attach to their building. Payments for fire marks supported the firefighting companies. If protected property had a fire, the appropriate firefighting company was notified. Once the fire mark was identified, the fire was fought. Presumably, there were cases of improper companies being notified, of "wrong" fire brigades being closer to the loss, or of uninsured property being allowed to burn while firefighters stood by, all of which caused bad public relations for the fire mark system. Municipal and rural fire departments supported by taxes were more logical solutions to firefighting.

1943 New York Standard Fire Insurance Policy (SFP)

Fire insurance based on contracts between insureds and insurers became widely accepted after the 1906 San Francisco earthquake and fire.[1] Property values were greater than most families could afford to lose, and lenders needed the security that insurance provided for credit transactions. At first, fire insurers wrote their own contracts and presumably developed their own premium rates. Subsequently, fire insurance contracts were standardized. The **1943 New York Standard Fire Insurance Policy (SFP)** was the basis for all fire insurance in this country for the following thirty years. This policy is no longer in common use, but its component parts, and especially the legal precedents associated with this policy, still are very much a feature in current insurance policies covering the fire peril.

---

[1] Readers can find some interesting reading on this topic at the San Francisco Museum Web site: (*http://www.sfmuseum.org/hist1/index0.1.html/*).

Definition of Fire

One of the first steps in providing any type of insurance is defining the coverage in such a careful way that there should be no disagreement about whether there has been a covered loss. Readers might think defining the covered loss would be an easy assignment, especially in the case of fire, because most people are familiar with the peril. We shall see, however, that even in the case of a peril as familiar as fire, defining the loss is not always easy.

Fire

Hostile fire

Friendly fire

Fire is not defined in insurance policies, perhaps because its meaning is well established by the courts. For a peril to qualify as a **fire**, there must be a clearly visible flame or glow and the fire must be hostile. A **hostile fire** is one that is unconfined and beyond its designated boundaries. A **friendly fire** is one deliberately ignited and remaining within desired boundaries. It makes no difference if a fire begins as friendly and subsequently becomes hostile or if it is hostile from the beginning. If an insured is to collect for a fire loss, the proximate cause must be a hostile fire.

Here are some useful examples of relevant issues. In each case, the pivotal point is the definition of fire:

- *Heater Malfunction*: Assume that the thermostat controlling a furnace malfunctions. The furnace continues heating the building's interior until there is significant damage. Would a fire insurance policy cover this claim? Unless additional perils were specified, such as malfunction of heating equipment, a policy covering only the fire peril would not cover this loss because the fire in the furnace is friendly.

- *Smoke Damage*: Assume that property sustains smoke damage because a fireplace damper is thoughtlessly left closed. A wood fire in a stone fireplace on a chilly Wisconsin evening is a beautiful sight. If it causes smoke damage because the damper is left closed when the fire is started, however, a policy specifying only the fire peril would not cover the loss because the fire is friendly and remained so despite the smoke damage.

As a third example, assume that a neighbor's leaf fire sends a burning leaf through an open window, causing fire and smoke damage to the home's interior. What began as a friendly fire became hostile, and subsequent damage would be covered. Furthermore, if water damage were sustained when the fire department extinguished the fire, the proximate cause of the water damage would be the hostile fire, and this damage also would be covered by a fire policy.

I include these examples to show you how important it is to define the insured peril precisely. Using English (or any other language) to achieve a specific contractual aim is not an easy task. Fortunately for most property owners, fire insurance usually is purchased in packages specifying other related perils, so the legal issues confronted historically by insureds purchasing only "fire" insurance should not be frequently encountered.

Reporting Forms

Many firms have wide swings in their inventory during the course of an operating cycle. For example, department stores build inventory before the Christmas season, and canning companies carry more stock after the harvest. To solve the insurance problems presented by variation in inventory values, insurers use reporting forms. With this coverage, a maximum amount of insurance is purchased and an initial premium set. Subsequently, the insured reports the actual amount of inventory held (on a weekly, monthly, or quarterly basis) and the premium is adjusted based on these reports. Students frequently ask what happens if the insured underreports the inventory to reduce the premium. Reporting forms require the insured to be scrupulously honest. If the insurer audits the insured's records (most likely after a loss), and if the insured's records do not support the amount of inventory claimed by the most recent report, the insured will collect only the proportion of the insured claim that the amount of inventory reported bore to the actual amount of inventory on hand. Thus, if only three-quarters of the actual inventory was reported, only three-quarters of the loss will be covered by insurance. This penalty clause presumably reduces the moral hazard.

Business Income (BI) Coverage

The Business Income Form of the CPP may be used to cover indirect losses. Determining the amount of coverage a business needs and explaining how the Business Income Form is filled out involve interesting accounting issues, but they are beyond the scope of this textbook. An Internet search on the keywords "business income insurance" will produce more information for readers needing technical details.[2]

Indirect losses   **Indirect losses** occur after insured physical damage. Insurers categorize these losses as follows:

1. *Loss of Income*: For example, if fire destroys a clothing store, the loss of the building and inventory is a direct loss. The income lost while the building is rebuilt and the business reestablished is an indirect loss.
2. *Continuing Expenses*: While a business is being reestablished, fixed expenses such as bond interest payments, property taxes, and salary for indispensable employees continue. Insurance that replaced only lost net income would not cover these expenses. Business income, as defined in this policy, includes **continuing expenses**.
3. *Extra Expenses*: For some businesses, such as television stations, bakeries, and banks, operations must be uninterrupted. These businesses will not suffer lost income after a direct loss because they will keep operating. They are likely to incur **extra expenses** to stay in operation, and business income insurance can cover these extra costs.
4. *Leasehold Interest*: This loss is calculated as the net present value of rent differential between the preloss and postloss rent paid by the insured, and it also would include any unamortized acquisition costs, improvements, or prepaid rent.

Continuing expenses

Extra expenses

The trigger for BI coverage is the necessary suspension of operations caused by direct physical loss of or damage to property at the premises described in the declarations. The policy covers the actual loss of business income consisting of net income and continuing normal operating expenses. The insurance covers the period beginning 72 hours after the loss and ending when the damaged property could be repaired with reasonable speed and similar quality. Insureds can also purchase an "Extended Period of Indemnity," which can result in an additional period of coverage in exchange for an additional premium.

Business Income from Dependent Properties

In some cases, a business suffers no direct physical damage, but its operations still may be halted because other businesses or the transportation system sustain physical loss. Consider the following examples:

- After the 1994 Northridge earthquake in California, several especially well constructed buildings survived, but because the interstate highways leading to them were destroyed, operations in these buildings still had to be suspended.

---

[2] This Web site describes in detail some of the issues associated with the business interruption claims following Hurricane Katrina: (*http://www.abanet.org/litigation/committee/insurance/katrina/businter_list.pdf/*).

- Consider the problem of tenants in a shopping mall if the lead department store in the mall has a fire. Traffic to the other occupants likely will decline even if they are undamaged.
- Several years ago, a fire at a telephone switching station in a Chicago suburb disrupted service for more than a month, causing business losses and extra expenses estimated to be in the millions of dollars.
- Assume that the New York Shirt Company buys all its buttons from the New Jersey Button Company. If a tornado destroys the button company, the shirt company also may shut down until it can find a new supplier of buttons that meet its specifications. Finally, if we reverse the previous example, we can see a situation where a manufacturer depends on one customer to purchase all its output. If the customer were to be destroyed by fire, the manufacturer likely would suffer significant income loss despite remaining physically intact. The **dependent properties** business income form can cover these contingencies.

Dependent properties

Additional Forms

Insurers use additional forms to provide commercial property insurance. For example, insurers use specific policies for commercial condominium owners, contractors, and businesses making substantial leasehold improvements. Describing these policies is beyond the scope of an introductory textbook, but an Internet search can provide more comprehensive information.

Property Insurance Rating

Rate

Premium

A property insurance **rate** is the cost per hundred dollars of exposed value. Insurers calculate the **premium** by multiplying the rate by the number of hundreds of dollars of value of exposed property. For example, assume that the property insurance rate is $0.80 per each $100 of value. A $16 million factory has 160,000 such units. Therefore, the premium will be 160,000 multiplied by $0.80, or $128,000.

Class rating

How was this $0.80 property insurance rate developed? Property insurers commonly use two different methods to produce rates: class rating and schedule rating. **Class rating** operates by placing comparable units into a group and then charging a class rate reflecting the expected loss experience and expenses of the group. This approach is especially useful with relatively homogeneous property, such as residential homes, small apartment buildings, or churches. Factors that influence a class rate include the following:

- Construction of the building (e.g., wood or brick frame).
- Occupancy (e.g., owner-occupied or not).
- Community firefighting capability. (Typically insurers use a 1-to-10 scale to grade a fire protection district. The grade reflects an evaluation of several factors including the equipment, personnel training, and water availability.)
- External surrounding exposures (e.g., are nearby structures especially flammable and in such proximity that fires will spread quickly to the insured property?).

Figure 18–2 illustrates some possible class rates reflecting these factors. Assume that an apartment owner with a wooden frame structure, in a medium-sized city with an average fire department, whose property was not closely surrounded by homes or businesses, wanted to purchase a property insurance policy. The agent or the home-office underwriter would look in a rate manual (most likely on a computer) until he or she finds the combination of factors that relates to this particular property. Assume that this combination produces a rate of $0.90. If the apartment owner has a $1 million

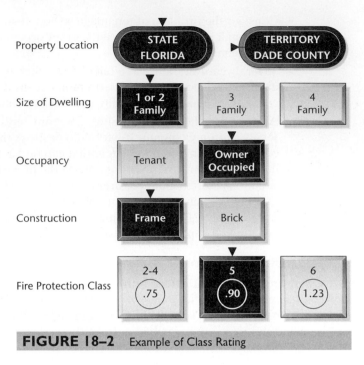

FIGURE 18–2   Example of Class Rating

structure and wants to insure its full value against property damage, it will cost $9,000 a year ($1,000,000/100 × $0.90 = $9,000).

Schedule rating

Schedule rating analyzes each property individually and is used primarily in rating commercial buildings. This procedure begins with a rate for a standard building (for example, $0.60 per each $100 of value) in the same city as the building under consideration. Next, charges (for more hazardous conditions) and credits (for less hazardous conditions) are combined, producing a rate for this specific building.

Examples of construction features that would produce schedule rating charges for a building are more flammable floors, walls, or roof than the standard building. Occupancy by a mattress factory, where there is the possibility of combustible dust, is an example of a use that would produce a charge. Credits would be granted for such features as a fire sprinkler system, fire doors, and smoke alarms. By giving careful consideration to the construction, use, and fire prevention devices of a particular building, a unique rate applicable to that building and use is developed. An example of a schedule rate is presented in Table 18–1.

TABLE 18–1	Illustration of Schedule Rating (Based on Universal Mercantile System)	
Base rate		$0.60
Charges		
Construction:		
Wooden floors	$0.10	
Deficient floor	$0.20	
Use		
Mattress factory	$0.20	
Total		$1.10
Credits		
Fire sprinkler (20% credit)		($0.22)
Rate		$0.88

This description of rate making might lead you to conclude that property insurance rating is scientific and precise. This conclusion is not quite right. Judgment still must be used in the schedule-rating approach to produce fair charges and credits. Class rating is fairly mechanical, but constant revision of class rates is called for as new loss patterns develop or as a community's firefighting ability improves. Competitive considerations often enter into the decisions as well. In general, insurance rates are based on shared loss data and estimates. While the mathematical estimating process is refined, insurance rates still involve actuarial and underwriting judgment and estimates.

TRANSPORTATION INSURANCE

Ocean Marine Insurance

History

Ocean marine insurance

Ocean marine insurance is one of the earliest forms of insurance. Commerce by ship was well established in the Mediterranean Sea before the year 2,000 B.C. The Babylonians, Phoenicians, Greeks, and Romans were great sea traders. Coincident with the development of this trade, insurance transactions emerged as distinct commercial agreements. *Bottomry* was a transaction that protected an owner from financial loss if his ship was destroyed. If the shipowner acquired the ship by means of a loan, an interest rate was paid to a moneylender. The moneylender, for a premium beyond the ordinary interest rate, would agree to forgive the loan if the ship was destroyed.

The bottomry loan was an early forerunner of ocean marine insurance. Recalling the elements of an ideally insurable exposure from Chapter 2, "Defining the Insurable Event," we can see that (1) similar units (ships) were exposed to similar perils; (2) nonaccidental, self-inflicted losses were presumably excluded from coverage; (3) losses were definite and measurable; and (4) catastrophes were not likely. We can see transfer and pooling in the bottomry loan, because the moneylender charged each shipowner a premium that presumably was sufficient to pay for the few loans that would have to be forgiven.

Nevertheless, some elements of the modern insurance transaction were missing. Actuarial science was not practiced, although the Phoenicians were noted mathematicians, so premiums were probably not based on mathematical estimates but on intuition. Today, judgmental estimates remain the basis of marine underwriting. The early sea traders and moneylenders also lacked a highly developed body of law like that providing the environment for the modern insurance transaction.

Respondentia loans were comparable to bottomry loans, but the difference lay in the subject of the loan. In the case of respondentia loans, the ship's cargo, rather than the ship itself, was the subject of the loan. Otherwise, the transaction was comparable. A merchant, placing cargo on a ship, would take out a loan using the cargo as collateral. The moneylender, for a premium in addition to the regular interest charged, agreed to forgive the loan if the cargo were lost. Again, as we will see shortly, modern ocean marine cargo insurance is very similar to the respondentia loan.

Today, as in historical times, ocean marine insurance is essential to international commerce. The worldwide shipping of petroleum products, manufactured goods, and agricultural products creates a great need for ocean marine insurance. Many people who never think about this insurance actually pay the premiums because they are included in the price of foreign petroleum, imported automobiles, and other imported products.

Ocean Marine Coverages

Hull, cargo, and freight losses

Liability loss

Four distinct types of loss exposures—**hull, cargo, and freight losses** and **liability loss**—are insured by ocean marine insurance polices, as follows:

- The *hull* exposure includes the value of the ship and its equipment. This coverage is comparable to the bottomry loan in that the insurer agrees to pay the shipowner if the ship is lost while the policy is in force.

- The *cargo* exposure is the value of the goods being shipped. This coverage is comparable to respondentia loans in that the shipper is compensated for losses suffered while the goods are being shipped.

- The loss of *freight* is the loss of income that the shipowner would have earned if the cargo (or passengers) had been delivered rather than lost. This coverage is comparable to the business income consequential loss coverage of property insurance.

- The *liability* loss exposure is the loss that a shipowner would suffer if the ship were held to be legally responsible for negligently injuring other people or their property.

Particular average

General average

Much ocean marine insurance terminology is quaint by today's standards, especially that used to describe losses. **Particular average** losses are those borne by the owners of the ship or cargo due to direct damage to their property. **General average** is the loss attributed to the owners of property where there was not necessarily a loss to their property, but other property was thrown overboard to save the ship and the loss was borne proportionately by all who had property exposed to loss during the voyage. For example, if Mr. Washington's $100,000 worth of gears and wheels were thrown overboard to save the ship during a storm, the loss would be shared by all those having an interest in the voyage. The shipowner and the others whose goods were not lost would (or their insurers would on their behalf) have to contribute a proportionate share of the loss. Ocean marine insurance policies may cover either particular or general average losses, as well as freight and liability losses.

The perils covered by an ocean marine insurance policy are quite broad. The traditional Lloyd's of London marine insurance policy includes the following:

> Touching the adventures and perils which we the assurers are contented to bear and take upon us in this voyage; they are of the seas, men of war, fire, enemies, pirates, rovers, thieves, jettisons, letters of mart and countermart, surprises, taking at sea, arrests, restraints, and detainments of all kings, princes, and people, of what nation, condition, or quality soever, barratry of the master and the mariners, and of all other perils, losses, and misfortunes, that have or shall come to the hurt, detriment, or damage of the said goods and merchandise, and ship, etc., or any part thereof.

This list of perils, many of which are less likely today than when the policy was first used at Lloyd's, is very broad, and for good reason. If the perils were specific and narrow, rather than "all other perils, losses, and misfortunes," it would be very hard to collect insurance coverage for losses because the peril that caused a loss is difficult or even impossible to establish when the ship is at the bottom of the ocean.

Even though the list of perils mentioned is comprehensive, current ocean marine policies do not cover all risks. Losses resulting from war or fraud generally are not covered. (War losses can be covered for an extra premium.) Nor will the insurance proceeds be paid if the conditions of the policy are breached by the insured.

Ocean Marine Insurance Rating

Unlike property insurance, ocean marine insurance rates mostly are based on the judgment of the underwriters. There are no rate manuals or schedules. Rather, an underwriter, such as one operating at Lloyd's of London or a U.S. insurer, will quote an applicant a rate based on a subjective estimate of the risk involved in the particular case. The following factors usually are considered:

- The seaworthiness of the ship
- The experience and ability of the captain and crew
- The potential for loss of the cargo—$1 million of glass crystal having more potential for loss than $1 million of sheet steel
- The scheduled route and the season of the year
- The coverage provided by the policy

Competition in the ocean marine insurance marketplace and the potential for war damage (if not excluded by the policy) also would be factors to consider in developing a final premium in ocean marine insurance. Some ocean marine policies are written to cover only one voyage, others cover a specific time period, and some are written on an open-ended basis and are good until canceled.

Inland Marine Insurance[3]

Inland marine insurance is less familiar to most readers than many other property insurance types. This section begins, therefore, with some historical background and a definition of this category of coverage. The diagram's purpose is to remind you that inland marine coverage is one component of the commercial package policy.

Commercial Package Insurance

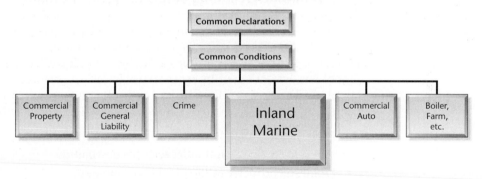

Inland marine insurance is written as an open-perils contract. This type of coverage provides insurance against "risks of direct physical loss," and then limits the coverage by specific exclusions. Open-perils contracts put the legal burden on the insurer to prove that an exclusion applies if it wants to deny a claim. War, nuclear hazard, wear and tear, and government action are among several exclusions that apply to inland marine insurance policies. The peril causing the largest amount of inland marine losses is theft.

---

[3] Web-based information about inland marine insurance can be found at the Web site of the Inland Marine Underwriting Association (IMUA; *http://www.imua.org/*). The IMUA describes itself as follows: "Founded in 1930, Inland Marine Underwriters Association (IMUA) is the national association for the inland marine insurance industry. IMUA serves as the voice of the inland marine industry, with more than 400 member companies representing over 90 percent of all inland marine insurers. The association provides its members with comprehensive training and educational programs, including research papers and bulletins, industry analysis, and seminars on current inland marine issues."

History

Inland marine insurance

Inland marine insurance is essentially an American distinction. Other countries have not separated the underwriting powers of insurers to the extent it is done in the United States. That is, in other countries, if an insurer (underwriter) wants to write property insurance, marine insurance, or perhaps even life insurance, it is a private decision, and the insurer may proceed unconstrained by law. In the United States, however, there was an early tradition of allowing fire insurers to write fire insurance exclusively and marine insurers to write marine coverage exclusively. This separation of underwriting power led to a separation of inland from ocean marine insurance. In the United States, the distinction between the two marine branches remains.

After the Industrial Revolution began in the 19th century, commerce moved progressively inland. Canal barges, railroads, and trucks became the vehicles of commerce. At first, the warehouse-to-warehouse approach of the ocean marine policy appeared adequate to meet the needs of insureds and insurers. Over time, however, the differences in the perils, salvage potential, and loss investigation potential led to the development of inland marine as a separate branch of marine insurance.

The distinction between fire and inland marine insurance is not as clear as that between fire and ocean marine insurance. In the early 20th century, jurisdictional questions led to considerable controversy between fire and inland marine insurers. The rather mechanical rating approach of the fire insurers was in sharp contrast to the judgmental rating approach of the inland marine insurers. The latter had much more flexibility in providing coverage and determining premiums. The fire insurers did not like losing business to the inland marine insurers. The inventory of chain stores is an example of the type of property that was subject to jurisdictional dispute.

Nationwide Definition of Inland Marine Insurance

Nationwide definition

The 1933 **Nationwide Definition** of marine insurance was developed to settle the dispute between the fire and the inland marine insurers. (For the purpose of historical accuracy, the first title was the "Nationwide Definition and Interpretation of the Insuring Powers of Marine and Transportation Underwriters.") This definition, in the form of a model law, was adopted by most states. In 1953, a second nationwide definition was adopted. This second definition, currently effective in a majority of states, provides for five types of property to be the proper subject of inland marine insurance:

- Property designated for export
- Imported property until it reaches its destination
- Domestic property in the process of shipment
- Property used to facilitate (instrumentalities of) transportation, such as bridges, tunnels, pipelines, and electrical transmission towers
- Personal property that is moved easily and is typically of significant value, such as jewelry, furs, and cameras

The states have made further modifications of the Nationwide Definition to broaden the earlier definitions, especially to include computers.

The Importance of Inland Marine Insurance

It is very difficult to think of any other type of insurance coverage that is less well known or understood by the general public than inland marine insurance. This lack of recognition cannot be attributed to the subject's lack of importance. On the contrary, inland marine insurance is one of our most important types of insurance.

Can you think of any of your property that has not been the subject of inland marine insurance? Consider your blue jeans. Presumably they are made of blue cotton denim. The cotton bales, frequently transported from location to location, were the subject of inland marine insurance. The processed cotton was probably subject to *cotton buyers' transit insurance*, a special type of inland marine coverage. The finished jeans, when shipped from manufacturer to wholesaler or directly to a chain or department store, most likely were covered by an *annual transit policy*. This very basic and important type of inland marine policy insures incoming or outgoing merchandise against most losses. The *department store transit policy* is used to provide coverage when merchandise is shipped within one company from location to location. As you can see, your blue jeans probably were the subject of not one but several different types of inland marine insurance before you bought them. The same reasoning will reveal that most of the property we own was likewise the subject of inland marine insurance because almost everything we own has been transported on a truck or train several times before its purchase.

Here are some interesting data that demonstrate the importance of inland marine insurance:[4]

- In one recent year, 13.2 billion tons of freight were moved within the United States. Sixty percent of this total was moved by trucks.
- In this year, trucks traveled about 215 million miles, an increase of 60 percent in a decade.
- Trucking companies report that their insurance premiums account for about 3 percent of their operating expenses.
- Federal law requires trucks carrying goods over state lines to have at least $750,000 in liability insurance and $5,000 in cargo insurance.

Additional Inland Marine Coverages

In addition to the various types of transportation insurance, inland marine insurance policies include bailees' customers' policies, instrumentalities of transportation policies, and personal and commercial property floaters.

Bailment

Bailment   In a **bailment**, property belonging to one party (the bailor) is temporarily in the possession of a second party (the bailee), but ultimate possession is to return to the first party. This very common arrangement describes such situations as parking a car in a public garage, leaving clothes at a dry cleaner, shipping goods on a truck, or lending a lawnmower to a neighbor. Although not owning the property in temporary possession, the bailee is legally responsible for its safe return to the bailor. Even if not legally responsible, the bailee may feel morally responsible and not wish to jeopardize public goodwill. Because of these obligations, the bailee often insures the bailed property while it is in its possession. A **bailees' customers' insurance policy** (such as those purchased by dry cleaners or furriers) will pay the bailee if the property is lost, not returned, or damaged. After a loss of customer property, the insurer pays the bailee's (cleaner's) claim, then the bailee will reimburse the bailor (customer) to be relieved of legal liability or moral obligation for the damaged property.

Bailees' customers' insurance policy

Annual transit policy

Shipping Cargo on Common Carriers   The **annual transit policy** protects the interest of the shipper (bailor). The **motor truck cargo insurance** (a form of bailee's liability coverage) protects the interest of the trucking company. For example, if a loss occurs

Motor truck cargo insurance

---

[4] These data and other interesting information can be found at the Web site of the Federal Highway Administration (*http://www.fihwa.dot.gov/*).

while merchandise is being transported by truck, the insured shipper will usually look to its own inland marine insurer for payment. After payment, the shipper's insurer will then seek payment from the motor carrier, which in turn will look to its own inland marine insurer for payment of the loss.

The following example outlines this relationship:

---

1. The Blue Jeans Company places $1 million worth of jeans on a truck.
2. While aboard the truck, the cargo is destroyed because of the trucker's negligence.
3. The Blue Jeans Company looks to its own insurer for payment for the $1 million loss.
4. The insurer pays the Blue Jeans Company under its annual transit inland marine policy.
5. The insurer is subrogated (substituted) to the Blue Jeans Company's right to sue the trucker.
6. The trucker's insurer pays the Blue Jeans Company's insurer on behalf of the trucker because this loss is covered by the trucker's motor cargo insurance policy.

Readers may ask why the shipper needs transit insurance, because payment for losses could presumably be sought from the motor carrier that caused the damage. The annual transit policy serves several purposes. Getting payment from the trucker may be slow and involve legal complications. For example, questions of facts surrounding the loss might have to be litigated. Also, the trucker might go bankrupt after the loss. Or the loss might have been due to an "act of God" (an unfortunate phrase describing such things as tornadoes, floods, and other natural calamities) for which the trucker was not legally responsible and hence would not have to pay. For all these reasons, it is simpler for the shipper to purchase an independent policy for the goods, collect payment from the insurer if a loss occurs, and allow the insurer to try to collect from the trucking company through a legal doctrine known as *subrogation*.

Because the shipper's insurer often will succeed in recovering from truckers (or their insurers), transit insurance is less costly than would otherwise be the case. The relatively low price is another argument for the shipper to purchase a transit insurance policy.

Instrumentalities of transportation

Property Used in Transportation and Communication **Instrumentalities of transportation** may cover a variety of different structures, including bridges, tunnels, piers, pipelines, wharves, dams, and traffic signals. Also covered by inland marine policies, because they are in many respects similar to the foregoing, are television and radio transmission towers and electrical power transmission towers. The inland marine coverage on this property is generally broader (open perils) than is that provided by property insurance.

Floater policies

Personal articles floater

Blanket floaters

Scheduled floaters

Floater Policies Inland marine insurance **floater policies** cover property that is easily and frequently moved and is generally of high value. The two basic types of floaters are personal and commercial. One type of personal floater, the **personal articles floater**, covers valuable assets such as cameras, jewelry, furs, guns, stamp and coin collections, and silverware. **Blanket floaters** are used when the property as a whole is valuable (e.g., silverware), but no one item is of outstanding value. **Scheduled floaters** can cover items of significant individual value, such as medical equipment, salesperson's samples, livestock, fine art, and other valuable commercial property that may be transported easily.

AVIATION INSURANCE[5]

Aircraft owners and operators, airport operators, and companies that build and supply parts for aircraft (including their navigation equipment) purchase aviation insurance. Not all firms build, own, or operate aircraft, but a significant number of organizations do. The term *aircraft* as used in insurance is quite broad. In addition to airplanes, private and commercial, the term also applies to helicopters, hot air balloons, hang gliders, and space satellites.

Aircraft hull policy

Open-perils coverage

Aircraft owners purchase both property insurance to protect against loss caused by physical damage to the plane and liability insurance to protect against lawsuits. Insurers call the airplane itself, including its electronic equipment, a *hull*. An **aircraft hull policy** provides protection, either for damage caused by specified perils or on an open-perils basis. Remember that **open-perils coverage** does not mean that all losses will be covered. It means that, unless otherwise excluded, all losses will be covered. Typically excluded would be losses due to war or wear and tear. On the other hand, the loss of a plane that simply vanishes (perhaps over the ocean or in Alaska) would be covered by an open-perils policy. The core insurance problem that faces aviation insurers is that the small number of exposure units weakens the application of the law of large numbers, while any single exposure unit is capable of causing a catastrophic loss.

The cost of aircraft insurance is a function of the perils covered. For example, open-perils coverage is more expensive than specified-perils coverage, while ground and flight coverage is more expensive than a not-in-motion policy. The latter coverage would provide property loss damage coverage but not liability coverage. Commercial airlines pay more for liability coverage because their planes generally are in the air more than private planes and represent a significantly greater exposure to loss because of the number of people onboard a commercial aircraft. On the other hand, light planes are more susceptible to damage or theft while on the ground, which raises the rate for their property coverage. Another important factor that insurers consider when setting rates for a particular exposure is the health, experience, and training of the airplane's pilot(s).

AUTOMOBILE PROPERTY INSURANCE

Figure 18–3 summarizes the types of damage caused by automobile accidents. In this section, we briefly describe the automobile *property* loss exposure. Chapter 19, "Commercial Liability Insurance," describes automobile *liability* insurance.

Almost all business organizations own, operate, or authorize the use of vehicles. Thus, every comprehensive risk management plan must consider potential losses caused or sustained by business vehicles. In many cases, large firms will self-insure vehicle property damage. However, they generally insure some or all of the liability exposure associated with vehicles. Businesses wanting to insure their vehicle exposure can add the commercial auto component to their CPP.

Business Automobile Insurance

The commercial auto component of the CPP provides both liability and property coverage. Special forms are available to firms in the automobile business. Business automobiles are classified in nine different categories, including owned and nonowned vehicles, private passenger cars, and other-than-private passenger autos.

---

[5] Entering the keywords "commercial aviation" and "aviation insurance" into an Internet search engine produces current information on this topic.

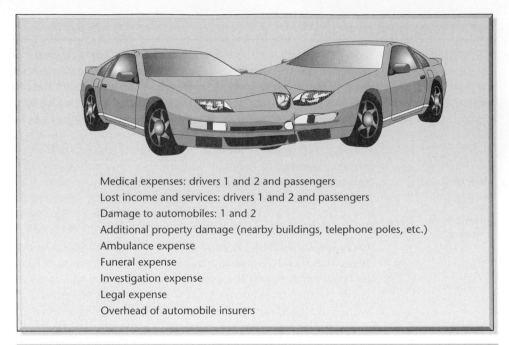

Medical expenses: drivers 1 and 2 and passengers
Lost income and services: drivers 1 and 2 and passengers
Damage to automobiles: 1 and 2
Additional property damage (nearby buildings, telephone poles, etc.)
Ambulance expense
Funeral expense
Investigation expense
Legal expense
Overhead of automobile insurers

FIGURE 18–3   Damage Caused by Automobile Accidents

Commercial Package Insurance

```
                    Common Declarations

                    Common Conditions

Commercial   Commercial   Crime   Inland   Commercial   Boiler,
Property     General               Marine   Auto         Farm,
             Liability                                    etc.
```

The Cause of the Loss

When providing physical damage coverage, insurers make an important distinction based on the cause of the loss. A loss is caused by collision or it is not. Thus, the definition of the term *collision* in automobile insurance takes on similar importance to the definition of the term *fire* in the property insurance policy.

To get a complete program of automobile property insurance, a business must purchase collision coverage, in which the insurer agrees to pay "for loss caused by collision," and a second part, sometimes referred to as comprehensive coverage, in which the insurer agrees to pay "for loss caused other than by collision." Each of these coverages may be purchased separately (if state law permits), but in so doing a consumer may unknowingly create a serious gap in automobile property insurance protection.

Collision   **Collision** means collision (striking) of an automobile with another object (a car, a tree, or even standing water). The word *object* has a quite broad meaning in this context, and it includes almost anything that can be seen or felt. Losses clearly not caused by collision include theft, vandalism, fire, and windstorm. As might be expected, gray areas exist. If a car is stolen and the thief has a collision, is the loss caused by theft or collision? If a car in Miami, Florida, is under a coconut tree during a storm and a coconut falls and breaks the windshield, was the loss caused by collision? If a car hits a pheasant, causing the bird to disintegrate on the windshield and in turn causing the driver to leave the road and hit a tree, was the loss due to collision (car hits bird or car hits tree)? ISO automobile policy forms deal with this issue with the following wording:

> For the purpose of this coverage, breakage of glass and loss caused by missile, falling objects, fire, theft or larceny, explosion, earthquake, windstorm, hail, water, flood, malicious mischief or vandalism, riot or civil commotion, or colliding with a bird or animal shall not be deemed to be loss caused by collision.

You might wonder why it makes a difference if a loss is a collision or not. Frequently, different loss settlement provisions, such as the dollar amount deducted from the loss before the insurer must pay, make this distinction important. The distinction also would be important if one or the other but not both coverages were purchased.

SUMMARY

Commercial property insurance is provided as one part of a seven-part commercial property package (CPP). Property coverage falls into three categories: buildings, personal business property, and property of others. Fire and ten other perils are specified causes of loss in the basic form. Coverage that is more extensive is available in the broad and special forms.

Fire insurance has an interesting history in the United States, starting with the fire marks of the Ben Franklin era. For more than 30 years, the 1943 New York Standard Fire Insurance Policy provided the backbone of U.S. fire insurance contracts. The term *fire* is defined as a chemical reaction producing heat and a flame or glow. Hostile fires are those that burn beyond designated boundaries.

Indirect loss coverage is available for income lost and extra expenses following a direct loss. Income lost because of direct losses at dependent properties also can be insured. Reporting forms are used in cases of widely varying inventory values.

Property insurance rates usually are determined on a schedule or a class-rating basis. Scheduled rating requires comparing property to a standard exposure and increasing or decreasing the premium for desirable or undesirable features. Class rating involves placing property in a class with similarly situated exposures.

Transportation insurance generally covers mobile property. Ocean marine insurance provides very broad peril coverage if the loss is to the ship (hull), cargo, or freight (the carrier's earnings for transporting cargo), or if it is a liability claim. Inland marine coverage also is used for instrumentalities of transportation and small and expensive personal property, such as furs and jewelry.

Aircraft property insurance protects airplane (and other aircraft) owners from loss of their property (aircraft hull). The coverage may be for all risks (with some perils, such as wear and tear, excluded) or the coverage may protect only if specifically named perils cause the loss.

Automobile property insurance protects car owners against loss to their property. A key factor in providing this coverage is the definition of *collision*.

REVIEW TERMS

- 1943 New York Standard Fire Insurance Policy
- Aircraft hull policy
- Annual transit policy
- Bailment
- Blanket floaters
- Building and personal property coverage form
- Business personal property
- Causes-of-loss form
- Class rating
- Collision
- Commercial insurance
- Commercial package policy (CPP)
- Conditions
- Continuing expenses

- Declarations
- Dependent properties
- Extra expenses
- Fire
- Fire marks
- Floater policies
- Friendly fire
- General average
- Hostile fire
- Hull, cargo, and freight losses
- Indirect losses
- Inland marine insurance
- Instrumentalities of transportation
- Insurance Services Office (ISO)
- Intangible property

- Liability loss
- Motor truck cargo insurance
- Nationwide Definition
- Ocean marine insurance
- Open-perils coverage
- Particular average
- Personal articles floater
- Personal insurance
- Personal property
- Premium
- Rate
- Real property
- Schedule rating
- Scheduled floaters
- Tangible property

REVIEW

1. What is the difference between real and personal property? Why is this difference important in insurance underwriting and pricing (rating)?
2. Briefly explain the format and content of the ISO CPP.
3. Identify several different types of organizations that might purchase a CPP.
4. What role does the ISO play in the commercial property insurance market? Does it set rates for insurance companies?
5. Why do insurers insist on exact identification of an insured's covered property?
6. Identify some property that is excluded from coverage under the building and personal property coverage form.
7. What is business personal property?
8. Distinguish a friendly fire from a hostile fire.
9. List the 11 perils covered in the basic cause-of-loss form.
10. Explain the difference between extra expenses and continuing expenses in business income coverage.
11. Give some examples of a need for coverage of business income from dependent properties.
12. What is a reporting form, and what purpose does it serve?

13. Describe schedule and class ratings.
14. Describe the loss exposures insured by hull, cargo, and freight policies in ocean marine insurance.
15. Why is ocean marine coverage so broad in scope? What are the limits on ocean marine coverage with respect to losses not covered?
16. Identify some items in your possession that have been covered by inland marine insurance at some point in time. Identify some items that have not been insured by inland marine insurance.
17. What factors are considered when insurers develop a rate for an ocean marine exposure?
18. What is the Nationwide Definition?
19. What kinds of property are covered by floater policies?
20. What is a bailment? Describe three bailments in which you have been involved.
21. Describe the difference between the annual transit policy and the motor truck cargo policy.
22. What is the difference between blanket and scheduled floaters?
23. Define the term *collision*.

OBJECTIVE QUESTIONS

1. The basic form of business property coverage provides protection against all the following perils except:
   a. Lightning
   b. Smoke
   c. Theft of currency
   d. Vandalism

2. If a business has large differences in the value of the inventory it has on hand during the year, the cost of its insurance requires the _____ form of insurance policy.
   a. Reporting
   b. Variation

c. Inventory cycle
d. Double reduction
3. Choose the true statement.
    a. Ocean marine insurance is a relatively new form of coverage appearing slightly more than 100 years ago.
    b. Ocean and inland marine insurance cover about the same losses and are used for about the same purposes.
    c. Inland marine insurance is found mostly in Europe.
    d. Inland marine insurance is used mostly in the United States.
4. Floater policies:
    a. Cover property usually associated with ships
    b. Cover all property that moves on water
    c. Cover property that is easily and frequently moved
    d. Cover property only when it moves within a warehouse
5. Property that is permanently attached to land, such as buildings, is called:
    a. Real property
    b. Permanent property

c. Intangible property
d. Collective property
6. A hostile fire is defined as one that:
    a. Causes a loss
    b. Was set deliberately
    c. Is unconfined and beyond designated boundaries
    d. Is without a known cause or origin
7. Categories of indirect losses include all the following except:
    a. Loss of income
    b. Advertising
    c. Extra expenses
    d. Continuing expenses
8. A property insurance _____ is the cost per each $100 of exposed value.
    a. Premium
    b. Charge
    c. Fund
    d. Rate

DISCUSSION QUESTIONS

1. Why do you think so many expensive fires occur each year in the United States despite technology to prevent or reduce fire loss? Prepare a report on several large fire losses that occurred in the past few years.
2. Why do you think so much economic damage continues to be caused by automobiles each year? Prepare a report on damage caused by or sustained by commercial vehicles.
3. Do you think most small manufacturers adequately cover losses from dependent properties in their risk management plans? Explain your answer by developing a case study for a hypothetical mail-order clothing company.

INTERNET RESEARCH ASSIGNMENTS

1. "Once the ISO evaluates a community's building codes and establishes a classification, how often can the classification change?" Start your search at this site: (*http://www.iso.com/*).
2. How many civilians were killed or injured by fire in the most recent year for which data are available at this site: (*http://www.usfa.fema.gov/statistics/*)?
3. Perform an Internet search to identify the names of some specific inland marine insurance contracts.
4. For an interesting view of early fire insurance and firefighting, perform an Internet search for the history of fire marks and the history of firefighting. Do collectors trade fire marks on the Internet, and if so, how and where?

CHAPTER 19

Commercial Liability Insurance

After studying this chapter, you should be able to:

■ Explain the function of liability insurance

■ Explain how organizations insure their general liability exposures

■ Describe the umbrella liability policy and explain its function in a risk management program

■ Describe the difference between claims-made and occurrence-based liability insurance policies

■ Explain the role of insurance in transferring costs arising from environmental damage

■ Identify who benefits from products liability insurance and who pays the cost

■ Describe professional liability insurance and identify who needs to purchase it

■ Discuss some possible solutions to problems caused by the errors of health care practitioners

■ Identify some of the sources of liability employers face in their personnel management activities

■ Explain the purposes of the Americans with Disabilities Act (ADA)

■ Explain how nuclear liability insurance is provided

I n Chapter 18, "Commercial Property Insurance," we explained how risk managers could insure their firms' exposure to property losses. In this chapter, we examine insurance arrangements made to compensate businesses if they are sued.

While all organizations and individuals face loss caused by their general liability exposure, many risk managers report spending a great deal of time dealing with special liability exposures, including the following five specialized areas:

Environmental impairment liability (EIL)

Products liability

Professional liability

Employment practices liability

Nuclear liability

- **Environmental impairment liability (EIL)** describes a class of legal claims against individuals and organizations whose actions damage the environment.
- **Products liability**, sometimes called *product liability*, arises when a manufactured item injures a consumer.
- **Professional liability**, sometimes called *malpractice liability* or *errors and omissions coverage*, is caused by errors committed by professionals.
- **Employment practices liability** arises from injuries arising out of the hiring, supervising, and terminating of employees.
- **Nuclear liability** arises from damage caused by nuclear radiation.

BUSINESS GENERAL LIABILITY INSURANCE

Given the wide scope of most business activities and the ever-fertile imaginations of plaintiffs and their attorneys, the possibility of a business being sued is great. Many businesses and other organizations will insure their exposure to general liability lawsuits using the commercial package policy we began to discuss in Chapter 18. The following logo shows that liability coverage is an integral part of this package.

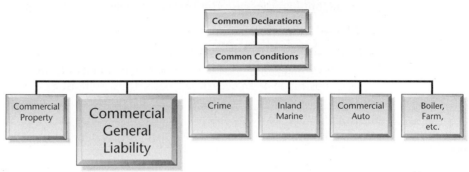

Commercial Package Insurance

Exposures

We can categorize business general liability exposures as follows:

- Direct liability
- Vicarious liability
- Contractual liability

Direct Liability

Direct liability

Direct liability arises out of a firm's own actions. Most of these exposures, except damage done by vehicles, fall into the following three subcategories:

- *Premises and Operations.* Many lawsuits result from the ownership, use, and maintenance of business buildings and grounds. For example, assume that an employee neglects to clean an oil spill from a floor, resulting in a patron's slipping and being injured. The patron then sues the firm, alleging the injury resulted from the firm's negligence. Other examples might involve an elevator accident that injures a shopper or an attack on a shopper in a poorly lit parking lot.
- *Products Liability.* Many lawsuits allege that a firm's products caused injuries to users.
- *Completed Operations.* Many service firms, including contractors, plumbers, and insect exterminators, are sued when plaintiffs claim that their work was improperly done or left undone, resulting in an injury. Note that these losses generally occur away from the firm's premises, so specific coverage is needed for this exposure.

Vicarious Liability

Vicarious liability

Vicarious liability, also called *indirect liability*, most often arises when a firm hires an independent subcontractor. If the independent subcontractor injures a third party, the firm that hired the contractor may find itself named in the lawsuit along with the independent contractor. The plaintiff would claim that the firm was negligent in hiring, informing, or supervising the contractor.

Contractual Liability

Contractual liability occurs if a firm accepts by contract a liability that it otherwise would not have. For example, to get the Rockenroll Railroad to build a track to its warehouse, the Big Tree Lumber Mill agrees to sign a **hold-harmless agreement**. This agreement relieves Rockenroll of liability arising from the use of the tracks on Big Tree's property and places the liability for accidents on the tracks with Big Tree. In this example, Big Tree needs liability insurance for the exposure that it assumed from Rockenroll. If a Rockenroll train engineer negligently destroys a truck or injures somebody on Big Tree's property, then the injured party may sue either Big Tree or the Rockenroll railroad, but in either case Big Tree (or its insurer) will satisfy the legal judgment.

Contractual liability

Hold-harmless agreement

CLAIMS-MADE AND OCCURRENCE POLICIES

Insurers make an important distinction in liability insurance between policies written on a claims-made or an occurrence basis. Thus, we must examine this important distinction.

Claims-Made Policies

Claims-made basis

If a policy is written on a **claims-made basis**, the insurer will be liable to provide coverage only if the following two conditions are met:

1. The claim arises from a covered event that occurs after the beginning date (or a retroactive date if retroactive coverage is purchased) and before the end of the policy period.
2. The claim is made between the policy's beginning date and its expiration date.

Retroactive date

Policy period

Tail period

Extended reporting period

The policy's *beginning date* will be the first day the coverage is in force after the purchase. The policy *coverage period* may start at an earlier time, called the *retroactive date*. The **retroactive date** is a date preceding the beginning date that is mutually agreed upon and for which coverage is provided for an additional premium. For example, a policy might be acquired and have a beginning date of January 1, 2006, while the retroactive date might be January 1, 2002. A two-year policy period would end two years after the beginning date (that is, on December 31, 2008). Therefore, the **policy period** is January 1, 2006 until December 31, 2008. The period in which claims may be reported can be extended by the purchase of tail coverage. The **tail period**, which insurers also call the **extended reporting period**, extends the time during which a claim may be filed for a loss that occurs during the policy period. For example, assume that tail coverage is purchased for three years, making the expiration date of the policy December 31, 2011. The tail coverage will provide insurance for losses occurring after the retroactive date but before December 31, 2008, and reported between December 31, 2006, and December 31, 2011. Both the retroactive date (the earliest date for a covered occurrence) and the tail period (the ending date of the reporting period) are subject to negotiation between the insurer and insured. Figure 19–1 presents this complicated terminology graphically.

As an example, assume that Leaky Louis, the plumber, installs a gas water heater during September 2005. On January 1, 2006, he purchases a one-year claims-made liability insurance policy with a retroactive date of June 1, 2005. The one-year policy ends on January 1, 2007, and has no tail coverage. On February 1, 2006, the water heater that Louis installed explodes, destroying the house and killing a cat. Leaky Louis is sued within an hour of the explosion for $1 million, half of which represented emotional damages from the cat's death. In August 2008, a jury awards the victim $1 million. Because the occurrence took place after the retroactive date and the claim was filed during the policy coverage period, the insurer is obligated to defend the suit and pay the judgment. The award of the judgment after the policy period expired does not affect the insurer's liability in this case.

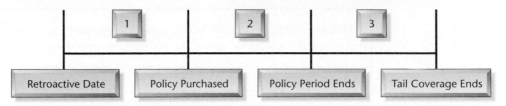

1. If a loss occurs between the retroactive date and the beginning date, **and** is first reported during the policy period, there is coverage.
2. If a loss occurs and is reported during the policy period, there is coverage.
3. If a loss occurs after the retroactive date and before the policy period ends, and is reported during the tail period, there is coverage. There is no coverage for losses occurring during the tail period.

FIGURE 19–1   Claimes-Made Policy Terminology

Occurrence-Based Policies

Occurrence-based liability policy

If a policy is written as an **occurrence-based liability policy**, the insurer is liable to make payment if its policy was in force when the negligence occurred. For example, assume that Dr. Pasteur delivered a baby, Napoleon, in 2004. At the time, he was insured on an occurrence basis by the French Insurance Company. In 2007, Napoleon's family sues Dr. Pasteur, alleging that negligence during the delivery caused Napoleon to have a pointed head and diminished mental capacities. Assume further that in 2007, Dr. Pasteur no longer is insured by the French Insurance Company because he retired. Nevertheless, the French Insurance Company must defend the doctor against the claim and pay any adverse judgment because the injury occurred during the period in which the French Insurance Company provided coverage. Because it was written on an occurrence basis, the French Insurance Company's liability is open-ended. This indefinitely long liability exposure is spoken of as the "long tail of claims."

As a second example, again assume that in 2007, Dr. Pasteur is sued by Napoleon's family for the 2004 injury and that he had not purchased medical malpractice liability insurance before 2004. In 2007, even though he retired, he purchased three years of professional liability tail coverage from the Austrian Insurance Company on a *claims-made* basis. The tail coverage would end in 2010. Assume that this policy had a 2005 retroactive date. In this instance, because the alleged injury occurred before the retroactive date, there would be no coverage for the 2004 injury claim. However, if Dr. Pasteur's alleged negligence caused an injury after 2005 that was reported between 2007 and 2010, the tail coverage policy would be available to pay a successful lawsuit.

Next, assume that the Austrian Insurance Company's liability insurance coverage had a retroactive date of January 1, 1999, and a termination date of December 31, 2003. Because it is responsible only for claims made while the policy is in force, after 2003, the Austrian Insurance Company is not responsible for a 2004 (or later) claim against Dr. Pasteur.

One reason for describing this legally important but complex terminology is to alert the reader to the essential work of the risk manager in arranging liability insurance coverage carefully. Likewise, the insurance company must underwrite and price liability insurance carefully based on clearly understood contractual language.

COMPREHENSIVE GENERAL LIABILITY (CGL) POLICY CONTRACT

Comprehensive general liability (CGL)

Claims-made form

The current Insurance Services Office (ISO) **comprehensive general liability (CGL)** policies have two formats: (1) an occurrence form and (2) a claims-made form. The **claims-made form** obligates the insurer to pay only for claims first made against the insured during the policy period and arising from incidents occurring after the retroactive date stated on the policy. The policy states:

> This insurance applies to bodily injury or property damage only if the injury or damage did not occur before the retroactive date, if any, shown in the declarations.

Claims-made forms allow the insurer to close the book on the business after the policy period has expired and also relieve the insurer of responsibility for injuries sustained before the retroactive date.

The CGL has the following five sections:

Section 1. In Section 1, Coverage A, the insurer agrees to cover claims alleging accidental bodily injury or property damage. The insurer agrees to provide a legal defense for the insured, and the cost of the defense does not reduce the amount available for paying covered losses. If a business loses an $850,000 judgment and the defense costs $150,000, the insurer bears the full $1 million cost even though the coverage limit of the policy was $850,000. The CGL contains a general aggregate limit of insurance that puts a cap on the amount that a policy can pay on behalf of the insured. Under previous versions of the CGL, a loss payment did not reduce the amount of coverage available for future occurrences. Under the current CGL, each loss payment under Coverages A, B, or C reduces the amount available to pay future claims. For example, assume that an insured has an aggregate limit of $500,000. If three $250,000 losses occur, the insurer will pay for only the first two, for a total of $500,000. After the second $250,000 payment, the aggregate limit of coverage is exhausted. This example provides a good argument for buying high limits of liability coverage.

Each of the fourteen exclusions found in Section 1, Coverage A are important.

Exclusions

Exclusions state that the insurer does not pay for losses arising from intentional acts, workers' compensation claims, pollution and cleanup costs, or damage to the insured's own products. (A liability policy generally does not cover losses to an insured's property; property insurance provides this coverage.) Also not covered are claims arising from contractual liability, liquor liability, and accidents involving aircraft, automobiles, or watercraft.

Section 1, Coverage B, protects the firm if the plaintiff alleges personal or advertising injury. Included in this category of torts are false arrest or imprisonment, libel or slander, copyright infringement, and invasion of privacy.

Section 1, Coverage C, provides medical payments to injured plaintiffs (who are not "insureds" under the policy) regardless of the insured's legal liability. This coverage allows the insured business to provide first aid to injured people before questions of fault are litigated. The injury must be the result of an accident, which means the injury was neither expected nor intended by the insured.

Section 2. Section 2 of the CGL specifies whom the policy covers. Possibilities include owners of proprietorships, partners, and officers and directors of corporations. The policy also covers employees acting within the scope of their employment.

Section 3. Section 3 of the CGL limits the insurer's liability after a loss. The policy has overall (aggregate) limits and sublimits. The risk manager will determine these limits before the policy is purchased. Of course, the greater the coverage purchased, the higher the premium.

Section 4. Section 4 of the CGL presents the policy conditions and explains such things as what the insured must do if it is sued or if it decides to cancel the policy.

Section 5. Section 5 is the policy's glossary. Here the policy provides definitions of terms that appear throughout the policy.

BUSINESS LIABILITY UMBRELLA POLICIES

Umbrella policy

Excess liability insurance

As the risk manager contemplates worst-case possibilities, surely the possibility of being sued successfully for an amount in excess of available policy limits must be considered. To deal with this possibility, a commercial **umbrella policy** can be purchased to provide coverage after underlying liability policies have been exhausted.[1] In this case, the umbrella policy is called **excess liability insurance** because the umbrella policy pays only for losses in excess of the underlying limits. For example, assume the Green Bean Factory is held responsible for injuring William M. Rice, a visiting salesperson. The jury returns a $10 million verdict in favor of Mr. Rice. Green Bean's CGL Coverage A limit is $1 million for such bodily injuries. If Green Bean has a $10 million liability umbrella, it would pay $9 million of the award (the excess of the award over the underlying coverage), which, along with the CGL coverage of $1 million, would compensate Mr. Rice fully.

The commercial umbrella policy also may cover some exposures left uncovered by underlying policies if the insured absorbs the first dollars of such a loss. Typically, the insured's retention limits must be at least $10,000 (and often a larger amount) for cases when the umbrella policy is providing the initial coverage rather than an underlying liability insurance policy. In all cases, umbrella policies require the insured to maintain minimum amounts of underlying liability insurance coverage. Naturally, the insurer providing the umbrella coverage realizes its loss potential is less when the insured has more underlying liability coverage.

AUTOMOBILE LIABILITY INSURANCE

Americans annually do an alarming amount of economic damage with their automobiles. They injure each other and damage property amounting to billions of dollars each year. Compensation for the damage done to others comes through the tort liability system, except in no-fault jurisdictions. Most people rely on a personal automobile insurance policy, which was described in Chapter 11, "The Personal Auto Policy," to protect them against being sued because of an automobile accident.

Commercial Automobile Insurance

Business auto coverage form

Risk managers of most businesses need to consider the liability loss potential presented by the ownership, maintenance, or use of vehicles. As we stated in Chapter 18, in many cases, large firms will self-insure vehicle property damage. They almost always will seek to insure some of or all the vehicle liability exposure. Firms wanting to insure their vehicle exposure can add the **business auto coverage form** to their commercial property package.

The business auto coverage form can be used by most firms, except those engaged in the automobile business. This latter group includes garages, repair shops, and car dealerships. These firms must use a special *garage coverage form*. The business auto coverage form provides liability coverage for insureds who face claims arising from an automobile accident. Like the CGL, the insurer agrees to pay to defend the insured and such legal defense costs do not reduce the amounts available to satisfy judgments. Many of this policy's provisions are comparable to those found in the Personal Auto Policy (PAP) discussed in Chapter 11.

---

[1] The umbrella coverage also can be exhausted. However, risk managers generally select a high umbrella policy limit so that there is a low probability of a loss greater than the policy limit.

ENVIRONMENTAL IMPAIRMENT LIABILITY (EIL)

Pollution

Environmental impairment liability (EIL)

Pollution is a word that Americans read or hear frequently. The term implies destruction of the environment by the introduction of toxic substances, heat, or noise. Attorneys identify the legal liability arising from such acts as **environmental impairment liability (EIL)**. No event better marks our national concern with pollution and its effects than the publication of the book *Silent Spring* by Rachel Carson in 1962. Since that date, we have recognized that past and present industrial practices have resulted and continue to result in serious environmental damage.

Industrial processes have affected air, water, and land adversely. Everything from the ozone in the upper atmosphere to the water in the deepest ocean depths has been exposed to impurities introduced by humans. Because of deliberate (though often uninformed) actions, an untold amount of damage has been done and an untold amount of money will have to be spent to reverse the process if we are to survive.

Both the scope of pollution damage and the possibility of using the earth's resources at an unsustainable rate have received global attention. Many serious attempts to repair environmental damage already have occurred. However, some problems seem to be getting worse. In the United States, tens of millions of dollars have been spent (some readers might prefer "wasted") on legal battles to determine responsibility for cleanup costs.

Superfund or CERCLA

Several different federal laws have been enacted to promote a cleaner environment, including the Clean Air Act, the Clean Water Act, the Toxic Substances Control Act, the Comprehensive Environmental Response, Compensation Liability Act of 1980 (also known as **Superfund or CERCLA**), and the Superfund Amendments and Reauthorization Act of 1986 (SARA).[2] Risk managers must be familiar with the requirements of these and all other relevant federal and state environmental legislation for two reasons. First, many corporations willingly accept the responsibility of good corporate citizenship, including the responsibility of protecting the environment. Thus, loss prevention activities to protect the environment are an integral part of the corporate strategic business plan. Second, many of these laws provide for significant fines and penalties. Environmental critics of government policy maintain that some of these laws, and the government agencies responsible for their enforcement, actually have contributed to aggravating the problem. It also should be noted that some of the state-level environmental protection laws have stricter standards than the comparable federal statutes.

One necessary question we now face is: How will the financial cost of cleaning up the environment be distributed? We cannot very well require previous generations of taxpayers or insurance purchasers to pay their "fair" share. So this question really becomes: How will the burden be shared between current and future generations? The insurance mechanism usually results in shifting the loss cost to consumers because producers include insurance costs in pricing their goods and services. That is, if an insurance company increases a chemical company's insurance premium because of a large claim, this cost will be reflected in higher prices for chemicals. Taxation and other transfer schemes may have different economic effects than insurance, and legislators must consider carefully the economic effects of each approach.

---

[2] Current information on this legislation and related issues can be found at the Environmental Protection Agency (EPA) Web site: (*http://www.epa.gov/superfund/*).
[3] For a comprehensive review of the issues raised in this section, see George B. Flanigan, "A Perspective on General Liability Insurance and the Pollution Hazard: Exposures and Contracts," *Journal of Insurance Regulation*, Spring 2002: 296–337.

Insurance History[3]

Since 1966, firms and other organizations that face either lawsuits from injured third parties or large cleanup costs imposed by regulatory agencies have looked for insurance coverage from their CGL. From 1970 until 1985, the CGL contained an exclusion for discharges of pollutants that are not "sudden and accidental." Since 1985, liability policies have contained what is believed to be an absolute exclusion for most pollution damage. Because the CGL was issued on an occurrence basis prior to 1985, and because injuries still being litigated trace their origin back to that period, the meaning of that policy and its pollution exclusion continue to be a concern.

An examination of the wording of the relevant exclusion contained in the ISO CGL issued between 1973 and 1985 provides a very instructive lesson about insurance policy construction, the exact use of English, and how litigation between insureds and insurers develops. This often-litigated pollution exclusion reads as follows:

> This insurance does not apply . . . (f) to bodily injury or property damage arising out of the discharge, dispersal, release or escape of smoke, vapors, soot fumes, acids, alkalis, toxic chemicals, liquids or gases, waste materials or other irritants, contaminants or pollutants into or upon land, the atmosphere or any water course or body of water, *but this exclusion does not apply if such discharge, dispersal, release or escape is sudden and accidental.* [Emphasis added.]

This language may seem clear to readers, but it has not seemed clear to insurers, insureds, or to the courts. Insurers claim the words mean that the policy covers only damage that occurs without warning, is of short duration, and is neither expected nor intended by the insured, nor otherwise excluded. Insureds argue that the word *sudden* means unexpected or unintended without regard to duration, as is implied in the term *sudden death*, in which case the duration is not short.

For example, from the insurer's standpoint, if a valve were to malfunction accidentally and a chemical plant were to release a cloud of corrosive gas that ruined some car finishes or killed some people, presumably the CGL would cover this occurrence. However, if a leaking valve caused a continuing release of small amounts of gas over a period of years that discolored all the homes near the plant, the exclusion would apply because the damage was not sudden and accidental. From the insured's standpoint, if a vandal were to enter the property and loosen a valve, causing a chemical tank to leak toxic chemicals into the ground for months before being discovered, the CGL with the pollution exclusion in effect should cover the damage because the ensuing groundwater pollution was neither expected nor intended by the insured and the onset was sudden.

Consider the possibility of a gasoline leak from an underground tank if the tank is ruptured by an external force such as being run over by a heavy bulldozer. Assume that the leak goes undiscovered for months or years. Is the resulting damage the result of a sudden and accidental event? What if the tank deteriorates with age, producing the same amount of damage as in the first instance? What if it cannot be factually determined if the tank was ruptured by external force or deteriorated with age? Courts typically have to address these questions when determining the meaning of **sudden and accidental**.

These brief examples give you a sample of the arguments that have arisen in the courts. The various state courts have not been consistent in their interpretation of the language in question. Some courts have determined that *sudden and accidental* means "of a short duration," while others have held that the words mean "an event that begins abruptly

Sudden and accidental

without previous notice, regardless of whether the event's duration is short or long." The difference in interpretation can mean millions of dollars of legal responsibility.

One interesting legal case that deals with the issue of the meaning of sudden and accidental and the effect of this exception to the CGL pollution exclusion is *Jackson Township Municipal Utilities Authority* v. *Hartford Accident & Indemnity Co.* (186 NJ Super 156, 451 A2d 900, NJ Super 1982). In this case, the municipality operated a landfill and hauled waste to the site. Over time, toxic chemicals leaked from the dump and polluted the water table. Because of the pollution, nearby residents sued the city, alleging negligent site selection, design, and operation of the dump. The city's insurer denied that its policy covered this occurrence because the damage was neither sudden nor accidental. (The term *accident* is especially difficult to apply in many cases when deliberate actions lead to an unintended result.) The court held that the policy did provide coverage because the damage was neither expected nor intended. The court reasoned that the CGL policy language was ambiguous on the question of pollution coverage, and ambiguities should be resolved in favor of the insured.

Risk Management Strategy

Insureds not wanting to rely on court interpretations of pre-1985 CGL coverage can try to purchase EIL policies. Such policies are not always available or priced affordably and are subject to negotiation. Among the issues that must be negotiated are the following:

1. The availability of retroactive coverage and, if available, the length of time of retroactive coverage. EIL policies are issued on a claims-made basis, so retroactive coverage can be both valuable and expensive.
2. Whether defense costs reduce policy limits. In one instance, a company reported its estimated defense costs were between $5 and $10 million, exceeding the estimated cleanup costs.
3. Whether cleanup costs are covered for the insured's premises as well as injured third-party premises.
4. The amount of coverage for insurer-provided loss prevention services.

Insurance Principles and EIL Coverage

Consider the criteria presented in Chapter 2, "Defining the Insurable Event," for an ideal insurance transfer in relation to the EIL exposure and you will understand why insurers either have severely restricted their underwriting or stopped writing this coverage. First, loss potential can be catastrophic. Some EIL claims have been over $1 billion; however, most claims are not this large. Second, loss potential is unpredictable because it is often difficult to estimate the cost to complete a cleanup of an affected site. However, in recent years, new engineering and ground mapping tools have allowed better evaluations of potential problems.

Environmental Remediation Stop Loss

Cleanup Cost Cap

Pollution Legal Liability

One result of several decades of experience with pollution problems and EIL claims has been the introduction of new risk transfer and financing options. **Environmental Remediation Stop Loss** or **Cleanup Cost Cap** policies provide coverage for the costs of cleaning up known contamination problems. These policies provide payment to an insured if the costs of cleaning of a site exceed a budget agreed to by regulators. **Pollution Legal Liability** policies provide protection associated with the cleanup of previously unknown pollution sites, such as would arise if a purchaser of land discovered after the purchase the property was polluted. Thus, EIL insurance policies are evolving, and will continue to do so as experience with remediation accumulates and new engineering solutions develop.

PRODUCTS LIABILITY INSURANCE[4]

The special area of products liability insurance continues to receive public attention, perhaps because of the novelty of some of the reported claims that have been made and paid. Perhaps some of the notoriety is due to the large dollar amounts some juries have awarded plaintiffs. In fact, since a court rendered the first $1 million personal injury award in 1963, hundreds of $1 million (and greater) awards have been made in favor of plaintiffs in products liability lawsuits.[5] For these and other reasons, products liability insurance remains a subject of considerable interest and importance.

The manufacturer of a product has a legal duty to design and produce a product that will not injure people from normal use. Some courts have held producers liable if their product "failed to perform as safely as an ordinary consumer would expect when used in an intended or reasonably foreseeable manner." Other courts have held producers liable if the injured person can show "that the product is unreasonably dangerous and that a reasonable alternative design could have reduced foreseeable risks of harm." Both of these definitions of liability raise questions of fact (that is, "What do "ordinary" consumers expect?" or "What is a "reasonable" alternative design?") that may require courtroom arguments.

In addition to careful designing and manufacturing, products must be packaged carefully and accompanied by adequate instructions and warnings so consumers may use them properly and avoid injury. If any of these duties are not fulfilled and the result is an injured user, potential for a products liability lawsuit exists. Moreover, not merely the manufacturer or processor may be named defendants in a products liability lawsuit, but the vendor of a product, such as a drugstore or automobile dealer, also may be named.

Asbestos Litigation

To bring the subject of products liability into focus, we will analyze one particular problem. The liability arising out of the use of asbestos now has a long and complex legal history.[6] More importantly, litigation and legislative proposals relating to asbestos production and use continue today. Asbestosis and other diseases caused by exposure to hazardous substances may be recognized only decades after the initial exposure. A worker may have been exposed to some disease-causing chemical from 1955 until 1985, but the first symptoms of disease may not have appeared until 1985. Death may not have occurred until 1995, when the worker was 70 years old. During this period, the employer, its suppliers, and its customers may have had a dozen different insurers that provided products liability insurance. Moreover, the injured employee may have had several different employers during his career and may have smoked two packs of cigarettes a day for many years.

Like pollution coverage, products liability insurance traditionally has been provided to manufacturers as part of the CGL policy. One problem with this policy is that it does not make clear which insurer is liable for the loss. At least three possibilities exist: (1) the insurer whose policy was in force when the first exposure occurred (the exposure

---

[4] For a comprehensive review of this topic, see David W. Lannetti, "Toward a Revised Definition of 'Product' Under the Restatement (Third) of Torts: Products Liability," *Tort and Insurance Law Journal*, Summer 2000 (Vol. 35, p. 4).

[5] The awards and negotiated settlements involving tobacco products were in the billions of dollars. The fast-food obesity lawsuits raise many interesting points and are discussed by Caleb E. Mason, "Doctrinal Considerations for Fast-Food Obesity Suits," *Tort Trial and Insurance Practice Law Journal*, Fall 2004, pp. 75–106.

[6] Entering the keywords "asbestos lawsuits" into a search engine produces a great deal of current information about this issue. The following Web site, maintained by the Congressional Budget Office (CBO), provides a review of the problem and attempts at a legislative solution: (*http://www.cbo.gov/publications/collections/asbestos.cfm/*).

theory); (2) the insurer whose policy was in force when the disease was first recognized (the manifestation theory); and (3) the insurer whose policy was in force when the disease developed (the exposure-in-residence period theory). In one relevant case, *Keene v. INA*,[7] the court dealt with the issue of which insurer was responsible for the loss. The court ruled that if several insurance policies were in force when a developing injury is in progress, all the insurers would be responsible for providing coverage. (This decision is called the **triple-trigger theory**. The three triggers are exposure, manifestation, and exposure-in-residence period.) In the Keene case, the court allowed the insurers to determine among themselves how the loss would be shared. It also placed the burden of proof on any insurer that claimed its policy did not apply.

Triple-trigger theory

A key question in products liability cases is whether the plaintiff has the burden of establishing the defendant's negligence (as is usually the case in negligence suits) or whether the defendant has the burden of proving a lack of negligence on its part. If the court applies the doctrine of ***res ipsa loquitur*** ("the thing speaks for itself"), the burden is on the defendant. If the court adopts the *strict liability* approach, the burden also is on the defendant. That is, the producer still can defend itself, for example, by establishing that the injured party modified the product in some irresponsible way or failed to give heed to clearly stated and conspicuous warnings, but in the absence of a valid defense, the producer will be held liable. In several areas of the country, especially in cases involving food and drugs, courts have been moving in the direction of strict liability. Arguments the courts have used that favor imposing strict liability on producers include the following:

Res ipsa loquitur

- The party best able to detect and eliminate defects should be responsible for injuries caused by the product.
- The party best able to absorb the costs should be held liable.
- Injured parties often have too difficult a burden proving negligence in product liability cases.

Courts that impose strict liability on producers recognize that ultimately, the consumers of a product bear the cost of victims injured by that product. This result occurs if the producers purchase insurance and include the cost in the product price. Injured consumers also bear the cost if no insurance is purchased and the producer is bankrupted by liability claims.

The problem of unavailability of certain vaccines and medicines and the increase in cost of those still available is one aspect of the products liability problem that has received Congressional attention. Although these health-related dislocations caused by potential products liability claims indeed are serious, many products manufacturers face comparable problems. Some companies report abandoning research and development of new products. Because many U.S. companies must compete with foreign firms that do not have to build the costs of products liability lawsuits into the price of their products, the U.S. firms may face a competitive disadvantage in the world market.

Risk Management Strategy

Products liability insurance protects manufacturers or vendors that have been sued. The insurer agrees to pay the plaintiff on behalf of the insured defendant and to pay the insured defendant's legal defense costs. This coverage is found in Section 1, Coverage

---

[7] D.C. Cir. (October 1, 1981), No. 81.

A, of the CGL policy. Insurers consider the type of products made and the insured's claims history when pricing this coverage.

The Controversy

Because the products liability question has been so controversial, it has been the subject of investigation by legislative commissions at the state and federal levels. Many changes in existing laws have been suggested, and many changes in state laws were implemented in the late 1980s. Some unions and consumer groups have supported stricter standards of performance for producers. Some businesses and their insurers have suggested that laws must be changed to stop the trend toward ever-higher burdens placed on producers.

Among the tort reform measures being considered or that have already been enacted by some states are the following:

- A statute of limitations (or repose) so the manufacturer of an item would not be indefinitely liable for injuries that it caused.

Joint-and-several liability

- Elimination or modification of **joint-and-several liability**. This legal doctrine causes a defendant to be responsible for an entire damage award if other defendants are unable to pay their share of the claim, regardless of the extent of its particular contribution to the injury. In practical terms, this doctrine means large corporations or those with adequate insurance often pay claims for which they are only slightly responsible.

- Limitations on payments for such noneconomic damages as pain and suffering.

- Limitations on punitive damage awards, except in cases in which gross negligence can be established convincingly.

Contingency fees for attorneys

- Limitations on **contingency fees for attorneys**, by which an attorney is paid only if the case is won. With such an arrangement, the plaintiff incurs little or no cost when a suit against a manufacturer is lost. An end to the contingency fee arrangement might be expected to reduce the number of lawsuits brought against manufacturers. Commentators who favor the current system argue that ending contingency fees will deprive poor people, who could not bear the cost of litigation, of the possibility of recovering for their injuries.

- An end to *state-of-the-art evidence*. In some instances, when manufacturers have improved their products by making them safer, their own improvements have been used as evidence to prove the original product was unsafe.

- Producers probably would favor a *state-of-the-art defense*. With this defense, if a producer could show the product that caused the injury incorporated all the technological advances then known and customarily in use, then subsequent advances in technology could not be held out as a standard. Thus, 2003 cars would have to be measured against 2003 standards for safety rather than against subsequent standards.

- An increase in protection for vendors and other distributors, eliminating them from many lawsuits.

Proponents of the current tort liability system have different views of each of these arguments. They argue that consumers are safer because manufacturers must think very carefully about the design and production process in light of the litigation potential. With some justification, they point to many products that have improved safety features as the result of litigation initiated by injured victims. They also argue that manufacturers of defective products should be punished and victims should receive full compensation for all injuries that they sustained because of defective products.

PROFESSIONAL LIABILITY INSURANCE

Who Is a Professional?

Professional

The term **professional** refers to a person with special skills, education, or knowledge compensated to provide a service to the public. In many cases, professionals are licensed by the states. Originally the term was restricted to people employed in the areas of theology, law, and medicine, but today the term is applied more widely. Professional liability insurance is a necessary purchase for accountants, actuaries, architects, directors of corporations, pharmacists, hairstylists, insurance agents and brokers, and other professions that require special education or a license.

Professional liability insurance

Malpractice insurance

Errors and omissions insurance

Sometimes **professional liability insurance** is called **malpractice insurance** or **errors and omissions insurance**. However designated, such insurance typically commits an insurer to pay *all sums that the insured becomes legally obligated to pay as damages* resulting from providing or failing to provide professional services.

Coverage Clause

The language of the coverage clause of a professional liability policy for lawyers makes the insurer's intentions clear. The following is some typical language from a modern policy:

> Your professional liability insurance is written on a "claims-made" basis and only applies to those claims first made against you while this insurance is in force. No coverage exists for claims first made against you after the end of the policy term unless and to the extent an extension of coverage applies.
>
> We will pay all amounts, up to our limit of liability, which you become legally obligated to pay as a result of a wrongful act by you.

Claims Settlement

The legal obligation to pay damages implies litigation establishing the professional's negligence. Professional liability policies, unlike personal liability policies, generally do not give the insurer the right to settle suits without the insured's consent. The reason for the difference between the two policies is that the professional's reputation and future earnings could be affected adversely by settling negligence claims even though sometimes it might be expedient for the insurer to offer a settlement. The professional would not want an insurer to settle all claims, especially so-called nuisance claims, because too many settlements would imply professional incompetence.

If an insured professional wants to contest a suit that the insurer wants to settle without litigation, some insurance companies insert a contractual agreement that causes their insureds to bear any loss above the amount for which the insurer could settle the claim. This type of clause creates a dilemma for the insured; on the one hand, the insured could allow the insurer to settle nuisance or other claims, thereby risking injury to his or her reputation. On the other hand, the insured could contest such claims and be exposed to the very financial loss for which the insurance was purchased.

Types of Professional Liability Coverage

When a certified public accountant (CPA) certifies that financial statements are a fair representation of a company's financial performance and situation, the CPA becomes liable if people who relied on such statements suffer losses because the statements subsequently prove inaccurate. This type of claim arose in the widely publicized collapse of both Enron and WorldCom. In these instances, billions of dollars in losses were sustained by investors. It seems unlikely these losses ultimately will be borne by the accountants or their insurers. It is more likely the accountants will pass their increased insurance costs along to their customers, who in turn will pass them along to consumers. This same argument applies to economic loss caused by incompetent attorneys, architects, and insurance agents and brokers. In all these cases, the cost of the economic loss is likely to be borne by the professional's clients, who in turn pass it along to all consumers.

Among the different professional liability policies available, the more frequently purchased are the following:

Physicians', surgeons', and dentists' liability policy

- **Physicians', surgeons', and dentists' liability policy**. These policies are often written with a $1 million limit per incident and a $3 million limit for the policy period. Policy costs are a function of the city and state of the physician's practice and medical specialty—with surgeons and obstetricians among the most expensive classes. Insurance rates generally are not a function of the practitioner's history, but a poor claims history can lead to nonrenewal or denial of coverage. We address the serious societal issue of medical liability shortly.

Hospital liability policy

- **Hospital liability policy**. This type of policy covers hospitals for tort and vicarious liability arising from the operation of its facilities.

Druggists' liability policy

- **Druggists' liability policy**. This type of policy covers a pharmacist for liability arising from the actions as a druggist, such as dispensing the wrong medication or the wrong dose of medication, or improper compounding of drugs and solutions that require manual compounding.

Directors' and officers' liability insurance

D&O insurance

- **Directors' and officers' liability insurance**. This type of insurance covers directors of corporations and other organizations. It is used to protect directors and officers from liability arising from their mismanagement and failure to carry out their duties with due care. **D&O insurance**, as it is called, is used to attract people to serve on boards of directors. This coverage helps board members protect their personal assets which are subject to liability claims.

   The Enron collapse, as well as other corporate scandals of recent years, illustrates the need for and uses of D&O insurance. If courts decide that investors were injured by various boards of directors breaching their fiduciary duty to oversee management actions, D&O insurance may provide coverage for the directors. However, if courts decide the injuries resulted from intentional or criminal acts, the D&O insurers may not have to pay the claims. Moreover, some insurers who issued D&O coverage to some of these collapsed corporations claim that they were defrauded when the insurance applications were based on deceptive accounting statements that subsequently were restated. Again, it will take time and litigation to resolve the contentious issues raised between D&O insurers and their insureds.

Sarbanes-Oxley Act of 2002 (SOX)

   To battle corporate corruption, the **Sarbanes-Oxley Act of 2002 (SOX)** added clearly stated responsibilities for directors, auditors, and attorneys of publicly traded companies. The law makes the directors and managers responsible for the effectiveness and efficiency of operations, for the reliability of financial reporting, and for compliance with applicable laws and regulations. Under this law, knowingly certifying a false financial report can lead to large fines and prison. Because this law is relatively new, implementation of its requirements by management, as well as the testing of its meaning by the courts, are in the early stages of development. Already, company managements, including insurance company managements, are providing investors more information on the risks associated with company activities.

Errors and omissions insurance

Completed operations insurance

- **Errors and omissions insurance**. Many professions, such as real estate agents, insurance agents, accountants, and architects, need this type of liability protection to cover clients' claims alleging professional negligence.

- **Completed operations insurance**. This type of policy covers claims from injuries that arise after a service is rendered and the property's control is returned to the owner. This coverage would help Leaky Louis, the plumber, whose negligence caused a water heater to explode.

Medical Liability[8]

One key part of the continuing health care debate in the United States has been the effect of medical malpractice and medical malpractice insurance. Therefore, we will give special attention to this type of professional liability.

Physicians' and hospitals' liability insurance

In the 1970s the cost of **physicians' and hospitals' liability insurance**, which is also called *medical malpractice insurance*, rose rapidly as the number of successful lawsuits against medical practitioners grew both in number and in the size of awards won by successful plaintiffs. Professional liability insurance was always expensive, but for some physicians, it was not even available, causing them to risk the possibility of losing their practices after a liability suit. The years following 1970 saw several cycles in the medical liability insurance market. The early years of this decade once again saw problems, as some states saw doctors going on strike, emergency rooms of hospitals shutting down, and women having to drive more than fifty miles to be seen by the nearest obstetrician/gynecologist.

The debate about whether the current medical liability system benefits society continues. Proponents of the medical tort laws, especially trial lawyers, argue that the current system discourages poor healthcare practices, compensates victims of medical negligence, and penalizes negligent providers. Opponents claim that the system is very expensive, with the costs being borne by the public. Opponents also cite a reduction in medical services, especially in areas that award large judgments to injured plaintiffs.

The number of liability cases brought in recent years certainly suggests the possibility of a large number of medical mistakes, with the most frequent claims against physicians including failure to diagnose correctly, failed surgery, and improper treatment.[9] A report by the Institute of Medicine estimated that 98,000 people die each year due to preventable medical errors; that averages 268 per day.[10] The institute also estimated 1.5 million injuries caused by medication mistakes each year.[11] However, the Congressional Budget Office (CBO) notes, "Malpractice costs amounted to an estimated $24 billion in 2002, but that figure represents less than 2 percent of overall health care spending."[12]

The costs of medical malpractice fall into the following categories:

- *Medical liability insurance*: Commercial insurance premiums, self-insurance contributions, and uninsured losses. The impact of investment earnings on

---

[8] For an extended discussion of several issues raised in this section of the chapter, see Louis A. Trosch and Mark S. Dorfman, "An Analysis of Proposals to Reform the Medical Malpractice Liability Crisis," *Business Law Review,* Spring 2004, Vol. 37, pp. 81–101.

[9] A CBO study, "Limiting Tort Liability for Medical Malpractice" (January 8, 2004), stated: "Each year, about 15 malpractice claims are filed for every 100 physicians, and about 30 percent of those claims result in an insurance payment." p. 4. The subject is discussed further in a CBO background paper, "Medical Malpractice Tort Limits and Health Care Spending," April 2006.

[10] 148 Cong. Rec. at S9075 (statement of Sen. Nelson, quoting a 1999 study).

[11] Institute of Medicine, July 20, 2006. (*http://www.iom.edu/CMS/3809/22526/35939/35943.aspx*).

[12] CBO study, 2004, p. 6.

malpractice insurance premiums is significant because an average of five years elapses between the time premiums are paid and claims are settled. This length of time allows good or bad investment earnings to have a noticeable impact on the cost of coverage.

- *Defensive medical costs*: Costs for diagnostic tests and treatments that physicians would not make if there were no threat of lawsuit. Critics have noted that some defensive medical costs are motivated by the income it generates for health care providers, and that savings from reducing "defensive medicine" may not be great.

- *Liability-related administrative costs*: Costs incurred to minimize liability exposure including extra record keeping, and time-consuming activities such as participating in the various stages of litigation. Experts have attributed some of these costs to attorneys who file frivolous lawsuits, but the large number of cases and high dollar judgments won by plaintiffs' attorneys suggests that attorneys generally have pursued legitimate complaints.

- *Medical device and pharmaceutical liability costs*: Insurance and self-insurance costs of drug firms and manufacturers of medical equipment.

Since 1970, many people and groups have suggested solutions for dealing with the medical tort liability problem, including the following:

- A limitation of the amount of money a jury can award as a judgment. One of President George W. Bush's proposed remedies for the nation's medical liability crisis is a $250,000 cap on noneconomic damages in medical malpractice claims. This cap on noneconomic damages, such as jury awards for pain and suffering, mirrors a California law.[13] Opponents of caps on medical malpractice judgments have noted that in 2002, about two decades after the California law became effective, the average actual premium in California is higher than the average of all states without caps on noneconomic damages.[14]

- A redefinition of the word *negligence* so that every minor mistake would not result in a negligence lawsuit.

- A limitation on contingency fees for the plaintiff's attorney.

- Development of state-operated medical malpractice insurance pools.

- Precertification of lawsuits by an expert panel. This reform requires the plaintiff to submit the claim to a panel of experts (typically doctors, health care administrators, and attorneys) who determine if the claim has merit. The plaintiff may ignore adverse judgments of this panel, but the panel's findings become admissible as evidence if the matter is litigated.

These suggested solutions deal with certain legal and insurance aspects of the problem. They do not deal with the underlying problem of professional incompetence. Unless adequate measures are taken to protect the public from incompetent professionals, no solutions to the insurance or legal problems will provide much more than a redistribution of the costs of negligence. If society wishes to reward injured plaintiffs richly, it must consider the source of the payments. It is unlikely the costs will be borne by the professionals or their insurers.

---

[13] California Civil Code § 3333.2, better known as the Medical Injury Compensation Reform Act.
[14] See the Trosch and Dorfman article (cited in footnote 8), Tables 1 and 2, for average malpractice insurance costs of states with and without medical caps.

EMPLOYMENT PRACTICES LIABILITY

Americans with Disabilities Act of 1990 (ADA)

Another area of liability losses arises when a local or state government or the federal government creates rights for special classes of citizens and then allows these citizens to sue organizations that abridge these newly created rights. The **Americans with Disabilities Act of 1990 (ADA)** (Public Law 101-336) is a classic example of this type of legislation. Three similarly purposed federal laws protect the rights of minorities, women, and the aged: the *Civil Rights Act of 1964* (Title VII) [42 U.S.C. 2000 *et seq.*] the *Age Discrimination in Employment Act of 1967* [29 U.S.C. 621 *et seq.*], and the *Civil Rights Act of 1991* [42 U.S.C. 12101 *et seq.*].[15] Many federal and state laws contain whistleblower and anti-retaliation provisions to protect the rights of injured workers and their colleagues further.

One reason for these laws is to improve the "fabric of society" so that more than 280 million Americans can live together in a more peaceful and productive way. For example, before the ADA, many capable workers who could contribute positively to society often were denied the opportunity to prove their worth to an employer. Moreover, because they had no opportunity to have a job, they were denied access to employer-provided insurance benefits, including health insurance. Thus, the ADA created a circumstance where disabled people had the legal right to prove their ability to participate in the economy.

Because these laws have a big impact on an employer's personnel administration practices, they can influence costs greatly. Moreover, some employers believe that the rules sometimes lead to fraud, legal "blackmail," and other abuses. In the first full year of the ADA's enforcement, 25,000 lawsuits were filed. The legal cost to defend an employer charged with a violation of an employee's rights ranges from $20,000 to $200,000 depending on where the legal process stops. Legal defense costs will be incurred in cases where the plaintiff's allegations are true, false, or even frivolous. The costs of this type of litigation also must include the time and stress on the supervisors directly involved in the legal defense. The added costs of complying with these laws are likely passed forward to consumers, and these costs must be compared with the benefits that society receives from the passage of this legislation.

Laws now govern an employer's actions between the time a position is created (including rules governing the advertising of the position and the interviewing of job applicants) and the time the position is eliminated. Legal requirements and accompanying litigation potential govern promotion policy, pay increases or decreases, and allowing or contributing to an atmosphere where sexual harassment occurs. The following list illustrates some of the reasons employers have been sued:

Negligent hiring

- **Negligent hiring** (to cite an extreme example, when inadequate investigation during the job interview allows the employment of a psychopath who subsequently kills one or more coworkers).

Invasion of privacy

- **Invasion of privacy** (too much pre-employment investigation causing emotional distress to a job applicant).

Negligent supervision

- **Negligent supervision** (a frequent contention in harassment cases where, even if employers did not know of the offensive activity, juries have held that they should have known about it).

Negligent discharge

- **Negligent discharge** (claims of age, gender, religious, and sexual orientation discrimination, infliction of emotional distress, and other lines of legal argument surrounding the discharge of an employee).

Wrongful discipline and negligent evaluation

- **Wrongful discipline and negligent evaluation** (also including failure to promote).

---

[15] Refer to the U.S. Justice Department Web site (*http://www.usdoj.gov/crt/ada/adahom1.htm/*) for specific information on the Americans with Disabilities Act (ADA) and the Equal Employment Opportunity Commission Web site (*http://www.eeoc.gov/*) for information about employment and civil rights law.

Americans with Disabilities Act (ADA)

The following brief discussion of the ADA highlights some of the responsibilities that this type of legislation creates for risk managers. Congress passed the ADA in response to the problems of an estimated 43 million Americans with disabilities. Congress found that these citizens had been isolated and segregated, faced restrictions and limitations, occupied an inferior status, and had been seriously disadvantaged relative to other citizens. Therefore, these citizens were entitled to the protection of a specific law designed to put them in a position equal to nondisabled citizens. An essential element of this law defines the protected group. The ADA defines **disability** as:

Disability

- A physical or mental impairment that substantially limits one or more of the major life activities
- A record of such an impairment
- Being regarded as having such an impairment

The act then prohibits discrimination by either state or local governments or private businesses against disabled persons in the areas of employment and access to public services (including transportation), public accommodations (for example, restaurants and hotels), and telecommunications. In the area of employment, employers must make reasonable accommodations for disabled current employees or qualified job applicants who are otherwise capable of performing a specific task or occupation. The reasonableness of the accommodations required by the ADA may be a question of fact, but special furniture and computer equipment are examples of items that employers might provide disabled people so they can work. In the area of public access, for example, firms must assist disabled people by removing physical barriers, providing convenient restrooms, posting readable signs (including Braille lettering), and providing assistive listening devices where appropriate. If an organization breaches its duties as specified by the ADA, one possible outcome is a lawsuit and subsequent damage award. Even if a court finds that an organization did not discriminate against a disabled plaintiff, the legal defense of such an allegation may cost tens of thousands of dollars. Thus, the risk manager faced with an exposure to liability losses such as those created by the ADA must work to be sure the organization avoids prohibited behaviors and conforms to ADA requirements, and, furthermore, that its efforts to comply with the law are well documented. Figure 19–2 presents a checklist summarizing the risk management approach to the potential for legal liability created by the ADA or similar laws.

Applying the general rules presented in Figure 19-2 to the specific issue of sexual harassment, two researchers identified the following elements needed in an effective sexual harassment policy:[16]

- A statement of zero tolerance
- A description of conduct that constitutes sexual harassment
- A complaint procedure
- A statement that the employer will investigate complaints thoroughly promptly
- A statement regarding the confidential nature of the investigation
- A no-retaliation statement
- A statement that offenders will be subject to corrective action, including discipline, up to and including termination

[16] William J. Warfel, and J. Tim Query, "Sex Ed: Insulating Yourself from Sexual Hara *Risk Management Magazine*, February 2005, pp. 14–20.

► *Know the Meaning and Application of the Law*: The risk management and the human resources (personnel) departments should maintain current knowledge of how the law is being interpreted and enforced.

► *Self-evaluation*: Organizations should conduct an initial audit to honestly assess their personnel policies. Thereafter, audits for compliance should be done routinely.

► *Loss Prevention*:
  ► Prepare a manual to describe procedures needed for compliance with the specific law. The manual should be available to all affected employees of the organization.
  ► Organizations should have a stated policy that they offer equal opportunities for employment and advancement to all qualified individuals regardless of age, gender, race, religion, sexual orientation, or other factors.
  ► Work with legal counsel to prepare procedures and written material. Guidelines should be very specific in defining discrimination or harassment, for example. Guidelines should be prepared outlining steps to be followed after a complaint is filed. The rights of accuser and accused must be protected.
  ► Educate people responsible for compliance, including executive management. Controversial compliance issues may need to be addressed in detail.
  ► Identify a contact person should questions arise in specific cases.
  ► Develop monitoring programs to ensure company policy is being followed.

► *Loss Reduction*:
  ► Operate on the basis that litigation is inevitable. However, not every incident or complaint must result in litigation.
  ► Develop an early warning plan to identify and evaluate potential problems at a stage when remediation is possible.
  ► Develop documentation or recordkeeping procedures to assist with legal defense when litigation arises.

► *Insurance*: In a recent year about a dozen companies offered nonstandard policies covering an employer's liability arising from the following events: unintentional discrimination, wrongful termination, sexual harassment, hiring, promotion and demotion practices, and wrongful discipline. This coverage appeared in the early 1990s. Most of the insurers providing this coverage agree to pay legal judgments, back pay, and defense costs. Most carriers exclude coverage for punitive damage awards and acts of malicious intent or willful violations of the law.

FIGURE 19–2   Checklist for Compliance with Nondiscrimination Laws

NUCLEAR LIABILITY INSURANCE

The question of how to provide energy to an industrialized society (or to a nonindustrial society, for that matter) is a perplexing challenge. No simple answers are available. Every form of energy has advantages and drawbacks. The problems in energy production range from economic (including capital requirements, balance-of-trade deficits, and inflationary impact) to technological (including acid rain, coal mine fatalities, massive oil spills, smog and other air pollution, and nuclear catastrophe). As society develops solutions to the problems, the role that insurance will play will be better defined. The following is an overview of the role of insurance in the production of energy by nuclear reaction.

In March 1979, a nuclear reactor operated by Metropolitan Edison at Three Mile Island in Pennsylvania malfunctioned. Almost three decades after the accident, the radioactive contamination still has not been cleaned up completely. The utility continues to replace the power lost during the shutdown of the plant by purchasing power from other companies. (The utility did not have extra-expense or business-interruption insurance, either or both of which would have been most useful.) A total of 3,000 families were evacuated during the crisis, at a cost of about $1.5 million, and about $55 million has been paid to people for losses ranging from loss of use of property to injury caused by emotional stress.

Despite this damage, the physical integrity of the plant apparently was not breached by the accident. It is no wonder, then, that a malfunction resulting in the release of radioactivity in large amounts would be a catastrophe. Although a reactor cannot explode like a bomb, the release of large amounts of radioactivity during a malfunction could make large areas of land uninhabitable for thousands of years. The question arises: Can our society—or any society—absorb such a loss? A second critical question also must be answered: Who should bear the financial burden of such a loss?

Price-Anderson Act

In 1957, Congress passed the **Price-Anderson Act**, which limits the total amount of liability borne by the operator of a nuclear power plant. Furthermore, the act determines how the cost of a nuclear accident shall be distributed among operators, consumers, and property owners. In August 1988, President Ronald Reagan signed legislation that renewed the Price-Anderson Act for another 15 years. Before this extension was granted, it was hotly debated. On one side were people in favor of ending all nuclear power generation of electricity. These people argued for unlimited liability for operators of nuclear-generating stations. Such a position would be unacceptable to utility operators. On the other side were the utilities and their insurers, who argued the country needs the power provided by nuclear plants and that the generation of this power is relatively safe.

In the Energy Policy Act of 2005, the Price-Anderson Act was renewed to 2025.[17] The revised Act provides for private insurance to bear the first level of loss. Two pools of insurers (the Mutual Atomic Energy Liability Underwriters and American Nuclear Insurers) provide a total of $160 million in coverage to owners and operators of nuclear reactors. This insurance provides both property and liability insurance to the operators of reactors. Through the line of reasoning presented in Chapter 1, "Fundamentals and Terminology," about who actually bears the cost of insurance, one concludes the insurance cost is borne by the utility consumer, because as a regulated monopoly, a utility presumably can pass all its costs forward to consumers.

As a second source of compensation for injured victims, the Price-Anderson Act also provides for a $66 million assessment for each operating reactor in the event the insurance coverage is inadequate to meet claims. There are more than 100 nuclear plants now operating in the United States, so the assessment fund would be about $7 billion. The cost of these assessments would likely be borne by the consumers of the utilities who paid the assessments, although the stockholders of the companies might also bear part of the burden. Damage in excess of $7 billion apparently will be borne by the unfortunate property owners or others injured by the peril. Most property insurance policies specifically exclude damage from the peril of nuclear accidents. The intent of the Price-Anderson Act is that people injured by a nuclear reactor malfunction be compensated by the industry essentially on a no-fault basis.

SUMMARY

Firms are exposed to different types of liability lawsuits arising from the following sources: direct liability, premises and operations liability, products liability, completed operations liability, vicarious liability, and contractual liability. The basic business liability insurance policy is the commercial general liability insurance policy (CGL), which can provide coverage against the previously listed categories of liability exposure. The CGL contains many exclusions from coverage, including an exclusion against losses caused by pollution.

A commercial umbrella policy provides coverage after underlying liability policies have been exhausted. The umbrella policy is called *excess liability*

---

[17] For more information about the renewal of the Price-Anderson Act, see (*http://www.ans.org/pi/ps/docs/ps54-bi.pdf*) and (*http://professionals.pr.doe.gov/ma5/MA-5Web.nsf/WebAttachments/AL2005-15/$File/AL2005-15.doc*).

insurance because the umbrella policy pays only for losses in excess of the underlying limits.

Both individual and firms must purchase insurance to protect themselves from liability claims arising from the ownership, maintenance, or use of automobiles. Individuals purchase such insurance protection using the Personal Auto Policy (PAP), which was described in Chapter 11. Firms purchase the business auto coverage form, which provides liability protection needed by commercial vehicle operators.

Any profit or nonprofit institution that makes, uses, or disposes of hazardous substances can be sued if these actions lead to property damage or bodily injury to others. The costs of such lawsuits can be extremely high, as is the cost of government-mandated cleanup responsibility. Risk managers must use all available tools to deal with the potential for environmental impairment litigation. The risk management problem is complicated because courts have differed about the meaning of the "sudden and accidental" language found in the historic CGL. The pre-1986 policy has been held to provide coverage in some jurisdictions, but not in others. Currently, manuscripted or custom-written EIL policies can be used to provide insurance against some types of environmental impairment lawsuits.

When people are injured as a result of using a defective product (for example, cars with easily ruptured gas tanks or improperly processed soup or baby formula), they are entitled to collect compensation for the damage done. Producers, processors, manufacturers, and vendors can purchase products liability insurance as part of their commercial general liability insurance to pay injured parties on their behalf when a court awards judgments in favor of injured parties.

When physicians, lawyers, accountants, or other professionals injure people through professional negligence, the injured victims often will seek to recover damages. The professionals can purchase professional liability insurance to protect themselves against having to pay court-awarded damages because such insurance policies agree to pay such claims on the insured's behalf.

Organizations that hire, supervise, or terminate personnel must do so with caution. Both federal and state governments have created protected classes of citizens whose rights must be scrupulously protected through laws such as the Americans with Disabilities Act of 1990 (ADA). Should an employer abridge these rights, one result can be expensive litigation and expensive adverse legal judgments.

If a nuclear reactor malfunctions, the potential for economic damage is hard to imagine, let alone calculate. To encourage nuclear power, Congress passed the Price-Anderson Act. This act limits a utility's nuclear liability and shifts the burden of paying costs to private insurers, operators of nuclear generating facilities and their consumers, and property owners.

REVIEW TERMS

- Americans with Disabilities Act of 1990 (ADA)
- Business auto coverage form
- Claims-made basis
- Commercial General Liability policy (CGL)
- Completed operations insurance
- Comprehensive General Liability policy (CGL)
- Contingency fees for attorneys
- Contractual liability
- Direct liability
- Directors' and officers' liability insurance
- Disability
- Druggists' liability policy
- Employment practices liability
- Environmental impairment liability (EIL)
- Errors and omissions insurance
- Excess liability insurance
- Hospital liability policy
- Invasion of privacy
- Joint-and-several liability
- Long-tail claims
- Malpractice insurance
- Negligent discharge
- Negligent hiring
- Negligent supervision
- No-fault automobile insurance
- Nuclear liability
- Occurrence-based liability policy
- Physicians', surgeons', and dentists' liability policy
- Pollution
- Price-Anderson Act
- Products liability
- Professional
- Professional liability insurance
- *Res ipsa loquitur*
- Retroactive date
- Sudden and accidental
- Superfund or CERCLA
- Tail coverage
- Triple-trigger theory
- Umbrella policy
- Vicarious liability
- Wrongful discipline and negligent evaluation

REVIEW

1. How can one person be held responsible for another's actions? What is this type of legal responsibility called?
2. Does an umbrella liability policy require other insurance policies to cover an insured loss first?
3. Identify three categories of direct liability exposures.
4. Explain contractual liability and the nature of a hold-harmless agreement.
5. What is the retroactive date in a claims-made CGL form? Why is that date important?
6. How can tail coverage help an attorney who has just retired from active practice?
7. What are the requirements for coverage for an incident to be covered under a claims-made liability policy? How do these requirements differ from an occurrence-based policy?
8. How does the retroactive date differ from the tail period in a claims-made liability policy?
9. What are the names of some of the federal legislation designed to deal with the pollution problem?
10. Why are claims still filed under CGL policies written before 1985?
11. What are two different court-accepted definitions of "sudden and accidental?"
12. Do environmental impairment insurance policies violate the standards of an ideally insurable exposure?
13. List several types of organizations that need EIL coverage. Why would a university need this protection?
14. What is products liability insurance designed to do?
15. Which insurance companies were held liable in the *Keene* case? How did the court reach this decision?
16. Several suggestions have been made to improve the current tort liability system as it relates to products and services. Explain some of these suggestions.
17. Describe the Price-Anderson Act. What role does this act provide for private insurers?
18. How do the insurer's interests sometimes conflict with the professional's interest with respect to the opportunity to settle malpractice suits?
19. Give some reasons why each of the following might be sued for professional malpractice: lawyer, accountant, architect, and insurance agent.
20. What are some of the major costs from health care professionals' errors and omissions?
21. Identify some of the major federal laws affecting employment practices.
22. List some of the reasons employers have been sued with respect to the managing of their employees.
23. How does the ADA define disability?
24. Describe some loss prevention activities a risk manager can use to reduce the potential for liability lawsuits from disabled customers or job applicants.

OBJECTIVE QUESTIONS

1. Dr. Xavier Self, M.D., purchases a one-year, claims-made, professional liability policy on June 1, 2003. It has a retroactive date of June 1, 2000. It also has two years of tail coverage that ends on June 1, 2006. Which of the following incidents would be covered by this policy?
   a. Patient injured December 31, 2003; claim filed July 1, 2005
   b. Patient injured December 31, 1999; claim filed July 1, 2000
   c. Patient injured December 31, 2000; claim filed July 1, 2006
   d. Patient injured December 31, 2003; claim filed July 1, 2006
2. Business general liability includes each of the following categories except:
   a. Direct liability
   b. Vicarious liability
   c. Professional liability
   d. Contractual liability
3. An umbrella policy:
   a. Covers wet marine exposures
   b. Covers property exposures
   c. Provides excess liability coverage
   d. Is only available if inland marine insurance has been purchased first
4. Firms engaged in the automobile business must purchase _____ to cover their liability exposure.
   a. Commercial automobile open-perils coverage
   b. Garage coverage form
   c. Retroactive commercial automobile policy
   d. Dealers and Auto Mechanics Specific Coverage Policy (DAMSCP)
5. The words that courts have found controversial and difficult to define in environmental impairment litigation are:
   a. Separate but equal
   b. Long-lasting and effective control
   c. Deep and penetrating
   d. Sudden and accidental
6. A(n) _____ policy requires the insurance company providing the coverage at the time of the negligence to pay the claim.
   a. Occurrence-based liability insurance
   b. Claims-made liability insurance
   c. Sequential claims liability insurance
   d. Double indemnity liability insurance

7. Insurers call claims filed many years after the alleged negligence:
   a. Stale claims
   b. Long-tail claims
   c. Out-of-warranty claims
   d. Extended claims

8. Professional liability insurance policies would include each of the following except:
   a. Hospital liability policy
   b. Druggists' liability policy
   c. Lumberjack cutoff policy
   d. Errors and omissions insurance

DISCUSSION QUESTIONS

1. Explain in detail who you think bears the ultimate costs of:
   a. Pollution
   b. Compensating victims of poorly manufactured products
   c. Compensating victims of medical malpractice
   d. Compensating victims of employer abuse
   e. Negligent operation of nuclear generators

2. Do you think an injured party should have the burden of proving a company was guilty of negligence to collect damages? Should the burden be on the company to prove the consumer was negligent for the company to avoid having to pay the victim?

3. Explain the definition of vicarious liability and give an example of when you think this legal doctrine produces unfair results.

INTERNET RESEARCH ASSIGNMENTS

1. What is the most recent estimate of the cost of the U.S. tort system? Start your search at this site: (*http://www.towersperrin.com/tillinghast/*). Type "tort liability reform" in the SEARCH window.

2. Use a search engine and get some recent information about asbestos lawsuits.

3. Use a search engine and get some recent information about pollution lawsuits.

4. What were some of the largest damage awards in sex discrimination or sexual harassment lawsuits? Start your search at this site: (*http://library.findlaw.com/*).

5. What is the minimum amount of automobile liability insurance required by your state? Start your search at this site: (*http://info.insure.com/auto/minimum.html/*).

CASE FOR DISCUSSION

Ed "Bonzo" Jones was a college student. He played outfielder on his fraternity's softball team. A home run was hit, and the ball went into an area of electrical transformers operated by the local utility, Total Power and Light Company. The electrical transformers were surrounded by a five-foot-high wire fence that Jones climbed to retrieve the ball. Warning signs were posted by the utility indicating that the area was dangerous. It was later determined that the gate to the area was left unlocked, although Jones did not use it to gain access. In retrieving the ball, Jones made contact with some equipment and was severely burned by the electricity. He was hospitalized for three months and suffered permanent disfigurement. His medical bills amounted to $300,000.

1. What arguments would you make for plaintiff Jones if he were to sue Total Power for his injuries?
2. What arguments would you make if you were planning the legal defense of Total Power and Light Company?
3. If you were on the jury in this case, would you award a judgment for damages to Jones? Explain your reasons.

CHAPTER 20

Bonding, Crime Insurance, and Reinsurance

After studying this chapter, you should be able to:

■ Explain the use and value of surety bonds

■ Describe the difference between a fidelity and surety bond

■ Explain the role of crime insurance in a comprehensive risk management plan

■ Explain the importance of reinsurance to smaller insurance companies

■ Describe how losses are shared between reinsurers

Bonding and crime insurance both provide financial guarantees of human performance or indemnity payments in cases where people fail to perform honestly. Fidelity bonds protect a firm against losses caused by dishonest employees. Crime insurance covers losses caused by nonemployees (that is, the public). A comprehensive risk management plan must consider potential losses caused by human failure to act honestly because such losses can destroy a business as surely as physical damage or liability claims. Enterprises with significant amounts of cash or valuable inventory make a tempting target for criminals. If such assets are handled by employees, an organization needs both crime and fidelity coverage.

Business organizations infrequently engage in large-scale construction projects. Thus, most firms do not have the expertise to investigate, direct, and supervise contractors. Without adequate oversight, a multimillion-dollar construction project could produce substantial problems and large losses. The surety bond removes uncertainty from these transactions. The surety guarantees the contractor's performance or stands prepared to make a payment to the firm that needs the construction completed.

Employees of banks and real estate firms should be familiar with the principles and vocabulary of surety and fidelity bonding. Many students have found interesting careers in the bonding/insurance industry because the services provided by this industry are essential to the U.S. economy.

The final topic covered in this chapter, reinsurance, is not directly related to bonding or crime insurance. Reinsurance is a transaction engaged in by two insurance companies who agree to share premiums and losses. Many times, the original purchaser of insurance may not even be aware of this second transaction. It is sufficiently important that we could give it comprehensive treatment in its own chapter. However, while it is an important topic to understand, and reinsurance vocabulary can be quite interesting, it is not in keeping with my purpose of writing a user-friendly introductory textbook to exhaust this relatively narrow topic. This chapter explains briefly how reinsurance benefits small and large insurance companies and their insureds.

SURETY BONDING

Introductory Terminology

Surety bond

Surety

Obligee

Principal

A surety bond involves three distinct parties. The designation of the three parties involves some unusual names for most students of insurance. The **surety bond**, or suretyship contract, requires the **surety** to pay a second party (the **obligee**) if a third party (the **principal**) fails to fulfill an obligation to the obligee. This triangular relationship is illustrated in Figure 20–1.

To illustrate this relationship, assume that the Flimsy Construction Company agrees to build a school building for the Cook County School Board. The obligee is the school board. Flimsy Construction Company, the principal, owes the obligation. The surety is the RealDeal Surety Company. The surety bond requires RealDeal to pay the school board if Flimsy fails to perform its obligation as specified in the construction contract. Two separate contracts exist in this arrangement. First, a construction contract exists between the school board and the contractor. Second, a surety bond (suretyship contract) exists among all three parties.

The Reasons for Surety Bonding

One may question why a surety bond is useful in the arrangement between the Cook County School Board and Flimsy Construction Company. If Flimsy failed to perform its contractual obligations, couldn't the board file a lawsuit seeking legal satisfaction for the damages caused by the breach of contract? This option is certainly open to the school board. But rather than illustrating the elimination of the need for a surety bond, the court approach highlights the necessity for the bond. The school board wants a school built; it does not want to participate in breach of contract litigation, which, even

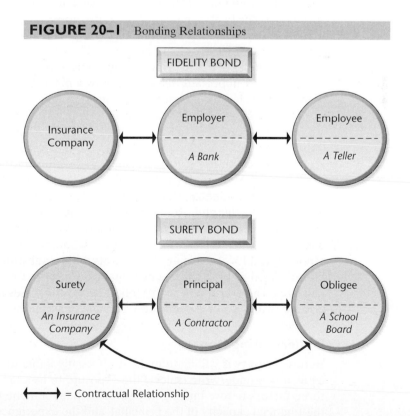

FIGURE 20–1   Bonding Relationships

FIDELITY BOND

Insurance Company ⟷ Employer — — — A Bank ⟷ Employee — — — A Teller

SURETY BOND

Surety — — — An Insurance Company ⟷ Principal — — — A Contractor ⟷ Obligee — — — A School Board

⟷ = Contractual Relationship

if successful, may be lengthy and expensive and probably will not result in the school being built when needed. In contrast, a surety bond allows the school board to avoid this problem. When the breach of contract occurs, the board looks to the surety for satisfaction of its claim, which the surety normally provides rapidly. The board avoids litigation and can use the money from the surety to hire a new contractor to complete the school in a timely fashion. The surety then will seek compensation from the contractor, but this is not the school board's problem. From the board's perspective, certainty has been substituted for uncertainty—the hallmark of the insurance transaction.

The surety has facilitated the construction of the school by providing two basic services. It lends its financial strength and credit to the principal (contractor). Also, it thoroughly investigates the principal's financial position and reputation prior to writing the bond, something a prudent obligee (school board) would have to do in the absence of the surety bond.

The Difference Between Suretyship and Insurance

If an author is not careful, either too much or too little can be made of the technical differences between suretyship and insurance. At least two of the differences are important enough to discuss.

A surety bond involves three parties—the surety, the principal, and the obligee. An insurance contract generally involves two parties—the insurer and the insured. This distinction has importance because of its effect on misrepresentation, concealment, or other fraud. In an insurance contract, if an insured attempts to defraud an insurer by misrepresenting a material fact, the insurance contract generally becomes void and unenforceable. Thus, if the insured commits arson for profit, the insurer with evidence of the crime will not pay for the loss. With a surety bond, even if the contractor tried to defraud the school board (for example, by substituting lower-quality materials than those specified in the contract or lying about previously completed assignments), the surety's liability to the obligee remains. In fact, protection against fraud or dishonesty may be a primary reason for requiring the bond. The only time that fraud will void the surety arrangement is when the principal and obligee conspire to defraud the surety.

A second important distinction between suretyship and insurance exists with respect to the relationship between the insurer (surety) and the insured (principal). If an insured's negligence results in a claim against the insurer (an insured's house is destroyed negligently by fire for which the insured was responsible, or a pedestrian is struck negligently by an automobile driven by the insured), the insurer normally has no recourse, or claim for damages, against its own insured. It pays the insured's claim, regardless of the insured's (nonfraudulent) contribution to the loss. This result does not occur in surety bonding. If a contractor's negligence or fraud results in the surety paying a claim to the obligee, the surety in turn will look to the contractor for whatever satisfaction it can get. This satisfaction may come from a lawsuit that alleges breach of contract between the contractor and the school board. Because it already has paid the school board for the damages, the surety will be substituted (subrogated) to the school board's legal right to sue the principal (the surety's own insured, in one sense) for the damages. The ability to seek reimbursement for losses from its own insured is an important distinction between suretyship and insurance.

Underwriting Bonds

Before a surety is willing to make itself legally liable to an obligee on behalf of a principal, it will underwrite (select) the exposure to loss carefully. The surety will evaluate three factors before making any suretyship agreement: the character of the principal, the financial capacity of the principal, and the experience of the principal.

The character, or reputation, of the principal is important for obvious reasons. Has the principal paid its bills in a timely fashion? Have the principal's banking relationships reflected integrity? Have the principal's employee relations reflected fairness and stability? These are the types of questions a surety will want answered thoroughly before guaranteeing performance. Financial capacity may be assessed by referring to the principal's financial statements. Are the assets adequate? Is there too much debt relative to the amount of assets? Is there adequate net working capital (current assets minus current liabilities)? The surety undoubtedly will do a thorough analysis of any applicant for a surety bond before agreeing to act as surety.

A surety also will consider the experience, or history of performance, of the principal. Have projects comparable to the one under contract between the principal and obligee been completed successfully in the past? Are the factors in the assignment being considered, such as supervisory personnel or geography, comparable to previous experience? For example, a contractor that successfully builds houses and gas stations may not have the expertise to complete an airport assignment. "Nothing succeeds like success" is a truism that applies to getting a surety bond.

Only after it has thoroughly investigated all the various factors identified will a surety add its name and financial resources to a bond arrangement. Without a bond, a contractor will not be able to compete successfully for assignments in which a bond is a precondition to submitting a bid. Thus, the importance of establishing and maintaining a bondable status is very important in many businesses, particularly in construction.

Types of Bonds

Surety Bonds

Surety bonds — *Surety bonds*, as distinguished from fidelity bonds, guarantee the performance of the principal. This performance includes, but is not limited to, a principal's honesty. In this category are contract bonds, judicial bonds, license and permit bonds, and public official bonds. The nature of contract bonds has been developed by the example of the Cook County School Board and the Flimsy Construction Company. There are numerous variations of contract bonds, but the most important is the performance bond, in which the surety guarantees that the work will be completed according to contract specifications.

Judicial bonds — **Judicial bonds** are required by various courts to guarantee the performance of litigants or others involved in a court-related function. For example, the probate court generally will require an executor or administrator of an estate to post a bond. These people have numerous responsibilities, such as distributing assets, liquidating assets, and paying taxes, which must be handled with skill and integrity. A bond guarantees this result. If not, the surety must make good all losses. Similar requirements for performance hold true for trustees and guardians of minors or the insane, so their performance also will be bonded. In many cases, specific instructions relieving executors from having to post a bond are given in a will. Often, a close family relation will be acting in the trusted capacity, eliminating the need for a bond. But the bond guarantees (insures) results and is a prudent arrangement to make in many instances.

Public official bonds — **Public official bonds** are required for such positions as state or local treasurer, whose function is to manage public funds. Tax collectors, auditors, and sheriffs also may need to post a bond guaranteeing their performance. License and permit bonds often are required of firms if state, local, or federal law requires a license to operate. Liquor and tobacco manufacturers, plumbers, electricians, and public warehouse operators are required to provide bonds before operating.

Fidelity Bonds

Fidelity bonds — A basic distinction is made between fidelity and surety bonds. In contrast with surety bonds, **fidelity bonds** protect employers from loss caused by dishonest acts of employees.

Consistent with our earlier terminology, the employee is the principal who owes the duty of honest performance to the obligee, the employer. The surety stands behind the principal's duty and agrees to indemnify the employer if a loss results from an employee's dishonesty.

Dishonesty

Dishonesty is a general term that is given specific application in a fidelity bond. Included in this term are larceny, theft, embezzlement, forgery, misappropriation of funds, and other fraudulent or dishonest acts. (I recommend a legal dictionary if readers need precise definitions of these terms.)

Financial institutions are likely to purchase fidelity bonds. Banks, security dealers, credit unions, and similar institutions where employees have access to valuable assets need this protection. Nonfinancial business organizations, such as educational institutions, fraternities, and churches, also might purchase commercial fidelity bonds. Even though the organization's primary mission is not handling financial assets, if one or more employees handle significant amounts of money, it creates a need for fidelity bond coverage.

CRIME INSURANCE[1]

Crime insurance

Theft

Robbery

Burglary

It is not a long jump from fidelity bonding to crime insurance. In essence, a fidelity bond provides payment if a dishonest employee causes a loss. **Crime insurance** covers losses caused by people outside the firm. Crime insurance typically covers **theft** (taking property without permission); **robbery** (taking property from a person with a threat of violence); and **burglary** (breaking into a premises and removing property).

Commercial Package Insurance

The appearance of the commercial package policy (CPP) diagram reminds us that businesses can purchase crime insurance as part of the Insurance Service Offices (ISO) CPP. We introduced this package policy in Chapter 18, "Commercial Property Insurance." The **crime coverage forms** can be purchased individually or as part of the CPP. Fourteen perils can be covered, including the following:

Crime coverage forms

- Employee dishonesty
- Forgery
- Theft, disappearance, and destruction
- Robbery and safe burglary
- Computer fraud
- Extortion

---

[1] The following Web address provides crime statistics: (*http://www.ojp.usdoj.gov/bjs/*).

When attached to the CPP, the crime forms have their own separate declarations, their own limits of coverage, and their own exclusions. Among the more important exclusions are losses resulting from an insured's dishonesty and indirect losses.

Banks, by their nature, present a special need for crime insurance and loss prevention. Not only do they need coverage for burglary and robbery, but they also need to cover liability for property placed in their safety deposit boxes. The recent growth of automatic teller machines (ATMs) at remote locations has created an additional need for crime coverage. Banks may use standard policies or, through a broker, may negotiate with underwriters for individual policies suited to their needs. Banks can purchase a **blanket coverage fidelity bond**, which protects the bank from losses caused by any employee. Alternatively, banks can purchase a **scheduled fidelity bond** in which specifically named people or specific positions are identified as being capable of causing an insured loss.

Blanket coverage fidelity bond

Scheduled fidelity bond

REINSURANCE[2]

Introductory Terminology

Reinsurance

As stated earlier in this chapter, **reinsurance** is a transaction between two insurance companies in which one insurance company purchases insurance from another insurance company. Both life and nonlife insurance companies engage in reinsurance transactions.

Primary insurer

Ceding company

Reinsurer

We call the company that originally writes the insurance the **primary insurer** or **ceding company**. We call the insurance company from which the primary insurer purchases insurance the **reinsurer**. The reinsurer agrees to indemnify the primary insurer as specified in the reinsurance contract.

Here is the definition of the term *reinsurance* used by the Reinsurance Association of America: "A transaction whereby the assuming reinsurer, for a payment, agrees to indemnify the ceding insurer against all, or a part, of the loss which the latter may sustain under the policy or policies which it has issued."

An example will clarify the reinsurance concept. Assume that the Nevada Mutual Property Insurance Company writes a $225 million property insurance policy for the Miseryloves Company. Assume that the Nevada Company reinsures a part of this coverage with the Colorado Reinsurance Company. In this example, the Nevada Mutual Property Insurance Company is the primary insurer (and also the ceding company), and the Colorado Reinsurance Company is the reinsurer. If an insured loss occurs at the Miseryloves Company, it reports the claim to the Nevada Company. The Nevada Company pays the claim and, assuming that the claim is sufficiently large, the primary insurer (Nevada Company) in turn seeks payment from its reinsurer, the Colorado Reinsurance Company. Figure 20–2 illustrates this relationship.

Reinsurance Arrangements

We call the two basic arrangements between primary companies and reinsurers *facultative* or *treaty* reinsurance. A **facultative reinsurance** arrangement occurs when a primary insurer makes a separate agreement each time it needs reinsurance. Each time it needs reinsurance, the primary company enters the reinsurance market and negotiates the terms of the coverage and the premium it will pay.

Facultative reinsurance

A **treaty reinsurance** arrangement, also called **automatic reinsurance**, involves a standing relationship between a primary insurer and a reinsurer in which a portfolio of the primary insurer's exposures is covered by reinsurance, without specific arrangements for any particular exposure. The treaty between the primary insurer and the reinsurer is subject to renewal or nonrenewal, but in general, while the treaty is in

Treaty reinsurance

Automatic reinsurance

---

[2] Information about reinsurance can be obtained at the Reinsurance Association of America Web site: (*http://reinsurance.org/*).

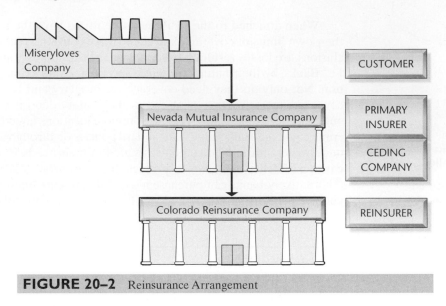

FIGURE 20–2 Reinsurance Arrangement

force, the primary insurer is committed to cede and the reinsurer is committed to accept all the business covered by the treaty.

Reinsurance Coverage

Reinsurance coverages can have some elaborate and strange-sounding names, such as *pro rata quota share treaty reinsurance* or *excess-of-loss per risk reinsurance*. When reduced to simple and understandable dimensions, there are two types of reinsurance arrangements: (1) proportional coverages, known as *pro rata reinsurance*; and (2) excess-of-loss coverage.

Pro rata reinsurance means that the losses, premiums, and expenses are divided proportionately by the primary insurer and the reinsurer. For example, the primary insurer may retain 40 percent of the coverage and cede the remaining 60 percent. Income and expenses are shared in the same proportions. This concept is illustrated in Figure 20–3.

In contrast to pro rata reinsurance, in which the reinsurer shares part of every loss, **excess-of-loss reinsurance** coverage commits the reinsurer to pay part of a claim only after the primary insurer's coverage has been exhausted. The reinsurer pays only the excess of loss beyond what the primary insurer has retained. This concept also is illustrated in Figure 20–3. The amount of coverage the reinsurer provides and its remoteness from the underlying layer of coverage determine its share of the income and expenses.

The following example illustrates the difference between the two types of coverage. Assume, in both cases, that a $1 million factory is insured and it sustains a $400,000 loss. In the first case, pro rata coverage exists, in which the primary insurer retains 30 percent of the coverage and the reinsurer provides 70 percent of the coverage. In this case, the primary insurer pays $120,000 (0.30 × $400,000 = $120,000, or percent retained × amount of loss = amount of payment). Using the same mathematical approach, the reinsurer will pay $280,000, or 70 percent of the $400,000 loss.

In the second case, assume that the primary insurer purchased excess-of-loss coverage, in which the reinsurer agrees to pay for all losses in excess of $300,000. (The loss retained by the primary company may be expressed either as a dollar amount or as a percentage of the exposure.) The primary insurer will pay $300,000, its retention limit.

Pro rata reinsurance

Excess-of-loss reinsurance

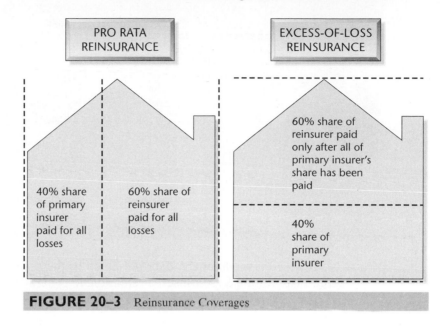

FIGURE 20–3 Reinsurance Coverages

The reinsurer will pay $100,000 ($400,000 − $300,000, or the total loss minus the primary insurance amount). The reinsurer pays only the excess of the loss beyond the amount retained by the primary insurer.

The insured most likely would be unaware of any reinsurance coverage arrangements made by the primary insurer, as mentioned earlier. In the event of a loss, the insured will receive only one check for payment, from the primary insurer. The primary insurer and the reinsurer will handle the reinsurance settlement, without the participation or even the knowledge of the insured.

It also should be pointed out that pro rata coverage can be arranged on a facultative or a treaty basis. The same is true of excess-of-loss coverage. Thus, one might describe a *pro rata facultative reinsurance arrangement* or a *pro rata treaty reinsurance arrangement*.

Catastrophe Reinsurance

Catastrophe reinsurance

One particular type of excess-of-loss reinsurance arrangement deserves special attention. **Catastrophe reinsurance** is distinguished by very high retentions by the primary carriers and other reinsurers before the catastrophe reinsurer becomes liable. Catastrophe reinsurance also has very high upper limits on the reinsurance policy, with increments of coverage often expressed in the millions of dollars. For example, a policy might provide $10 million of coverage after a $5 million loss has been incurred and paid by the primary insurer or the insured. Part of the primary insurer's retention with respect to the catastrophe reinsurance frequently may be reinsured, creating layers of coverage.

For example, assume that the primary insurer provides $40 million of the $100 million of coverage required by an oil refinery. The primary insurer purchases reinsurance for losses in excess of $15 million and less than $40 million. If a $100 million loss occurs, the primary insurer would pay $15 million. The first reinsurer would pay $25 million: $40 million (its upper limit) − $15 million (the primary insurer's retention). The catastrophe reinsurer would pay $60 million: $100 million (size of loss) − $40 million (the amount of coverage provided by the primary insurer and its reinsurer). Figure 20–4 illustrates this result.

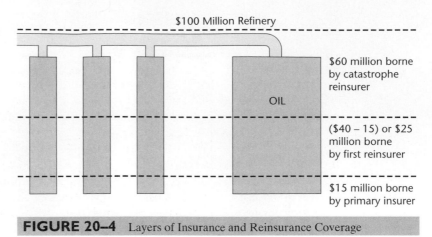

FIGURE 20–4 Layers of Insurance and Reinsurance Coverage

Table 20–1 modifies the data presented in the preceding figure, showing the insured's (oil company) self-insured retention. In general, the first layer of loss for large industrial exposures typically is borne by the insured.

Reasons for Reinsurance

Reinsurance arrangements allow (smaller) primary insurers to use the marketing, actuarial, or other expertise of the (larger) reinsurer, as well as the financial strength of the reinsurer, to enhance their presence in the market.

Reinsurance allows the primary insurer to keep its exposures similar in size. After the primary insurer sets an internal retention limit, it retains all exposures up to this limit and reinsures amounts that exceed this limit. For example, a life insurer may retain a maximum of $100,000 of insurance on any one life. If it were to sell a policy in an amount greater than $100,000, it would reinsure the difference. By keeping its exposures similar in size through the use of reinsurance, no single loss can upset the insurer's loss predictions. Imagine what would happen to an insurer with 999 lives insured for $100,000 and the 1,000th life insured for $10 million. If the 1,000th life were the one lost, the insurer's predictions for loss payments would be inaccurate. In more formal terms, the variation in loss potential is greatly increased if greatly disproportional coverage is written on just a few lives. Thus, reinsurance allows stability in operating results.

Another reason for an insurance company to reinsure is that reinsurance reduces the primary insurer's need to maintain loss and unearned premium reserves. When the primary insurer purchases reinsurance, it reduces the size of its potential loss and thereby reduces the size of the reserves it must maintain. Limiting the amount of reserves it must maintain can be an important consideration for a small but growing insurer. Thus, reinsurance facilitates growth.

In recent years, critics have raised some questions about the solvency of reinsurers, especially some offshore (alien) reinsurers that some U.S. insurers have used. While U.S. companies are subject to regulatory inspection, alien reinsurers often are not

TABLE 20–1 Layers of Coverage for $100 Million Refinery (Amounts in $ Millions)

Catastrophe (top) layer	60, excess of 40
First excess layer	25, excess of 15
Primary coverage	10, excess of 5
Self-insured retention	5, per occurrence

subject to the same level of regulation. If a large claim resulted in a primary insurer looking for reimbursement from an insolvent reinsurer, the primary insurer, not the original insured, would have to bear the additional loss. Thus, the solvency of the primary insurer can be threatened if the reinsurer is not financially sound. Moreover, it has been suggested that if U.S. primary insurers were unable to spread their losses abroad, many domestic insurance companies might not be able to remain solvent if several catastrophic occurrences struck within a short time.

Finally, a reinsurance arrangement allows a primary insurer with limited surplus to accept the larger-sized exposures that, in the absence of the reinsurance arrangement, it could not accept. Accepting a wider range of exposures is a valuable service to be able to offer a company's insureds. Also, a company's field agents can find it useful to be able to accept a wide range of exposures because the agents thereby can compete for more business. In this sense, reinsurance improves relations between a company and its agents.

Reinsurance and Risk Management

Fronting arrangements

Many risk managers of larger firms have incorporated reinsurance arrangements into their risk financing plans. Risk managers call these reinsurance agreements *fronting arrangements*. When risk managers develop **fronting arrangements**, they start their own insurance company with the intention of ceding all or a large portion of the business to a reinsurer. Unfortunately, not all reinsurers have proven financially sound, and while primary companies are monitored carefully by state regulators, critics claim that reinsurers have not been subjected to equal scrutiny. Both the tax and solvency issues raised by fronting arrangements have attracted regulatory attention at the state and federal levels.

Some risk managers and their primary insurers also have begun to substitute complex financial instruments and derivative securities for traditional reinsurance arrangements. Some of these arrangements were described in Chapter 17, "Advanced Topics in Risk Management," where we described financial risk management and the transfer of catastrophic exposures.

Providers of Reinsurance

Professional reinsurance companies engage only in reinsurance transactions. These companies provide a large share of the reinsurance market. In one recent year, the world's two largest reinsurers were Swiss Re Group (*http://www.swissre.com/*) and Munich Re Group (*http://www.munichre.com/*). Many primary insurers also accept reinsurance from other primary insurers. Thus, insurance companies can be both primary and reinsurance companies. Another type of competitor in the reinsurance market is self-insurance subsidiaries of noninsurance companies. In addition to providing insurance for the parent company, these companies also provide reinsurance facilities.

Concluding Comments

Reinsurance works for the benefit of consumers because the financial strength of the reinsurer bolsters the primary insurer. Reinsurance also allows the primary insurer to predict operating results more accurately and manage growth more efficiently. Reinsurance works for the benefit of the reinsurer, allowing it to profit from the insurance transaction without necessarily marketing a product to the public.

Retrocession

Because reinsurance has proven to be such a workable idea, it is not surprising that reinsurers themselves engage in the practice. When a reinsurer purchases reinsurance, we call it **retrocession**.

SUMMARY

A surety bond is used when one party wants to guarantee the performance of a second party that is obligated to the first party. For example, a school board may want to insure that a contractor completes a school building according to contract specifications and in a timely fashion. The contractor is called the *principal* and the school board is called the *obligee*. The surety bond relieves the obligee of having to sue the principal in the event that the obligation is not performed. It also puts the financial strength of the surety behind the contract.

Several differences between suretyship and insurance exist. A surety contract involves three parties, whereas an insurance contract involves two parties. A surety can attempt to recover damages from the principal, whereas an insurer generally cannot recover from its insureds. In underwriting surety bonds, the surety evaluates the principal's financial strength, past performance, and character.

Fidelity bonds are used when an employer wants to insure against losses caused by an employee's dishonesty. Banks, stockbrokers, and other firms whose employees handle valuable assets often purchase fidelity bonds. Fidelity bonds provide coverage for crime losses caused by employees, whereas crime insurance is used to cover losses caused by people other than employees.

A reinsurance relationship exists when an insurance company in turn purchases insurance on some exposure. Thus, Company 1 may insure a sausage factory for $1 million. Company 1 then may purchase reinsurance from Company 2. The reinsurance contract may provide that Company 2 pay a percentage of all insured losses at the sausage factory; we call this arrangement *pro-rata reinsurance*. An alternative arrangement may provide that Company 2 pay Company 1 only when insured losses exceed some specified amount; we call this arrangement *excess-of-loss reinsurance*.

We call a standing agreement between a primary insurer and a reinsurer to reinsure all the former's contracts a *treaty reinsurance arrangement*. We call a reinsurance agreement requiring separate negotiations for each case *facultative reinsurance*. Reinsurance in amounts greater than $50 million is referred to as *catastrophe reinsurance*.

Reinsurance is purchased to improve the predictability of operating results for the primary insurer and to allow loss exposure sizes to be similar. It also allows younger or smaller insurers to grow more rapidly and to accept exposures they otherwise might have to decline. Reinsurance is provided by companies writing reinsurance exclusively, by those writing both primary and reinsurance, and by large international insurance companies.

REVIEW TERMS

- Automatic reinsurance
- Blanket coverage fidelity bond
- Burglary
- Catastrophe reinsurance
- Ceding company
- Crime coverage forms
- Crime insurance
- Dishonesty
- Excess-of-loss reinsurance
- Facultative reinsurance
- Fidelity bonds
- Fronting arrangements
- Judicial bonds
- Obligee
- Primary insurer
- Principal
- Pro rata reinsurance
- Public official bonds
- Reinsurance
- Reinsurer
- Retrocession
- Robbery
- Scheduled fidelity bond
- Surety
- Surety bond
- Theft
- Treaty reinsurance

REVIEW

1. Define the terms *obligee*, *principal*, and *surety*.
2. What are the two important services that the surety provides the obligee?
3. Develop some examples in which a surety bond would be useful.
4. Explain why fraud against the obligee by the principal does not violate a surety bond.
5. List the important factors a surety will consider before offering a contractor a construction bond.
6. Under what circumstances are judicial bonds used?

7. Which public officials are likely to need a bond? Explain your answer.
8. What kinds of offenses are included in the definition of dishonesty?
9. Develop some examples in which a fidelity bond would be needed.
10. What are the similarities between suretyship and insurance? What are the differences?
11. List some perils covered by the crime coverage form of the commercial package policy.
12. How do banks typically protect themselves from crime?

13. What are the reasons that reinsurance is so widely purchased by insurers?
14. Develop some mathematical examples illustrating pro rata reinsurance and excess-of-loss reinsurance.
15. What is the difference between a facultative and a treaty reinsurance arrangement?
16. What does "25, excess of 15" mean in a reinsurance arrangement?
17. Define the term *fronting arrangement*.
18. What type of exposures would encourage a life insurance company to purchase catastrophe reinsurance?

OBJECTIVE QUESTIONS

1. One usual type of bond needed by a building contractor is a:
   a. Performance bond
   b. Practice bond
   c. Development bond
   d. James bond
2. Robbery means:
   a. Stealing
   b. Taking property from a person with the threat of violence
   c. Theft
   d. Breaking and entering
3. The insurance company purchasing insurance from the reinsurer is called:
   a. The first insurer
   b. The selling insurance company
   c. The ceding insurance company
   d. The retrocessionaire
4. Pro rata reinsurance occurs:
   a. If the reinsurance is automatic
   b. If the reinsurance must be negotiated each time it is purchased
   c. If the reinsurer pays only for losses in excess of the stated amount
   d. If the reinsurer and primary insurer share losses on a proportional basis
5. _____ is a transaction engaged in by two insurance companies who agree to share premiums and losses.
   a. Suretyship
   b. Reinsurance

c. Bonding
d. Primary insurance
6. Which of the following parties is not part of the surety bond contract?
   a. Principal
   b. Obligee
   c. Surety
   d. Discussant
7. Assume an excess-of-loss reinsurance arrangement with the primary insurer retaining the first $10 million of loss, and assume that a $50 million covered loss occurs. (Choose the true statement.)
   a. The primary insurer and reinsurer each pays $25 million for the loss.
   b. The primary insurer pays $40 million; the reinsurer pays $10 million.
   c. The primary insurer pays $10 million; the reinsurer pays $40 million.
   d. The primary insurer and reinsurer each pays $50 million, and the insured collects $100 million.
8. Treaty reinsurance means:
   a. The primary insurer must cede business and the reinsurer must accept business during the period covered by the treaty.
   b. Each case of reinsurance requires separate negotiations.
   c. The primary insurer and the reinsurer must sign the International Reinsurance treaty.
   d. All losses must be settled by the terms of the U.S. pro rata treaty.

DISCUSSION QUESTIONS

1. Why would a new contractor have a more difficult time getting bonded than a contractor with a proven record? What problems does getting bonded present to people trying to begin a construction firm, especially minority contractors?

2. Should we bond all public officials, including state governors? Who would bear the cost of the bonds? How many elected officials (state, local, and federal) were convicted of felonies in a recent year for which you can obtain data?

3. If you were a large business owning $10 million worth of property, would you want your primary insurer to purchase reinsurance? Explain your reasons. Would you prefer to deal with a small primary insurer who reinsured your risk, or a large primary insurer who did not purchase reinsurance?

INTERNET RESEARCH ASSIGNMENTS

1. How much in premiums did the Swiss Re company earn in the most recent year for which it provides data? How much did it earn in non-life insurance, and how much did it earn in life insurance? Start your search at this site: (*http://www.swissre.com/*). While you are at this site, review the topics covered in their Sigma research series.

2. What is the amount of surety and fidelity bond written premiums reported in the most recent year for which data is provided at this Web site: (*http://www.surety.org/*).

(Hint: use the "About the Industry" tab on this site to find this information.)

3. Refer to the American Bankers Association's Web site. Perform a search with the keywords "fidelity checklist" and "crime prevention checklist." What can you conclude about the need for crime loss or fidelity loss protection?

4. Search the Internet for the keywords "bail bond." What is a bail bond, and how does it differ from a surety bond? Do insurance companies sell bail bonds?

CHAPTER 21

Employee Benefits

After studying this chapter, you should be able to:

■ Identify the main nonwage benefits offered to workers in the United States

■ Describe the role employee benefits play for employers who offer them

■ Explain why and how the federal government encourages employers to offer nonwage benefits

■ Identify the purpose of group life insurance

■ Identify the limitations of group health insurance

■ Describe how employees benefit from three federal laws: the Consolidated Omnibus Budget Reconciliation Act of 1985 (COBRA), the Family and Medical Leave Act (FMLA), and the Health Insurance Portability and Accountability Act (HIPPA)

■ Describe two ways that pension benefits are determined

■ Identify several types of tax-favored pension and profit-sharing plans for individuals and small businesses

Employee benefits

Employers define **employee benefits** as anything of value received by an employee other than wages. Included in this category are the following (not all of which are offered by all employers):

- Government-mandated benefits: Social Security, workers' compensation, and unemployment insurance (we describe these benefits in Chapters 22 and 23)
- Group life insurance plans
- Group disability income insurance plans
- Group health insurance plans
- Pension plans
- All other benefits, including vacations, day care, employee discounts, and reimbursement for educational expenses

The first five benefit categories involve the application of insurance principles to fund the benefit, which is why we cover this topic in this risk management and insurance textbook. Figure 21–1 presents these benefit categories graphically.

THE INCREASING IMPORTANCE OF THIS CHAPTER

Understanding employee benefits is becoming increasingly important. Stories about employee benefits appear in the news frequently, and recently many of these stories had negative implications for employees. For example, in recent years, some employers have reduced health insurance and pension benefits for their employees, and there

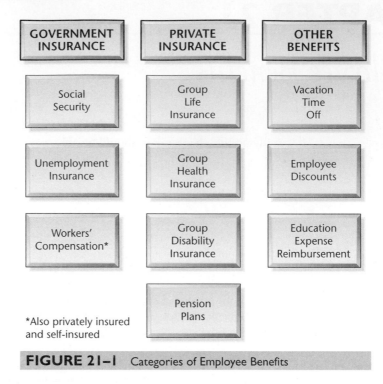

FIGURE 21–1   Categories of Employee Benefits

Pension Benefit Guarantee Corporation (PBGC)

Tripod of economic security

Government Accountability Office (GAO)

have been reports of bankrupt firms transferring their underfunded pension liabilities to the **Pension Benefit Guarantee Corporation (PBGC)**. There also has been much discussion and analysis of the consequences for society of an aging population, global competition, and health care cost increases. Each of these issues has a direct impact on employee benefits. Many commentators believe we have reached a turning point in the United States, away from the traditional **tripod of economic security**. This historic tripod anticipated that the employer, the government, and the individual each would provide roughly one-third of the individual's economic security. Today, however, some experts believe the employer-sponsored portion of the tripod may not be sustainable, in part because productivity growth cannot support the rising cost of benefits. We discuss some of these current benefits issues later in this chapter.

Table 21-1 and Figure 21-2 from a recent U.S. **Government Accountability Office (GAO)** report present a clear picture of the increase in benefit costs to employers over a recent fifteen-year period.[1] The main driver of this increase has been rising health

---

TABLE 21–1   Employers' Real Average Hourly Costs for Employee Total Compensation, Wages, and Total Benefits for All Workers, 1991 to 2005

	1991	*2005*	*Percentage change*
Total compensation	$20.83	$23.39	12
Wages and salaries	$15.07	$16.60	10
Total benefits	$ 5.77	$ 6.79	18

SOURCE: GAO analysis of Bureau of Labor Statistics (BLS) data from the National Compensation Survey (NCS).

---

[1] U.S. Government Accountability Office (GAO), "Employee Compensation" (February 2006), GAO-06-285. Table, p. 8; graph, p. 10.

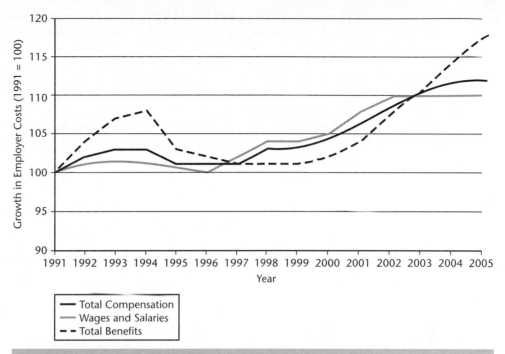

FIGURE 21–2   Growth in Real Employer Hourly Costs for Employee Total Compensation, Wages, and Total Benefits for All Workers, 1991 to 2005

SOURCE: GAO analysis of Bureau of Labor Statistics (BLS) data from the National Compensation Survey (NCS).

insurance costs, but the cost of funding retirement income also has contributed to the increase.[2]

The material presented in this chapter is especially important because no other society relies as much on the private market to deliver the basic framework of economic security to its citizens as the United States.

THE GOALS OF THE GOVERNMENT, EMPLOYER, AND EMPLOYEE

The Government

Working people in the farming societies that were prevalent in the United States and elsewhere before the twentieth century were assumed to be self-sufficient. If disaster (such as premature death or disability) occurred, the remaining members of the family assumed responsibility. Few people lived long enough to retire from work, and extended families lived close enough to help one another. Industrialization destroyed this agrarian pattern, however. People left the land and lost their self-sufficiency. Society became interdependent and relied on a monetary exchange system for transactions. Families were more likely to be separated geographically. Improved sanitation and health care increased life expectancy. The result was a potentially long retirement period that often involved economic and physical dependency. The use of machinery and fossil fuel

---

[2] A good source of data on employee benefits is the Bureau of Labor Statistics Web site: (*http://www. bls.gov/*).

shortened workweeks, providing leisure time. Society was revolutionized, and so was the method of providing economic security to its members. Instead of the family, the government assumed the responsibility for providing economic security to its citizens. These changes, as well as the change from the view of individual responsibility for one's welfare to collective or social responsibility, did not happen suddenly. Today, however, in all industrialized societies, the government provides some level of economic security for its citizens.

Each society approaches the problem of providing economic security differently. The democratic socialist approach found in Western European countries involves some measure of free enterprise but with heavy government intervention, regulation, and taxation. These governments also provide economic security directly to their citizens in the form of health care, pension payments, childcare allowances, and disability income payments. Because government bureaucrats do not have the competitive incentive to perform, and because the government controls vast amounts of capital to fund benefit plans, the efficiency and quality of this approach are open to question. But one advantage of the democratic socialist approach is universal coverage for all citizens.

The U.S. approach relies on free enterprise, with a foundation of government-provided benefits and extensive regulation, to provide the framework of the national economic security program. This system has many advantages. The competition of free enterprise promotes efficiency. When numerous insurers, hospitals, and health maintenance organizations (HMOs) each can provide coverage and compete for business in terms of price and quality, society benefits from the invisible hand of competition. The large amount of capital required to fund pension plans also remains in private hands, which is consistent with our political philosophy. Taxes are lower than would be the case if government benefits were substituted for benefits coming from the private sector.

The free enterprise system also has several disadvantages. The unemployed, part-time employees, and employees of companies with no (or minimum) benefit programs may be cut off from essential services. Health care access is an especially troublesome social issue. The tax revenues forgone when the government induces employers to provide employee benefits by granting tax breaks also means somebody's taxes must go up if the government is to raise the revenue needed for social programs. Critics maintain that such a tax policy often benefits the upper-income and middle-income citizens at the expense of lower-income people.

With this background, we can identify three advantages that our government receives from the private employee benefits system in addition to the economic efficiency associated with free enterprise. First, fewer people depend on the government for support (that is, welfare). Second, the burden on the Social Security program is reduced if people also have private pensions and life insurance. Third, government control of the economy is avoided if the funds that finance the benefits system remain in private hands.

The Employer

If an employer was given the option of paying employees either $14 an hour in wages or $10 an hour in wages and $4 in benefits, why might it choose the second alternative? First, the government provides some tax benefits for the second approach. In both cases, the employer's costs would be deductible from income so long as the compensation was reasonable; therefore, there is no direct tax advantage in the deductibility of expenses. Assume that the employer had a goal of providing a given dollar amount of pension benefit to each employee, such as $500 a month. Then, because there is no tax payable on the investment income during the employee's working years if there is a qualified plan, the employer does not have to put as much into the fund to accumulate the desired amount.

Second, it is argued that employee benefits allow the employer to attract, retain, and motivate employees better than straight wages. In a competitive job market, if one employer's total compensation package is viewed as less desirable than all others, presumably that employer will have difficulty finding and keeping good workers. On the other hand, if one employer has a better compensation program than others, it might be able to hire the best workers. So long as employees view the combination of wages and employee benefits as more desirable than wages alone, competitive employers must provide them to attract the best people.

Third, an efficient pension plan allows employers to facilitate the retirement of older workers, whose salaries *might* be much greater than needed to attract younger workers. Younger workers also might have more recent job skills, better health, and more enthusiasm for work. Of course, not all young workers have as good job skills, good work habits, or other desirable attributes as older workers. However, many employers believe that orderly retirements allow regular promotions throughout the workforce and can be a useful part of a well-designed human resources program.

The Employee

For several years, I asked my students, "Which would you rather have, $14 an hour in wages or $10 an hour in wages and $4 an hour in benefits?" The second choice was by far the most popular, for reasons such as I already have described.

Tax deferral

Some benefits are received tax-free, including premiums spent on group health insurance, which often amount to thousands of dollars for workers and their families. Other benefits receive the significant advantage of **tax deferral**. That is, although the employer gets an immediate income tax deduction when contributions are made to a pension plan, the employee does not have to report the income until the pension is received, which may be forty years after the employer's payment is made.

Tax deferral provides several advantages. First, postponing tax payment allows interest to be earned on dollars "owed" to the government. This is the present value advantage of deferring taxes. The employee also may be in a lower tax bracket upon receiving the distribution. Also, deferral allows the compound interest to accumulate on a tax-deferred basis. To understand the importance of these advantages, compare the position of Joe Green, who must pay taxes on his marginal $1,000 of income at a 30 percent rate. He can invest $700 after taxes. Each year, he also must pay 30 percent of his investment earnings in taxes. Sue Blue, in contrast, postpones the taxes on the marginal $1,000 contributed to her pension plan. The full $1,000 is invested. Furthermore, she also postpones the taxes on all the income the $1,000 produces. In the long run, even though she owes taxes when withdrawals are made, Sue's position will be superior to Joe's. The appendix to this chapter illustrates the advantages of tax deferral in detail.

The tax advantages of the current employee benefits system are very valuable to employees. These advantages may be even more valuable when the employer and employee are the same person, as is often the case in professional corporations (such as those formed by physicians and lawyers) and in small businesses.

Employees receive other advantages from employee benefit programs. These include (1) forced saving for retirement; (2) obtaining insurance coverage for lower cost than if similar coverage were purchased individually; and (3) obtaining insurance coverage when it might be unavailable individually.

INSURED EMPLOYEE BENEFITS

Qualification Rules

The government's philosophy is that when it grants tax breaks for employee benefit plans, it also provides regulations to ensure that the employer distributes these benefits fairly to all employees. Put another way, the government does not want to forgo tax revenue to subsidize plans benefiting only upper-income employees. The desire for nondiscriminatory benefits has resulted in complex benefit plan regulations because benefit plan providers, their salespeople, and their attorneys have been very creative in developing strategies designed to get around the spirit of the rules.

Internal Revenue Code (IRC)

Employee Retirement Income Security Act of 1974 (ERISA)

Qualification rules

A significant portion of the federal regulations applying to employee benefits is found in the **Internal Revenue Code (IRC)** and the **Employee Retirement Income Security Act of 1974 (ERISA)**. These laws have two areas of emphasis: qualification rules and nondiscrimination rules. The **qualification rules** appear straightforward, detailing what employers must do to receive tax benefits. The rules require the following:

- The plan must be in writing.
- The plan must create legally enforceable rights for employees.
- The plan must be for the exclusive benefit of employees.
- The plan must be expected to last indefinitely.

Nondiscrimination rules

The **nondiscrimination rules** are not easily summarized. Using guidelines, formulas, and "safe harbor" provisions, the government tries to ensure that employee benefits do not discriminate in favor of the highly compensated group and against the lower-paid workers.

General Features

Group insurance

When an insurer provides coverage for many people under one master contract, the result is called **group insurance**. Typical groups covered include the employees of one employer or all the members of a labor union. Group insurance can be written on all the debtors (credit card holders with outstanding balances) of one creditor (bank, credit union, or department store). Group coverage also has been offered to all members of social fraternities, sororities, or the alumni of a particular university. To prevent adverse selection, the most important characteristic of the covered group is that the reason for its existence is something other than the purchase of group insurance.

Certificate of participation

Group life, disability, and health insurance require a contract between an employer and an insurer. With an insured plan, each employee receives a **certificate of participation** and an explanation of the benefits provided, but the insured technically is the employer.

Third-party administrator (TPA)

Rather than purchase insurance, many employers currently self-fund their health benefits. The employer with a self-funded health benefit typically hires a **third-party administrator (TPA)**, which might be an insurance company or a Blue Cross plan, to administer the program. The TPA administers the program, but the payments to providers come from the employer. Self-funding health benefits has become increasingly popular for financial and other reasons. For example, some court decisions have recognized the right of employers with self-funded plans to reduce benefits for specific diseases, a strategy not possible with insured plans. Some self-funded plans also use insurance arrangements to provide coverage if a given year produces losses far greater than expected.

Group insurance is lower in cost than comparable individual insurance. Several reasons explain the cost difference. In most group insurance cases, no medical examination is required, though an examination may be required for groups with few members (typically, ten or fewer). The insured often provides administrative services, including collecting premiums when employees contribute to the cost. The acquisition cost to the insurer, including the commission paid to the selling agent, is lower than if a comparable amount of individual coverage is sold. For these reasons, the insurer can offer group coverage for a lower price than individual coverage.

Group insurance involves underwriting the group as a whole. Group demographics, size, and stability are important factors in developing a premium. Depending on the type of coverage—life, disability, or health—insurers will adjust the premium if there are large percentages of men or women and old or young people. The insurer also will be interested in the stability of the group. Is there an above-average rate of leaving and joining? Most underwriters also are not favorably impressed in cases in which the insured has switched insurers two or more times in the last five years.

Experience-rated premiums

Credibility

If the group is large, the insurer will offer **experience-rated premiums**. In this case, once the employer's data have **credibility** because of the large number of observations, the insurer has confidence in tailoring the premium to the particular group's outcome. Once a group has credibility, if there are fewer deaths, disabilities, or hospitalizations in a policy year, the group receives lower premiums in future years. An employer with fewer employees may have to wait several years before its data are given sufficient credibility by the insurer to experience rate premiums. Before a group achieves statistical credibility, the insurer determines its rates using group averages.

GROUP LIFE INSURANCE

Group term life insurance

Perhaps the easiest employee benefit to understand is **group term life insurance**. This contract provides a death benefit for a specified period, typically one year. When the term expires, the policy can be renewed. If an employer offers this benefit, when a covered employee dies, a beneficiary (identified in the enrollment card filled out by the employee) receives the death benefit.

The insurer bases the premiums for group term life insurance on the average age of the covered employees. Unlike an individual, a group's average age does not necessarily increase every calendar year. In fact, if several older employees were to retire and were replaced by younger employees, the average age of the group would go down. Thus, the age and number of employees entering and leaving immediately affect the average age of a group.

Most employers offering this benefit cover only full-time workers, but some also may offer the coverage to part-time employees. Some employers also offer coverage, often in reduced amounts, to retired employees.

The amount of insurance may be a *flat amount*. For example, each beneficiary receives $25,000 if a covered worker dies. Alternatively, the amount of insurance may be based on a *position schedule*. In this case, the benefit may be $40,000 for salaried workers and $20,000 for hourly workers. The amount of insurance also may be a *percentage of earnings*. For example, each employee's benefit equals one year's salary or, perhaps, 150 percent of annual salary. Combinations of these approaches are possible. For example, in one company, benefits equal 200 percent of annual salary for upper-level managers, 150 percent for middle managers, and 100 percent for all other employees.

The employee generally is allowed free choice when designating a beneficiary and may assign contract rights if proper notification is given to the insurer. The employee or beneficiary has several settlement options, comparable with the settlement options available with individual insurance: namely, lump-sum payment, lifetime income, or payments for a limited period.

Most contracts allow for conversion of the group insurance coverage to individual insurance if the employee leaves the group. This right is exercised rarely except by people otherwise uninsurable. One reason for the relatively small number of conversions is that the conversion must be from the group term policy to a cash-value type of coverage with premiums calculated at the insured's age at the time of conversion. If the employee is older when converting from group term to individual coverage, these premiums tend to be relatively high. If the employee leaves one employer's group to enter another employer's group, an expensive conversion would be unattractive. If the employee left the group and is unemployed, an expensive conversion may not even be affordable.

The federal income taxation of group term life insurance allows the employer a deduction for premiums paid, so long as an employee's total compensation is reasonable. The employee does not have to report the premium paid as income, so long as the insurance benefit is less than $50,000. If the benefit is greater than $50,000, the premium for the insurance in excess of $50,000 is included in the employee's taxable income.

Most financial advisors recommend that people not rely entirely on group term life insurance, or even a combination of group term life insurance and Social Security survivor benefits, for their life insurance program. Several reasons exist for this advice. First, the benefits may be inadequate to meet all financial needs and goals. This outcome is likely because employers determine benefit amounts without considering employee needs. Second, the benefits may be unavailable if employment ends or the employer cancels the plan because of bankruptcy, merger, or other reasons. We already explained why the conversion of group insurance to individual insurance is unlikely. Third, group term life insurance involves no savings, and this feature of individual cash-value life insurance may be important to some people. Thus, most people will recognize employer-provided life insurance as one leg of a tripod, with Social Security and individual life insurance as the other two legs.

GROUP DISABILITY INCOME INSURANCE

If an employee is disabled by a work-related accident or illness, workers' compensation benefits are available to provide indemnity and rehabilitation payments. Workers' compensation benefits, however, generally are inadequate to replace all lost income. Moreover, not all permanent disabilities are work-related. Thus, for work-related or non-work-related disability, many people need disability income insurance to provide economic security. Insurers categorize these programs as short-term or long-term programs.

Sick-leave plans

Short-term programs continue the employee's salary for six or fewer months. Employers often call these plans **sick-leave plans**, and usually they are not insured. Employers that offer this benefit credit employees with a certain number of sick days for a given period worked. For example, an employee may earn one sick day for each month of employment. If more sick days are taken than are earned, the employee's pay is reduced accordingly. Some employers coordinate a sick-leave plan with an insured short-term disability income plan that provides covered employees with up to six months of coverage.

Long-Term Disability

Long-term disability benefits, when offered by an employer, typically will be insured. Long-term benefits may begin after a (six-month) waiting period and last for a period of years (for example, five or ten years) or until a specified age (for example, age 65) is reached.

Permanent disability

Several problems must be solved when offering long-term disability insurance. The plan must define **permanent disability**. Definitions may be liberal (unable to perform the tasks of the occupation for which the person is trained), or strict (unable to perform the tasks of any occupation for which the person might be trained in the future). Some policies combine definitions, applying the liberal definition for the first few years of disability and then shifting to the strict definition if the disability persists. Thus, a teacher who suffers a permanent voice loss may meet the liberal definition but may not be able to continue to qualify for disability benefits under the strict definition if the requirements of an administrative position could be met.

Integrated plans

The compensation provided must not be so great as to encourage malingering. The usual approach to achieving this goal is to limit the compensation paid to some percentage of the predisability income, such as 66 percent. Generally, the employer considers all sources of disability income, including Social Security, when calculating the amount of disability insurance benefit provided. Plans that consider Social Security benefits when determining disability insurance benefits are called **integrated plans**.

Only a few exclusions are likely to be found in group disability contracts. Typical exclusions are (1) losses arising out of self-inflicted injuries (including suicide attempts); (2) losses arising out of the commission of a felony; and (3) losses arising out of war.

The federal taxation of disability income benefits allows the employer to deduct the cost of purchasing the insurance coverage. The employee does not have to report the cost of the employer's contribution as taxable income. If the employee receives payments as a result of disability, however, these payments are included in the employee's taxable income in the year received. There is an exception to this rule. If the employee paid the premium for the disability income protection, then there is no federal income tax on the benefits. If the premiums were paid in part by the employer and in part with employee contributions, then the amount of disability income attributed to the employee's contribution is not subject to income tax. For example, if the employer paid 60 percent of the premium and the employee paid 40 percent, then only 60 percent of the disability income payments the employee receives is included in taxable income.

GROUP HEALTH INSURANCE

Health Insurance Contracts

Employers providing group health insurance typically cover the employee and eligible dependents. Eligible dependents include a spouse, if the employee and spouse are not separated, and children under a specified age, such as 19.

Health maintenance organizations (HMOs)

Preferred provider organizations (PPOs)

Capitation payments

Insurers provide group health insurance benefits under a basic medical or a major medical insurance policy. **Health maintenance organizations (HMOs)** and **preferred provider organizations (PPOs)** provide alternatives to the traditional insured plans. HMOs provide extensive health care, including physical examinations, in exchange for monthly payments made by the employer called **capitation payments**. Once the HMO sets the capitation payment (such as $400 each month for each employee), the amount does not change because of use. The HMO will use this rate for a specified period such as six months or a year. PPOs, such as hospitals, provide services on a contract basis to employers. They do not provide prepaid benefits like HMOs, but they bill the user (employer) at prearranged (discounted) prices when service is rendered.

Employers use disincentives, such as reduced coverage if employees use a non-PPO provider, to encourage employees to get their health care needs met by the PPO. For example, if the employee uses the PPO hospital and physicians for a medical condition, the bill may be $10,000, and the employee may be reimbursed for 90 percent of this amount, or $9,000. If the employee uses non-PPO providers, however, the bill may be 20 percent higher, or $12,000, because the PPO agreed to reduce its charges to secure the employer's business. Moreover, the reimbursement for the non-PPO providers may be at a lower level than the PPO provider, say 60 percent rather than 90 percent. A 60 percent level of reimbursement provides payment of $7,200 (0.6 × 12,000) rather than the $9,000 paid when the PPO provider is used. Thus, using the PPO costs the employee $1,000 ($10,000 − $9,000), while using the non-PPO costs him or her $4,800 ($12,000 − $7,200). Plans using PPOs to control costs, however, usually provide a strong financial incentive to use the preferred providers.

Chapter 16, "Medical Expense and Disability Income Insurance," presented the features and provisions of individual health insurance contracts. This chapter presents only a brief review of this material because group and individual insurance contracts are comparable in most important respects.

Basic Medical Insurance

Basic medical insurance provides a limited amount of insurance (for example, $5,000 or $10,000) for expenses incurred if the insured is hospitalized. Covered hospital expenses include room charges, X-ray films and supplies, and charges for use of special facilities such as the intensive care unit. Physicians' charges for services delivered in the hospital also are covered. Reimbursement of physicians is based on either the reasonable and customary charge or a scheduled approach. The insurer bases reasonable and customary payments on geographic areas. In most cases, physicians accept this amount as payment in full. The scheduled approach lists the payments available for every service a physician may perform. If the scheduled approach results in an insurance payment that is less than the physician charged, the insured must pay the difference.

Basic medical policies provide first-dollar coverage, usually without any participation by the insured. That is, there is no deductible or coinsurance provision. Thus, if the insured incurs a $1,470 fee for using the emergency room, the insurance will pay the full amount.

Major Medical Insurance

Group major medical insurance

Group major medical insurance generally has high policy limits, or sometimes no maximum limits. It also has a deductible provision and a participation provision. These two provisions cause the insured to pay an initial amount for covered claims and also to pay a percentage of all claims in excess of the deductible. Caps (limits) are placed on the total amount an insured must pay each year. If the sum of the deductible and the participation payments exceed the cap (for example, $1,000), the major medical insurance pays 100 percent of the excess up to the policy limits.

As an example of how a major medical insurance policy might respond to an insured's claim, consider the information in Table 21–2. The insured has $50,000 in covered expenses in one calendar year. The policy has a $250 deductible, an 80-20 copay (participation) provision, and a $1,000 cap on the insured's annual payments.

General Provisions of Group Health Insurance Contracts

Several exclusions generally apply to group health insurance policies. Typical exclusions include the following:

- *No Coverage of Custodial Care.* This generally means there is no coverage when the insured is in a facility that is not trying to improve the status of the patient's health. A nursing home is an example of such a facility.

TABLE 21–2   Calculation of a Major Medical Insurance Claim

Covered expenses	$50,000
(less) deductible	250
Total	$49,750
For the next $3,750 of the claim,	
the insured pays 20% ($750)	
and the insurer pays 80% ($3,000)[a]	
80% coinsurance until cap	3,000
100% insurance after cap	46,000
Total paid by insurer	49,000
Total paid by employee (250 + 750)	1,000

[a] *The algebraic solution is 0.2(x) + $250 = $1,000; where (x) is the maximum amount of the claim that the insured must participate in. In this example, it is $3,750. Eighty percent of this amount is the $3,000 paid by the insurer shown in the table. When the claim exceeds $3,750, the insurer pays 100% of the remainder (50,000 − 250 − 3,750 = 46,000).*

- *No Coverage of Physical Examinations.* Unlike HMOs, traditional indemnity plans and Blue Cross plans generally do not pay for regular examinations such as an annual physical.
- *No Elective Cosmetic Surgery.* Generally this is not covered.
- *No Coverage for Preexisting Conditions.* The definition of the term *preexisting conditions* varies, but it generally means conditions for which the employee was being treated before the employment (and hence the insurance coverage) began.

Most group health insurance policies place limits on the amounts they will pay for mental health problems and payments for health problems arising from substance abuse.

Coordination of benefits

Another area of concern in group health insurance policies is **coordination of benefits**. With many families having two working spouses and medical expense coverage provided by personal automobile policies, when hospitalization results from automobile accidents, insurers need to determine which policy pays first (provides primary coverage) and which policy pays second (provides excess coverage). Either the policies themselves or an appropriate state law will determine the issue. The purpose of these rules is to allow the insured to be indemnified but not allow more compensation than the costs incurred.

Cost-containment or cost-shifting measures have become increasingly common in recent years. Such measures as wellness programs (including emphasis on physical fitness and elimination of smoking and drinking), precertification before surgery (when a medical technician reviews and approves the anticipated length of stay), second opinions before surgery, and postclaim audits of medical bills all have been tried to reduce the rapid rise in employers' health care costs. Despite all these measures, employers' health insurance premiums have continued to rise at steep rates in recent years.

Three Federal Regulations

Many federal and state regulations affect group health insurance plans. This introductory risk management and insurance textbook is not the place to explore the depth and breadth of these regulations.[3] However, we will devote special attention to the

---

[3] An Internet search with the various acts as keywords will provide extensive details on the respective legislation. An advanced course in employee benefits is also a good place to learn about the significance of these laws.

of employment would receive 40 percent (1 percent × 40 years) of final salary under this formula. With a defined-benefit plan, the pension (output) is predetermined, and the employer must provide adequate input to achieve the promised result.

Cash balance plan

The **cash balance plan** is a special, or hybrid, type of defined benefit plan. The inputs are a specified percentage of the employee's annual salary while working, such as 5 percent, plus a guaranteed interest credit on the employee's hypothetical account. The account is hypothetical because the employer actually pools all employees' accounts. The employer guarantees the interest credit and bears the investment risk if actual earnings are less than the guaranteed percentage. If actual earnings exceed the guaranteed rate, the employer can adjust future deposits.[4]

Defined-contribution plan

Money purchase plan

A **defined-contribution plan** requires the employer to make a specified input payment. Unlike defined benefit plans, including cash balance plans, defined contributions plan makes no promises regarding output. The simplest type of defined contribution plan is the **money purchase plan**. A money purchase plan, for example, may call for the employer to deposit 6 percent of the employee's annual salary into the plan. The investment earnings on a money purchase plan could vary widely over a working career, and the employer guarantees no particular rate of return. At retirement, the employee receives the sum of all the input amounts plus the investment earnings. Each employee has a separate account and the employee bears the investment risk.

In the past two decades or so, the popularity of defined benefit plans has decreased while the popularity of contribution plans has increased. We discuss some of the reasons and consequences of this shift in the section of this chapter called "Current Issues in Pension Planning," which follows shortly. We have postponed this discussion, however, to allow for the presentation of more vocabulary and concepts.

Requirements for Qualified Plans

The requirements for plan qualification can be understood in terms of two overriding government goals:

1. Plans should not discriminate in favor of highly compensated employees. This goal is enforced primarily by IRC regulations. IRC regulations also place maximum limits on contributions to pension plans and provide other rules to limit the revenue loss to the government.
2. Plans should be operated in a financially sound manner. This goal is achieved primarily by ERISA regulations.

Actual IRC and ERISA regulations are complex. The four general requirements that follow are just summaries of these complex requirements:

- *Eligibility.* Plans should cover all full-time employees over age 21 with one full year of service.
- *Nondiscrimination.* Plans should not provide unfairly large benefits to highly compensated employees. Employer contributions to the plan also must not be unfair. The Internal Revenue Service (IRS) determines the meaning of "unfair" using formulas and safe harbor provisions.
- *Funding.* Defined-benefit plans must be funded in advance according to the requirements of ERISA. Regular payments must be made to defined-contribution plans. The employer must give up control of any funds used to finance qualified pension plans.

---

[4] For more information on this type of plan, see U.S. Government Accountability Office (GAO), "Private Pensions: Information of Cash Balance Pension Plans," November 2005 (GAO-06-42).

- *Vesting.* After a specified period, the employee is given a right to the employer's contribution to the pension plan. That is, if the employee leaves employment after the period when pension benefits are 100 percent vested, the employee can assume that any contributions made by the employer belong to the employee. For example, a plan may provide for no vested benefits before five years of service are completed, with 100 percent vesting thereafter. This is called *five-year cliff vesting.* One purpose of the vesting requirement is to discourage employers from firing employees with many years of service just before retirement.

Vesting

Vesting does not mean that employees may take their benefits in cash at the point of termination, though this may be allowed in the case of a small amount of benefits. Generally, if benefits are vested, the employee will be eligible for whatever pension benefit is called for at the normal retirement age.

As an example of vesting, assume that Annette worked for twenty years before leaving her employer at age 50. Annette is fully vested in her pension benefit when she leaves her employer, but she must wait until she is 65 to begin to receive her pension. Her employer's pension plan formula specified that her pension is calculated as 1 percent of her final year's salary (assume that it was $50,000) for each year she worked (twenty years). So her annual pension when she reaches age 65 (the plan's normal retirement age) would be 20 percent of $50,000, or $10,000.

Federal Regulation of Pension Plans[5]

An author of an introductory insurance textbook accepts the responsibility to summarize and explain vast and complex issues. The reader should realize that summary presentations omit complexities that may have important implications for some issues. You are advised that the preceding material and the following discussion are only summaries of long and complex legislation and court decisions, congressional hearings, and administrative interpretations of these laws. Moreover, it is likely that changes will be made in some particulars after this book is in print.

The Employee Retirement Income Security Act of 1974 (ERISA)[6]

ERISA is the most far-reaching federal law covering pension plans. Its overall purpose is to protect the rights of pension plan participants. To accomplish this goal, it has four core features:

1. Reporting and disclosure requirements—that is, employers are required to provide employees with easily understood plan descriptions and benefit statements.
2. Fiduciary requirements, so that those responsible for holding and investing pension assets must be careful to protect the assets and minimize risk of loss.
3. Minimum plan requirements (the requirements for qualification just discussed previously).

Pension Benefit Guarantee Corporation (PBGC)

4. Plan termination insurance. This part of ERISA created the **Pension Benefit Guarantee Corporation** (**PBGC**; *http://www.pbgc.gov/*). The PBGC is a government agency that collects an insurance premium from all plan sponsors and in return stands ready to assume the liabilities of insolvent plans. Only defined-benefit plans create liabilities of the type the PBGC assumes. In recent

---

[5] On August 17, President George W. Bush signed the Pension Protection Act (PPA) of 2006 into law. The PPA was designed to strengthen the Pension Benefit Guaranty Corporation (PBGC) and to ensure that employers improve how they value and fund their defined benefit pension plans.
[6] The Web site (*http://www.dol.gov/dol/topic/health-plans/erisa.htm#doltopics/*) provides information from the Department of Labor concerning ERISA. Also see (*http://www.dol.gov/dol/topic/*).

years, the bankruptcies of several large steel companies and airlines have caused significant financial problems for the PBGC. We discuss these problems in the "Current Issues in Pension Planning" section of this chapter, which follows shortly.

Age Discrimination in Employment Act of 1967 (ADEA) (as amended)[7]

The purpose of the Age Discrimination in Employment Act (ADEA) is to prohibit discrimination against employees in the protected age group (ages 40 to 70). This act prevents employers from forcing employees to retire before age 70. It also prevents plan provisions, such as those relating to contributions or benefits, from discriminating against individuals in the protected group.

The Civil Rights Act of 1964 (as amended)[8]

This act prevents employers from discriminating in pension plan benefits based on gender or race. As a result of U.S. Supreme Court rulings, pension plans may not collect unequal contributions or pay unequal benefits based on gender considerations.

The Retirement Equity Act of 1984 (REA)

This law requires married workers to take their pension benefit as a joint-and-survivor annuity unless the nonemployee spouse consents to another type of distribution. This law prevents, for example, the retired employee from taking a lump-sum payment or a single-life annuity unless the spouse agrees, in writing, to this alternative.

The Role of Insurance in Pension Plans

The material on pensions presented thus far covers concepts unique to pensions, rules for qualification, and some relevant federal laws. This is an insurance textbook, though, and you might be wondering what role insurance plays in pension plans. Insurance is one of two ways employers may fund their pension plans. The other arrangement involves trusts.

Recall from the discussion of annuities that the initial phase, the *accumulation period*, is followed by the second phase, the *liquidation period*. A similar situation occurs in pension plans. During the period of active employment (the accumulation period), money is contributed to the pension plan. After retirement (the liquidation period), payments are received from the pension plan. Employers can use the services of an insurance company in one or both phases of a pension plan. That is, the insurer can provide services during the accumulation phase, the liquidation phase, or both. Before we proceed with this description, some definition of vocabulary terms is again necessary.

Allocated funding

Unallocated funding

If a worker's pension benefit balance is funded individually while the benefit is accumulating, insurers call the pension benefit an *allocated benefit*. When an employer purchases an annuity or a life insurance policy for each employee, this is called **allocated funding** of a pension plan. Allocated funding is associated with small employers. Large employers typically do not allocate their pension funds; rather, they contribute an actuarially determined amount to a pool of assets held in trust. At an employee's retirement, the trust makes payments from the pool of assets. When such a pool of money receives pension plan contributions and individual balances are not kept, the pension-funding method is called **unallocated funding**. Employers use trusts to hold the unallocated funds because they can accommodate more benefit and investment changes than insurance contracts.

To compete with trusts, insurance companies offer unallocated funding alternatives called *group deposit administration contracts* and *immediate participation guarantee*

---

[7] For more information, see the Web site (*http://www.eeoc.gov/*).
[8] For more information, see the Web site (*http://www.usdoj.gov/crt/cor/coord/titlevi.htm/*).

Group deposit administration contract

Immediate participation guarantee contract

contracts. The **group deposit administration contract** is just a pool of money until the worker retires, at which time an individual annuity is purchased. The **immediate participation guarantee contract** remains unallocated even after the employee retires. Even in retirement, pension payments come directly from the pension assets, without the guarantees associated with the purchase of an annuity. If the assets are inadequate to make the promised payments in any unallocated funding approach, the employer is legally responsible for making up any deficit. When employers use insurance contracts in an allocated plan, the insurance company guarantees mortality, expense, and investment risks.

Insurance Contracts

As we noted, allocated funding can use individual annuities or individual life insurance contracts. Deferred annuities are designed to provide retirement income, and their use to fund pension obligations makes sense. When insurance contracts and annuities are used to fund pensions, the insurer provides guarantees, and the employer is relieved of further liability for pension benefits as long as the premiums are paid. For example, if employees lived unexpectedly long lives or if investment returns were less than expected, the insurer (not the employer) bears the costs when the funding is allocated. The drawbacks to using insurance contracts involve less flexibility in changing benefit amounts and in investment alternatives.

If a pension plan is funded with life insurance rather than deferred annuities, IRS rules limit the type of life insurance contracts used. If life insurance policies are used, the death benefit must be "incidental" to the pension benefit. *Incidental* means that the death benefit should not be more than 100 times greater than the monthly pension benefit. For example, if the monthly pension benefit is $400, no more than $40,000 in cash-value life insurance can be used to fund the benefit. Most traditional whole life contracts cannot meet the incidental death-benefit test and still provide the required pension benefit. Thus, if whole life insurance is used to fund a pension, the employer also must contribute to a side fund used to supplement the cash values funding the pension. When a side fund is used to supplement a whole life insurance policy, insurers call the plan a *combination plan*.

Retirement income policies

As an alternative to whole life insurance, **retirement income policies** build up cash values more rapidly than whole life policies. Insurers designed retirement income policies to meet the need for an individual life insurance contract that funds a pension benefit with only incidental death benefits. Retirement income policies have not been popular in recent years because they have noncompetitive rates of return and are less flexible than alternatives. When retirement income or whole life insurance policies are used, medical examinations may be required. If an employee cannot meet underwriting standards, the death benefit of the insurance policy is reduced or eliminated, but the cash values continue to accumulate according to schedule, and the annuity (pension) benefits remain the same.

CURRENT ISSUES IN PENSION PLANNING

Many pension plan issues have appeared in the press, in academic literature, and in Congress in recent years. We have chosen to summarize the following three issues because they seem most relevant to this textbook:

- The decline of defined benefit plans
- The underfunding of pension plans
- The insolvency of the PBGC

The Decline of Defined Benefit Plans

As we discussed earlier in this chapter, the number of defined benefits plans has been on a long-run decline since the mid-1980s. Some experts believe this shift is an expected result of the increasing mobility of the work force, because defined contribution plans generally are more appealing to workers who change jobs frequently. Another factor promoting this trend is global competition, which causes employers to reduce costs and liabilities. Other commentators have expressed concern that the defined contribution plan requires more attention from a more educated participant than does the defined benefit plan. If workers do not manage their defined contribution options well, if they fail to participate fully, or fail to leave the money inside their retirement plan, the results are likely to prove far less desirable than those achieved by the defined benefit plan. Another concern of commentators has centered on the risk of increasing longevity, which employers bear in defined benefit plans and which employees bear in defined contribution plans. That is, when an employer promises a worker "half your final annual wage in retirement," the employer bears the longevity risk. When the employer says, "you can have the balance in your individual retirement fund when you reach retirement," the employee is responsible for liquidating this amount over his or her lifetime.

Whether or not the trend from defined benefit to defined contribution plans is desirable remains an issue; what is no longer a question is whether the trend has occurred. Review the following quotation from a PBGC report:

> Traditional defined benefit pension plans, based on years of service and either final salary or a flat-dollar benefit formula, provide a stable source of retirement income to supplement Social Security. The number of private-sector defined benefit plans reached a peak of 112,000 in the mid-1980s. At that time, about one-third of American workers were covered by defined benefit plans. The number of plans now stands at about 30,000. In recent years, many employers have chosen not to adopt defined benefit plans, and others have chosen to terminate their existing defined benefit plans. From 1986 to 2004, 101,000 single-employer plans with about 7.5 million participants were terminated. In about 99,000 of these terminations, the plans had enough assets to purchase annuities in the private sector to cover all benefits earned by workers and retirees (a "standard termination"). In the remaining 2,000 cases, companies with underfunded plans shifted their pension liabilities to the PBGC.[9]

Some Reasons for the Shift from Defined Benefit to Defined Contribution Plans

The following reasons explain the increasing popularity of defined contributions plans with employers:

- Once the employer has made its contribution to the defined contribution plan, it has no further liability. The employer guarantees no future benefit.
- The employee bears the investment risk. Because the output is not guaranteed, if investment earnings are large, small, or even negative, the results affect only the worker's individual account.
- Defined contribution plans tend to be simpler to administer than defined benefit plans. Actuaries are not needed to determine if the plan is overfunded or underfunded.

---

[9] Pension Benefit Guarantee Corporation (PBGC), "An Analysis of Frozen Defined Benefit Plans," December 2005, p. 1.

- Defined contribution plans incur no PBGC premium cost. Because they do not create liabilities for unfunded promises, these plans are not subject to PBGC control.

If a defined contribution plan is substituted for a defined benefit plan, the employer gives up some of the following advantages.

- Because the defined benefit plan generally has a target replacement ratio sufficient to support a worker in retirement when supplemented by Social Security and individual resources, it facilitates the retirement of older workers. In contrast, if an older worker's defined contribution plan has an "inadequate" account balance, perhaps because of poor investment results, the worker well may continue working long after the employer wishes.
- The tax benefits, particularly for small firms, may be greater with a defined benefit plan than with a defined contribution plan.

As the data showing the decline in defined benefit plans reveal, the advantages of the shift from defined benefit to defined contribution plans have far outweighed the disadvantages for many employers.

The Underfunding of Defined Benefit Pension Plans

Consider the following equation that actuaries use to determine the financial soundness of a defined benefit pension plan:

Formula 21 – 1

Assets on hand + PV of future contributions = PV of promised benefits

PV = present value

To see how this equation works, we will consider the very simple case of a one-employee pension plan. The employee, Hailey, begins work at age 25, and her employer promises her a pension equal to half her final salary when she reaches age 65. The employer will fund the pension with regular contributions throughout Hailey's career. At age 25, no assets are on hand to fund Hailey's pension, but the company expects to make forty years of contributions. Because the employer's liability to Hailey is forty years in the future, it is very small when Hailey begins employment. Assume that, as planned, the employer contributes to the plan and the assets on hand grow over time. Then the present value of the future contributions will decrease each year after the employer makes the required contribution. Likewise, as Hailey steadily approaches age 65, the present value of her promised benefits increases. However, if the assets on hand fail to grow at the assumed rate, or if they shrink due to poor investment choices, then the employer either must increase future contributions or add more assets to the plan to keep the equation balanced. (In fact, in two recent years, plan sponsors have added more than $100 billion to meet federal minimum funding levels.)

Many actuarial assumptions are implied in this simple example, including assumptions about employee turnover, employee mortality before and after retirement, and investment earnings—the present value (PV) factor in the formula. Here we will focus only on the PV factor. If a high rate is assumed, the PV of the employer's future contributions and the pension liability will be smaller than if a low rate is assumed. But, if a high rate is assumed, then the plan must earn this rate, or there will be insufficient assets on hand when Hailey retires. Thus, a pension plan is **underfunded** when the sum of the assets on hand plus future contributions are inadequate to pay the promised

Underfunded

benefits. Deciding the correct interest rate to use when valuing pension plan assets and liabilities has been a subject for debate among accountants, actuaries and politicians because using the relatively low rates specified by current pension legislation has left many pension plans underfunded. As this material is being written, Congress is still debating the best way to deal with this underfunding.

The Financial Condition of the PBGC[10]

What happens if the government agency that guarantees pension payments to employees of insolvent pension plans is insolvent itself? Although President George W. Bush signed the Pension Protection Act in August 2006, much controversy still surrounds this topic. Consider the following two quotations:

> In 2004, the single-employer insurance program posted its largest loss and largest year-end shortfall in the agency's 30-year history. For the year, completed and probable pension plan terminations required PBGC to record financial losses totaling $14.7 billion. By year-end, these losses had more than doubled the program's deficit to $23.3 billion.[11]
>
> The PBGC estimates that, measured on a termination basis, total underfunding in the single-employer defined benefit plans it insures exceeded $450 billion as of September 30, 2005.[12]

The $450 billion figure is an estimate, and as the preceding material in this section described, many actuarial and statistical assumptions were used to develop this estimate. Moreover, this estimate likely will change several times before this textbook is printed. Moreover, not all currently underfunded pension plans will become PBGC liabilities. Nevertheless, the reader can assume that in the absence of a further legislative solution to the problem, at some point the PBGC's assets will be insufficient to pay all future pension benefits guaranteed by the PBGC.

The Pension Protection Act of 2006 raised the annual per-participant premium for single employer plans from $19 to $30. Future premium rates will be indexed to wage inflation beginning in 2007. This legislation also required employers emerging from bankruptcy to pay the PBGC a $1,250 per-participant fee annually for three years.

In addition to raising the employers' premium costs, other solutions to the PBGC's problems that Congress likely will consider include lowering guaranteed benefits to eligible retired workers or using general tax revenue to support the program. Each of these suggestions raises its own set of problems. For example, raising the PBCG premium causes employers with solvent defined benefit pension plans to subsidize employers with insolvent plans. Moreover, raising premiums likely will accelerate the move from defined benefit to defined contribution plans. Lowering benefits to retired workers is likely to be politically unpopular. Finally, with government deficits growing for the near future, adding an additional amount even close to the $450 billion PBGC projection would be economically undesirable. Another suggestion, raising the interest rate used to evaluate the solvency of pension plans as we discussed in the preceding section, will reduce the underfunding problem on paper, but if the pension plans do not earn the increased investment returns, this "solution" will only postpone dealing with this serious issue.

---

[10] For comprehensive background and current information on this topic, search the following Web site maintained by the Congressional Budget Office (CBO), (*http://www.cbo.gov/search.htm*), using the keywords "Pension Benefit Guarantee Corporation."

[11] *2004 Annual Report of the Pension Benefit Guarantee Corporation*, p. 4.

[12] "Understanding the Financial Condition of the Pension Insurance Program" (*http://www.pbgc.gov/media/key-resources-for-the-press/content/page15247.html/*).

PROFIT-SHARING, 401(K), 403(B), KEOGH, AND CAFETERIA PLANS

Profit-Sharing Plans

Profit-sharing plans are one type of defined-contribution plan. Unlike money purchase plans, the employer is not committed to a regular annual contribution. Rather, in years when the firm's profits permit, the employer credits each employee with a share of the profit. The payments may be in cash or may be deferred (like pension plans). Deferred profit-sharing plans may be qualified like pension plans. If they are qualified, they get the same tax-deferral advantages and must meet similar qualification requirements as pension plans. Because profit-sharing plans do not produce predictable benefits on which to base retirement income, they usually supplement other pension plans. The maximum tax-deductible contribution is 25 percent of an eligible employees' compensation, subject to a contribution limit that is indexed annually for inflation. Under limited circumstances, profit-sharing plans also may allow employees to receive distributions while working.

401(k) Plans

Most employers, including nonprofit organizations (except state and local governments), can establish a 401(k) plan. A 401(k) plan allows an employee a choice between taking income in cash or deferring the income by putting it in a qualified plan. If the employee chooses to put the income in a qualified 401(k) plan, all the advantages of tax deferral are available. That is, the employee can make contributions on a pretax basis, which lowers current taxable income. Tax law limits the annual contributions to 401(k) plans to $15,000 in 2006.[13] Once funds are deposited in this arrangement, withdrawals before age 59½ are subject to a 10 percent penalty unless attributed to the employee's death, disability, or hardship. Some employers match all or part of their employee's contributions, presumably as an inducement to increase plan participation. Some plans allow employees to borrow from their 401(k) accounts. Some plans also allow hardship withdrawals for emergency medical expenses, college tuition, or to purchase a home.

403(b) Plans or Tax-Deferred Annuities (TDAs)

The employees of nonprofit (tax-exempt) organizations such as universities, schools, hospitals, and museums have a special section of the IRC devoted to them. Congress justifies this special tax advantage because nonprofit employers do not have the same tax incentives as taxpaying employers to provide for their employees' welfare.

Originally, the law allowed the employees of the specified nonprofit institutions to reduce their salaries (and their income tax liability) voluntarily to purchase deferred annuities. Subsequently, the law was amended to allow contributions to be made to mutual funds. Money placed into tax-deferred annuities (TDAs) has all the advantages of tax deferral discussed throughout this chapter. There are limits on the amounts an employee can contribute to a TDA—$15,000 in 2006. Early withdrawal from these plans results in a 10 percent penalty.

Keogh Plans

Before 1983, Keogh plans were used to provide retirement benefits to the self-employed because qualified plans at that time had restrictions that applied to pensions

---

[13] These limits are subject to change by Congress. Readers can find current information at this Web site: (*http://www.irs.ustreas.gov/*). Use "401(k) contribution limits" as the keywords in the Search box on this site. Roth 401(k)s now exist. In general, deposits to these accounts are made with after-tax dollars, and if certain requirements are met, the distributions are not taxable.

for partners and sole proprietors. These restrictions no longer apply, and many partnerships and proprietorships use qualified plans for all employees, including the owners. Some smaller employers still use defined-benefit Keogh plans to fund pensions, however, because they allow considerable tax-shelter advantages when older owners are covered. The rules governing the amounts deposited in these plans are complicated.

Cafeteria Plans

In the past few years, some employers have given employees a choice of benefits by giving them an amount of money to spend, with minimum participation required in each alternative. Such choice-oriented plans may allow an employee, for example, to trade a higher deductible on the major medical plan in exchange for a dependent-care allowance. Each person or family will have a different priority of needs, and the flexibility of having a larger or smaller major medical deductible in exchange for a day care allowance can be valuable. Because of administrative difficulties and some issues involving taxation, cafeteria plans have not yet been widely adopted. Cafeteria plans are also known as **flexible benefit plans**, or **Section 125 plans**. One recent application of these plans has allowed employees to reduce their salaries voluntarily to fund dependent-care costs or medical benefits not covered by group health insurance. Using this approach, deductible and participation amounts and services not covered by group plans (such as regular medical examinations or orthodontia) can be financed on a tax-advantaged basis.

Flexible benefit plans

Section 125 plans

INDIVIDUAL RETIREMENT ACCOUNTS (IRAS)

Individual Retirement Account (IRA)

The federal government wants to encourage people to save for retirement and has passed several laws to achieve this result. One tax law allows qualified people to make limited tax-deductible contributions to an **Individual Retirement Account (IRA)**.[14] This provision of the tax code allows IRA accounts to earn tax-deferred investment income. Congress passed the original IRA provisions as part of ERISA.

Current tax rules distinguish between deductible and nondeductible IRA contributions. Deductible contributions can be made only by people in categories to be described shortly. Other people can make nondeductible contributions. Deductible contributions lower taxable income in the year made. The advantage of making nondeductible contributions lies in the tax deferral that is accorded to the investment income.

The maximum limits on contributions are the same for deductible and nondeductible contributions. The maximum limits, which are subject to change, rise to $5,000 in 2008. After 2008, the limit will be indexed to inflation and increase in $500 increments.[15]

Eligibility for Deductible Contributions

Currently, people in the following categories can make deductible IRA contributions:

- Single people not covered by an employer-provided pension.
- Married couples where neither spouse is covered by an employer-provided pension.

---

[14] Entering the keywords "Individual Retirement Account" or "IRA" into a search engine will produce a large number of interesting Web sites with information on this topic.

[15] As we previously noted, changing these limits is subject to the political process, and current limits and program features should be reviewed on the Internet at the IRS Web site (*http://irs.ustreas.gov/*).

TABLE 21–3 The Advantages of Contributing to an IRA

	IRA	*No IRA*
Gross income	$55,000	$55,000
IRA contribution [a]	(4,000)	0
Adjusted gross income	51,000	55,000
Personal exemption [a]	(3,500)	(3,500)
Standard deduction [a]	(5,000)	(5,000)
Taxable income	42,500	46,500
Income tax [b]	(6,375)	(6,975)
Disposable income	36,125	39,525

[a]*This is a hypothetical number. The actual number is indexed for inflation and changes each year.*
[b]*A 15 percent rate is used for the purpose of illustration.*

- Single people or married couples covered by an employer-provided pension but with lower or middle incomes may make deductible IRA contributions determined by a formula tied to their total income.

As an example of how an IRA can benefit a worker, consider Al Goma, who earned $55,000 in a recent year. His employer provided no pension plan for his employees. Al wants to save $4,000 for his retirement. He is considering using an IRA and uses Table 21–3 to evaluate the results.

Note that if Al makes the IRA contribution, his disposable income is $36,125, but he has $4,000 in an IRA for a total of $40,125. This amount is slightly greater than his disposable income if the IRA contribution is not made. Moreover, Al continues to earn tax-deferred income until he withdraws the money from the IRA. Note that the taxes are deferred, not eliminated. Also, if Al makes the IRA contribution, he cannot withdraw the money without penalty before age 59½. Because he is 55 now, the early withdrawal penalty is not troublesome. Younger people, however, may feel differently.

Investment Alternatives

IRA funds must be held by qualified trustees or by a life insurance company. If a life insurance company holds the funds, the IRA contracts must be in the form of annuities and no death benefit may be provided. Qualified trustees include banks, other savings institutions (including federal credit unions), mutual funds, and stock brokerages that provide self-directed IRA accounts. Most of the investment alternatives provided by these institutions are available for IRA use.

Rollovers

Rollover

Money may be placed in an IRA by a rollover. A **rollover** occurs when money from an IRA or other retirement plan is placed with a new trustee. For example, a rollover occurs if an investor takes IRA funds from one mutual fund and places them with another fund. Rollovers may occur when an employee switches jobs and takes vested retirement benefits from a pension plan, or when an employer terminates a pension plan and makes payments of vested benefits to individual employees. If the employee takes the vested benefits and places them in an IRA, this transaction is considered a rollover. A rollover also would occur if a person switched from one investment medium to another, such as from a mutual fund to a bank. In general, a person has sixty days to move funds from one IRA trustee to another without recognizing taxable income on the exchange.

Taxation

IRA withdrawals are taxed as ordinary income in the year received. Any portion of a payment attributed to a nondeductible contribution is not taxed a second time. In other words, only deductible contributions and tax-deferred interest are taxed.

In general, age 59½ is the earliest date of withdrawal without penalty. Early withdrawal from an IRA causes a 10 percent tax penalty in addition to the ordinary income tax arising when the withdrawal is added to the person's taxable income. Withdrawal of funds must begin by age 70½. Exceptions to the premature withdrawal penalty exist in cases of death or disability before age 59½.

Roth IRA

The preceding material describes what now has come to be known as the "traditional IRA." A more recent version of the IRA is known as the "Roth IRA." Contributions to a Roth IRA are not tax deductible, but the funds in the account are tax-free when withdrawn. Under current rules, withdrawals of contributions at any time are not subject to tax, as would be expected because the contributions were made with after-tax dollars. Withdrawals of investment earnings also are tax-free if IRC rules are followed. To avoid taxation, withdrawals of investment earnings must occur after the taxpayer is at least 59½ years old, and the Roth IRA must have existed for at least five years before that. Tax-free withdrawals of investment earnings also are possible if the Roth IRA has existed for at least five years, and the taxpayer becomes disabled, has died, or uses up to $10,000 for qualified first-time home-buyer expenses.

Table 21–4 provides a comparison of the major features of a traditional IRA and the Roth IRA.

TABLE 21–4   A Comparison of an IRA and a Roth IRA

Feature	Traditional IRA	Roth IRA
Eligibility	Working taxpayers under age 70½ can contribute up to $4,000 (2005). *Phase-out rules and limits may apply.*	Up to $4,000 (2005) of earned income may be contributed. *Phase-out rules and limits may apply.*
Tax deductibility of contributions	Yes, subject to income limits and phase-out restrictions and if a person is not a participant in an employer's plan.	None
Taxation of annual investment earnings	None	None
Maximum age for contributions	70½	None
Mandatory age for withdrawals	April 1 of the year after the year in which the taxpayer reaches 70½.	None
Taxation upon distribution	All taxed at ordinary income tax rates.	No tax if account is five years old and withdrawn after 59½.
Penalty for early withdrawal	10% on amount of distribution before 59½ (unless exception applies)	Contributions may be removed with no tax penalty or tax if account is open five years or more.
		10% penalty on amount of earnings distributed before 59½ (unless exception applies). Income tax also applies to earnings withdrawn prematurely.

SUMMARY

Employers define the term *employee benefits* as anything of value received by an employee other than wages. Major employer-provided benefits include the following:

- Government-mandated benefits: Social Security, workers' compensation, and unemployment insurance
- Group life insurance plans
- Group disability income insurance plans
- Group health insurance plans
- Pension plans
- All other benefits, including vacations, day care, employee discounts, and reimbursement for educational expenses

Proponents argue that employee benefits allow the employer to attract, retain, and motivate the employee better than straight wages. Employees receive many advantages from employee benefit programs, including (1) forced saving for retirement accompanied by professional money management; (2) getting insurance coverage for lower cost than if purchased individually; and (3) getting insurance coverage when it might be totally unavailable individually.

Employee benefit plans must not discriminate in favor of highly compensated employees. Several federal laws, including ERISA and the IRC, are designed to prevent such discrimination with tax-subsidized dollars.

A pension plan is designed to provide employees with retirement income. A pension plan may be qualified or nonqualified. If it qualifies under relevant sections of the IRC, the employer and employee receive substantial tax advantages centering on tax deferral. If the plan does not qualify, the employee reports income as soon as the employer makes a payment to the pension.

The following federal laws regulate pension plans:

- Employee Retirement Income Security Act of 1974 (ERISA)
- Age Discrimination in Employment Act of 1967 (ADEA) (amended in 1986)
- Civil Rights Act of 1964 (amended in 1978)
- Retirement Equity Act of 1984

The chapter also described profit-sharing plans, IRAs, and 401(k) plans, among other investment options.

REVIEW TERMS

- Age Discrimination in Employment Act of 1967 (ADEA)
- Allocated funding
- Basic medical insurance
- Capitation payments
- Certificate of participation
- Coordination of benefits
- Credibility
- Defined-benefit plan
- Defined-contribution plan
- Employee benefits
- Employee Retirement Income Security Act of 1974 (ERISA)
- Experience-rated premium
- Flexible benefit plans
- Government Accountability Office (GAO)
- Group deposit administration contract
- Group insurance
- Group major medical insurance
- Group term life insurance
- Health Insurance Portability and Accountability Act of 1996 (HIPAA)
- Health maintenance organizations (HMOs)
- Immediate participation guarantee contract
- Individual Retirement Account (IRA)
- Integrated plans
- Money purchase plan
- Nondiscrimination rules
- Nonqualified pension plans
- Normal retirement age
- Pension Benefit Guarantee Corporation (PBGC)
- Pension plan
- Permanent disability
- Preferred provider organizations (PPOs)
- Qualification rules
- Qualified pension plans
- Replacement ratio
- Retirement
- Retirement Equity Act of 1984 (REA)
- Retirement income policies
- Rollover
- Section 125 plans
- Sick-leave plans
- Tax deferral
- Unallocated funding
- Vesting

REVIEW

1. Define the term *employee benefits* and describe some of the benefits included in this category.
2. Why is it important to learn about employee benefits?
3. Identify nine federal laws governing employee benefit plans.
4. How does the U.S. approach to providing society with economic security differ from other national governments' approaches?
5. Describe the employer's goals in offering employee benefits.
6. Why do employees prefer employee benefits to straight wage income?
7. What are two main objectives of federal employee-benefits legislation? Briefly describe how these purposes are achieved.
8. Describe the four basic requirements for a benefit plan to be qualified for tax benefits.
9. Explain some important characteristics of group insurance.
10. List three different approaches for determining a group life insurance benefit.
11. How is group term life insurance taxed while the insured is alive?
12. Most financial planners do not recommend that employees rely exclusively on group life insurance for family survivor death benefits. Explain their reasons.
13. What is an integrated group disability plan?
14. Give two different definitions of permanent disability.
15. What are some of the differences between basic medical and major medical insurance policies?
16. Identify some expenses typically excluded by group health insurance contracts.
17. Describe several categories of workers who might benefit from the COBRA provisions.
18. Describe some benefits provided by the FMLA.
19. Describe the main reason for qualifying pension plans from the government's standpoint and from the employer's standpoint.
20. Explain the difference between defined-benefit and defined-contribution pension plans.
21. List four requirements for qualifying a pension plan.
22. Describe four of the federal laws that apply to pension plans.
23. Describe an important difference between pension plans funded with insurance contracts and those funded using trusts.
24. What is the general rule regarding the taxation of pension benefits?
25. Describe the groups that are supposed to benefit from Keogh plans, 401(k) plans, and 403(b) plans.
26. Describe two important tax advantages accruing to people making IRA contributions. Why would an employee be willing to make a nondeductible contribution to an IRA?
27. What is an IRA rollover?

OBJECTIVE QUESTIONS

1. All the following rules apply to qualifying a benefit plan except:
   a. The employee must receive all the tax benefits.
   b. The plan must be in writing.
   c. The plan must be for the exclusive benefit of employees.
   d. The plan must be expected to last indefinitely.
2. "Credibility" with respect to experience-rated group insurance premiums means:
   a. The employer is well known to the insurer.
   b. The employer has a minimum number of employees.
   c. The insurer has charged the lowest rates permitted by regulation.
   d. The insurer has observed the employer's loss data for a sufficiently long period to have confidence in the results.
3. All the following exclusions are common in group health insurance plans except:
   a. No coverage of cosmetic surgery
   b. No coverage of the expenses of the emergency room
   c. No coverage for preexisting conditions
   d. No coverage of custodial care
4. In a defined benefit plan:
   a. The employee's pension is determined by a formula.
   b. The employer makes a flat amount annual payment for each employee.
   c. The employer receives no immediate tax advantage but gets a deduction after the employee retires.
   d. The employee makes the investment choices and bears the investment risk.
5. One advantage of tax deferral on qualified pension plan contributions is:
   a. The employee never has to pay taxes on the contribution.
   b. Taxes are deferred until withdrawal and investment income can be earned on money that would otherwise have been paid in taxes.
   c. Only the employer can earn tax-free investment income; the employee pays taxes immediately but at a reduced rate.

d. The employee pays taxes in the year the employer makes contributions, but then taxes on investment earnings are deferred until withdrawn in retirement.
6. HMOs charge employers a monthly fee called:
   a. A coverage fee
   b. The pro rata plan fee
   c. The subrogation payment
   d. The capitation payment
7. When an insurer provides coverage for many people under one master contract, the result is called:

a. Reinsurance
b. Multiple insurance
c. Group insurance
d. Combination plan
8. In group health insurance, a disease for which the employee was being treated before the employment began is called:
   a. A pretreated disease
   b. An undiscovered ailment
   c. A preexisting condition
   d. A known disorder

DISCUSSION QUESTIONS

1. What are the advantages and disadvantages of using the free enterprise system to provide economic security to society?
2. What are some of the important problems encountered in delivering health care to society? Do you think it is the government's responsibility to provide health care to all citizens?
3. Would you prefer a 10 percent increase in your before-tax salary or 10 percent of your salary contributed to a qualified pension plan? Explain your choice. (If you are a typical unemployed student, assume that you are working full time and making an average salary in your chosen profession.)

INTERNET RESEARCH ASSIGNMENTS

1. What does the PBGC guarantee? What does it not guarantee? What are the current monthly maximum amounts guaranteed by the PBGC? Start your search at this site: (*http://www.pbgc.gov/*).
2. Collect some recent data on the U.S. employee benefit system. Start your search at this site: (*http://www.ebri.org/*). (Hint: use the Publications and Data Book tabs at this site.)
3. Determine the current IRS contribution limits for some of the pension plans described in this chapter.

(Hint: use "contribution limits" in a keyword search on the IRS Web site (*http://irs.gov/*).
4. Investigate how a Roth 401(k) works if employers choose to offer one in addition to the regular 401(k) plan. Determine when the Roth 401(k) plan is set to expire—that is, when it no longer will have favorable tax status.

Appendix: Tax Deferral

The benefit of tax deferral is critical to the understanding of qualified pension plans. Figure 21–1 and Table 21–4, earlier in the chapter, might help some readers to understand the significance of the process.

Again, assume that Joe Green and Sue Blue each receives $1,000 in marginal income. Joe takes his income in cash. Sue takes hers in some qualified plan. Joe and Sue each pay 30 percent in taxes. Each earns 8 percent on investments.

At the end of year 1, Joe paid $300 in taxes on his $1,000 in income, and $16.80 in taxes on the $56 dollars of investment income. He begins year 2 with $739.20. Sue earned $80 in income on the $1,000. She has no tax liability until the money is withdrawn. Figure 21–3 shows these data.

The Advantages of Tax Deferral

Once you have mastered the concept presented in Figure 21–3, examine Table 21–5. It shows the process repeated for thirty years. Note that Sue must pay taxes at the 30 percent rate at the end of the period, whereas Joe pays annual taxes. Even after paying taxes, the balance in Sue's account is about double that in Joe's. This is due to the advantage of tax deferral. Sue earned income on dollars that otherwise would have been paid in taxes (the initial $300). She also earned income on the portion of the annual investment returns that otherwise would have been paid in taxes.

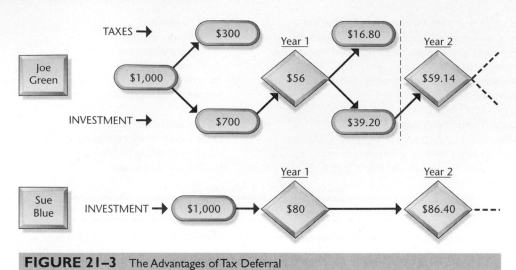

FIGURE 21–3 The Advantages of Tax Deferral

TABLE 21–5 30 Years of Tax Deferral

	Joe Green					Sue Blue				
Year	Deposit	Taxes	Interest	Taxes	Fund Balance	Deposit	Interest	Fund Balance	Taxes	Balance After Tax
1	1,000.00	300	56.00	16.80	739.20	1,000.00	80.00	1,080.00		
2			59.14	17.74	780.60		86.40	1,166.40		
3			62.45	18.73	824.31		93.31	1,259.71		
4			65.94	19.78	870.47		100.78	1,360.49		
5			69.64	20.89	919.22		108.84	1,469.33		
6			73.54	22.06	970.69		117.55	1,586.87		
7			77.66	23.30	1,025.05		126.95	1,713.82		
8			82.00	24.60	1,082.45		137.11	1,850.93		
9			86.60	25.98	1,143.07		148.07	1,999.00		
10			91.45	27.43	1,207.08		159.92	2,158.92		
11			96.57	28.97	1,274.68		172.71	2,331.64		
12			101.97	30.59	1,346.06		186.53	2,518.17		
13			107.68	32.31	1,421.44		201.45	2,719.62		
14			113.72	34.11	1,501.04		217.57	2,937.19		
15			120.08	36.03	1,585.10		234.98	3,172.17		
16			126.81	38.04	1,673.87		253.77	3,425.94		
17			133.91	40.17	1,767.60		274.08	3,700.02		
18			141.41	42.42	1,866.59		296.00	3,996.02		
19			149.33	44.80	1,971.12		319.68	4,315.70		
20			157.69	47.31	2,081.50		345.26	4,660.96		
21			166.52	49.96	2,198.06		372.88	5,033.83		
22			175.85	52.75	2,321.16		402.71	5,436.54		
23			185.69	55.71	2,451.14		434.92	5,871.46		
24			196.09	58.83	2,588.40		469.72	6,341.18		
25			207.07	62.12	2,733.35		507.29	6,848.48		
26			218.67	65.60	2,886.42		547.88	7,396.35		
27			230.91	69.27	3,048.06		591.71	7,988.06		
28			243.84	73.15	3,218.75		639.04	8,627.11		
29			257.50	77.25	3,399.00		690.17	9,317.27		
30			271.92	81.58	3,589.35		745.38	10,062.66	3,018.80	7,043.86

CHAPTER 22

Social Security

After studying this chapter, you should be able to:

- Explain why the Social Security system was developed

- Describe the benefits that Social Security provides

- Describe how Social Security benefits are financed

- List eligible recipients of Social Security benefits

- Describe how the amount of a worker's benefits are calculated

- Describe the benefits provided by Medicare

- Discuss some of the issues facing the Social Security system

At the end of 2005, 48 million people were receiving benefits: 33 million retired workers and their dependents, 7 million survivors of deceased workers, and 8 million disabled workers and their dependents. During the year an estimated 159 million people had earnings covered by Social Security and paid payroll taxes. Total benefits paid in 2005 were $521 billion. Income was $702 billion, and assets held in special issue U.S. Treasury securities grew to $1.9 trillion.[1]

As the preceding quotation shows, the Social Security program affects virtually all Americans, either as beneficiaries or as covered workers. The designers intended this essential social insurance program to be the floor of protection for the financial security of our society. Thus, questions about its solvency, its efficiency, and its future are of the utmost importance. In recent years, these very questions have been at the forefront of public debate. This chapter provides a comprehensive description of the Social Security program and provides the background needed to understand critical but complex arguments about the future economic security of Americans.[2]

The Social Security program has been operating for more than seventy years and most commentators agree that this program has served the country well. Social Security's future, however, is less clear. Many critics have serious concerns about the system's stability. Some people believe the system is inadequately financed and in the long run will be unable to deliver all the benefits promised unless substantial changes are made in the near future. Many young workers believe Social Security will not provide them with benefits. Conversely, other critics believe the system currently is accumulating too large a

---

[1] *The 2006 Annual Report of the Board of Trustees of the Federal Old-Age and Survivors Insurance and Disability Insurance Trust Funds*, p. 2. To see the document, check the following Web sites: (*http://www. socialsecurity.gov/OACT/TRSUM/trsummary.html*) and (*http://www.socialsecurity.gov/OACT/TR/*).
[2] The Social Security Administration (SSA) Web site (*http://www.ssa.gov/*) provides current data and information on this all-important part of the U.S. social safety net. Readers can find current Medicare information at (*http://www.medicare.gov/*).

surplus. Some critics find the benefits too liberal; others believe the benefits are inadequate. Some politicians suggest that people be given the option of substituting private insurance and savings programs for compulsory participation in Social Security. We will discuss these interesting questions in this chapter, but we will not provide the answers to these suggestions or criticisms. Instead, our aim is to give the background so readers can understand the issues raised by the system's critics and defenders and form their own opinions about these important issues.

SOCIAL INSURANCE BACKGROUND

During the Industrial Revolution, the economy changed from an agricultural to an industrial basis. This change occurred first in Europe, in the latter half of the nineteenth century. There were several distinct characteristics of this revolution, including the appearance of steam-powered machinery, a movement of the population from the country to the city, and a devotion to applied technological research, so rapid change bred on itself. Among the changes in society caused by this revolution were a separation of people from the land and growing interdependence among people, with far fewer families capable of self-sufficiency. Moreover, laborers living in rapidly growing urban areas often no longer could look to their relatives for financial or other support. Industrial society therefore created greater economic insecurity.

To note that the Industrial Revolution caused great suffering as well as delivering great material benefits is to state the obvious. Today's relatively high standard of living, which machinery and scientific advances made possible, follows a period of great economic distress for many workers. Low wages and unsanitary living conditions preceded the greatly increased life span and the amount of leisure time people presently enjoy. The widespread human suffering associated with the Industrial Revolution, combined with the decline of self-sufficiency and the great disparities in wealth between the upper and lower classes, led to the introduction of social insurance as well as the socialist political philosophy.

Interestingly, social insurance was developed as a response to socialism rather than being a part of it. The most conspicuous man in the early development and implementation of a social insurance system was Otto von Bismarck, the chancellor of Germany. As chancellor, he saw growing opposition to his party from the socialist movement. The economic misery of the masses of people was what fed the socialist cause in Germany and elsewhere in Europe. Bismarck, viewed by some as the devil, by others as a diplomatic and political genius, was unrelenting in his approach to opponents. After an unsuccessful attempt to destroy the socialist movement by force, he changed tactics and implemented the first Social Security system. The purpose of his scheme was to cut at the taproot of the economic problems that fed the socialist political party. Funding his program by taxing current workers, he accomplished his goal of undermining the socialists without cost to the wealthy members of society who supported his party.

Bismarck's system became law in stages. Medical insurance was provided in 1883, accident insurance in 1884, and old-age and disability insurance in 1889. Unemployment insurance was not a part of Bismarck's program. The rest of industrialized Europe, which faced the same political and economic problems, soon followed Bismarck's lead. At the beginning of the twentieth century, social insurance programs were the rule in European industrialized countries.

In the United States, we refer to the time of our most serious economic problems as the Great Depression. The stock market crash of 1929 was a dramatic and clearly identifiable symptom of the problem. From an economic standpoint, however, the greatest number of people felt the worst consequences in the early 1930s. President Franklin D. Roosevelt responded with the New Deal program. Part of this program was the Social Security Act. More formally, the program was called the Old-Age Benefits Program. Today the program is known as the **Old-Age, Survivors, Disability Insurance—Hospital Insurance Program (OASDI-HI)**. Congress passed the Social Security Act in 1935 and the program took effect in 1937. Thus, some forty-five years after the implementation of Bismarck's program, the U.S. government began to apply the principles of insurance to the solution of society's greatest economic problem—the provision of economic security.

Old-Age, Survivors, Disability Insurance— Hospital Insurance Program (OASDI-HI)

The History and Philosophy of the U.S. Social Security System

In the Depression of the 1930s, about 25 percent of all Americans were unemployed. Many banks failed, and people lost not only their current income but past savings as well. No wonder the term *Social Security* was chosen rather than *social insurance*. In those troubled days, people needed the promise and hope of economic security.

The Social Security Act represented a great break with past political philosophy in the United States. The principle of individual responsibility typified the prevailing political philosophy before 1935. Each family was responsible for its own financial security. However, moving from the farm to the city substituted economic interdependency for self-sufficiency. Thus, a vacuum existed in society's economic safety net, and after 1935, the government assumed part of the family's role in providing economic security.

The Social Security Act of 1935 marked the federal government's acceptance of some of the responsibility for the provision of individual economic security. The key word here is *some*. According to the original concept of Social Security, benefits were to be the floor upon which people were to complete the remainder of their economic building. While the *floor-of-protection* concept remains the current philosophy of the program, the appropriate height of the floor is subject to debate. Some people want a relatively high level of benefits; others prefer a more moderate level. Those critics who continue to stress individual responsibility favor a relatively low level of benefits.

Over the years since 1935, the expansion of the original program has been continuous. New groups, such as physicians and members of the armed forces, have been added to the program. New benefits, disability coverage, and health insurance for the aged, were added. The amount of benefits has increased steadily. In one recent year, the dollars spent for the Social Security program represented about 21 percent of all the dollars spent by the federal government. Today almost all Americans either pay Social Security taxes or are eligible to receive benefits.

Social Security Is Not a Public Assistance Program

Public assistance programs

Both **public assistance programs** and Social Security are solutions to social and economic problems, but public assistance, or welfare, is not social insurance. What these two government programs have in common is that they both are government-operated transfer payment systems. The government takes money from all taxpayers to fund welfare payments to people in need, and the government takes money from the currently employed to fund benefits for eligible workers and their dependents. In each case, the government takes money from one group and gives it to another group.

Two characteristics distinguish public assistance from Social Security. First, people who receive Social Security benefits made contributions for their benefits, as is the case with any insurance program. No such payment is expected of welfare recipients. Second, recipients of Social Security do not have to demonstrate financial need to receive benefits. Social Security benefits are a legal right for all eligible people. The wealthiest

Americans are entitled to Social Security benefits as soon as their eligibility, which is *not* a function of financial need, is established.

While Social Security and public assistance are different types of programs, they share some common threads. That is, some aspects of the Social Security system spring from the same goals as a welfare program. For example, the total amount of survivor benefits a family receives is determined in part by the number of dependent children. Thus, the greater the need, the greater the benefits paid. Also, the current Social Security benefit structure provides lower-income people more than their actuarially fair share of the benefits. Providing benefits based in part on need reflects the goal of supplying **socially adequate** benefits. Paying benefits based on individual earnings, regardless of need, reflects the goal of providing **individual equity** in benefits.

Socially adequate

Individual equity

Social Security and Private Insurance Are Different

Several important distinctions can be made between private insurance and Social Security, including the following:

- Participation in Social Security is compulsory; private insurance purchases are a matter of free choice.
- Social Security benefits are predetermined by a formula; private insurance benefits are a matter of choice.
- The Social Security system, with the taxing power of the government behind it, can operate on a self-supporting, pay-as-you-go basis. To protect the public against insolvencies, regulators demand private insurance companies be fully funded. Theoretically, a private life insurance company could be liquidated at any point and all its liabilities could be met. By contrast, the Social Security system never has been fully funded.
- Benefits of the Social Security program can be changed (either increased or decreased) by legislation; private, contractual benefits generally are not subject to change.

Social Security Is an Insurance System

Social Security is unique. It is not a public assistance program, and it is different from private insurance. It is a social insurance program operated by the federal government. The major perils covered by the Social Security program are premature death, disability, outliving one's income, and medical expenses of the aged. These are the same perils insured by private life insurance companies. The Social Security system, as is true of all insurance systems, transfers costs from the few people who experience losses to all who are exposed to them. The system uses the pooling technique of combining loss exposures and then using actuarial statistics to predict losses. If the system predicts losses accurately, it can operate on a financially sound basis even though it is not fully funded.

Because the essential features of an insurance system underlie its operations, insurance experts conclude that the Social Security program is an insurance program, despite having some aspects comparable to public assistance. Because the government operates the Social Security system and because it is different from private insurance in several important respects, we call Social Security a social insurance program. A **social insurance program** is a government-run insurance program operated soundly using actuarial techniques but funded primarily by current contributions while relying on the taxing power of the government to guarantee solvency. Table 22–1 reviews some of these ideas.

Social insurance program

TABLE 22–1   Comparison of Social Security, Private Insurance, and Public Assistance

	Social Security	*Private Insurance*	*Public Assistance*
Recipient pays for benefits	Yes	Yes	No
Benefits subject to change	Yes	No	Yes
Compulsory program	Yes	No	No
General tax support	No	No	Yes
Fully funded program	No	Yes	No
Losses predicted Exposed to perils	Yes	Yes	No, transferred to all
Benefits based on need	No	No	Yes

THE OPERATION OF THE SOCIAL SECURITY PROGRAM

People writing about the "current" Social Security system must realize that their work likely will be obsolete, at least in some respects, before it is published. Therefore, especially with respect to any numbers cited in this chapter, I advise readers to check the Social Security Web site cited earlier or with the nearest Social Security branch office before making any personal financial decisions or giving any speeches. Although the numbers change regularly, the general ideas and rules forming the Social Security program change much less frequently.

The Program Is Compulsory for Almost Every Worker

Federal Insurance Contributions Act (FICA)

Since it began in 1935, the Social Security program has considerably expanded the scope of covered employment. Today almost every wage earner pays the Social Security tax, the **Federal Insurance Contributions Act (FICA)** deduction from paychecks. The program now covers wage earners, self-employed people, members of the U.S. armed forces, farmers, and people whose income comes from tips. It is easier to cite the few groups excluded from the program than to cite the covered groups. Full-time civilian employees of the federal government who were hired before 1984 are not covered. Special provisions of the Social Security law also allow employees of a few state and local governments, specified religious occupations, and children under 18 working for a parent to avoid participation in the program.

A Tax on Wages Is the Main Source of Funds

Covered maximum wage

Where does the government get the money to pay Social Security benefits? Almost all the money comes from a tax on the wages of covered employees. The tax applies only until a covered maximum wage is reached. The **covered maximum wage** is subject to change each year to allow for inflation. For example, in 2006, the covered maximum wage was $94,200. Both the employer and employee pay the Social Security tax. In a recent year, each party paid 7.65 percent of the covered wage up to the covered maximum. Employees who earn more than the covered maximum pay 1.45 percent of all additional earnings to support the hospital insurance (HI) portion of the Social Security program. The tax on self-employed people is 15.3 (2×7.65) percent.

As an example of how the Social Security tax applies to earned income, consider three brothers. The first, Dick Shun, a speech therapist at a hospital, earned $40,000 in 2006 and paid $3,060 ($0.0765 \times 40,000$) in Social Security taxes. The hospital also paid $3,060 in Social Security taxes for its employee. His brother, Moe Shun, an airline pilot, earned $100,000 in 2006, when the maximum covered wage was $94,200. Moe's Social

Security tax is calculated as follows:

$$0.0765 \times 94{,}200 = \$7{,}206$$
$$0.0145 \times (100{,}000 - 94{,}200) = \underline{84}$$
$$\text{Total tax} = \$7{,}290$$

The third Shun brother, Penn, is retired. He received $25,000 in dividend and interest income in 2006 but had no wages (earned income). Because the Social Security tax applies only to earned income, Penn pays no Social Security tax.

Benefits Are Not Fully Funded

The government operates Social Security on a pay-as-you-go or current-income basis. The taxes collected from currently employed workers and their employers are used to pay benefits to the current recipients. Unlike private life insurance companies, the invested assets of the Social Security system are small relative to the system's liabilities. Therefore, investment earnings play a much smaller role in financing Social Security benefits than they do in financing private life insurance benefits.

Since the late 1980s, the system has accumulated a surplus that will be used to cushion the impact of the retirement of the baby-boom workers who were born after 1946 and will begin to retire around the year 2013. These accumulating funds are invested in government securities as required by law. The securities issued to the Social Security system earn interest based on the prevailing rate that the U.S. government pays to borrow money from other sources.

General tax revenue plays almost no part in providing funds to the system. One exception is the government contribution toward Part B benefits of the Medicare program. Social Security was designed originally, and continues to be operated, as a self-supporting, pay-as-you-go system.

Insured Status and Eligibility for Benefits

Eligible

To be **eligible** for benefits, a person must be (1) fully insured, (2) currently insured, or (3) disability insured.

Fully insured

People are **fully insured** after they accumulate forty quarters (ten years) of covered employment. Once attained, fully insured status cannot be lost. A person is **currently insured** if six of the thirteen quarters prior to death were in covered employment. Currently insured status makes a worker eligible for survivor benefits but not retirement benefits. To be **disability insured**, the worker must have been in covered employment for twenty of the forty quarters before disability and be fully insured. Special provisions apply to relatively young or old workers.

Currently insured

Disability insured

Quarters of Coverage (QC)

Quarter of coverage (QC)

Workers earn one **quarter of coverage (QC)** when their covered earnings exceed a stated minimum. In the year 2006, $970 in wage or self-employment income was required for each QC earned. Workers earning $3,880 or more during this year earned four QCs. No more than four QCs can be earned in one year. Workers do not need to earn covered income in four separate quarters to receive four QCs; some baseball players could earn four QCs in one inning. The amount required to earn one QC is subject to change annually.

Calculation of Benefits

Covered earnings

The amount of Social Security benefits paid to recipients and their families is based on the amount of **covered earnings**—earnings on which Social Security taxes have been paid. Not all earnings are subject to the Social Security tax. Only the earnings up to a stated maximum are subject to the tax. The maximum earnings amount has changed in each of the past several years. Earnings in excess of these amounts do not count in a determination of the amount of Social Security benefits a worker receives.

Since 1977, workers' wages have been indexed to allow for the effects of inflation. Explaining the actual mathematical procedure underlying the indexing is beyond the scope of this introductory book. Rather, we examine a shortened and simplified view of how a benefit is calculated:[3]

- *Step 1.* The number of years after 1950 (or a person's 21st birthday, if later) up to but not including the year of death, disability, or 62nd birthday (whichever comes first) is calculated.
- *Step 2.* Five years are subtracted from the forgoing total, allowing elimination of the five years of lowest earnings.
- *Step 3.* The actual earnings for the remaining years are entered, limited by the maximum amount of covered earnings.
- *Step 4.* The earnings are then indexed.
- *Step 5.* The total earnings, after indexation, are divided by the total number of months in the worker's career. For example, assume that in Step 4, the worker's total indexed earnings equal $1 million over a thirty-five-year career. Thirty-five years equals 420 months. The formula calls for $1,000,000 / 420, or about $2,381.

Average indexed monthly earnings (AIME)

Primary insurance amount (PIA)

Maximum family benefit

Cost-of-living adjustment (COLA)

Consumer price index (CPI)

The $2,381 outcome is called the worker's **average indexed monthly earnings (AIME).** The AIME is then used to determine the worker's **primary insurance amount (PIA).** The transformation from the AIME to the PIA is done by a formula that is updated annually. Retirement, disability, and survivor benefits are expressed as a percentage of the worker's PIA. The PIA also determines the **maximum family benefit,** the greatest amount payable on one Social Security account. Thus, if Johann Bach died leaving twenty dependent children, each child's benefit and the widow's benefit would have to be reduced proportionally so that the maximum family benefit is not exceeded.

Since 1975, Social Security benefits have received annual increases called a **cost-of-living adjustment (COLA).** That is, each year Social Security benefits increase by the same percentage as the increase in the **consumer price index (CPI).** Such annual increases allow Social Security recipients to maintain their purchasing power.

CATEGORIES OF BENEFITS

Social Security benefits fall into the following four broad categories:

- Retirement benefits
- Survivor benefits
- Disability benefits
- Medical care benefits for the aged and disabled

Retirement Benefits

Worker

Retirement benefit

The **retirement benefit** is similar to a pure annuity—that is, Social Security sends out regular monthly checks during the recipient's lifetime. A full retirement benefit is

---

[3] The SSA Web site (*http://www.ssa.gov/*) includes a benefits calculator that people can use to estimate their benefits.

available to *fully insured* workers at the "**normal retirement age**." An increase in the normal retirement age from 65 to 67 began to be phased in 2003 (67 is the normal retirement age for people born in 1960 or later). For simplicity's sake, however, we will continue to illustrate examples using age 65 as the normal retirement age. When a worker retires between the ages of 62 and 65, a reduced retirement benefit is available. The reduction is based on actuarial statistics.

Spouse

If the retired worker is married, the spouse, if age 65, is entitled to a retirement benefit equal to 50 percent of the worker's benefit. If the spouse is 62 to 64, an actuarially reduced benefit is available. If the spouse also is entitled to a benefit due to his or her own covered employment, he or she may take the larger of the two benefits but not both.

For example, assume both John and Gail Adams are employed and are entitled to Social Security retirement benefits based on their own employment records. If John's monthly benefit is $800 and Gail's is $650, Gail will have the choice of $400 (half of $800) or $650. Clearly, she will choose her own retirement benefit. Had she worked only intermittently and therefore earned a minimum monthly benefit of $350, she still would be able to receive $400, which is one-half of her husband's benefit. If the retired

worker has a **dependent child**—one who is younger than 18—the child also is entitled to a monthly benefit equal to 50 percent of the worker's benefit.

Benefit Example

To illustrate the retirement benefit provisions and calculations, assume that Francis Bacon, a swine breeder, retires in 2007 with a PIA of $1,500. If he is age 65, he can receive $1,500 per month as a retirement benefit. His wife, Etta (if she is 65 or older), can receive a monthly benefit of $750 (half of $1,500) based on her husband's earnings and PIA. If Francis is 62, his benefit is reduced to $1,200 (80 percent of $1,500). If Etta is 62, her benefit is reduced to $562.50 (75 percent of $750). For ages between 62 and 65, benefits are reduced by 5/9 of 1 percent for each month that the worker is under age 65. Therefore, retirement 36 months early causes a 20 percent reduction in benefits (5/9 × 36 = 20). A spouse's benefit is reduced by 25/36 of 1 percent for each month the spouse is under 65.

Table 22–2 provides a review of the retirement benefits available from Social Security.

Survivor Benefits

If fully insured or currently insured workers die, their survivors are entitled to Social Security benefits. These benefits do not take the form of a single cash payment, which is the typical way life insurance policy death claims are paid. Rather, Social Security survivor benefits involve a regular monthly check paid to the dependent survivors. The only one-time payment that Social Security makes is a $255 lump-sum death benefit, which is one feature of the program that has not changed.

TABLE 22–2 Social Security Retirement Benefits

Worker:	
Normal retirement age	100% of PIA
Age 62–65	PIA reduced
Spouse:	
Normal retirement age	50% of worker's PIA
Age 62–65	50% of PIA reduced
Eligible child	50% each

A mother's or father's benefit is payable as long as the parent is caring for a dependent child—defined in this case as someone younger than 16. A dependent child's benefit is payable as long as the child is younger than 18 (unless attending high school and then benefits last until age 19), or over 18 but disabled before age 22. A widow's or widower's benefit is payable at and after age 60. If the deceased worker's parents depended on the worker, they are eligible to receive benefits when they are 62 or older.

Benefit Example

Returning to our previous example of Francis and Etta Bacon, assume that instead of retiring at age 65, Francis Bacon died prematurely at age 45, with the same PIA of $1,500. In this case, Etta Bacon receives a survivor's widow's benefit of 75 percent of her husband's PIA, or $1,125, so long as she is caring for a child under age 16. Each child also receives a benefit of $1,125 while under age 18. To illustrate just this set of facts, assume that there is a maximum family benefit of $1,875, so if there are two or more children, each beneficiary's benefit will be reduced so as not to exceed the maximum family benefit.

The Blackout Period

A review of the combination of retirement and survivor benefits reveals a potentially serious gap in the coverage provided by the Social Security program. Retirement benefits are first fully payable at age 65. They are payable at age 62 on a reduced basis. Survivor benefits are payable only so long as the mother or father is caring for a child younger than 16 or disabled before 22. There is a potential time gap between the receipt of these two benefits, as illustrated in the following example.

Assume that Jacob and Rachel are both age 25. They have one son, Joseph, who is 2 years old. If Jacob were to die at age 25, Rachel would receive survivor benefits for as long as Joseph was under age 16—that is, 14 years. When Joseph reaches age 16, Rachel would be 39 years old and the survivor benefits would end. At age 60, Rachel would be eligible for a widow's benefit. If she were permanently disabled, she could receive benefits as early as age 50. There would be a period from age 39 until benefits are resumed when Rachel would receive no benefits from the Social Security system. This gap in income, often called the **blackout period**, can be bridged with a private life insurance purchase.

Blackout period

The Earnings Test

A reduction of survivor benefits occurs when a beneficiary under age 65 earns more than the permissible limit, which is subject to annual change. Each $2 of earnings beyond the limit reduces benefits by $1. If one survivor loses benefits because of earned income, however, it does not affect other survivors. Thus, if Rachel goes to work after Jacob's death, she may lose her survivor benefits, but Joseph would continue to receive his.

Earnings test

The effect of the **earnings test** is to reduce the cost of the Social Security program. The cost is reduced when people who are willing and able to earn substantial wages forgo their Social Security benefits.

Table 22–3 provides a review of Social Security survivor benefits.

Disability Benefits

In 1956, Congress added disability benefits to the old-age and survivor benefits of Social Security. What had been OASI became OASDI. Since 1956, the original disability program has been broadened several times. Currently, if a worker is fully insured and was in covered employment for twenty of the forty quarters preceding total disability,

Disability

TABLE 22–3 Social Security Survivor Benefits	
Spouse:	
Caring for dependent child	75% deceased worker's PIA
Starting at age 65	100% deceased worker's PIA
Age 60–64	Deceased worker's PIA, reduced
Disabled, 50–65	50% + deceased worker's PIA
Child	75% deceased worker's PIA
Dependent Parent	
One	82.5% deceased worker's PIA
Two	75% PIA, each

that person is entitled to Social Security disability benefits. Special, more liberal provisions apply to younger workers. In addition to the eligible worker, the spouse and dependent children of a disabled worker also are entitled to benefits (subject to a maximum limit on a family's total benefits).

In an individually purchased disability insurance policy, the definition of the term *disability* is a key feature. The definition of **disability** used in the Social Security program is "the inability to engage in any substantial gainful activity by reason of any medically determinable physical or mental impairment which can be expected to last for a continuous period of not less than twelve months." This definition is not as favorable as a definition such as, "unable to engage in one's own occupation." Determinations of disability are made by state agencies, not by the Social Security Administration (SSA); thus, there may not be national uniformity in applying the definition of disability.

If workers are disabled by a work-related accident, they usually will be entitled to workers' compensation benefits. Social Security and workers' compensation benefits are coordinated, which limits the total amount an injured worker can receive from both systems. Thus, if the total benefit available from both sources exceeds 80 percent of the average earnings before the disability, Social Security benefits are reduced until the 80 percent level is reached.

Like retirement and survivor benefits, only limited amounts of earnings are permitted for totally disabled workers, with one very important exception. As an incentive for personal rehabilitation efforts, the program provides a twenty-four-month trial work period.

Social Security pays disability benefits at any age and benefits continue until the worker recovers, dies, or reaches age 65. At age 65, the disabled worker's disability benefits stop and retirement benefits begin. The insured will never know the difference, but the accounting requirements of the Social Security system direct this change. Table 22–4 outlines Social Security disability benefits.

Medicare (Health Insurance for the Aged and Disabled)

In 1965, Congress passed the Medicare program and OASDI became Old-Age, Survivors, Disability and Hospital Insurance (OASDI-HI). If one considers the OASDI program to be a jungle of rules, regulations, interpretations, exceptions, and questions,

TABLE 22–4 Social Security Disability Benefits	
Disabled worker	100% PIA
Spouse:	
Caring for dependent child	75% disabled worker's PIA
Age 65	50% disabled worker's PIA
Age 62–65	50% disabled worker's PIA, reduced
Eligible child	50% disabled worker's PIA

the Medicare program is a jungle within a jungle. In keeping within the scope and the purpose of this text, we will present only the broad outline of the program. Readers who want detailed information will find many details on the Internet. The following two Web sites are good places to begin a search: (*http://ssa.gov/*) and (*http://www.medicare.gov/*).

The Medicare program now has three main parts:

- Part A: basic hospital insurance benefits
- Part B: voluntary supplementary medical benefits
- Part D: Medicare prescription drug coverage

In general, insureds who are eligible to receive Social Security benefits because they are 65 or older or because they are disabled are eligible to participate in the Medicare program. Special provisions apply to those insureds with chronic kidney disease. Part A is compulsory and requires no premium payment from most insureds, but Parts B and D are voluntary and require premium payments that are subject to annual change.[4]

Part A — Hospital Insurance Benefits
This coverage provides the following inpatient hospital service benefits:

- Room and board in a semiprivate hospital room
- Nursing services
- Drugs furnished in the hospital
- Operating room costs

In addition to these benefits, the program also provides coverage for some outpatient expenses, including the following:

- *Skilled Nursing Care.* A physician must certify that skilled nursing care is needed following a condition that was treated in a hospital. Long-term custodial care is not provided.
- *Home Health Care Benefits.* If a patient can be treated at home rather than in a hospital or nursing facility, Part A pays the full cost for an unlimited number of visits by a home health agency.
- *Hospice Benefits.* If a person is terminally ill and certified to be within six months of death, Part A will pay for hospice care.

Part B — Voluntary Supplementary Medical Insurance Benefits
Part B provides benefits for medical expenses not covered by Part A, especially payment for physician's services. Participation in the program is voluntary, and insureds must pay a monthly premium. One interesting aspect of this program is that, while the participant pays a premium, the government uses general tax revenues to subsidize at least half the cost. Thus, this part of the Medicare program is not funded directly by taxes on current workers but by premiums paid in part by the insureds and in part by the government. Should a person participate and then drop out, strict reinstatement restrictions prevent adverse selection.

The benefits provided by Part B of Medicare include payments for the following medical services:

- Doctors' bills
- Hospital diagnostic studies

[4] Part C offers the health maintenance organization (HMO) option as a substitute for Parts A and B.

- Dental surgery
- Outpatient care
- Home health care
- Blood transfusions (with the restriction that you pay for the first three pints of blood)

Although Part B covers a broad range of services, several important exclusions apply to this coverage, including the following expenses:

- Routine physical exams
- Dental care
- Eyeglasses and hearing aids

Medicare Supplemental Insurance Policies (Medigap Insurance)

Medicare recipients often purchase Medicare supplemental insurance to cover the deductibles, coinsurance requirements, and other provisions of the Medicare program requiring cash outlays by insureds. The deductible and coinsurance requirements are complex and subject to annual change. The deductibles and copayments can involve expenses of hundreds of dollars each day, and many thousands of dollars during one spell of illness, which makes Medicare supplemental insurance an expensive, but often necessary, purchase by Medicare insureds.

Managed Care and Medicare

Medicare Advantage Plans

Managed care is another Medicare option available to recipients living in large cities where health maintenance organizations (HMOs) exist. The 2006 Medicare Handbook identifies several managed care plans, including Medicare HMOs and Medicare preferred provider organizations (PPOs) as **Medicare Advantage Plans**. If an insured is willing to accept coverage by an HMO or PPO as a replacement for traditional benefits (including the new prescription drug benefit), the insured generally can avoid the deductibles and most of the copayment provisions of Medicare. However, many insureds object to having to accept care from only the HMO physicians and other providers because they already have long-standing relationships with health care providers who are not part of the HMO. Other people have objected to the "long lines" and waiting time at some HMOs. Moreover, many HMOs have not found the reimbursement schedule provided by Social Security to be adequate or attractive. Therefore, the majority of Medicare participants have not chosen these alternatives to the traditional program.

Part D: Prescription Drug Coverage

Medicare Prescription Drug Improvement and Modernization Act of 2003

In December 2003, the **Medicare Prescription Drug Improvement and Modernization Act of 2003** became law. This law provides for limited coverage of a Medicare beneficiary's prescription drug bills subject to a deductible amount and a sequence of different copayment percentages. Beneficiaries also must pay a monthly premium for coverage. In addition to its complexity and cost to the government, among the other controversial points relating to this bill is a provision that prevents the U.S. government from bargaining with pharmaceutical companies to lower the price of drugs, as often is done by the U.S. Veterans Administration and by foreign governments. The government's cost to offer this program has been the subject of controversy as well. The following Congressional Budget Office (CBO) Web site provides background and current information on this issue: (*http://www.cbo.gov/publications/collections/prescriptiondrugs.cfm/*).

The following description summarizes some of the law's provisions. Personal decisions regarding participation in the program should not be made without consulting a competent advisor and the Medicare Web site (*http://www.medicare.gov/*), which has several relevant tool kits, including one that estimates drug costs. This site also provides answers to frequently asked questions about the new program.

The basic facts of the program are the following:

- Everyone with Medicare coverage is eligible for it, regardless of income, health status, or current prescription expenses.
- People get coverage by joining a Medicare prescription drug plan or by joining a Medicare health plan that offers drug coverage.
- The following data on copayment and deductible provisions may vary by plan and premium payments and are subject to change:
  - $35 monthly cost
  - $250 deductible
  - 25% copay between $250 and $2,250
  - 100% between $2,250–$5,100
  - Medicare pays 95% of costs when they exceed $5,100

With a total prescription cost of $5,100, the participant will have an out-of-pocket expense of $3,600, not including the monthly premium, as shown here:

Drug Costs $	Plan Pays	Individual Pays	Out of Pocket $
250	0%	250.00	250
251–2250	75%	25%	500
2,250–5,100	0%	100%	2,850
		total 3600	3,600
above 5,100	95%	5%	5% above 5,100

- The hypothetical calculation of benefit for a person with $4,000 in annual prescription medicine cost based on preceding plan provisions would be as follows:

Premium payment ($35 × 12) =	$ 420
Deductible =	$ 250
Copayment = .25 [($2,250 − $250) = $2,000] =	$ 500
Corridor deductible = ($4,000 − $2,250) =	$1,750
Total paid by participant =	$2,920

With a plan having these features, if the participant has $4,000 in prescription medicine cost, this benefit saves ($4,000 − $2,920) = $1,080.

In the period when this benefit was introduced, many potential participants reported difficulty in deciding whether or not to participate and in choosing a particular plan that was right for them. As is the case with other types of insurance coverage, some plans charged higher premiums and provided improved benefits including eliminating the corridor (or "gap") deductible between $2,250 and $5,100. Some potential participants were concerned about the integration of the new Medicare prescription drug plan with their current employer-provided medical benefits. The safest conclusion to be drawn regarding participation is that it is an individual decision that involves estimates of future prescription drug costs and the specific drugs that an individual takes. Most experts recommend that people should make this decision in consultation with health care and other competent advisors.

SOME CURRENT ISSUES FACING THE SOCIAL SECURITY SYSTEM

For many years, it has been apparent to experts that the Social Security system will have problems paying benefits at some time in the future. Many recent books and articles describe the problem and suggest solutions. President George W. Bush made reformation of the Social Security program, in part by introducing private accounts for covered workers, a high priority of his second term. To date, neither a majority of Congress nor a majority of the public have accepted his ideas. However, his intentions to reform the program have focused needed attention to a looming problem. The following Web site, maintained by the CBO, provides a good deal of background and current information on this controversial topic: (*http://www.cbo.gov/publications/collections/socialsecurity.cfm/*).

This section of the chapter provides a summary of some core concepts surrounding this ongoing discussion. Experts have made more suggestions to solve the problem than can be covered appropriately in an introductory risk management and insurance textbook.[5] Many of these arguments require actuarial mathematics to understand. Moreover, this topic no doubt will generate additional publications after this edition of the textbook appears. Thus, readers interested in the latest information on this topic should do a Web search using "Social Security system" as the keywords, and visit a library as well. We begin with a quotation from David M. Walker, Comptroller General of the United States, presented before a Special Committee of the U.S. Senate:

> Our Social Security challenge is more urgent that it may appear. Failure to take remedial action will, in combination with other entitlement spending, lead to a situation unsustainable both for the federal government and, ultimately, the economy. This problem is about more than finances. It is also about maintaining an adequate safety net for American workers against loss of income from retirement, disability, or death; Social Security provides a foundation of retirement income for millions of Americans and has prevented many former workers and their families from living their retirement years in poverty.[6]

Will Social Security "Be There" for Young and Middle-Aged Americans?

The problem concerning many experts is that long-run, seventy-five-year projections reveal an imbalance between the inflow and outflow of dollars funding Social Security.

The *2006 Annual Report* of the trustees of the Social Security program stated the following:

> Annual cost will exceed tax income starting in 2017 at which time the annual gap will be covered with cash from net redemptions of special obligations of the Treasury, until these assets are exhausted in 2040. (p. 2)

This quotation makes an interesting point: even if no changes are made in the program, all benefits will be paid until the year 2040. After 2040, about 70 percent of all benefits still will be covered by then-current cash inflow. Clearly, 70 percent is not 100 percent, but it is also far from zero.

---

[5] The author suggests the book *Saving Social Security: A Balanced Approach* by Peter A. Diamond and Peter R. Orszag (Brookings Institution Press, 2003) as a good introduction to the issues summarized in this section.
[6] U.S. General Accounting Office (GAO), *Statement of David M. Walker, January 15, 2003*, (GAO-03-376T), p. 3.

The financial problems facing the Medicare program will have a more immediate and dramatic impact, according to the SSA:

> As we reported last year, Medicare's financial difficulties come sooner—and are much more severe—than those confronting Social Security. While both programs face demographic challenges, the impact is more severe for Medicare because health care costs increase at older ages. Moreover, underlying health care costs per enrollee are projected to rise faster than the wages per worker on which the payroll tax is paid and on which Social Security benefits are based. As a result, while Medicare's annual costs were 2.7 percent of GDP in 2005, or over 60 percent of Social Security's, they are now projected to surpass Social Security expenditures in a little more than 20 years and reach 11 percent of GDP in 2080.[7]

The Causes: Demographic Trends

Two demographic trends, a low birth rate and increased longevity, will have a substantial impact on the program. If the United States continues to have a low birth rate, and if longevity continues to increase, the ratio of current workers to retired workers will continue to decrease. After 2015, when the post–World War II baby-boom generation retires, a relatively smaller number of employed workers will be supporting a relatively larger number of retired workers. Some demographic estimates suggest that about 20 percent of the population will be age 65 or older by 2020, with the fastest growing segment of this group being over age 85. Because the main source of money for retired workers' benefits is a tax on current workers and their employers, the source of the projected imbalance between the inflow and outflow is apparent.

Evaluating Social Security Reform Proposals

Because the debate over reforming Social Security remains unresolved, having a framework to judge different possible solutions is most valuable. David Walker's testimony, from which we quoted earlier, suggests the following three basic criteria to assess reform proposals:

- The extent to which a proposal achieves sustainable solvency and how it would affect the economy and federal budget
- The relative balance struck between the goals of individual equity and income adequacy
- How readily a proposal could be implemented, administered, and explained to the public[8]

Possible Solutions: Raise Taxes, Lower Benefits[9]

Experts have suggested several alternative strategies to ensure the system's financial stability. These suggestions include lowering benefits, increasing the tax rate paid by employees and employers, removing the limit on covered earnings (subjecting more of the income of the highest wage earners to the Social Security tax), and subjecting Social Security benefits to the income tax. Each of these remedies has potential negative consequences. Perhaps the most significant negative result will be the lack of coordination between the time the money is raised and when it will be needed. That is,

---

[7] *Summary of 2006 Annual Trustees Report*, p. 2.
[8] *Ibid.*, p. 14.
[9] A good academic discussion of these important issues can be found in this article: Peter A. Diamond, "The Public Pension Reform Debate in the United States and International Experience," *Risk Management and Insurance Review*, Spring 2006, pp. 9–35.

raising taxes now will increase today's already growing Social Security surplus, which many critics think is a bad idea for reasons we will explain shortly. Moreover, raising taxes never has been an easy or popular political undertaking.

Lowering benefits might be accomplished by raising the normal retirement age from the scheduled age of 67 to, for example, age 70. Other suggestions of how to lower benefits include lowering the benefits calculated by the PIA formula by a set percentage or by tying the indexing formula to prices instead of wages. Another suggestion is to limit the annual COLA increases. As with raising taxes, lowering benefits may have some unintended and undesired consequences, such as producing inadequate benefit levels for a large number of people.

Possible Solution: Allow Investments in the Private Securities Markets

One frequently discussed suggestion to change the Social Security program is to allow workers to invest some limited amount of Social Security funds in the private securities markets. The argument favoring this strategy is straightforward: The Social Security system historically has invested all surplus funds in U.S. Treasury securities, and the historical risk and return on these securities is significantly less than the returns achieved in equity investments in the private capital markets. The arguments raised in opposition to this suggestion also are substantial. Opponents to private investment raise the following questions: Who will do the investing, the SSA, or individuals directing their own accounts? If the government does the investing, to what extent will government political goals affect private companies and their managers? If the government is a passive owner of "private" enterprise, will it insulate management from market discipline? If the stock market turns down, how will shortfalls in benefits be funded? How are all the participants to be educated to make sound investment choices, and if workers make poor investment choices, or are defrauded and perhaps lose all their money, who will pay for their benefits? What will the administrative costs be for individuals investing their funds? What will be the effects on the U.S. capital markets if billions of dollars are redirected from Treasury securities to the equities market? It should be clear to readers that the suggestion to privatize some part of the Social Security program is complex and that any changes to the Social Security system affect too many people to be made without careful thought and debate.

Another serious set of questions deals with the funding effects of the partial privatization process. Will the private accounts be supplemental to the existing program, or a substitute for the worker's scheduled contribution to the program? If supplemental, the effect is to increase the worker's Social Security tax rate and reduce discretionary income. If money put in a worker's private account is a portion of their scheduled contribution, where will the money come from to pay all the benefits promised to currently retired workers? The funding questions might involve trillions of dollars, and they were never addressed in President Bush's reform proposals, which might, in part, explain why those proposals have not been adopted.

The Social Security Surplus and the Federal Deficit

Despite concerns for the Social Security system's long-term survival, for many years the system has been accumulating large surpluses. The purpose of the surplus accumulation is to provide a buffer to help balance the inadequate cash inflow projected after 2020. Some critics believe the current annual Social Security surplus is a serious problem that hides the actual amount of the current federal deficit because Social Security funds are integrated with all other government cash flows. These critics believe the current Social Security surplus removes some restraint against deficit spending. Moreover, these critics maintain that because the taxpayers must redeem the Treasury securities being accumulated by the Social Security system, the process currently in place distorts both current federal spending and the future performance of the Social Security system.

Other Criticism

In addition to concerns about the financial stability of the Social Security system, other critics have expressed concern about the impact of Social Security taxes on the national economy. With about 15 percent of payroll costs represented by the combined taxes on employees and employers, a considerable amount of capital is removed from the private economy and administered by the federal government.

Other critics complain that some aspects of the program produce unfairly low benefits for the poor, minorities, and women. The concern is that the average shorter lives of the poor and minorities result in shorter retirement periods, and hence they will receive less retirement benefits than people with longer lives. In contrast, different critics are concerned that higher-income wage earners, the healthy, and the young are not getting as good a deal from Social Security as they could get in the private market and should have the option of withdrawing from the Social Security system.

I hope that readers who have studied the material in this section of the chapter understand the following conclusions:

- The funding problems facing Social Security are serious, but they are long-run problems.
- Academic and other experts have presented and discussed many alternative solutions to these problems without reaching general agreement.
- Politicians have not reached general agreement on solutions, either.
- The debate continues, and all Americans have a vital stake in the outcome of this argument. Therefore, everybody should remain informed on the topic.

SUMMARY

Social insurance first appeared in Germany in the late nineteenth century. In an effort to stop the growth of the Socialist Democratic Party, Chancellor Otto von Bismarck introduced a social insurance plan designed to reduce the economic hardship caused by the Industrial Revolution.

President Franklin D. Roosevelt proposed the Social Security Act of 1935 as a part of the New Deal economic plan designed to cure the economic problems of the United States. The program was designed as a "floor of protection" for U.S. workers. Constant expansion has taken place from the beginning: New groups of workers have been added to the program, new types of benefits have been added, and benefit amounts have been raised regularly.

Social Security is neither a welfare program nor a private insurance system. Unlike welfare, benefits are not based solely on economic need. The more survivors or dependents a worker has, the greater the benefits received (up to the family maximum).

Unlike private insurance, benefits are not based on a contract but on a law; neither is the system operated on a fully funded basis. Social Security is an insurance system that combines U.S. workers exposed to the perils of premature death, disability, and outliving financial assets and transfers the costs of losses to the covered workers and their employers.

Social Security provides four categories of benefits for eligible recipients: (1) retirement benefits, (2) survivor benefits, (3) disability benefits, and (4) Medicare benefits. For the first three categories, the benefits a worker receives are determined by the amount of average monthly earnings. The average monthly earnings, in turn, determine the worker's primary insurance amount.

Social Security operates on a self-supporting, current-income basis. The system currently is building up surplus funds to be used when workers born between 1946 and 1964 (the so-called baby boomers) begin to retire. Some critics feel these surplus funds encourage federal deficit spending and distort the safety of the Social Security system.

Certain questions about the Social Security program (including Medicare) continue to receive public attention. How should the system be financed? Will a declining birth rate combined with increased longevity destroy the self-supporting operations of the system? Some experts estimate that the open-ended Medicare promises will cause greater funding problems than the better defined and more controllable portions of Social Security. Debate on these and other issues should focus the public's attention on a very important part of its financial security program.

REVIEW TERMS

- Average indexed monthly earnings (AIME)
- Blackout period
- Cost of living adjustment (COLA)
- Covered earnings
- Covered maximum wage
- Currently insured
- Dependent child
- Disability

- Disability insured
- Earnings test
- Eligible
- Federal Insurance Contributions Act (FICA)
- Fully insured
- Maximum family benefit
- Normal retirement age

- Old-Age, Survivors, Disability Insurance—Hospital Insurance Program (OASDI-HI)
- Primary insurance amount (PIA)
- Public assistance program
- Quarter of coverage (QC)
- Retirement benefit
- Social insurance program

REVIEW

1. What is the connection between a society that moves from an agricultural to an industrial base and the development of a social insurance system?
2. Who was Otto von Bismarck? What role did he play in the development of social insurance?
3. When was the Social Security Act passed? What was the political philosophy that determined its level of benefits, both initially and currently?
4. What aspects of Social Security are similar to a welfare program? How is Social Security different from public assistance?
5. List four similarities and differences between Social Security and private insurance.
6. What is FICA? And what role does it play in the Social Security program?
7. What is the covered maximum wage?
8. Using the same factors that applied in the Shun brothers example, calculate the Social Security tax for Larry (earned wages of $60,000), Michael (earned salary of $2 million), and Sam (dividend income of $25 million).
9. Describe two major categories of insured status and their requirements.
10. What role does general tax revenue play in funding Social Security benefits?

11. What does "pay as you go" mean with respect to Social Security retirement benefits?
12. Identify three different categories of insured status for Social Security benefits.
13. What is an AIME? Describe a PIA.
14. Who is entitled to retirement benefits under the Social Security system? Who is entitled to survivor benefits? Disability benefits? Medicare benefits?
15. What is meant by the blackout period for Social Security benefits?
16. Identify the different types of benefits provided by the hospital insurance part of Medicare and by the supplementary medical insurance portion of the program. What are the deductible and participation provisions of these programs?
17. What problems will a declining birth rate and increasing longevity cause for the Social Security system?
18. Why do some critics argue that building up Social Security surplus funds might not be a good solution to the system's future financing needs?
19. Identify some solutions that have been offered to help maintain the Social Security system's solvency.

OBJECTIVE QUESTIONS

1. The man whose name is associated with the development of the first social insurance program is:
   a. Philip Morris
   b. Albrecht Durer
   c. Rolf von Winkle
   d. Otto von Bismarck

2. The main source of funding for the Social Security program is:
   a. The federal income tax
   b. The federal estate and gift tax
   c. A tax on wages
   d. The capital gains tax

3. To be fully insured requires how many quarters of coverage?
   a. 60
   b. 55
   c. 40
   d. 25
4. All the following are main categories of benefits provided by Social Security except:
   a. Welfare benefits for poor people
   b. Retirement benefits
   c. Survivors benefits
   d. Disability benefits
5. The U.S. Social Security program has been operating for more than _____ years.
   a. 65
   b. 75
   c. 85
   d. 105
6. Choose the false statement regarding the Social Security program.

a. Participation in Social Security is compulsory.
b. Social Security benefits are predetermined by a formula.
c. Social Security operates mostly on the pay-as-you-go basis.
d. Social Security benefits cannot be changed by legislation.

7. The acronym for the Social Security tax deduction is:
   a. SSTX
   b. FICA
   c. FDIC
   d. SPCA
8. The funds accumulating as Social Security surpluses are invested in:
   a. The U.S. stock market
   b. U.S. government securities that earn interest
   c. U.S. government securities that do not earn interest
   d. Certificates of deposit

DISCUSSION QUESTIONS

1. Do you think Social Security retirement benefits will be there for you when you retire? Argue both sides of this question.
2. Do you think people who can show evidence that they have made substitute arrangements in the private insurance market should be allowed to drop out of the Social Security system?
3. Do you think that Social Security should have a greater welfare component, less welfare, or about the same? Explain your reasons. Cite specific changes you would like to see made.

INTERNET RESEARCH ASSIGNMENTS

1. Gather some of the most recent statistics about the Social Security program. Start your search at this site: (*http://www.ssa.gov/policy/docs/quickfacts/stat_snapshot/index.html/*).
2. Retrieve the most recent data available on the benefits provided by Medicare. Start your search at this site: (*http://www.medicare.gov/*).

Monetary policy

employment **monetary policy**. For many complicated reasons, including the psychological effect of consumer expectations, government actions to "fine tune" the national economy do not always produce the theoretical effects within the expected time frame.

Transfer payments

A third way for the government to assist the economy is through **transfer payments**, defined as taking money from one group of citizens and giving it to another group. If the group receiving the money is more likely to spend it than the group from whom the money was taken, demand for consumer goods will increase, with the result being more employment in industries that produce consumer goods. Because Social Security, public assistance, and unemployment insurance all follow this pattern, they result in the stabilization of consumption.

The unemployment insurance program is designed to meet the peril of short-term unemployment caused by the business cycle and other factors over which workers have little control. Because unemployment insurance checks allow the unemployed worker to maintain some purchasing power, aggregate demand for consumer goods does not begin as severe a downward spiral as otherwise would be the case. A severe downward spiral begins with a lack of demand for consumer goods caused by some unemployed people, who in turn are unable to purchase goods, causing additional groups of workers to be laid off, with the process building momentum at each downward turn. The unemployment insurance program automatically acts to counter the effects of a downturn in the economy by softening the effects on consumer demand. Thus, unemployment

Automatic stabilizer

insurance is known as an **automatic stabilizer**, one requiring no additional government action to be put into effect. During periods of severe unemployment, Congress can extend the short-term (twenty-six-week) benefit period to soften the impact of unemployment on families and the national economy.

The administration of Franklin D. Roosevelt decided that, to avoid a political and legal challenge to the constitutionality of the unemployment insurance program, it should be separated from the rest of the Social Security program. Thus, the federal government now imposes an unemployment tax on employers but allows a credit for up to 90 percent of the federal tax if employers pay a state unemployment tax. In effect, the federal government encourages the states to impose their own unemployment tax. Under this arrangement, the states determine who is eligible for benefits, how long benefits last, and the amount of benefit payments. In one recent year, the various state programs covered about 129 million workers and paid a total of about $41 billion in benefits to about 9 million workers.[3]

Some employers give permanently terminated employees an amount of money beyond their final wages. Such payment, called *severance pay*, allows workers time to find new jobs. It also allows the unemployed to maintain their purchasing power for a limited time. Yet private approaches to the unemployment problem, however helpful they are in individual instances, are inadequate to deal with the national problem of unemployment because they lack the government's control over monetary and fiscal policy.

Operations of the Unemployment Insurance Program

Currently, the unemployment insurance program is a joint federal-state program. The U.S. Department of Labor administers the federal portion of the program (*http://www.dol.gov/*). The Department of Labor is responsible for ensuring that the states operate their unemployment programs efficiently and also provides the states technical assistance and training.

---

[3] Data on the unemployment insurance program and related issues can be found at the Economic Policy Institute's Web site (*http://www.epinet.org/Issueguides/unemployment/*). Also see Government Accountability Office, "Unemployment Insurance: Factors Associated with Benefit Receipt" (March 2006), GAO-06-341, for an interesting statistical analysis of this program.

The unemployment insurance program is financed by a 6.2 percent federal tax on covered wages. The federal tax is offset up to 90 percent if an employer must pay a tax to a state unemployment insurance program. The federal covered maximum wage for unemployment insurance taxation is $7,000, an amount far less than the Social Security maximum.[4] State unemployment tax collections allow the states to fund their unemployment insurance programs. If a state unemployment insurance fund is inadequate to continue paying benefits, the states then can borrow money from the federal government without paying interest. Some penalties are involved if the loan balance is not reduced, however.

An interesting question arises concerning who ultimately pays the unemployment insurance tax. Three possibilities exist: (1) the employer, through lower profits; (2) the employee, through lower wages; or (3) the consumer, through higher prices. Some combination of the three is the probable answer, but this answer raises difficulties in analyzing the transfer caused by the insurance mechanism. In an insurance operation, all exposed to the potential loss (the whole work force) should share the costs of the unfortunate few who experience the loss (the unemployed). This outcome cannot be established with unemployment insurance, which leads to the following question.

Is Unemployment Insurance Really Insurance?

This question has two sides. In Chapter 1, "Fundamentals and Terminology," we identified an insurance system as one that transfers the cost of loss from the few who experience it to the many who are exposed to it. The transfer is made using a contract between the insured and insurer. Unemployment insurance fails both these tests. There is a legal rather than a contractual right to benefits and the effects of the transfer are not clear-cut, as we explained. The unemployment insurance operation lacks predictive accuracy and faces the possibility of catastrophic losses. Both private insurance and the Social Security system have predictive accuracy and do not face catastrophic loss potential. Thus, some critics think the term *unemployment compensation* is more descriptive than *unemployment insurance*.

The unemployment program, however, does have some aspects of an insurance program. Payments for losses are funded in advance, although the program is not funded actuarially because losses cannot be predicted accurately. Generally, the payments provided do not replace the total amount of wages lost. Like other insurance transfers, the program makes compensation payments only to those workers who suffer losses from a specified peril: short-term unemployment from causes beyond the recipient's control. These payments are a matter of right and are not based on need. The next section of this chapter describes eligibility requirements to participate in the program and disqualification provisions that preclude adverse selection. Both the eligibility requirements and disqualification provisions have counterparts in private group insurance programs.

Experience rating

Perhaps the most interesting resemblance to a private insurance operation is the experience-rating pricing approach found in almost all state plans. **Experience rating** means the insurer looks backward over time to determine if an insured has paid a fair premium. For example, if an insured's loss experience was favorable, experience rating results in a refund of a portion of the premium. Experience rating is quite common in private group life and health insurance.

Careful analysis of an experience-rating plan reveals an effect that is just the opposite of the insurance transfer. That is, while insurance transfers the cost of losses

---

[4] Some states have higher tax rates and some have higher covered-wage bases. Information on the various state programs can be found on the Department of Labor Web site (*http://www.dol.gov/*).

from the fortunate many to the unfortunate few, experience-rating refunds transfer money to the fortunate employers with good loss records and not to the employers with average or poor loss records.

The justification given for experience rating is that it encourages or promotes a stable work force. An employer is put in the position of having to balance the savings from laying off employees for short periods against the increase in the employer's unemployment insurance costs. While promoting a stable work force is a worthy objective, the effect of experience rating may be just the opposite of what the economy needs. When the economy is going strong, unemployment insurance premiums are reduced because employers have relatively good loss experience. When the economy is weak, unemployment premiums go up because employers have relatively poor loss experience. Thus, with experience rating, the insurance system takes more money out of the economy during a downswing in the cycle than during an upswing. More logically, the program should take more money out during the upswing, when business is good, than during the periods when business is relatively poor.

The safest answer one may give to the question posed at the beginning of this section is that unemployment insurance is a government-operated transfer payment scheme having some, but not all, elements in common with private group and individual insurance programs.

General Provisions of State Programs

All state unemployment insurance programs have provisions that cover eligibility to participate in the program, actions that disqualify workers from receiving benefits, and provisions for determining the amount of benefits an unemployed worker receives.

Eligibility

Waiting period

States have three general requirements relating to **eligibility** to receive benefits: (1) a waiting period, (2) an earnings record, and (3) a continuing interest in employment. A one-week **waiting period** is a typical requirement before unemployment benefits are available. A previous earnings record is stated in terms of some minimum dollar amount, such as earnings of at least $1,000 in the past twelve months. A continuing interest in employment means the worker must be both able and available to work. These three requirements are designed to keep people who have not worked recently (including people who have already received the maximum coverage from their unemployment insurance), or who do not intend to work in the near future, from collecting unemployment insurance.

Certain actions may disqualify a worker from receiving benefits even if the three eligibility tests are met. Disqualification for benefits results if a worker (1) has left employment voluntarily, (2) was fired for misconduct, (3) refuses suitable work, (4) is not legally eligible to work, or (5) is unemployed owing to a labor dispute. Several of these points involve questions of fact. Was the employee really fired for misconduct? Was an employee who "voluntarily quit" really forced out? Is the (noncitizen) worker legally eligible to work? States can make exceptions to these general rules on disqualification.

Traditionally, unemployment claims had to be made in person at state employment offices. Recently, some states have allowed claims submissions over the telephone or Internet. After the claim is filed, the state sends a form to the unemployed worker's former employer requesting verification of earnings and the reason for their leaving employment. Each state determines the amount of benefits to which an unemployed worker is entitled. Benefits are subject to federal income taxes. States typically use a formula based on previous earnings. Some states grant dependents' allowances as an increase in the weekly benefit. The states also determine the duration of benefits; most states grant twenty-six weeks. This restriction is in keeping with the principle that unemployment insurance should compensate for short-term unemployment. During periods of high unemployment, however, a federal-state program provides for an extension of benefits beyond the maximum set by the states. This program has some automatic provisions that are activated when national unemployment exceeds a stated level.

Summary—Unemployment Insurance

Unemployment is an awful peril to which all workers are exposed. The results of this peril are lost income, frustration, and possible depression. Much unemployment is due to causes beyond the worker's control. The swings of the economic cycle, changes in methods of production, and new inventions all have caused unemployment. Some unemployment is not beyond a worker's control, and unemployment insurance is not designed to compensate workers for such losses.

The current federal-state approach to unemployment insurance appeared as a part of the Social Security Act of 1935. The unemployment insurance provisions of the federal program were separated from the other coverages to avoid a constitutional challenge. Under the current approach, employers can offset up to 90 percent of the federal unemployment tax if they pay a state unemployment tax. This approach allows the various states rather than the federal government to determine eligibility requirements and the amount of benefits paid.

Unemployment insurance has some features comparable to private insurance programs and others that are quite different. Unlike private insurance, there is no contract between insured and insurer, nor is the loss necessarily transferred from those who experience it to those who are exposed to it, because both employers and customers may be paying for the loss. Also, unlike a private insurance arrangement, the unemployment insurance program lacks predictive accuracy and may experience catastrophic losses. Funds for making payment for losses, however, are collected in advance, and requirements restrict the program to cover a specified peril: short-term unemployment arising from causes beyond the worker's control. Many states have experience-rating plans, whereby those employers who have a good record receive the benefit of lower insurance premiums. While the experience-rating plan may encourage a stable employment policy, it has economic implications that can be undesirable.

All states have their own general provisions covering eligibility for benefits. The states also determine certain conditions and circumstances that would disqualify workers from receiving benefits. The states determine both the amount and the duration of unemployment insurance benefits.

WORKERS' COMPENSATION[5]

Among the problems that arose when the economy changed from an agricultural to an industrial basis were work-related injuries and illnesses. Agriculture historically was, and remains, a relatively dangerous occupation. However, the move from farm to factory exposed many more workers to new and dangerous occupations and unsafe working environments. The problem in the United States probably reached its peak during the period between 1900 and 1910. New members of the labor force, many from agricultural backgrounds, and many women and children were exposed to machinery for the first time. Under such conditions as then prevailed—long hours, long work weeks, and dangerous working conditions—many factories saw relatively high injury rates.

The cry for reform followed public awareness of the problem. One widely read book, Upton Sinclair's *The Jungle* (1906), dealt with industrial accidents in the meatpacking

---

[5] For the most recent workers' compensation insurance data and information, see the following Web site: (*http://www.ncci.com/*).

industry. As was the case with several other economic problems related to the Industrial Revolution, Europeans provided Americans with workable solutions. Compensation for industrial accidents was a part of German chancellor Otto von Bismarck's social insurance program, and other European countries subsequently followed the German pattern.

The Problem

Work-related accidents and illnesses are an unfortunate part of the industrial economy. In addition to physical and emotional problems, industrial accidents cause workers two types of economic problems: (1) medical, rehabilitative, or funeral expenses, and (2) lost wages. The important economic and social question presented by these occurrences is "Who shall bear the economic burden of these costs?" Before workers' compensation laws were enacted, the answer was almost always the injured worker and the family. One objective of the new laws was to transfer this cost from the injured worker to other parties. As we have noted several times throughout this textbook, one of the most effective and efficient means of transferring the cost of losses is through the insurance mechanism. Therefore, it should not be surprising that insurance was the device used to achieve this new objective.

Why were injured workers bearing the cost of most industrial accidents? In essence, it was because of the common-law legal doctrine that prevailed in the United States before the enactment of workers' compensation laws. As a rule, whenever a person is injured because of another's negligence, that person can sue the negligent party for the damage sustained. The defendant in such a case has the right to try to establish that its actions were not responsible for the plaintiff's injuries. Before the enactment of workers' compensation laws, the injured worker had a legal right to sue the employer, and the employer had a right to a defense.

Such a legal system, although seeming fair on the surface, really was very lopsided in favor of the employer, thus producing unfair results. In many cases, employees would not or could not sue their employer because they had no money or they feared losing jobs they might never replace. Fellow workers were not eager to testify against their employers for the same reasons. Assuming one did sue one's employer, the employer had three lines of defense to assert. Establishing any of these defenses would stop an injured worker's recovering from the employer.

Contributory negligence

Fellow servant rule

Assumption-of-risk defense

The employer could claim **contributory negligence**—that is, the worker's own actions contributed to the injury. The employer might establish that another worker, not the employer, was responsible for the injury—the **fellow servant rule**. The employer also might establish that a reasonable person should have known a line of work such as meatpacking presented some chance of injury. If the worker knew that a job was dangerous before accepting it, the employer could invoke the **assumption-of-risk defense** because the employer compensated the employee for the inherent danger. Thus, the chances of an injured worker collecting damages from an employer under the prevailing legal doctrines at the time varied from slim to none.

The Solution

Faced with public indignation and the European example, the various states enacted legislation that changed this situation. The new workers' compensation laws substituted the employer's liability without fault for the prevailing common-law doctrine of negligence, and the current program is a form of "no fault" insurance. Under the new laws, the employee could not sue the employer to collect for work-related injuries. The workers' compensation claim payment was the **exclusive remedy** available to the injured worker. The employer had to pay the worker for the damages regardless of fault, but the employer then was protected from employees' civil claims that arose from work-related injuries.

Exclusive remedy

It is unlikely that the employer ultimately bears all the cost of a worker's injuries. More likely, the consumer pays the cost through higher prices. Because the employer treats workers' compensation insurance premiums as another cost of doing business, these expenses are included in the cost of producing goods and in the price charged for the goods. The result of including claims for workers' injuries in the price of goods is that goods that are relatively dangerous to produce have an additional element of cost that goods that are relatively safe to produce do not have.

Workers' compensation laws established the employer's liability in cases of work-related injury. Employers, exposed to this peril of liability losses, purchase insurance to cover their exposure. Workers' compensation insurance policies promise to pay on behalf of the employer "any sums for which the employer is legally liable because of injuries to employees arising out of the course of their employment." Premiums for this insurance transfers money to those employers who experience such losses from all the employers exposed to such losses.

As in the case of unemployment insurance, insurance companies use experience rating to adjust an insured's premiums. Thus, employers with good safety records will pay lower insurance rates than employers with poor safety records. Experience rating rewards loss prevention and loss reduction efforts. Generally, only larger employees receive significant benefits from experience-rated premiums because insurers do not give the data from small employers much credibility.

The Purposes of Workers' Compensation Laws

The National Commission on State Workmen's Compensation Laws completed and presented a comprehensive study of existing workers' compensation laws to the president and Congress in 1972.[6] Though it is now more than thirty years old, the objectives in the report still provide the focus for a modern workers' compensation program. These objectives were expressed as the commission's opinion of what an ideal workers' compensation program should accomplish, as follows:

- Broad coverage of employees and work-related injuries and diseases
- Substantial protection against loss of income
- Sufficient medical care and rehabilitation services
- Encouragement of safety
- An effective delivery system for workers' compensation

Broad Coverage of Employees and Work-related Injuries and Diseases

Coverage should be provided for all U.S. workers. Many states have exclusions applying to small businesses, agricultural workers, government workers, household workers, and other groups. Such exclusions are undesirable, in the commission's opinion. Likewise, the commission argued that all occupational diseases should be covered, not just specified illnesses as is the current practice. Such an objective presents problems. How does one determine whether high blood pressure, ulcers, and so forth are work-related illnesses? Presumably, an administrative body would have to judge each case individually. More discussion of the cumulative injury problem follows later in this chapter.

Substantial Protection Against Loss of Income

Benefits should be equated with the total remuneration of the injured worker. Such things as overtime, employee benefits, and vacation pay should be considered in addition to basic wages and salaries. Minimum and maximum benefit totals should be developed, but the goal should be a close approximation of indemnity. In addition to

---

[6] *The Report of the National Commission on State Workmen's Compensation Laws* (Washington, D.C.: U.S. Government Printing Office, 1972).

lost income, indemnity payments would include payment for medical expenses caused by injury or disease. With rapid inflation, benefits should be increased regularly to keep pace with cost-of-living increases.[7]

Sufficient Medical Care and Rehabilitation Services

This goal reflects the point that an injured worker is entitled to prompt and continuous medical care, combined with postaccident physical therapy, if necessary, until productive employment can be resumed. The workers' compensation system should provide incentives to restore injured workers to useful lives.

Encouragement of Safety

This objective seems to require a retrospective rating system as an economic incentive for employers to encourage safety.

An Effective Delivery System for Workers' Compensation

This objective reinforces the four goals previously noted. The commission thought that an adequate number of attorneys, physicians, and state administrators was needed to maintain the workers' compensation system's efficiency and effectiveness.

Because there is a current discussion of the desirability of continuing to provide workers' compensation under more than fifty different administrative jurisdictions, the normative goals set forth by this commission probably will serve as a benchmark in evaluating the existing state programs. Many people believe workers' compensation should be administered on a federal basis, arguing that the current system produces inadequate and often unfair results. The commission's report has been a useful source of ideas and information for this debate.

Operations of Workers' Compensation Systems

Including Puerto Rico, Washington, D.C., and other territories under U.S. control, there are more than fifty different jurisdictions that administer workers' compensation laws. We present the general features of these programs in this section. The answers to specific questions about a given state's program should be sought at local administrative offices.

Each state's workers' compensation program has criteria for determining a worker's eligibility to receive benefits. The general test that must be satisfied is that an employee in covered employment (defined by state law) must suffer a work-related injury or illness. The injury must be caused by an accident arising out of employment and in the course of such employment. The "course of employment" rule generally requires that the injury occur on the employer's premises and during working hours. This rule eliminates coverage for employees traveling to and from work. However, employees who are injured away from the employer's premises, such as delivery drivers, are likely to receive coverage.

The following exclusions generally disqualify workers from compensation: (1) injuries that result from intoxication, (2) injuries that are willfully self-inflicted, and (3) injuries that arise from a willful failure to follow safety precautions.

Workers' compensation insurance provides three types of benefits after eligibility has been established:

- Cash payments to replace lost income
- Full payment of medical expenses
- Payment for rehabilitation services

Cash benefits generally begin after injury and a waiting period, typically one week. Cash benefits are determined using three different factors. Some percentage of weekly

---

[7] The following book covers this issue extensively: H. Allan Hunt, ed., *Adequacy of Earnings Replacement in Workers' Compensation Programs,* (Kalamazoo, MI: W. E. Upjohn Institute for Employment Research, 2004).

income, often two-thirds, is paid to injured employees who are unable to work. In addition, there may be a schedule of cash benefits for accidents involving permanent impairment, such as paralysis or loss of a finger or an eye. Third, if a worker is killed because of an accident, survivors generally are entitled to a lump-sum benefit prescribed by law. Workers' compensation income benefits are coordinated with Social Security disability benefits, so a total of no more than 80 percent of a worker's average monthly wage is paid from both sources.

Workers' compensation insurance covers medical expenses for accidents without the worker having to pay for deductible, copayments, or upper limits on coverage. However, medical expenses arising from occupational illness often are not covered completely. This lack of complete medical coverage for occupational illnesses is another complaint about current plans.

Injured workers generally are entitled to rehabilitation after an industrial accident. **Rehabilitation programs** teach workers how to use injured arms and legs or provide training with prosthetic devices. Some of the program's critics think more can and should be done to improve state rehabilitation programs.

The providers of workers' compensation insurance vary from jurisdiction to jurisdiction. Some states require that employers purchase insurance from a state-operated workers' compensation fund. Other states allow competition between private insurers and state-operated funds. Some states have no state-operated funds and private insurers provide all the coverage. Still other states allow employers with large work forces and established financial assets to operate self-insurance programs.

In all cases, the insurance premium is based on an employer's payroll. Experience-rating formulas may reduce the premiums. Insurers classify employers by industry, giving recognition to the fact that some industries involve more danger to workers than others. An employer in a relatively dangerous industry would pay a higher rate than an employer in a relatively safe industry. Experience rating provides rewards for employers with good safety records, regardless of an industry's accident record.

If an injured employee thinks an insurer has not handled his or her case fairly, most states provide for settlement of the dispute by a workers' compensation board. Some states have designated a court to oversee the administration of workers' compensation disputes. Workers' compensation boards may judge questions relating to whether an injury was work-related, whether the injured worker was acting within the scope of his or her assignment, or the severity of the injury. One of the original purposes of the workers' compensation laws, however, was to eliminate litigation and provide prompt and fair settlement of claims. Thus, voluminous litigation is to be neither an expected nor a desired part of an effective workers' compensation program.

Some Current Concerns About Workers' Compensation[8]

Financing the cost of injured workers presents an ongoing problem to many risk managers and insurers. On average, employers reported that costs rose from about 1 percent of payroll in the 1970s to about 3 percent of payroll in recent years. The driving force behind this increase in expense has been increases in health care costs.

In addition to health care costs, other factors causing prices to rise include the following:

- The lack of a requirement for injured or disabled employees to pay even a small part of their health care costs because workers' compensation benefits have no

Left margin note: **Rehabilitation programs**

---

[8] The description of issues in this section is current as of the time this chapter was prepared (late 2006). An Internet search will provide ongoing discussions of these issues, which continue to receive attention from academicians, industry experts, and politicians.

deductible or copayment requirements like those found in individual and group health insurance policies. Because employees do not spend any of their own funds, employers and their insurers believe more services are used.

Permanent partial disability

Temporary partial disability

Temporary total disability

Permanent total disability

- More frequent categorization of injuries as "permanent partial disability," a designation that increases both the amount of money received by the employee and the employer's cost. **Permanent partial disability** means that the employee has suffered some permanent injury, such as the loss of an eye or a limb, but still can work. Some "repetitive motion" injuries that affect office workers, butchers, and other workers who perform the same task throughout the day have been categorized as permanent partial injuries. These painful conditions have been difficult to prevent, and employers have found it expensive to rehabilitate the injured workers. Other loss categories include **temporary partial disability** (the worker will recover and can work part time while disabled), **temporary total disability** (the worker will recover but can do no work until disability ends), and **permanent total disability** (the worker has suffered permanent injury and can no longer work).

- A large number of fraudulent claims.

- A continuing indifference to potentially hazardous working conditions by some employers.

- The practice of some health care providers to charge more for services when treating workers' compensation patients than for other patients with the same diagnosis. Such differential charges are especially likely to occur in cases where Medicare pays for service, on the one hand, and workers' compensation insurance, on the other. Some commentators describe this problem as *cost shifting* from the government (Medicare) to private (workers' compensation) insurers.

While employers and their insurers were expressing great concern about the costs of providing workers' compensation coverage, many employees felt their benefits were inadequate. In some states, benefits were significantly less than 80 percent of pre-disability income, which is an accepted target replacement ratio. Thus, all concerned parties—employers, insurers, and employees—have expressed dissatisfaction with the workers' compensation system: Employers felt the system was too costly, insurers found the business unprofitable, and many employees felt they were under-compensated for their injuries.

Cumulative injuries

A second issue that affects the provision of workers' compensation insurance is how to compensate victims of cumulative injuries and stress-related claims. **Cumulative injuries** are job-related disabilities that result over many years of employment. Black lung, to cite one example, is a cumulative illness that affects coal miners, and workers' compensation programs compensate injured victims with this disease. Some workers have claimed that their heart attacks or deafness also are job-related cumulative injuries, which raises the issue of how workers' compensation boards should distinguish job-related heart attacks or deafness from non-job-related events. Surely some people would become deaf or have high blood pressure, regardless of their employment. This problem causes some commentators to recommend that employers combine their health insurance and workers' compensation insurance, providing twenty-four-hour coverage for all accidents and illnesses. These programs are called *24-hour plans*.

In recent years, many jurisdictions have recognized job-related stress as a compensable cause of a work-related injury, entitling affected workers to compensation benefits. The number of these claims and the associated expenses has increased in recent years. One effect of these claims is to cause employers to handle terminations carefully and sensitively; another is to make the workers' compensation burden that consumers bear even greater.

Summary—Workers' Compensation

Each year, thousands of workers die or are injured permanently, and more than 2 million miss one or more days of work because of job-related injuries and diseases. As a result of workers' compensation laws, the economic cost of these injuries no longer falls on the unfortunate worker. Before the Industrial Revolution, the worker and his or her family bore the burden of industrial accidents. Workers had the right to sue employers, and employers had the right to defend themselves against the claim of negligence. Three almost-sure defenses were available to employers: (1) contributory negligence (workers contributed to their own loss), (2) fellow servant rules (the injury was caused by a fellow worker, not the employer), and (3) assumption of the risk (the employee should have known the employment was inherently dangerous when accepting the work). Because of the prevailing legal doctrines, injured workers rarely collected for injuries.

Workers' compensation legislation created liability for employers, regardless of fault. At the same time, it took the right to sue away from the employee. The transfer of the cost of injuries probably went from the worker to the consumer because the employer passes along all costs, including the costs for workers' compensation insurance, to the consumer.

A national commission outlined the following objectives for a modern compensation program:

- Broad coverage of employees and work-related injuries and diseases
- Substantial protection against loss of income
- Sufficient medical care and rehabilitation services
- Encouragement of safety
- An effective delivery system for workers' compensation

Under current state administration, each workers' compensation program has criteria for determining eligibility and for exclusions from coverage. The types of benefits currently available under workers' compensation programs are (1) cash benefits, (2) medical expenses, and (3) rehabilitation services. State-operated funds or private insurers may provide workers' compensation insurance. In all cases, the premium is based on the amount of payroll and the relative danger to employees in the industry. Experience ratings recognize the safety efforts of particular employers. In the case of a dispute between an injured employee and an insurer, workers' compensation boards are available to settle disputes. Workers' compensation laws were designed to minimize litigation, however, and legal disputes should not be an outcome of these laws.

Current concerns about the workers' compensation program include the rapidly increasing costs of health care; the spreading cost of cumulative injuries, especially those arising from stress; and inadequate rates for insurers.

REVIEW TERMS

- Assumption-of-risk defense
- Automatic stabilizer
- Contributory negligence
- Cumulative injuries
- Eligibility
- Exclusive remedy
- Experience rating
- Fellow servant rule
- Fiscal policy
- Monetary policy
- Permanent partial disability
- Permanent total disability
- Rehabilitation programs
- Temporary partial disability
- Temporary total disability
- Transfer payments
- Waiting period
- Workers' compensation insurance policies

REVIEW

1. Describe some causes of unemployment. Separate your list into causes beyond the worker's control and those under the worker's control. Can you identify some gray areas in these causes?
2. What alternatives are available to the government for dealing with unemployment?
3. What do Social Security, public assistance, and unemployment insurance have in common?
4. Explain why a downward cycle of unemployment is likely to develop without government action.
5. How does unemployment insurance help to reverse the downward spiral of unemployment? Why is unemployment insurance called an *automatic stabilizer*?
6. What parts do the state and federal governments play in providing the unemployment insurance program?
7. Who do you think ultimately pays the cost for the unemployment insurance program?
8. Why does experience rating reverse the insurance transfer process? What is the explanation for experience rating in unemployment insurance?
9. What are the general provisions of state unemployment insurance programs?
10. Identify four reasons that may disqualify a worker from receiving unemployment benefits.
11. Under our current workers' compensation laws, are employers, employees, or consumers most likely to bear the costs of work-related injuries?
12. What was the fellow servant rule? What role did it play in the development of workers' compensation laws?
13. Why is workers' compensation known as the exclusive remedy?
14. List the five purposes of workers' compensation laws as outlined by the National Commission on State Workmen's Compensation Laws.
15. Identify three reasons an injured worker may be excluded from workers' compensation coverage despite being injured while at work.
16. If a worker is killed while at work, what is the typical workers' compensation benefit?
17. Identify the three general types of workers' compensation benefits.
18. Describe the role that insurance plays in distributing the cost of work-related injuries.
19. If an injured worker thinks that the compensation for the injuries sustained is unfair, what course of action may be pursued to attempt to correct the problem?
20. Give an example of a permanent partial disability.

OBJECTIVE QUESTIONS

1. "Fiscal policy" describes direct government actions to:
   a. Put money into or take money out of the economy
   b. Raise interest rates
   c. Regulate insurance transactions
   d. Increase the supply of money
2. Unemployment insurance is called an *automatic stabilizer* because:
   a. It reduces the tax rates on the unemployed.
   b. It gives purchasing power to people who would not be able to make purchases without these payments.
   c. It transfers money from the upper to the lower income brackets.
   d. It generally reduces the federal deficit in most years.
3. States have three general requirements relating to eligibility to receive unemployment benefits. These requirements include all the following except:
   a. A waiting period
   b. An earnings record
   c. A continuing interest in employment
   d. Fully insured status for Social Security benefits
4. All the following were legal defenses used by employers before workers' compensation laws existed, allowing employers to avoid making payments to injured workers, except:
   a. The fellow servant rule
   b. Assumption of the risk
   c. Dishonorable discharge of duties
   d. Contributory negligence
5. The workers' compensation claim payment is the _____ available to the injured worker.
   a. Exclusive remedy
   b. Government contribution
   c. Agreed amount
   d. Principal sum
6. _____ is designed to reward loss prevention and loss reduction efforts.
   a. Reduced credibility
   b. Warranty reduction factors
   c. Experience rating
   d. Ex-post factoring
7. Currently, workers' compensation programs are administered by:
   a. The federal government
   b. The state governments
   c. City governments
   d. Labor unions
8. Each of the following is an excluded injury under workers' compensation insurance programs except:
   a. Injuries resulting from intoxication
   b. Injuries willfully self-inflicted
   c. Injuries suffered traveling to or from work
   d. Injuries caused by a fellow employee

DISCUSSION QUESTIONS

1. Do you think that the cumulative-illness doctrine, which spread workers' compensation coverage from accidents to work-related illnesses, is desirable? What are some of the problems with this broadening of workers' compensation coverage? Who will bear the costs of this approach?

2. In recent years, states have done a great deal of borrowing from the federal government to finance unemployment insurance payments. Do you think the political climate has changed sufficiently since 1935 to allow the federal government to take over this program and combine it with Social Security? Do you think such a change would be a good idea or a bad idea?

3. Do you think the federal government should take over the workers' compensation program? Explain your reasons.

INTERNET RESEARCH ASSIGNMENTS

1. Using the most recent available data, discover how many people made initial claims for unemployment benefits in your state of residence. What is the exhaustion ratio for your state? Define the term *exhaustion ratio*. Start at this Web site to find the answer: (*http://www.dol.gov/dol/topic/unemployment-insurance/index.htm/*).

2. Collect some of the most recent data available on workers' compensation insurance. Start your search at this site: (*http://www.ncci.com/*).

3. How is workers' compensation handled in your state? Is there private insurance, state-run pools, or both?

4. Does your state have a second injury fund? What is a second injury fund designed to do? How does it work?

Glossary

This section of the text is neither an exhaustive dictionary of insurance terms nor a complete listing of all the definitions used in this text. Rather, it will help readers who want to look up insurance terms that can be explained by short definitions. Readers can find definitions of other terms requiring longer explanations using the index.

Abandonment Turning over damaged property to an insurer. The Standard Fire Policy states, "There can be no abandonment to this Company of any property." In marine insurance, the insurer will accept abandoned property.

Absolute liability A legal doctrine that causes one party always to be responsible for payment of damage claims, regardless of the circumstances causing the loss. This doctrine has been applied to those using explosives or keeping dangerous animals as pets.

Acceptance A required act in the formation of a contract. Acceptance of a contractual offer means complete agreement with the proposed terms.

Accidental death benefit See: *Double indemnity.*

Accumulation period The time period when payments flow from the owner of a deferred annuity to the insurance company and remain on deposit, prior to the liquidation period. See also: *Liquidation period.*

Act of God A misnomer that refers to a natural disaster such as a flood or tornado. See also: *Catastrophe.*

Activities of daily living (ADLs) The usual activities of mobile individuals, including bathing, eating, and dressing. The typical insured peril in long-term care insurance is the inability to perform a specified number of ADLs.

Actual cash value (ACV) An amount typically calculated as the replacement cost of property at the time of the loss, minus an allowance for depreciation. Using this definition, property that could be replaced for $100 and that had been used for one-quarter of its expected life would have an ACV of $75 ($100 − $25).

Actuary An insurance company mathematician who compiles statistics of losses, develops insurance rates, calculates dividends, and evaluates the financial standing of an insurance company.

Additional living expenses (loss of use) The extra costs of food and lodging incurred after an insured loss while the homeowner's property is being replaced or repaired.

Adjuster The person whom an insurance company appoints to determine the value of an insured's claim for loss recovery.

Admitted assets Those assets that the state allows an insurer to use in meeting tests of solvency. Typically, these assets can be realized easily as cash and used to pay claims. Nonadmitted assets are things that ordinarily could not be used to satisfy insureds' claims, such as home-office furniture.

Admitted insurer An insurer licensed to conduct business in a state. See also: *Surplus line.*

Advance premium mutual In terms of volume of insurance written, the most important kind of mutual insurance company. Under the advance premium system, policyholders pay their premiums when their insurance begins and become eligible for a dividend (and often the subsequent premium is reduced) when the insurance period ends.

Adverse selection Selection against the insurer. The tendency of less desirable exposures to loss, such as people in poor health or people with bad driving records, to try to purchase insurance protection at standard (average) rates. One possible result of asymmetric possession of information.

Agent A person authorized to act for another person, known as a *principal.* In the typical insurance transaction, the individual dealing with the consumer is an agent acting for the insurer, the principal.

Aleatory contract A contract in which both parties know from the inception that the monetary value exchanged will not be equal. Insurance is an aleatory contract in which the insured can receive more or less than the premium paid for the coverage.

Alien insurance company An insurer from another country. Contrast this with a *foreign* insurance company, which is one doing business in a state other than the one in which it is incorporated. An Ohio-based insurer doing business in Indiana is a foreign insurer in Indiana, while a Canadian insurer doing business in Indiana is an alien insurer.

All risks policy See: *Open perils.*

Allocated funding If a worker's pension benefit balance is funded for each individual and the worker has a claim on specific assets while the benefit is accumulating, insurers call the pension benefit an *allocated benefit.* When an employer purchases an annuity or a life insurance policy for each employee, this is called *allocated funding of a pension plan.*

Ambiguity A word or phrase that can have more than one meaning. For example, the word *war* may mean "fighting by large groups of armed men" to some, but it may be interpreted to mean a "fight between two or more sovereign powers" to others. The rule in insurance is that ambiguities are construed against the party writing the contract. See also: *Contract of adhesion rule*.

American Lloyds An insurance organization patterned after Lloyd's of London, which is permitted to operate in some states.

Amount at risk The amount of the insurer's exposure to loss. This amount may be different from the face amount of insurance in cash value life insurance contracts because some of the death benefits received by the beneficiary may be considered as arising from the savings value of the contract. Thus, the amount at risk ($700) is the difference between the face amount of insurance ($1,000) and the cash value ($300).

Annual transit policy An inland marine policy that covers all shipments made during a specified year.

Annuity A regular series of payments (sometimes called *rent*). If payments are made for a lifetime, the contract is called a *pure annuity* or a *straight life annuity*. If payments are guaranteed for a specified period, regardless of the annuitant's survival or death, the arrangement is called an *annuity certain*. If payments are guaranteed for a lifetime or a certain period, whichever event is last, the arrangement is called a *life annuity, period certain*. Annuities covering two or more lives are called *joint life annuities* if payments end at the first death. If payments end at the second of two deaths, the contract is called a *joint-and-last-survivor annuity*. Contracts that call for a refund when the total amount of rent received by the annuitant (for example, $25,000) is less than the premium paid for the contract (for example, $60,000) are called *refund annuities*. If the refund is made in a lump sum ($35,000 in this example), the contract is called a *cash refund annuity*. If the refund is made by continuing the regular installment payments (for example, $6,000 a year until the $35,000 refund is paid) to contingent beneficiaries, the contract is called an *installment refund annuity*.

Antirebating laws Laws that forbid agents from sharing their commissions with an insured.

Appleton rule A part of the New York insurance code that states that insurance companies doing any business in the state of New York must be in substantial compliance with all New York's rules in whatever state they do business.

Arson The deliberate destruction of property by fire. Arson for profit involves fraud against an insurer. Arson losses also may be caused by vandals or children.

Assessment mutual An insurer with the legal right to demand additional premium payments from its insureds if insufficient funds are available to meet the insurer's obligations to claimants. These mutuals are sometimes called *farm mutuals*.

Assigned risk An applicant for insurance that could not get coverage in the voluntary market and thus was assigned by state law to an insurer that otherwise would not accept the insured. This arrangement is found predominantly in the high-risk automobile insurance market.

Assignment The legal transfer of contractual rights and duties from one party to another. Assignment may or may not involve consideration. Assignment of insurance contracts is governed by policy language. Assignment of fire insurance policies is possible only with the consent of the insurer. Assignment of life insurance policies requires only the proper notification of the insurer.

Assumption of risk A legal defense in negligence litigation. When the plaintiff knew, or should have known, that a course of behavior could lead to his or her own injury, and persisted in such behavior despite this knowledge, the defendant can assert this defense in attempting to avoid compensating the plaintiff for injuries sustained.

Automatic premium loan (APL) An optional contractual feature of cash value life insurance policies. The insurer agrees to make a loan equal to any missed premiums to keep a policy in force. The total amount of loans made, plus interest, must be supported by the available cash values of the contract.

Automobile insurance plans The result of state rules that force insurers to insure some percentage of poor drivers who are unable to buy insurance from other sources. The percentage of bad drivers assigned to an insurer by the automobile insurance plan typically is determined by the insurance written voluntarily. Some plans are known as *assigned risk plans*.

Bailment Possession of property by a party other than the owner, with the intent of the property being returned to the owner. Examples of bailments include property left with dry cleaners, stored in warehouses, or placed on common carriers. The party owning the property is the *bailor*; the party in temporary possession of the property is the *bailee*.

Basic medical expense insurance Medical expense insurance policies historically providing coverage only when the insured was hospitalized; now most policies cover outpatient treatment as well.

Beneficiary The person who is designated to receive the proceeds of a life insurance policy.

Binder A temporary insurance contract used to provide property insurance coverage until the actual contract can be issued. See also: *Conditional receipt for a comparable life insurance term*.

Blanket coverage An insurance policy covering more than one item of property at one or more locations.

Bond A contractual arrangement, similar to insurance, in which one party (the surety) agrees to provide payment to another party (the obligee) if this party is injured by the acts, omissions, or dishonesty of someone else who owes the obligee a duty (the principal, or an employee). If a bond guarantees the performance of a principal, it is called a *surety bond*. If the bond guarantees the honesty of an employee or a fiduciary, it is called a *fidelity bond*.

Breach of contract A failure, without legal excuse, to fulfill one's contractual duties.

Broker An agent of the applicant for insurance. The broker may be authorized to design coverages and/or shop for insurance coverage.

Burglary Breaking and entering a person's property to commit a crime such as theft.

Burial insurance Life insurance sold in relatively small amounts to fund funeral expenses. See also: *Industrial life insurance*.

Business income (interruption) insurance This coverage provides protection from indirect losses, such as lost profits or extra expenses, that arise after a direct loss of property.

Buy-and-sell agreement An arrangement made to allow the continuation of a partnership or a close corporation after the death of one of the owners. The agreement sets the price at which the sale will be made. It also forces the owners to sell and the buyers to buy the property at this price. Such an agreement is often accompanied by the purchase of life insurance, which provides the funds to complete the transaction.

Capacity (1) The legal ability to make a binding contract. (2) The amount of insurance an insurance company can write. (3) The ability of the property-casualty insurance industry to pay claims in the event of a catastrophe.

Captive insurer An insurance company operated by a (manufacturing) company or group of companies to insure its own risks. A part of a self-insurance plan.

Cash value The saving feature associated with permanent life insurance. The result of an initial period when premium payments exceed mortality and other charges.

Cash-refund annuity See: *Annuity*.

Catastrophe An incident or series of closely related incidents that causes extremely large amounts of property losses. Floods, earthquakes, and volcanoes can produce natural catastrophes, which makes them generally uninsurable by private insurers.

Catastrophe bonds Risk-based securities that provide investors with relatively high interest rates and provide insurers with a source of funds in the event of a specified catastrophe. An alternative to traditional reinsurance arrangements.

Catastrophe modeling Using computers to integrate the frequency and severity of loss (hurricane or other catastrophic occurrence) data with proprietary insurance company data, such as number of policies written and aggregate amount of insurance written in a geographic area for the purpose of measuring an insurance company's loss potential in the specified area.

Catastrophe reinsurance An excess-of-loss reinsurance arrangement distinguished by very high retentions by the primary insurer before the reinsurer becomes liable. Catastrophe reinsurance also has very high upper limits on the reinsurance policy, with increments of coverage often being expressed in the millions of dollars.

Ceding company See: *Primary insurer*.

Claim A demand for payment made for a covered loss by an insured on an insurer.

Claims-made form A type of liability policy in which the insurer agrees to pay only for claims made during the period covered by the policy. Thus, this format is designed to eliminate coverage for incidents that occur during the policy period but which result in litigation after the policy period expires. This format is the opposite of an occurrence-basis liability policy, which pays for losses occurring during the policy period regardless of when the claim is filed.

Coinsurance A requirement in an insurance policy that the insured pay a portion of a claim if the insured purchases an inadequate amount of insurance.

Collision In automobile insurance, this term means contact of the vehicle with another object. However, several types of vehicle/object contacts, such as contact with a bird or animal, are deemed not to be collision in the personal auto policy (PAP). These events are covered by the other-than-collision provisions.

Combined ratio The sum of the loss and the expense ratio. It is calculated roughly as the sum of the losses and expenses divided by the premiums for a given period of time.

Commercial general liability (CGL) insurance An Insurance Services Office (ISO) package policy that covers many different liability exposures of small and large businesses.

Commercial insurance Insurance for businesses, governmental units, or nonprofit organizations.

Comparative negligence A modification of the contributory negligence doctrine. The comparative negligence doctrine allows the plaintiff some recovery for injuries sustained despite the fact that the plaintiff contributed slightly to the loss.

Concealment Silence when obligated to speak. A duty is imposed on applicants for insurance to reveal all material facts even if specific information is not requested by the insurer. Neglect of this duty is called *concealment*.

Condition precedent A duty required to be fulfilled by one party to a contract before the other party is required to perform. For example, the insured must file a timely notice of loss with the insurer before the insurer must pay a claim.

Condition subsequent Action (or lack of action) that destroys contractual rights. For example, the failure of an insured to begin a lawsuit against an insurer within the time specified by the contract destroys the right of the insured to sue the insurer.

Conditional receipt An arrangement used in life insurance to provide coverage to an applicant before an actual contract can be issued. These agreements typically require the applicant to submit the first premium payment and are conditioned on the insured meeting all the requirements for acceptance by the insurer, including passing a medical examination.

Consolidated Omnibus Budget Reconciliation Act of 1986 (COBRA) A federal law that affects a large number of matters, including rules requiring employers to extend group health insurance coverage to qualified employees for up to thirty-six months after a qualifying event such as a spouse's death, divorce, or separation from employment.

Consideration The amount of economic value given up in making a valid contract.

Continuing care retirement community A group living arrangement for the elderly with independent living units and a nursing facility. Admission usually involves a large front-end fee.

Contract An agreement between two parties. A valid contract is one whose terms a court will enforce. A void contract lacks one or more requirements of a valid contract. A voidable contract is one that has been breached by one of the parties.

Contract of adhesion rule A rule pertaining to insurance law that construes any ambiguities found in an insurance contract against the writer of the contract.

Contributory negligence A legal doctrine applied in negligence litigation that allows the defendant to avoid payment for the plaintiff's injuries once it is established that some action of the plaintiff (however slight) contributed to the loss.

Conversion privilege A contractual right of the employee to convert group life insurance into an individual (permanent) policy after terminating employment. This privilege also applies to some group health contracts.

Convertible term life insurance A term insurance policy that allows the insured to convert to a permanent form of insurance without providing evidence of insurability.

Coordination of benefits (COB) clause A clause found in health insurance policies that prevents insureds from collecting a full insurance recovery from each of several insurers covering the same loss exposure. The COB clause is designed to limit the total recovery to the amount of damage sustained and determines which insurance contract or contracts pay for the loss.

Countersignature law A state law requiring that a licensed resident agent sign policy forms sold to in-state residents by out-of-state agents.

Covered earnings A Social Security term describing the amount of earnings subject to taxation. In recent years, this amount has been indexed for inflation.

Credibility An actuarial concept used in experience-rated group insurance. The more reliable an employer's loss data, the more its peculiar results are reflected in its premium calculations.

Credit life insurance A type of group life insurance that covers all the debtors of one creditor—a retail store or automobile financing company, for example. The purpose of this coverage is to repay unpaid credit balances if the debtor dies with an outstanding loan balance.

Credit risk Loss potential caused by a borrower defaulting on a loan.

Crime insurance Insurance that provides payments when a crime loss (such as theft or burglary) is caused by nonemployees. Fidelity bonds cover employee-caused crime losses.

Criminal act An act in violation of penal law. An offense against the state.

Currency risk The risk of loss associated with fluctuations in one currency's value against other currencies. Importers and exporters face this risk.

Currently insured An insured status category of the Social Security program providing survivor benefits to dependents of workers with covered earnings in six of the thirteen quarters prior to death. See also: *Fully insured*.

Custodial care Care for the activities of daily living (bathing, dressing, and toileting, for example). There is no expectation that this care will improve a person's health. It is designed to maintain a person at his or her current level. Providing this care requires no medical training. To be covered by insurance, custodial care requires a doctor's orders.

Debit life insurance A form of life insurance typically sold in amounts of less than $1,000, with premiums collected at the insured's home on a weekly or monthly basis. Also known as *home service life insurance* and *burial life insurance*.

Declarations The first part of the insurance policy, in which the property, people, and insurance coverages purchased are set forth.

Decreasing term life insurance A term insurance policy that has a level premium but provides regular reductions in the face amount of coverage. This coverage often is used to repay the decreasing balance on home mortgage loans if the homeowner dies prematurely.

Deductible The first dollars of loss that the insurance contract causes to be borne by the insured. For example, if a policy has a $250 deductible and there is a covered loss amounting to $10,000, the insured collects $9,750. Deductibles may be worded in terms of a dollar amount or as a percentage of the loss.

Deep-pocket defendant A defendant in a liability suit with large financial resources or large amounts of insurance.

Defendant The party allegedly causing the plaintiff's loss in a negligence suit.

Defensive medicine Medical procedures or tests that would not be carried out in the absence of potential legal liability litigation.

Deferred annuity A contract in which payments to the annuitant begin some time after the premium payments to the insurer have ended. Thus, a person age 40 who purchases an annuity with payments to begin on his 65th birthday has purchased a deferred annuity.

Defined-benefit plan A pension plan in which the employee's benefit is predetermined by a formula. The defined benefit in turn determines the actuarial contributions required to fund the benefit.

Defined-contribution plan A pension plan in which the employer's contribution is established by a formula but no predetermined benefit amount is guaranteed.

Demutualization The process of converting a mutual insurance company to the stock form of ownership.

Dependent properties A nonowned property whose loss would interrupt or reduce an insured's profitability. For example, the loss at a supplier's (or customer's) premises could interrupt an insured's operations if inputs could not be delivered or output could not be shipped. This exposure can be insured with dependent properties coverage.

Difference-in-conditions (DIC) insurance A separate insurance policy, often used in providing international coverage, which fills in gaps in underlying alien insurance coverage. This umbrella-type coverage provides a level of uniformity when property is owned in several different foreign locations and insured with several different foreign insurers.

Direct liability Legal liability arising from one's own actions. See also: *Vicarious liability*.

Direct loss The physical damage that occurs as a consequence of a covered peril, such as the damage to property caused by a fire. See also: *Indirect loss*.

Direct writer An insurer marketing products that uses employees as agents.

Disability (total) This term is subject to different definitions by different insurers and in different policies. One of the strictest definitions is "the inability to engage in any gainful employment." A more liberal definition would be "the inability to engage in the employment one is trained for."

Disability income riders An extra-cost option that can be added to life insurance policies that provides payment if an insured meets the definition of disability found in the contract. For example, a disability income rider may provide $10 per month of income for each $1,000 face amount of life insurance.

Disability insurance This coverage replaces lost income while an insured is unable to work (that is, meeting the definition of disability found in the contract).

Dividend An amount paid on participating insurance policies. When dividends are paid to policyholders of mutual insurers, the dividends represent a nontaxable return. Dividends also are paid to owners of stock insurers; such dividends are a taxable return on their investment.

Double indemnity An option on some life insurance contracts that causes the insurer to pay twice the face of the policy if death is caused by a specified circumstance, such as an accident. This coverage is also called an *accidental death benefit*.

Earned premium The percentage of an advanced premium belonging to the insurer, based on the passage of time. For example, if the insured pays an annual premium in advance, the insurer earns one-twelfth of the premium each month.

Economic damages A measurement used in negligence cases to compensate a plaintiff for monetary costs of an injury. Examples include medical bills and loss of income. *Noneconomic damages*, in contrast, are a measurement used for losses such as pain and suffering, where there have been no out-of-pocket costs.

Elimination period A time specified by disability income insurance policies that must pass before the insured is entitled to benefits.

Embezzlement Fraudulent taking of another's property entrusted to one's care.

Employee benefits Any nonwage benefit provided by an employer to employees, including pensions, life, health, and disability insurance.

Employment Retirement Security Act of 1974 (ERISA) Federal legislation designed to guarantee certain aspects of pension plans of private employers.

Endorsement A written modification of an insurance policy that changes the original (often standardized) contract of insurance. Endorsements may either broaden or narrow the original policy language.

Endowment life insurance   A contract that promises to pay proceeds to a beneficiary if the insured dies before the end of the endowment period, or to pay the insured if the insured survives the specified period. A *pure endowment*, on the other hand, promises payment only if the insured survives the specified period.

Entire-contract provision   A clause required by state law to appear in life insurance policies, which makes the printed contract and the application attached thereto the entire contract between the parties. The purpose of this provision is to prevent incorporation of other documents (such as a corporate charter) by reference.

Environmental impairment insurance (EIL)   A coverage that provides protection to manufacturers, transporters, disposal firms, municipalities, or others for legal liability arising from activities resulting in the destruction of the environment.

Errors and omissions insurance   Liability coverage designed to protect professionals, such as accountants or insurance agents, from claims that their professional actions resulted in losses to their clients.

Estate planning   The development of a financial plan designed to cover the liquidation and disposal of assets before and at a person's death. Such a plan may involve living considerations (gifts), death considerations (identifying in a will which people will receive property), and tax considerations (including the federal unified transfer tax).

Estoppel   A common-law doctrine that prevents a person from asserting a known right when such an assertion is inconsistent with the person's past actions. For example, if an insurer issues a policy knowing that the insured is ineligible for the coverage, it may be estopped from denying a claim because of the initial ineligibility.

Evidence of insurability   In life insurance, whatever evidence an applicant for insurance must provide to induce an insurer to offer a life insurance contract. The term includes, but is not limited to, good health.

Excess of loss reinsurance   A contract in which the reinsurer must pay the primary insurer only for the amount of loss in excess of the retention limit of the primary insurer (also known as the *ceding company*). For example, if the primary insurer retains $40,000 of a $100,000 exposure, ceding the remainder on an excess of loss basis, and if a $60,000 loss occurs, then the reinsurer must pay only $20,000 ($60,000 − $40,000).

Exclusion   A clause in an insurance policy in which the insurer specifies losses (circumstances, types of property, ineligible people, etc.) not covered by the policy.

Exclusive remedy   A workers' compensation rule making workers' compensation the sole source of funds for injured workers. This rule provides for the absolute liability of employers and eliminates the need (ability) of employees to recover damages by litigation.

Expense ratio   The ratio of all the expenses (such as sales commissions or credit investigations, but not including the costs of covered losses) incurred in writing insurance, divided by the premiums realized from selling the insurance.

Experience rating   A plan found in group insurance that gives recognition in premium costs to the specific claims of the particular group being insured.

Extended-term option   A nonforfeiture option found in life insurance policies that provides for the continuation of the face amount of coverage for a period funded by available cash values.

Face amount   The initial amount of life insurance scheduled to be paid at the insured's death. The face amount may not be the amount that the beneficiary receives because of outstanding loans at the time of the insured's death (which decrease the death benefit) or because of the inclusion of paid-up additions in the proceeds (which increases the death benefit).

Factory mutual   An insurer specializing in highly protected risks. These organizations put great emphasis on loss prevention technology and inspections.

Facultative reinsurance   A reinsurance arrangement in which the reinsurer has the right to reject submissions of business from the primary insurer.

Fair Access to Insurance Requirements (FAIR) plan   A plan adopted in several states that requires insurers to offer insurance if applicants meet specific requirements. Reasons for rejecting business must be stated and are limited by state law.

Family and Medical Leave Act of 1993 (FMLA)   This law requires employers with fifty or more employees to offer up to twelve weeks of unpaid leave to eligible employees for the birth or adoption of a child, to care for a sick family member, or for the employee's own illness.

Federal Insurance Contributions Act (FICA)   Provides for the familiar Social Security tax deduction on paychecks.

Fiduciary   A person who acts on behalf of another person. A fiduciary is held by law to the highest standards of ethical conduct. Examples of fiduciaries are trustees and executors.

Financial responsibility laws   State laws that require drivers to show proof that they can satisfy legal judgments arising out of negligence in operating their motor vehicles.

Financial risk management   A branch of risk management dealing with loss exposures associated with fluctuations in financial markets—in particular, losses associated with interest rate changes and currency fluctuations.

Fire For insurance purposes, a fire is a chemical reaction that produces heat, light, or a glow and must be considered hostile when doing damage. *Hostile* means that the fire has gone beyond designated boundaries. Fires that are not hostile are designated *friendly*, and even though friendly fires may do considerable damage, insurance policies often do not provide compensation for such claims. Damage caused by a properly functioning stove, when left unattended for a long period of time, is an example of damage from a friendly fire.

Flexible premium deferred annuity An annuity in which accumulations result from a series of payments prior to liquidation. For example, some policies allow owners to make monthly payments (of irregular amounts) for many years prior to liquidation during retirement.

Floater A type of inland marine insurance policy that covers mobile property. Floaters may be scheduled (specific property is identified, as by serial number) or nonscheduled (the type of property covered is identified, but individual items are not).

Foreign Credit Insurance Association (FCIA) Established in 1961 as part of the Export-Import Bank. The FCIA is the most important source of export credit insurance for small U.S. exporters.

Foreign insurance company See: *Alien insurance company*.

Fortuitous Occurring by chance.

Forward contracts Contracts similar to futures contracts, but forward contracts are not traded on organized exchanges. See also: *Futures contracts*.

Fraud An act, such as lying or other deception, designed to cheat an insurer. Fraud against an insurer generally allows the insurer to void the insurance contract.

Fronting arrangement An agreement that typically involves a self-insurance risk financing plan. Under this type of agreement, the fronting insurance company agrees to issue a policy but cedes all or most of the business to a reinsurer.

Fully insured A category of the Social Security program that provides a broad range of benefits to workers accumulating at least forty quarters of covered earnings. Special rules allow younger workers to attain fully insured status before acquiring forty quarters of coverage. See also: *Currently insured*.

Futures contracts Contracts for orders to be placed in advance to buy or sell a commodity or financial asset at a specified price.

Grace period A limited period of time, such as thirty days, in which an insured can pay a past-due life insurance premium without having to go through the formalities of reinstating the policy.

Gramm-Leach-Bliley Act (1999) Federal legislation that allows the formation of financial service holding companies with component parts that may include commercial banks, insurance companies, and securities dealers. This act revoked the Glass-Steagall Act, legislation passed in the 1930s that separated commercial banking from other financial services.

Gross estate The property owned by a decedent at death. For federal estate tax purposes, this amount may include some transfers made within three years of death.

Gross premium A mathematical concept that recognizes all costs of marketing the coverage, including a reserve for unexpected losses. See also: *Net premium*.

Guaranteed insurability option A life insurance provision that allows insureds to purchase additional coverage, regardless of their insurability, at specified intervals (for example, the fifth policy anniversary) or at specified events (for example, the birth of a child or a marriage).

Guaranteed renewable A health insurance term that recognizes the insurer's limited rights to cancel in-force contracts. These are renewable at the insured's option to a certain age, but the premium can be changed (for the entire class of insureds) by the insurer.

Hazard A circumstance that increases either the frequency or the severity of losses.

Health Insurance Portability and Accountability Act (HIPAA) This federal act, passed in 1996, was designed to promote labor mobility. One main feature of the act was to allow workers to change jobs without the preexisting conditions exclusion of group health insurance to be applied. See also: *Preexisting conditions*.

Health maintenance organization (HMO) A medical organization that typically allows subscribers (usually members of employee groups) to pay one annual fee in exchange for the right to all needed health care services. HMOs stress preventive care (loss prevention). See also: *Preferred provider organization (PPO)*.

Hedging Taking two simultaneous and offsetting positions so that an increase in one position is matched by a decrease in the other position. This action usually is taken to reduce risk.

Highly protected risk An exposure to loss, such as a warehouse or factory, which incorporates a significant amount of loss prevention and loss reduction technology.

Hold-harmless agreement A contract transferring one party's legal liability to another. For example, a railroad may ask a lumberyard to sign a hold-harmless agreement before building a spur on the yard's site.

The agreement would transfer the railroad's liability for accidents on the spur to the lumberyard.

Home office The headquarters of an insurance company. The home office of an insurer determines the state in which it is domiciled.

Hospice A facility that cares for the terminally ill, usually for only a brief period (such as six months before death).

Hull coverage Marine and aircraft insurance that provides payment for direct losses of the ship or aircraft. Separate coverage is needed for losses of cargo or liability losses.

Immediate annuity A contract in which the first payment begins after only a short delay, such as one payment period.

Immediate notice A property and liability insurance policy provision that requires insureds to notify the insurer as soon as practicable that a covered event has occurred. Determining whether the insured has satisfied this provision sometimes requires litigation.

Incidents of ownership Any economic benefit in a life insurance policy, including the right to designate a beneficiary, make a policy loan, or receive the cash surrender value (if any exists) from a life insurance policy.

Incontestable clause A part of the life insurance contract that prevents the insurer from denying a claim for alleged fraud occurring at the policy's inception. The insurer has a limited period of time to discover any such fraud, after which time there can be no defense for nonpayment by the insurer. This means the insurer must pay even if fraud can be proved after this time has elapsed.

Increase in hazard An action by the insured that materially increases the chance of loss. In fire insurance, increases of hazard suspend the coverage.

Indemnity A payment by the insurer to the insured that leaves the insured in the same financial position occupied before the covered loss took place.

Independent adjuster A person who acts as an agent for an insurer but is not an employee of the insurer. Insurers use independent adjusters because it would not be practical or cost-effective to send employees to all loss locations.

Independent agent (independent agency system) An approach to marketing property insurance in which the selling agent is not an employee of an insurance company but rather represents several insurers and owns the business placed with any one company. See also: *Direct writer.*

Indirect loss The loss of income following a direct loss. For example, if fire destroys a motel, the structural damage is the direct loss; the lost income, continuing expenses, or extra expenses to keep operating are the indirect losses.

Industrial life insurance See: *Debit life insurance.*

Injury A wrong done to another, including damaging a person's body, property, reputation, or rights.

Inland marine insurance Provides coverage on property to be exported or imported, small valuable items (such as furs and jewelry), property being transported, and bridges and tunnels (instruments of transportation).

Insolvency (guaranty) fund A state-operated insurance fund operated for the purpose of guaranteeing the promises of insolvent insurers. The money to operate the fund comes from assessments on solvent insurers.

Installment refund annuity See: *Annuity.*

Insurable interest The ability to demonstrate that the insured event is capable of causing a financial loss to the person owning the insurance. To collect from a property insurance contract, the insurable interest must be demonstrated at the time of the loss. In life insurance, the insurable interest must exist when the policy is begun.

Insurance (1) A contractual relationship between two parties in which one party, the *insurer*, is paid a premium by the other party, the *insured*. In return for the premium, the insurer promises to indemnify the insured in the event of a covered loss. (2) A money transfer scheme in which those exposed to a loss voluntarily put money into a pool from which losses are paid to those pool members that experience loss.

Insurance Services Office (ISO) The national property and liability statistical collection and dissemination organization in the United States and its territories. The ISO develops model policy forms and publishes statistics for its member companies to use in their rate-making process.

Insuring agreement The part of the insurance contract that describes the insurer's duty to indemnify the insured.

Intentional injury A deliberate act resulting in another's injury, also known as *intentional interference*. False imprisonment of suspected shoplifters and libelous advertising are business examples of intentional injuries.

Interest-adjusted method A mathematical procedure for calculating a cost index that allows the logical comparison of cash value life insurance policies.

Interest option A life insurance settlement option that provides payments to the beneficiary derived from the interest earned on the death benefit. Any remaining principal (if principal amounts were withdrawn) is paid to a second beneficiary at the first beneficiary's death.

Interest rate risk An exposure to losses caused by changes in prevailing interest rates. See also: *Financial risk management.*

Intermediate care   Occasional nursing and rehabilitative care ordered by a physician. This level of care is performed under the supervision of skilled medical personnel.

Interpleader   A legal method for an insurance company to avoid litigation by remitting insurance proceeds to a court, allowing the court to determine rightful ownership of the proceeds.

Irrevocable beneficiary   A beneficiary in a life insurance policy whose rights cannot be impaired by the policyowner without the beneficiary's permission.

Joint-and-several liability   A legal rule that allows a plaintiff to collect the full amount of damages from one defendant if other defendants have inadequate resources to pay the judgment. The defendant from whom the damages are collected will be one of several parties responsible for injuring the plaintiff. This rule allows complete recovery even from defendants whose contribution to the injury was slight, if the other defendants have inadequate resources to pay the claim.

Joint-and-last-survivor annuity   A type of life income annuity that is based on two lives, with payments while both people are alive and ending when the last survivor dies.

Joint-life annuity   An annuity in which payments end at the death of the first of two covered lives. See also: *Annuity*.

Judgment   The finding of the court in a lawsuit (such as a suit seeking damages due to negligence).

Key employee life insurance   Coverage purchased by a business to indemnify it if a key employee dies prematurely.

Lapse   The expiration of a life insurance policy because of nonpayment of the premium.

Lapse ratio   The number of policies lapsed in a year divided by the number of policies in force at the beginning of the year.

Last clear chance   A legal doctrine that creates liability for the party with the "last clear chance" to avoid injuring another. The rule is applied, for example, after a defendant establishes that the plaintiff contributed to a loss. The last clear chance doctrine allows the plaintiff to collect, even if the plaintiff contributed to the loss, if the defendant had the last clear chance to avoid the injury.

Law of large numbers   When an event based on chance is observed, the larger the number of observations, the more likely it is that the actual result will coincide with the expected result.

Lease   A legal agreement giving one party (the tenant) the right to enjoy another party's (landlord's) property for a predetermined length of time. Possession of a leasehold interest can create an insurable interest in property.

Legal liability   A liability recognized and enforced by a court. In insurance, legal liability often results from an insured's (defendant's) negligence that results in a court-awarded judgment for an injured third party (plaintiff). The liability insurer agrees to pay its insured's legal judgment.

Legal reserve   The reserve (liability) required by state law to promote the solvency of life insurers. The reserve may be calculated on a prospective or retrospective basis and is a function of the insurer's contractual liabilities under the policies it has written.

Level-premium whole life insurance   A form of permanent, cash value life insurance that requires equal annual (or more frequent) premium payments for the insured's life or until the policy matures—for example, at age 100.

Life income option   A life insurance settlement option that provides annuity payments.

Life insurance trust   A form of trust often used in estate planning cases to decrease the federal transfer tax liability. The trust is the owner and beneficiary of a life insurance policy.

Limited payment whole life insurance   A form of permanent, cash value life insurance in which the number of premium payments is limited to a number of years (for example, eight years) or until a specified age (often age 65) is reached. When the payment period ends, the policy is designated as "paid-up."

Liquidation period   The period when payments flow from the insurer to the annuitant. See also: *Accumulation period*.

Liquidity risk   Loss potential caused by having to take a substantial discount to liquidate an investment quickly.

Lloyd's of London   An association of independent underwriters operating in Great Britain. Lloyd's of London is not an insurance company; rather, it is a marketplace for insurance where brokers representing applicants for insurance can contract with underwriters offering insurance.

Long-tail claims   In liability insurance, the result of occurrence-basis policies, in which the injury is discovered after the policy period ended, but the policy continues to provide coverage if the insured event or injury occurred during the period when the policy was in force.

Loss of use   A homeowners insurance provision that provides payment for the additional living expenses property owners experience after a covered loss. The term *loss of use* is also used to distinguish between direct and indirect losses.

Loss prevention   An activity designed to reduce the chance (frequency) of loss. Examples of loss prevention include driver training programs, better design of equipment, and better lighting in factories. See also: *Loss reduction.*

Loss ratio The amount of losses experienced in a year divided by the premiums earned from writing the insurance.

Loss reduction An activity designed to reduce the severity of losses. Examples of loss reduction include automatic fire sprinklers, directions for first aid found on containers of poisons, and separating a large exposure to loss into smaller units.

Major medical health insurance A contract typified by a large upper limit of coverage (such as $50,000), a participation provision (causing the insured to pay some percentage of the claim, such as 20 percent), and a deductible provision (such as $500).

Managed care A term used in health insurance to describe a system of providing health care with an emphasis on cost efficiency. Typical features of a managed care system include preventive examinations and controlled access to medical specialists, often through use of a "gatekeeper."

Market risk Loss potential caused by having to liquidate an investment during a downturn in the business cycle.

Maximum family benefit A Social Security provision that limits the total benefits received by a family unit with several eligible beneficiaries of one wage earner.

McCarran-Ferguson Act See: *Public Law 15.*

Medicaid A joint federal/state program providing health care to low-income people.

Medical Information Bureau (MIB) A nonprofit trade association of life insurance companies formed to conduct a confidential interchange of underwriting information. The purpose of the MIB is to prevent fraud.

Medicare A part of the Social Security program that provides health insurance to those receiving retirement benefits. See also: *Medigap insurance* and *Old-Age, Survivors, Disability Insurance—Hospital Insurance (OASDI-HI).*

Medigap insurance Private insurance designed to supplement Medicare by filling in or modifying some of the Medicare limitations and participation features.

Misstatement-of-age-provision A mandatory feature of life insurance contracts that causes insurers to adjust the amount of coverage to the appropriate benefit (given the paid premium) after a misstatement of age is discovered, rather than invalidating the entire contract.

Modified whole life insurance A type of permanent life insurance with the premiums increasing in a stair-step fashion during the early policy years. The initial premium will be less than the comparable level premium, but the modified premium climbs above the comparable level premium before leveling out for the duration of the contract.

Money purchase plan The most popular type of defined-contribution pension plan. The employer's responsibility ends after it makes the contribution, and no guaranteed benefit is provided.

Moral hazard A person who deliberately causes a loss or who exaggerates the size of a claim to defraud an insurer.

Morale hazard A person made indifferent to loss because of the purchase of insurance, thus causing the chance of loss to increase. The difference between the moral hazard and the morale hazard is seen in the difference between the arsonist who intentionally destroys property to defraud an insurer (moral hazard) and the individual who does little or nothing to protect property before a loss or to conserve property after a loss, thinking that the insurance will cover the loss.

Mortgage clause A homeowners (and other property) insurance provision that covers a lender by creating special rights and duties relative to the mortgaged property. For example, this clause precludes the insured's actions from depriving the lender of coverage; it also commits the lender to paying unpaid premiums if the lender wants the coverage to continue.

Multiple-line insurers Insurers that offer several distinct lines of insurance, such as fire, marine, liability, and workers' compensation.

Mysterious disappearance Loss of property from a known location, but without a known cause. For example, assume that a dress is left in a motel room. When the owner returns, the dress is missing, without explanation.

Named insured The individual insured(s) whose name(s) appear(s) on the declarations page.

Negligence Doing something a reasonable person would not do (for example, speeding in a car) or failing to do something a reasonable person would do (for example, removing a hazardous amount of snow or ice from a sidewalk), which act or omission results in injury to another.

Net premium A mathematical concept used to illustrate only the loss costs in developing insurance premiums. No overhead or other expenses are included.

No-fault insurance A first-party compensation scheme in which the insurer agrees to compensate its own insured regardless of whose negligence caused a loss. Various forms of no-fault automobile insurance plans operate in about sixteen states.

Noncancellable A health insurance term that recognizes the insurers' limited rights to cancel in-force contracts. The contract must be renewed to a specified age at the insured's option, and premiums may not be changed. See also: *Guaranteed renewable*.

Nonforfeiture value The amount to which the insured is entitled upon surrender of a cash value life insurance policy. The nonforfeiture options include a lump sum of cash (the cash surrender value), extended term insurance, or a reduced amount of paid-up whole life insurance.

Nonindemnity coverage A catastrophic reinsurance or financial arrangement in which the insurer receives a payment in the event of a covered loss that may be more or less than the damage that the insurer must pay its insureds. Payment may be triggered by such things as an industry loss index or maximum wind speed in a hurricane.

Nonparticipating (nonpar) insurance A for-profit insurance scheme that does not provide for dividend payments to policyholders. Nonpar insurance uses more realistic projections of losses and expenses than does participating insurance; thus initial premiums for nonpar insurance typically are lower than participating premiums. See also: *Participating insurance*.

Nonqualified pension plan A pension plan that does not meet federal requirements for tax advantages. In most cases, these plans discriminate in favor of highly compensated employees. Because they are nonqualified, the year in which the employer recognizes the compensation expense is the year the employee must report taxable income.

Obligee The party protected by a bond. See also: *Bond*.

Occupational illness (disease) Sickness arising out of employment in some way. Some occupational disease has long been recognized, such as black lung disease. Stress-related complaints are a newer form of occupational illness recognized in some states.

Occurrence-basis form See also: *Claims-made form*.

Old-Age, Survivors, Disability Insurance—Hospital Insurance (OASDI-HI) Better known as Social Security, this is a federal insurance program begun in 1935 that provides death, retirement, survivors', disability, and health insurance benefits to qualified recipients.

Open cargo marine insurance policies These policies provide automatic coverage for importers or exporters for all shipments reported to the insurer. Premiums may be calculated based on monthly reports or may require a year-end adjustment of the initial premium.

Open perils A term used in newer property insurance contracts to replace the term *all risks*. These policies cover a broad range of perils on a nonspecified basis but contain explicit exclusions restricting coverage for specific reasons.

Ordinance-or-law exclusion A property insurance provision that excludes coverage for losses to undamaged portions of buildings when total destruction of property is required by law, or if current zoning laws prevent rebuilding.

Ordinary life insurance A term that describes individual life insurance purchases in relatively large amounts paid for with annual (or more frequent) premiums. Ordinary life insurance is distinguished from debit or group life insurance.

Paid-up life insurance A whole life policy that has no additional premium payments due.

Participating insurance An insurance scheme that allows the policyholder to share in the favorable or unfavorable operating results of the insurance company. The policyholder/owner is entitled to an annual distribution of dividends based on the company's operating results. Typically, unrealistically high initial estimates are made of expected losses and expenses; when actual results are more favorable than the initial estimates, dividends are paid to the policyholders.

Participation provision A major medical insurance policy clause that causes insureds to pay a portion of each claim. It is sometimes identified as a *coinsurance provision*, but the parallels are not exact, because the coinsurance penalty (property insurance) can be avoided, while the participation provision (health insurance) payments cannot.

Pension Benefit Guarantee Corporation (PBGC) A federal agency established by the Employee Retirement Income Security Act of 1974 (ERISA), whose purpose is to guarantee that payments are made to retired workers covered by defined-benefit pension plans.

Pension plan A benefit plan designed primarily to provide retirement income to individuals. These plans commonly are tied to employment and included in an employee's benefit plan. Some pension plans include ancillary benefits, but the main focus of pension plans is providing income to retirees.

Peril The cause of a loss.

Permanent disability A term defined in a disability income policy. Some definitions of this term can be relatively liberal (e.g., "unable to engage in one's own profession"), while others can be relatively strict (e.g., "unable to engage in any profession").

Perpetual mutual A relatively rare type of insurer that provides an indeterminate period of coverage in exchange for one large initial premium. Earnings on the premium deposit fund loss payments.

Personal injury A broader description of injuries sustained by victims of negligence than *bodily injury*.

Personal injury can include lost wages and economic damage to reputations, while bodily injury pertains closely to medical expenses and related losses.

Personal property floater   An inland marine coverage that protects the insured for loss of valuable items, such as furs, jewelry, guns, and silverware.

Plaintiff   The individual alleging injury in a negligence lawsuit.

Policy   The contract between the insurer and insured.

Preexisting conditions   A health insurance policy provision that excludes coverage for health care problems experienced (diagnosed) before the policy became effective.

Preferred provider organization (PPO)   An organization of doctors, hospitals, and other medical providers that are contracted to provide health care for an employer group or insurer at reduced rates. Financial incentives are provided to encourage participants to use services in the network; for example, services provided outside the network cost more than those provided within the network. *See also: Health maintenance organization (HMO).*

Premium   The payment made by insureds to insurers for their policies.

Price-Anderson Act   A federal law that determines the legal liability of nuclear power plant operators in the event of a catastrophic loss.

Primary insurance amount (PIA)   A Social Security term that describes the basis of all a worker's benefits. That is, benefits are described as a percentage of the worker's PIA. For example, a retirement benefit at age 65 is 100 percent of the worker's PIA.

Primary insurer   The insurer who first markets the insurance to a consumer/insured. The primary insurer, also known as the *ceding company*, in turn purchases insurance in an arrangement known as *reinsurance.*

Principal   The party that must perform a duty for the obligee in a bonding arrangement. See also: *Bond.*

Prior approval   An approach to state insurance rate regulation that requires insurers to gain approval for proposed rates before implementing them.

Products liability   The liability of manufacturers and vendors that arises from products that injure people who use them. Products liability claims arise from claims of negligent design, manufacture, or failure to provide adequate warnings, packaging, or instructions. Sometimes called just *product liability.*

Professional liability   The legal liability of people with special knowledge, training, or a license to practice who injure clients in the course of providing their service.

Proximate cause   The first cause in an unbroken chain of events leading to a loss; also, the cause without which the loss would not have occurred.

Public adjuster   An individual who works for an insured after a loss has occurred to arrive at a fair claims settlement.

Public Law 15   A federal law that authorizes the continuation of state regulation of insurance so long as state regulation continues to be held in the public interest. Also known as the McCarran-Ferguson Act. Public Law 15 is reproduced in its entirety at the end of Chapter 7, "Insurance Regulation."

Punitive damages   Damages awarded by courts in addition to the compensatory damages, for cases in which the defendant's outrageous conduct requires special punishment. The purpose of punitive damages, in part, is to discourage similar future conduct.

Pure risk   A loss exposure in which the only outcome is a loss or no change in condition.

Qualified pension plan   A pension plan that meets federal nondiscrimination laws, funding requirements, and other requirements. Qualified pension plans receive valuable tax benefits not available to nonqualified plans, such as allowing the employer to recognize the pension plan payment as an expense in the year made but not requiring the beneficiary to recognize income until the year received.

Rating bureau   An organization that collects insurance data from member companies and that uses these data to develop insurance rates for the member companies. In other industries, this action would be considered a violation of antitrust laws, but it is allowed in insurance.

Real property   Land and anything permanently attached to the land.

Reasonable person   A legal standard applied in negligence cases that allows the court to evaluate the facts in particular cases.

Reciprocal exchange   A type of insurer that is unincorporated and operates on a nonprofit basis. Each insured provides insurance to all other members of the reciprocal exchange.

Recision   Canceling a contract by mutual consent or because one party made an obvious mistake. In the case of an obvious mistake, the law allows the contract to be canceled to prevent the other party from taking unfair advantage of the mistake. See also: *Reformation.*

Reduced paid-up life insurance option   A nonforfeiture option (of a permanent life insurance contract having a cash surrender value) that provides the policyowner with a lower face amount of life insurance but relieves him or her of the need to pay further premiums.

Reformation   The authorized rewriting of a contract when the written document does not reflect the intentions of both parties.

Reinstatement   The right of a life insurance policy-holder to return a lapsed contract to its original terms. Reinstatement must occur within the specified time limits provided in the policy. Reinstatement requires evidence of insurability and payment of all policy financial obligations, such as outstanding loan balances and missed premium payments. See also: *Lapse* and *Evidence of insurability*.

Reinsurance   The purchase of insurance on some portion of a covered exposure by an insurance company. The company purchasing the insurance is called the *primary insurer* or *ceding company*; the company providing the insurance is called the *reinsurer*. Two typical reinsurance arrangements are *pro rata reinsurance* (both the premiums and losses are shared on a proportional basis) and *excess-of-loss reinsurance* (the reinsurer pays only when covered losses exceed some predetermined amount, and then pays only the excess above this amount).

Renewable term life insurance   A policy that the insured can renew without presenting evidence of insurability.

Replacement-cost insurance   A property insurance policy in which the insured pays for the replacement cost of the insured property rather than the actual cash value. A typical requirement causes the insured actually to repair or replace the damaged property in order to receive this amount.

Replacement ratio   The ratio of retirement to preretirement income.

Representation   A statement made by an applicant in an insurance application. The insurer relies on the truth of the applicant's representations in underwriting the policy. A material misrepresentation generally allows the insurer to avoid the contract.

Reservation of rights   Notice from the insurer to the insured that the insurer is not certain that coverage exists but plans to proceed with the loss adjustment, and perhaps the legal defense, as if the coverage existed, but that certain events may occur in the future that may cause the insurer to reevaluate its position.

Res ipsa loquitur   Literally meaning "the thing speaks for itself," a legal doctrine applied in negligence cases in which the only explanation for the plaintiff's injuries is the defendant's actions. For example, the doctrine is often applied in commercial airplane accidents, in which passengers could not conceivably have contributed to the loss. The application of the doctrine relieves the plaintiff of the duty to establish the defendant's negligence, but it does not preclude the defendant from establishing a defense.

Retention   The amount of insurance kept by the primary insurer in a reinsurance arrangement. See also: *Primary insurer* and *Reinsurance*.

Retroactive date   In a claims-made liability policy, the retroactive date determines the first point in time where a covered loss may occur. The retroactive date may be subject to change or negotiation.

Retrocession   The purchase of reinsurance by a reinsurer.

Robbery   A felony involving the taking of another's property by force or threat of force.

Salvage   The amount recovered from the sale of damaged property.

Schedule rating   An approach to property insurance rate making in which the specific characteristics of the covered property are compared to a standard, and then credits or charges are applied for above or below standard features when developing a final rate.

Scheduled property   The specifically identified property (such as cameras or jewelry) in an inland marine personal property floater or other policy that requires a listing of property.

Short-rate cancellation schedule   The short-rate cancellation schedule applies when an insured cancels a property insurance policy. The short-rates are higher than pro rata cancellation rates to allow the insurer to recover the acquisition expenses and recognize the potential for adverse selection. For example, the short rates may credit the insurer with earning 5 percent of the premium after one day of coverage, while the pro rata rates would credit the insurer with only 1/365 of the premium for the same period.

Skilled-nursing care   Daily nursing and rehabilitative care ordered by a physician. This level of care is performed under the supervision of skilled medical personnel.

Skilled-nursing facility   A state-licensed facility.

Social Security   See: *Old-Age, Survivors, Disability Insurance—Hospital Insurance (OASDI-HI)*.

Speculative risk   An exposure to loss that could result in a loss, gain, or no change as a result of fortuitous circumstances. Investing in common stocks creates a speculative risk.

Split-dollar life insurance   A method of paying for permanent life insurance coverage in which two parties (often an employer and employee) each pays a portion of the annual premium, with one party paying an amount equal to the increase in cash value in a given year (the employer) and the other party (the employee) paying the remainder.

Stare decisis   The legal principle of abiding by already decided cases, which provides continuity to legal decisions. The decision of the court when it first encounters a particular set of circumstances sets a precedent for deciding future cases that involve similar circumstances.

Statute of limitations A law that defines a specific period of time during which a lawsuit can be brought. For example, the law may allow an injured party three years from the time an injury was discovered to file suit. If the injured party does not begin the lawsuit within the specified time period, that party loses the right to bring the suit.

Stock insurance company An insurer organized as a for-profit venture, with owners who are not necessarily policyholders.

Strict liability Liability without fault. This rule of law creates a heavy burden for defendants in liability suits.

Structured settlements In negligence cases, instead of the defendant paying a lump sum to a plaintiff, the defendant (using the services of an insurer) promises a series of annuity payments to the injured party.

Subrogation The substitution of one party (the insurer) for another party (the insured) in that party's rights. The substitution occurs because the first party has made a payment for which another is responsible. In insurance, subrogation occurs when the insurer pays a claim while the insured has a right of action against a third party for causing a loss. After making the claims payment, the insurer is subrogated to the insured's right to sue the third party.

Subsidization A result of insurance operations when one group of insureds pays more than its mathematically fair share of losses, while another group pays less than its mathematically fair share.

Surety bond See: *Bond*.

Surplus line Insurance on an exposure for which no coverage is available in the normal market.

Survivor life insurance A life insurance policy covering two lives that provides a death payment at the second death. (If more than two lives are covered, payment is made at the last person's death.) Survivor life insurance frequently is used in estate planning cases based on plans leaving the entire estate at the first death to the surviving spouse, with life insurance proceeds providing liquidity for estate taxes at the second death. (Also known as *second-to-die life insurance*.)

Swap A transaction in which two companies lend to each other different currencies (a currency swap) or at different interest rates, one fixed and one floating (an interest rate swap).

Theft A broad term that describes the taking of another's property with the intent of depriving the owner of the property. Burglary and embezzlement are types of theft.

Time element coverage See: *Business income (interruption) insurance*.

Tontine A money transfer scheme, now illegal in the United States, where all money transferred to a pool is given to the last survivor(s) of the pool.

Tort A wrongful act, other than a breach of contract, that results in another's injury.

Traded option The creation of a legal right to buy or sell a commodity or a financial asset at an agreed-upon price for a specific time period.

Twisting An illegal replacement of life insurance based on incomplete or deceptive comparisons between existing and proposed policies.

Uberrima fides Literally translated as "utmost good faith," this term refers to the standard of behavior imposed on the insured by an insurance contract—that is, the requirement that the insured deal with the insurer without making material misrepresentations or concealing material facts.

Umbrella liability policy A policy, usually with large limits, that covers losses in excess of the limits provided by underlying liability insurance. For example, a personal umbrella liability insurance policy provides people with excess coverage over the liability coverage provided by their homeowners and automobile insurance policies.

Underinsurance Having less insurance than is required by the policy provisions, especially the coinsurance provision. See also: *Coinsurance*.

Underinsured motorists' insurance An automobile insurance policy option that provides payment when the insured is injured by a negligent motorist who has less insurance than the insured, and the insured cannot recover for all damage sustained because of the defendant's inadequate coverage.

Underwriting The process of selecting and rating applicants for insurance for the purpose of calculating a premium.

Unearned premium The percentage of an advance premium not yet earned by the insurer by the passage of time. For example, assume that an insured pays a one-year premium for a policy in advance. After the policy has been in force for two months, ten-twelfths of the premium remains unearned.

Uniform transfer tax The combination of the federal gift and estate taxes.

Universal life insurance A type of life insurance policy that allows the insured flexibility in choosing premium payments and death benefits during the contract period.

Unlimited marital deduction A provision of the federal estate tax that allows the first spouse to die to transfer an unlimited amount of assets to the surviving spouse without incurring an estate tax liability.

Unoccupied A situation that arises when an insured leaves possessions in a residence but is temporarily absent from the premises. See also: *Vacant*.

Vacant The situation where a building is completely empty and without contents. See also: *Unoccupied*.

Valued policy A type of insurance policy in which the insurer agrees to pay the face amount in the event of a total loss, regardless of the actual damage sustained. Valued insurance policies often are used to insure artwork and similar items because the market value at the time of loss may be difficult to estimate when the insurance policy begins.

Vandalism The malicious destruction of another's property.

Variable annuity An annuity with a flexible liquidation payment determined by the performance of an underlying (common stock) investment portfolio.

Variable life insurance A type of cash value life insurance policy that gives the insured flexibility in choosing the underlying investment media.

Vested benefit The right of an employee to the employer's contribution to a pension plan. Federal law specifies vesting schedules for qualified pension plans.

Vicarious liability Legal liability that arises out of another's actions. For example, a contractor may have vicarious liability if a subcontractor injures another party.

Waiver Giving up a known contractual right.

Waiver-of-premium option An extra-cost life insurance policy provision that provides for the insurer to forgo collecting premiums while the insured is permanently disabled. Despite the forgone premiums, the policy remains in force, with benefits calculated as if premiums had been paid.

Warranty A statement made by an insured that induces the insurer to enter into the insurance contract. The statement must be absolutely true or the insurer can avoid its contractual obligations. If the statement covers the future (for example, "there always will be at least two guards on duty"), it is a *promissory warranty*. If the statement represents a current condition (for example, "this ship is seaworthy"), it is an *affirmative warranty*.

Whole life insurance A contract that promises payment whenever death occurs, or at age 100. Whole life contracts involve savings and often are called *permanent insurance*.

Wrongful death lawsuit Litigation that arises when a defendant's alleged actions resulted in a plaintiff's death.

Homeowners Insurance Policies HO-2 and HO-3

These sample policies are Copyright Insurance Services Office 2000 and are used with its permission.

HOMEOWNERS 2—BROAD FORM

AGREEMENT

We will provide the insurance described in this policy in return for the premium and compliance with all applicable provisions of this policy.

DEFINITIONS

A. In this policy, "you" and "your" refer to the "named insured" shown in the Declarations and the spouse if a resident of the same household. "We", "us" and "our" refer to the Company providing this insurance.

B. In addition, certain words and phrases are defined as follows:

1. "Aircraft Liability", "Hovercraft Liability", "Motor Vehicle Liability" and "Watercraft Liability", subject to the provisions in b. below, mean the following:

   a. Liability for "bodily injury" or "property damage" arising out of the:

   (1) Ownership of such vehicle or craft by an "insured";

   (2) Maintenance, occupancy, operation, use, loading or unloading of such vehicle or craft by any person;

   (3) Entrustment of such vehicle or craft by an "insured" to any person;

   (4) Failure to supervise or negligent supervision of any person involving such vehicle or craft by an "insured"; or

   (5) Vicarious liability, whether or not imposed by law, for the actions of a child or minor involving such vehicle or craft.

   b. For the purpose of this definition:

   (1) Aircraft means any contrivance used or designed for flight, except model or hobby aircraft not used or designed to carry people or cargo;

   (2) Hovercraft means a self-propelled motorized ground effect vehicle and includes, but is not limited to, flarecraft and air cushion vehicles;

   (3) Watercraft means a craft principally designed to be propelled on or in water by wind, engine power or electric motor; and

   (4) Motor vehicle means a "motor vehicle" as defined in 7. below.

2. "Bodily injury" means bodily harm, sickness or disease, including required care, loss of services and death that results.

3. "Business" means:

   a. A trade, profession or occupation engaged in on a full-time, part-time or occasional basis; or

   b. Any other activity engaged in for money or other compensation, except the following:

   (1) One or more activities, not described in (2) through (4) below, for which no "insured" receives more than $2,000 in total compensation for the 12 months before the beginning of the policy period;

   (2) Volunteer activities for which no money is received other than payment for expenses incurred to perform the activity;

   (3) Providing home day care services for which no compensation is received, other than the mutual exchange of such services; or

   (4) The rendering of home day care services to a relative of an "insured".

4. "Employee" means an employee of an "insured", or an employee leased to an "insured" by a labor leasing firm under an agreement between an "insured" and the labor leasing firm, whose duties are other than those performed by a "residence employee".

5. "Insured" means:

   a. You and residents of your household who are:

   (1) Your relatives; or

   (2) Other persons under the age of 21 and in the care of any person named above;

   b. A student enrolled in school full time, as defined by the school, who was a resident of your household before moving out to attend school, provided the student is under the age of:

   (1) 24 and your relative; or

   (2) 21 and in your care or the care of a person described in a.(1) above;

   c. Under Section II:

   (1) With respect to animals or watercraft to which this policy applies, any person or organization legally responsible for these animals or watercraft which are owned by you or any person included in a. or b. above. "Insured" does not mean a person or organization using or having custody of these animals or watercraft in the course of any "business" or without consent of the owner; or

(2) With respect to a "motor vehicle" to which this policy applies:

(a) Persons while engaged in your employ or that of any person included in a. or b. above; or

(b) Other persons using the vehicle on an "insured location" with your consent.

Under both Sections I and II, when the word an immediately precedes the word "insured", the words an "insured" together mean one or more "insureds".

6. "Insured location" means:

a. The "residence premises";

b. The part of other premises, other structures and grounds used by you as a residence; and

(1) Which is shown in the Declarations; or

(2) Which is acquired by you during the policy period for your use as a residence;

c. Any premises used by you in connection with a premises described in a. and b. above;

d. Any part of a premises:

(1) Not owned by an "insured"; and

(2) Where an "insured" is temporarily residing;

e. Vacant land, other than farm land, owned by or rented to an "insured";

f. Land owned by or rented to an "insured" on which a one, two, three or four family dwelling is being built as a residence for an "insured";

g. Individual or family cemetery plots or burial vaults of an "insured"; or

h. Any part of a premises occasionally rented to an "insured" for other than "business" use.

7. "Motor vehicle" means:

a. A self-propelled land or amphibious vehicle; or

b. Any trailer or semitrailer which is being carried on, towed by or hitched for towing by a vehicle described in a. above.

8. "Occurrence" means an accident, including continuous or repeated exposure to substantially the same general harmful conditions, which results, during the policy period, in:

a. "Bodily injury"; or

b. "Property damage".

9. "Property damage" means physical injury to, destruction of, or loss of use of tangible property.

10. "Residence employee" means:

a. An employee of an "insured", or an employee leased to an "insured" by a labor leasing firm, under an agreement between an "insured" and the labor leasing firm, whose duties are related to the maintenance or use of the "residence premises", including household or domestic services; or

b. One who performs similar duties elsewhere not related to the "business" of an "insured".

A "residence employee" does not include a temporary employee who is furnished to an "insured" to substitute for a permanent "residence employee" on leave or to meet seasonal or short-term workload conditions.

11. "Residence premises" means:

a. The one family dwelling where you reside;

b. The two, three or four family dwelling where you reside in at least one of the family units; or

c. That part of any other building where you reside;

and which is shown as the "residence premises" in the Declarations. "Residence premises" also includes other structures and grounds at that location.

DEDUCTIBLE

Unless otherwise noted in this policy, the following deductible provision applies:

Subject to the policy limits that apply, we will pay only that part of the total of all loss payable under Section I that exceeds the deductible amount shown in the Declarations.

SECTION I—PROPERTY COVERAGES

A. Coverage A—Dwelling

1. We cover:

a. The dwelling on the "residence premises" shown in the Declarations, including structures attached to the dwelling; and

b. Materials and supplies located on or next to the "residence premises" used to construct, alter or repair the dwelling or other structures on the "residence premises".

2. We do not cover land, including land on which the dwelling is located.

B. Coverage B—Other Structures

1. We cover other structures on the "residence premises" set apart from the dwelling by clear space. This includes structures connected to the dwelling by only a fence, utility line, or similar connection.

2. We do not cover:

a. Land, including land on which the other structures are located;

b. Other structures rented or held for rental to any person not a tenant of the dwelling, unless used solely as a private garage;

c. Other structures from which any "business" is conducted; or

d. Other structures used to store "business" property. However, we do cover a structure that contains "business" property solely owned by an "insured" or a tenant of the dwelling provided that "business" property does not include gaseous or liquid fuel, other than fuel in a permanently installed fuel tank of a vehicle or craft parked or stored in the structure.

3. The limit of liability for this coverage will not be more than 10% of the limit of liability that applies to Coverage A. Use of this coverage does not reduce the Coverage A limit of liability.

C. Coverage C—Personal Property

1. **Covered Property**

We cover personal property owned or used by an "insured" while it is anywhere in the world. After a loss and at your request, we will cover personal property owned by:

a. Others while the property is on the part of the "residence premises" occupied by an "insured"; or

b. A guest or a "residence employee", while the property is in any residence occupied by an "insured".

2. **Limit For Property At Other Residences**

Our limit of liability for personal property usually located at an "insured" residence, other than the "residence premises", is 10% of the limit of liability for Coverage C, or $1,000, whichever is greater. However, this limitation does not apply to personal property:

a. Moved from the "residence premises" because it is being repaired, renovated or rebuilt and is not fit to live in or store property in; or

b. In a newly acquired principal residence for 30 days from the time you begin to move the property there.

3. **Special Limits Of Liability**

The special limit for each category shown below is the total limit for each loss for all property in that category. These special limits do not increase the Coverage C limit of liability.

a. $200 on money, bank notes, bullion, gold other than goldware, silver other than silverware, platinum other than platinumware, coins, medals, scrip, stored value cards and smart cards.

b. $1,500 on securities, accounts, deeds, evidences of debt, letters of credit, notes other than bank notes, manuscripts, personal records, passports, tickets and stamps. This dollar limit applies to these categories regardless of the medium (such as paper or computer software) on which the material exists.

This limit includes the cost to research, replace or restore the information from the lost or damaged material.

c. $1,500 on watercraft of all types, including their trailers, furnishings, equipment and outboard engines or motors.

d. $1,500 on trailers or semitrailers not used with watercraft of all types.

e. $1,500 for loss by theft of jewelry, watches, furs, precious and semiprecious stones.

f. $2,500 for loss by theft of firearms and related equipment.

g. $2,500 for loss by theft of silverware, silverplated ware, goldware, gold-plated ware, platinumware, platinum-plated ware and pewterware. This includes flatware, hollowware, tea sets, trays and trophies made of or including silver, gold or pewter.

h. $2,500 on property, on the "residence premises", used primarily for "business" purposes.

i. $500 on property, away from the "residence premises", used primarily for "business" purposes. However, this limit does not apply to loss to electronic apparatus and other property described in Categories j. and k. below.

j. $1,500 on electronic apparatus and accessories, while in or upon a "motor vehicle", but only if the apparatus is equipped to be operated by power from the "motor vehicle's" electrical system while still capable of being operated by other power sources.

Accessories include antennas, tapes, wires, records, discs or other media that can be used with any apparatus described in this Category j.

k. $1,500 on electronic apparatus and accessories used primarily for "business" while away from the "residence premises" and not in or upon a "motor vehicle". The apparatus must be equipped to be operated by power from the "motor vehicle's" electrical system while still capable of being operated by other power sources.

Accessories include antennas, tapes, wires, records, discs or other media that can be used with any apparatus described in this Category k.

4. **Property Not Covered**

We do not cover:

a. Articles separately described and specifically insured, regardless of the limit for which they are insured, in this or other insurance;

b. Animals, birds or fish;

c. "Motor vehicles".

(1) This includes:

(a) Their accessories, equipment and parts; or

(b) Electronic apparatus and accessories designed to be operated solely by power from the electrical system of the "motor vehicle". Accessories include antennas, tapes, wires, records, discs or other media that can be used with any apparatus described above.

The exclusion of property described in (a) and (b) above applies only while such property is in or upon the "motor vehicle".

(2) We do cover "motor vehicles" not required to be registered for use on public roads or property which are:

(a) Used solely to service an "insured's" residence; or

(b) Designed to assist the handicapped;

d. Aircraft meaning any contrivance used or designed for flight including any parts whether or not attached to the aircraft.

We do cover model or hobby aircraft not used or designed to carry people or cargo;

e. Hovercraft and parts. Hovercraft means a self-propelled motorized ground effect vehicle and includes, but is not limited to, flarecraft and air cushion vehicles;

f. Property of roomers, boarders and other tenants, except property of roomers and boarders related to an "insured";

g. Property in an apartment regularly rented or held for rental to others by an "insured", except as provided under E.10. Landlord's Furnishings under Section I—Property Coverages;

h. Property rented or held for rental to others off the "residence premises";

i. "Business" data, including such data stored in:

(1) Books of account, drawings or other paper records; or

(2) Computers and related equipment.

We do cover the cost of blank recording or storage media, and of prerecorded computer programs available on the retail market;

j. Credit cards, electronic fund transfer cards or access devices used solely for deposit, withdrawal or transfer of funds except as provided in E.6. Credit Card, Electronic Fund Transfer Card Or Access Device, Forgery And Counterfeit Money under Section I-Property Coverages; or

k. Water or steam.

D. Coverage D—Loss Of Use

The limit of liability for Coverage D is the total limit for the coverages in 1. Additional Living Expense, 2. Fair Rental Value and 3. Civil Authority Prohibits Use below.

1. Additional Living Expense

If a loss covered under Section I makes that part of the "residence premises" where you reside not fit to live in, we cover any necessary increase in living expenses incurred by you so that your household can maintain its normal standard of living.

Payment will be for the shortest time required to repair or replace the damage or, if you permanently relocate, the shortest time required for your household to settle elsewhere.

2. Fair Rental Value

If a loss covered under Section I makes that part of the "residence premises" rented to others or held for rental by you not fit to live in, we cover the fair rental value of such premises less any expenses that do not continue while it is not fit to live in.

Payment will be for the shortest time required to repair or replace such premises.

3. Civil Authority Prohibits Use

If a civil authority prohibits you from use of the "residence premises" as a result of direct damage to neighboring premises by a Peril Insured Against, we cover the loss as provided in 1. Additional Living Expense and 2. Fair Rental Value above for no more than two weeks.

4. Loss Or Expense Not Covered

We do not cover loss or expense due to cancellation of a lease or agreement.

The periods of time under 1. Additional Living Expense, 2. Fair Rental Value and 3. Civil Authority Prohibits Use above are not limited by expiration of this policy.

E. Additional Coverages

1. Debris Removal

a. We will pay your reasonable expense for the removal of:

(1) Debris of covered property if a Peril Insured Against that applies to the damaged property causes the loss; or

(2) Ash, dust or particles from a volcanic eruption that has caused direct loss to a building or property contained in a building.

This expense is included in the limit of liability that applies to the damaged property. If the amount to be paid for the actual damage to the property plus the debris removal expense is more than the limit of liability for the damaged property, an additional 5% of that limit is available for such expense.

b. We will also pay your reasonable expense, up to $1,000, for the removal from the "residence premises" of:

(1) Your tree(s) felled by the peril of Windstorm or Hail or Weight of Ice, Snow or Sleet; or

(2) A neighbor's tree(s) felled by a Peril Insured Against under Coverage C; provided the tree(s):

(3) Damage(s) a covered structure; or

(4) Does not damage a covered structure, but:

(a) Block(s) a driveway on the "residence premises" which prevent(s) a "motor vehicle", that is registered for use on public roads or property, from entering or leaving the "residence premises"; or

(b) Block(s) a ramp or other fixture designed to assist a handicapped person to enter or leave the dwelling building.

The $1,000 limit is the most we will pay in any one loss regardless of the number of fallen trees. No more than $500 of this limit will be paid for the removal of any one tree.

This coverage is additional insurance.

2. Reasonable Repairs

a. We will pay the reasonable cost incurred by you for the necessary measures taken solely to protect covered property that is damaged by a Peril Insured Against from further damage.

b. If the measures taken involve repair to other damaged property, we will only pay if that property is covered under this policy and the damage is caused by a Peril Insured Against. This coverage does not:

(1) Increase the limit of liability that applies to the covered property; or

(2) Relieve you of your duties, in case of a loss to covered property, described in B.4. under Section I—Conditions.

3. Trees, Shrubs And Other Plants

We cover trees, shrubs, plants or lawns, on the "residence premises", for loss caused by the following Perils Insured Against:

a. Fire or Lightning;

b. Explosion;

c. Riot or Civil Commotion;

d. Aircraft;

e. Vehicles not owned or operated by a resident of the "residence premises";

f. Vandalism or Malicious Mischief; or

g. Theft.

We will pay up to 5% of the limit of liability that applies to the dwelling for all trees, shrubs, plants or lawns. No more than $500 of this limit will be paid for any one tree, shrub or plant. We do not cover property grown for "business" purposes.

This coverage is additional insurance.

4. Fire Department Service Charge

We will pay up to $500 for your liability assumed by contract or agreement for fire department charges incurred when the fire department is called to save or protect covered property from a Peril Insured Against. We do not cover fire department service charges if the property is located within the limits of the city, municipality or protection district furnishing the fire department response.

This coverage is additional insurance. No deductible applies to this coverage.

5. Property Removed

We insure covered property against direct loss from any cause while being removed from a premises endangered by a Peril Insured Against and for no more than 30 days while removed.

This coverage does not change the limit of liability that applies to the property being removed.

6. Credit Card, Electronic Fund Transfer Card Or Access Device, Forgery And Counterfeit Money

a. We will pay up to $500 for:

(1) The legal obligation of an "insured" to pay because of the theft or unauthorized use of credit cards issued to or registered in an "insured's" name;

(2) Loss resulting from theft or unauthorized use of an electronic fund transfer card or access device used for deposit, withdrawal or transfer of funds, issued to or registered in an "insured's" name;

(3) Loss to an "insured" caused by forgery or alteration of any check or negotiable instrument; and

(4) Loss to an "insured" through acceptance in good faith of counterfeit United States or Canadian paper currency.

All loss resulting from a series of acts committed by any one person or in which any one person is concerned or implicated is considered to be one loss.

This coverage is additional insurance. No deductible applies to this coverage.

b. We do not cover:

(1) Use of a credit card, electronic fund transfer card or access device:

(a) By a resident of your household;

(b) By a person who has been entrusted with either type of card or access device; or

(c) If an "insured" has not complied with all terms and conditions under which the cards are issued or the devices accessed; or

(2) Loss arising out of "business" use or dishonesty of an "insured".

c. If the coverage in a. applies, the following defense provisions also apply:

(1) We may investigate and settle any claim or suit that we decide is appropriate. Our duty to defend a claim or suit ends when the amount we pay for the loss equals our limit of liability.

(2) If a suit is brought against an "insured" for liability under a.(1) or (2) above, we will provide a defense at our expense by counsel of our choice.

(3) We have the option to defend at our expense an "insured" or an "insured's" bank against any suit for the enforcement of payment under a.(3) above.

7. Loss Assessment
   a. We will pay up to $1,000 for your share of loss assessment charged during the policy period against you, as owner or tenant of the "residence premises," by a corporation or association of property owners. The assessment must be made as a result of direct loss to property, owned by all members collectively, of the type that would be covered by this policy if owned by you, caused by a Peril Insured Against under Coverage A, other than:
   (1) Earthquake; or
   (2) Land shock waves or tremors before, during or after a volcanic eruption.
   The limit of $1,000 is the most we will pay with respect to any one loss, regardless of the number of assessments. We will only apply one deductible, per unit, to the total amount of any one loss to the property described above, regardless of the number of assessments.
   b. We do not cover assessments charged against you or a corporation or association of property owners by any governmental body.
   c. Paragraph P. Policy Period under Section I—Conditions does not apply to this coverage.
   This coverage is additional insurance.

8. Collapse
   a. With respect to this Additional Coverage:
   (1) Collapse means an abrupt falling down or caving in of a building or any part of a building with the result that the building or part of the building cannot be occupied for its current intended purpose.
   (2) A building or any part of a building that is in danger of falling down or caving in is not considered to be in a state of collapse.
   (3) A part of a building that is standing is not considered to be in a state of collapse even if it has separated from another part of the building.
   (4) A building or any part of a building that is standing is not considered to be in a state of collapse even if it shows evidence of cracking, bulging, sagging, bending, leaning, settling, shrinkage or expansion.
   b. We insure for direct physical loss to covered property involving collapse of a building or any part of a building if the collapse was caused by one or more of the following:
   (1) The Perils Insured Against;
   (2) Decay that is hidden from view, unless the presence of such decay is known to an "insured" prior to collapse;
   (3) Insect or vermin damage that is hidden from view, unless the presence of such damage is known to an "insured" prior to collapse;

   (4) Weight of contents, equipment, animals or people;
   (5) Weight of rain which collects on a roof; or
   (6) Use of defective material or methods in construction, remodeling or renovation if the collapse occurs during the course of the construction, remodeling or renovation.
   c. Loss to an awning, fence, patio, deck, pavement, swimming pool, underground pipe, flue, drain, cesspool, septic tank, foundation, retaining wall, bulkhead, pier, wharf or dock is not included under b. (2) through (6) above, unless the loss is a direct result of the collapse of a building or any part of a building.
   d. This coverage does not increase the limit of liability that applies to the damaged covered property.

9. Glass Or Safety Glazing Material
   a. We cover:
   (1) The breakage of glass or safety glazing material which is part of a covered building, storm door or storm window;
   (2) The breakage of glass or safety glazing material which is part of a covered building, storm door or storm window when caused directly by earth movement; and
   (3) The direct physical loss to covered property caused solely by the pieces, fragments or splinters of broken glass or safety glazing material which is part of a building, storm door or storm window.
   b. This coverage does not include loss:
   (1) To covered property which results because the glass or safety glazing material has been broken, except as provided in a.(3) above; or
   (2) On the "residence premises" if the dwelling has been vacant for more than 60 consecutive days immediately before the loss, except when the breakage results directly from earth movement as provided in a.(2) above. A dwelling being constructed is not considered vacant.
   c. This coverage does not increase the limit of liability that applies to the damaged property.

10. Landlord's Furnishings
   We will pay up to $2,500 for your appliances, carpeting and other household furnishings, in each apartment on the "residence premises" regularly rented or held for rental to others by an "insured", for loss caused by a Peril Insured Against other than Theft.
   This limit is the most we will pay in any one loss regardless of the number of appliances, carpeting or other household furnishings involved in the loss.

This coverage does not increase the limit of liability applying to the damaged property.

11. **Ordinance Or Law**

a. You may use up to 10% of the limit of liability that applies to Coverage A for the increased costs you incur due to the enforcement of any ordinance or law which requires or regulates:

(1) The construction, demolition, remodeling, renovation or repair of that part of a covered building or other structure damaged by a Peril Insured Against;

(2) The demolition and reconstruction of the undamaged part of a covered building or other structure, when that building or other structure must be totally demolished because of damage by a Peril Insured Against to another part of that covered building or other structure; or

(3) The remodeling, removal or replacement of the portion of the undamaged part of a covered building or other structure necessary to complete the remodeling, repair or replacement of that part of the covered building or other structure damaged by a Peril Insured Against.

b. You may use all or part of this ordinance or law coverage to pay for the increased costs you incur to remove debris resulting from the construction, demolition, remodeling, renovation, repair or replacement of property as stated in a. above.

c. We do not cover:

(1) The loss in value to any covered building or other structure due to the requirements of any ordinance or law; or

(2) The costs to comply with any ordinance or law which requires any "insured" or others, to test for, monitor, clean up, remove, contain, treat, detoxify or neutralize, or in any way respond to, or assess the effects of, pollutants in or on any covered building or other structure.

Pollutants means any solid, liquid, gaseous or thermal irritant or contaminant, including smoke, vapor, soot, fumes, acids, alkalis, chemicals and waste. Waste includes materials to be recycled, reconditioned or reclaimed.

This coverage is additional insurance.

12. **Grave Markers**

We will pay up to $5,000 for grave markers, including mausoleums, on or away from the "residence premises" for loss caused by a Peril Insured Against.

This coverage does not increase the limits of liability that apply to the damaged covered property.

SECTION I—PERILS INSURED AGAINST

We insure for direct physical loss to the property described in Coverages A, B and C caused by any of the following perils unless the loss is excluded under Section I— Exclusions.

1. **Fire Or Lightning**

2. **Windstorm Or Hail**

This peril includes loss to watercraft of all types and their trailers, furnishings, equipment, and outboard engines or motors, only while inside a fully enclosed building.

This peril does not include loss to the inside of a building or the property contained in a building caused by rain, snow, sleet, sand or dust unless the direct force of wind or hail damages the building causing an opening in a roof or wall and the rain, snow, sleet, sand or dust enters through this opening.

3. **Explosion**

4. **Riot Or Civil Commotion**

5. **Aircraft**

This peril includes self-propelled missiles and spacecraft.

6. **Vehicles**

This peril does not include loss to a fence, driveway or walk caused by a vehicle owned or operated by a resident of the "residence premises".

7. **Smoke**

This peril means sudden and accidental damage from smoke, including the emission or puffback of smoke, soot, fumes or vapors from a boiler, furnace or related equipment.

This peril does not include loss caused by smoke from agricultural smudging or industrial operations.

8. **Vandalism Or Malicious Mischief**

This peril does not include loss to property on the "residence premises", and any ensuing loss caused by any intentional and wrongful act committed in the course of the vandalism or malicious mischief, if the dwelling has been vacant for more than 60 consecutive days immediately before the loss. A dwelling being constructed is not considered vacant.

9. **Theft**

a. This peril includes attempted theft and loss of property from a known place when it is likely that the property has been stolen.

b. This peril does not include loss caused by theft:

(1) Committed by an "insured";

(2) In or to a dwelling under construction, or of materials and supplies for use in the construction until the dwelling is finished and occupied;

(3) From that part of a "residence premises" rented by an "insured" to someone other than another "insured"; or

(4) That occurs off the "residence premises" of:

(a) Trailers, semitrailers and campers;

(b) Watercraft of all types, and their furnishings, equipment and outboard engines or motors; or

(c) Property while at any other residence owned by, rented to, or occupied by an "insured", except while an "insured" is temporarily living there. Property of an "insured" who is a student is covered while at the residence the student occupies to attend school as long as the student has been there at any time during the 60 days immediately before the loss.

10. Falling Objects

This peril does not include loss to the inside of a building or property contained in the building unless the roof or an outside wall of the building is first damaged by a falling object. Damage to the falling object itself is not included.

11. Weight Of Ice, Snow Or Sleet

This peril means weight of ice, snow or sleet which causes damage to a building or property contained in a building.

This peril does not include loss to an awning, fence, patio, pavement, swimming pool, foundation, retaining wall, bulkhead, pier, wharf, or dock.

12. Accidental Discharge Or Overflow Of Water Or Steam

a. This peril means accidental discharge or overflow of water or steam from within a plumbing, heating, air conditioning or automatic fire protective sprinkler system or from within a household appliance. We also pay to tear out and replace any part of the building, or other structure, on the "residence premises", but only when necessary to repair the system or appliance from which the water or steam escaped. However, such tear out and replacement coverage only applies to other structures if the water or steam causes actual damage to a building on the "residence premises".

b. This peril does not include loss:

(1) On the "residence premises", if the dwelling has been vacant for more than 60 consecutive days immediately before the loss. A dwelling being constructed is not considered vacant;

(2) To the system or appliance from which the water or steam escaped;

(3) Caused by or resulting from freezing except as provided in Peril Insured Against 14. Freezing;

(4) On the "residence premises" caused by accidental discharge or overflow which occurs off the "residence premises"; or

(5) Caused by mold, fungus or wet rot unless hidden within the walls or ceilings or beneath the floors or above the ceilings of a structure.

c. In this peril, a plumbing system or household appliance does not include a sump, sump pump or related equipment or a roof drain, gutter, downspout or similar fixtures or equipment.

d. Section I—Exclusion 3. Water Damage, Paragraphs a. and c. that apply to surface water and water below the surface of the ground do not apply to loss by water covered under this peril.

13. Sudden And Accidental Tearing Apart, Cracking, Burning Or Bulging

This peril means sudden and accidental tearing apart, cracking, burning or bulging of a steam or hot water heating system, an air conditioning or automatic fire protective sprinkler system, or an appliance for heating water.

This peril does not include loss caused by or resulting from freezing except as provided in Peril Insured Against 14. Freezing below.

14. Freezing

a. This peril means freezing of a plumbing, heating, air conditioning or automatic fire protective sprinkler system or of a household appliance but only if you have used reasonable care to:

(1) Maintain heat in the building; or

(2) Shut off the water supply and drain all systems and appliances of water.

However, if the building is protected by an automatic fire protective sprinkler system, you must use reasonable care to continue the water supply and maintain heat in the building for coverage to apply.

b. In this peril, a plumbing system or household appliance does not include a sump, sump pump or related equipment or a roof drain, gutter, downspout or similar fixtures or equipment.

15. Sudden And Accidental Damage From Artificially Generated Electrical Current

This peril does not include loss to tubes, transistors, electronic components or circuitry that are a part of appliances, fixtures, computers, home entertainment units or other types of electronic apparatus.

16. Volcanic Eruption

This peril does not include loss caused by earthquake, land shock waves or tremors.

SECTION I—EXCLUSIONS

We do not insure for loss caused directly or indirectly by any of the following. Such loss is excluded regardless of any other cause or event contributing concurrently or in any sequence to the loss. These exclusions apply whether or not the loss event results in widespread damage or affects a substantial area.

 HO 00 02 05 01

1. Ordinance Or Law

Ordinance or Law means any ordinance or law:

a. Requiring or regulating the construction, demolition, remodeling, renovation or repair of property, including removal of any resulting debris. This Exclusion 1.a. does not apply to the amount of coverage that may be provided for in E.11. Ordinance Or Law under Section I—Property Coverages;

b. The requirements of which result in a loss in value to property; or

c. Requiring any "insured" or others to test for, monitor, clean up, remove, contain, treat, detoxify or neutralize, or in any way respond to, or assess the effects of, pollutants.

   Pollutants means any solid, liquid, gaseous or thermal irritant or contaminant, including smoke, vapor, soot, fumes, acids, alkalis, chemicals and waste. Waste includes materials to be recycled, reconditioned or reclaimed.

This Exclusion 1. applies whether or not the property has been physically damaged.

2. Earth Movement

Earth Movement means:

a. Earthquake, including land shock waves or tremors before, during or after a volcanic eruption;

b. Landslide, mudslide or mudflow;

c. Subsidence or sinkhole; or

d. Any other earth movement including earth sinking, rising or shifting;

caused by or resulting from human or animal forces or any act of nature unless direct loss by fire or explosion ensues and then we will pay only for the ensuing loss.

   This Exclusion 2. does not apply to loss by theft.

3. Water Damage

Water Damage means:

a. Flood, surface water, waves, tidal water, overflow of a body of water, or spray from any of these, whether or not driven by wind;

b. Water or water-borne material which backs up through sewers or drains or which overflows or is discharged from a sump, sump pump or related equipment; or

c. Water or water-borne material below the surface of the ground, including water which exerts pressure on or seeps or leaks through a building, sidewalk, driveway, foundation, swimming pool or other structure;

caused by or resulting from human or animal forces or any act of nature.

   Direct loss by fire, explosion or theft resulting from water damage is covered.

4. Power Failure

Power Failure means the failure of power or other utility service if the failure takes place off the "residence premises". But if the failure results in a loss, from a Peril Insured Against on the "residence premises", we will pay for the loss caused by that peril.

5. Neglect

Neglect means neglect of an "insured" to use all reasonable means to save and preserve property at and after the time of a loss.

6. War

War includes the following and any consequence of any of the following:

a. Undeclared war, civil war, insurrection, rebellion or revolution;

b. Warlike act by a military force or military personnel; or

c. Destruction, seizure or use for a military purpose.

Discharge of a nuclear weapon will be deemed a warlike act even if accidental.

7. Nuclear Hazard

This Exclusion 7. pertains to Nuclear Hazard to the extent set forth in M. Nuclear Hazard Clause under Section I—Conditions.

8. Intentional Loss

Intentional Loss means any loss arising out of any act an "insured" commits or conspires to commit with the intent to cause a loss.

   In the event of such loss, no "insured" is entitled to coverage, even "insureds" who did not commit or conspire to commit the act causing the loss.

9. Governmental Action

Governmental Action means the destruction, confiscation or seizure of property described in Coverage A, B or C by order of any governmental or public authority.

   This exclusion does not apply to such acts ordered by any governmental or public authority that are taken at the time of a fire to prevent its spread, if the loss caused by fire would be covered under this policy.

SECTION I—CONDITIONS

A. Insurable Interest And Limit Of Liability

Even if more than one person has an insurable interest in the property covered, we will not be liable in any one loss:

1. To an "insured" for more than the amount of such "insured's" interest at the time of loss; or

2. For more than the applicable limit of liability.

B. Duties After Loss

In case of a loss to covered property, we have no duty to provide coverage under this policy if the failure to comply with the following duties is prejudicial to us. These duties must be performed either by you, an "insured" seeking coverage, or a representative of either:

1. Give prompt notice to us or our agent;

2. Notify the police in case of loss by theft;

3. Notify the credit card or electronic fund transfer card or access device company in case of loss as provided for in E.6. Credit Card, Electronic Fund Transfer Card Or Access Device, Forgery And Counterfeit Money under Section I—Property Coverages;

4. Protect the property from further damage. If repairs to the property are required, you must:
   a. Make reasonable and necessary repairs to protect the property; and
   b. Keep an accurate record of repair expenses;

5. Cooperate with us in the investigation of a claim;

6. Prepare an inventory of damaged personal property showing the quantity, description, actual cash value and amount of loss. Attach all bills, receipts and related documents that justify the figures in the inventory;

7. As often as we reasonably require:
   a. Show the damaged property;
   b. Provide us with records and documents we request and permit us to make copies; and
   c. Submit to examination under oath, while not in the presence of another "insured," and sign the same;

8. Send to us, within 60 days after our request, your signed, sworn proof of loss which sets forth, to the best of your knowledge and belief:
   a. The time and cause of loss;
   b. The interests of all "insureds" and all others in the property involved and all liens on the property;
   c. Other insurance which may cover the loss;
   d. Changes in title or occupancy of the property during the term of the policy;
   e. Specifications of damaged buildings and detailed repair estimates;
   f. The inventory of damaged personal property described in 6. above;
   g. Receipts for additional living expenses incurred and records that support the fair rental value loss; and
   h. Evidence or affidavit that supports a claim under E.6. Credit Card, Electronic Fund Transfer Card Or Access Device, Forgery And Counterfeit Money under Section I—Property Coverages, stating the amount and cause of loss.

C. **Loss Settlement**
   In this Condition C., the terms "cost to repair or replace" and "replacement cost" do not include the increased costs incurred to comply with the enforcement of any ordinance or law, except to the extent that coverage for these increased costs is provided in E.11. Ordinance Or Law under Section I—Property Coverages. Covered property losses are settled as follows:

1. Property of the following types:
   a. Personal property;
   b. Awnings, carpeting, household appliances, outdoor antennas and outdoor equipment, whether or not attached to buildings;
   c. Structures that are not buildings; and
   d. Grave markers, including mausoleums;
   at actual cash value at the time of loss but not more than the amount required to repair or replace.

2. Buildings covered under Coverage A or B at replacement cost without deduction for depreciation, subject to the following:
   a. If, at the time of loss, the amount of insurance in this policy on the damaged building is 80% or more of the full replacement cost of the building immediately before the loss, we will pay the cost to repair or replace, after application of any deductible and without deduction for depreciation, but not more than the least of the following amounts:
      (1) The limit of liability under this policy that applies to the building;
      (2) The replacement cost of that part of the building damaged with material of like kind and quality and for like use; or
      (3) The necessary amount actually spent to repair or replace the damaged building.
      If the building is rebuilt at a new premises, the cost described in (2) above is limited to the cost which would have been incurred if the building had been built at the original premises.
   b. If, at the time of loss, the amount of insurance in this policy on the damaged building is less than 80% of the full replacement cost of the building immediately before the loss, we will pay the greater of the following amounts, but not more than the limit of liability under this policy that applies to the building:
      (1) The actual cash value of that part of the building damaged; or
      (2) That proportion of the cost to repair or replace, after application of any deductible and without deduction for depreciation, that part of the building damaged, which the total amount of insurance in this policy on the damaged building bears to 80% of the replacement cost of the building.
   c. To determine the amount of insurance required to equal 80% of the full replacement cost of the building immediately before the loss, do not include the value of:
      (1) Excavations, footings, foundations, piers, or any other structures or devices that support all or part of the building, which are below

the undersurface of the lowest basement floor;

(2) Those supports described in (1) above which are below the surface of the ground inside the foundation walls, if there is no basement; and

(3) Underground flues, pipes, wiring and drains.

d. We will pay no more than the actual cash value of the damage until actual repair or replacement is complete. Once actual repair or replacement is complete, we will settle the loss as noted in 2.a. and b. above.

However, if the cost to repair or replace the damage is both:

(1) Less than 5% of the amount of insurance in this policy on the building; and

(2) Less than $2,500;

we will settle the loss as noted in 2.a. and b. above whether or not actual repair or replacement is complete.

e. You may disregard the replacement cost loss settlement provisions and make claim under this policy for loss to buildings on an actual cash value basis. You may then make claim for any additional liability according to the provisions of this Condition C. Loss Settlement, provided you notify us of your intent to do so within 180 days after the date of loss.

D. Loss To A Pair Or Set

In case of loss to a pair or set we may elect to:

1. Repair or replace any part to restore the pair or set to its value before the loss; or

2. Pay the difference between actual cash value of the property before and after the loss.

E. Appraisal

If you and we fail to agree on the amount of loss, either may demand an appraisal of the loss. In this event, each party will choose a competent and impartial appraiser within 20 days after receiving a written request from the other. The two appraisers will choose an umpire. If they cannot agree upon an umpire within 15 days, you or we may request that the choice be made by a judge of a court of record in the state where the "residence premises" is located. The appraisers will separately set the amount of loss. If the appraisers submit a written report of an agreement to us, the amount agreed upon will be the amount of loss. If they fail to agree, they will submit their differences to the umpire. A decision agreed to by any two will set the amount of loss.

Each party will:

1. Pay its own appraiser; and

2. Bear the other expenses of the appraisal and umpire equally.

F. Other Insurance And Service Agreement

If a loss covered by this policy is also covered by:

1. Other insurance, we will pay only the proportion of the loss that the limit of liability that applies under this policy bears to the total amount of insurance covering the loss; or

2. A service agreement, this insurance is excess over any amounts payable under any such agreement. Service agreement means a service plan, property restoration plan, home warranty or other similar service warranty agreement, even if it is characterized as insurance.

G. Suit Against Us

No action can be brought against us unless there has been full compliance with all of the terms under Section I of this policy and the action is started within two years after the date of loss.

H. Our Option

If we give you written notice within 30 days after we receive your signed, sworn proof of loss, we may repair or replace any part of the damaged property with material or property of like kind and quality.

I. Loss Payment

We will adjust all losses with you. We will pay you unless some other person is named in the policy or is legally entitled to receive payment. Loss will be payable 60 days after we receive your proof of loss and:

1. Reach an agreement with you;

2. There is an entry of a final judgment; or

3. There is a filing of an appraisal award with us.

J. Abandonment Of Property

We need not accept any property abandoned by an "insured".

K. Mortgage Clause

1. If a mortgagee is named in this policy, any loss payable under Coverage A or B will be paid to the mortgagee and you, as interests appear. If more than one mortgagee is named, the order of payment will be the same as the order of precedence of the mortgages.

2. If we deny your claim, that denial will not apply to a valid claim of the mortgagee, if the mortgagee:

a. Notifies us of any change in ownership, occupancy or substantial change in risk of which the mortgagee is aware;

b. Pays any premium due under this policy on demand if you have neglected to pay the premium; and

c. Submits a signed, sworn statement of loss within 60 days after receiving notice from us of your failure to do so. Paragraphs E. Appraisal, G. Suit Against Us and I. Loss Payment under Section I—Conditions also apply to the mortgagee.

3. If we decide to cancel or not to renew this policy, the mortgagee will be notified at least 10 days before the date cancellation or nonrenewal takes effect.

4. If we pay the mortgagee for any loss and deny payment to you:

  a. We are subrogated to all the rights of the mortgagee granted under the mortgage on the property; or

  b. At our option, we may pay to the mortgagee the whole principal on the mortgage plus any accrued interest. In this event, we will receive a full assignment and transfer of the mortgage and all securities held as collateral to the mortgage debt.

5. Subrogation will not impair the right of the mortgagee to recover the full amount of the mortgagee's claim.

L. No Benefit To Bailee

We will not recognize any assignment or grant any coverage that benefits a person or organization holding, storing or moving property for a fee regardless of any other provision of this policy.

M. Nuclear Hazard Clause

1. "Nuclear Hazard" means any nuclear reaction, radiation, or radioactive contamination, all whether controlled or uncontrolled or however caused, or any consequence of any of these.

2. Loss caused by the nuclear hazard will not be considered loss caused by fire, explosion, or smoke, whether these perils are specifically named in or otherwise included within the Perils Insured Against.

3. This policy does not apply under Section I to loss caused directly or indirectly by nuclear hazard, except that direct loss by fire resulting from the nuclear hazard is covered.

N. Recovered Property

If you or we recover any property for which we have made payment under this policy, you or we will notify the other of the recovery. At your option, the property will be returned to or retained by you or it will become our property. If the recovered property is returned to or retained by you, the loss payment will be adjusted based on the amount you received for the recovered property.

O. Volcanic Eruption Period

One or more volcanic eruptions that occur within a 72 hour period will be considered as one volcanic eruption.

P. Policy Period

This policy applies only to loss which occurs during the policy period.

Q. Concealment Or Fraud

We provide coverage to no "insureds" under this policy if, whether before or after a loss, an "insured" has:

1. Intentionally concealed or misrepresented any material fact or circumstance;

2. Engaged in fraudulent conduct; or

3. Made false statements;

relating to this insurance.

R. Loss Payable Clause

If the Declarations show a loss payee for certain listed insured personal property, the definition of "insured" is changed to include that loss payee with respect to that property.

If we decide to cancel or not renew this policy, that loss payee will be notified in writing.

SECTION II—LIABILITY COVERAGES

A. Coverage E—Personal Liability

If a claim is made or a suit is brought against an "insured" for damages because of "bodily injury" or "property damage" caused by an "occurrence" to which this coverage applies, we will:

1. Pay up to our limit of liability for the damages for which an "insured" is legally liable. Damages include prejudgment interest awarded against an "insured"; and

2. Provide a defense at our expense by counsel of our choice, even if the suit is groundless, false or fraudulent. We may investigate and settle any claim or suit that we decide is appropriate. Our duty to settle or defend ends when our limit of liability for the "occurrence" has been exhausted by payment of a judgment or settlement.

B. Coverage F—Medical Payments To Others

We will pay the necessary medical expenses that are incurred or medically ascertained within three years from the date of an accident causing "bodily injury". Medical expenses means reasonable charges for medical, surgical, x-ray, dental, ambulance, hospital, professional nursing, prosthetic devices and funeral services. This coverage does not apply to you or regular residents of your household except "residence employees". As to others, this coverage applies only:

1. To a person on the "insured location" with the permission of an "insured"; or

2. To a person off the "insured location", if the "bodily injury:"

  a. Arises out of a condition on the "insured location" or the ways immediately adjoining;

  b. Is caused by the activities of an "insured";

  c. Is caused by a "residence employee" in the course of the "residence employee's" employment by an "insured"; or

  d. Is caused by an animal owned by or in the care of an "insured."

   HO 00 02 05 01

SECTION II—EXCLUSIONS

A. "Motor Vehicle Liability"

1. Coverages E and F do not apply to any "motor vehicle liability" if, at the time and place of an "occurrence", the involved "motor vehicle":

   a. Is registered for use on public roads or property;

   b. Is not registered for use on public roads or property, but such registration is required by a law, or regulation issued by a government agency, for it to be used at the place of the "occurrence"; or

   c. Is being:

      (1) Operated in, or practicing for, any prearranged or organized race, speed contest or other competition;

      (2) Rented to others;

      (3) Used to carry persons or cargo for a charge; or

      (4) Used for any "business" purpose except for a motorized golf cart while on a golfing facility.

2. If Exclusion A.1. does not apply, there is still no coverage for "motor vehicle liability" unless the "motor vehicle" is:

   a. In dead storage on an "insured location";

   b. Used solely to service an "insured's" residence;

   c. Designed to assist the handicapped and, at the time of an "occurrence," it is:

      (1) Being used to assist a handicapped person; or

      (2) Parked on an "insured location";

   d. Designed for recreational use off public roads and:

      (1) Not owned by an "insured"; or

      (2) Owned by an "insured" provided the "occurrence" takes place on an "insured location" as defined in Definitions B. 6.a., b., d., e. or h.; or

   e. A motorized golf cart that is owned by an "insured," designed to carry up to 4 persons, not built or modified after manufacture to exceed a speed of 25 miles per hour on level ground and, at the time of an "occurrence," is within the legal boundaries of:

      (1) A golfing facility and is parked or stored there, or being used by an "insured" to:

         (a) Play the game of golf or for other recreational or leisure activity allowed by the facility;

         (b) Travel to or from an area where "motor vehicles" or golf carts are parked or stored; or

         (c) Cross public roads at designated points to access other parts of the golfing facility; or

      (2) A private residential community, including its public roads upon which a motorized golf cart can legally travel, which is subject to the authority of a property owners association and contains an "insured's" residence.

B. "Watercraft Liability"

1. Coverages E and F do not apply to any "watercraft liability" if, at the time of an "occurrence," the involved watercraft is being:

   a. Operated in, or practicing for, any prearranged or organized race, speed contest or other competition. This exclusion does not apply to a sailing vessel or a predicted log cruise;

   b. Rented to others;

   c. Used to carry persons or cargo for a charge; or

   d. Used for any "business" purpose.

2. If Exclusion B.1. does not apply, there is still no coverage for "watercraft liability" unless, at the time of the "occurrence", the watercraft:

   a. Is stored;

   b. Is a sailing vessel, with or without auxiliary power, that is:

      (1) Less than 26 feet in overall length; or

      (2) 26 feet or more in overall length and not owned by or rented to an "insured"; or

   c. Is not a sailing vessel and is powered by:

      (1) An inboard or inboard-outdrive engine or motor, including those that power a water jet pump, of:

         (a) 50 horsepower or less and not owned by an "insured"; or

         (b) More than 50 horsepower and not owned by or rented to an "insured"; or

      (2) One or more outboard engines or motors with:

         (a) 25 total horsepower or less;

         (b) More than 25 horsepower if the outboard engine or motor is not owned by an "insured";

         (c) More than 25 horsepower if the outboard engine or motor is owned by an "insured" who acquired it during the policy period; or

         (d) More than 25 horsepower if the outboard engine or motor is owned by an "insured" who acquired it before the policy period, but only if:

            (i) You declare them at policy inception; or

            (ii) Your intent to insure them is reported to us in writing within 45 days after you acquire them.

   The coverages in (c) and (d) above apply for the policy period.

   Horsepower means the maximum power rating assigned to the engine or motor by the manufacturer.

C. **"Aircraft Liability"**

This policy does not cover "aircraft liability".

D. **"Hovercraft Liability"**

This policy does not cover "hovercraft liability".

E. **Coverage E — Personal Liability And Coverage F — Medical Payments To Others**

Coverages E and F do not apply to the following:

1. **Expected Or Intended Injury**

   "Bodily injury" or "property damage" which is expected or intended by an "insured" even if the resulting "bodily injury" or "property damage":

   a. Is of a different kind, quality or degree than initially expected or intended; or

   b. Is sustained by a different person, entity, real or personal property, than initially expected or intended.

   However, this Exclusion E.1. does not apply to "bodily injury" resulting from the use of reasonable force by an "insured" to protect persons or property;

2. **"Business"**

   a. "Bodily injury" or "property damage" arising out of or in connection with a "business" conducted from an "insured location" or engaged in by an "insured", whether or not the "business" is owned or operated by an "insured" or employs an "insured".

   This Exclusion E.2. applies but is not limited to an act or omission, regardless of its nature or circumstance, involving a service or duty rendered, promised, owed, or implied to be provided because of the nature of the "business".

   b. This Exclusion E.2. does not apply to:

   (1) The rental or holding for rental of an "insured location";

   (a) On an occasional basis if used only as a residence;

   (b) In part for use only as a residence, unless a single family unit is intended for use by the occupying family to lodge more than two roomers or boarders; or

   (c) In part, as an office, school, studio or private garage; and

   (2) An "insured" under the age of 21 years involved in a part-time or occasional, self-employed "business" with no employees;

3. **Professional Services**

   "Bodily injury" or "property damage" arising out of the rendering of or failure to render professional services;

4. **"Insured's" Premises Not An "Insured Location"**

   "Bodily injury" or "property damage" arising out of a premises:

   a. Owned by an "insured";

   b. Rented to an "insured"; or

   c. Rented to others by an "insured";

   that is not an "insured location";

5. **War**

   "Bodily injury" or "property damage" caused directly or indirectly by war, including the following and any consequence of any of the following:

   a. Undeclared war, civil war, insurrection, rebellion or revolution;

   b. Warlike act by a military force or military personnel; or

   c. Destruction, seizure or use for a military purpose.

   Discharge of a nuclear weapon will be deemed a warlike act even if accidental;

6. **Communicable Disease**

   "Bodily injury" or "property damage" which arises out of the transmission of a communicable disease by an "insured";

7. **Sexual Molestation, Corporal Punishment Or Physical Or Mental Abuse**

   "Bodily injury" or "property damage" arising out of sexual molestation, corporal punishment or physical or mental abuse; or

8. **Controlled Substance**

   "Bodily injury" or "property damage" arising out of the use, sale, manufacture, delivery, transfer or possession by any person of a Controlled Substance as defined by the Federal Food and Drug Law at 21 U.S.C.A. Sections 811 and 812. Controlled Substances include but are not limited to cocaine, LSD, marijuana and all narcotic drugs. However, this exclusion does not apply to the legitimate use of prescription drugs by a person following the orders of a licensed physician.

Exclusions A. "Motor Vehicle Liability", B. "Watercraft Liability", C. "Aircraft Liability", D. "Hovercraft Liability" and E.4. "Insured's" Premises Not An "Insured Location" do not apply to "bodily injury" to a "residence employee" arising out of and in the course of the "residence employee's" employment by an "insured".

F. **Coverage E — Personal Liability**

Coverage E does not apply to:

1. Liability:

   a. For any loss assessment charged against you as a member of an association, corporation or community of property owners, except as provided in D. Loss Assessment under Section II — Additional Coverages;

   b. Under any contract or agreement entered into by an "insured". However, this exclusion does not apply to written contracts:

   (1) That directly relate to the ownership, maintenance or use of an "insured location"; or

   (2) Where the liability of others is assumed by you prior to an "occurrence";

   unless excluded in a. above or elsewhere in this policy;

2. "Property damage" to property owned by an "insured". This includes costs or expenses incurred by an "insured" or others to repair, replace, enhance, restore or maintain such property to prevent injury to a person or damage to property of others, whether on or away from an "insured location;"

3. "Property damage" to property rented to, occupied or used by or in the care of an "insured". This exclusion does not apply to "property damage" caused by fire, smoke or explosion;

4. "Bodily injury" to any person eligible to receive any benefits voluntarily provided or required to be provided by an "insured" under any:
   a. Workers' compensation law;
   b. Non-occupational disability law; or
   c. Occupational disease law;

5. "Bodily injury" or "property damage" for which an "insured" under this policy:
   a. Is also an insured under a nuclear energy liability policy issued by the:
      (1) Nuclear Energy Liability Insurance Association;
      (2) Mutual Atomic Energy Liability Underwriters;
      (3) Nuclear Insurance Association of Canada; or any of their successors; or
   b. Would be an insured under such a policy but for the exhaustion of its limit of liability; or

6. "Bodily injury" to you or an "insured" as defined under Definitions 5.a. or b.
   This exclusion also applies to any claim made or suit brought against you or an "insured":
   a. To repay; or
   b. Share damages with;
   another person who may be obligated to pay damages because of "bodily injury" to an "insured".

G. Coverage F—Medical Payments To Others
Coverage F does not apply to "bodily injury":
1. To a "residence employee" if the "bodily injury":
   a. Occurs off the "insured location"; and
   b. Does not arise out of or in the course of the "residence employee's" employment by an "insured";
2. To any person eligible to receive benefits voluntarily provided or required to be provided under any:
   a. Workers' compensation law;
   b. Non-occupational disability law; or
   c. Occupational disease law;
3. From any:
   a. Nuclear reaction;
   b. Nuclear radiation; or
   c. Radioactive contamination;
   all whether controlled or uncontrolled or however caused; or
   d. Any consequence of any of these; or

4. To any person, other than a "residence employee" of an "insured", regularly residing on any part of the "insured location".

SECTION II—ADDITIONAL COVERAGES

We cover the following in addition to the limits of liability:
A. Claim Expenses
We pay:
1. Expenses we incur and costs taxed against an "insured" in any suit we defend;
2. Premiums on bonds required in a suit we defend, but not for bond amounts more than the Coverage E limit of liability. We need not apply for or furnish any bond;
3. Reasonable expenses incurred by an "insured" at our request, including actual loss of earnings (but not loss of other income) up to $250 per day, for assisting us in the investigation or defense of a claim or suit; and
4. Interest on the entire judgment which accrues after entry of the judgment and before we pay or tender, or deposit in court that part of the judgment which does not exceed the limit of liability that applies.

B. First Aid Expenses
We will pay expenses for first aid to others incurred by an "insured" for "bodily injury" covered under this policy. We will not pay for first aid to an "insured".

C. Damage To Property Of Others
1. We will pay, at replacement cost, up to $1,000 per "occurrence" for "property damage" to property of others caused by an "insured."
2. We will not pay for "property damage":
   a. To the extent of any amount recoverable under Section I;
   b. Caused intentionally by an "insured" who is 13 years of age or older;
   c. To property owned by an "insured";
   d. To property owned by or rented to a tenant of an "insured" or a resident in your household; or
   e. Arising out of:
      (1) A "business" engaged in by an "insured";
      (2) Any act or omission in connection with a premises owned, rented or controlled by an "insured", other than the "insured location"; or
      (3) The ownership, maintenance, occupancy, operation, use, loading or unloading of aircraft, hovercraft, watercraft or "motor vehicles".
         This exclusion e.(3) does not apply to a "motor vehicle" that:
         (a) Is designed for recreational use off public roads;

(b) Is not owned by an "insured"; and

(c) At the time of the "occurrence", is not required by law, or regulation issued by a government agency, to have been registered for it to be used on public roads or property.

D. Loss Assessment

1. We will pay up to $1,000 for your share of loss assessment charged against you, as owner or tenant of the "residence premises", during the policy period by a corporation or association of property owners, when the assessment is made as a result of:

a. "Bodily injury" or "property damage" not excluded from coverage under Section II—Exclusions; or

b. Liability for an act of a director, officer or trustee in the capacity as a director, officer or trustee, provided such person:

(1) Is elected by the members of a corporation or association of property owners; and

(2) Serves without deriving any income from the exercise of duties which are solely on behalf of a corporation or association of property owners.

2. Paragraph I. Policy Period under Section II—Conditions does not apply to this Loss Assessment Coverage.

3. Regardless of the number of assessments, the limit of $1,000 is the most we will pay for loss arising out of:

a. One accident, including continuous or repeated exposure to substantially the same general harmful condition; or

b. A covered act of a director, officer or trustee. An act involving more than one director, officer or trustee is considered to be a single act.

4. We do not cover assessments charged against you or a corporation or association of property owners by any governmental body.

SECTION II—CONDITIONS

A. Limit Of Liability

Our total liability under Coverage E for all damages resulting from any one "occurrence" will not be more than the Coverage E limit of liability shown in the Declarations. This limit is the same regardless of the number of "insureds", claims made or persons injured. All "bodily injury" and "property damage" resulting from any one accident or from continuous or repeated exposure to substantially the same general harmful conditions shall be considered to be the result of one "occurrence".

Our total liability under Coverage F for all medical expense payable for "bodily injury" to one person

as the result of one accident will not be more than the Coverage F limit of liability shown in the Declarations.

B. Severability Of Insurance

This insurance applies separately to each "insured". This condition will not increase our limit of liability for any one "occurrence".

C. Duties After "Occurrence"

In case of an "occurrence", you or another "insured" will perform the following duties that apply. We have no duty to provide coverage under this policy if your failure to comply with the following duties is prejudicial to us. You will help us by seeing that these duties are performed:

1. Give written notice to us or our agent as soon as is practical, which sets forth:

a. The identity of the policy and the "named insured" shown in the Declarations;

b. Reasonably available information on the time, place and circumstances of the "occurrence"; and

c. Names and addresses of any claimants and witnesses;

2. Cooperate with us in the investigation, settlement or defense of any claim or suit;

3. Promptly forward to us every notice, demand, summons or other process relating to the "occurrence";

4. At our request, help us:

a. To make settlement;

b. To enforce any right of contribution or indemnity against any person or organization who may be liable to an "insured";

c. With the conduct of suits and attend hearings and trials; and

d. To secure and give evidence and obtain the attendance of witnesses;

5. With respect to C. Damage To Property Of Others under Section II—Additional Coverages, submit to us within 60 days after the loss, a sworn statement of loss and show the damaged property, if in an "insured's" control;

6. No "insured" shall, except at such "insured's" own cost, voluntarily make payment, assume obligation or incur expense other than for first aid to others at the time of the "bodily injury".

D. Duties Of An Injured Person—Coverage F—Medical Payments To Others

1. The injured person or someone acting for the injured person will:

a. Give us written proof of claim, under oath if required, as soon as is practical; and

b. Authorize us to obtain copies of medical reports and records.

2. The injured person will submit to a physical exam by a doctor of our choice when and as often as we reasonably require.

© ISO Properties, Inc., 2000   **HO 00 02 05 01**

E. Payment Of Claim—Coverage F—Medical Payments To Others

Payment under this coverage is not an admission of liability by an "insured" or us.

F. Suit Against Us

1. No action can be brought against us unless there has been full compliance with all of the terms under this Section II.
2. No one will have the right to join us as a party to any action against an "insured".
3. Also, no action with respect to Coverage E can be brought against us until the obligation of such "insured" has been determined by final judgment or agreement signed by us.

G. Bankruptcy Of An "Insured"

Bankruptcy or insolvency of an "insured" will not relieve us of our obligations under this policy.

H. Other Insurance

This insurance is excess over other valid and collectible insurance except insurance written specifically to cover as excess over the limits of liability that apply in this policy.

I. Policy Period

This policy applies only to "bodily injury" or "property damage" which occurs during the policy period.

J. Concealment Or Fraud

We do not provide coverage to an "insured" who, whether before or after a loss, has:

1. Intentionally concealed or misrepresented any material fact or circumstance;
2. Engaged in fraudulent conduct; or
3. Made false statements;

relating to this insurance.

SECTIONS I AND II—CONDITIONS

A. Liberalization Clause

If we make a change which broadens coverage under this edition of our policy without additional premium charge, that change will automatically apply to your insurance as of the date we implement the change in your state, provided that this implementation date falls within 60 days prior to or during the policy period stated in the Declarations.

This Liberalization Clause does not apply to changes implemented with a general program revision that includes both broadenings and restrictions in coverage, whether that general program revision is implemented through introduction of:

1. A subsequent edition of this policy; or
2. An amendatory endorsement.

B. Waiver Or Change Of Policy Provisions

A waiver or change of a provision of this policy must be in writing by us to be valid. Our request for an appraisal or examination will not waive any of our rights.

C. Cancellation

1. You may cancel this policy at any time by returning it to us or by letting us know in writing of the date cancellation is to take effect.
2. We may cancel this policy only for the reasons stated below by letting you know in writing of the date cancellation takes effect. This cancellation notice may be delivered to you, or mailed to you at your mailing address shown in the Declarations. Proof of mailing will be sufficient proof of notice.
   a. When you have not paid the premium, we may cancel at any time by letting you know at least 10 days before the date cancellation takes effect.
   b. When this policy has been in effect for less than 60 days and is not a renewal with us, we may cancel for any reason by letting you know at least 10 days before the date cancellation takes effect.
   c. When this policy has been in effect for 60 days or more, or at any time if it is a renewal with us, we may cancel:
      (1) If there has been a material misrepresentation of fact which if known to us would have caused us not to issue the policy; or
      (2) If the risk has changed substantially since the policy was issued.
      This can be done by letting you know at least 30 days before the date cancellation takes effect.
   d. When this policy is written for a period of more than one year, we may cancel for any reason at anniversary by letting you know at least 30 days before the date cancellation takes effect.
3. When this policy is canceled, the premium for the period from the date of cancellation to the expiration date will be refunded pro rata.
4. If the return premium is not refunded with the notice of cancellation or when this policy is returned to us, we will refund it within a reasonable time after the date cancellation takes effect.

D. Nonrenewal

We may elect not to renew this policy. We may do so by delivering to you, or mailing to you at your mailing address shown in the Declarations, written notice at least 30 days before the expiration date of this policy. Proof of mailing will be sufficient proof of notice.

E. Assignment

Assignment of this policy will not be valid unless we give our written consent.

F. Subrogation

An "insured" may waive in writing before a loss all rights of recovery against any person. If not waived, we may require an assignment of rights of recovery for a loss to the extent that payment is made by us.

If an assignment is sought, an "insured" must sign and deliver all related papers and cooperate with us.

Subrogation does not apply to Coverage F or Paragraph C. Damage To Property Of Others under Section II—Additional Coverages.

G. Death

If any person named in the Declarations or the spouse, if a resident of the same household, dies, the following apply:

1. We insure the legal representative of the deceased but only with respect to the premises and property of the deceased covered under the policy at the time of death; and

2. "Insured" includes:

   a. An "insured" who is a member of your household at the time of your death, but only while a resident of the "residence premises"; and

   b. With respect to your property, the person having proper temporary custody of the property until appointment and qualification of a legal representative.

HOMEOWNERS 3—SPECIAL FORM

AGREEMENT

We will provide the insurance described in this policy in return for the premium and compliance with all applicable provisions of this policy.

DEFINITIONS

A. In this policy, "you" and "your" refer to the "named insured" shown in the Declarations and the spouse if a resident of the same household. "We", "us" and "our" refer to the Company providing this insurance.

B. In addition, certain words and phrases are defined as follows:

1. "Aircraft Liability", "Hovercraft Liability", "Motor Vehicle Liability" and "Watercraft Liability", subject to the provisions in b. below, mean the following:

   a. Liability for "bodily injury" or "property damage" arising out of the:

   (1) Ownership of such vehicle or craft by an "insured";

   (2) Maintenance, occupancy, operation, use, loading or unloading of such vehicle or craft by any person;

   (3) Entrustment of such vehicle or craft by an "insured" to any person;

   (4) Failure to supervise or negligent supervision of any person involving such vehicle or craft by an "insured"; or

   (5) Vicarious liability, whether or not imposed by law, for the actions of a child or minor involving such vehicle or craft.

   b. For the purpose of this definition:

   (1) Aircraft means any contrivance used or designed for flight except model or hobby aircraft not used or designed to carry people or cargo;

   (2) Hovercraft means a self-propelled motorized ground effect vehicle and includes, but is not limited to, flarecraft and air cushion vehicles;

   (3) Watercraft means a craft principally designed to be propelled on or in water by wind, engine power or electric motor; and

   (4) Motor vehicle means a "motor vehicle" as defined in 7. below.

2. "Bodily injury" means bodily harm, sickness or disease, including required care, loss of services and death that results.

3. "Business" means:

   a. A trade, profession or occupation engaged in on a full-time, part-time or occasional basis; or

   b. Any other activity engaged in for money or other compensation, except the following:

   (1) One or more activities, not described in (2) through (4) below, for which no "insured" receives more than $2,000 in total compensation for the 12 months before the beginning of the policy period;

   (2) Volunteer activities for which no money is received other than payment for expenses incurred to perform the activity;

   (3) Providing home day care services for which no compensation is received, other than the mutual exchange of such services; or

   (4) The rendering of home day care services to a relative of an "insured".

4. "Employee" means an employee of an "insured", or an employee leased to an "insured" by a labor leasing firm under an agreement between an "insured" and the labor leasing firm, whose duties are other than those performed by a "residence employee".

5. "Insured" means:

   a. You and residents of your household who are:

   (1) Your relatives; or

   (2) Other persons under the age of 21 and in the care of any person named above;

   b. A student enrolled in school full time, as defined by the school, who was a resident of your household before moving out to attend school, provided the student is under the age of:

   (1) 24 and your relative; or

   (2) 21 and in your care or the care of a person described in a.(1) above; or

   c. Under Section II:

   (1) With respect to animals or watercraft to which this policy applies, any person or organization legally responsible for these animals or watercraft which are owned by you or any person included in a. or b. above. "Insured" does not mean a person or organization using or having custody of these animals or watercraft in the course of any "business" or without consent of the owner; or

(2) With respect to a "motor vehicle" to which this policy applies:

    (a) Persons while engaged in your employ or that of any person included in a. or b. above; or

    (b) Other persons using the vehicle on an "insured location" with your consent.

Under both Sections I and II, when the word an immediately precedes the word "insured", the words an "insured" together mean one or more "insureds".

6. "Insured location" means:

  a. The "residence premises";

  b. The part of other premises, other structures and grounds used by you as a residence; and

    (1) Which is shown in the Declarations; or

    (2) Which is acquired by you during the policy period for your use as a residence;

  c. Any premises used by you in connection with a premises described in a. and b. above;

  d. Any part of a premises:

    (1) Not owned by an "insured"; and

    (2) Where an "insured" is temporarily residing;

  e. Vacant land, other than farm land, owned by or rented to an "insured";

  f. Land owned by or rented to an "insured" on which a one, two, three or four family dwelling is being built as a residence for an "insured";

  g. Individual or family cemetery plots or burial vaults of an "insured"; or

  h. Any part of a premises occasionally rented to an "insured" for other than "business" use.

7. "Motor vehicle" means:

  a. A self-propelled land or amphibious vehicle; or

  b. Any trailer or semitrailer which is being carried on, towed by or hitched for towing by a vehicle described in a. above.

8. "Occurrence" means an accident, including continuous or repeated exposure to substantially the same general harmful conditions, which results, during the policy period, in:

  a. "Bodily injury"; or

  b. "Property damage".

9. "Property damage" means physical injury to, destruction of, or loss of use of tangible property.

10. "Residence employee" means:

  a. An employee of an "insured", or an employee leased to an "insured" by a labor leasing firm, under an agreement between an "insured" and the labor leasing firm, whose duties are related to the maintenance or use of the "residence premises", including household or domestic services; or

  b. One who performs similar duties elsewhere not related to the "business" of an "insured".

A "residence employee" does not include a temporary employee who is furnished to an "insured" to substitute for a permanent "residence employee" on leave or to meet seasonal or short-term workload conditions.

11. "Residence premises" means:

  a. The one family dwelling where you reside;

  b. The two, three or four family dwelling where you reside in at least one of the family units; or

  c. That part of any other building where you reside;

and which is shown as the "residence premises" in the Declarations.

    "Residence premises" also includes other structures and grounds at that location.

DEDUCTIBLE

Unless otherwise noted in this policy, the following deductible provision applies:

Subject to the policy limits that apply, we will pay only that part of the total of all loss payable under Section I that exceeds the deductible amount shown in the Declarations.

SECTION I—PROPERTY COVERAGES

A. Coverage A—Dwelling

1. We cover:

  a. The dwelling on the "residence premises" shown in the Declarations, including structures attached to the dwelling; and

  b. Materials and supplies located on or next to the "residence premises" used to construct, alter or repair the dwelling or other structures on the "residence premises".

2. We do not cover land, including land on which the dwelling is located.

B. Coverage B—Other Structures

1. We cover other structures on the "residence premises" set apart from the dwelling by clear space. This includes structures connected to the dwelling by only a fence, utility line, or similar connection.

2. We do not cover:

  a. Land, including land on which the other structures are located;

  b. Other structures rented or held for rental to any person not a tenant of the dwelling, unless used solely as a private garage;

  c. Other structures from which any "business" is conducted; or

  d. Other structures used to store "business" property. However, we do cover a structure that contains "business" property solely owned by an "insured" or a tenant of the dwelling provided that "business" property does not include gaseous or liquid fuel, other than fuel in a permanently installed fuel tank of a vehicle or craft parked or stored in the structure.

3. The limit of liability for this coverage will not be more than 10% of the limit of liability that applies to Coverage A. Use of this coverage does not reduce the Coverage A limit of liability.

C. Coverage C—Personal Property

1. Covered Property

We cover personal property owned or used by an "insured" while it is anywhere in the world. After a loss and at your request, we will cover personal property owned by:

a. Others while the property is on the part of the "residence premises" occupied by an "insured"; or

b. A guest or a "residence employee", while the property is in any residence occupied by an "insured".

2. Limit For Property At Other Residences

Our limit of liability for personal property usually located at an "insured's" residence, other than the "residence premises", is 10% of the limit of liability for Coverage C, or $1,000, whichever is greater. However, this limitation does not apply to personal property:

a. Moved from the "residence premises" because it is being repaired, renovated or rebuilt and is not fit to live in or store property in; or

b. In a newly acquired principal residence for 30 days from the time you begin to move the property there.

3. Special Limits Of Liability

The special limit for each category shown below is the total limit for each loss for all property in that category. These special limits do not increase the Coverage C limit of liability.

a. $200 on money, bank notes, bullion, gold other than goldware, silver other than silverware, platinum other than platinumware, coins, medals, scrip, stored value cards and smart cards.

b. $1,500 on securities, accounts, deeds, evidences of debt, letters of credit, notes other than bank notes, manuscripts, personal records, passports, tickets and stamps. This dollar limit applies to these categories regardless of the medium (such as paper or computer software) on which the material exists.

This limit includes the cost to research, replace or restore the information from the lost or damaged material.

c. $1,500 on watercraft of all types, including their trailers, furnishings, equipment and outboard engines or motors.

d. $1,500 on trailers or semitrailers not used with watercraft of all types.

e. $1,500 for loss by theft of jewelry, watches, furs, precious and semiprecious stones.

f. $2,500 for loss by theft of firearms and related equipment.

g. $2,500 for loss by theft of silverware, silver-plated ware, goldware, gold-plated ware, platinumware, platinum-plated ware and pewterware. This includes flatware, hollowware, tea sets, trays and trophies made of or including silver, gold or pewter.

h. $2,500 on property, on the "residence premises", used primarily for "business" purposes.

i. $500 on property, away from the "residence premises", used primarily for "business" purposes. However, this limit does not apply to loss to electronic apparatus and other property described in Categories j. and k. below.

j. $1,500 on electronic apparatus and accessories, while in or upon a "motor vehicle", but only if the apparatus is equipped to be operated by power from the "motor vehicle's" electrical system while still capable of being operated by other power sources.

Accessories include antennas, tapes, wires, records, discs or other media that can be used with any apparatus described in this Category j.

k. $1,500 on electronic apparatus and accessories used primarily for "business" while away from the "residence premises" and not in or upon a "motor vehicle". The apparatus must be equipped to be operated by power from the "motor vehicle's" electrical system while still capable of being operated by other power sources.

Accessories include antennas, tapes, wires, records, discs or other media that can be used with any apparatus described in this Category k.

4. Property Not Covered

We do not cover:

a. Articles separately described and specifically insured, regardless of the limit for which they are insured, in this or other insurance;

b. Animals, birds or fish;

c. "Motor vehicles".

(1) This includes:

(a) Their accessories, equipment and parts; or

(b) Electronic apparatus and accessories designed to be operated solely by power from the electrical system of the "motor vehicle". Accessories include antennas, tapes, wires, records, discs or other media that can be used with any apparatus described above.

The exclusion of property described in (a) and (b) above applies only while such property is in or upon the "motor vehicle".

(2) We do cover "motor vehicles" not required to be registered for use on public roads or property which are:

(a) Used solely to service an "insured's" residence; or

(b) Designed to assist the handicapped;

d. Aircraft meaning any contrivance used or designed for flight including any parts whether or not attached to the aircraft.

We do cover model or hobby aircraft not used or designed to carry people or cargo;

e. Hovercraft and parts. Hovercraft means a self-propelled motorized ground effect vehicle and includes, but is not limited to, flarecraft and air cushion vehicles;

f. Property of roomers, boarders and other tenants, except property of roomers and boarders related to an "insured";

g. Property in an apartment regularly rented or held for rental to others by an "insured", except as provided in E.10. Landlord's Furnishings under Section I—Property Coverages;

h. Property rented or held for rental to others off the "residence premises";

i. "Business" data, including such data stored in:

(1) Books of account, drawings or other paper records; or

(2) Computers and related equipment.

We do cover the cost of blank recording or storage media, and of prerecorded computer programs available on the retail market;

j. Credit cards, electronic fund transfer cards or access devices used solely for deposit, withdrawal or transfer of funds except as provided in E.6. Credit Card, Electronic Fund Transfer Card Or Access Device, Forgery And Counterfeit Money under Section I—Property Coverages; or

k. Water or steam.

D. Coverage D—Loss Of Use

The limit of liability for Coverage D is the total limit for the coverages in 1. Additional Living Expense, 2. Fair Rental Value and 3. Civil Authority Prohibits Use below.

1. Additional Living Expense

If a loss covered under Section I makes that part of the "residence premises" where you reside not fit to live in, we cover any necessary increase in living expenses incurred by you so that your household can maintain its normal standard of living.

Payment will be for the shortest time required to repair or replace the damage or, if you permanently relocate, the shortest time required for your household to settle elsewhere.

2. Fair Rental Value

If a loss covered under Section I makes that part of the "residence premises" rented to others or held for rental by you not fit to live in, we cover the fair rental value of such premises less any expenses that do not continue while it is not fit to live in.

Payment will be for the shortest time required to repair or replace such premises.

3. Civil Authority Prohibits Use

If a civil authority prohibits you from use of the "residence premises" as a result of direct damage to neighboring premises by a Peril Insured Against, we cover the loss as provided in 1. Additional Living Expense and 2. Fair Rental Value above for no more than two weeks.

4. Loss Or Expense Not Covered

We do not cover loss or expense due to cancellation of a lease or agreement.

The periods of time under 1. Additional Living Expense, 2. Fair Rental Value and 3. Civil Authority Prohibits Use above are not limited by expiration of this policy.

E. Additional Coverages

1. Debris Removal

a. We will pay your reasonable expense for the removal of:

(1) Debris of covered property if a Peril Insured Against that applies to the damaged property causes the loss; or

(2) Ash, dust or particles from a volcanic eruption that has caused direct loss to a building or property contained in a building.

This expense is included in the limit of liability that applies to the damaged property. If the amount to be paid for the actual damage to the property plus the debris removal expense is more than the limit of liability for the damaged property, an additional 5% of that limit is available for such expense.

b. We will also pay your reasonable expense, up to $1,000, for the removal from the "residence premises" of:

(1) Your tree(s) felled by the peril of Windstorm or Hail or Weight of Ice, Snow or Sleet; or

(2) A neighbor's tree(s) felled by a Peril Insured Against under Coverage C; provided the tree(s):

(3) Damage(s) a covered structure; or

(4) Does not damage a covered structure, but:

    (a) Block(s) a driveway on the "residence premises" which prevent(s) a "motor vehicle", that is registered for use on public roads or property, from entering or leaving the "residence premises"; or

    (b) Block(s) a ramp or other fixture designed to assist a handicapped person to enter or leave the dwelling building.

The $1,000 limit is the most we will pay in any one loss regardless of the number of fallen trees. No more than $500 of this limit will be paid for the removal of any one tree.

This coverage is additional insurance.

2. Reasonable Repairs

  a. We will pay the reasonable cost incurred by you for the necessary measures taken solely to protect covered property that is damaged by a Peril Insured Against from further damage.

  b. If the measures taken involve repair to other damaged property, we will only pay if that property is covered under this policy and the damage is caused by a Peril Insured Against. This coverage does not:

    (1) Increase the limit of liability that applies to the covered property; or

    (2) Relieve you of your duties, in case of a loss to covered property, described in B.4. under Section I—Conditions.

3. Trees, Shrubs And Other Plants

We cover trees, shrubs, plants or lawns, on the "residence premises", for loss caused by the following Perils Insured Against:

  a. Fire or Lightning;

  b. Explosion;

  c. Riot or Civil Commotion;

  d. Aircraft;

  e. Vehicles not owned or operated by a resident of the "residence premises";

  f. Vandalism or Malicious Mischief; or

  g. Theft.

We will pay up to 5% of the limit of liability that applies to the dwelling for all trees, shrubs, plants or lawns. No more than $500 of this limit will be paid for any one tree, shrub or plant. We do not cover property grown for "business" purposes.

This coverage is additional insurance.

4. Fire Department Service Charge

We will pay up to $500 for your liability assumed by contract or agreement for fire department charges incurred when the fire department is called to save or protect covered property from a Peril Insured Against. We do not cover fire department service charges if the property is located within the limits of the city, municipality or protec-tion district furnishing the fire department response.

This coverage is additional insurance. No deductible applies to this coverage.

5. Property Removed

We insure covered property against direct loss from any cause while being removed from a premises endangered by a Peril Insured Against and for no more than 30 days while removed.

This coverage does not change the limit of liability that applies to the property being removed.

6. Credit Card, Electronic Fund Transfer Card Or Access Device, Forgery And Counterfeit Money

  a. We will pay up to $500 for:

    (1) The legal obligation of an "insured" to pay because of the theft or unauthorized use of credit cards issued to or registered in an "insured's" name;

    (2) Loss resulting from theft or unauthorized use of an electronic fund transfer card or access device used for deposit, withdrawal or transfer of funds, issued to or registered in an "insured's" name;

    (3) Loss to an "insured" caused by forgery or alteration of any check or negotiable instrument; and

    (4) Loss to an "insured" through acceptance in good faith of counterfeit United States or Canadian paper currency.

All loss resulting from a series of acts committed by any one person or in which any one person is concerned or implicated is considered to be one loss.

This coverage is additional insurance. No deductible applies to this coverage.

  b. We do not cover:

    (1) Use of a credit card, electronic fund transfer card or access device:

      (a) By a resident of your household;

      (b) By a person who has been entrusted with either type of card or access device; or

      (c) If an "insured" has not complied with all terms and conditions under which the cards are issued or the devices accessed; or

    (2) Loss arising out of "business" use or dishonesty of an "insured".

  c. If the coverage in a. above applies, the following defense provisions also apply:

    (1) We may investigate and settle any claim or suit that we decide is appropriate. Our duty to defend a claim or suit ends when the amount we pay for the loss equals our limit of liability.

(2) If a suit is brought against an "insured" for liability under a.(1) or (2) above, we will provide a defense at our expense by counsel of our choice.

(3) We have the option to defend at our expense an "insured" or an "insured's" bank against any suit for the enforcement of payment under a.(3) above.

7. Loss Assessment

a. We will pay up to $1,000 for your share of loss assessment charged during the policy period against you, as owner or tenant of the "residence premises", by a corporation or association of property owners. The assessment must be made as a result of direct loss to property, owned by all members collectively, of the type that would be covered by this policy if owned by you, caused by a Peril Insured Against under Coverage A, other than:

(1) Earthquake; or

(2) Land shock waves or tremors before, during or after a volcanic eruption.

The limit of $1,000 is the most we will pay with respect to any one loss, regardless of the number of assessments. We will only apply one deductible, per unit, to the total amount of any one loss to the property described above, regardless of the number of assessments.

b. We do not cover assessments charged against you or a corporation or association of property owners by any governmental body.

c. Paragraph **P.** Policy Period under Section I—Conditions does not apply to this coverage.

This coverage is additional insurance.

8. Collapse

a. With respect to this Additional Coverage:

(1) Collapse means an abrupt falling down or caving in of a building or any part of a building with the result that the building or part of the building cannot be occupied for its current intended purpose.

(2) A building or any part of a building that is in danger of falling down or caving in is not considered to be in a state of collapse.

(3) A part of a building that is standing is not considered to be in a state of collapse even if it has separated from another part of the building.

(4) A building or any part of a building that is standing is not considered to be in a state of collapse even if it shows evidence of cracking, bulging, sagging, bending, leaning, settling, shrinkage or expansion.

b. We insure for direct physical loss to covered property involving collapse of a building or any part of a building if the collapse was caused by one or more of the following:

(1) The Perils Insured Against named under Coverage C;

(2) Decay that is hidden from view, unless the presence of such decay is known to an "insured" prior to collapse;

(3) Insect or vermin damage that is hidden from view, unless the presence of such damage is known to an "insured" prior to collapse;

(4) Weight of contents, equipment, animals or people;

(5) Weight of rain which collects on a roof; or

(6) Use of defective material or methods in construction, remodeling or renovation if the collapse occurs during the course of the construction, remodeling or renovation.

c. Loss to an awning, fence, patio, deck, pavement, swimming pool, underground pipe, flue, drain, cesspool, septic tank, foundation, retaining wall, bulkhead, pier, wharf or dock is not included under b.(2) through (6) above, unless the loss is a direct result of the collapse of a building or any part of a building.

d. This coverage does not increase the limit of liability that applies to the damaged covered property.

9. Glass Or Safety Glazing Material

a. We cover:

(1) The breakage of glass or safety glazing material which is part of a covered building, storm door or storm window;

(2) The breakage of glass or safety glazing material which is part of a covered building, storm door or storm window when caused directly by earth movement; and

(3) The direct physical loss to covered property caused solely by the pieces, fragments or splinters of broken glass or safety glazing material which is part of a building, storm door or storm window.

b. This coverage does not include loss:

(1) To covered property which results because the glass or safety glazing material has been broken, except as provided in a.(3) above; or

(2) On the "residence premises" if the dwelling has been vacant for more than 60 consecutive days immediately before the loss, except when the breakage results directly from earth movement as provided in a.(2) above. A dwelling being constructed is not considered vacant.

c. This coverage does not increase the limit of liability that applies to the damaged property.

10. **Landlord's Furnishings**

We will pay up to $2,500 for your appliances, carpeting and other household furnishings, in each apartment on the "residence premises" regularly rented or held for rental to others by an "insured", for loss caused by a Peril Insured Against in Coverage C, other than Theft.

This limit is the most we will pay in any one loss regardless of the number of appliances, carpeting or other household furnishings involved in the loss.

This coverage does not increase the limit of liability applying to the damaged property.

11. **Ordinance Or Law**

a. You may use up to 10% of the limit of liability that applies to Coverage A for the increased costs you incur due to the enforcement of any ordinance or law which requires or regulates:

(1) The construction, demolition, remodeling, renovation or repair of that part of a covered building or other structure damaged by a Peril Insured Against;

(2) The demolition and reconstruction of the undamaged part of a covered building or other structure, when that building or other structure must be totally demolished because of damage by a Peril Insured Against to another part of that covered building or other structure; or

(3) The remodeling, removal or replacement of the portion of the undamaged part of a covered building or other structure necessary to complete the remodeling, repair or replacement of that part of the covered building or other structure damaged by a Peril Insured Against.

b. You may use all or part of this ordinance or law coverage to pay for the increased costs you incur to remove debris resulting from the construction, demolition, remodeling, renovation, repair or replacement of property as stated in a. above.

c. We do not cover:

(1) The loss in value to any covered building or other structure due to the requirements of any ordinance or law; or

(2) The costs to comply with any ordinance or law which requires any "insured" or others to test for, monitor, clean up, remove, contain, treat, detoxify or neutralize, or in any way respond to, or assess the effects of, pollutants in or on any covered building or other structure.

Pollutants means any solid, liquid, gaseous or thermal irritant or contaminant, including smoke, vapor, soot, fumes, acids, alkalis, chemicals and waste. Waste includes materials to be recycled, reconditioned or reclaimed.

This coverage is additional insurance.

12. **Grave Markers**

We will pay up to $5,000 for grave markers, including mausoleums, on or away from the "residence premises" for loss caused by a Peril Insured Against under Coverage C.

This coverage does not increase the limits of liability that apply to the damaged covered property.

SECTION I—PERILS INSURED AGAINST

A. **Coverage A—Dwelling And Coverage B—Other Structures**

1. We insure against risk of direct physical loss to property described in Coverages A and B.

2. We do not insure, however, for loss:

a. Excluded under Section I—Exclusions;

b. Involving collapse, except as provided in E.8. Collapse under Section I—Property Coverages; or

c. Caused by:

(1) Freezing of a plumbing, heating, air conditioning or automatic fire protective sprinkler system or of a household appliance, or by discharge, leakage or overflow from within the system or appliance caused by freezing. This provision does not apply if you have used reasonable care to:

(a) Maintain heat in the building; or

(b) Shut off the water supply and drain all systems and appliances of water.

However, if the building is protected by an automatic fire protective sprinkler system, you must use reasonable care to continue the water supply and maintain heat in the building for coverage to apply.

For purposes of this provision a plumbing system or household appliance does not include a sump, sump pump or related equipment or a roof drain, gutter, downspout or similar fixtures or equipment;

(2) Freezing, thawing, pressure or weight of water or ice, whether driven by wind or not, to a:

(a) Fence, pavement, patio or swimming pool;

(b) Footing, foundation, bulkhead, wall, or any other structure or device that supports all or part of a building, or other structure;

(c) Retaining wall or bulkhead that does not support all or part of a building or other structure; or

(d) Pier, wharf or dock;

(3) Theft in or to a dwelling under construction, or of materials and supplies for use in the construction until the dwelling is finished and occupied;

(4) Vandalism and malicious mischief, and any ensuing loss caused by any intentional and wrongful act committed in the course of the vandalism or malicious mischief, if the dwelling has been vacant for more than 60 consecutive days immediately before the loss. A dwelling being constructed is not considered vacant;

(5) Mold, fungus or wet rot. However, we do insure for loss caused by mold, fungus or wet rot that is hidden within the walls or ceilings or beneath the floors or above the ceilings of a structure if such loss results from the accidental discharge or overflow of water or steam from within:

    (a) A plumbing, heating, air conditioning or automatic fire protective sprinkler system, or a household appliance, on the "residence premises"; or

    (b) A storm drain, or water, steam or sewer pipes, off the "residence premises".

For purposes of this provision, a plumbing system or household appliance does not include a sump, sump pump or related equipment or a roof drain, gutter, downspout or similar fixtures or equipment; or

(6) Any of the following:

    (a) Wear and tear, marring, deterioration;

    (b) Mechanical breakdown, latent defect, inherent vice, or any quality in property that causes it to damage or destroy itself;

    (c) Smog, rust or other corrosion, or dry rot;

    (d) Smoke from agricultural smudging or industrial operations;

    (e) Discharge, dispersal, seepage, migration, release or escape of pollutants unless the discharge, dispersal, seepage, migration, release or escape is itself caused by a Peril Insured Against named under Coverage C.

       Pollutants means any solid, liquid, gaseous or thermal irritant or contaminant, including smoke, vapor, soot, fumes, acids, alkalis, chemicals and waste. Waste includes materials to be recycled, reconditioned or reclaimed;

    (f) Settling, shrinking, bulging or expansion, including resultant cracking, of bulkheads, pavements, patios, footings, foundations, walls, floors, roofs or ceilings;

    (g) Birds, vermin, rodents, or insects; or

    (h) Animals owned or kept by an "insured".

Exception To c.(6)

Unless the loss is otherwise excluded, we cover loss to property covered under Coverage A or B resulting from an accidental discharge or overflow of water or steam from within a:

    (i) Storm drain, or water, steam or sewer pipe, off the "residence premises"; or

    (ii) Plumbing, heating, air conditioning or automatic fire protective sprinkler system or household appliance on the "residence premises". This includes the cost to tear out and replace any part of a building, or other structure, on the "residence premises", but only when necessary to repair the system or appliance. However, such tear out and replacement coverage only applies to other structures if the water or steam causes actual damage to a building on the "residence premises".

We do not cover loss to the system or appliance from which this water or steam escaped.

    For purposes of this provision, a plumbing system or household appliance does not include a sump, sump pump or related equipment or a roof drain, gutter, down spout or similar fixtures or equipment.

Section I—Exclusion A.3. Water Damage, paragraphs a. and c. that apply to surface water and water below the surface of the ground do not apply to loss by water covered under c.(5) and (6) above.

    Under 2.b. and c. above, any ensuing loss to property described in Coverages A and B not precluded by any other provision in this policy is covered.

B. Coverage C—Personal Property

We insure for direct physical loss to the property described in Coverage C caused by any of the following perils unless the loss is excluded in Section I—Exclusions.

  1. Fire Or Lightning

  2. Windstorm Or Hail

This peril includes loss to watercraft of all types and their trailers, furnishings, equipment, and outboard engines or motors, only while inside a fully enclosed building.

    This peril does not include loss to the property contained in a building caused by rain, snow, sleet, sand or dust unless the direct force of wind or hail damages the building causing an opening in a roof or wall and the rain, snow, sleet, sand or dust enters through this opening.

  3. Explosion

  4. Riot Or Civil Commotion

  5. Aircraft

This peril includes self-propelled missiles and spacecraft.

6. **Vehicles**

7. **Smoke**

This peril means sudden and accidental damage from smoke, including the emission or puffback of smoke, soot, fumes or vapors from a boiler, furnace or related equipment.

This peril does not include loss caused by smoke from agricultural smudging or industrial operations.

8. **Vandalism Or Malicious Mischief**

9. **Theft**

   a. This peril includes attempted theft and loss of property from a known place when it is likely that the property has been stolen.

   b. This peril does not include loss caused by theft:

   (1) Committed by an "insured";

   (2) In or to a dwelling under construction, or of materials and supplies for use in the construction until the dwelling is finished and occupied;

   (3) From that part of a "residence premises" rented by an "insured" to someone other than another "insured"; or

   (4) That occurs off the "residence premises" of:

      (a) Trailers, semitrailers and campers;

      (b) Watercraft of all types, and their furnishings, equipment and outboard engines or motors; or

      (c) Property while at any other residence owned by, rented to, or occupied by an "insured", except while an "insured" is temporarily living there. Property of an "insured" who is a student is covered while at the residence the student occupies to attend school as long as the student has been there at any time during the 60 days immediately before the loss.

10. **Falling Objects**

This peril does not include loss to property contained in a building unless the roof or an outside wall of the building is first damaged by a falling object. Damage to the falling object itself is not included.

11. **Weight Of Ice, Snow Or Sleet**

This peril means weight of ice, snow or sleet which causes damage to property contained in a building.

12. **Accidental Discharge Or Overflow Of Water Or Steam**

   a. This peril means accidental discharge or overflow of water or steam from within a plumbing, heating, air conditioning or automatic fire protective sprinkler system or from within a household appliance.

   b. This peril does not include loss:

   (1) To the system or appliance from which the water or steam escaped;

   (2) Caused by or resulting from freezing except as provided in Peril Insured Against 14. Freezing;

   (3) On the "residence premises" caused by accidental discharge or overflow which occurs off the "residence premises"; or

   (4) Caused by mold, fungus or wet rot unless hidden within the walls or ceilings or beneath the floors or above the ceilings of a structure.

   c. In this peril, a plumbing system or household appliance does not include a sump, sump pump or related equipment or a roof drain, gutter, downspout or similar fixtures or equipment.

   d. Section I—Exclusion A.3. Water Damage, Paragraphs a. and c. that apply to surface water and water below the surface of the ground do not apply to loss by water covered under this peril.

13. **Sudden And Accidental Tearing Apart, Cracking, Burning Or Bulging**

This peril means sudden and accidental tearing apart, cracking, burning or bulging of a steam or hot water heating system, an air conditioning or automatic fire protective sprinkler system, or an appliance for heating water.

We do not cover loss caused by or resulting from freezing under this peril.

14. **Freezing**

   a. This peril means freezing of a plumbing, heating, air conditioning or automatic fire protective sprinkler system or of a household appliance but only if you have used reasonable care to:

   (1) Maintain heat in the building; or

   (2) Shut off the water supply and drain all systems and appliances of water.

   However, if the building is protected by an automatic fire protective sprinkler system, you must use reasonable care to continue the water supply and maintain heat in the building for coverage to apply.

   b. In this peril, a plumbing system or household appliance does not include a sump, sump pump or related equipment or a roof drain, gutter, downspout or similar fixtures or equipment.

15. **Sudden And Accidental Damage From Artificially Generated Electrical Current**

This peril does not include loss to tubes, transistors, electronic components or circuitry that are a part of appliances, fixtures, computers, home entertainment units or other types of electronic apparatus.

16. Volcanic Eruption

This peril does not include loss caused by earthquake, land shock waves or tremors.

SECTION I—EXCLUSIONS

A. We do not insure for loss caused directly or indirectly by any of the following. Such loss is excluded regardless of any other cause or event contributing concurrently or in any sequence to the loss. These exclusions apply whether or not the loss event results in widespread damage or affects a substantial area.

1. Ordinance Or Law

Ordinance Or Law means any ordinance or law:

a. Requiring or regulating the construction, demolition, remodeling, renovation or repair of property, including removal of any resulting debris. This Exclusion A.1.a. does not apply to the amount of coverage that may be provided for in E.11. Ordinance Or Law under Section I—Property Coverages;

b. The requirements of which result in a loss in value to property; or

c. Requiring any "insured" or others to test for, monitor, clean up, remove, contain, treat, detoxify or neutralize, or in any way respond to, or assess the effects of, pollutants.

Pollutants means any solid, liquid, gaseous or thermal irritant or contaminant, including smoke, vapor, soot, fumes, acids, alkalis, chemicals and waste. Waste includes materials to be recycled, reconditioned or reclaimed.

This Exclusion A.1. applies whether or not the property has been physically damaged.

2. Earth Movement

Earth Movement means:

a. Earthquake, including land shock waves or tremors before, during or after a volcanic eruption;

b. Landslide, mudslide or mudflow;

c. Subsidence or sinkhole; or

d. Any other earth movement including earth sinking, rising or shifting;

caused by or resulting from human or animal forces or any act of nature unless direct loss by fire or explosion ensues and then we will pay only for the ensuing loss.

This Exclusion A.2. does not apply to loss by theft.

3. Water Damage

Water Damage means:

a. Flood, surface water, waves, tidal water, overflow of a body of water, or spray from any of these, whether or not driven by wind;

b. Water or water-borne material which backs up through sewers or drains or which overflows or

is discharged from a sump, sump pump or related equipment; or

c. Water or water-borne material below the surface of the ground, including water which exerts pressure on or seeps or leaks through a building, sidewalk, driveway, foundation, swimming pool or other structure; caused by or resulting from human or animal forces or any act of nature.

Direct loss by fire, explosion or theft resulting from water damage is covered.

4. Power Failure

Power Failure means the failure of power or other utility service if the failure takes place off the "residence premises". But if the failure results in a loss, from a Peril Insured Against on the "residence premises", we will pay for the loss caused by that peril.

5. Neglect

Neglect means neglect of an "insured" to use all reasonable means to save and preserve property at and after the time of a loss.

6. War

War includes the following and any consequence of any of the following:

a. Undeclared war, civil war, insurrection, rebellion or revolution;

b. Warlike act by a military force or military personnel; or

c. Destruction, seizure or use for a military purpose.

Discharge of a nuclear weapon will be deemed a warlike act even if accidental.

7. Nuclear Hazard

This Exclusion A.7. pertains to Nuclear Hazard to the extent set forth in M. Nuclear Hazard Clause under Section I—Conditions.

8. Intentional Loss

Intentional Loss means any loss arising out of any act an "insured" commits or conspires to commit with the intent to cause a loss.

In the event of such loss, no "insured" is entitled to coverage, even "insureds" who did not commit or conspire to commit the act causing the loss.

9. Governmental Action

Governmental Action means the destruction, confiscation or seizure of property described in Coverage A, B or C by order of any governmental or public authority.

This exclusion does not apply to such acts ordered by any governmental or public authority that are taken at the time of a fire to prevent its spread, if the loss caused by fire would be covered under this policy.

B. We do not insure for loss to property described in Coverages A and B caused by any of the following.

However, any ensuing loss to property described in Coverages A and B not precluded by any other provision in this policy is covered.

1. Weather conditions. However, this exclusion only applies if weather conditions contribute in any way with a cause or event excluded in A. above to produce the loss.

2. Acts or decisions, including the failure to act or decide, of any person, group, organization or governmental body.

3. Faulty, inadequate or defective:

   a. Planning, zoning, development, surveying, siting;

   b. Design, specifications, workmanship, repair, construction, renovation, remodeling, grading, compaction;

   c. Materials used in repair, construction, renovation or remodeling; or

   d. Maintenance;

   of part or all of any property whether on or off the "residence premises".

SECTION I—CONDITIONS

A. Insurable Interest And Limit Of Liability

Even if more than one person has an insurable interest in the property covered, we will not be liable in any one loss:

1. To an "insured" for more than the amount of such "insured's" interest at the time of loss; or

2. For more than the applicable limit of liability.

B. Duties After Loss

In case of a loss to covered property, we have no duty to provide coverage under this policy if the failure to comply with the following duties is prejudicial to us. These duties must be performed either by you, an "insured" seeking coverage, or a representative of either:

1. Give prompt notice to us or our agent;

2. Notify the police in case of loss by theft;

3. Notify the credit card or electronic fund transfer card or access device company in case of loss as provided for in E.6. Credit Card, Electronic Fund Transfer Card Or Access Device, Forgery And Counterfeit Money under Section I—Property Coverages;

4. Protect the property from further damage. If repairs to the property are required, you must:

   a. Make reasonable and necessary repairs to protect the property; and

   b. Keep an accurate record of repair expenses;

5. Cooperate with us in the investigation of a claim;

6. Prepare an inventory of damaged personal property showing the quantity, description, actual cash value and amount of loss. Attach all bills, receipts and related documents that justify the figures in the inventory;

7. As often as we reasonably require:

   a. Show the damaged property;

   b. Provide us with records and documents we request and permit us to make copies; and

   c. Submit to examination under oath, while not in the presence of another "insured", and sign the same;

8. Send to us, within 60 days after our request, your signed, sworn proof of loss which sets forth, to the best of your knowledge and belief:

   a. The time and cause of loss;

   b. The interests of all "insureds" and all others in the property involved and all liens on the property;

   c. Other insurance which may cover the loss;

   d. Changes in title or occupancy of the property during the term of the policy;

   e. Specifications of damaged buildings and detailed repair estimates;

   f. The inventory of damaged personal property described in 6. above;

   g. Receipts for additional living expenses incurred and records that support the fair rental value loss; and

   h. Evidence or affidavit that supports a claim under E.6. Credit Card, Electronic Fund Transfer Card Or Access Device, Forgery And Counterfeit Money under Section I—Property Coverages, stating the amount and cause of loss.

C. Loss Settlement

In this Condition C., the terms "cost to repair or replace" and "replacement cost" do not include the increased costs incurred to comply with the enforcement of any ordinance or law, except to the extent that coverage for these increased costs is provided in E.11. Ordinance Or Law under Section I—Property Coverages. Covered property losses are settled as follows:

1. Property of the following types:

   a. Personal property;

   b. Awnings, carpeting, household appliances, outdoor antennas and outdoor equipment, whether or not attached to buildings;

   c. Structures that are not buildings; and

   d. Grave markers, including mausoleums;

at actual cash value at the time of loss but not more than the amount required to repair or replace.

2. Buildings covered under Coverage A or B at replacement cost without deduction for depreciation, subject to the following:

   a. If, at the time of loss, the amount of insurance in this policy on the damaged building is 80% or more of the full replacement cost of the building immediately before the loss, we will pay the cost to repair or replace, after application of any deductible and without deduction for depreciation, but not more than the least of the following amounts:

(1) The limit of liability under this policy that applies to the building;

(2) The replacement cost of that part of the building damaged with material of like kind and quality and for like use; or

(3) The necessary amount actually spent to repair or replace the damaged building.

If the building is rebuilt at a new premises, the cost described in (2) above is limited to the cost which would have been incurred if the building had been built at the original premises.

b. If, at the time of loss, the amount of insurance in this policy on the damaged building is less than 80% of the full replacement cost of the building immediately before the loss, we will pay the greater of the following amounts, but not more than the limit of liability under this policy that applies to the building:

(1) The actual cash value of that part of the building damaged; or

(2) That proportion of the cost to repair or replace, after application of any deductible and without deduction for depreciation, that part of the building damaged, which the total amount of insurance in this policy on the damaged building bears to 80% of the replacement cost of the building.

c. To determine the amount of insurance required to equal 80% of the full replacement cost of the building immediately before the loss, do not include the value of:

(1) Excavations, footings, foundations, piers, or any other structures or devices that support all or part of the building, which are below the undersurface of the lowest basement floor;

(2) Those supports described in (1) above which are below the surface of the ground inside the foundation walls, if there is no basement; and

(3) Underground flues, pipes, wiring and drains.

d. We will pay no more than the actual cash value of the damage until actual repair or replacement is complete. Once actual repair or replacement is complete, we will settle the loss as noted in 2.a. and b. above.

However, if the cost to repair or replace the damage is both:

(1) Less than 5% of the amount of insurance in this policy on the building; and

(2) Less than $2,500;

we will settle the loss as noted in 2.a. and b. above whether or not actual repair or replacement is complete.

e. You may disregard the replacement cost loss settlement provisions and make claim under this policy for loss to buildings on an actual cash value basis. You may then make claim for any additional liability according to the provisions of this Condition C. Loss Settlement, provided you notify us of your intent to do so within 180 days after the date of loss.

D. Loss To A Pair Or Set

In case of loss to a pair or set we may elect to:

1. Repair or replace any part to restore the pair or set to its value before the loss; or

2. Pay the difference between actual cash value of the property before and after the loss.

E. Appraisal

If you and we fail to agree on the amount of loss, either may demand an appraisal of the loss. In this event, each party will choose a competent and impartial appraiser within 20 days after receiving a written request from the other. The two appraisers will choose an umpire. If they cannot agree upon an umpire within 15 days, you or we may request that the choice be made by a judge of a court of record in the state where the "residence premises" is located. The appraisers will separately set the amount of loss. If the appraisers submit a written report of an agreement to us, the amount agreed upon will be the amount of loss. If they fail to agree, they will submit their differences to the umpire. A decision agreed to by any two will set the amount of loss.

Each party will:

1. Pay its own appraiser; and

2. Bear the other expenses of the appraisal and umpire equally.

F. Other Insurance And Service Agreement

If a loss covered by this policy is also covered by:

1. Other insurance, we will pay only the proportion of the loss that the limit of liability that applies under this policy bears to the total amount of insurance covering the loss; or

2. A service agreement, this insurance is excess over any amounts payable under any such agreement. Service agreement means a service plan, property restoration plan, home warranty or other similar service warranty agreement, even if it is characterized as insurance.

G. Suit Against Us

No action can be brought against us unless there has been full compliance with all of the terms under Section I of this policy and the action is started within two years after the date of loss.

H. Our Option

If we give you written notice within 30 days after we receive your signed, sworn proof of loss, we may repair or replace any part of the damaged property with material or property of like kind and quality.

I. Loss Payment

We will adjust all losses with you. We will pay you unless some other person is named in the policy or is legally entitled to receive payment. Loss will be payable 60 days after we receive your proof of loss and:

1. Reach an agreement with you;
2. There is an entry of a final judgment; or
3. There is a filing of an appraisal award with us.

J. Abandonment Of Property

We need not accept any property abandoned by an "insured".

K. Mortgage Clause

1. If a mortgagee is named in this policy, any loss payable under Coverage A or B will be paid to the mortgagee and you, as interests appear. If more than one mortgagee is named, the order of payment will be the same as the order of precedence of the mortgages.

2. If we deny your claim, that denial will not apply to a valid claim of the mortgagee, if the mortgagee:

   a. Notifies us of any change in ownership, occupancy or substantial change in risk of which the mortgagee is aware;

   b. Pays any premium due under this policy on demand if you have neglected to pay the premium; and

   c. Submits a signed, sworn statement of loss within 60 days after receiving notice from us of your failure to do so. Paragraphs E. Appraisal, G. Suit Against Us and I. Loss Payment under Section I—Conditions also apply to the mortgagee.

3. If we decide to cancel or not to renew this policy, the mortgagee will be notified at least 10 days before the date cancellation or nonrenewal takes effect.

4. If we pay the mortgagee for any loss and deny payment to you:

   a. We are subrogated to all the rights of the mortgagee granted under the mortgage on the property; or

   b. At our option, we may pay to the mortgagee the whole principal on the mortgage plus any accrued interest. In this event, we will receive a full assignment and transfer of the mortgage and all securities held as collateral to the mortgage debt.

5. Subrogation will not impair the right of the mortgagee to recover the full amount of the mortgagee's claim.

L. No Benefit To Bailee

We will not recognize any assignment or grant any coverage that benefits a person or organization holding, storing or moving property for a fee regardless of any other provision of this policy.

M. Nuclear Hazard Clause

1. "Nuclear Hazard" means any nuclear reaction, radiation, or radioactive contamination, all whether controlled or uncontrolled or however caused, or any consequence of any of these.

2. Loss caused by the nuclear hazard will not be considered loss caused by fire, explosion, or smoke, whether these perils are specifically named in or otherwise included within the Perils Insured Against.

3. This policy does not apply under Section I to loss caused directly or indirectly by nuclear hazard, except that direct loss by fire resulting from the nuclear hazard is covered.

N. Recovered Property

If you or we recover any property for which we have made payment under this policy, you or we will notify the other of the recovery. At your option, the property will be returned to or retained by you or it will become our property. If the recovered property is returned to or retained by you, the loss payment will be adjusted based on the amount you received for the recovered property.

O. Volcanic Eruption Period

One or more volcanic eruptions that occur within a 72 hour period will be considered as one volcanic eruption.

P. Policy Period

This policy applies only to loss which occurs during the policy period.

Q. Concealment Or Fraud

We provide coverage to no "insureds" under this policy if, whether before or after a loss, an "insured" has:

1. Intentionally concealed or misrepresented any material fact or circumstance;
2. Engaged in fraudulent conduct; or
3. Made false statements;

relating to this insurance.

R. Loss Payable Clause

If the Declarations show a loss payee for certain listed insured personal property, the definition of "insured" is changed to include that loss payee with respect to that property.

If we decide to cancel or not renew this policy, that loss payee will be notified in writing.

SECTION II—LIABILITY COVERAGES

A. Coverage E—Personal Liability

If a claim is made or a suit is brought against an "insured" for damages because of "bodily injury" or "property damage" caused by an "occurrence" to which this coverage applies, we will:

1. Pay up to our limit of liability for the damages for which an "insured" is legally liable. Damages

include prejudgment interest awarded against an "insured"; and

2. Provide a defense at our expense by counsel of our choice, even if the suit is groundless, false or fraudulent. We may investigate and settle any claim or suit that we decide is appropriate. Our duty to settle or defend ends when our limit of liability for the "occurrence" has been exhausted by payment of a judgment or settlement.

B. Coverage F—Medical Payments To Others

We will pay the necessary medical expenses that are incurred or medically ascertained within three years from the date of an accident causing "bodily injury". Medical expenses means reasonable charges for medical, surgical, x-ray, dental, ambulance, hospital, professional nursing, prosthetic devices and funeral services. This coverage does not apply to you or regular residents of your household except "residence employees". As to others, this coverage applies only:

1. To a person on the "insured location" with the permission of an "insured"; or

2. To a person off the "insured location", if the "bodily injury":

   a. Arises out of a condition on the "insured location" or the ways immediately adjoining;

   b. Is caused by the activities of an "insured";

   c. Is caused by a "residence employee" in the course of the "residence employee's" employment by an "insured"; or

   d. Is caused by an animal owned by or in the care of an "insured".

SECTION II—EXCLUSIONS

A. "Motor Vehicle Liability"

1. Coverages E and F do not apply to any "motor vehicle liability" if, at the time and place of an "occurrence", the involved "motor vehicle":

   a. Is registered for use on public roads or property;

   b. Is not registered for use on public roads or property, but such registration is required by a law, or regulation issued by a government agency, for it to be used at the place of the "occurrence"; or

   c. Is being:

      (1) Operated in, or practicing for, any prearranged or organized race, speed contest or other competition;

      (2) Rented to others;

      (3) Used to carry persons or cargo for a charge; or

      (4) Used for any "business" purpose except for a motorized golf cart while on a golfing facility.

2. If Exclusion A.1. does not apply, there is still no coverage for "motor vehicle liability" unless the "motor vehicle" is:

   a. In dead storage on an "insured location";

   b. Used solely to service an "insured's" residence;

   c. Designed to assist the handicapped and, at the time of an "occurrence", it is:

      (1) Being used to assist a handicapped person; or

      (2) Parked on an "insured location";

   d. Designed for recreational use off public roads and:

      (1) Not owned by an "insured"; or

      (2) Owned by an "insured" provided the "occurrence" takes place on an "insured location" as defined in Definitions B.6.a., b., d., e. or h.; or

   e. A motorized golf cart that is owned by an "insured", designed to carry up to 4 persons, not built or modified after manufacture to exceed a speed of 25 miles per hour on level ground and, at the time of an "occurrence", is within the legal boundaries of:

      (1) A golfing facility and is parked or stored there, or being used by an "insured" to:

         (a) Play the game of golf or for other recreational or leisure activity allowed by the facility;

         (b) Travel to or from an area where "motor vehicles" or golf carts are parked or stored; or

         (c) Cross public roads at designated points to access other parts of the golfing facility; or

      (2) A private residential community, including its public roads upon which a motorized golf cart can legally travel, which is subject to the authority of a property owners association and contains an "insured's" residence.

B. "Watercraft Liability"

1. Coverages E and F do not apply to any "watercraft liability" if, at the time of an "occurrence", the involved watercraft is being:

   a. Operated in, or practicing for, any prearranged or organized race, speed contest or other competition. This exclusion does not apply to a sailing vessel or a predicted log cruise;

   b. Rented to others;

   c. Used to carry persons or cargo for a charge; or

   d. Used for any "business" purpose.

2. If Exclusion B.1. does not apply, there is still no coverage for "watercraft liability" unless, at the time of the "occurrence", the watercraft:

   a. Is stored;

b. Is a sailing vessel, with or without auxiliary power, that is:
   (1) Less than 26 feet in overall length; or
   (2) 26 feet or more in overall length and not owned by or rented to an "insured"; or
c. Is not a sailing vessel and is powered by:
   (1) An inboard or inboard-outdrive engine or motor, including those that power a water jet pump, of:
      (a) 50 horsepower or less and not owned by an "insured"; or
      (b) More than 50 horsepower and not owned by or rented to an "insured"; or
   (2) One or more outboard engines or motors with:
      (a) 25 total horsepower or less;
      (b) More than 25 horsepower if the outboard engine or motor is not owned by an "insured";
      (c) More than 25 horsepower if the outboard engine or motor is owned by an "insured" who acquired it during the policy period; or
      (d) More than 25 horsepower if the outboard engine or motor is owned by an "insured" who acquired it before the policy period, but only if:
         (i) You declare them at policy inception; or
         (ii) Your intent to insure them is reported to us in writing within 45 days after you acquire them.
   The coverages in (c) and (d) above apply for the policy period.
   Horsepower means the maximum power rating assigned to the engine or motor by the manufacturer.

C. "Aircraft Liability"
This policy does not cover "aircraft liability".

D. "Hovercraft Liability"
This policy does not cover "hovercraft liability".

E. Coverage E—Personal Liability And Coverage F—Medical Payments To Others
Coverages E and F do not apply to the following:
   1. Expected Or Intended Injury
   "Bodily injury" or "property damage" which is expected or intended by an "insured" even if the resulting "bodily injury" or "property damage:"
   a. Is of a different kind, quality or degree than initially expected or intended; or
   b. Is sustained by a different person, entity, real or personal property, than initially expected or intended.
   However, this Exclusion E.1. does not apply to "bodily injury" resulting from the use of reason-

able force by an "insured" to protect persons or property;
   2. "Business"
   a. "Bodily injury" or "property damage" arising out of or in connection with a "business" conducted from an "insured location" or engaged in by an "insured", whether or not the "business" is owned or operated by an "insured" or employs an "insured".
      This Exclusion E.2. applies but is not limited to an act or omission, regardless of its nature or circumstance, involving a service or duty rendered, promised, owed, or implied to be provided because of the nature of the "business".
   b. This Exclusion E.2. does not apply to:
      (1) The rental or holding for rental of an "insured location";
         (a) On an occasional basis if used only as a residence;
         (b) In part for use only as a residence, unless a single family unit is intended for use by the occupying family to lodge more than two roomers or boarders; or
         (c) In part, as an office, school, studio or private garage; and
      (2) An "insured" under the age of 21 years involved in a part-time or occasional, self-employed "business" with no employees;
   3. Professional Services
   "Bodily injury" or "property damage" arising out of the rendering of or failure to render professional services;
   4. "Insured's" Premises Not An "Insured Location"
   "Bodily injury" or "property damage" arising out of a premises:
   a. Owned by an "insured";
   b. Rented to an "insured"; or
   c. Rented to others by an "insured";
   that is not an "insured location";
   5. War
   "Bodily injury" or "property damage" caused directly or indirectly by war, including the following and any consequence of any of the following:
   a. Undeclared war, civil war, insurrection, rebellion or revolution;
   b. Warlike act by a military force or military personnel; or
   c. Destruction, seizure or use for a military purpose.
   Discharge of a nuclear weapon will be deemed a warlike act even if accidental;
   6. Communicable Disease
   "Bodily injury" or "property damage" which arises out of the transmission of a communicable disease by an "insured";

7. Sexual Molestation, Corporal Punishment Or Physical Or Mental Abuse

"Bodily injury" or "property damage" arising out of sexual molestation, corporal punishment or physical or mental abuse; or

8. Controlled Substance

"Bodily injury" or "property damage" arising out of the use, sale, manufacture, delivery, transfer or possession by any person of a Controlled Substance as defined by the Federal Food and Drug Law at 21 U.S.C.A. Sections 811 and 812. Controlled Substances include but are not limited to cocaine, LSD, marijuana and all narcotic drugs. However, this exclusion does not apply to the legitimate use of prescription drugs by a person following the orders of a licensed physician.

Exclusions A. "Motor Vehicle Liability", B. "Watercraft Liability", C. "Aircraft Liability", D. "Hovercraft Liability" and E.4. "Insured's" Premises Not An "Insured Location" do not apply to "bodily injury" to a "residence employee" arising out of and in the course of the "residence employee's" employment by an "insured".

F. Coverage E—Personal Liability

Coverage E does not apply to:

1. Liability:
   a. For any loss assessment charged against you as a member of an association, corporation or community of property owners, except as provided in D. Loss Assessment under Section II—Additional Coverages;
   b. Under any contract or agreement entered into by an "insured". However, this exclusion does not apply to written contracts:
      (1) That directly relate to the ownership, maintenance or use of an "insured location"; or
      (2) Where the liability of others is assumed by you prior to an "occurrence";
      unless excluded in a. above or elsewhere in this policy;

2. "Property damage" to property owned by an "insured". This includes costs or expenses incurred by an "insured" or others to repair, replace, enhance, restore or maintain such property to prevent injury to a person or damage to property of others, whether on or away from an "insured location";

3. "Property damage" to property rented to, occupied or used by or in the care of an "insured". This exclusion does not apply to "property damage" caused by fire, smoke or explosion;

4. "Bodily injury" to any person eligible to receive any benefits voluntarily provided or required to be provided by an "insured" under any:
   a. Workers' compensation law;

b. Non-occupational disability law; or
   c. Occupational disease law;

5. "Bodily injury" or "property damage" for which an "insured" under this policy:
   a. Is also an insured under a nuclear energy liability policy issued by the:
      (1) Nuclear Energy Liability Insurance Association;
      (2) Mutual Atomic Energy Liability Underwriters;
      (3) Nuclear Insurance Association of Canada; or any of their successors; or
   b. Would be an insured under such a policy but for the exhaustion of its limit of liability; or

6. "Bodily injury" to you or an "insured" as defined under Definitions 5.a. or b.
   This exclusion also applies to any claim made or suit brought against you or an "insured":
   a. To repay; or
   b. Share damages with;
   another person who may be obligated to pay damages because of "bodily injury" to an "insured".

G. Coverage F—Medical Payments To Others

Coverage F does not apply to "bodily injury":

1. To a "residence employee" if the "bodily injury":
   a. Occurs off the "insured location"; and
   b. Does not arise out of or in the course of the "residence employee's" employment by an "insured";

2. To any person eligible to receive benefits voluntarily provided or required to be provided under any:
   a. Workers' compensation law;
   b. Non-occupational disability law; or
   c. Occupational disease law;

3. From any:
   a. Nuclear reaction;
   b. Nuclear radiation; or
   c. Radioactive contamination;
   all whether controlled or uncontrolled or however caused; or
   d. Any consequence of any of these; or

4. To any person, other than a "residence employee" of an "insured", regularly residing on any part of the "insured location".

SECTION II—ADDITIONAL COVERAGES

We cover the following in addition to the limits of liability:

A. Claim Expenses

We pay:

1. Expenses we incur and costs taxed against an "insured" in any suit we defend;

2. Premiums on bonds required in a suit we defend, but not for bond amounts more than the Coverage E limit of liability. We need not apply for or furnish any bond;

3. Reasonable expenses incurred by an "insured" at our request, including actual loss of earnings (but not loss of other income) up to $250 per day, for assisting us in the investigation or defense of a claim or suit; and

4. Interest on the entire judgment which accrues after entry of the judgment and before we pay or tender, or deposit in court that part of the judgment which does not exceed the limit of liability that applies.

B. First Aid Expenses

We will pay expenses for first aid to others incurred by an "insured" for "bodily injury" covered under this policy. We will not pay for first aid to an "insured".

C. Damage To Property Of Others

1. We will pay, at replacement cost, up to $1,000 per "occurrence" for "property damage" to property of others caused by an "insured".

2. We will not pay for "property damage":
   a. To the extent of any amount recoverable under Section I;
   b. Caused intentionally by an "insured" who is 13 years of age or older;
   c. To property owned by an "insured";
   d. To property owned by or rented to a tenant of an "insured" or a resident in your household; or
   e. Arising out of:
      (1) A "business" engaged in by an "insured";
      (2) Any act or omission in connection with a premises owned, rented or controlled by an "insured", other than the "insured location"; or
      (3) The ownership, maintenance, occupancy, operation, use, loading or unloading of aircraft, hovercraft, watercraft or "motor vehicles".

         This exclusion e.(3) does not apply to a "motor vehicle" that:
      (a) Is designed for recreational use off public roads;
      (b) Is not owned by an "insured"; and
      (c) At the time of the "occurrence", is not required by law, or regulation issued by a government agency, to have been registered for it to be used on public roads or property.

D. Loss Assessment

1. We will pay up to $1,000 for your share of loss assessment charged against you, as owner or tenant of the "residence premises", during the policy period by a corporation or association of property owners, when the assessment is made as a result of:
   a. "Bodily injury" or "property damage" not excluded from coverage under Section II—Exclusions; or
   b. Liability for an act of a director, officer or trustee in the capacity as a director, officer or trustee, provided such person:
      (1) Is elected by the members of a corporation or association of property owners; and
      (2) Serves without deriving any income from the exercise of duties which are solely on behalf of a corporation or association of property owners.

2. Paragraph I. Policy Period under Section II—Conditions does not apply to this Loss Assessment Coverage.

3. Regardless of the number of assessments, the limit of $1,000 is the most we will pay for loss arising out of:
   a. One accident, including continuous or repeated exposure to substantially the same general harmful condition; or
   b. A covered act of a director, officer or trustee. An act involving more than one director, officer or trustee is considered to be a single act.

4. We do not cover assessments charged against you or a corporation or association of property owners by any governmental body.

SECTION II—CONDITIONS

A. Limit Of Liability

Our total liability under Coverage E for all damages resulting from any one "occurrence" will not be more than the Coverage E limit of liability shown in the Declarations. This limit is the same regardless of the number of "insureds", claims made or persons injured. All "bodily injury" and "property damage" resulting from any one accident or from continuous or repeated exposure to substantially the same general harmful conditions shall be considered to be the result of one "occurrence".

Our total liability under Coverage F for all medical expense payable for "bodily injury" to one person as the result of one accident will not be more than the Coverage F limit of liability shown in the Declarations.

B. Severability Of Insurance

This insurance applies separately to each "insured". This condition will not increase our limit of liability for any one "occurrence".

C. Duties After "Occurrence"

In case of an "occurrence", you or another "insured" will perform the following duties that apply. We have no duty to provide coverage under this policy if your failure to comply with the following duties is prejudicial to us. You will help us by seeing that these duties are performed:

1. Give written notice to us or our agent as soon as is practical, which sets forth:
   a. The identity of the policy and the "named insured" shown in the Declarations;
   b. Reasonably available information on the time, place and circumstances of the "occurrence"; and
   c. Names and addresses of any claimants and witnesses;
2. Cooperate with us in the investigation, settlement or defense of any claim or suit;
3. Promptly forward to us every notice, demand, summons or other process relating to the "occurrence";
4. At our request, help us:
   a. To make settlement;
   b. To enforce any right of contribution or indemnity against any person or organization who may be liable to an "insured";
   c. With the conduct of suits and attend hearings and trials; and
   d. To secure and give evidence and obtain the attendance of witnesses;
5. With respect to C. Damage To Property Of Others under Section II—Additional Coverages, submit to us within 60 days after the loss, a sworn statement of loss and show the damaged property, if in an "insured's" control;
6. No "insured" shall, except at such "insured's" own cost, voluntarily make payment, assume obligation or incur expense other than for first aid to others at the time of the "bodily injury".

D. Duties Of An Injured Person—Coverage F—Medical Payments To Others
1. The injured person or someone acting for the injured person will:
   a. Give us written proof of claim, under oath if required, as soon as is practical; and
   b. Authorize us to obtain copies of medical reports and records.
2. The injured person will submit to a physical exam by a doctor of our choice when and as often as we reasonably require.

E. Payment Of Claim—Coverage F—Medical Payments To Others
Payment under this coverage is not an admission of liability by an "insured" or us.

F. Suit Against Us
1. No action can be brought against us unless there has been full compliance with all of the terms under this Section II.
2. No one will have the right to join us as a party to any action against an "insured".

3. Also, no action with respect to Coverage E can be brought against us until the obligation of such "insured" has been determined by final judgment or agreement signed by us.

G. Bankruptcy Of An "Insured"
Bankruptcy or insolvency of an "insured" will not relieve us of our obligations under this policy.

H. Other Insurance
This insurance is excess over other valid and collectible insurance except insurance written specifically to cover as excess over the limits of liability that apply in this policy.

I. Policy Period
This policy applies only to "bodily injury" or "property damage" which occurs during the policy period.

J. Concealment Or Fraud
We do not provide coverage to an "insured" who, whether before or after a loss, has:
1. Intentionally concealed or misrepresented any material fact or circumstance;
2. Engaged in fraudulent conduct; or
3. Made false statements;
relating to this insurance.

SECTIONS I AND II—CONDITIONS

A. Liberalization Clause
If we make a change which broadens coverage under this edition of our policy without additional premium charge, that change will automatically apply to your insurance as of the date we implement the change in your state, provided that this implementation date falls within 60 days prior to or during the policy period stated in the Declarations.

This Liberalization Clause does not apply to changes implemented with a general program revision that includes both broadenings and restrictions in coverage, whether that general program revision is implemented through introduction of:
1. A subsequent edition of this policy; or
2. An amendatory endorsement.

B. Waiver Or Change Of Policy Provisions
A waiver or change of a provision of this policy must be in writing by us to be valid. Our request for an appraisal or examination will not waive any of our rights.

C. Cancellation
1. You may cancel this policy at any time by returning it to us or by letting us know in writing of the date cancellation is to take effect.
2. We may cancel this policy only for the reasons stated below by letting you know in writing of the date cancellation takes effect. This cancellation notice may be delivered to you, or mailed to you at your mailing address shown in the Declarations. Proof of mailing will be sufficient proof of notice.

a. When you have not paid the premium, we may cancel at any time by letting you know at least 10 days before the date cancellation takes effect.

b. When this policy has been in effect for less than 60 days and is not a renewal with us, we may cancel for any reason by letting you know at least 10 days before the date cancellation takes effect.

c. When this policy has been in effect for 60 days or more, or at any time if it is a renewal with us, we may cancel:

   (1) If there has been a material misrepresentation of fact which if known to us would have caused us not to issue the policy; or

   (2) If the risk has changed substantially since the policy was issued.

   This can be done by letting you know at least 30 days before the date cancellation takes effect.

d. When this policy is written for a period of more than one year, we may cancel for any reason at anniversary by letting you know at least 30 days before the date cancellation takes effect.

3. When this policy is canceled, the premium for the period from the date of cancellation to the expiration date will be refunded pro rata.

4. If the return premium is not refunded with the notice of cancellation or when this policy is returned to us, we will refund it within a reasonable time after the date cancellation takes effect.

D. Nonrenewal

We may elect not to renew this policy. We may do so by delivering to you, or mailing to you at your mailing address shown in the Declarations, written notice at least 30 days before the expiration date of this policy. Proof of mailing will be sufficient proof of notice.

E. Assignment

Assignment of this policy will not be valid unless we give our written consent.

F. Subrogation

An "insured" may waive in writing before a loss all rights of recovery against any person. If not waived, we may require an assignment of rights of recovery for a loss to the extent that payment is made by us.

If an assignment is sought, an "insured" must sign and deliver all related papers and cooperate with us.

Subrogation does not apply to Coverage F or Paragraph C. Damage To Property Of Others under Section II—Additional Coverages.

G. Death

If any person named in the Declarations or the spouse, if a resident of the same household, dies, the following apply:

1. We insure the legal representative of the deceased but only with respect to the premises and property of the deceased covered under the policy at the time of death; and

2. "Insured" includes:

   a. An "insured" who is a member of your household at the time of your death, but only while a resident of the "residence premises"; and

   b. With respect to your property, the person having proper temporary custody of the property until appointment and qualification of a legal representative.

APPENDIX B

Personal Auto Policy

This sample policy is Copyright Insurance Services Office 1997 and is used with its permission.

PERSONAL AUTO POLICY
AGREEMENT

In return for payment of the premium and subject to all the terms of this policy, we agree with you as follows:

DEFINITIONS

A. Throughout this policy, "you" and "your" refer to:
  1. The "named insured" shown in the Declarations; and
  2. The spouse if a resident of the same household.

If the spouse ceases to be a resident of the same household during the policy period or prior to the inception of this policy, the spouse will be considered "you" and "your" under this policy but only until the earlier of:
  1. The end of 90 days following the spouse's change of residency;
  2. The effective date of another policy listing the spouse as a named insured; or
  3. The end of the policy period.

B. "We", "us" and "our" refer to the Company providing this insurance.

C. For purposes of this policy, a private passenger type auto, pickup or van shall be deemed to be owned by a person if leased:
  1. Under a written agreement to that person; and
  2. For a continuous period of at least 6 months.

Other words and phrases are defined. They are in quotation marks when used.

D. "Bodily injury" means bodily harm, sickness or disease, including death that results.

E. "Business" includes trade, profession or occupation.

F. "Family member" means a person related to you by blood, marriage or adoption who is a resident of your household. This includes a ward or foster child.

G. "Occupying" means:
  1. In;
  2. Upon; or
  3. Getting in, on, out or off.

H. "Property damage" means physical injury to, destruction of or loss of use of tangible property.

I. "Trailer" means a vehicle designed to be pulled by a:
  1. Private passenger auto; or
  2. Pickup or van.

It also means a farm wagon or farm implement while towed by a vehicle listed in 1. or 2. above.

J. "Your covered auto" means:
  1. Any vehicle shown in the Declarations.
  2. A "newly acquired auto".
  3. Any "trailer" you own.
  4. Any auto or "trailer" you do not own while used as a temporary substitute for any other vehicle described in this definition which is out of normal use because of its:
      a. Breakdown;
      b. Repair;
      c. Servicing;
      d. Loss; or
      e. Destruction.

This Provision (J.4.) does not apply to Coverage For Damage To Your Auto.

K. "Newly acquired auto":
  1. "Newly acquired auto" means any of the following types of vehicles you become the owner of during the policy period:
      a. A private passenger auto; or
      b. A pickup or van, for which no other insurance policy provides coverage, that:
        (1) Has a Gross Vehicle Weight Rating of 10,000 lbs. or less; and
        (2) Is not used for the delivery or transportation of goods and materials unless such use is:
          (a) Incidental to your "business" of installing, maintaining or repairing furnishings or equipment; or
          (b) For farming or ranching.
  2. Coverage for a "newly acquired auto" is provided as described below. If you ask us to insure a "newly acquired auto" after a specified time period described below has elapsed, any coverage we provide for a "newly acquired auto" will begin at the time you request the coverage.
      a. For any coverage provided in this policy except Coverage For Damage To Your Auto, a "newly acquired auto" will have the broadest coverage we now provide for any vehicle shown in the Declarations. Coverage begins on the date you become the owner. However, for this coverage to apply to a "newly acquired auto" which is in addition to any vehicle shown in the Declarations, you must ask us to insure it within 14 days after you become the owner.

      If a "newly acquired auto" replaces a vehicle shown in the Declarations, coverage is provided for this vehicle without your having to ask us to insure it.

b. Collision Coverage for a "newly acquired auto" begins on the date you become the owner. However, for this coverage to apply, you must ask us to insure it within:

(1) 14 days after you become the owner if the Declarations indicate that Collision Coverage applies to at least one auto. In this case, the "newly acquired auto" will have the broadest coverage we now provide for any auto shown in the Declarations.

(2) Four days after you become the owner if the Declarations do not indicate that Collision Coverage applies to at least one auto. If you comply with the 4 day requirement and a loss occurred before you asked us to insure the "newly acquired auto", a Collision deductible of $500 will apply.

c. Other Than Collision Coverage for a "newly acquired auto" begins on the date you become the owner. However, for this coverage to apply, you must ask us to insure it within:

(1) 14 days after you become the owner if the Declarations indicate that Other Than Collision Coverage applies to at least one auto. In this case, the "newly acquired auto" will have the broadest coverage we now provide for any auto shown in the Declarations.

(2) Four days after you become the owner if the Declarations do not indicate that Other Than Collision Coverage applies to at least one auto. If you comply with the 4 day requirement and a loss occurred before you asked us to insure the "newly acquired auto", an Other Than Collision deductible of $500 will apply.

PART A—LIABILITY COVERAGE

INSURING AGREEMENT

A. We will pay damages for "bodily injury" or "property damage" for which any "insured" becomes legally responsible because of an auto accident. Damages include prejudgment interest awarded against the "insured". We will settle or defend, as we consider appropriate, any claim or suit asking for these damages. In addition to our limit of liability, we will pay all defense costs we incur. Our duty to settle or defend ends when our limit of liability for this coverage has been exhausted by payment of judgments or settlements. We have no duty to defend any suit or settle any claim for "bodily injury" or "property damage" not covered under this policy.

B. "Insured" as used in this Part means:

1. You or any "family member" for the ownership, maintenance or use of any auto or "trailer".

2. Any person using "your covered auto".

3. For "your covered auto", any person or organization but only with respect to legal responsibility for acts or omissions of a person for whom coverage is afforded under this Part.

4. For any auto or "trailer", other than "your covered auto", any other person or organization but only with respect to legal responsibility for acts or omissions of you or any "family member" for whom coverage is afforded under this Part. This Provision (B.4.) applies only if the person or organization does not own or hire the auto or "trailer".

SUPPLEMENTARY PAYMENTS

We will pay on behalf of an "insured":

1. Up to $250 for the cost of bail bonds required because of an accident, including related traffic law violations. The accident must result in "bodily injury" or "property damage" covered under this policy.

2. Premiums on appeal bonds and bonds to release attachments in any suit we defend.

3. Interest accruing after a judgment is entered in any suit we defend. Our duty to pay interest ends when we offer to pay that part of the judgment which does not exceed our limit of liability for this coverage.

4. Up to $200 a day for loss of earnings, but not other income, because of attendance at hearings or trials at our request.

5. Other reasonable expenses incurred at our request.

These payments will not reduce the limit of liability.

EXCLUSIONS

A. We do not provide Liability Coverage for any "insured":

1. Who intentionally causes "bodily injury" or "property damage".

2. For "property damage" to property owned or being transported by that "insured".

3. For "property damage" to property:

a. Rented to;

b. Used by; or

c. In the care of;

that "insured".

This Exclusion (A.3.) does not apply to "property damage" to a residence or private garage.

4. For "bodily injury" to an employee of that "insured" during the course of employment. This Exclusion (A.4.) does not apply to "bodily injury" to a domestic employee unless workers' compensation benefits are required or available for that domestic employee.

5. For that "insured's" liability arising out of the ownership or operation of a vehicle while it is being used as a public or livery conveyance. This Exclusion (A.5.) does not apply to a share-the-expense car pool.

6. While employed or otherwise engaged in the "business" of:
   a. Selling;
   b. Repairing;
   c. Servicing;
   d. Storing; or
   e. Parking;
   vehicles designed for use mainly on public highways. This includes road testing and delivery. This Exclusion (A.6.) does not apply to the ownership, maintenance or use of "your covered auto" by:
   a. You;
   b. Any "family member"; or
   c. Any partner, agent or employee of you or any "family member".

7. Maintaining or using any vehicle while that "insured" is employed or otherwise engaged in any "business" (other than farming or ranching) not described in Exclusion A.6.
   This Exclusion (A.7.) does not apply to the maintenance or use of a:
   a. Private passenger auto;
   b. Pickup or van; or
   c. "Trailer" used with a vehicle described in a. or b. above.

8. Using a vehicle without a reasonable belief that that "insured" is entitled to do so. This Exclusion (A.8.) does not apply to a "family member" using "your covered auto" which is owned by you.

9. For "bodily injury" or "property damage" for which that "insured":
   a. Is an insured under a nuclear energy liability policy; or
   b. Would be an insured under a nuclear energy liability policy but for its termination upon exhaustion of its limit of liability.
   A nuclear energy liability policy is a policy issued by any of the following or their successors:
   a. Nuclear Energy Liability Insurance Association;
   b. Mutual Atomic Energy Liability Underwriters; or
   c. Nuclear Insurance Association of Canada.

B. We do not provide Liability Coverage for the ownership, maintenance or use of:
   1. Any vehicle which:
      a. Has fewer than four wheels; or
      b. Is designed mainly for use off public roads.
      This Exclusion (B.1.) does not apply:
      a. While such vehicle is being used by an "insured" in a medical emergency;

      b. To any "trailer"; or
      c. To any non-owned golf cart.
   2. Any vehicle, other than "your covered auto", which is:
      a. Owned by you; or
      b. Furnished or available for your regular use.
   3. Any vehicle, other than "your covered auto", which is:
      a. Owned by any "family member"; or
      b. Furnished or available for the regular use of any "family member".
      However, this Exclusion (B.3.) does not apply to you while you are maintaining or "occupying" any vehicle which is:
      a. Owned by a "family member"; or
      b. Furnished or available for the regular use of a "family member".
   4. Any vehicle, located inside a facility designed for racing, for the purpose of:
      a. Competing in; or
      b. Practicing or preparing for;
      any prearranged or organized racing or speed contest.

LIMIT OF LIABILITY

A. The limit of liability shown in the Declarations for each person for Bodily Injury Liability is our maximum limit of liability for all damages, including damages for care, loss of services or death, arising out of "bodily injury" sustained by any one person in any one auto accident. Subject to this limit for each person, the limit of liability shown in the Declarations for each accident for Bodily Injury Liability is our maximum limit of liability for all damages for "bodily injury" resulting from any one auto accident.

The limit of liability shown in the Declarations for each accident for Property Damage Liability is our maximum limit of liability for all "property damage" resulting from any one auto accident.

This is the most we will pay regardless of the number of:
   1. "Insureds";
   2. Claims made;
   3. Vehicles or premiums shown in the Declarations; or
   4. Vehicles involved in the auto accident.

B. No one will be entitled to receive duplicate payments for the same elements of loss under this coverage and:
   1. Part B or Part C of this policy; or
   2. Any Underinsured Motorists Coverage provided by this policy.

OUT OF STATE COVERAGE

If an auto accident to which this policy applies occurs in any state or province other than the one in which "your covered auto" is principally garaged, we will interpret your policy for that accident as follows:

A. If the state or province has:

    1. A financial responsibility or similar law specifying limits of liability for "bodily injury" or "property damage" higher than the limit shown in the Declarations, your policy will provide the higher specified limit.

    2. A compulsory insurance or similar law requiring a nonresident to maintain insurance whenever the nonresident uses a vehicle in that state or province, your policy will provide at least the required minimum amounts and types of coverage.

B. No one will be entitled to duplicate payments for the same elements of loss.

FINANCIAL RESPONSIBILITY

When this policy is certified as future proof of financial responsibility, this policy shall comply with the law to the extent required.

OTHER INSURANCE

If there is other applicable liability insurance we will pay only our share of the loss. Our share is the proportion that our limit of liability bears to the total of all applicable limits. However, any insurance we provide for a vehicle you do not own, including any vehicle while used as a temporary substitute for "your covered auto", shall be excess over any other collectible insurance.

PART B—MEDICAL PAYMENTS COVERAGE

INSURING AGREEMENT

A. We will pay reasonable expenses incurred for necessary medical and funeral services because of "bodily injury":

    1. Caused by accident; and

    2. Sustained by an "insured".

We will pay only those expenses incurred for services rendered within 3 years from the date of the accident.

B. "Insured" as used in this Part means:

    1. You or any "family member":

      a. While "occupying"; or

      b. As a pedestrian when struck by;

    a motor vehicle designed for use mainly on public roads or a trailer of any type.

    2. Any other person while "occupying" "your covered auto".

EXCLUSIONS

We do not provide Medical Payments Coverage for any "insured" for "bodily injury":

    1. Sustained while "occupying" any motorized vehicle having fewer than four wheels.

    2. Sustained while "occupying" "your covered auto" when it is being used as a public or livery conveyance. This Exclusion (2.) does not apply to a share-the-expense car pool.

    3. Sustained while "occupying" any vehicle located for use as a residence or premises.

    4. Occurring during the course of employment if workers' compensation benefits are required or available for the "bodily injury".

    5. Sustained while "occupying", or when struck by, any vehicle (other than "your covered auto") which is:

      a. Owned by you; or

      b. Furnished or available for your regular use.

    6. Sustained while "occupying", or when struck by, any vehicle (other than "your covered auto") which is:

      a. Owned by any "family member"; or

      b. Furnished or available for the regular use of any "family member".

    However, this Exclusion (6.) does not apply to you.

    7. Sustained while "occupying" a vehicle without a reasonable belief that that "insured" is entitled to do so. This Exclusion (7.) does not apply to a "family member" using "your covered auto" which is owned by you.

    8. Sustained while "occupying" a vehicle when it is being used in the "business" of an "insured". This Exclusion (8.) does not apply to "bodily injury" sustained while "occupying" a:

      a. Private passenger auto;

      b. Pickup or van; or

      c. "Trailer" used with a vehicle described in a. or b. above.

    9. Caused by or as a consequence of:

      a. Discharge of a nuclear weapon (even if accidental);

      b. War (declared or undeclared);

      c. Civil war;

      d. Insurrection; or

      e. Rebellion or revolution.

    10. From or as a consequence of the following, whether controlled or uncontrolled or however caused:

      a. Nuclear reaction;

      b. Radiation; or

      c. Radioactive contamination.

    11. Sustained while "occupying" any vehicle located inside a facility designed for racing, for the purpose of:

      a. Competing in; or

      b. Practicing or preparing for;

    any prearranged or organized racing or speed contest.

LIMIT OF LIABILITY

A. The limit of liability shown in the Declarations for this coverage is our maximum limit of liability for each person injured in any one accident. This is the most we will pay regardless of the number of:

1. "Insureds";
2. Claims made;
3. Vehicles or premiums shown in the Declarations; or
4. Vehicles involved in the accident.

B. No one will be entitled to receive duplicate payments for the same elements of loss under this coverage and:

1. Part A or Part C of this policy; or
2. Any Underinsured Motorists Coverage provided by this policy.

OTHER INSURANCE

If there is other applicable auto medical payments insurance we will pay only our share of the loss. Our share is the proportion that our limit of liability bears to the total of all applicable limits. However, any insurance we provide with respect to a vehicle you do not own including any vehicle while used as a temporary substitute for "your covered auto", shall be excess over any other collectible auto insurance providing payments for medical or funeral expenses.

PART C—UNINSURED MOTORISTS COVERAGE

INSURING AGREEMENT

A. We will pay compensatory damages which an "insured" is legally entitled to recover from the owner or operator of an "uninsured motor vehicle" because of "bodily injury":

1. Sustained by an "insured"; and
2. Caused by an accident.

The owner's or operator's liability for these damages must arise out of the ownership, maintenance or use of the "uninsured motor vehicle".

Any judgment for damages arising out of a suit brought without our written consent is not binding on us.

B. "Insured" as used in this Part means:

1. You or any "family member".
2. Any other person "occupying" "your covered auto".
3. Any person for damages that person is entitled to recover because of "bodily injury" to which this coverage applies sustained by a person described in 1. or 2. above.

C. "Uninsured motor vehicle" means a land motor vehicle or trailer of any type:

1. To which no bodily injury liability bond or policy applies at the time of the accident.
2. To which a bodily injury liability bond or policy applies at the time of the accident. In this case its limit for bodily injury liability must be less than the minimum limit for bodily injury liability specified by the financial responsibility law of the state in which "your covered auto" is principally garaged.
3. Which is a hit-and-run vehicle whose operator or owner cannot be identified and which hits:
   a. You or any "family member";
   b. A vehicle which you or any "family member" are "occupying"; or
   c. "Your covered auto".

4. To which a bodily injury liability bond or policy applies at the time of the accident but the bonding or insuring company:
   a. Denies coverage; or
   b. Is or becomes insolvent.

However, "uninsured motor vehicle" does not include any vehicle or equipment:

1. Owned by or furnished or available for the regular use of you or any "family member".
2. Owned or operated by a self-insurer under any applicable motor vehicle law, except a self-insurer which is or becomes insolvent.
3. Owned by any governmental unit or agency.
4. Operated on rails or crawler treads.
5. Designed mainly for use off public roads while not on public roads.
6. While located for use as a residence or premises.

EXCLUSIONS

A. We do not provide Uninsured Motorists Coverage for "bodily injury" sustained:

1. By an "insured" while "occupying", or when struck by, any motor vehicle owned by that "insured" which is not insured for this coverage under this policy. This includes a trailer of any type used with that vehicle.
2. By any "family member" while "occupying", or when struck by, any motor vehicle you own which is insured for this coverage on a primary basis under any other policy.

B. We do not provide Uninsured Motorists Coverage for "bodily injury" sustained by any "insured":

1. If that "insured" or the legal representative settles the "bodily injury" claim and such settlement prejudices our right to recover payment.
2. While "occupying" "your covered auto" when it is being used as a public or livery conveyance. This Exclusion (B.2.) does not apply to a share-the-expense car pool.

3. Using a vehicle without a reasonable belief that that "insured" is entitled to do so. This Exclusion (B.3.) does not apply to a "family member" using "your covered auto" which is owned by you.

C. This coverage shall not apply directly or indirectly to benefit any insurer or self-insurer under any of the following or similar law:
1. Workers' compensation law; or
2. Disability benefits law.

D. We do not provide Uninsured Motorists Coverage for punitive or exemplary damages.

LIMIT OF LIABILITY

A. The limit of liability shown in the Declarations for each person for Uninsured Motorists Coverage is our maximum limit of liability for all damages, including damages for care, loss of services or death, arising out of "bodily injury" sustained by any one person in any one accident. Subject to this limit for each person, the limit of liability shown in the Declarations for each accident for Uninsured Motorists Coverage is our maximum limit of liability for all damages for "bodily injury" resulting from any one accident.

This is the most we will pay regardless of the number of:
1. "Insureds";
2. Claims made;
3. Vehicles or premiums shown in the Declarations; or
4. Vehicles involved in the accident.

B. No one will be entitled to receive duplicate payments for the same elements of loss under this coverage and:
1. Part A. or Part B. of this policy; or
2. Any Underinsured Motorists Coverage provided by this policy.

C. We will not make a duplicate payment under this coverage for any element of loss for which payment has been made by or on behalf of persons or organizations who may be legally responsible.

D. We will not pay for any element of loss if a person is entitled to receive payment for the same element of loss under any of the following or similar law:
1. Workers' compensation law; or
2. Disability benefits law.

OTHER INSURANCE

If there is other applicable insurance available under one or more policies or provisions of coverage that is similar to the insurance provided under this Part of the policy:
1. Any recovery for damages under all such policies or provisions of coverage may equal but not exceed the highest applicable limit for any one vehicle under any insurance providing coverage on either a primary or excess basis.

2. Any insurance we provide with respect to a vehicle you do not own, including any vehicle while used as a temporary substitute for "your covered auto", shall be excess over any collectible insurance providing such coverage on a primary basis.
3. If the coverage under this policy is provided:
    a. On a primary basis, we will pay only our share of the loss that must be paid under insurance providing coverage on a primary basis. Our share is the proportion that our limit of liability bears to the total of all applicable limits of liability for coverage provided on a primary basis.
    b. On an excess basis, we will pay only our share of the loss that must be paid under insurance providing coverage on an excess basis. Our share is the proportion that our limit of liability bears to the total of all applicable limits of liability for coverage provided on an excess basis.

ARBITRATION

A. If we and an "insured" do not agree:
1. Whether that "insured" is legally entitled to recover damages; or
2. As to the amount of damages which are recoverable by that "insured";

from the owner or operator of an "uninsured motor vehicle", then the matter may be arbitrated. However, disputes concerning coverage under this Part may not be arbitrated.

Both parties must agree to arbitration. If so agreed, each party will select an arbitrator. The two arbitrators will select a third. If they cannot agree within 30 days, either may request that selection be made by a judge of a court having jurisdiction.

B. Each party will:
1. Pay the expenses it incurs; and
2. Bear the expenses of the third arbitrator equally.

C. Unless both parties agree otherwise, arbitration will take place in the county in which the "insured" lives. Local rules of law as to procedure and evidence will apply. A decision agreed to by at least two of the arbitrators will be binding as to:
1. Whether the "insured" is legally entitled to recover damages; and
2. The amount of damages. This applies only if the amount does not exceed the minimum limit for bodily injury liability specified by the financial responsibility law of the state in which "your covered auto" is principally garaged. If the amount exceeds that limit, either party may demand the right to a trial. This demand must be made within 60 days of the arbitrators' decision. If this demand is not made, the amount of damages agreed to by the arbitrators will be binding.

PART D—COVERAGE FOR DAMAGE TO YOUR AUTO

INSURING AGREEMENT

A. We will pay for direct and accidental loss to "your covered auto" or any "non-owned auto", including their equipment, minus any applicable deductible shown in the Declarations. If loss to more than one "your covered auto" or "non-owned auto" results from the same "collision", only the highest applicable deductible will apply. We will pay for loss to "your covered auto" caused by:

1. Other than "collision" only if the Declarations indicate that Other Than Collision Coverage is provided for that auto.

2. "Collision" only if the Declarations indicate that Collision Coverage is provided for that auto.

If there is a loss to a "non-owned auto", we will provide the broadest coverage applicable to any "your covered auto" shown in the Declarations.

B. "Collision" means the upset of "your covered auto" or a "non-owned auto" or their impact with another vehicle or object.

Loss caused by the following is considered other than "collision":

1. Missiles or falling objects;
2. Fire;
3. Theft or larceny;
4. Explosion or earthquake;
5. Windstorm;
6. Hail, water or flood;
7. Malicious mischief or vandalism;
8. Riot or civil commotion;
9. Contact with bird or animal; or
10. Breakage of glass.

If breakage of glass is caused by a "collision", you may elect to have it considered a loss caused by "collision".

C. "Non-owned auto" means:

1. Any private passenger auto, pickup, van or "trailer" not owned by or furnished or available for the regular use of you or any "family member" while in the custody of or being operated by you or any "family member"; or

2. Any auto or "trailer" you do not own while used as a temporary substitute for "your covered auto" which is out of normal use because of its:
   a. Breakdown;
   b. Repair;
   c. Servicing;
   d. Loss; or
   e. Destruction.

TRANSPORTATION EXPENSES

A. In addition, we will pay, without application of a deductible, up to a maximum of $600 for:

1. Temporary transportation expenses not exceeding $20 per day incurred by you in the event of a loss to "your covered auto". We will pay for such expenses if the loss is caused by:
   a. Other than "collision" only if the Declarations indicate that Other Than Collision Coverage is provided for that auto.
   b. "Collision" only if the Declarations indicate that Collision Coverage is provided for that auto.

2. Expenses for which you become legally responsible in the event of loss to a "non-owned auto". We will pay for such expenses if the loss is caused by:
   a. Other than "collision" only if the Declarations indicate that Other Than Collision Coverage is provided for any "your covered auto".
   b. "Collision" only if the Declarations indicate that Collision Coverage is provided for any "your covered auto".

However, the most we will pay for any expenses for loss of use is $20 per day.

B. Subject to the provisions of Paragraph A., If the loss is caused by:

1. A total theft of "your covered auto" or a "non-owned auto", we will pay only expenses incurred during the period:
   a. Beginning 48 hours after the theft; and
   b. Ending when "your covered auto" or the "non-owned auto" is returned to use or we pay for its loss.

2. Other than theft of a "your covered auto" or a "non-owned auto", we will pay only expenses beginning when the auto is withdrawn from use for more than 24 hours.

C. Our payment will be limited to that period of time reasonably required to repair or replace the "your covered auto" or the "non-owned auto".

EXCLUSIONS

We will not pay for:

1. Loss to "your covered auto" or any "non-owned auto" which occurs while it is being used as a public or livery conveyance. This Exclusion (1.) does not apply to a share-the-expense car pool.

2. Damage due and confined to:
   a. Wear and tear;
   b. Freezing;
   c. Mechanical or electrical breakdown or failure; or
   d. Road damage to tires.

This Exclusion (2.) does not apply if the damage results from the total theft of "your covered auto" or any "non-owned auto".

3. Loss due to or as a consequence of:
   a. Radioactive contamination;
   b. Discharge of any nuclear weapon (even if accidental);
   c. War (declared or undeclared);
   d. Civil war;
   e. Insurrection; or
   f. Rebellion or revolution.
4. Loss to any electronic equipment that reproduces, receives or transmits audio, visual or data signals. This includes but is not limited to:
   a. Radios and stereos;
   b. Tape decks;
   c. Compact disc systems;
   d. Navigation systems;
   e. Internet access systems;
   f. Personal computers;
   g. Video entertainment systems;
   h. Telephones;
   i. Televisions;
   j. Two-way mobile radios;
   k. Scanners; or
   l. Citizens band radios.
   This Exclusion (4.) does not apply to electronic equipment that is permanently installed in "your covered auto" or any "non-owned auto".
5. Loss to tapes, records, disks or other media used with equipment described in Exclusions 4-6. A total loss to "your covered auto" or any "non-owned auto" due to destruction or confiscation by governmental or civil authorities.
6. This Exclusion (6.) does not apply to the interests of Loss Payees in "your covered auto".
7. Loss to:
   a. A "trailer", camper body, or motor home, which is not shown in the Declarations; or
   b. Facilities or equipment used with such "trailer", camper body or motor home. Facilities or equipment include but are not limited to:
      (1) Cooking, dining, plumbing or refrigeration facilities;
      (2) Awnings or cabanas; or
      (3) Any other facilities or equipment used with a "trailer", camper body, or motor home.
   This Exclusion (7.) does not apply to a:
   a. "Trailer", and its facilities or equipment, which you do not own; or
   b. "Trailer", camper body, or the facilities or equipment in or attached to the "trailer" or camper body, which you:
      (1) Acquire during the policy period; and
      (2) Ask us to insure within 14 days after you become the owner.
8. Loss to any "non-owned auto" when used by you or any "family member" without a reasonable belief that you or that "family member" are entitled to do so.
9. Loss to equipment designed or used for the detection or location of radar or laser.
10. Loss to any custom furnishings or equipment in or upon any pickup or van. Custom furnishings or equipment include but are not limited to:
    a. Special carpeting or insulation;
    b. Furniture or bars;
    c. Height-extending roofs; or
    d. Custom murals, paintings or other decals or graphics.
       This Exclusion (10.) does not apply to a cap, cover or bedliner in or upon any "your covered auto" which is a pickup.
11. Loss to any "non-owned auto" being maintained or used by any person while employed or otherwise engaged in the "business" of:
    a. Selling;
    b. Repairing;
    c. Servicing;
    d. Storing; or
    e. Parking;
    vehicles designed for use on public highways. This includes road testing and delivery.
12. Loss to "your covered auto" or any "non-owned auto", located inside a facility designed for racing, for the purpose of:
    a. Competing in; or
    b. Practicing or preparing for;
    any prearranged or organized racing or speed contest.
13. Loss to, or loss of use of, a "non-owned auto" rented by:
    a. You; or
    b. Any "family member";
    if a rental vehicle company is precluded from recovering such loss or loss of use, from you or that "family member", pursuant to the provisions of any applicable rental agreement or state law.

LIMIT OF LIABILITY

A. Our limit of liability for loss will be the lesser of the:
   1. Actual cash value of the stolen or damaged property; or
   2. Amount necessary to repair or replace the property with other property of like kind and quality.
   However, the most we will pay for loss to:
   1. Any "non-owned auto" which is a trailer is $1500.
   2. Electronic equipment that reproduces, receives or transmits audio, visual or data signals, which is permanently installed in the auto in locations not used by the auto manufacturer for installation of such equipment, is $1,000.

B. An adjustment for depreciation and physical condition will be made in determining actual cash value in the event of a total loss.

C. If a repair or replacement results in better than like kind or quality, we will not pay for the amount of the betterment.

PAYMENT OF LOSS

We may pay for loss in money or repair or replace the damaged or stolen property. We may, at our expense, return any stolen property to:

1. You; or
2. The address shown in this policy.

If we return stolen property we will pay for any damage resulting from the theft. We may keep all or part of the property at an agreed or appraised value.

If we pay for loss in money, our payment will include the applicable sales tax for the damaged or stolen property.

NO BENEFIT TO BAILEE

This insurance shall not directly or indirectly benefit any carrier or other bailee for hire.

OTHER SOURCES OF RECOVERY

If other sources of recovery also cover the loss, we will pay only our share of the loss. Our share is the proportion that our limit of liability bears to the total of all applicable limits. However, any insurance we provide with respect to a "non-owned auto" shall be excess over any other collectible source of recovery including, but not limited to:

1. Any coverage provided by the owner of the "non-owned auto";
2. Any other applicable physical damage insurance;
3. Any other source of recovery applicable to the loss.

APPRAISAL

A. If we and you do not agree on the amount of loss, either may demand an appraisal of the loss. In this event, each party will select a competent and impartial appraiser. The two appraisers will select an umpire. The appraisers will state separately the actual cash value and the amount of loss. If they fail to agree, they will submit their differences to the umpire. A decision agreed to by any two will be binding. Each party will:

1. Pay its chosen appraiser; and
2. Bear the expenses of the appraisal and umpire equally.

B. We do not waive any of our rights under this policy by agreeing to an appraisal.

PART E—DUTIES AFTER AN ACCIDENT OR LOSS

We have no duty to provide coverage under this policy if the failure to comply with the following duties is prejudicial to us:

A. We must be notified promptly of how, when and where the accident or loss happened. Notice should also include the names and addresses of any injured persons and of any witnesses.

B. A person seeking any coverage must:

1. Cooperate with us in the investigation, settlement or defense of any claim or suit.
2. Promptly send us copies of any notices or legal papers received in connection with the accident or loss.
3. Submit, as often as we reasonably require:
   a. To physical exams by physicians we select. We will pay for these exams.
   b. To examination under oath and subscribe the same.
4. Authorize us to obtain:
   a. Medical reports; and
   b. Other pertinent records.

5. Submit a proof of loss when required by us.

C. A person seeking Uninsured Motorists Coverage must also:

1. Promptly notify the police if a hit-and-run driver is involved.
2. Promptly send us copies of the legal papers if a suit is brought.

D. A person seeking Coverage For Damage To Your Auto must also:

1. Take reasonable steps after loss to protect "your covered auto" or any "non-owned auto" and their equipment from further loss. We will pay reasonable expenses incurred to do this.
2. Promptly notify the police if "your covered auto" or any "non-owned auto" is stolen.
3. Permit us to inspect and appraise the damaged property before its repair or disposal.

PART F—GENERAL PROVISIONS

BANKRUPTCY

Bankruptcy or insolvency of the "insured" shall not relieve us of any obligations under this policy.

CHANGES

A. This policy contains all the agreements between you and us. Its terms may not be changed or waived except by endorsement issued by us.

B. If there is a change to the information used to develop the policy premium, we may adjust your premium. Changes during the policy term that may result in a premium increase or decrease include, but are not limited to, changes in:

1. The number, type or use classification of insured vehicles;
2. Operators using insured vehicles;
3. The place of principal garaging of insured vehicles;
4. Coverage, deductible or limits.

If a change resulting from A. or B. requires a premium adjustment, we will make the premium adjustment in accordance with our manual rules.

C. If we make a change which broadens coverage under this edition of your policy without additional premium charge, that change will automatically apply to your policy as of the date we implement the change in your state. This Paragraph (C.) does not apply to changes implemented with a general program revision that includes both broadenings and restrictions in coverage, whether that general program revision is implemented through introduction of:

1. A subsequent edition of your policy; or
2. An Amendatory Endorsement.

FRAUD

We do not provide coverage for any "insured" who has made fraudulent statements or engaged in fraudulent conduct in connection with any accident or loss for which coverage is sought under this policy.

LEGAL ACTION AGAINST US

A. No legal action may be brought against us until there has been full compliance with all the terms of this policy. In addition, under Part A, no legal action may be brought against us until:

1. We agree in writing that the "insured" has an obligation to pay; or
2. The amount of that obligation has been finally determined by judgment after trial.

B. No person or organization has any right under this policy to bring us into any action to determine the liability of an "insured".

OUR RIGHT TO RECOVER PAYMENT

A. If we make a payment under this policy and the person to or for whom payment was made has a right to recover damages from another we shall be subrogated to that right. That person shall do:

1. Whatever is necessary to enable us to exercise our rights; and
2. Nothing after loss to prejudice them.

However, our rights in this Paragraph (A.) do not apply under Part D, against any person using "your covered auto" with a reasonable belief that that person is entitled to do so.

B. If we make a payment under this policy and the person to or for whom payment is made recovers damages from another, that person shall:

1. Hold in trust for us the proceeds of the recovery; and
2. Reimburse us to the extent of our payment.

POLICY PERIOD AND TERRITORY

A. This policy applies only to accidents and losses which occur:

1. During the policy period as shown in the Declarations; and
2. Within the policy territory.

B. The policy territory is:

1. The United States of America, its territories or possessions;
2. Puerto Rico; or
3. Canada.

This policy also applies to loss to, or accidents involving, "your covered auto" while being transported between their ports.

TERMINATION

A. Cancellation

This policy may be cancelled during the policy period as follows:

1. The named insured shown in the Declarations may cancel by:
   a. Returning this policy to us; or
   b. Giving us advance written notice of the date cancellation is to take effect.
2. We may cancel by mailing to the named insured shown in the Declarations at the address shown in this policy:
   a. At least 10 days notice:
   (1) If cancellation is for nonpayment of premium; or

(2) If notice is mailed during the first 60 days this policy is in effect and this is not a renewal or continuation policy; or

b. At least 20 days notice in all other cases.

3. After this policy is in effect for 60 days, or if this is a renewal or continuation policy, we will cancel only:

a. For nonpayment of premium; or

b. If your driver's license or that of:

(1) Any driver who lives with you; or

(2) Any driver who customarily uses "your covered auto";

has been suspended or revoked. This must have occurred:

(1) During the policy period; or

(2) Since the last anniversary of the original effective date if the policy period is other than 1 year; or

c. If the policy was obtained through material misrepresentation.

B. Nonrenewal

If we decide not to renew or continue this policy, we will mail notice to the named insured shown in the Declarations at the address shown in this policy. Notice will be mailed at least 20 days before the end of the policy period. Subject to this notice requirement, if the policy period is:

1. Less than 6 months, we will have the right not to renew or continue this policy every 6 months, beginning 6 months after its original effective date.

2. 6 months or longer, but less than one year, we will have the right not to renew or continue this policy at the end of the policy period.

3. 1 year or longer, we will have the right not to renew or continue this policy at each anniversary of its original effective date.

C. Automatic Termination

If we offer to renew or continue and you or your representative do not accept, this policy will automatically terminate at the end of the current policy period. Failure to pay the required renewal or continuation premium when due shall mean that you have not accepted our offer.

If you obtain other insurance on "your covered auto", any similar insurance provided by this policy will terminate as to that auto on the effective date of the other insurance.

D. Other Termination Provisions

1. We may deliver any notice instead of mailing it. Proof of mailing of any notice shall be sufficient proof of notice.

2. If this policy is cancelled, you may be entitled to a premium refund. If so, we will send you the refund. The premium refund, if any, will be computed according to our manuals. However, making or offering to make the refund is not a condition of cancellation.

3. The effective date of cancellation stated in the notice shall become the end of the policy period.

TRANSFER OF YOUR INTEREST IN THIS POLICY

A. Your rights and duties under this policy may not be assigned without our written consent. However, if a named insured shown in the Declarations dies, coverage will be provided for:

1. The surviving spouse if resident in the same household at the time of death. Coverage applies to the spouse as if a named insured shown in the Declarations; and

2. The legal representative of the deceased person as if a named insured shown in the Declarations. This applies only with respect to the representative's legal responsibility to maintain or use "your covered auto".

B. Coverage will only be provided until the end of the policy period.

TWO OR MORE AUTO POLICIES

If this policy and any other auto insurance policy issued to you by us apply to the same accident, the maximum limit of our liability under all the policies shall not exceed the highest applicable limit of liability under any one policy.

APPENDIX C

Sample Whole Life Insurance Policy and Application

This sample policy was provided by the American Council of Life Insurance, and used with its permission.

SAMPLE

THE COUNCIL LIFE INSURANCE COMPANY

The Council Life Insurance Company agrees to pay the benefits provided in this policy, subject to its terms and conditions. Executed at New York, New York on the Date of Issue.

David Olson

Secretary

Barbara Sloan

President

Life Policy — Participating

Amount payable at death of Insured $10,000.

Premiums payable to age 90.

Schedule of benefits and premiums page 2.

Right to Examine Policy—Please examine this policy carefully. The Owner may return the policy for any reason within ten days after receiving it. If returned, the policy will be considered void from the beginning and any premium paid will be refunded.

A GUIDE TO THE PROVISIONS OF THIS POLICY

Accidental Death Benefit	12
Beneficiaries	7
Cash Value, Extended Term and Paid-Up Insurance	5
Change of Policy	6
Contract	3
Dividends	4
Loans	6
Ownership	3
Premiums and Reinstatement	4
Specification	2
Waiver of Premium Right	11

Endorsements Made At Issue Appear After "General Provisions." Additional Benefits, If Any, Are Provided By Rider.

Specifications

Plan and Additional Benefits	Amount	Premium	Years Payable
Whole Life (Premiums payable to age 90)	$10,000	$229.50	55
Waiver of Premium (To age 65)		4.30	30
Accidental Death (To age 70)	10,000	7.80	35

A premium is payable on the policy date and every 12 policy months thereafter. The first premium is $241.60.

TABLE OF GUARANTEED VALUES

END OF POLICY YEAR	CASH OR LOAN VALUE	PAID-UP. INSURANCE	EXTENDED TERM INSURANCE YEARS	DAYS
1	$ 14	$ 30	0	152
2	174	450	4	182
3	338	860	8	65
4	506	1,250	10	344
5	676	1,640	12	360
6	879	2,070	14	335
7	1,084	2,500	16	147
8	1,293	2,910	17	207
9	1,504	3,300	18	177
10	1,719	3,690	19	78
11	1,908	4,000	19	209
12	2,099	4,300	19	306
13	2,294	4,590	20	8
14	2,490	4,870	20	47
15	2,690	5,140	20	65
16	2,891	5,410	20	66
17	3,095	5,660	20	52
18	3,301	5,910	20	27
19	3,508	6,150	19	358
20	3,718	6,390	19	317
AGE 60	4,620	7,200	18	111
AGE 65	5,504	7,860	16	147

Paid-up additions and dividend accumulations increase the cash values; indebtedness decreases them.

The percentage referred to in section 5.6 is 83.000%.

Direct Beneficiary   Helen M. Benson, wife of the insured

Owner   Thomas A. Benson, the insured

Insured	Thomas A. Benson	**Age and Sex**	37 Male
Policy Date	November 1, 1980	**Policy Number**	000/00
Date of Issue	November 1, 1980		

2

SECTION 1. THE CONTRACT

1.1 LIFE INSURANCE BENEFIT

The Council Life Insurance Company agrees, subject to the terms and conditions of this policy, to pay the Amount shown on page 2 to the beneficiary upon receipt at its Home Office of proof of the death of the Insured.

1.2 INCONTESTABILITY

This policy shall be incontestable after it has been in force during the lifetime of the Insured for two years from the Date of Issue.

1.3 SUICIDE

If within two years from the Date of Issue the Insured dies by suicide, the amount payable by the Company shall be limited to the premiums paid.

1.4 DATES

The contestable and suicide periods commence with the Date of Issue. Policy months, years and anniversaries are computed from the Policy Date. Both dates are shown on page 2 of this policy.

1.5 MISSTATEMENT OF AGE

If the age of the Insured has been misstated, the amount payable shall be the amount which the premiums paid would have purchased at the correct age.

1.6 GENERAL

This policy and the application, a copy of which is attached when the policy is issued, constitute the entire contract. All statements in the application are representations and not warranties. No statement shall void this policy or be used in defense of a claim under it unless contained in the application.

Only an officer of the Company is authorized to alter this policy or to waive any of the Company's rights or requirements.

All payments by the Company under this policy are payable at its Home Office.

SECTION 2. OWNERSHIP

2.1 THE OWNER

The Owner is as shown on page 2, or his successor or transferee. All policy rights and privileges may be exercised by the Owner without the consent of any beneficiary. Such rights and privileges may be exercised only during the lifetime of the Insured and thereafter to the extent permitted by Sections 8 and 9.

2.2 TRANSFER OF OWNERSHIP

The Owner may transfer the ownership of this policy by filing written evidence of transfer satisfactory to the Company at its Home Office and, unless waived by the Company, submitting the policy for endorsement to show the transfer.

2.3 COLLATERAL ASSIGNMENT

The Owner may assign this policy as collateral security. The Company assumes no responsibility for the validity or effect of any collateral assignment of this policy. The Company shall not be charged with notice of any assignment unless the assignment is in writing and filed at its Home Office before payment is made.

The interest of any beneficiary shall be subordinate to any collateral assignment made either before or after the beneficiary designation.

A collateral assignee is not an Owner and a collateral assignment is not a transfer of ownership.

SECTION 3. PREMIUMS AND REINSTATEMENT

3.1 PREMIUMS

(a) Payment. All premiums after the first are payable at the Home Office or to an authorized agent. A receipt signed by an officer of the Company will be provided upon request.

(b) Frequency. Premiums may be paid annually, semiannually, or quarterly at the published rates for this policy. A change to any such frequency shall be effective upon acceptance by the Company of the premium for the changed frequency. Premiums may be paid on any other frequency approved by the Company.

(c) Default. If a premium is not paid on or before its due date, this policy shall terminate on the due date except as provided in Sections 3.1(d), 5.3 and 5.4.

(d) Grace Period. A grace period of 31 days shall be allowed for payment of a premium not paid on its due date. The policy shall continue in full force during this period. If the Insured dies during the grace period, the overdue premium shall be paid from the proceeds of the policy.

(e) Premium Refund at Death. The portion of any premium paid which applies to a period beyond the policy month in which the Insured died shall be refunded as part of the proceeds of this policy.

3.2 REINSTATEMENT

If the policy has not been surrendered for its cash value, it may be reinstated within five years after the due date of the unpaid premium provided the following conditions are satisfied:

(a) Within 31 days following expiration of the grace period, reinstatement may be made without evidence of insurability during the lifetime of the Insured by payment of the overdue premium.

(b) After 31 days following expiration of the grace period, reinstatement is subject to:

(i) receipt of evidence of insurability of the Insured satisfactory to the Company;

(ii) payment of all overdue premiums with interest from the due date of each at the rate of 6% compounded annually; or any lower rate established by the Company.

Any policy indebtedness existing on the due date of the unpaid premium, together with interest from that date, must be repaid or reinstated.

SECTION 4. DIVIDENDS

4.1 ANNUAL DIVIDENDS

This policy shall share in the divisible surplus, if any, of the Company. This policy's share shall be determined annually and credited as a dividend. Payment of the first dividend is contingent upon payment of the premium or premiums for the second policy year and shall be credited proportionately as each premium is paid. Thereafter, each dividend shall be payable on the policy anniversary.

4.2 USE OF DIVIDENDS

As directed by the Owner, dividends may be paid in cash or applied under one of the following:

(a) Paid-Up Additions. Dividends may be applied to purchase fully paid-up additional insurance. Paid-up additions will also share in the divisible surplus.

(b) Dividend Accumulations. Dividends may be left to accumulate at interest. Interest is credited at a rate of 3% compounded annually, or any higher rate established by the Company.

(c) Premium Payment. Dividends may be applied toward payment of any premium due within one year, if the balance of the premium is paid. If the balance is not paid, or if this policy is in force as paid-up insurance, the dividend will be applied to purchase paid-up additions.

If no direction is given by the Owner, dividends will be applied to purchase paid-up additions.

4.3 USE OF ADDITIONS AND ACCUMULATIONS

Paid-up additions and dividend accumulations increase the policy's cash value and loan value and are payable as part of the policy proceeds. Additions may be surrendered and accumulations withdrawn unless required under the Loan, Extended Term Insurance, or Paid-up Insurance provisions.

4.4 DIVIDEND AT DEATH

A dividend for the period from the beginning of the policy year to the end of the policy month in which the Insured dies shall be paid as part of the policy proceeds.

4

SECTION 5. CASH VALUE, EXTENDED TERM AND PAID-UP INSURANCE

5.1 CASH VALUE

The cash value, when all premiums due have been paid, shall be the reserve on this policy less the deduction described in Section 5.5, plus the reserve for any paid-up additions and the amount of any dividend accumulations.

The cash value within three months after the due date of any unpaid premium shall be the cash value on the due date reduced by any subsequent surrender of paid-up additions or withdrawal of dividend accumulations. The cash value at any time after such three months shall be the reserve on the form of insurance then in force, plus the reserve for any paid-up additions and the amount of any dividend accumulations.

If this policy is surrendered within 31 days after a policy anniversary, the cash value shall be not less than the cash value on that anniversary.

5.2 CASH SURRENDER

The Owner may surrender this policy for its cash value less any indebtedness. The policy shall terminate upon receipt at the Home Office of this policy and a written surrender of all claims. Receipt of the policy may be waived by the Company.

The Company may defer paying the cash value for a period not exceeding six months from the date of surrender. If payment is deferred 30 days or more, interest shall be paid on the cash value less any indebtedness at the rate of 3% compounded annually from the date of surrender to the date of payment.

5.3 EXTENDED TERM INSURANCE

If any premium remains unpaid at the end of the grace period, this policy shall continue in force as nonparticipating extended term insurance. The amount of insurance shall be the amount of this policy, plus any paid-up additions and dividend accumulations, less any indebtedness. The term insurance shall begin as of the due date of the unpaid premium and its duration shall be determined by applying the cash value less any indebtedness as a net single premium at the attained age of the Insured. If the term insurance would extend to or beyond attained age 100, paid-up insurance under Section 5.4 below will be provided instead.

5.4 PAID-UP INSURANCE

In lieu of extended term insurance this policy may be continued in force as participating paid-up life insurance.

Paid-up insurance may be requested by written notice filed at the Home Office before, or within three months after, the due date of the unpaid premium. The insurance will be for the amount that the cash value will purchase as a net single premium at the attained age of the Insured. Any indebtedness shall remain outstanding.

5.5 TABLE OF GUARANTEED VALUES

The cash values, paid-up insurance, and extended term insurance shown on page 2 are for the end of the policy year indicated. These values are based on the assumption that premiums have been paid for the number of years stated and are exclusive of any paid-up additions, dividend accumulations, or indebtedness. During the policy year allowance shall be made for any portion of a year's premium paid and for the time elapsed in that year. Values for policy years not shown are calculated on the same basis as this table and will be furnished on request. All values are equal to or greater than those required by the State in which this policy is delivered.

In determining cash values a deduction is made from the reserve. During the first five policy years, the deduction for each $1,000 of Amount is $9 plus $.15 for each year of the Insured's issue age. After the fifth policy year, the deduction decreases yearly by one-fifth of the initial deduction until there is no deduction in the tenth and subsequent policy years. If the premium paying period is less than ten years, there is no deduction in the last two policy years of the premium paying period or thereafter.

5.6 RESERVES AND NET PREMIUMS

Reserves, net premiums and present values are determined in accordance with the Commissioners 1958 Standard Ordinary Mortality Table and 3% interest, except that for the first five years of any extended term insurance, the Commissioners 1958 Extended Term Insurance Table is used. All reserves are based on continuous payment of premiums and immediate payment of claims. Net annual premiums are the same in each policy year, except that if premiums are payable for more than 20 years, the net annual premium in the 21st and subsequent policy years is determined by applying the percentage shown on page 2 to the net annual premium for the 20th policy year. On the Policy Date, the present value of all future guaranteed benefits equals the present value of all future net annual premiums. The reserve at the end of any policy year is the excess of the present value of all future guaranteed benefits over the present value of all future net annual premiums. The reserve is exclusive of any additional benefits.

SECTION 6. LOANS

6.1 POLICY LOAN

The Owner may obtain a policy loan by assignment of this policy to the Company. The amount of the loan, plus any existing indebtedness, shall not exceed the loan value. No loan shall be granted if the policy is in force as extended term insurance. The Company may defer making a loan for six months unless the loan is to be used to pay premiums on policies issued by the Company.

6.2 PREMIUM LOAN

A premium loan shall be granted to pay an overdue premium if the premium loan option is in effect. If the loan value, less any indebtedness, is insufficient to pay the overdue premium, a premium will be paid for any other frequency permitted by this policy for which the loan value less any indebtedness is sufficient. The premium loan option may be elected or revoked by written notice filed at the Home Office.

6.3 LOAN VALUE

The loan value is the largest amount which, with accrued interest, does not exceed the cash value either on the next premium due date or at the end of one year from the date of the loan.

6.4 LOAN INTEREST

Interest is payable at the rate of 8% compounded annually, or at any lower rate established by the Company for any period during which the loan is outstanding.

The Company shall provide at least 30 days written notice to the Owner (or any other party designated by the Owner to receive notice under this policy) and any assignee recorded at the Home Office of any increase in interest rate on loans outstanding 40 or more days prior to the effective date of the increase.

Interest accrues on a daily basis from the date of the loan on policy loans and from the premium due date on premium loans, and is compounded annually. Interest unpaid on a loan anniversary is added to and becomes part of the loan principal and bears interest on the same terms.

6.5 INDEBTEDNESS

Indebtedness consists of unpaid policy and premium loans on the policy including accrued interest. Indebtedness may be repaid at any time. Any unpaid indebtedness will be deducted from the policy proceeds.

If indebtedness equals or exceeds the cash value, this policy shall terminate. Termination shall occur 31 days after a notice has been mailed to the address of record of the Owner and of any assignee recorded at the Home Office.

SECTION 7. CHANGE OF POLICY

7 CHANGE OF PLAN

The Owner may change this policy to any permanent life or endowment plan offered by the Company on the Date of Issue of this policy. The change may be made upon payment of any cost and subject to the conditions determined by the Company. For a change made after the first year to a plan having a higher reserve, the cost shall not exceed the difference in cash values or the difference in reserves, whichever is greater, plus 3½% of such difference.

SECTION 8. BENEFICIARIES

8.1 DESIGNATION AND CHANGE OF BENEFICIARIES

(a) By Owner. The Owner may designate and change direct and contingent beneficiaries and further payees of death proceeds:

(1) during the lifetime of the Insured.

(2) during the 60 days following the date of death of the Insured, if the Insured immediately before his death was not the Owner. Any such designation of direct beneficiary may not be changed. If the Owner is the direct beneficiary and elects a payment plan, any such designation of contingent beneficiaries and further payees may be changed.

(b) By Direct Beneficiary. The direct beneficiary may designate and change contingent beneficiaries and further payees if:

(1) the direct beneficiary is the Owner.

(2) at any time after the death of the Insured, no contingent beneficiary or further payee is living, and no designation is made by the Owner under Section 8.1 (a) (2).

(3) the direct beneficiary elects a payment plan after the death of the Insured, in which case the interest in the share of such direct beneficiary or any other payee designated by the Owner shall terminate.

(c) By Spouse (Marital Deduction Provision). Notwithstanding any provision of Section 8 or 9 of this policy to the contrary, if the Insured immediately before death was the Owner and if the direct beneficiary is the spouse of the Insured and survives the Insured, such direct beneficiary shall have the power to appoint all amounts payable under the policy either to the executors or administrators of the direct beneficiary's estate or to such other contingent beneficiaries and further payees as he may designate. The exercise of that power shall revoke any then existing designation of contingent beneficiaries and further payees and any election of a payment plan applying to them.

(d) Effective Date. Any designation or change of beneficiary shall be made by the filing and recording at the Home Office of a written request satisfactory to the Company. Unless waived by the Company, the request must be endorsed on the policy. Upon the recording, the request will take effect as of the date it was signed. The Company will not be held responsible for any payment or other action taken by it before the recording of the request.

8.2 SUCCESSION IN INTEREST OF BENEFICIARIES

(a) Direct Beneficiaries. The proceeds of this policy shall be payable in equal shares to the direct beneficiaries who survive to receive payment. The unpaid share of any direct beneficiary who dies while receiving payment shall be payable in equal shares to the direct beneficiaries who survive to receive payment.

(b) Contingent Beneficiaries. At the death of the last surviving direct beneficiary, payments due or to become due shall be payable in equal shares to the contingent beneficiaries who survive to receive payment. The unpaid share of any contingent beneficiary who dies while receiving payment shall be payable in equal shares to the contingent beneficiaries who survive to receive payment.

(c) Further Payees. At the death of the last to survive of the direct and contingent beneficiaries, the proceeds, or the withdrawal value of any payments due or to become due if a payment plan is in effect, shall be paid in one sum:

(1) in equal shares to the further payees who survive to receive payment; or
(2) if no further payees survive to receive payment, to the executors or administrators of the last to survive of the direct and contingent beneficiaries.

(d) Estate of Owner. If no direct or contingent beneficiaries or further payees survive the Insured, the proceeds shall be paid to the Owner or the executors or administrators of the Owner.

8.3 GENERAL

(a) Transfer of Ownership. A transfer of ownership will not change the interest of any beneficiary.

(b) Claims of Creditors. So far as permitted by law, no amount payable under this policy shall be subject to the claims of creditors of the payee.

(c) Succession under Payment Plans. A direct or contingent beneficiary succeeding to an interest in a payment plan shall continue under such plan subject to its terms, with the rights of transfer between plans and of withdrawal under plans as provided in this policy.

SECTION 9. PAYMENT OF POLICY BENEFITS

9.1 PAYMENT

Payment of policy benefits upon surrender or maturity will be made in cash or under one of the payment plans described in Section 9.2, if elected.

If policy benefits become payable by reason of the Insured's death, payment will be made under any payment plan then in effect. If no election of a payment plan is in effect, the proceeds will be held under the Interest Income Plan (Option A) with interest accumulating from the date of death until an election or cash withdrawal is made.

9.2 PAYMENT PLANS

(a) Interest Income Plan (Option A). The proceeds will earn interest which may be received in monthly payments or accumulated. The first interest payment is due one month after the plan becomes effective. Withdrawal of accumulated interest as well as full or partial proceeds may be made at any time.

(b) Installment Income Plans. Monthly installment income payments will be made as provided by the plan elected. The first payment is due on the date the plan becomes effective.

(1) Specified Period (Option B). Monthly installment income payments will be made providing for payment of the proceeds with interest over a specified period of one to 30 years. Withdrawal of the present value of any unpaid installments may be made at any time.

(2) Specified Amount (Option D). Monthly installment income payments will be made for a specified amount of not less than $5 per $1,000 of proceeds. Payments will continue until the entire proceeds with interest are paid, with the final payment not exceeding the unpaid balance. Withdrawal of the unpaid balance may be made at any time.

(c) Life Income Plans. Monthly life income payments will be made as provided by the plan elected. The first payment is due on the date the plan becomes effective. Proof of date of birth satisfactory to the Company must be furnished for any individual upon whose life income payments depend.

(1) Single Life Income (Option C). Monthly payments will be made for the selected certain period, if any, and thereafter during the remaining lifetime of the individual upon whose life income payments depend. The selections available are:

    (i) no certain period,
    (ii) a certain period of 10 or 20 years, or
    (iii) a refund certain period such that the sum of the income payments during the certain period will be equal to the proceeds applied under the plan, with the final payment not exceeding the unpaid balance.

(2) Joint and Survivor Life Income (Option E). Monthly payments will be made for a 10 year certain period and thereafter during the joint lifetime of the two individuals upon whose lives income payments depend and continuing during the remaining lifetime of the survivor.

(3) Withdrawal. Withdrawal of the present value of any unpaid income payments which were to be made during a certain period may be made at any time after the death of all individuals upon whose lives income payments depend.

(d) Payment Frequency. In lieu of monthly payments a quarterly, semiannual or annual frequency may be selected.

9.3 PAYMENT PLAN RATES

(a) Interest Income and Installment Income Plans. Proceeds under the Interest Income and Installment Income plans will earn interest at rates declared annually by the Company, but not less than a rate of 3% compounded annually. Interest in excess of 3% will increase payments, except that for the Installment Income Specified Amount Plan (Option D), excess interest will be applied to lengthen the period during which payments are made.

The present value for withdrawal purposes will be based on a rate of 3% compounded annually.

The Company may from time to time also make available higher guaranteed interest rates under the Interest Income and Installment Income plans, with certain conditions on withdrawal as then published by the Company for those plans.

(b) Life Income Plans. Life Income Plan payments will be based on rates declared by the Company. These rates will provide not less than 104% of the income provided by the Company's Immediate Annuities being offered on the date the plan becomes effective. The rates are based on the sex and age nearest birthday of any individual upon whose life income payments depend, and adjusted for any certain period and the immediate payment of the first income payment. In no event will payments under these rates be less than the minimums described in Section 9.3(c).

(c) Minimum Income Payments. Minimum monthly income payments for the Installment Income Plans (Options B and D) and the Life Income Plans (Options C and E) are shown in the Minimum Income Table. The minimum Life Income payments are determined as of the date the payment plan becomes effective and depend on the age nearest birthday adjusted for policy duration.

The adjusted age is equal to the age nearest birthday decreased by one year if more than 25 years have elapsed since the Policy Date, two years if more than 35 years have elapsed, three years if more than 40 years have elapsed, four years if more than 45 years have elapsed or five years if more than 50 years have elapsed.

8

9.4 ELECTION OF PAYMENT PLANS

(a) **Effective Date.** Election of payment plans for death proceeds made by the Owner and filed at the Home Office during the Insured's lifetime will be effective on the date of death of the Insured. All other elections of payment plans will be effective when filed at the Home Office, or later if specified.

(b) **Death Proceeds.** Payment plans for death proceeds may be elected:

(1) by the Owner during the lifetime of the Insured.

(2) by the Owner during the 60 days following the date of death of the Insured, if the Insured immediately before his death was not the Owner. Any such election may not be changed by the Owner.

(3) by a direct or contingent beneficiary to whom such proceeds become payable, if no election is then in effect and no election is made by the Owner under Section 9.4(b) (2).

(c) **Surrender or Maturity Proceeds.** Payment plans for surrender or maturity proceeds may be elected by the Owner for himself as direct beneficiary.

(d) **Transfers Between Payment Plans.** A direct or contingent beneficiary receiving payment under a payment plan with the right to withdraw may elect to transfer the withdrawal value to any other payment plan then available.

(e) **Life Income Plan Limitations.** An individual beneficiary may receive payments under a Life Income Plan only if the payments depend upon his life. A corporation may receive payments under a Life Income Plan only if the payments depend upon the life of the Insured, or a surviving spouse or dependent of the Insured.

(f) **Minimum Amounts.** Proceeds of less than $5,000 may not be applied without the Company's approval under any payment plan except the Interest Income Plan (Option A) with interest accumulated. The Company retains the right to change the payment frequency or pay the withdrawal value if payments under a payment plan are or become less than $25.

9.5 INCREASE OF MONTHLY INCOME

The direct beneficiary who is to receive the proceeds of this policy under a payment plan may increase the total monthly income by payment of an annuity premium to the Company. The premium, after deduction of charges not exceeding 2% and any applicable premium tax, shall be applied under the payment plan at the same rates as the policy proceeds. The net amount so applied may not exceed twice the proceeds payable under this policy.

MINIMUM INCOME TABLE

Minimum Monthly Income Payments Per $1,000 Proceeds

INSTALLMENT INCOME PLANS (Options B and D)

PERIOD (YEARS)	MONTHLY PAYMENT	PERIOD (YEARS)	MONTHLY PAYMENT	PERIOD (YEARS)	MONTHLY PAYMENT
1	$84.50	11	$8.86	21	$5.32
2	42.87	12	8.24	22	5.15
3	29.00	13	7.71	23	4.99
4	22.07	14	7.26	24	4.84
5	17.91	15	6.87	25	4.71
6	15.14	16	6.53	26	4.59
7	13.17	17	6.23	27	4.48
8	11.69	18	5.96	28	4.37
9	10.54	19	5.73	29	4.27
10	9.62	20	5.51	30	4.18

MINIMUM INCOME TABLE

Minimum Monthly Income Payments Per $1,000 Proceeds

LIFE INCOME PLANS

SINGLE LIFE MONTHLY PAYMENTS (Option C)					
ADJUSTED AGE		CERTAIN PERIOD			
MALE	FEMALE	NONE	10 YEARS	20 YEARS	REFUND
50	55	$ 4.62	$4.56	$4.34	$4.36
51	56	4.72	4.65	4.40	4.44
52	57	4.83	4.75	4.46	4.52
53	58	4.94	4.85	4.53	4.61
54	59	5.07	4.96	4.59	4.69
55	60	5.20	5.07	4.66	4.79
56	61	5.33	5.19	4.72	4.88
57	62	5.48	5.31	4.78	4.99
58	63	5.64	5.43	4.84	5.09
59	64	5.80	5.57	4.90	5.20
60	65	5.98	5.70	4.96	5.32
61	66	6.16	5.85	5.02	5.44
62	67	6.36	5.99	5.07	5.57
63	68	6.57	6.14	5.13	5.71
64	69	6.79	6.30	5.17	5.85
65	70	7.03	6.45	5.22	6.00
66	71	7.28	6.62	5.26	6.15
67	72	7.54	6.78	5.30	6.31
68	73	7.83	6.95	5.33	6.48
69	74	8.13	7.11	5.36	6.66
70	75	8.45	7.28	5.39	6.85
71	76	8.79	7.45	5.41	7.05
72	77	9.16	7.62	5.43	7.26
73	78	9.55	7.79	5.45	7.48
74	79	9.96	7.95	5.46	7.71
75	80	10.41	8.11	5.48	7.95

JOINT AND SURVIVOR MONTHLY PAYMENTS (Option E)

ADJUSTED AGE   JOINT PAYEE ADJUSTED AGE

MALE		45	50	55	60	65	70	75
	FEMALE	50	55	60	65	70	75	80
45	50	$3.68	$3.80	$3.90	$3.97	$4.02	$4.06	$4.10
50	55	3.80	3.97	4.13	4.25	4.34	4.41	4.46
55	60	3.90	4.13	4.35	4.56	4.72	4.84	4.92
60	65	3.97	4.25	4.56	4.86	5.13	5.33	5.48
65	70	4.02	4.34	4.72	5.13	5.51	5.85	6.10
70	75	4.06	4.41	4.84	5.33	5.85	6.33	6.73
75	80	4.10	4.46	4.92	5.48	6.10	6.73	7.28

10

WAIVER OF PREMIUM BENEFIT

1. THE BENEFIT

If total disability of the Insured commences before the policy anniversary nearest his 60th birthday, the Company will waive the payment of premiums becoming due during total disability of the Insured.

If total disability of the Insured commences on or after the policy anniversary nearest his 60th birthday but before the policy anniversary nearest his 65th birthday, the Company will waive the payment of premiums becoming due during total disability of the Insured and before the policy anniversary nearest his 65th birthday.

The Company will refund that portion of any premium paid which applies to a period of total disability beyond the policy month in which the disability began.

The premium for this benefit is shown on page 2.

2. DEFINITION OF TOTAL DISABILITY

Total disability means disability which:

(a) resulted from bodily injury or disease;
(b) began after the Date of Issue of this policy and before the policy anniversary nearest the Insured's 65th birthday;
(c) has existed continuously for at least six months; and
(d) prevents the Insured from engaging in an occupation. During the first 24 months of disability, occupation means the occupation of the Insured at the time such disability began; thereafter it means any occupation for which he is reasonably fitted by education, training or experience, with due regard to his vocation and earnings prior to disability.

The total and irrecoverable loss of the sight of both eyes, or of speech or hearing, or of the use of both hands, or of both feet, or of one hand and one foot, shall be considered total disability, even if the Insured shall engage in an occupation.

3. PROOF OF DISABILITY

Before any premium is waived, proof of total disability must be received by the Company at its Home Office:

(a) during the lifetime of the Insured;
(b) during the continuance of total disability; and
(c) not later than one year after the policy anniversary nearest the Insured's 65th birthday.

Premiums will be waived although proof of total disability was not given within the time specified, if it is shown that it was given as soon as reasonably possible, but not later than one year after recovery.

4. PROOF OF CONTINUANCE OF DISABILITY

Proof of the continuance of total disability may be required once a year. If such proof is not furnished, no further premiums shall be waived. Further proof of continuance of disability will no longer be required if, on the policy anniversary nearest the Insured's 65th birthday, the Insured is then and has been totally and continuously disabled for five or more years.

5. PREMIUMS

Any premium becoming due during disability and before receipt of proof of total disability is payable and should be paid. Any such premiums paid shall be refunded by the Company upon acceptance of proof of total disability. If such premiums are not paid, this benefit shall be allowed if total disability is shown to have begun before the end of the grace period of the first unpaid premium.

If on any policy anniversary following the date of disablement the Insured continues to be disabled and this benefit has not terminated, an annual premium will be waived.

6. TERMINATION

This benefit shall be in effect while this policy is in force, but shall terminate on the policy anniversary nearest the Insured's 65th birthday unless the Insured is then totally disabled and such disability occurred prior to the policy anniversary nearest the Insured's 60th birthday. It may also be terminated within 31 days of a premium due date upon receipt at the Home Office of the Owner's written request.

ACCIDENTAL DEATH BENEFIT

1. THE BENEFIT

The Company agrees to pay an Accidental Death Benefit upon receipt at its Home Office of proof that the death of the Insured resulted, directly and independently of all other causes, from accidental bodily injury, provided that death occurred while this benefit was in effect.

2. PREMIUM AND AMOUNT OF BENEFIT

The premium for and the amount of this benefit are shown on page 2. This benefit shall be payable as part of the policy proceeds.

3. RISKS NOT ASSUMED

This benefit shall not be payable for death of the Insured resulting from suicide, for death resulting from or contributed to by bodily or mental infirmity or disease, or for any other death which did not result, directly and independently of all other causes, from accidental bodily injury.

Even though death resulted directly and independently of all other causes from accidental bodily injury, this benefit shall not be payable if the death of the Insured resulted from:

(a) Any act or incident of war. The word "war" includes any war, declared or undeclared, and armed aggression resisted by the armed forces of any country or combination of countries.

(b) Riding in any kind of aircraft, unless the Insured was riding solely as a passenger in an aircraft not operated by or for the Armed Forces, or descent from any kind of aircraft while in flight. An Insured who had any duties whatsoever at any time on the flight or any leg of the flight with respect to any purpose of the flight or to the aircraft or who was participating in training shall not be considered a passenger.

4. TERMINATION

This benefit shall be in effect while this policy is in force other than under the Extended Term Insurance or Paid-up Insurance provisions, but shall terminate on the policy anniversary nearest the Insured's 70th birthday. It may also be terminated within 31 days of a premium due date upon receipt at the Home Office of the Owner's written request.

David Olson
Secretary
THE COUNCIL LIFE INSURANCE COMPANY

RECEIPT FOR PAYMENT AND CONDITIONAL LIFE INSURANCE AGREEMENT

THOMAS A. BENSON $10,000   LIFE POLICY - PARTICIPATING
Name of Proposed Insured   Face Amount   Plan
Received of ___ THOMAS A. BENSON ___
the sum of $ __241.60__ for the policy applied for in the application to THE COUNCIL INSURANCE COMPANY (CL) with the same date and number as this receipt. Checks, drafts, and money orders are accepted subject to collection.

NEW YORK, N.Y., Nov 1 19 80 . J.R. Washington ___ Agent.
Place and Date

CONDITIONAL LIFE INSURANCE AGREEMENT

I. **No Insurance Ever in Force.** No insurance shall be in force at any time if the proposed insured is not an acceptable risk on the Underwriting Date for the policy applied for according to CL's rules and standards. No insurance shall be in force under an Additional Benefit for which the proposed insured is not an acceptable risk.

II. **Conditional Life Insurance.** If the proposed insured is an acceptable risk on the Underwriting Date, the insurance shall be in force subject to the following maximum amounts if the proposed insured dies before the policy is issued:

When premium is paid at the time of application, complete this Agreement and give to the Applicant. No other Agreement will be recognized by the Company. If premium is not paid—do not detach.

Life Insurance			Accidental Death Benefit	
Age at Issue	Policies Issued at Standard Premiums	Policies Issued at Higher Premiums	Age at Issue	Maximum Amount
0-24	$ 500,000	$250,000	0-14	$ 25,000
25-45	1,000,000	500,000	15-19	50,000
46-55	800,000	400,000	20-24	75,000
56-65	400,000	200,000	25-60	150,000
66-70	200,000	100,000	Over 60	-0-
Over 70	-0-	-0-		

Reduction in Maximum Amounts. The maximum amounts set forth in the preceding table shall be reduced by any existing CL insurance on the life of the proposed insured with an Issue Date within 90 days of the date of this Agreement or by any pending prepaid applications for CL insurance on the life of the proposed insured with an Underwriting Date within 90 days of the date of this Agreement.

Termination of Conditional Life Insurance. If the proposed insured is an acceptable risk for the policy applied for according to CL's rules and standards only at a premium higher than the premium paid, any insurance under this Agreement shall terminate on the date stated in a notice mailed by CL to the applicant unless by such date the applicant accepts delivery of the policy and pays the additional premium required.

Underwriting Date. The Underwriting Date is the date of page 2 (90-2) of the application or the date of the medical examination [if required, otherwise the date of the nonmedical, page 4 (90-4)], whichever is the later.

III. **Premium Adjustment.** If the proposed insured is an acceptable risk for the policy applied for only at a premium higher than the premium paid and dies before paying the additional premium required, that additional premium shall be subtracted from the insurance benefit payable to the beneficiary.

IV. **Premium Refund.** Any premium paid for any insurance or Additional Benefit not issued or issued at a higher premium but not accepted by the applicant shall be returned to the applicant.

NOT A "BINDER"—NO INSURANCE WHERE SECTION I APPLIES—NO AGENT MAY MODIFY.

PART I   Life Insurance Application To *The COUNCIL Life Insurance Company*

IMPORTANT NOTICE—This application is subject to approval by the Company's Home Office. Be sure all questions in all parts of the application are answered completely and accurately, since the application is the basis of the insurance contract and will become part of any policy issued.

1. Insured's Full Name (Please Print-Give title as Mr., Dr., Rev., etc.)

MR. THOMAS A. BENSON

Single ☐   Married ☑   Widowed ☐   Divorced ☐   Separated ☐

Mo., Day, Yr. of Birth	Ins. Age	Sex	Place of Birth	Social Security No.
APRIL 6, 1943	37	M	BOSTON, MASS.	000-00-0000

2. Addresses last 5 yrs.

		Number	Street	City	State	Zip Code	County	Yrs.
Mail to ☐ Home:	Present	217	E. 62 STREET	NEW YORK, N.Y.		10017	NEW YORK	6
	Former							
☑ Business:	Present	PEPPER, GRINSTEAD, & CROUCH 55 E. 49TH ST				10017	NEW YORK	7
	Former							

3. Occupation

	Title	Describe Exact Duties	Yrs.
Present	ATTORNEY	REPRESENTS CLIENTS IN LEGAL MATTERS	7
Former			

4. a) Employer

b) Any change contemplated? Yes ☐ (Explain in Remarks)   No ☑

5. Have you ever   Yes   No

a) been rejected, deferred or discharged by the Armed Forces for medical reasons or applied for a government disability rating? ☐ ☑

b) applied for insurance or for reinstatement which was declined, postponed, modified or rated? ☐ ☑

c) used LSD, heroin, cocaine or methadone? ☐ ☑

6. a) In the past 3 years have you

(i) had your driver's license suspended or revoked or been convicted of more than one speeding violation? ☐ ☑

(ii) operated, been a crew member of, or had any duties aboard any kind of aircraft? ☐ ☑

(iii) engaged in underwater diving below 40 feet, parachuting, or motor vehicle racing? ☐ ☑

b) In the future, do you intend to engage in any activities mentioned in (ii) and (iii) of a) above? ☐ ☑
(If "Yes" to 5a or any of 6, complete Supplemental Form 3375)

7. Have you smoked one or more cigarettes within the past 12 months? ☑ ☐

8. Are other insurance applications pending or contemplated? ☐ ☑

9. Do you intend to go to any foreign country? ☑ ☐

10. Will coverage applied for replace or change any life insurance or annuities? (If "Yes", submit Replacement Form) ☐ ☑

11. Total Life Insurance in force $ 35,000   None ☐

12. Face Amount $ 10,000   Plan WL

Accidental Death ☑   Waiver of Premium ☐

Purchase Option   Regular ☐   Preferred ☐   PEP ☐   GOR ☐

_____ units of Wife's Term - name: _____

$ _____ initial amount Decreasing Term, _____ Years

(Joint ☐)   (Mot. Pro. ☐)   (Straight Line ☐)

Children's Term ☐   Other: _____

13. Auto. Prem. Loan provision operative if available? Yes ☐   No ☑

14. Dividend Option

Additions (for other than Term policies) ☐   Deposits ☐

Reduce premium, if applicable, otherwise cash ☑

Supplemental Protection (Keyman only) ☐

1 Year Term—any balance to

Deposits ☐   Additions ☐   Reduce prem. (cash if mo.) ☐

15. Beneficiary - for children's, wife's or joint insurance as provided in contract; for other insurance as follows, subject to policy's beneficiary provisions.

	(Name)	(Relationship to Insured)	
1st	HELEN M. BENSON	WIFE	if living, if not
2nd	DAVID A. BENSON	SON	if living, if not
3rd			if living, if not

the executors or administrators of: Insured ☑   Other (use Remarks) ☐
(Joint beneficiaries will receive equally or survivor, unless otherwise specified.)

16. Flexible Plan settlement (personal beneficiary only) ☐

17. Rights During Insured's lifetime all rights belong to

Insured ☑   Other: _____

Trustee ☐
(attach Trust)
(After Insured's death as provided in contract on wife's insurance.)

18. Premium—Frequency ANNUAL Amt. Paid $ 241.60   None ☐
Have you received a Conditional Receipt? Yes ☑   No ☐

REMARKS [Include details (company, date, amt., etc.) for all "Yes" answers to questions 4b, 5b, 5c, 8, 9 and 10]

Q9: PLANS VACATION IN SWITZERLAND

I agree that: (1) No one but the Company's President, a Vice-President or Secretary has authority to accept information not contained in the application, to modify or enlarge any contract, or to waive any requirement. (2) Except as otherwise provided in any conditional receipt issued, any policy issued shall take effect upon its delivery and payment of the first premium during the lifetime of each person to be insured. Due dates of later premiums shall be as specified in the policy.

Dated at NEW YORK, N.Y. on NOVEMBER 1 19 80   Signature of Insured Thomas A. Benson

Signature of Applicant (if other than Insured) who agrees to be bound by the representations and agreements in this and any other part of this application _____

     (Name)   (Relationship)   (Complete address of Applicant)

Countersigned by Ed Haley

     Field Underwriter (Licensed Resident Agent)

13

PART 1A	Statements Forming Part Of Application To *The COUNCIL Life Insurance Company*
	[Complete this Part if any Non-Medical or Family Insurance is Applied For]

1. Name of Insured *THOMAS A. BENSON*   Ins. Age *37*   Height *6* ft. *1* in.   Weight *185* lbs.

2. If Family, Children's, Wife's or Joint Insurance desired, other family members proposed for insurance:

Wife (include maiden name)	Ins. Age	Mo., Day, Yr. of Birth	Height ft. in.	Weight lbs.	Life in Force $	Place of Birth

Children	Sex	Ins. Age	Mo., Day, Yr. of Birth	Children	Sex	Ins. Age	Mo., Day, Yr. of Birth

3. Has any eligible dependent (a) been omitted from 2? Yes ☐ No ☐ (b) applied for insurance or for reinstatement which was declined, postponed, modified or rated or had a policy cancelled or renewal refused? Yes ☐ No ☐ (Give name, date, company in 8)

4. Have you or anyone else proposed for insurance, so far as you know, ever been treated for or had indication of (underline applicable item)

		Yes	No
a)	high blood pressure? (If "Yes", list drugs prescribed and dates taken.)	☐	☑
b)	chest pain, heart attack, rheumatic fever, heart murmur, irregular pulse or other disorder of the heart or blood vessels?	☐	☑
c)	cancer, tumor, cyst, or any disorder of the thyroid, skin, or lymph glands?	☐	☑
d)	diabetes or anemia or other blood disorder?	☐	☑
e)	sugar, albumin, blood or pus in the urine, or venereal disease?	☐	☑
f)	any disorder of the kidney, bladder, prostate, breast or reproductive organs?	☐	☑
g)	ulcer, intestinal bleeding, hepatitis, colitis, or other disorder of the stomach, intestine, spleen, pancreas, liver or gall bladder?	☐	☑
h)	asthma, tuberculosis, bronchitis, emphysema or other disorder of the lungs?	☐	☑
i)	fainting, convulsions, migraine headache, paralysis, epilepsy or any mental or nervous disorder?	☐	☑
j)	arthritis, gout, amputation, sciatica, back pain or other disorder of the muscles, bones or joints?	☐	☑
k)	disorder of the eyes, ears, nose, throat or sinuses?	☐	☑
l)	varicose veins, hemorrhoids, hernia or rectal disorder?	☐	☑
m)	alcoholism or drug habit?	☐	☑

5. Have you or anyone else proposed for insurance, so far as you know, (underline applicable item)

		Yes	No
a)	consulted or been examined or treated by any physician or practitioner in the past 5 years?	☑	☐
b)	had, or been advised to have, an x-ray, cardiogram, blood or other diagnostic test in the past 5 years?	☑	☐
c)	been a patient in a hospital, clinic, or other medical facility in the past 5 years?	☐	☑
d)	ever had a surgical operation performed or advised?	☑	☐
e)	ever made claim for disability or applied for compensation or retirement based on accident or sickness?	☐	☑

6. Are you or any other person proposed for insurance, so far as you know, in impaired physical or mental health, or under any kind of medication?   Yes ☐ No ☑

7. Weight change in last 6 months of adults proposed for insurance: *N.A.*

Name	Gain	Loss	Cause

8. Details of all "Yes" answers. For any checkup or routine examination, indicate what symptoms, if any, prompted it and include results of the examination and any special tests. Include clinic number if applicable.

Question No.	Name of Person	Illness & Treatment	No. of Attacks	Dates: Onset-Recovery	Doctor, Clinic or Hospital and Complete Address
5a	THOMAS A. BENSON	ANNUAL CHECKUP	—	—	LIFE EXTENSION INSTITUTE
5b	THOMAS A. BENSON	ROUTINE OF ANNUAL CHECKUP	—	—	"
5d	THOMAS A. BENSON	TONSILLECTOMY-AGE 5	1	JUNE 1949	BOSTON HOSPITAL 2 PITTS STREET, BOSTON, MASS.

So far as may be lawful, I waive for myself and all persons claiming an interest in any insurance issued on this application, all provisions of law forbidding any physician or other person who has attended or examined, or who may attend or examine, me or any other person covered by such insurance, from disclosing any knowledge or information which he thereby acquired.

I represent the statements and answers in this and in any other part of this application to be true and complete to the best of my knowledge and belief, and offer them to the Company for the purpose of inducing it to issue the policy or policies and to accept the payment of premiums thereunder. I also agree that payment of the first premium (if after this date) shall be a representation by me that such statements and answers would be the same if made at the time of such payment.

Dated at *NEW YORK, N.Y.* on *NOV.1* 19 *80*   Signature of Insured *Thomas A. Benson*

Witnessed by *Ed Hooley*   Signature of Wife (if insured) _____
Field Underwriter (Licensed Resident Agent)

AUTHORIZATION

For purposes of determining my eligibility for insurance, I hereby authorize any physician, practitioner, hospital, clinic, institution, insurance company, Medical Information Bureau, or other organization or person that has records or knowledge of me or my health to give any such information to the Council Life Insurance Company.

If application is made to The Council Life Insurance Company for insurance on any member of my family, this authorization also applies to such member. A photostatic copy of this authorization shall be as valid as the original.

Signed on *NOVEMBER 1* , 19 *80*   *Thomas A. Benson*
Signature of Insured

APPENDIX D

Answers to Objective Questions

				Question				
Chapter	1	2	3	4	5	6	7	8
1	C	A	D	C	D	A	A	B
2	C	A	B	C	D	C	C	A
3	D	C	A	A	B	D	A	C
4	B	C	D	C	A	B	A	C
5	B	A	A	D	D	A	C	B
6	A	B	C	B	D	B	A	C
7	D	C	C	B	B	D	A	D
8	C	A	D	A	B	A	C	B
9	A	A	D	C	D	B	B	A
10	Answers to odd-numbered questions appear in the text.							
11	Answers to odd-numbered questions appear in the text.							
12	C	A	C	C	B	A	D	A
13	B	A	C	C	D	B	D	A
14	B	D	A	A	C	A	D	A
15	A	C	C	B	D	A	B	C
16	C	B	D	A	C	A	D	B
17	A	C	B	B	A	C	A	D
18	C	A	D	C	A	C	B	D
19	A	C	C	B	D	A	B	C
20	A	B	C	D	B	D	C	A
21	A	D	B	A	B	D	C	C
22	D	C	C	A	A	D	B	B
23	A	B	D	C	A	C	B	D

Index

Numbers

165 lines, 170
1943 New York Standard Fire Insurance Policy (SFP), 170, 352
2001 Commissioners Standard Ordinary Mortality Table, 269
403(b) plans, 243, 425
401(k) plans, 243, 425

A

Ab initio, 156
Accelerated death benefits, 246–247
Acceptance
    of contracts, 146
    of risk, 229
Access to health care, 306
Accidental losses, 19, 39
Accidental smoke damage, 190–191
Accidents
    definition of, 18
    disability income insurance, 310–312
    double-indemnity option, 283
    duties after, 220–221
    faked, 89
Accountants, 94–95
Accounting
    disposal of property, 339
    standards, 77, 95
Accounts
    catastrophe bonds, 329
    reserves
        life insurance, 134–135
        property insurance, 133–134
    separate, 263
    trusts, 243
Accumulation period, annuities, 290
Activities
    investments, 138
    regulated, 132–140
Activities of daily living (ADL), 315
Actual authority, 83
Actual cash value (ACV), 145, 150–151, 219
Actual number of losses, 5
Actuarial data, Eastern Europe, 77–78
Actuarial Standard of Practice Number Twelve, 28
Actuaries, 95–96
Additional coverage
    definition of, 188
    homeowners (HO) insurance, 182
Adelman, Saul W., 82
Adequate rates, 137
Adequate water supply, 46
Adhesion, contracts, 145, 153–155, 162–163

Adjusted cost basis, 229
Adjusters, 90–91
    licensing qualifications, 138–140
Adjustment bureaus, 90
Admitted assets, 133
Admitted insurers, 139, 337
Adult day care, 315
Advance funding, 17
Advance premium mutual, 68–69, 73
Adverse selection, 18, 27, 92
Affirmative warranty, 156
Affirming contracts, 147
Affordability, 110
    of premiums, 18
After-market repair parts, 220
Age
    effect on annuity benefits, 295
    misstatement of, 320
Age Discrimination in Employment Act of 1967 (ADEA), 420
Agency law, 82–84
Agents, 79–81, 82–84
    adjusters, 90
    duties of, 88–89
    ethics, 101–105
    independent, 86
    insurance, 86–87
    legal issues facing, 100
    licensing
        qualifications, 138–140
        requirements, 86
    life insurance, 87
    selection of, 112, 113
Aggregate retention, 330
Agreements
    hold-harmless, 370
    insuring, 165, 167–168
Agricultural commodities, 8
Aid Association for Lutherans, 71
AIDS, high cost of health care, 302
Air conditioners, 191
Aircraft
    commercial package policy (CPP), 352
    perils, 190
Alcohol abuse, 302
Aleatory, contracts, 145, 159
Alien insurance, 139
Allocated funding, 420
All-risk policies, 153
All risks coverage, 189
Alternative risk transfer (ART) market, 324
A.M. Best Company, 112
Ambiguous contracts, 153
American Association of Insurance Services, 166
American College of Financial Planning, 228
American Council of Life Insurance, 275

American Institute of Certified Public Accountants, 228
American Medical Association (AMA), 154
Americans with Disabilities Act (ADA), 385–386
Amount at risk, universal life insurance, 260
Amount of benefits, disability income insurance, 311
Amount of insurance, selection of, 114–115
Amount of net worth, 332
Andrew (Hurricane), 21
    ordinance or law exclusion, 193
Annual apportionment of divisible surplus, 277
Annual gift tax exclusion, 241
Annually renewable term life insurance, 253
Annual-premium annuities, 289
Annual transit policy, 361
Annuitants
    definition of, 287
    number of, 293–294
Annuities
    benefits, 289–290, 293–294
    classification of, 289–294
    definitions, 287–289
    effect of age and gender, 295
    equity-indexed, 300
    Guaranteed Minimum Death Benefit (GMDB), 298–299
    Guaranteed Minimum Income Benefit (GMIB), 299
    Guaranteed Minimum Withdrawal Benefit (GMWB), 300
    guarantees, purchasing, 300
    life insurance, conversion to, 280
    liquidation distributions, 295–296
    number of annuitants, 293–294
    premiums, 287, 289
    promises purchased, 291–293
    role of during middle years, 240
    suitability issues, 288–289
    tax-deferred annuities (TDAs), 425
    taxes, 259, 295–296
    uses of, 288–289
    variable, 293, 298–300
    withdrawal before annuitization, 295
Antiselection, 27, 92
Anti-stacking provisions, 221
Antitrust, 137–138
Apparent (implied) authority, 83
Appleton rule, 130
Applicants, genetic testing of, 30
Applications
    whole life policy example, 531–545

W

Waiting periods
  disability income insurance, 311
  unemployment insurance, 456
Waiver-of-premium option, 283
Waivers, 91
War
  exclusions, 193
  restrictions, life insurance, 278
Warfel, William J., 385
Warranty
  breach of, 163
  contracts, 145, 156
Water damage
  exclusions, 192, 194–195
  perils, 191
Water heaters, 191
Water Pollution Control Act, 54
Weather-related insurance, 32
Wedding insurance, 33

Weight of ice, snow or sleet, 191
Whole life insurance, 256–260
  ledger sheets, 259–260
  loans, 276
  policy example, 531–545
  savings plans, 257
  single-premium, 272
  types of, 257–259
  uses of, 259
Wills, 241
Wilma (Hurricane), 17
Windstorms
  commercial package policy (CPP), 352
  perils, 190
Withdrawals
  before annuitization, 295
  Guaranteed Minimum Withdrawal
    Benefit (GMWB), 300
Wives, life insurance for, 236
Workers' Compensation insurance, 24,
  452, 457–463

Workplace safety, 7
WorldCom, 380
World Trade Center attacks, 106
Worth, net, 332
Wright, Elizur, 279
Written premiums, 10, 11
Wrongful discipline and negligent
  evaluation, 384
Wrongful hiring, 51

Y

Yearly renewable term life insurance, 253
You, definition of, 210
Your covered auto, definition of, 210

Z

Zero-coupon Treasury securities, 329